T0271291

Trade Links

The World Trade Organization is undergoing an existential crisis. Trade links the world not only through the flow of international commerce in goods, services, and ideas, but also through its economic, environmental, and social impacts. Trade links are supported by a WTO trading system founded on rules established in the twentieth century that do not account for all the modern changes in the global economy. James Bacchus, a founder of the WTO, posits that this global organization can survive and continue to succeed only if the trade links among WTO members are revitalized and reimagined. He explains how to bring the WTO into the twenty-first century, exploring the ways it can be utilized to combat future pandemics and climate change and advance sustainable development, all while continuing to foster free trade. This book is among the first to explain comprehensively the new trade rules needed for our new world.

JAMES BACCHUS is Distinguished University Professor of Global Affairs and Director of the Center for Global Economic and Environmental Opportunity at the University of Central Florida. While a member of the Congress of the United States, he helped create the World Trade Organization. He was a founding judge and the chief judge for the WTO during its first decade. Among his previous books is *The Willing World: Shaping and Sharing a Sustainable Global Prosperity*, published by Cambridge University Press in 2018 and named by the *Financial Times* as one of the "Best Books of the Year."

Trade Links

New Rules for a New World

JAMES BACCHUS
University of Central Florida

CAMBRIDGE
UNIVERSITY PRESS

Shaftesbury Road, Cambridge CB2 8EA, United Kingdom

One Liberty Plaza, 20th Floor, New York, NY 10006, USA

477 Williamstown Road, Port Melbourne, VIC 3207, Australia

314–321, 3rd Floor, Plot 3, Splendor Forum, Jasola District Centre, New Delhi – 110025, India

103 Penang Road, #05–06/07, Visioncrest Commercial, Singapore 238467

Cambridge University Press is part of Cambridge University Press & Assessment, a department of the University of Cambridge.

We share the University's mission to contribute to society through the pursuit of education, learning and research at the highest international levels of excellence.

www.cambridge.org
Information on this title: www.cambridge.org/9781009098106

DOI: 10.1017/9781009105941

First published 2022

A catalogue record for this publication is available from the British Library

ISBN   978-1-009-09810-6   Hardback

For my mother,
who taught me to read and took me to the Maitland Public Library.

Contents

Introduction

Fraying Links

No one knows how it started. No one knows precisely when it started. No one knows for certain exactly where it started. What is known is that sometime in late 2019, the novel coronavirus that causes the disease since named COVID-19 leaped from an animal – maybe a monkey or perhaps a small, scaled, anteater-like mammal called a pangolin – and possibly one of these animals or some other animal that had first been infected by a bat – into a human in the city of Wuhan in Hubei Province in central China.[1] Wuhan is a major metropolis, home to ten million people – three million more than New York City. The deadly new virus spread rapidly throughout the city and the surrounding province, without warning, without a vaccine, and without any cure. By late January 2020, Wuhan had been quarantined in a lockdown by the Chinese government. By then, at least 4,000 people (officially) in Wuhan had died, and the virus had reached other parts of China, which were likewise locked down.[2] On January 30, 2020, the World Health Organization declared the outbreak a "Public Health Emergency of International Concern."[3]

The arrival of COVID-19 highlighted all the varied links that bind the world. In centuries past, the viruses that carried plagues took years, even decades, to travel from one part of the world to another.[4] In today's globalized world, despite belated but extensive governmental efforts to contain the contagion in China, the new virus "boarded a 747" and quickly spread overseas.[5] Thousands soon died in Iran and in Italy, Spain, the United Kingdom, and other countries in Europe. The first case of the deadly new virus in the United States was reported in Washington State in late January 2020. Within weeks, COVID-19 appeared and surged in New York City, and Americans began to die in growing numbers as well. The new disease spread steadily elsewhere in the United States, at first in the major metropolitan areas and then in the smaller cities and the countryside. Traveling invisibly and inexorably from China, from Europe, and from North America, COVID-19 soon began to arrive and thrive lethally in the less affluent developing countries of South Asia, Southeast Asia, Latin America, and sub-Saharan Africa. On March 11, 2020, the World Health Organization characterized the global health situation as a pandemic.[6]

As the global search by scientists for a vaccine for the virus began, death tolls from the shifting epicenters of the new virus rose daily. Within weeks, total deaths from COVID-19 exceeded the annual death totals from influenza and other common and seasonal viruses. Within months, they exceeded the total number of deaths from recent wars and other global devastations. Counting methods within countries and among countries have not been uniform. Without question, the numbers of infections and deaths have been understated. In the United States alone, health officials think the true number of infections from COVID-19 has been about ten times higher than the official count.[7] Researchers at the Massachusetts Institute of Technology have concluded that, for each reported infection, twelve infections have gone unrecorded, and that for every two deaths from COVID-19, a third death has been attributed mistakenly to other causes.[8]

With these qualifications, as of this writing, officially, worldwide, there have been about 248 million infections and about five million deaths from COVID-19.[9] The largest numbers of infections and deaths in the world have been in the United States, which has recorded more than 46 million infections and has suffered 748,643 deaths.[10] With just 4 percent of the world's population, the United States has accounted for about 18 percent of all the world's official infections and about 15 percent of all the world's official deaths from COVID-19. These tragic numbers rose daily as 2020 turned into 2021 and the pandemic entered and continued through its second year.[11] Almost 3,000 people were killed by the terrorist attacks on September 11, 2001.[12] On many days during the pandemic, more Americans died from COVID-19 than were killed on 9/11.

The pain of the pandemic came not only from the growing numbers of infections and deaths. During 2019, in the absence of a vaccine, COVID-19 also took a rising economic toll amid the shock of a "global sudden stop."[13] Keeping people a safe distance of six feet or so apart – an epidemiological concept soon known to everyone everywhere as "social distancing" – was, scientists said, the best means available for slowing the spread of the virus.[14] Governments throughout the world shut down their economies to save lives. At one point, more than four billion people were subject to some sort of stay-at-home order.[15] Social distancing did save lives.[16] But it did so at a considerable global economic cost. The livelihoods of those whose lives were saved and of untold millions more were sacrificed, at least temporarily, to contain the pandemic and to preserve public health. In some parts of the world, many people were largely confined to their homes, unable to venture out for fear of infection, and shorn of many of their family and community ties.

In the first months of the pandemic, and, in many places, for maddening months afterward, grim evidence of the impact of COVID-19 was everywhere. Borders were closed. Schools and universities were shut down. Factories were shuttered. Oil and other commodity prices plummeted. Cranes and oil drilling rigs collected dust.[17] Airplanes sat empty on quiet runways. Amusement parks were silent. Grocery shelves were bare. Food lines grew. Medical masks became common sights on barren streets. Hospital wards and intensive care units were filled with afflicted patients struggling to breathe. And many people never made it to the hospital wards. They died at home and often alone.

As the new virus spread, the numbers of infections rose and fell and then rose again and yet again in different places. The erratic pattern of ascending and ebbing infections was a result in part of the inconsistencies of governmental precautions and reactions in different countries and within different countries. Because the disease was new, no one really knew exactly how to respond to it. Some countries shut down their economies. Others did not. Many sought an elusive balance between protecting health and maintaining jobs. Countries looked, mostly vainly, for "middle-ground measures" that would "prevent the disease from overwhelming hospitals while loosening some of the heaviest restrictions."[18] As the months passed and the contagion continued, the novel coronavirus surged more, and then still more, and it did so with a vengeance in some places where it had earlier been contained. Among the most vulnerable, and therefore among the most infected, were the half of humanity without access to essential health services.[19]

"The scale and the severity" of the COVID-19 pandemic was "unprecedented."[20] The United Nations described it as "the greatest test that we have faced since the formation of the United Nations" in 1945.[21] In a triumph of science, a tribute to the dedication of scientists, and a testimony to the liberating powers of innovation, the first vaccines were discovered by year-end 2020; but vaccine production was woefully slow, distribution by overwhelmed governments was slower, and the virus continued to prevail while billions of people waited for months for doses of the vaccines. Ominously, new strains of the virus began to appear as it mutated and, although the best of the new vaccines seemed to provide protection against them, infections from these virus variants surged in one country after another around the world.[22]

Surprisingly, in the United States, which, with its wealth, had been assumed by much of the rest of the world to be better prepared to fight a pandemic than perhaps any other country, the struggle to contain and combat COVID-19 was quickly caught up in the worsening political division and dysfunction that had increasingly gripped the country and put American representative democracy to the test. From the outset in 2020, political calculations prevailed in the White House of President Donald Trump. Hard facts about the virus were countered by phony propaganda. Scientific advice was disparaged or ignored. The severity of COVID-19 was downplayed by President Trump and his political appointees initially and at every twisted turn. Sometimes it was dismissed as a "hoax." At other times, it was said to be simply another form of the familiar seasonal flu. At all times, it was not treated as the deadly pandemic it quickly became.

There was no national strategy in the United States for fighting the pandemic. Cities and states were left to cope mostly on their own. So, too, were millions of Americans. The country locked down too late, opened again too soon, and plunged deeper into political impasse, an impasse made worse by the indecision and the incompetence at the highest levels of governance. Decades of reckless and relentless "anti-government" rhetoric in the pursuit of political power had resulted in a climate of distrust in which President Trump was able to succeed in simultaneously minimizing the threat of the virus and demonizing the struggles of many state and local governments to deal with it. He turned the simple and sensible health precaution of requiring the wearing of a mask to protect others into a supposed act of governmental oppression and suppression of personal freedom.

As the mortalities mounted, the fatal consequences of mixing an ersatz populism with a dangerous concoction of nihilism and "know-nothing-ism" were made manifest by the failure of the president of the United States and his sycophantic administration to mount anything even approaching a national response in confronting the pandemic. Thousands of Americans died who need not have. Shortly after President Trump was defeated for reelection, the British medical journal *The Lancet* published a "damning assessment" of his stewardship during the long night of the pandemic, concluding that 40 percent of the nearly 500,000 COVID-19 deaths in the United States while he was president were avoidable.[23] Disproportionately, the Americans who died from the coronavirus were Blacks, Hispanics, and members of other minority groups. One in every 1,000 African Americans was killed because of the coronavirus.[24]

With the shutdowns, much of global economic activity abruptly collapsed. Where it continued, there was a gaping societal divide. This divide had previously existed, largely unnoticed; now COVID-19 put it in a glaring spotlight. The pandemic "revealed deep flaws in our society that have been festering for decades."[25] This was perhaps most immediately evident in the differing impact of the shutdowns on workers with differing skills. Worldwide, two in five workers were able to work from home.[26] But most could not. Those in the workforce who could work remotely were more likely to be those with higher skilled, higher paying jobs in higher income countries. Those workers with lower skilled, lower paying jobs, especially in lower income countries, were more likely to have to leave home to work, which increased their exposure to COVID-19. Thus, the pandemic added to the polarizing division in the global labor market between high-skilled and low-skilled jobs, "with opportunities declining for those with a moderate level of skills."[27]

The lucky labored on laptops, safe at home. The unlucky labored outside of home amid the widening contagion of the office, the shop, and the sun. Or, left jobless, they sought work but usually could not find it. In the poorer places and poorer countries, fewer people were able to work remotely. Especially in the poorest of countries, more people worked in an informal economy and lived day-to-day. If they did not find work on any given day, then they and their families did not eat that day. Everywhere, those who could not work from home, were forced to choose between locking themselves and their families away from the spreading pandemic or inviting the possibility of immiseration and hunger by leaving home to work. Where faced with this dilemma, most people chose to leave home and keep working while clinging ever more precariously and ever more perilously to the steepening cliff of global economic decline.

Global economic integration had proceeded apace in the first years following the fall of the Berlin Wall in 1989 and the collapse of the Soviet Union in 1991. But, by the end of the twentieth century, a backlash against economic globalization had begun. Globalization vastly increased global economic growth, benefiting untold millions of people; yet, in many countries, the gains from that growth were not widely, or fairly, shared. Instead of focusing on the hard task of ensuring that all could share in the gains from globalization, that all could profit from continued global engagement, political leaders in an increasing number of countries chose instead to ignore the mounting inequities while emphasizing only the overall growth. Their seeming indifference to these inequities created a political opening for those who denounced the disruptive economic effects of globalization while denying its enormous and unprecedented economic benefits.

The backlash against economic globalization intensified in the wake of the global financial crisis of 2008, a crisis that undermined much of what remained of public trust in public leadership after years of political and economic disappointments that were often magnified by self-seeking demagogues such as Trump. On the eve of the COVID-19 outbreak in Wuhan, globalization was already in retreat for the first time since the Second World War.[28] The widening global contagion of the virus only added "further momentum to the deglobalization trend."[29] As the Organization for Economic Co-operation and Development – a Paris-based international institution comprised of the world's wealthiest countries – summed up this change, "The pandemic ... accelerated the shift from 'great integration' to 'great fragmentation.'"[30] Suddenly forgotten were the bounties of economic globalization; remembered only was the weight of its transitional burdens.

Worldwide, the impacts of COVID-19 on jobs and employment were "deep, far-reaching and unprecedented."[31] The recession that followed the financial crisis of 2008 had devastated much of the global economy. It was followed by a slow, modest, and uneven but largely sustained recovery. In the United States, the post-recession recovery continued for longer than any previous sustained period of growth in American history. Despite this, by 2020, the economic gains from the recovery, for most people, still had not offset their economic losses in the recession. Now, with the shocking arrival of COVID-19, for many people, their hard-won gains since the recession, such as they were, evaporated almost overnight.

Countries in every region of the world plunged into recession.[32] Worker income worldwide declined by one tenth.[33] The number of job losses in the first few months of the pandemic was ten times greater than in the first months of the 2008 financial crisis.[34] Total hours worked around the world dropped in the second quarter of 2020 by more than 10 percent, a number "equivalent to" job losses for "305 million workers with a 48-hour workweek" – fifteen times the job losses in the 2008 financial crisis.[35] The International Monetary Fund said the global economic crisis caused by the pandemic was "unlike anything the world has seen before."[36] The World Bank blamed the novel coronavirus for "the most adverse peacetime shock to the global economy in a century," the first recession "since 1870 to be triggered solely by a pandemic."[37] The Bank's economists predicted "the deepest global recession in eight decades," one three times the depth of the recession that followed the 2008 financial crisis.[38] Most national economies were expected to experience their largest declines in per capita output since 1870.[39] Emerging market and developing economies were expected to contract by 2.5 percent – their first decline in sixty years.[40] The OECD forecast that, even with some measure of an anticipated recovery, total global output in 2021 would remain below that of 2019.[41]

In the United States, as the virus and the layoffs spread, the unemployment rate rose in April 2020 to 14.7 percent.[42] Millions more jobless Americans were not counted in the official statistics.[43] The Federal Reserve reported that, during the first, long year of the pandemic, the number of US business establishments that closed permanently was about 200,000 more than the previous annual historical levels.[44] All told, economists David Cutler and Lawrence Summers of Harvard University estimated that the cumulative financial costs of the COVID-19 pandemic to the American people would be more than $16 trillion, or about 90 percent of annual American GDP. Of this amount, they attributed about half to the economic effects of the economic recession caused by COVID-19, and about half to the economic effects of "shorter and less healthy lives" due to the health consequences of the pandemic.[45] The nonpartisan US Congressional Budget Office calculated that, over the next decade, the pandemic would shrink the size of the American economy by about $8 trillion.[46]

In the United States and throughout the world, disproportionately, those left jobless and living even closer to the edge by the heedless march of the virus were minorities, women, young people, and workers without high-tech skills.[47] The sharp contraction of the global economy hurt them first and worst. It quickly stripped bare any lingering pretense of a patina of fairness in the disparate economic arrangements of humanity. COVID-19 "exposed and intensified deep-seated inequity, thrusting many of the world's most vulnerable into more precarious situations" and revealing their plight to a much greater public awareness.[48] No longer could the eyes of the complacent and the willfully ignorant be easily averted from the persistence of sexism, racism, and agism, or from the vast and growing gaps between rich and poor.

The global societal divide uncovered by COVID-19 disclosed many divisions. Common to them all was a striking and disturbing inequality. The inequality of humanity had been there before, but now it was much harder to ignore. Unequal incidence of the virus. Unequal access to health care. Unequal access to economic relief. Unequal access to justice. Unequal access to political power. Perhaps most telling, "some of the worst affected countries (were) among the world's most unequal."[49] They were also among the world's most lacking in the necessities of health care infrastructure. South Africa, Kenya, Brazil, Peru, Indonesia – in these developing countries and more, inequalities increased the health and economic impacts of the coronavirus crisis.[50] In India, for instance, a national lockdown of 1.4 billion people with just four hours' notice made no provision for the 90 percent of Indians in the country's informal work force. When, suddenly, jobless workers left the contagious cities to return to their original rural homes, the lockdown "set off the largest migration since the traumatic events of the partition (of India and Pakistan) in 1947."[51]

This economic pain was happening despite the salve of an unprecedented outpouring of state spending that totaled trillions of dollars worldwide. Advocacy of austerity seemed ancient history. Fiscal conservatives across the world bowed, at least temporarily, to the urgent logic of unprecedented deficit spending. Even the ardently anti-government Ayn Rand Institute in the United States sought and accepted a governmental bailout.[52] Countries throughout the world simply printed money and handed it out to individuals and to businesses alike in hopes of saving their sinking economies. In 2020, total public debt worldwide soared to $9 trillion and topped 103 percent of global GDP – an historic rise of more than 10 percent in just one year.[53] Few people anywhere seemed to give much thought to how or when the ever-growing mountain of public debt would be repaid. With customary caution widely abandoned in the dire and demanding circumstances created by COVID-19, it was "the age of magic money."[54]

Poorer countries, with less fiscal latitude and less potential financial credit, lined up to ask for global aid. The IMF estimated that developing countries needed $2.5 trillion to address the impacts of the pandemic.[55] In many places, the help that came was too little and too late, following in the wake of damage that was already done. After the financial crisis of 2008, poorer countries had turned more and more to private investors as public assistance proved harder to come by. In April of 2020, with the virus spreading, the Group of 20 major economies – the G20 – urged global private investors to join them in a moratorium on debt payments for the world's poorest counties for the remainder of the year. But this plan was "paralyzed" when credit-rating firms replied that restructuring private-sector borrowing could count as a default.[56] Without debt concessions or debt forgiveness from public and private creditors, in 2021, countries in Africa, Latin America, and elsewhere faced a "debt tsunami."[57]

Further complicating matters for many of the poorer countries amid this "debt tsunami" were the added pressures they faced because they owed increasing billions of dollars in outstanding debts to Chinese banks and to Chinese state-owned enterprises from loans made to finance local infrastructure as part of China's Belt and Road Initiative. In one way or another, the Chinese infrastructure project affected more than 130 countries.[58] By one estimate, governments and state-owned enterprises in Africa alone had received about $143 billion in loans from China since 2000 – much of which they could not afford to repay. Thus, the poorer countries got poorer as their economies continued to sink while, at the same time, the economic leverage of China over many of them increased.[59]

The prolonged recession that followed the financial crisis of 2008 had, for the most part, hit developed countries the hardest, and had harmed the "emerging economies" and the other affected developing countries mainly by lowering, temporarily, their rates of growth. The recession that came with COVID-19 was less discriminating and more pervasive. Countries suffered in different ways and to differing extents as the virus crossed the world and then crossed it again. But, this time, all countries suffered. As the lost year of 2020 went on, developed countries and developing countries alike struggled in their own ways to come up with just the right combination of economic boosts and health safeguards to avert the worst of the dire predictions that kept coming from the scientists and the economists.

With 2020 over at last but with the pandemic still spreading, in January 2021, looking ahead, the World Bank predicted that global growth between 2021 and 2030 would average only half of the global growth in the previous decade – and would be further cut in half in the absence of a successful global vaccination.[60] Delays in vaccinations, the bank foresaw, would make economic (as well as health) matters worse – for everyone. Plus, while economies would resume their previous growth, new growth would be measured against the shrunken economic production of 2020, and would therefore, at a superficial glance, seem stronger than it truly was in the real workaday world. Although hopeful, the bank warned that, for the global economy, the years 2021 through 2030 could be a "lost decade."[61] Meanwhile, the global health care industry prepared for a "permawar" against COVID-19, its various emerging new strains, and its possible successors in a new pandemic world.[62]

But also, in the final months of 2020, medicine makers on several continents announced the discovery of new vaccines to prevent infections by COVID-19. Developed by private firms in record time, the new vaccines were at first available in only a handful of developed countries. Though barely tested, they were deployed, some with much success. As vaccinations increased, some confidence was regained, and economic activity was revived in those places where vaccinations were initially available and successful. As 2020 became 2021, even as the pandemic continued, some of the economies of the world started to show signs of recovery.

Struck first, China recovered first. Having locked down in tight quarantine in early 2020 to limit the virus after first failing to contain it, China largely opened up in midyear and managed an annual GDP growth of 2.3 percent, making it the only major economy in the world that expanded during the plague year.[63] In April 2021, the Chinese government announced that its economic growth in the first quarter of 2021 was an "eye-popping" record of 18.3 percent higher than during the first quarter of 2020.[64] Given that COVID-19 had caused a decline of 6.8 percent in Chinese economic growth during the first quarter of 2020, this number was not as striking as it seemed.[65] Also, the first quarter growth in 2021 was only 0.6 percent above the growth in the last quarter of 2020, perhaps suggesting "waning momentum."[66] Later in the year, the spread of the delta variant of the virus threatened China anew.

Such as it was, the Chinese recovery was uneven, and the underlying vulnerabilities of China's statist economy remained unaltered. The population was aging, and the workforce was shrinking. The dependency on export-led growth was constraining the growth of the domestic consumer market. Consumer credit remained limited. A reassertion of state direction of the economy threatened the job-producing enterprise in the private market. Not least, the Chinese government had pumped huge amounts of money into the domestic economy to support growth in 2020, and, especially, there were fears "about the asset bubbles caused by excess liquidity."[67] Although China continued to narrow its economic gap with the United States, mounting debt and a tightening state stranglehold over the private sector threaten China's prospects for long-term growth.

The US economy began to recover slowly in late 2020 as Americans dealt with the turbulent conduct and aftermath of a divisive presidential election. By March 2021, with Donald Trump banned from Twitter and Joe Biden settled into the White House, the official unemployment rate was down to 6.0 percent.[68] This jobless number, however, did not count the more than four million Americans who had dropped out of the labor force since the beginning of the pandemic. Taking them into account, the actual unemployment rate was estimated by the Pew Research Center at 50 percent higher than the official number. Moreover, Black and Hispanic workers were represented disproportionately among the unemployed.[69]

The combination of significant improvements in the distribution of COVID-19 vaccines in the United States by the new Biden administration and the added stimulus of the new president's $1.9 trillion "American Rescue Plan," enacted in March, transformed the gradual growth into turbo-charged growth, and the American economic recovery took off.[70] Bank of America foresaw the US economic "flood gates" as opening and estimated US GDP growth would be 6.5 percent in 2021.[71] Goldman Sachs forecast 2021 US growth at 8 percent.[72] Equally bullish, Morgan Stanley predicted the US growth rate for the year would be 8.1 percent.[73] For the first time in decades, the United States seemed poised to outpace the annual growth rate of China, although, as in China, the rapid spread of the delta variant later in the year ended up curbing US growth.

In March 2021, the International Monetary Fund projected that global economic growth would be 6 percent in 2021 – the most since 1980 – and 4.4 percent in 2022.[74] In revising their previous projections upward, economists for the IMF pointed to the extent of "additional fiscal support in a few large economies"; an anticipated "vaccine-powered recovery" during the second half of the year; and "continued adaptation of economic activity to subdued mobility."[75] In plainer words, the governments of the largest economies were printing and spending unprecedented amounts of money, more people were being vaccinated, and people were learning how to be productive even though they were limited in moving around. The IMF identified the United States and China as the two key drivers of a resurgent global economy. With respect to the United States, it said, "the Biden administration's new fiscal package is expected to deliver a strong boost to growth in the United States in 2021 and provide sizable positive spillovers to trading partners."[76]

But the United States seemed likely to grow faster than either Europe or Japan. Likewise, other developing countries were expected to grow much slower than China. Laden with debt, most countries in the world looked to fall farther behind the most economically advanced countries after decades of toil in closing the development gap. In India, 32 million people had been driven out of the middle class and back into poverty, "undoing decades of progress for a country that in fits and starts has brought hundreds of millions of people out of poverty."[77] Similarly, poverty was rising anew in Brazil, where, according to the World Bank, the pandemic was "jeopardizing years of progress in poverty reduction and human capital accumulation."[78]

As the economies of China and the United States grew even amid the continuing pandemic, the virus raged in India, Brazil, Indonesia, Peru, and other developing countries. In India, thousands of bloated bodies of COVID-19 victims washed up on the shores of the sacred Ganges River.[79] The dearth of vaccine doses in the developing countries cost untold lives – and cast doubt on predictions of their resumed growth. Worse, public health experts warned that the ever-evolving new strains of the virus could cause new and more serious infections and upend hopes for health and recovery. And, of course, looming on the horizon was the prospect of more pandemics to come.

Like the Indigenous peoples of the Americas half a millennium ago, who greeted the conquistadores and the colonists from faraway Europe when they came ashore, those everywhere who gazed out on the sea of an unknown future did not know what fate awaited them. Would it be a dark decimation by disease? Or would it be a return to life and – just possibly – a beginning of a better, brighter way of life? With the advent of COVID-19, the world had changed. It had changed forever.

For just a moment in the spring of 2020, there was the fond thought that there might at least be some consolation for the ravages of the virus in its results for global climate change. There was the hope that the economic decline caused by the pandemic would have the ironic salutary effect of a significant decline also in the carbon dioxide and other greenhouse gas emissions driving the rapid acceleration of climate change. Perhaps, some surmised, this would be a "bright spot" in an otherwise gloomy global prospect.[80] There was in fact a temporary slowing of increased emissions. Emissions continued but at a slower rate. But then emissions surged back in the summer of 2020 as, with the deceptive ebb of the initial outbreaks of the virus, economies began to reopen and to churn out more carbon and other greenhouse gases.[81]

All the while, climate scientists and climate activists urged that the same intensity be shown in battling climate change as in battling the virus. To save the climate, there was, they urged, equal need for declaration of a "planetary emergency."[82] Global carbon dioxide emissions were about 7 percent lower in 2020 than in 2019.[83] This temporary decline, though, was only a small fraction of the drop in global emissions needed to slow global warming, which continued to accelerate.[84] Despite the hopes of the spring, in the trajectory of atmospheric CO_2 levels over the long term, the impact of the emissions reductions in 2020 was negligible.[85] Global warming continued, and 2020 matched 2016 as the hottest year on record.[86] By April 2021, the International Energy Agency was predicting that the projected 4.6 percent rise in energy demand in a recovering global economy in 2021 would trigger the second largest annual increase in carbon emissions in history.[87] The leading reinsurance firm Swiss Re reported that the effects of climate change could be expected to reduce global economic output by between 11 and 14 percent of what growth would have been without climate change – a prospective loss of $23 trillion by 2050.[88] As greenhouse gas emissions continued to accumulate in the atmosphere, United Nations Secretary-General Antonio Guterres warned world leaders that, "We are on the verge of the abyss."[89]

Global warming was but one of the ecological challenges the world continued to face during the novel coronavirus pandemic, all of which were worsened by the onrush of climate change.[90] Hurricanes and other storms were more frequent and more intensified. Floods drowned lives and futures. Droughts lengthened on parched land. Scorching wildfires spread in woodlands brittle from the sweltering heat. Animal species of all kinds suffered and died from habitat loss and extreme weather events.[91] Nearly three billion animals were killed or displaced by "devastating bushfires" in Australia.[92] Rare species of one-horned rhinos perished in massive floods in northeast India.[93] Gopher tortoises were sacrificed to urban sprawl in Florida.[94]

As the COVID-19 pandemic devastated human civilization, the reckless human destruction and "degradation of the ecosystems on which all life depends" continued.[95] Having caused the loss of 83 percent of all wild animals and 50 percent of all plants since human civilization had begun, humanity seemed unable to stop itself.[96] Scientists reported that, largely due to habitat loss and to a wider use of pesticides, there were nearly three billion fewer birds in North America than there had been half a century before.[97] The skies were "emptying out."[98] Birdsong was fading. Of all the birds left on Earth, 70 percent were farmed poultry – chickens and other foul grown for human consumption.[99] Nature was stripped bare and, in retaliation, stripped humanity bare. As if symbolic, biblical swarms of locusts devoured crops across East Africa.[100]

Amid all else that transpired in the wake of the spreading pandemic, one alarming indicator of the unraveling of international economic integration was that international trade "collapsed."[101] During the recession that began in 2008, trade declined for six months before turning upward. A dozen years later, in the face of the COVID-19 pandemic, trade fell even more. The cost of shipping a container of goods tripled.[102] Cargo vessels sat offshore for weeks without being able to dock in port. Planes, when they flew, had cargo holds that were empty. World merchandise trade fell 5.3 percent in 2020. An increase of 8 percent from this lower base was projected for 2021.[103] But projections of trade growth were "subject to an unusually high degree of uncertainty" and depended on "the evolution of the pandemic and government responses to it."[104] Moreover, even if this optimistic projection proved accurate, world trade in 2021 would still be less than it had been in 2019, the year before the pandemic.[105]

Trade links the world. It links the world through the fertile flow of international commerce in goods, services, and ideas. It is a means of both commerce and communication. Trade links the world through its vast economic, environmental, and social impacts. It contributes to the economic wealth of humanity and provides the material underpinning for much else that we do for human well-being. Trade links the world, too, through competition. The need to meet and outpace competition spurs the urge for the innovation from which more economic wealth is derived. Trade links the world also through much else that we do domestically and internationally to connect to others. It makes the world smaller and brings people throughout the world closer together. Distance dies and differences fade. Total strangers become trading partners.

To increase the flow of trade and thus secure more gains from trade, the trading nations of the world have long recognized the necessity for trade links. Toward this end, they have forged links in the form of a global trading system founded on agreed rules. They have spent the past three-quarters of a century, since the end of the Second World War, building this "multilateral" trading system, which has gradually expanded over the decades to include 164 member countries. About 98 percent of all world trade occurs among the members of this system.[106] This multilateral system furthers the flow of trade within the agreed rules framework of an international institution established by treaty in 1995 that is called the World Trade Organization. This institution is commonly known as the "WTO."

The multilateral trading system of the WTO is often described as a "rule-based" system. This is simply another way of saying that it is a "law-based" system.[107] WTO trade rules are laws. The WTO is an international legal framework that is part of the broader sum of public international law established by the nearly 200 sovereign nation-states into which the world is divided. WTO rules therefore bind WTO members as a matter of law. Being sovereign, the states that have agreed to abide by WTO rules can, of course, choose to ignore their WTO treaty commitments; but, when they choose to do so, they violate the international law they helped to make, and, under that law, they stand to lose some of the considerable trade benefits they obtain from being a part of the multilateral trading system.

Like all laws, WTO rules acquire solidity as laws by being upheld through the rule of law. This occurs through the willing compliance by WTO members with almost all WTO rules almost all the time – a fact often neglected in debates over international trade. This occurs also through the peaceful settlement of international trade disputes when, unavoidably, disputes arise about the correct meanings of the rules during the exchanges of global commerce. Where there is the rule of law, the rules are written and agreed in advance. They are written to apply to all equally, and all are equal under the law and before the law. Nothing less than this can rightly be called the rule of law. Confidence in the rule of law creates certainty in the conduct of trade. This certainty provides "security and predictability" to the trading system, which in turn permits trade to flourish.[108]

As with so many other aspects of how we live and work together in the world, and of how we share the global abundance we have accumulated, the arrival of the novel coronavirus has shorn the deceptive surface and revealed to all the full extent of the underlying tensions that grip the WTO-based trading system. Despite the more than seven decades of success of the WTO and its predecessor, the General Agreement on Tariffs and Trade (the GATT), in helping generate vastly more economic growth worldwide, the multilateral trading system was already at risk before the arrival of COVID-19 in late 2019. In perhaps the most telling of the many manifestations of the increasing global skepticism of additional economic integration, in the quarter of a century since the creation of the WTO, the countries that are members of the WTO system have found it nearly impossible to conclude new global agreements to stimulate trade flows and strengthen trade links by freeing more trade.

In many ways, the WTO still functions. For the most part, WTO members still comply with WTO rules. For the most part, too, WTO rules still advance world trade. Along the ragged edges of the global economy, the WTO still settles many disputes and still makes some improvements. Yet the controversies at the core of global economic concern seem beyond the current capacity of the WTO to resolve, or even to confront, in a mutually acceptable way. And there is less and less support everywhere for the WTO as a forum and framework for trade governance. Why has all this happened? The editorial writers of the *Financial Times* have rightly summed up our collective international failure on trade as a "failure to understand the benefits of trade, failure to share its gains, failure to help those adversely affected, failure to update the global rules, and failure to sustain essential cooperation."[109]

This failure is global; no one country alone is responsible for it. But, in recent years, it has been worsened immeasurably by the actions of the United States of America during the presidency of Donald Trump. One of the saddest signs of the precarious vulnerability of the rule–based WTO trading system has been the retreat of the largest trading country in the world from the international rule of law in trade.[110] Long a global champion of the rule of law, the United States, with Trump as president, became a legal pariah in international trade, adhering to WTO rules selectively, and ignoring or flouting WTO rules whenever it wished. When President Trump left the White House (reluctantly) in January 2021 following his defeat by former Vice President Joe Biden, he left not only his own country, but also the WTO, in turmoil. This turmoil in the multilateral trading system only intensified as the pandemic pulled the world farther apart.

The very survival of the multilateral trading system is in question in part because the WTO has not fulfilled some of the original expectations of its founders in 1995. For the most part, the WTO has been successful in the peaceful settlement of international trade disputes that have arisen under the existing rules. It has not been successful, however, in keeping the rules up to date with the requirements of an ever-changing global economy. Originally, the WTO was envisaged by those who negotiated and approved the WTO treaty as an ongoing global forum and framework for addressing new commercial developments and challenges in the world as they arose. It was intended to be built around and bound by an ever-evolving set of agreed rules. It has fallen considerably short of that. WTO rules seem frozen in time, and that time is 1995.

The rules of the multilateral trading system largely do not address the rapid transformation of the global economy since then and up until the global shock of the pandemic. Nor do they reflect any of the new and lasting changes made in the world by the disruptive impacts of the pandemic. WTO rules were written in and for the world of the twentieth century. In the twenty-first century, many of these trade rules are still fit for purpose. They still work. They should be upheld so that they can continue to work. But many other trade rules are outdated. They no longer work. Moreover, many of the rules that are missing and are needed do not exist. The new rules that are required have yet to be written because they have not been negotiated and agreed. In some instances, the WTO has not even tried to negotiate them.

Decades-long efforts to eliminate the remaining tariffs and other distortive barriers to trade in manufactured and agricultural goods have stalled. Proposals to bring services trade, the trade-related aspects of intellectual property rights, and the trade dimensions of foreign direct investment more fully into the WTO–based trading system have faltered. At a time when – spurred still more by the pandemic – digital trade is utterly transforming the global economy, the WTO still has no specific rules on digital trade. At a time of growing worldwide concern about allegedly "unfair" trade, the topic of bringing competition policy – anti-trust policy – into the global trading system has not yet been placed on the WTO negotiating agenda. At a time when the economic rise of China has transformed world trade, it is unclear whether WTO rules are fit and sufficient to apply to China. And, at a time when eliminating the needless barriers to trade in medicines and other medical goods could hasten the end of the pandemic, WTO members have not even been able to come together to do that.

What is more, at a time of climate change and other ecological crises, WTO negotiators have, after decades of discussions, yet to deal seriously with the critical relationship between trade and the environment. The links between trade and climate change remain largely unexplored by the WTO; and despite the lofty promises made in the WTO treaty, WTO members have yet to begin to come to grips with the intricate links between trade and the far-ranging reach of the global environmental, economic, and social goals for achieving sustainable development on which they have all agreed as members of the United Nations. Now the pandemic has, as with so much else, revealed all too clearly to all the world just how far the WTO has fallen short of accomplishing all its initial ambitions.

Still more, the WTO has failed to come to grips with the widespread view in the world that freer trade helps the few but not the many. Throughout the world, there is a popular backlash against trade, born of the belief that the gains from trade go only to those at the top of the economic ladder, and at the price of pushing those on the bottom rungs off the ladder. Job losses are blamed on trade even when, as often, they have nothing to do with trade. The numerous job gains and other gains from trade are rarely attributed to trade. There is a broad popular feeling that those who would free more trade are unconcerned about economic inequities and indifferent to economic inclusion. As a result, there is little political appetite anywhere for moving forward on freeing trade.

The trade links of the World Trade Organization are frayed. Without reforms that produce the new and better rules needed in the new world of COVID-19, the WTO is at risk of increasing irrelevance. Its centrality to world trade is in doubt. Its rules for world trade are increasingly ignored. Its continued existence cannot be assumed. "At what point," asked one trade journalist in the midst of the pandemic, "is the World Trade Organization no longer relevant?"[111] The opponents of economic integration and other forms of globalization famously demonstrated against the WTO in the streets of Seattle in 1999. Now they no longer bother.

At this turning point in history, like much else that links us, like much else that is supposed to bind and unite us, the World Trade Organization is in existential crisis. This matters not only in world trade. It matters in all we do and in all we hope to do. The world can recover from the devastations of the COVID-19 pandemic only if the world economy recovers. The world economy can fully recover in this new pandemic world only if the countries of the world continue to trade and only if they trade more freely within a global framework of agreed rules. The rule-based trading system entrusted to the WTO can survive and succeed only with new rules that will serve the new world in which we now live. But, alas, as the pandemic continues, the fraying links that tie us together through international trade seem about to rip apart.

I

Links to the Global Economy

GLOBALIZATION IN THE NEW PANDEMIC WORLD

The yearning for a return to normal is universal. People everywhere wish for a return to the time when COVID-19 did not exist, when most people outside China had never heard of the city of Wuhan, and when few people had ever heard much, if anything, about the nomenclature and the nuances of the science of epidemiology. This yearning is understandable. It is also futile. The impact of the pandemic will be "felt for years to come."[1] The world cannot return to the "previous normal" after COVID-19.[2] The world cannot return to any semblance at all of normality unless and until the new vaccines that have been discovered in record time, and that can inoculate us against the disease, have been fully deployed worldwide. Even then, and from now on, we will live in a new pandemic world.

Even when everyone in the world has at last been vaccinated, there can be no reversing all the changes caused by the pandemic. Much has changed that cannot be unchanged. This pandemic may well be followed by others, which may be worse. Or it may be followed by something just as disruptive, perhaps a cyber breakdown or (lest we have forgotten) the quickly cascading consequences of climate change. The world we knew is the world of yesterday.[3] There can be no returning today or tomorrow to the now lost and vanished world of before the fateful events in Wuhan toward the end of 2019; for 2019 is akin to 1913, the year before the storm, the year before a "war to end all wars" swept away another lost and vanished world. As Amina Mohammed, the deputy secretary-general of the United Nations, has cautioned, even what may appear to be a return in some parts of the world to something resembling our previous reality "must not lull us into a false sense of security."[4] It must not blind us to the fact that the world is forever changed.[5]

What will the new world of COVID-19 be like? Much about the new world is still in the making. It is still unknown. Yet some characteristics of the new world are already apparent. For one, obviously, the pandemic world will be more virtual. Work will be more remote and more automated. While the disease remains a threat, and likely longer due to the threat of future similar diseases, there will be less travel and less human physical contact. Life will be lived more online. Commerce will occur more online. The COVID-19 world will gaze less often through an airplane window and more often through the video squares of a Zoom call. And life will be lived more at home. Even when we are all inoculated with a COVID-19 vaccine, we may find that we will need to wear masks in many places for mutual protection for some time to come. Rendered faceless by the novel coronavirus, the new world will be in search of new ways to see and construct the vital links of human connections.

The new world will include, for better and for worse, a larger role in society for the state. During the pandemic, more people everywhere have sought more security and a stronger social safety net from their government. There has been less emphasis on individual self-reliance and more stress on mutual aid through the machinery of government. The never-ending challenge in governance is to identify and implement the right mix between the two. Meeting this challenge has been made all the harder by the advent of COVID-19. In the new world, continued calls for governmental action to alleviate the medical, economic, and other pains of the pandemic will be heard and – in one way or another, and in different ways in different places – heeded. More and more, these actions by governments in response to these calls will raise fundamental questions about the best and fairest ways to structure human society. One basic question will be, can we be both safe and free?

Depending on the nature of the government, in some places, the state's larger role will enable human freedom; in others, it will diminish it. The power of the state can be employed to uphold human rights; encourage growth and innovation; stimulate new employment; and enforce new health and safety measures that fight the spread of COVID-19 and other diseases. The state can be a tool for helping humanity up. Yet the power of the state can be used instead to deny human rights; strangle the market; stifle human initiative; quell the expression of free speech; and erase the right of public assembly. In these and other ways, the state can be a tool for holding humanity down. New digital technologies, for instance, can help find vaccines and cures for new diseases. Yet they can also help impose pervasive and oppressive social control. The impact of the power of the state depends to a great extent on who is wielding that power and on how they came to wield it. Some leaders want to use power for good; others want only to possess power for the pleasure of possessing it. Democracy tends to serve freedom; dictatorship does not.

As we have already seen in the flurry of deficit spending sparked by the economic impacts of the pandemic, a larger role for the state will in many places be accompanied by a larger pile of accumulating public debt.

Worldwide, and especially in the wealthier countries, national currencies are being treated as if they were Monopoly money in "the whirring of the printing press."[6] By September 2020, national governments had committed $11.7 trillion – 12 percent of global output – to combating the economic downturn caused by the pandemic. Cumulative public debt neared 100 percent of global GDP.[7] The US debt rose by one-third under President Trump, mainly due first to his huge tax cut in 2017 and later to stimulus spending to fight the pandemic.[8] His successor, President Biden, began his term by proposing trillions of dollars in additional spending to help combat the virus and sustain the US economy until the pandemic subsides.[9] His subsequent spending proposals promised to push the budget deficit and the national debt even higher.

While the pandemic persists, there will be little political pushback against the incurrence of this debt. Thus far, and not without good reason, the coronavirus pandemic has produced a total victory for pump-priming Keynesianism. The trillions of dollars that have been printed and distributed by desperate governments throughout the world have helped prevent the impacts of the pandemic from becoming much worse than they are. The immediate imperative of getting through today has put off the eventual imposition of paying for tomorrow. Yet even Lord John Maynard Keynes himself might cringe at the rising height of the global mountain of debt.

What is more, there are downsides as well as upsides to printing more money to serve even the noblest of public purposes. As global economist Ruchir Sharma has advised,

A growing body of research shows that constant government stimulus (since the 2008 financial crisis) has been a major contributor to many of modern capitalism's most glaring ills. Easy money fuels the rise of giant firms and, along with crisis bailouts, keeps alive heavily indebted "zombie" firms at the expense of startups, which typically drive innovation. All of this leads to low productivity – the prime contributor to a slowdown in economic growth and a shrinking of the pie for everyone. At the same time, easy money has juiced up the value of stocks, bonds and other financial assets, which benefits mainly the rich, inflaming social resentment over growing inequalities in income and wealth.[10]

Added to these downsides to easy money must be the greater potential for public money to be misspent due to regulatory capture, crony capitalism, ill-considered subsidies, and more vulnerability to the siren song of trade protectionism. The likelihood is greater that the common public interest will be sacrificed to selfish private interests.

Irrespective of such cautions, and no matter their merits, fiscal demands for still more deficit spending are unlikely to subside. Yet fiscal procrastination about the extent of such spending cannot continue forever. Eventually, there will, in many countries, be a fiscal reckoning. Unless countered by the right kind of leadership, there will be every inclination in the new pandemic world to discard any fiscal thoughts of "intergenerational equity."[11] According to

Sharma, "What capitalism urgently needs is a new, more focused approach to government intervention – one that will ease the pain of disasters but leave economies free to grow on their own after the crises pass."[12] With a more focused approach, the extent of public debt could be constrained and perhaps diminished by a combination of more targeted and more accountable spending with some measure of income redistribution through fairer taxation. More likely, tomorrow will continue to be sacrificed for today because of a masked myopia that makes tomorrow a dim and distant blur.

The new pandemic world will be polarized politically even more than before. We have learned during the pandemic that "mustering a concerted and effective global response is nigh on impossible in a world of blustering demagogues and self-confident autocrats."[13] The unequal effects of the pandemic and the increased inequalities it has caused will drive still more divisive wedges between countries and between people within countries. Throughout the world, political elites will pay for their past failures and perceived complacencies. They will find it hard to unite their people, and harder to lead them. There will be little popular patience for reminders by elites of past accomplishments. There will be pressing demand instead for governments to stop reminding, stop pondering, stop deliberating, *and act*. The demand for governmental action will be made in many languages. It may be whispered or shouted, depending on where it is made. But everywhere people will ask of those who would deign to lead them, what will you do for me now?

Those making these demands will have little trust in those to whom their demands are made. Public trust is in short supply nowadays. Already, before the sudden shock of COVID-19, global surveys indicated that four out of every five people in Europe, China, India, the United States, and other countries believed that "the system" – whatever it was where they lived – was not working for them.[14] Amid the pandemic, in much of the world, "the system" seemed to be failing them once again, and with more fateful consequences. In the new pandemic world, the people who political elites wish to unite and to lead will tend to trust them even less than before. The people will seek solutions. But they will be more reluctant than ever to believe in solutions when they hear them. And they will be even more apt than they were before the pandemic to fall prey to the phony populism of those who are not truly seeking solutions but are seeking only to get and keep political power. In the United States, this situation is much worsened by the cumulative effects of several decades of steadily intensifying anti-government animus on the right of the American political spectrum.

Without electoral victories, responsible politicians of various stripes will be unable to find and apply solutions. Elections will be even harder to win for those who act responsibly in framing and proposing solutions. The cards of the COVID-19 world seem, in many places, to be stacked against the exercise of political responsibility. The urgency of now argues against the appreciation of nuance. The more fearful people are, the less accepting they are of the inconvenience of unwelcome facts, especially when these facts are contrary to their predispositions (however misguided) and may involve some personal sacrifices. They want solutions, but, when confronted with the facts about how best to achieve those solutions, they opt instead to cast their votes not for those who offer them the facts but for those who channel their anger and their resentment in fact-free demagoguery.

Making matters worse, in the fictive online world of social media, the COVID-19 pandemic has been accompanied by a highly contagious "info-demic" of "alternative facts" flowing out from a specious alternative reality that bears little or often no resemblance to what is happening in the real world.[15] In the United States, between 2016 and 2020, the amount of "fake news" that Americans consumed on Facebook and other social media sites tripled.[16] In the first few months following the outbreak of COVID-19, websites spreading health hoaxes drew an estimated 460 million views on Facebook.[17] In American politics, lies were uttered, circulated, and repeated endlessly to the credulous on social media. These lies revealed the fraught fault lines of the American democratic experiment, and, in the aftermath of a divisive national election, threatened to consume American democracy in conflagration. It is with the fantasies of this fabricated cyber world that facts must often compete.

The rejection of facts is indicative of "the rising rejection of the Enlightenment" commitment to reason, as reflected in the postmodernism of the vocal extremes of right and left alike on the political spectrum.[18] Postmodernism contends that there are no facts; there are only opinions.[19] In the absence of a common understanding of the facts, it becomes nigh impossible to find a mutual purchase on common ground. American historian Adam Garfinkle has pointed out that, in such circumstances, the "positive-sum" approach of the Enlightenment, in which institutions are built to serve all, and in which one person can profit without harming another, yields to a nihilistic "zero-sum" approach to everything, in which institutions are viewed as instruments of dominance and one person's gain must inevitably be another person's loss.[20] One casualty of such thinking, as conservative commentator George F. Will has noted, and as Donald Trump – the doyen of "zero-sum" thinking – has demonstrated, is the increasing inability of a fact-deprived populace to comprehend the proven mutual benefits of free trade.[21]

Martin Wolf, the eminent economic columnist for the *Financial Times*, of London, has rightly observed that the times "demand an alliance of politics with expertise, both domestically and globally, just as happened in the 1940s and 1950s."[22] And yet, in the new pandemic world, expertise has been devalued. Weariness with the high-handed hubris of some experts has led to wariness of all claimed expertise. Now, anyone with genuine expertise who has the temerity to endeavor to convey reliable information is immediately chal-lenged by hosts of self-appointed experts in the degraded public square of conventional and social media. Online, many people who may have barely passed high school biology have now morphed into self-certified epidemiologists. Online, on television, and on radio, imposters parade as sages in science, sociology, history, economics, finance, and, ubiquitously, international trade.[23]

In the new pandemic world, seemingly anyone can anoint themselves as an expert on almost anything. Likewise, anyone, however poorly informed, can feel free to reject the advice of an expert. The reactive reasoning goes, some experts have been wrong about some things; why then listen to any of them about anything? Dismissing expert advice with derisive disdain is a consoling way of appearing to assert personal control in a confusing world that seems beyond control. Given this devaluation of expertise, any public official so bold as to rely on expert advice and to tell people who do not want to hear it that they should follow it, will be told by pseudo-experts that they are, at best, deceived, or, at worst, prevaricating in pursuit of some elitist agenda.

It is all too clear from the dismaying quality of the debate on social media over the appropriate response to COVID-19 that, in the new pandemic world, the downward trajectory of recent years toward a widespread popular denial of the scientific method of testing by observation will continue and could descend to even more degraded depths. Social media savants will continue to multiply. Divisive viral images of "memes" and "GIFs," often originated by anonymous and foreign websites with dark agendas, will substitute for civil and reasoned discourse. And, borne of a widespread willful ignorance, more and more of the actual reality of the world will be seen by many as merely a concoction, merely a "hoax."

"These are dangerous times," laments the American arms control expert Tom Nichols in his book *The Death of Expertise.*

Never have so many people had so much access to so much knowledge and yet have been so resistant to learning anything. In the United States and other developed nations, otherwise intelligent people denigrate intellectual achievement and reject the advice of experts. Not only do increasing numbers of laypeople lack basic knowledge, they reject fundamental rules of evidence and refuse to learn how to make a logical argument. In doing so, they risk throwing away centuries of accumulated knowledge and undermining the practices and habits that allow us to develop new knowledge.[24]

Sadly, all too many people have not learned how to engage in the rational critical thinking that is a requisite of enlightened and effective citizenship. Without such skill, they are more likely to be confused by the complexities of their circumstances, and this leaves them more likely to believe the soothing simplicities of those who appeal to their baser instincts, and of those whose knowledge and whose wisdom are entirely of their own imagining. Unable to think critically, these generally good and well-intentioned people are often unable to discern the difference between a fake social media meme (perhaps produced by a Russian bot) and a reliable opinion. Unable to deal with the contemporary inevitability of complexity, they often fall prey to the divisive devices of those who pull us apart by stirring animosities and speaking darkly of conspiracy. It is easier for them to believe in conspiracy than to accept the fact that the fast-changing world around us is not simple but complex. The incendiary consequences of this shortage of critical thinking skills have been all too apparent during the pandemic, and they make it all the harder for public servants who truly try to lead to succeed.

Without question, the expert elites are not without fault for the travails that have befallen many people in the past generation and more. Far from it. The American invasion of Iraq in 2003 is a lasting example of how elites can fail; the run-up to the global financial crisis in 2008 is another. Yet this does not mean that expert advice is not worth hearing and, often, heeding. The key is to know when to ignore expert advice and when to listen to and follow it. Perhaps this is where we have failed the most in recent years. As conservative thinker David Brooks has concluded, "Our core problem is ignorance and incompetence and not an elite conspiracy."[25] In the United States, for instance, the problem is not a conspiratorial "deep state"; it is an ineffective state licensed and empowered by a public ignorance that has proven capable of entrusting the leadership of the state to unfit incompetents and unprincipled opportunists without even realizing it. This outcome is made more likely because the money spent to elect such adventurers is virtually unlimited and often undisclosed. And this democratically perilous situation threatens to worsen in the new COVID-19 world. Unable to think critically and thus unable to think for themselves, all too many people across the world are likely to be led astray by those who tell them lies and offer them only easy answers that are no answers at all.

The fear of disease exacerbates racial, religious, and ethnic tensions, and there is every danger, too, that these tensions will be much on display in the new world.[26] Fear is fodder for demagogues. In this new world, in a growing number of places, irresponsible demagogues of sundry dubious persuasions will offer stirring speeches that feed on fears. But they will not offer capable governance. They will not offer real answers. Without real answers to offer, they will look for scapegoats. In the new pandemic world, as before, these demagogues will find the scapegoats they seek among their fellow citizens who may look, act, think, and believe differently than they do. And they will find them beyond their borders by fomenting and exploiting the age-old irrational fear of the foreign and the foreigner.

In the United States, the times are even more dangerous because of the apprehension of many white Americans about the inexorable approach of a demographic destiny in which most Americans will not be white. A majority that will soon become a minority is more susceptible to demagoguery because they "feel their grip on power slipping away."[27] Americans are in the midst of a fundamental and far-reaching debate over whether America is an idea or an ethnic group. Demographic trends suggest that those Americans who see America as an idea – as a set of basic beliefs about individual rights and democratic self-governance belonging to all Americans, of whatever ethnicity or background – can prevail over time. The question is – will the idea of

America survive long enough to enable those who believe in the idea of America to prevail?

Disease-driven fear is combustible; it is tinder for violence. The imminent danger of contagion scorches the shallow surface of reasoned civilization and reveals the unreason below. For as long as such fear continues, power-seeking demagogues will spew a running sewer of isms – a foul flow comprised of a flammable combination of nativism, nationalism, isolationism, sexism, racism, and anti-intellectualism. To the extent that these foul emissaries for intolerance and for hate succeed, there will – both within countries and between countries – be more conflict and less cooperation. To that same extent, there will be less internationalism, less multilateralism, and an ever-rising crescendo of anomic and destructive attacks on the effective functioning of the WTO and the rest of the peaceful institutional apparatus of the postwar liberal world order. There will be more global distancing.

What, in this grave new world, will be the enduring effects of COVID-19 on trade? The atmosphere in the pandemic world is conducive to imposing new restrictions on international trade; it is amenable to protectionism. Amid all the upheavals of the pandemic, there is increasing apprehension everywhere about almost anything that is somehow different or that happens to be sent "here" – wherever "here" may be – from an alien somewhere else. Increasingly, many people around the world are fearful even of the supposed threats, invisible and otherwise, that they think will greet them if they so much as go outside their own home. Thus, there is little wonder that, stoked by the inflammatory divisiveness of self-serving demagogues, they are increasingly fearful, too, of much of all that originates outside their own borders – outside the borders of their neighborhood, their community, their city, their state or province, their country. Goods, services, people, ideas – all that is foreign is suddenly suspect.

The depth and intensity of these common fears will impede global recovery and progress on many economic and other fronts. It will prove no small obstacle to those who hope to revive world trade to its "previous normal" in the new pandemic world. Engulfed by the pandemic, those who seek to insulate themselves from the competition of foreign trade solely for self-interested economic reasons will now be inclined, all the more, to cloak their commercial interests in the local flag, whatever that flag may be. Amid "the legions of the anxious and the unemployed," these protectionists will be still more persuasive in doing so.[28] They will do all they can to disguise their selfish economic interests, cloak them in altruism, equate protectionism will patriotism, and make insulation from the competition of foreign trade seem a perfectly logical reaction to the changed nature of the surrounding world. Yet, if we descend worldwide into economic nationalism, if we rely on doses of the false economic cures of "Buy American," "Buy Chinese," "Buy Brazilian," "Buy Indian," and more, then, whatever the current forecasts, the decline in world trade since the onset of COVID-19 will be followed by an even steeper decline in the new pandemic world.

The decline in world trade during the pandemic did not begin with the pandemic. It had gone on for some years since soon after the turn of the century. As Douglas A. Irwin, a leading trade economist, has explained,

As measured by trade flows, this … era of globalization appears to have peaked in 2008 … [T]he world trade to GDP ratio has fallen since the Great Recession. World trade bounced back in 2010 from the sharp blow in 2009, but it has faltered ever since … While trade has tended in the past decades to grow more rapidly than world output, that is no longer the case. Instead, trade growth has been abnormally weak in recent years. World trade volume actually fell in 2019, even though the world economy grew steadily.[29]

By the time COVID-19 showed up, the heyday of ever-increasing international trade seemed just about over.

There were several causes for the decline in the growth of world trade preceding the pandemic. The growth in global supply chains subsided. The global agenda for lowering the remaining tariffs and other barriers to trade through further trade liberalization stalled. The number and scale of commercial conflicts between trading partners increased. The costly absence of much-needed new international trade rules and the inadequacies of the existing rules became more and more evident. The international trade flows that formerly seemed heralds of further increases in global wealth and prosperity now seem harbingers of a lesser world, a less optimistic and thus a less ambitious world, a fragile world of frayed trade rules in which it takes all of what remains of international cooperation to prevent the world from coming apart.

Added to the cause of this pre-pandemic decline in trade growth, too, must be the fact that, individually and collectively, we have been living since the global financial crisis of 2008 in "nervous states" characterized by a growing loss of confidence that our lives and our futures can be improved through more international trade and through other additional engagement with foreign "others" from elsewhere through globalization.[30] Increasingly, the festering feeling of many people in many parts of the world is that such engagement has not helped them; it has harmed them. It has, they feel, cost them jobs; it has shuttered factories and destroyed communities. It has, they think, caused vast increases in inequality. Better, it is felt, to trust only those who are near and not those who are far; better to trust only those who know and share the local ways. Where foreign trade is concerned, this feeling has been expressed in the belief of many that they are not beneficiaries of trade; they are trade's victims.

In recent years, the broad sharing of this feeling of victimization made it easier to blame much of all that went wrong in the world on foreign trade. It made little difference that this feeling about the results of trade was not true. Although the feeling of so many in the United States and throughout the world that they are victims of trade bears little resemblance to the actual reality of the actual results of increased trade, the feeling remains. The reality this feeling describes is a fiction; it exists only in the ether of the Internet and in the excited rallies of the demagogues. Nevertheless, this feeling describes the perception of reality as lived by those who strongly feel it. And, in politics, the perception of reality can often become the true reality at the ballot box.

Then came COVID-19. The arrival of the novel coronavirus accelerated this trend, and the world entered a new and current phase of economic integration that Irwin calls "slowbalization," a time when economic globalization persists but is assailed on all sides by economic and political forces that constrain and oppose it.[31] It is a time when many of the countries in the world are less inclined to engage even in the pretense of trying to reach any kind of new global agreements, including agreements on trade. It is a time when fewer countries in the world are willing to risk any of their dwindled store of political capital on defending international law, including the international law on trade. The new pandemic world is a world in which fewer and fewer are willing to think and act globally. Even in the wake of the pandemic, some as-yet unknown amount of economic globalization may continue in the altered world, albeit at a slower pace, but true international economic integration may not. One casualty of this "slowbalization" could be the WTO.

As a result of the pandemic, some foresee not only a slowing of globalization. They foresee an end to it. They anticipate not more unity but more division in the world. They await a sad but inevitable conclusion to the centuries-long idealistic quest to bring the nations of the world together as one to work together for one humanity. They have long seen the hopeful liberal internationalism that spun such dreams of international cooperation as doomed to fail. From the outset in 1945, they have seen the very notion of the United Nations as a supreme folly. Now they see humanity reawakening to the cruel Hobbesian world of all against all. Now they see the dream of so many of the founders of the WTO and other postwar international economic institutions – the dream of freer trade, a freer flow of capital, and open markets as liberating levers for open, peaceful, and cooperative societies in an open world – as over.[32]

In the new pandemic world, the optimists who have long dreamed these dreams are confronted by doubt. The pessimists who have long sought to dispel them feel vindicated. Global thinker Robert D. Kaplan, who has warned for decades about the smoldering divisions just beneath the veneer of global governance, cautions us that the new pandemic world "is about separating the globe into great-power blocs with their own burgeoning militaries and separate supply chains, about the rise of autocracies, and about social and class divides that have engendered nativism and populism, coupled with middle-class angst in Western democracies. In sum, it is a story about new and re-emerging global divisions, more friendly to pessimists."[33] There is no room in such a dog-eat-dog world for the lofty dreams of liberal internationalism.

One of the most persistent and eloquent of the pessimists, the British contrarian and political philosopher John Gray, predicts the final demise of liberal internationalism. He says,

The era of peak globalization is over. An economic system that relied on worldwide production and long supply chains is morphing into one that will be less interconnected. A way of life driven by unceasing mobility is shuddering to a stop. Our lives are going to be more physically constrained and more virtual than they were. A more fragmented world is coming into being ... Liberal capitalism is bust.[34]

Gray has long dismissed belief in progress as a pipe dream.[35] Now, for him and for the others who share his pessimism, the COVID-19 pandemic has dashed at last the hopes of the optimists for a bountiful and beneficent globalization.

For the pessimists, the bubble has at last burst on the airy illusions of all those who set out to shape new global economic governance for a peaceful and prosperous world at a conference in Bretton Woods, New Hampshire in 1944, toward the end of the Second World War, and of all those all over the world who have strived since then to achieve that abiding goal. Two enduring results of the conference at Bretton Woods were the World Bank and the International Monetary Fund. Another ultimate result of the conference was the General Agreement on Tariffs and Trade – the GATT – which eventually became the WTO. These three postwar Bretton Woods institutions have formed the fundamental international architecture that supports economic globalization.

Who is right about the fate of globalization in the pandemic world? Is it the optimists, who are still as confident as ever that an economically globalized world can become a better, brighter world for all? Or is it the pessimists, who have never thought that globalization could succeed or even last? How many times, and in how many ways, has this same question been posed in so many differing times and in so many differing circumstances in the past, long before the arrival of COVID-19? Human history never repeats itself in precisely the same way, but always there are recurring patterns. There are recurring patterns in history because human nature never changes. The recurrence of these historical patterns is evidence of our immutability as a species. At the same time, and at any given time, the variations in those patterns reveal whether we have displayed the best or the worst in our unchanging nature.

Whether by nature or by nurture, or perhaps by some mix of both, there are always optimists and there are always pessimists among humanity. Optimists always fire hope. Pessimists always pour cold water on hope. Yet, in all times, and in all circumstances, whether we are optimists or pessimists, the future is ours to shape. Who is right about the course of our future in any given time and in any given circumstance, is decided by who prevails then and there in seeing the future clearly enough to seize and shape it. We humans are autonomous agents of our own destiny. If human freedom means anything, it must mean that the future is not predetermined for us. It is always a consequence of the exercise of our free will. It is always open-ended. It is always ours to shape.

From time to time, fate may intervene with a pandemic or a crop failure, with a typhoon or a tornado, or with a rolling tsunami on the ocean tide. But the future depends in no small part on how we respond to such fateful events. In shaping our future, we must strive always to make the future better. Part of what makes us noteworthy as a species is that we can hope that the future will be better. And we are truest to the best in our humanity when we believe not only that we *can* hope, but also that we *must* hope. As the only species on earth that, so far as we now know, can foresee tomorrow, we have an obligation to believe in tomorrow. We have a duty of optimism.[36]

In the world of COVID-19, there is urgent need especially for fulfilling our duty of optimism in trade.

THE CONTINUED NECESSITY OF TRADE LINKS THROUGH THE WTO

The economic assumptions that underlie the rules of the multilateral trading system overseen by the WTO have not been altered in the new pandemic world. WTO rules are founded on basic principles of classical economics. Trade is a division of labor. Nationally and internationally, trade is linked through a division of labor. The production of wealth is multiplied by adding subdivisions to the division of labor. Artificial hindrances to the division of labor – such as import taxes called tariffs and the endlessly evolving host of nontariff trade barriers that amount to taxes – diminish the production of economic wealth. An ever-dividing and subdividing division of labor has for millennia been the wellspring of the flow of ever more human prosperity.

The notion that the division of labor is the foundation of the economy is the first principle of classical economics. It was the first lesson taught by the Scottish economist Adam Smith in the first chapter of his timeless treatise, *The Wealth of Nations*, published in the revolutionary year of 1776. Furthermore, Smith also taught that the division of labor is limited only by "the extent of the market."[37] During the centuries since 1776, and especially during the most recent age of globalization, we have learned over time that the extent of the market, and therefore the extent of the division of labor, can be worldwide. The cause of freeing trade to maximize the international division of labor is Smith's cause. The contemporary world of globalization through international economic integration is in many respects Smith's world.

Early in the nineteenth century, British economist David Ricardo built on Smith's insight about the division of labor when he introduced the counter-intuitive concept of "comparative advantage."[38] Ricardo explained that everyone can benefit from trade. No one needs to be *absolutely* the best at producing anything to benefit from trade. All of us can produce the most and thus profit the most from a division of labor when each of us does what we do *relatively* best when compared to others. Each of us, he explained, possesses a *comparative* advantage over others in the production of some good or service. And, if we each specialize where we have a comparative advantage, then we can all benefit from trade, both domestically and internationally. Ricardo's concept applies to individuals. It applies to firms. It applies also to countries. Thus, in the contemporary terms of game theory, trade is not a "zero-sum" game. When it is pursued consistently with comparative advantage, trade is a "win-win" for all.[39]

Later in the nineteenth century, another British political economist, John Stuart Mill, identified three different kinds of "gains from trade." First, he saw direct economic gains from the specializations in production derived from a division of labor. Trade enables more production through a more efficient allocation of limited resources. In this way, it magnifies overall national income and creates gains for consumers in the form of lower prices and broader choices. Second, Mill saw indirect economic gains in the ways trade makes limited resources more productive by stimulating innovations and enhancing the process of production and overall economic performance. Thus, trade contributes to the growth of productivity by increasing the ratio of what we produce to what goes into production.

Third, Mill contended, "the economical benefits of commerce are surpassed in importance by those of its effects which are intellectual and moral," such as supporting peace and speeding the spread of new ideas and useful knowledge.[40] Like Smith before him, Mill saw trade as a means not only of commerce but also of communication.

There is no specific mention of any of these underlying intellectual antecedents in the General Agreement on Tariffs and Trade of 1947, which was the ultimate trade product of the Bretton Woods conference in 1944 and doubled as a de facto trade institution for nearly half a century. Nor are any of them mentioned in the 1994 treaty that broadened the scope of the trade rules and transformed the GATT into the World Trade Organization in 1995. The WTO treaty is not a free trade agreement. The phrase "free trade" does not appear anywhere in the WTO treaty. Free trade is not mandated by WTO rules. Indeed, much that is entirely inconsistent with free trade is included in WTO rules (such as provisions permitting higher tariffs as economic "safeguards" when a domestic industry is seriously injured from a sudden surge of imports, but there is no allegation of unfair trade).[41] Instead, the WTO is a multilateral legal framework within which trading countries can, if they choose, agree on binding rules that reduce trade barriers, and thus result in freer trade under the rule of law. The WTO is a legal and institutional means of making more open economies and (the ultimate hope of many who made the WTO) more open societies.

The WTO treaty does not anywhere mention the link between trade and freedom. The existence of this liberating link is, however, a tacit but shared assumption of many of those from throughout the world who created and continue to support the WTO. These advocates of both trade and freedom believe that trade is about much more than merely commerce. For them, trade is also about individual freedom and the individual choices that are the essence of freedom. Being free is about being able to make as many personal choices as possible about how to live. The equation between trade and freedom is this: More trade equals more choices equals more opportunities for freedom. More trade does not guarantee more freedom, but it does create more opportunities for the full flourishing of freedom for all humanity. Without more trade, there are fewer opportunities for expanding freedom.[42]

None of the logic of this thinking about trade has been changed by COVID-19. If more human flourishing through more human freedom is the rightful global goal, then more trade links are needed. We must add further subdivisions to the division of labor. We must pursue comparative advantage. We must maximize the direct, indirect, and other gains from trade – even as we work to find better ways to help all of humanity share more fully and more fairly in those gains. If we do not, then we will not have all the personal choices we must have to make the most of our freedom. We will not prosper in the full enjoyment of freedom if we retreat from trade and from international cooperation on trade, and if we reject and undermine the trading rules on which we have long agreed to help govern globalization.[43]

Economists have found it difficult to quantify down to the last penny the benefits of belonging to the WTO-based multilateral trading system. How to determine the precise dollar value of sailing in smooth seas instead of stormy waters? How to express the monetary value of having what the WTO treaty calls "security and predictability" in world trade through global adherence to the rule of law in trade?[44] This said, in the now lost world before the outbreak of COVID-19, decades of successful efforts in freeing trade worldwide through liberalization of trade based on rules forbidding trade discrimination helped multiply global prosperity to unprecedented heights. Nobel Prize–winning economist Michael Spence maintains that,

The GATT was the beginning of the creation of what we now call the global economy . . . Together with cost-reducing technological advances in travel, transportation, and communication, the GATT was an essential catalyst to a second economic revolution, a much more inclusive one in which hundreds of millions of people started to experience the benefits, if also the turbulence, of growth. It is this revolution . . . that is shaping the way we live.[45]

For thousands of years, up until the dawn of the scientific age, the overall growth in human productivity was almost nil. Annual global rates of growth were consistently exceedingly small. Then new scientific discoveries and, along with them, new technologies began to change the world. The average global rate of growth annually was 0.3 percent from 1500 to 1820; 1.6 percent from 1820 to 1950; and 3.9 percent from 1950 to near the end of the twentieth century.[46] Few economists would contest the assertion that the tripling of the annual rate of global growth in the decades following the end of the Second World War was due in no small part to the lower barriers to trade and the more open economies in the growing and evolving multilateral trading system.

The fulfillment of, first, GATT, and now, WTO obligations, has led to direct and indirect advances for all the countries that are participants in the system. Directly, lower barriers to trade have increased market access and thus increased the volume of trade. This has, in turn, increased the gains from trade and, thus, the potential for more shared prosperity. Indirectly, the need to comply with agreed tariff cuts, transparency, nondiscrimination, and other international trade obligations has led to domestic reforms that have made national economies more open and, thus, more productive. One economic study has concluded, "Taking these (direct and indirect) effects into account suggests that, on average, GATT/WTO membership has increased trade between Members by 171% and trade between member and non-member countries by about 88%."[47]

According to Australian trade economist Kym Anderson, "While it remains difficult to attribute reforms directly to the GATT/WTO, the overall body of evidence . . . supports the economic professionals' consensus that this institution has contributed substantially to global economic welfare."[48] After reviewing all of the empirical studies by economists throughout the world on the economic impact of membership in the WTO, Anderson summarized succinctly the broad accomplishments of the WTO, which range beyond the economic: "[T]he lowering of trade distortions generally (although not in every case) has contributed to global economic welfare through, for example, improved efficiency of resource use, lower consumer prices, often more employment, faster economic growth, more sustainable development, nearly always less global income inequality and poverty and less conflict within and between nations."[49] This speaks to the value of the WTO as a global "public good" – a good that serves all of human society.

Although it is difficult to draw a straight line connecting the WTO through cause and effect to all of the worldwide economic advances between 1995 and the arrival of the novel coronavirus at the end of 2019, the increases in world trade during most of that time were unprecedented. The dollar value of world trade nearly quadrupled. The real volume of world trade expanded nearly threefold – 2.7 times. Average tariffs in the world were cut nearly in half, from 10.5 percent to 6.4 percent. During those same twenty-five years, the percentage of humanity living in extreme poverty fell from about one-third to less than 10 percent, not least due to the opening of the Chinese, Indian, and other rapidly growing developing country economies to the wider world, and to the resulting freer trade in the rules-based multilateral trading system.[50]

Consider the gains of trade under GATT and WTO rules of just one country, the United States. A recent study prepared for the Business Roundtable concluded that international trade supports nearly 39 million American jobs. One in every five American jobs is linked to imports and exports of goods and services. In the twenty-five years following the establishment of the WTO, trade-dependent jobs in the United States grew more than four times as fast as US jobs generally. Every one of the fifty US states realized net job gains that can be directly attributed to trade.[51] In another trade study, economists at the Peterson Institute for International Economics estimated "that the payoff to the United States from trade expansion – stemming from policy liberalization and improved transportation and communications technology – from 1950 to 2016 (was) roughly $2.1 trillion ... (and) that US GDP per capita and GDP per household accordingly increased by $7,014 and $18,131, respectively."[52] Further, "disproportionate gains probably accrue(d) to poorer households."[53]

The United States, of course, is far from the only country that has profited from participating in the WTO-based multilateral trading system. For Americans, though, it is worth noting that, according to a 2019 study by the Bertelsmann Foundation in Germany, membership in the WTO system has boosted annual US GDP by about $87 billion in the twenty-five years since the establishment of the WTO – *more than any other country*.[54] China was second in the annual benefits received from WTO membership, with about $85.5 billion, and Germany was third, with about $66 billion. Generally, countries, whatever their stage of development, have benefited from their participation in the rule-based multilateral trading system in rough equivalence with their percentage share of world trade.[55] Proportionately, no one country has benefited much more than any other, although it is certainly true that many developing countries could benefit more if they were more fully integrated into world trade.

In furthering transparency and facilitating trade liberalization, WTO rules promote openness. They do so because more openness to the world economy, including through trade, is necessary for economic growth and economic competitiveness. History demonstrates that no country has ever grown – *and continued to grow over time* – without opening economically to the wider world.[56] One common characteristic of all the high-growth economies in the past half-century has been that "[t]hey fully exploited the global economy."[57] Their "sustained growth became feasible only because the world economy became more open and more tightly integrated."[58] Over time, a country closed to the wider world will shrink and sink economically.

The need for rules that promote openness is borne out by the global experience with the most common of the many restrictions on trade – tariffs. In 2018, the International Monetary Fund studied the economic statistics from 151 countries over the course of more than half a century (from 1963 through 2014) and concluded that "tariff increases lead, in the medium term, to economically and statistically significant declines in domestic output and productivity as well as more unemployment and higher inequality."[59] Tariffs are popular with all of those who propose to put their own country "first" through economic nationalism; but, for any country, for all countries, imposing and raising tariffs lowers competitiveness.

Yet, while trade is necessary, an openness to trade is not enough. An increased openness to more trade and freer trade internationally must be matched domestically by actions that open the way for more free people to share fully in the gains of trade. Openness alone does not lead to success. "The competitiveness of economies in an integrated world [is determined by] how well they convert the potential created by access to global markets into opportunities for their ...

people."[60] The emphasis must be on creating the human capital of human capabilities.[61] Without domestic actions that increase the opportunities for individuals to become better prepared to compete, the gains derived from more and freer trade will be fewer, and those gains will be enjoyed by fewer people. The "distributive effects" from the trade gains – who gets them and how much of them they get – will be unfair. All too often, in America and elsewhere, this is precisely what has happened so far in this century.[62]

Open economies are enablers of growth. Closed economies decline and die. Competitiveness can only be maximized if there is openness.[63] The best path to competitiveness will vary from country to country with varying circumstances. Yet the basic ingredients of competitiveness are everywhere much the same. These ingredients include free trade, free investment, supportive laws and institutions that enable free and open markets, and, to glue it all together, the rule of law. Equally essential are financial stability and fiscal solvency. What is more, the basic ingredients of competitiveness everywhere include maximizing the potential gains from trade and from other economic endeavor – and thus the potential for the enjoyment of individual human freedom – by finding and combining the right mix of market and government actions.

The right line must be drawn everywhere between private and public – between markets and governments – between the necessity to preserve personal liberty and the necessity also to empower it. In always striving to find this right line, we must provide: innovative lifelong education for both work and citizenship, beginning with essential and cost-saving investments in early childhood development; practical, skills-based training and retraining and other forms of tested and proven unemployment and other transitional assistance such as wage insurance or refundable tax credits for workers; modern and environmentally friendly roads, transit systems, water systems, bridges, seaports, airports, spaceports, communications grids, power grids, and all other kinds of sustainable infrastructure; strong protections for civil rights and worker rights; a fair, limited, and broadly shared tax base; and a tax structure that does not undermine public trust by resulting in an obscene extent of income inequality.

This right line of a mixed public/private economy must be drawn also while providing ease of labor mobility; accessible and affordable universal health care; abundant basic scientific research and development; an ample and reliable social safety net; a sufficient but not counterproductive minimum wage; an enabling economic atmosphere that supports individual and cooperative initiative, incentive, and enterprise; antitrust laws that guard against economic monopolies and other predatory economic practices by assuring market competition; effective protection and preservation of the environment; and all else that is necessary to help make it possible for each and all to make the most of the opening of new economic opportunities through an open economy in an open society.

Yet no country can afford or provide the needed extent of all these domestic benefits if it does not have an open economy. No country can seize its fair share of the future if it clings stubbornly to a past that no longer exists. One essential ingredient of sustaining and strengthening competitiveness is thus an openness to economic change. The embrace of freedom demands a willingness to undergo "the ordeal of change" for the sake of a better future.[64] For any individual, any enterprise, or any country to be competitive in shaping such a future, there must be a firm and unwavering understanding that, as Spence has put it, "Sustained growth and structural change go hand in hand."[65] To be successful in generating economic growth, free markets must be free, if need be, to destroy the old so as to create the new.

The older sectors of an economy will always resist the "creative destruction" of capitalism.[66] They will resist the logic of comparative advantage – which teaches us that we prosper most when we specialize in producing what we produce relatively better than others. (Note the word "*relatively*" here – the oft-omitted core of the concept.) Those who derive power and profit from the way things are, will seek always to forestall the new way things could be. Those who own and control the less competitive parts of an economy, will resist yielding to the arrival of the new, and they will often seek to survive by securing the subsidizing support and other favoritism of government through profit-making from the largesse of political influence – through the "rent seeking" of unearned profits from "crony capitalism."

In the timeless words of Franklin Roosevelt in 1932, "The same man who tells us that he does not want to see the government interfere with business . . . is the first to go to the White House and ask the government for a prohibitive tariff on his product."[67] What was true then is true now. Entrenched economic interests that are no longer internationally competitive will do all they can to try to preserve their entrenchment while denying to themselves the incentivizing benefits of the competition offered by imports, and while denying to others the new opportunities that should be theirs to share in the gains from more trade and more investment. All of the other workers and the firms engaged in the broader economy will pay the opportunity costs of this protection of the old at the expense of the new through higher costs, higher taxes, lost innovation, and lost opportunities for jobs with a future.

In the United States, this was clearly illustrated in recent years by the costs of the unilateral 25 percent tariffs on imports of steel imposed by President Trump. US steel makers increased production to some extent after the tariffs were applied, largely because of increased domestic demand for steel. They did not, however, increase the number of steel workers. Instead, steel makers produced more steel from the modern and highly efficient mini-mills with electric-arc furnaces that require fewer workers than the older blast furnaces that date back to the fourteenth century.[68] Just 200 jobs were created in the US steel industry during the first year of the steel tariffs. The workers did not benefit much from the tariffs. Who did? As the editorial writers of the *Wall Street Journal* noted, the steel companies "are making more money as they benefit from their ability to raise prices in a protected market."[69] Trump's unilateral steel tariffs are "crony capitalism" in action.

Part of being competitive is being willing to compete. The spur of competition – both foreign and domestic – is necessary to the ongoing process of structural change. Growth involves a structural transformation that "is the result of competitive pressure."[70] Without the incentives from the pressures of competition, including open foreign competition, there will be less growth. Thus, "[g]overnments committed to growth must … liberalize product markets, allowing new, more productive firms to enter and obsolete firms to exit. They must also create room to maneuver in the labor market, so that new industries can quickly create jobs and workers can move freely to fill them."[71] Trying to protect and preserve jobs in uncompetitive sectors of the economy by insulating them from competition, Spence tells us, "is the functional equivalent of throwing sand in the gears of an otherwise well-oiled machine. It will negatively impact productivity and incomes – and, eventually, growth."[72]

As this image illustrates, comparative advantage "shifts continuously over time, in parallel with investment, human capital acquisition, and, ultimately, with prices and wages."[73] Competitiveness is everywhere and always about comparative advantage. To remain competitive, we must be willing to shift as comparative advantage shifts.[74] Some jobs will inevitably be lost along the way in these shifts because of the competition that comes from trade, both foreign and domestic. Yet, as Spence asserts, "The main job of government is to facilitate structural change by investing in human capital, protecting people in the transitions through income support and access to basic services, and then to let the market forces and investment incentives work."[75] Putting all this in one sentence, the best strategy to increase competitiveness is to protect people, not specific jobs. Strengthening international trade links helps implement this best strategy, and trade links are best strengthened through the multilateral trade framework called the WTO.

LINKS TO NATURE AND SUSTAINABLE DEVELOPMENT

Although COVID-19 has not changed our basic economic assumptions about the division of labor that is trade, the novel coronavirus has provided us with an all too revealing C-scan of how trade and other dimensions of the economy are linked, intricately and inextricably, to the environment, which contains the economy. The pandemic is not a punishment imposed (much as we may deserve it) by a judgmental Providence. Nor is it a random act of an indifferent nature. More accurately, the pandemic is nature's unconscious and unfeeling revenge for the heedless actions of humanity. As one global group of experts has explained, "Pandemics have their origins in diverse microbes carried by animal reservoirs, but their emergence is entirely driven by human activities."[76] The outbreak and spread of COVID-19 are linked directly to the human destruction of nature,[77] and this wanton destruction is linked in part to trade, both legal and illegal.

COVID-19 is only one of an untold number of zoonotic diseases that can potentially jump from animals to humans. Scientists report that "[a]n estimated 1.7 million currently undiscovered viruses are thought to exist in mammal and avian hosts. Of these, 631,000–827,000 could have the ability to infect humans."[78] Rats, bats, monkeys, and civets are among the animal species that host most of the known zoonotic viruses that can leap to humans. The likelihood of this lethal leap from these and other animal species is increasing because, throughout the world, "[h]uman activities are destroying, degrading, and fragmenting natural areas at an unprecedented rate. Habitat destruction and biodiversity loss are contributing to the rise in new diseases by undercutting the ability of ecosystems to reduce and regulate the risk of a pathogen spreading among wildlife."[79]

Thomas Lovejoy, the acclaimed conservation biologist who coined the phrase "biological diversity," has lamented that the rapid spread of COVID-19 is "the consequence of our persistent and excessive intrusion in nature and the vast illegal wildlife trade ... Habitat loss and overexploitation of wildlife – compounded by climate change – are driving factors in the disease boom."[80] Climate scientist Johan Rockstrom, who helped invent the notion of "planetary boundaries," has explained that, when we destroy more natural habitats and also hunt for more wildlife in what remains of those habitats, "the natural balance of species collapses due to loss of top predators and other iconic species, leading to an abundance of more generalized species adapted to live in human-dominated habitats."[81] This proximity promotes the spread of zoonotic diseases.

The human origins of COVID-19 and other zoonotic diseases have been summarized well by science writer Ferris Jabr: "Between 60 and 75 percent of emerging infectious diseases in humans come from other animals," including "rabies, Lyme, anthrax, mad cow disease, SARS, Ebola, West Nile, Zika," and now the novel coronavirus COVID-19.[82] He adds,

Zoonotic pathogens do not typically seek us out nor do they stumble onto us by pure coincidence. When diseases move from animals to humans, and vice versa, it is usually because we have reconfigured our shared ecosystems in ways that make the transition more likely. Deforestation, mining, intensive agriculture and urban sprawl destroy natural habitats, forcing wild creatures to venture into human communities. Excessive hunting, trade and consumption of wildlife significantly increase the probability of cross-species infection. Modern transportation can disperse dangerous microbes across the world in a matter of hours ... We drain the world's biological basins of the diversity that would ordinarily keep contagions in check. Other animals' diseases have not so much leapt onto us as flowed into us through channels we have supplied.[83]

Wildlife trade is frequently a source of human infection. The infection often occurs in the "wet" markets where much of such trade occurs, such as the Huanan market in Wuhan on which so much attention was centered in the early days of the COVID-19 pandemic. In these markets, human and disease-infected wild animals mingle in ways they never would otherwise. As Jabr has put it,

The wildlife trade is an ecological aberration: It thrusts species that would otherwise never meet into strained intimacy. Because captive animals are often undernourished and stressed, they are more susceptible to infection. When they are butchered on the spot, which happens in certain live-animal markets, their bespattered fluids potentially expose other animals as well as humans. It's an unparalleled crossroads for infectious pathogens.[84]

Various wildlife species are sold in these markets, mostly as sources of traditional medicines and exotic meat. But they can also be sources of human disease and death.

Like the Huanan market in Wuhan, these wildlife markets are found in many places in Central and South China. Likewise, they are found in many other places in Southeast Asia and Central Africa. And, as we have seen with COVID-19, new viruses can quickly spread from wildlife markets to humans and then to multiples of other humans, at first near and soon far. So long as we do little to address these and other sources of contagion, new zoonotic diseases are likely to spread. COVID-19 is the latest. It will not be the last. As one group of scientists has warned, the next plague from the next pandemic could potentially be "even more disruptive and lethal than Covid-19."[85]

Plagues are not new in the world.[86] The great Athenian statesman Pericles died during a plague that devastated Athens during the Peloponnesian War. Plagues slaughtered untold millions in the Rome of the Antonine emperors during the second century and the Byzantium of the emperor Justinian in the sixth century of the Common Era. The Black Death of the bubonic plague killed between 75 and 200 million people in Eurasia and North Africa in the fourteenth century. A renewed outbreak, the great plague of London, killed another 75,000 people in the seventeenth century. Fifty million people died worldwide from the Spanish Flu of 1918 and 1919 – far more than the 20 million deaths during the unprecedented carnage of the First World War. About 33 million people worldwide have died thus far from the HIV/AIDS epidemic that began in the Congo in the 1920s and was first recognized in the United States in the 1980s.[87] But plagues have never occurred previously in a world as thoroughly globalized as ours has become – a world in which our own actions are more likely than ever before to bring plagues upon us.

Contained as we humans are within the environment, we are likewise contained within the consequences of what we do to the environment. We are a part of all that surrounds us. All we do to all that surrounds us, we do also to ourselves. And yet, until now, we have long persisted in acting as if we, as a singular species, are a world unto our own, distinct from all the rest of nature. In our overweening pride, we have placed humanity alone on a pedestal, above all else, in control of all else, and untouched by all else. Amazingly, up until the advent of COVID-19, many of us extended this hubristic thinking even to public health, despite centuries of scientific evidence to the contrary. Health, we thought, came from exercise at the gym. Medicine, we believed, came from bottles.

But "[n]othing exists independent of the natural world."[88] And that includes us. Aaron Bernstein of Harvard University puts this point bluntly: "We swim in a common germ pool with other animals. If we stretch the fabric of life too far, things pop out of that germ pool and they land on us."[89] As disease ecologist Jonathan Epstein has explained, "We need to stop looking at people in a vacuum. Everything we do to disrupt natural systems, to manipulate the environment around us, influences our own health. We haven't thought about that carefully enough."[90] Nor have we thought carefully enough about all of the many other ways in which our occasionally noble, always striving, but ever-arrogant, species lives, not alone unto itself, and not within a vacuum, but, rather, within the ever-present constraints of the natural environment.

The human economy is one of those ways. The economy is a collective manifestation of humans working together in a shared effort to survive, thrive, and perpetuate ourselves as a sentient species. The economy is a way of paying for dinner this evening. It is a way of paying next month's bills. But, above all else, it is a means of preserving and passing on the human genetic code through human endurance and human flourishing. Looking at people in a vacuum, much of humanity has long tended to think of the environment as separate and distinct from the economic task. Now, in the pandemic world, looking at people anew as an embedded part of the natural world that surrounds us, we are impelled to see that the economy is enveloped by the environment. It is contained within it. The economy and the environment are not separate and distinct. They are one. They have always been one. They will always be one. We must internalize this basic, essential insight into all that we do, whether it be in fighting the pandemic, in furthering trade, or in forging the best links for accomplishing the global goals on which we have agreed for what we have described as "sustainable development."[91]

As a concept, "sustainable development" has been centuries in the making. Often called simply "sustainability," it has slowly emerged along with the slow awakening of humanity to the realization that human social and economic goals are not only linked to each other. The two are also unavoidably linked to the environment.[92] Indeed, there is a widespread but mistaken popular assumption that the idea of "sustainability" is exclusively about the environment. This, though, is not so. Sustainable development is holistic. It is an exercise in what might rightly be described as "systems thinking"; for it sees the world as an interrelated and mutually reinforcing system, and it sees humanity as one part of that system.[93] In this view, what the United Nations describes as the "three dimensions" of sustainable development – social, economic, and environmental – are interlinked. Each of these "three dimensions" is linked in ways that reinforce the other two. And each of the three must therefore be approached "in a balanced and integrated manner" to achieve "sustainable development."[94]

The most famous definition of "sustainable development" is in the 1987 report of the United Nations Commission on Environment and Development entitled "Our Common Future," commonly known as the Brundtland Report, after Gro Harlem Brundtland, the commission's chairwoman and the former three-time prime minister of Norway.[95] "Sustainable development" was famously defined in the Brundtland Report as "development that meets the needs of the present without compromising the ability of future generations to meet their own needs."[96] It was then explained in the report that the definition of sustainable development "contains within it two key concepts: the concept of 'needs,' in particular the essential needs of the world's poor, to which overriding priority should be given; and the idea of limitations imposed by the state of technology and social organization on the environment's ability to meet present and future needs."[97] Thus, the two linked "key concepts" of economic needs and environmental limits are entwined within the definition of "sustainable development" and within all that is done toward that end.

With this linked notion of "sustainable development" as their beckoning lodestar, in September 2015, 193 members of the United Nations adopted by consensus a declaration of their common goals to be accomplished by the year 2030 entitled "Transforming Our World: The 2030 Agenda for Sustainable Development." This document is not a treaty. It is not enforceable international law. Instead, it is an aspirational statement endorsed by all the members of the United Nations of where they all wish to go in furthering human flourishing. The global goals set out in the UN agenda are generally known as the "Sustainable Development Goals," or, in the acronymic UN argot, the "SDGs."[98] They are described in the UN 2030 agenda as "integrated and indivisible, global in nature and universally applicable," and as balancing "the three dimensions of sustainable development."[99] There are seventeen goals. There are 169 associated targets for achieving them. The goals are:

- Goal 1. End poverty in all its forms everywhere.
- Goal 2. End hunger, achieve food security and improved nutrition, and promote sustainable agriculture.
- Goal 3. Ensure healthy lives and promote well-being for all at all ages.
- Goal 4. Ensure inclusive and equitable quality education and promote lifelong learning opportunities for all.
- Goal 5. Achieve gender equality and empower all women and girls.
- Goal 6. Ensure availability and sustainable management of water and sanitation for all.
- Goal 7. Ensure access to affordable, reliable, sustainable and modern energy for all.
- Goal 8. Promote sustained, inclusive, and sustainable economic growth, full and productive employment and decent work for all.
- Goal 9. Build resilient infrastructure, promote inclusive and sustainable industrialization, and foster innovation.

- Goal 10. Reduce inequality within and among countries.
- Goal 11. Make cities and human settlements inclusive, safe, resilient, and sustainable.
- Goal 12. Ensure sustainable consumption and production patterns.
- Goal 13. Take urgent action to combat climate change and its impacts.[100]
- Goal 14. Conserve and sustainably use the oceans, seas, and marine resources for sustainable development.
- Goal 15. Protect, restore, and promote sustainable use of terrestrial ecosystems; sustainably manage forests; combat desertification; halt and reverse land degradation; and halt biodiversity loss.
- Goal 16. Promote peaceful and inclusive societies for sustainable development; provide access to justice for all; and build effective, accountable and inclusive institutions at all levels.
- Goal 17. Strengthen the means of implementation and revitalize the global partnership for sustainable development.

The members of the United Nations have agreed to achieve all seventeen of these ambitious goals by 2030. They have not agreed how to achieve them. The SDGs do not say how to achieve them. The intent is to "end poverty" and "end hunger." How this will be done is not specified. It is left to sovereign states to accomplish these worthy ends in their own chosen fashion. The SDGs do contemplate various means of implementation, such as, for example, overseas development assistance, international public finance, voluntary public reporting, and annual assessments in global gatherings at the United Nations. However, in the necessary process of "transforming our world," the members of the United Nations have together clearly acknowledged that "each country has primary responsibility for its own economic and social development."[101] Even in a world greatly transformed by globalization, national sovereignty still holds sway in shaping the course of a new kind of globalization as envisaged in the Sustainable Development Goals.

In bold words, the 193 countries that agreed to the SDGs stated,

We envisage a world free of poverty, hunger, disease and want, where all life can thrive. We envisage a world free of fear and violence ... We envisage a world of universal respect for human rights and human dignity, the rule of law, justice, equality, and non-discrimination ... We envisage a world in which every country enjoys sustained, inclusive and sustainable economic growth and decent work for all ... One in which humanity lives in harmony with nature and in which wildlife and other living species are protected.[102]

And this is only part of their lofty vision for 2030. Yet, more than seventy-five years after the establishment of the United Nations, it remains clear that the principal agent for achieving all that is promised in the SDGs remains the sovereign nation-state. International cooperation is sought. International cooperation is stressed as essential. Yet international cooperation is in no way mandated.

To spur cooperation for accomplishing the SDGs, the United Nations has established a "High-Level Political Forum on Sustainable Development" to monitor and mobilize continued support for the seventeen goals as a central part of the UN 2030 agenda. This forum has met annually since 2016 and, every four years, convenes as a meeting of heads of state. It is "voluntary and country-led" and features "reviews at regional and global levels" of national progress toward sustainable development.[103] At the meeting in New York in July 2020, forty-seven countries submitted "voluntary national reviews."[104] As COVID-19 spread, the vast majority of the countries that agreed to the Sustainable Development Goals in 2015 did not submit a self-review in 2020. Among them was the United States, which, while refraining from going so far as to renounce the SDGs, largely stopped participating in the SDG effort following the election of Donald Trump as president of the United States in 2016. In the first months that followed Joe Biden's inauguration to succeed him in January 2021, there was widespread expectation that the United States would once again become active in support of the Sustainable Development Goals. Without invoking them, Biden's initial legislative proposals seemed to echo the goals and the targets of the SDGs.

The United Nations has acknowledged that, even before the pandemic, "progress remained uneven" and "we were not on track" to achieve the Sustainable Development Goals by the target date of 2030.[105] As the United Nations Secretary-General Antonio Guterres has explained,

Some gains were visible: the share of children and youth out of school had fallen; the incidence of many communicable diseases was in decline; access to safely managed drinking water had been improved; and women's representation in leadership roles was increasing. At the same time, the number of people suffering from food insecurity was on the rise, the natural environment continued to deteriorate at an alarming rate, and dramatic levels of inequality persisted in all regions. Change was still not happening at the speed or scale required.[106]

Then, suddenly, at the beginning of 2020, the "modest progress of recent years" was erased.[107] In the space of a few weeks, the positive changes that had been happening were abruptly reversed, and the seventeen goals established in the SDGs seemed vastly farther away from any hope of accomplishment. Business leader Paul Polman, a global champion of the SDGs, has gone so far as to lament that "[t]he pandemic has put us back probably 20–30 years on the sustainable development goals."[108] Undaunted, the secretary-general has maintained that, "Far from undermining the case for the SDGs, the root cause and uneven impacts of COVID-19 demonstrate precisely why we need the" Sustainable Development Goals and the international agreements aimed at implementing them.[109] Other global leaders in the effort to achieve the SDGs have echoed him, insisting that

what we cannot afford to do, even in these crucial times, is shift resources away from crucial SDG actions. The response to the pandemic cannot be de-linked from the

SDGs ... After all, in a crisis we are only as strong as the weakest link. This is what the Sustainable Development Goals ... the global blueprint to end poverty, protect our planet and ensure prosperity, are all about.[110]

At the same time, some supporters of the Sustainable Development Goals have suggested that, in the wake of the pandemic, it may be time to "reset" the SDGs for the pandemic world by organizing a framework for fulfilling them.[111] From the outset, there has been uncertainty among the advocates of sustainable development about precisely how to go about organizing the SDGs to be best able to pursue them. In 2019, already concerned about the unwieldy structure of seventeen goals and 169 targets, a group of scientists advising the UN suggested reframing the SDGs through a half dozen categories called "entry points," while still endeavoring to achieve them all.[112] Also in 2019, leaders of the worldwide Sustainable Development Solutions Network set up by the UN to help spur local and national actions to achieve the SGS, proposed grouping the seventeen goals through six "transformations" in governance.[113] The SDSN proposal built on the similar proposal in 2018 by sixty authors and some 100 global experts engaged in the "World in 2050 Initiative" of the International Institute for Applied Systems Analysis, which was undertaken to provide scientific foundations for the 2030 agenda.[114]

Now, in the new world of the pandemic, some supporters of sustainable development have called for more than merely a reframing of the Sustainable Development Goals. They contend that COVID-19 makes the case for more fundamental thinking than is reflected in the SDGs. Environmental scientists Robin Naidoo and Brendan Fisher contend that the very premises of the SDGs have been undermined, and that, as a result, "Rosy hopes that globalization and economic growth would bankroll waves of green investment and development are no longer realistic ... The success of the SDGs depends on two big assumptions: sustained economic growth and globalization. COVID-19 has torn these to shreds."[115] Their alternatives? Foremost among them is: "Decouple development and growth"; that is, look at growth in a new and sustainable way.[116] In theirs and similar proposals, Ruchir Sharma's call for "a new, more focused approach to government intervention" as a means of making capitalism work again finds echoes in the call of many supporters of sustainable development for a "green recovery."[117]

LINKS TO A GREEN RECOVERY

In the new pandemic world, climate change continues to quicken. The industrial age began in the eighteenth century and greatly accelerated with James Watt's improvements in the steam engine. The steam engine was powered by the stored solar energy in coal, a fossil fuel. Since then, the advance of human civilization has largely been powered by fossil fuels, with carbon dioxide emissions piling up in the Earth's atmosphere, where they can linger for hundreds, if not thousands, of years. During Watt's time, global average carbon dioxide concentrations in the atmosphere were about 280 parts per million. In April 2021, CO_2 levels in the atmosphere were 420 parts per million – the highest total in human history.[118] This was despite the drop in carbon emissions during the previous year due to the reduced economic activity from the pandemic.[119]

There is more carbon dioxide in the atmosphere now than at any time in the past three million years.[120] Nobel Prize–winning economist Joseph Stiglitz has explained what this means for us: "As the atmospheric concentration of carbon increases, we are entering uncharted territory. Not since the dawn of humanity has there been anything like this. The models use the 'best estimate' of impacts, but as we learn more about climate change these best estimates keep getting revised, and, typically, in only one direction – more damage and sooner than expected."[121] According to James Hansen, the former NASA climate scientist who first brought the challenge of climate change to the attention of the Congress of the United States in the 1980s, "If humanity wishes to preserve a planet similar to that on which civilization developed and to which life on Earth is adapted ... CO_2 will need to be reduced ... to at most 350 ppm."[122]

The more carbon dioxide and other greenhouse gases there are in the atmosphere, the warmer the planet. Because of man-made alterations in the climate, the average temperature of the planet has already increased 1.2 degrees Celsius (nearly 2.2 degrees Fahrenheit) since 1880.[123] With the broadening scope of global industrial growth, two-thirds of this warming has occurred since 1975.[124] By the end of this century, in the year 2100, remedial climate mitigation and adaptation policies currently in place throughout the world are projected to reduce anticipated carbon dioxide and other greenhouse gas emissions sufficiently to limit global warming to about 3 degrees Celsius (about 5.4 degrees Fahrenheit) above preindustrial levels.[125] But that is all.

Climate scientists warn that this extent of warming would significantly exceed the amount of warming that can occur without imposing devastating harms on humanity and all else on the Earth.[126] Climatologists on the intergovernmental panel advising the United Nations on climate change tell us, "Continued emission of greenhouse gases will cause further warming and long-lasting changes in all components of the climate system, increasing the likelihood of severe, pervasive and irreversible impacts on people and ecosystems."[127] They predict with "high confidence" that, "Without additional mitigation efforts beyond those in place today, and even with adaptation, warming by the end of the 21st century will lead to high to very high risk of severe and irreversible impacts globally."[128] They add, ominously, that, "The risks of abrupt or irreversible changes increase as the magnitude of warming increases."[129]

Unless more changes – vastly more ambitious changes – are made now to curb global warming, the Earth's climate only a few decades from now will differ markedly from what it is today. To stabilize climate change, we must reduce net emissions of carbon dioxide to zero, and we must start yesterday;

for, as the World Bank has stated, "As long as we emit more than nature can absorb in its sinks (oceans, forests, and other vegetation), concentrations of CO_2 in the atmosphere will keep rising, and the planet will keep warming. And the decisions we make now will determine the planet's climate for centuries."[130]

We have done this to ourselves. We have denied the reality of climate change. We have delayed collective action on climate change for decades since we first became aware of the harm we have been doing to the climate. We have been content with hesitant and halting measures against climate change when we should have come together long ago to act boldly together in confronting the most serious threat in history to the future of humanity. The sad truth is, three decades on from the hopeful start of the human effort to fight climate change at the Earth Summit in Rio de Janeiro in 1992, so far not much has been accomplished to free humanity from our overwhelming dependence on fossil fuels for the energy that powers our economic production and perpetuates our civilization. For all the strides that have been made in recent years in developing renewable forms of energy, the source of more than 80 percent of global energy consumption remains oil, coal, or natural gas – the fossil fuels that have enabled human ingenuity to forge the transformations of the industrial revolution, but at a very high price.[131]

Closing in on nearly three centuries since the human creation of an economy based on carbon-fueled industrial production, we now know that the carbon and other emissions from the same fossil fuels that fired so many advances in human civilization are threatening to undermine and undo it by causing an increasingly rapid change in the climate of the planet. Motivated by the mounting scientific evidence of the reality and the impacts of climate change, the world has labored for several frustrating decades to engage in collective action. After nearly a quarter of a century of negotiations, 195 countries at long last concluded the Paris climate agreement in December 2015, three months after the global agreement on the Sustainable Development Goals.

The Paris climate agreement is only a start. Still, long years in coming, it is, at least, a start. The agreement mainly provides an international legal architecture to facilitate reducing carbon dioxide and other greenhouse gas emissions. It is legally binding; however, it is not an agreement containing many binding legal obligations. Apart from some reporting requirements, it does not mandate much at all. Notably, the Paris accord is not a "top-down" agreement that mandates across-the-board emissions cuts. It does not require countries to cut their carbon dioxide and other greenhouse gas emissions. It is, instead, a "bottom-up" agreement that provides a global legal framework in which countries can pledge to make such cuts voluntarily. The shared hope of the global climate negotiators has been that, in lieu of mandated emissions cuts, for which there is scant political support, particularly among major emitters, mutual peer pressure will, over time, encourage countries to ratchet up their ambitions for such cuts.[132]

In the Paris Agreement, the 195 countries announced as their ambition: "holding the increase in the global average temperature to well below 2C above pre-industrial levels and pursuing efforts to limit the temperature increase to 1.5C above pre-industrial levels."[133] Scientists say that holding the average temperature rise to no more than 2C is necessary to avoid the worst ravages of climate change. Initial voluntary national pledges made under the Paris Agreement fell far short of putting the world on a path to achieve either of these goals.[134] The United Nations Environment Programme warned in November 2019, not long before the outbreak of the novel coronavirus, that "even if all current unconditional commitments under the Paris Agreement are implemented, temperatures are expected to rise by 3.2C (by 2100)."[135] UNEP concluded that "[c]ollective ambition must increase more than fivefold over current levels to deliver the cuts needed over the next decade for the 1.5C goal."[136] To achieve this goal, global greenhouse gas emissions would need to fall by 7.6 percent each year between 2020 and 2030.[137]

The focus of UNEP on holding global warming to 1.5C instead of the less ambitious Paris goal of 2C was no doubt inspired by a special report in October 2018 in which the Intergovernmental Panel on Climate Change – the worldwide group of climate scientists that advise the United Nations – stressed that limiting warming to 1.5C (2.7 degrees Fahrenheit) by 2100 would be much safer than limiting it to 2C (3.6 degrees Fahrenheit).[138] "Climate-related risks to health, livelihoods, food security, water supply, human security, and economic growth are projected to increase with global warming of 1.5C and increase further with 2C," the climate scientists reported.[139] Global warming, they predicted, was likely to reach 1.5C between 2030 and 2052 at the current rate of temperature rise.[140] And the warming from human emissions "from the pre-industrial period to the present will persist for centuries to millennia and will continue to cause further long-term changes in the climate system."[141]

Due to decades of impasse and inaction, the opportunity to reverse global warming has passed. Our past carbon emissions are already in the atmosphere, where they will linger for centuries, and for perhaps as long as a thousand years.[142] Yet, the IPCC climate scientists stressed in their special report, limiting warming to 1.5C instead of 2C would have "clear and considerable benefits, such as significantly reducing the risks of water scarcity, ill-health, food insecurity, flood and drought, extreme heat, tropical cyclones, biodiversity loss, and sea level rise."[143] At 1.5C instead of 2C in warming, ten million fewer people could be at risk from sea level rise. The percentage of the world population exposed to water stress could be cut in half. The loss of 1.5 million tons of global annual catch for marine fisheries could be avoided. From 10 to 30 percent of coral reefs could be saved.[144] Global food scarcity would be less. Hundreds of millions of people, especially in poorer countries, would be at less risk of climate-related poverty. However, to accomplish these desirable ends by limiting global warming to 1.5C, the scientists explained, global greenhouse gas emissions would need to be reduced by 45 percent from 2010 levels by 2030, and by 100 percent – net zero – by 2050.[145]

What turned out to be the year of the pandemic, 2020, was supposed to be a turning point toward much more ambitious climate action. Under the Paris Agreement, countries pledged to submit new and updated voluntary national climate pledges by 2020.[146] For this reason, since the conclusion of the climate agreement in Paris in 2015, climate activists had been looking ahead to the global climate summit planned for 2020. The annual summit held in Madrid in December 2019 – COP25 – occurred just as the novel coronavirus began to make its way through Wuhan. COP25 was supposed to set the stage for the submission at COP26 in 2020 of much more ambitious national climate pledges, as envisaged in the Paris climate agreement. But little was achieved in Madrid,[147] and, amid the pandemic, the climate talks planned for COP26 in Glasgow were postponed until November 2021.[148]

Left in a negotiating limbo, climate activists worried that the fight against climate change would be forgotten in the fugue of a global preoccupation with the fight against the pandemic. These worries were complicated by the circumstances, in which temporary declines in emissions due to virus-related economic shutdowns led many people throughout the world to think, mistakenly, that the shutdowns were having the ironic effect of stopping climate change. Skies cleared, albeit briefly, in places where clear skies had not been seen in many years. Was the climate crisis not over? Likewise, sustainability activists fretted that the other Sustainable Development Goals would also be shunted to the sidelines in the scramble to get the global economy going again. As scholars at the Overseas Development Institute in the United Kingdom expressed this widespread concern, "The urgency of rapid economic recovery risks overshadowing the urgency of climate action and undermining sustainability commitments."[149]

As countries pondered how to resurrect their economies while also continuing to fight the pandemic, climate and sustainability activists urged that these aims be pursued while also facilitating the green economic transition needed to combat climate change and achieve sustainable development. The activists were not alone. In calling for a new approach, they were joined by scientists,[150] health care workers,[151] and business leaders,[152] among many others throughout the world. There was a compelling need, they all insisted, to "build back better" to increase resiliency in confronting future pandemics and future climate and other shocks.[153] According to the OECD, the notion of building back better meant "doing more than getting economies and livelihoods quickly back on their feet. Recovery policies also need to trigger investment and behavioural changes that will reduce the likelihood of future shocks and increase society's resilience to them when they do occur."[154]

Two British scholars, Eleanor Russell and Martin Parker, declared, "There is a real danger that the policy of bouncing back to a growth economy will simply overwhelm the necessity of reducing carbon emissions. This is the nightmare scenario, one in which Covid-19 is just a prequel to something much worse."[155] Understandably, the initial response of governments worldwide was focused on the most immediate tasks of human survival – delivering health care to victims of the virus and emergency aid to businesses that had been shuttered and to people who had been left without work by the social lockdowns that were intended to quell the virus. Little thought was given in the first round of public spending to anything else.

Subsequent spending by governments worldwide, however, has addressed the impact of the pandemic more broadly, and has included stimulus measures totaling trillions of dollars. The urgent need for these stimulus measures has created an unprecedented opportunity for fashioning a new approach, one in which governmental action would boost the economy *and* cut emissions, while also fulfilling all the other objectives of sustainable development. Climate scientists tell us that investing about 10 percent of stimulus funds in renewable energy would pay for the clean energy transition.[156] They also say that, among many other benefits for sustainable development, such an approach could avoid 0.3C of global warming by the middle of this century.[157]

At this historic turning point, there is the opportunity for a *green recovery*.

Not surprisingly, we are told by those with a vested interest in the oil-soaked status quo that a green recovery would be a jobless recovery. The scaremongering message of fossil fuel producers and other defenders of the carbon-based economy has long been that shifting from a carbon economy to a low-carbon and ultimately a no-carbon economy would cost workers untold millions of jobs. They warn that the price of going green would be going without work. Now, when many millions worldwide are out of work because of COVID-19, that message resonates even more with all too many anxious people living precariously on the economic edge. In the United States especially, where fossil fuel producers have spent untold millions of dollars disseminating misinformation that denies the very existence of climate change, and where their political shills have further confused a fretful public now concerned even more about their continued employment because of the pandemic, a candidate or an officeholder who truly seeks to level with the voters about the necessity for making a green transition is, indeed, an exemplar of political courage.

Yet now, too, there is accumulating evidence that going green can create new work and more work. The Global Commission on Economy and the Environment – comprised of former heads of state and finance ministers and leaders in economics, business, and finance, and chaired by former President Felipe Calderon of Mexico – concluded in 2018 that ambitious climate action "could generate over 65 million new low-carbon jobs in 2030, equivalent to today's entire workforces of the UK and Egypt combined, as well as avoid over 700,000 premature deaths from air pollution compared with business-as-usual."[158] Furthermore, the same global commission calculated, "Transitioning to this low-carbon, sustainable growth path could deliver a direct economic gain of US$26 trillion through to 2030," again, "compared to business-as-usual."[159]

In October 2020, in the midst of the pandemic, the International Monetary Fund forecast that "[t]he goal of bringing net carbon emissions to zero by 2050 can be achieved through a comprehensive policy package that is growth friendly (especially in the short term) and involves compensatory transfers to households to ensure inclusion."[160] As IMF economists pointed out, "A concern with decarbonization policies is that they will lead to job losses in carbon-intensive industries."[161] They concluded, however, that "[e]vidence from firms suggests that job losses in high-emission sectors (for example, high-emission manufacturing, transportation) in response to tighter environmental policies can be offset by job creation in low-emission sectors (for example, low-emission manufacturing and services)."[162] In the carbon-dominated energy sector alone, the International Energy Agency has estimated that, with a global annual investment of about $1 trillion over three years, about nine million jobs could be saved or created, as compared to the six million jobs at risk because of the COVID-19 pandemic.[163]

Precisely how to pursue this green transition through a green recovery has been a main topic during the pandemic. Part of the answer – an essential part of the answer – is putting a price on carbon. Another part of the answer is having the right mix of market initiatives and governmental regulations. Still another part is the basic research that helps lead to innovation. And a critical part, of course, is creating more and better jobs to replace those that are lost in the shift away from carbon. One study in 2020 – conducted by Joseph Stiglitz, former World Bank chief economist Lord Nicholas Stern, and leading economists from Oxford University – found that "a green recovery can produce higher returns on public spending and create more jobs in both the short term and the long term, compared to the alternative of pouring stimulus cash into the fossil fuel economy."[164] They contend that, as with the response to the coronavirus crisis, "Decisive state interventions are also required to stabilize the climate, by tipping energy and industrial systems toward newer, cleaner, and ultimately cheaper modes of production that become impossible to outcompete."[165]

This Oxford study "identifies stimulus policies that are perceived to deliver large economic multipliers, reasonably quickly, and shift our emissions trajectory towards net zero. The recovery packages can either kill these two birds with one stone – setting the global economy on a pathway towards net-zero emissions – or lock us into a fossil system from which it will be nearly impossible to escape."[166] The economists who conducted the study insist that "[r]ecovery policies can deliver both economic and climate goals," and they specify five types of policies that can do so:

- Clean physical infrastructure investment in the form of renewable energy assets, storage (including hydrogen), grid modernization, and carbon capture and storage technology.
- Building efficiency spending for renovations and retrofits, including improved insulation, heating, and domestic energy storage systems.

- Investment in education and training to address immediate unemployment from COVID-19 and structural shifts from decarbonization.
- Natural capital investment for ecosystem resilience and regeneration, including restoration of carbon-rich habitats and climate-friendly infrastructure.
- Clean research and development spending. (In many lower- and middle-income countries, the study suggests that clean R&D spending "might be replaced" with rural support scheme spending, particularly that associated with sustainable agriculture, ecosystem regeneration, or accelerating clean energy installations.[167]

To this list must be added the necessity of linking a green recovery to environmental justice.[168] Worldwide, minorities and the disadvantaged often bear the brunt of air, water, toxic, and hazardous waste pollution and other forms of environmental destruction.[169] In the United States and elsewhere, "the COVID-19 pandemic and recession have been particularly devastating for Black, Latino, and Indigenous communities."[170] Moreover, "[m]any of these same communities are disproportionately impacted by pollution, with significant public health and economic consequences."[171] A just transition in a green recovery must begin to remedy these contemporary and historical environmental injustices by investing in the environmental cleanups, energy efficiencies, green transit systems, and green housing much needed by these communities.

As precedent for their belief that their recommended approach will further the green transition while also fostering economic growth, the Oxford economists and other advocates of a green recovery pointed to the experience with the green provisions in some of the governmental stimulus packages in the aftermath of the 2008 financial crisis, when there were also calls for a green recovery. At the time, only about 16 percent of the global stimulus spending was deemed green.[172] This green spending on economic recovery a dozen years before the 2020 pandemic included "subsidies for renewably energy, seed funding for research and development, and new technology such as electric vehicles."[173]

Recalling this earlier experience, the Oxford study economists explained,

A lesson from the (global financial crisis) is that green stimulus policies often have advantages over traditional fiscal stimulus. For instance, renewable energy investment is attractive in both the short and the long run. Renewable energy generates more jobs in the short run (higher jobs multiplier), when jobs are scarce in the middle of a recession, which boosts spending and increases GDP multipliers (which are derived from expanding demand). In the long run, renewable energy conveniently requires less labour for operation and maintenance ... This frees up labour as the economy returns to capacity. The more efficient use of labour and the savings on fuel means that renewables are also able to offer higher long-run multipliers (which are derived from expanding supply.[174]

This earlier experience illustrates how the decisions made during the pandemic about the extent and the allocation of public spending "will lock in the world's development patterns for decades."[175] If we do not invest in renewable energy, we will have less of it. If current investments are the same as past investments, then we will have in the future only what we had in the past. What we had in the past may not be suitable for the future, given climate change and all its attendant consequences. Yet we will be "locked in" to the ways of the past and "locked out" of more suitable alternative solutions. To offer one example, turn a six-lane highway into a twelve-lane highway and more automobiles will travel it in a trail of path dependency. There will be less incentive to look for ways to travel other than by automobile. In the impacts of such choices, these pivotal pandemic spending decisions either will help perpetuate the carbon economy or will help put an end to it.

Thus far, have the decisions reflected in the recovery packages enacted in the new pandemic world kept us on the path of dependency on fossil fuels, or have they turned us toward a green path? For the most part, the early answer is, we are still traveling obliviously along the fossil fuel highway. In the months following the outbreak, nearly twice as much money was committed to fossil fuels as to clean energy in the recovery packages of the G20 leading industrial economies.[176] In June 2020, Bloomberg reported that, of the total $12 trillion in stimulus that had been by then enacted worldwide, less than two-tenths of 1 percent had been targeted toward climate priorities.[177]

Worse, we may be headed in the wrong direction. The scholars at one global think tank, Vivid Economics, claimed from their detailed analysis of national recovery plans that "30% of government stimulus from 17 major economies – roughly US$3.5 trillion – (was) going to support environmentally related sectors, and that most governments (were) failing to use this support to secure medium-term benefits to their citizens' welfare and the natural world around them." As a result, they concluded, "the vast majority of the money going to business in the short term could be risking future environmental sustainability."[178] So far, the governmental responses to the pandemic have, in their view, mimicked previous stimulus measures and disregarded "the broader sustainability and resilience impacts of their actions."[179]

In fact, in fourteen of the seventeen countries these scholars studied, "potentially damaging flows outweigh those supporting nature."[180] At the top of their list of those fourteen countries, posing the most danger to nature, is the United States, which "stands out as the largest scale risk."[181] Throughout most of 2020, while other countries were at least talking about a green recovery, the Trump administration in the United States was busy rolling back environmental protections.[182] The United States was, however, far from alone during that time in risking the environment while striving to recover from the impacts of the pandemic. Indonesia's stimulus plan eliminated environmental reviews for many new development projects, which risked the survival of primary rainforests that mitigate climate change by absorbing and storing carbon.[183] China's investment plans for economic recovery envisaged spending three times as much on fossil fuel projects as on low-carbon energy – casting considerable doubt on China's pledge in September 2020 to achieve "carbon neutrality" by 2060.[184]

All told, according to researchers for the Oxford University Economic Recovery Project, of the trillions of dollars in total spending of the world's largest fifty countries in 2020, only 2.5 percent was for green initiatives such as renewable energy generation, hydrogen power, transmission infrastructure, and battery and storage infrastructure.[185] In March 2021, they reported that, "Though some promising green recovery policy examples do exist, they have been overwhelmingly implemented by a small group of wealthy countries."[186] Even these initiatives by advanced economies were too little and too few. The global economic recovery that seemed to be gathering momentum in the spring of 2021 was, overall, far from green.

Some belated encouragement for those who sought a green recovery appeared in the bipartisan actions taken by the Congress of the United States in December 2020, soon after President Trump was defeated for reelection in November. A $900 billion COVID-19 relief bill included an unprecedented array of "green" climate actions, ranging from deep cuts in the use of climate-damaging hydrofluorocarbons (HFCs) to billions of dollars for research and development on solar energy, wind energy, carbon capture and storage, and energy storage; upgrades to the electric grid; energy-efficiency projects; and carbon-free nuclear energy.[187]

The election of President Biden added further encouragement as the new Biden administration, populated by ardent climate activists, set out to make combating climate change central to its whole approach to governance. On his first day as president, Biden reversed Trump's decision to withdraw the United States from the Paris climate agreement.[188] He underlined his support for the agreement by appointing former Secretary of State John Kerry, a dedicated climate advocate, as his "climate envoy" in charge of US international climate negotiations.[189] On Biden's first call as president to British Prime Minister Boris Johnson, he spoke of the need for a "green recovery."[190]

In April 2021, the new US president introduced what he described as a pillar of his plan for addressing climate change, a $2.3 trillion infrastructure package labeled the American Jobs Plan.[191] In addition to spending on such traditional infrastructure as roads, bridges, and ports, the Biden proposal included hundreds of billions of dollars of new spending on public transit, greener housing, electric vehicle manufacturing and infrastructure, resilience measures to prevent natural disasters, climate technology research and development, and other green initiatives. Climate campaigners praised the Biden plan while noting, with justification, that it did not go far enough in encouraging a societal shift away from carbon. The president's opponents denounced the bill for departing from the conventional concept of concrete infrastructure. With only a narrow majority in the House, an evenly divided Senate, and the prospect of no support from the opposing party, it was unclear whether the American Jobs Plan would be enacted. At this writing, the original Biden proposal has been reduced to

$1.2 trillion in spending over five years and narrowed in scope. The Senate has passed the plan with bipartisan support, and it awaits a vote by the House.[192]

Providing more encouragement was much of what was happening "in parts of Western Europe, South Korea and Canada," where the recovery plans offered "more promise with at least a portion of spending likely to be nature-friendly."[193] A new French plan for the national auto sector favored electric cars.[194] Canadian bailout money went only to firms that reported their climate risks.[195] Particularly encouraging was the "Next Generation EU" recovery plan of the European Union, which directed 30 percent of the total spending package of $830 billion to "green" initiatives, including targeted measures to reduce dependency on fossil fuels, improve energy efficiency, and invest in preserving and restoring the "natural capital" provided by natural resources.[196]

In the particulars of some of these proposals for a green recovery are the trade links. Proposals for a green recovery raise anew the age-old questions about the proper role for the state in relation to the economy. They revive – with a new rationale – the never-ending debate about the merits of a state-directed industrial policy, a debate dating back to before the back-and-forth between the free trader Adam Smith and the protection-minded mercantilists in eighteenth-century Great Britain. For centuries, this debate has always turned ultimately into one mainly over the merits of managed trade. All too often in the past, what has been proposed as an "industrial policy" by would-be reformers has been mostly a soothing synonym for a national policy of trade protectionism.

The reduction of an economic policy for recovery into mere protectionism must be avoided in the structuring of a green recovery. National policies aimed at achieving a green recovery surely will have many effects on trade. Through production subsidies, import tariffs, regulatory standards, and much more, trade measures will be employed to make climate and other sustainability measures more palatable politically with local voters. Understandably, domestic producers will not want to pay the costs and bear the consequences of national climate actions unless their competitors – including their foreign competitors – pay those same costs and bear those same consequences. Otherwise, they will be put at a competitive disadvantage. The question is, which green policies will be justified in the restrictions they impose on trade? And which policies, though they may be described as green policies, will in fact only be excuses for protecting domestic producers from fair foreign competition?

2

Links to the Pandemic

A WORLD TURNING INWARD

Turning inward and away from trade is nothing new. The notion that individuals and nations can be economically self-sufficient is an ancient illusion. In classical Greece, the early Athenians extolled the supposed societal virtues of "autarky," the Greek word for self-sufficiency. Greek philosophers looked down on the mundanities of mere commerce. Moreover, as Douglas Irwin has written, they "advocated restrictions on trade because of the moral and civic danger associated with it. They believed that contact with foreign strangers would be detrimental to law and order and could undermine the moral fabric of society."[1] For the ancient Greeks, as for so many provincial patriots throughout the world today, their "city was the only city, and her ways the only ways."[2] Certain as they were of their own superiority, they were suspicious of what they saw as inferior foreign "barbarians," and they believed in putting their city-states "first." Irwin has added, though, that, although "[s]elf-sufficiency was deemed far better than dependence on overseas trade ... self-sufficiency did not imply complete autarky because Greek philosophers reluctantly conceded that at least some foreign trade was imperative."[3]

A notable exception to the prevailing Greek philosophical aversion to trade was the Athenian Plato, who extolled the benefits of a division of labor in *The Republic*, noting that, "Quantity and quality are ... more easily produced when a man specializes appropriately on a single job for which he is naturally fitted, and neglects all others." In his ideal "republic," Plato went much too far in his embrace of specialization by structuring it within the construct of an ascribed and authoritarian society. Plato was no democrat. In places, his political thinking tended toward totalitarianism.[4] Nevertheless, his prescient insight was to perceive that the division of labor is, in fact, a trade in tasks. The goods and services that are exchanged are simply the results of this trade in tasks.

Looking around at the rocky terrain, the narrow coasts, the limited arable land, and the other scant natural resources of Greece, Plato observed, too, "[I]t is almost impossible to found a state in a place where it will not need imports."[5]

Plato's pupil Aristotle, who differed with his mentor on much else, generally agreed with him on the necessity of conducting at least some foreign trade. Assuming the taint of foreign traders could be minimized, he saw as advantageous for the Greek city-states "in respect of both security and the supply of necessary commodities . . . importation of commodities that they do not happen to have in their own country and the export of their surplus products are things indispensable."[6] Therefore, unable, practically, to be economically self-sufficient, the Athenians and the other Greeks were more open to trade than are most of the modern advocates of autarky. They traded to import what they needed but could not produce. Nevertheless, with their aversion to foreigners and to foreign thinking, they sought, to the extent they realistically could, to maintain the self-sufficiency of individuals and of the Greek city-states.[7] Autarky was considered a virtue for both.

Over time, of course, ancient Athens, blessed by a thriving port called Piraeus, became anything but an economic autarky. Athenian triremes plowed the middle sea, rowing from island to island, from port to port. The teeming market in Athens became a crossroads for the maritime trade throughout the Mediterranean and much of the Middle East. Athens, for example, imported most of the grain that fed a population that peaked in the classical period at about 300,000 people. Trade with other countries and with Greek islands and other Greek city-states fueled the rise of Athens as a beacon of art and culture and as a bastion of direct democracy. Today, what remains of the busy ancient Athenian agora is still marked by the stone paths of a far-flung trade.[8] Autarky may have been seen as a virtue by many Athenians, but it was not a philosophy by which they all lived and conducted commerce.

Much of what is being said today about trade is only an echo of what was said long ago by the ancient Greeks. More than two millennia later, the basic arguments for and against the illusion of an economic self-sufficiency remain much the same. Throughout all the centuries since Plato and Aristotle, the false but timeless appeal of autarky has continued to assail humanity. Insular medievalists, bullion-hungry mercantilists, Hitler's Germany, Mussolini's Italy, Franco's Spain, the Soviet Union, communist Albania, Cambodia under the Khmer Rouge, and, lately, the new latter-day exponents of a flag-waving economic nationalism – have all trumpeted, at one time or another, what they have perceived as the national benefits of an economic self-sufficiency achieved behind the walls of an economic isolation. Most of them have mischaracterized as "self-sufficiency" a combination of maximizing exports through protection of their domestic production from trade competition and soaking up raw materials needed as inputs for their domestic production from the natural resources of weaker countries through economic exploitation and military conquest.

All of these and other past experiments with differing versions of a would-be economic self-sufficiency ultimately failed. They failed because economic survival and more enduring economic success, is found only through economic interdependence derived from a division of labor – locally, nationally, and internationally. The notion of autarky is counterproductive to such economic success. When total national self-sufficiency is pursued, limited resources are not allocated most productively. Production is less than it would otherwise be, and it is less efficient. Productivity stops rising. Scarcities of all kinds result. Economic conflicts arise over these scarcities. These economic conflicts can then lead to sanguinary military conflicts. Resource wars can become shooting wars. Hitler and his supposedly self-sufficient Nazis did not invade Ukraine simply to secure another conquest; they invaded Ukraine because the rich Ukrainian soil grew wheat for making bread that could feed Hitler's armies and other Germans.[9]

The ancient Greeks who advocated autarky did not have the advantage of the insights of Adam Smith on the division of labor or David Ricardo on comparative advantage. Despite all their success with their own trade specialties, such as the making of their exquisite pottery as sturdy containers for their extensive seaborne trade, the Greeks did not generally make the key intellectual connection between divided labor and increased prosperity. In general, they had no commitment to increasing productivity through innovation.[10] Thus, they did not comprehend all those centuries ago that it is a specialization divided in accordance with comparative advantage, and not an illusory self-sufficiency, that results in the most efficient allocation of limited resources, natural and otherwise. Nor did they understand that it is a consistent commitment to comparative advantage that makes the utmost of specialization for both national and international economic gain.

The ancient Greek defenders of autarky did not realize – nor have any of their avowed autarkic successors realized since – the truth of one fundamental fact that refutes the entirety of the age-old argument for economic self-sufficiency: No one person and no one country has a sufficient amount or combination of resources to be self-sufficient in everything. This is true of every one of us as individuals. This is equally true of every one of the countries in which we may happen to live. Thus, for example, a country that decides, in a search for self-sufficiency, to impose restrictions on exports of one product, will soon learn that, to meet all its domestic needs, it will have to import other, different products from the very countries it has harmed with those export restrictions. Likewise, a country that pursues self-sufficiency by restricting imports in a move to spur domestic production of imported products will eventually discover that it cannot meet all its needs for domestic consumption solely from domestic production. This can be a hard lesson at any time. It can be the hardest of lessons during a pandemic.

To illustrate the absurdity of the pursuit of economic self-sufficiency: Even if I could somehow learn how to do so, do I, as an individual, really want to make all my own pencils? Do we as a country want to make all our own pencils?

What else could we be doing for much greater reward if we did not spend so much of our time making pencils? Moreover, do we happen to have the required resources readily available to make all our own pencils, now and from now on?[11] The writing core of a pencil is made from powdered graphite. Where is the nearest source of graphite ore? In addition to pencils, the same question might be posed about everything else we eat, wear, and use in the modern world.

Perhaps there was a lost time in a lost world long ago when we were all considerably more self-sufficient economically than we are now. Perhaps there was an Arcadian, pastoral time when we felled our own lumber, churned our own butter, sewed our own clothes, dug our own toilets, and delivered our own babies. But that was a Hobbesian time when life was shorter, harder, crueler, and decidedly more precarious for all of us. The modern world depends on specialization. So, too, do all the many blessings of the material bounty that come with the modern world – modern medicine, modern sanitation, modern communication, modern transportation, and so much more we would rather not live without. Few of us truly wish to return to that world we have lost, that world we have struggled so long and so hard to put forever behind us.[12] If not for our daily blood pressure pills, how many of us would no longer be here?

Despite these cautionary considerations, the world was, even before the COVID-19 pandemic, turning away from continued global economic progress and inward, if not toward a complete autarky, then toward something more philosophically akin to it than was the previously prevailing multilateral commitment to more liberalized trade. Between 1945 and 2008, international trade grew faster than GDP almost everywhere. In 2008, exports as a percentage of GDP reached a record high of 26 percent.[13] In recent years, this prolonged trend has reversed; trade has not grown faster than GDP. The volume of merchandise trade fell by 0.1 percent in 2019 while the value of that trade fell by 3 percent.[14] Amid the pandemic, this turn inward and away from the world has intensified. More countries, including many members of the WTO, are rediscovering the ancient allure of economic self-sufficiency, and they are tempted anew toward some contemporary semblance of autarky.

As Douglas Irwin has pointed out, in the pandemic world, "National security and public health concerns are providing new rationales for protectionism, especially for medical gear and food, and an emphasis on domestic sourcing."[15] The WTO reported that, during the first six months following the outbreak in Wuhan, WTO members and observers implemented 363 new trade and trade-related measures. Of this total, 165 restricted trade while 198 facilitated trade.[16] This mix was better than it might have been, given the pressures of the pandemic. The WTO, however, also noted that the trade coverage of the restrictive measures implemented since the depths of the financial crisis in 2009, and still in force, "continues to increase."[17]

Protectionism is proliferating. According to the WTO, 8.7 percent of world imports – valued at $1.7 trillion – "is affected by import-restrictive measures implemented since 2009 and still in force."[18] Many of these are measures against supposedly "unfair" trade, which often lies in the protectionist eyes of the competing beholder. And this sum does not include all the different kinds of trade barriers that were in place before 2009 and are still in place. "Between mid-October 2018 and mid-October 2019 (alone), the trade coverage of import-restrictive measures implemented by (WTO) members was estimated at USD 747 billion. This is the highest trade coverage recorded since October 2012 and represents an increase of 27% compared to the figure recorded in the previous annual overview (USD 588 billion)."[19]

The Swiss-based Global Trade Alert, which monitors the application of new restrictions on trade worldwide and tends to see trade restrictions more broadly than does the WTO, reported on the eve of the COVID-19 pandemic that, from January 1, 2017 to November 15, 2019, governments worldwide introduced 2,723 new trade distortions. The cumulative effect of those thousands of new distortions was to distort 40 percent of world trade.[20] During that three-year period, tariff increases affected 5.8 percent of world trade.[21] Government subsidies for domestic producers affected 9.2 percent of world trade – nearly twice as much as tariffs.[22] Locked in an increasingly bitter bilateral "trade war," China and the United States accounted for 23 percent of these trade-distorting measures.[23] Of the seventy-three new measures that distorted $10 million or more in world trade during that time, China implemented six and the United States implemented eighteen.[24]

Adding to the weighty bulk of the familiar protectionist rationalizations that seek to justify the discriminations in these new trade distortions, is a variation on the ancient prescription of autarky called "localism," which contends that "everything that can be produced locally should be produced locally."[25] Localism is superficially appealing. It is mainly a contemporary manifestation of British economist E. F. Schumacher's economic thesis of half a century ago, that "small is beautiful."[26] Without doubt, any advocate of a competitive economy would readily attest that small is, indeed, sometimes beautiful economically. Free competition is essential to the success of a free marketplace, and small businesses are an important part of ensuring free competition. In addition, there is nothing wrong with giving local businesses your custom. Nor is there anything wrong with buying fruits and vegetables that are grown locally. It is only natural to want to help your neighbor.

But the superficial appeal of localism is belied by the illogic of its underlying premises. Localists maintain, "If locally grown, GMO-free arugula costs more, so be it: it's good for the masses."[27] How, though, is it good for the "masses" if, because the arugula costs more, fewer of the masses can afford to buy it? And how much arugula will be grown locally in many parts of the world during the snowbound dead of winter or the scorched aridity of summer? The same questions might be asked of a commitment to buying "local" for any other good or service? How do we benefit from fewer choices at higher prices? If human freedom is defined as being able to make more personal decisions about how we wish to live, material and otherwise, then limiting our choices limits our freedom.[28] Only those who have more material choices because they have more money are likely to dismiss so cavalierly the prospect of higher prices.

Buying local may make us feel good about ourselves, but is it more ethical to buy locally instead of buying globally? We all live on the same planet. We are all part of the same species. On what moral basis do we owe more to those who live nearby than to those who live on the far side of the world? As the American libertarian economist Steven Horwitz has written,

It is not clear why people more near to us geographically should have (more) moral weight than those further away. Given the choice between helping a middle-class small businesswoman in our neighborhood or increasing the chances of better employment at a higher wage for much poorer men and women in China, why should we believe that the former is necessarily morally superior? If human beings deserve our moral consideration by virtue of their humanity, and if those who are worse off economically are deserving of more such consideration, then it would seem that if there is a moral case for anything, it's for buying in ways that help the least well-off, regardless of their nationality or ethnicity.[29]

Similarly, protecting local businesses and workers from foreign competition may be appealing as a political promise. Such promises routinely draw rounds of raucous applause on the political campaign trail, particularly with the "Buy American" exhortations (by Trump, Biden, and others) nowadays in the United States. But do American workers truly benefit overall when the employment prospects of the many Americans in the jobs of the future are sacrificed, through trade protection, to temporary job preservation for the relatively few Americans who are employed by firms and in sectors that, without trade protection, would not be able to compete with foreign products in either the American or the global marketplace? Similarly, over on the other side of the world, do the hundreds of millions of rural farmers in India engaged in back-breaking and brain-numbing small-scale bucolic toil truly benefit from perpetuation of an agricultural protectionism that continues to imprison them in agrarian subsistence at the price of forgone trade openings that could enable many of them to step up into the modern world?

Localism is aesthetically pleasing to a certain kind of romantic and reactionary thinker on both the right and the left of the political spectrum. Localists write some beautiful and thoughtful essays lamenting the alienation that often accompanies industrialization and extolling the wholeness of a life unadorned by the division of labor. In the United States, nearly a century ago, there were the essays written by the Nashville Agrarians.[30] Today, there are those written by the eloquent Wendell Berry, among others.[31] Yet, as an essayist with a sharply contrasting point of view, George Scialabba, has observed,

No amount of recycling, farming right, eating right, being neighborly, or being personally responsible in other ways will matter much if we don't subsidize solar and wind power, raise mileage requirements, steeply tax carbon, drastically reduce plastic production, kill coal, and provide jobs for all those whom these measures would disemploy ... [C]ultivating our own gardens and learning the virtues we have forgotten will not suffice to save the world, and is probably not even feasible.[32]

The French Enlightenment *philosophe* Voltaire might add that, like his Candide, if we do not also cultivate diligently the garden of the wider world, we will not be able to sit contentedly in the solace of our own garden "eating citrons and pistachios" (or, for that matter, arugula).[33] Localism is an altogether impractical rebellion against inescapable economic and other complexities of the modern world. It is nostalgia for a simpler world that no longer exists – if it ever did. The longings of localism can be lyrical, but this is not the same as being persuasive. Shorn of its atavistic and pseudo-altruistic trappings, and separated from its frail philosophical shorings, localism is mostly a rejection of modernism. Part of this rejection is a repudiation of the internationalism that accompanies modernism, including support for international trade.

Localism is just one more false justification for protectionism. Central to localism's economic blueprint of prioritizing the "near" in purchases and production is usually discriminating against the "far." To help those who are nearby, localism often favors erecting more barriers to trade with those who are not. Yet, in the ever more complex and interconnected twenty-first century, in the world that does exist, the world in which we all must live, we are much less likely than even the ancient Greeks to be able to depend entirely on local production. We are inescapably interdependent, and we must act in the knowledge that we are interdependent. In seeking the broadest public good in this unavoidably complicated real world, "The best path toward enriching everyone is allowing everyone to trade with everyone else."[34]

In any of its myriad forms, protectionism is contagious. In the darkest days of the 1930s, the contagion of protectionism spun out of control, and deepened and prolonged the Great Depression.[35] In the financial crisis of 2008, protectionism was largely contained, due in no small part to the existence and the actions of the WTO and other international institutions.[36] Today, we must, once again, keep from retreating economically from the rest of the world. The recent turn inward has been led by some of the countries that trade the most with other countries. Foremost among them, sadly, has been the United States of America, which is, ironically, the trading country with the least excuse for turning inward. When the United States concludes that, despite the constraints of WTO rules, it is free to distort trade, other countries soon begin to feel free to do the same. This is exactly what has been happening since the arrival of COVID-19 as protectionist measures, both legal and not, have continued to add up worldwide.

The growing global skepticism about trade certainly does not help us avert a headlong rush into a resurgent protectionism. Aiding and abetting domestic decisions to turn away from trade across the world has been the depth of the victimization that millions of workers feel because of trade. Many of these workers have been displaced. Many other workers are fearful that they soon will be displaced. All of them see the income gap within many countries widening and leaving them ever-farther behind in an increasingly unequal world. And all of them feel strongly that trade is a main source of these economic maladies, which have been worsened by the pandemic. Thus, not surprisingly, they believe the easiest cure for their economic peril is to restrict trade.

These feelings, though, are not based on facts. The vast majority of the displaced have not lost their jobs because of increased trade. They have lost their jobs because of new advances in technology. Douglas Irwin has explained that, in developed countries, "[a]lthough imports have put some people out of work, trade is far from the most important factor behind the loss of manufacturing jobs. The main culprit is *technology*. Automation and other new techniques have enabled vast productivity and efficiency improvements, but they have also made many blue-collar jobs obsolete."[37] He and other economists point in particular to one economic study that concluded that productivity growth due to automation and other technological improvements has accounted for more than 85 percent of US manufacturing job losses while only 13 percent of those job losses can be attributed to trade.[38] It is easier, though, when you lose your job, to blame a foreigner than a robot.

Just as mistaken is the widespread view that trade has done much to widen income inequality. The facts say otherwise. Elhanan Helpman, another of the world's leading scholars of international trade, has determined, after an exhaustive study of the empirical evidence, that,

[T]he prevalent view that globalization is primarily responsible for the large increase in the inequality of labor compensation has no basis in the evidence. Yes, globalization impacted the wages of different types of workers to different degrees, and yes, it contributed to an increase in the wages of skilled relative to unskilled workers through multiple channels. Yet, in sum, all these effects explain only a fraction of the rise in wage inequality in rich and poor countries alike.[39]

All in all, Helpman has concluded, "[G]lobalization in the form of foreign trade and offshoring has not been a large contributor to rising inequality."[40]

In addition to these mistaken views about the impacts of trade, there is another feeling that is not mistaken at all: the feeling that change is coming, that change is happening, and that the onrush of change cannot be avoided. Millions of people everywhere fear they are pawns of powerful impersonal forces that are coercing them into change. They fear that they will be discarded, that they will be cast away in torrents of economic change, of cultural change, and of other unwelcome changes to the way things are, the way things have always been, the way things ought to be. These fears are crystallized in a gripping "ordeal of change" that is characterized by an anxious apprehension of "other" people, other practices, and, most disturbing of all, the implicit challenges to received certainties posed by other ideas about how to live.[41] Thus, these pervasive fears readily fuse with the mistaken impression that more trade means more lost jobs and more inequality, and that, therefore, one necessary way to fight back against the uncertainties and the indignities occasioned by these forced changes is to fight against more trade.[42]

The cure for the fear of change is not to try to stop all change. If the long experience of history teaches us anything, it teaches us that there will always be change. Nor should we deceive ourselves into believing that all the changes that are pressing upon us are products of nefarious human actions. To be sure, avaricious actions abound. Many of the injustices in the world can be traced to an unchecked human greed. But not all. Climate change, for example, is a result of human actions; however, it was not until a few decades ago that we learned that in fueling our energy-eating economy with carbon we were also imperiling the future of our planet. Actions intended to perpetuate the human dependency on fossil fuels have only lately become nefarious.

Rather than trying to arrest change, we should be facing it rationally and realistically. The cure for the fear of change is to stop fearing it. The cure is for all people everywhere to work together to find our way safely through change to a better future we all can share. This task can only be accomplished by making a just transition to a green recovery in a sustainable world. Yet, for those who would presume to lead us, it is always easier to tell us that we need not change, that we can forestall change, that we can avoid facing it. For it is always easier for those seeking our political support to tell us what we want to hear instead of what we need to hear. And it is always easier to stoke fears than to dispel them.

When we add to these feelings – however much some of them may be mistaken – the all too real life-and-death fears of the pandemic, the mounting impetus worldwide for turning inward is not difficult to comprehend. Nowhere has the contrast between the visceral emotions underlying a self-sufficient autarky and the plain facts supporting more international economic integration coupled with more liberalized trade been presented more starkly than in the heated global debate weighing the costs against the considerable benefits of global supply chains, which has emerged amid the worldwide reaction to the COVID-19 pandemic.

THE EVOLUTION OF GLOBAL SUPPLY CHAINS

The rules of the World Trade Organization do not mandate global supply chains. The supply chains that circle the world are products purely of market forces. Market value is added at each stage of the supply chain by means that make the most economic sense. Global supply chains are often called global value chains because they convey not only value-added to the ultimate finished production of goods and services but also a wealth of technical knowledge and know-how for people throughout the world who have not been able to attain such skills before. Thus, production is no longer centered in one place; it is fragmented through an international division of labor. "A global value chain breaks up the production process across countries. Firms specialize in a specific task and do not produce the whole product."[43]

In an economy organized as a free market, decisions about whether and how to fragment the production process, and about where and how to locate the different pieces of production, are not made by governments. Such decisions are made instead by private firms in search of an ever-increasing productivity that will maximize production and profits. Arbitrary interference by government in making these decisions is a form of managed trade, attended by all the short-comings of managed trade. While WTO rules do not mandate global value chains, they do discipline some of the harmful interventions that governments might want to make to impede them. In particular, the trade rules constrain governmental measures that discriminate against foreign goods and services.

Up until the 1990s, international trade largely consisted of trade between buyers and sellers of basic commodities and finished products in different countries. Manufacturing production was largely located "at home" within a single country. Roughly coinciding with the transformation of the GATT into the WTO in 1995, two pivotal technological innovations led to the "unbundling" of this traditional form of international trade and production.[44] One was the increasingly widespread use of super-sized cargo ships carrying standardized containers to facilitate an exponential growth in global shipping.[45] The other was the development of the Internet and digital information and communications technology. The WTO was formed against the revolutionary backdrop of these signal innovations, which led to the death of distance. Today, 70 percent of all international trade is "for production in global value chains."[46]

As Richard Baldwin has noted of this historic transformation, "[R]adically better communications made it possible to coordinate complex activities at distance ... Today, it is almost costless to maintain a continuous, two-way flow of words, images, and data. For digitized ideas, distance truly died, or more precisely, the ICT revolution assassinated it."[47] Thus, "[p]arts and components began crisscrossing the globe as firms looked for efficiencies wherever they could find them."[48] Products were suddenly from nowhere and from everywhere. The "extent of the market" was now truly worldwide, and, with global value chains, large multinational corporations and other firms were able to trade in new ways they could never have envisaged before. Global trade expanded rapidly, and, as Adam Smith had predicted, so, too, did global wealth.

Baldwin has described this global economic phenomenon as "the great convergence."[49] As he has explained, while much of trade has remained unchanged, "[t]he most dynamic parts of today's trade flows ... are radically more complex and more entangled because of the changed organization of production. Specifically, he has written, twenty-first century trade reflects the intertwining of:

- Trade in parts and components.
- International movement of production facilities, personnel, and know-how.

- Services necessary to coordinate the dispersed production, especially infra-structure services such as telecoms, Internet, express parcel delivery, air cargo, trade-related finance, customs clearance, trade finance, and so on."[50]

As both production and knowledge fragmented, the death of distance gave birth to a dizzying multiplication of global value chains. According to the World Bank,

The growth of international trade and the expansion of global value chains (GVCs) over the last 30 years have had remarkable effects on development. Incomes have risen, productivity has gone up – particularly in developing countries – and poverty has fallen. The fragmentation of production and knowledge transfer inherent in GVCs are in no small part responsible for these advances. Hyperspecialization by firms at different stages of value chains enhances efficiency and productivity, and durable firm-to-firm relationships foster technology transfer and access to capital and inputs along value chains … Empirical evidence suggests that within three years of joining a manufacturing GVC, a country is more than 20 percent richer on a per capita basis.[51]

As only one example of the many benefits derived from participation in global value chains by people in the poorer parts of the world, "piggy-backing" on GVCs has helped add to the prosperity and opportunities of women in develop-ing countries.[52] Worldwide, firms that are part of global value chains hire more women than those that are not.[53] This is especially the case in developing countries. In the garment industry of Bangladesh, in the cut flower industry of Ethiopia, in the horticulture industry of Senegal, in the village industries of India, and in other local links of global value chains in the developing world, studies of GVCs have shown, not only that there are increases in income, which helps empower women especially, but also that "the chances of getting a job increase the returns to staying in school and improving literacy and numeracy," and the abilities to read and do math.[54] What is more, there are also "indirect positive effects" from employment in global value chains "on girls' school enrollment, nutrition, health, delayed marriage, and childbirth."[55]

Thus, supply chains deliver more than just goods and services. Consistent with the aims of Goal 8 of the Sustainable Development Goals, being a part of a global value chain can mean more and better choices in employment. It can also mean more and better choices in products and in prices. What is more, when assessing the overall worth of global value chains, the beneficial exposure that connecting to international commerce can bring to millions of people who have long been confined in rigid premodern regimes of living and thinking must not be underestimated. Global value chains can help pry open closed societies. For every person living fully within the new and open world of human freedom, there is another still imprisoned in the old and closed world where personal roles are assigned and where personal futures are ascribed. As Sir Karl Popper explained, in an open society, there are more personal choices about how to live.[56] Freedom is choosing. For some, the prospect of change engenders fear. For others, it offers liberation.

Most of world trade is trade in intermediate goods and services – the tangible and intangible inputs that go into the process of making finished products.[57] This is true of about half the trade of the United States. In form, international trade in the private sector is of two kinds. There are arms-length transactions between two different business firms in two different countries, and there are intra-firm transactions between two different affiliates of the same firm in two different countries. Unfortunately, trade statistics do not distinguish between these two forms of trade. Yet intra-firm trade – trade within the same company – is generally thought to comprise about one-third of all trade. These two facts – that so much of trade is in intermediate goods and, also, that so much of it is in intra-firm transactions – have added to the attraction of multinational firms to global value chains.[58]

Global value chains grew rapidly from 1990 to 2007 as the tasks of production were scattered increasingly across the planet.[59] That growth, however, has "leveled off since 2008, when GVCs peaked at 52 percent of world trade."[60] Leading up to 2020, GVC growth never quite recovered from the 2008 financial crisis. By the time the viral upheavals originated in Wuhan, the percentage of world trade that flowed through global value chains may even have declined.[61] According to the World Bank, "The reasons are complex. Slowing global growth and investment are one factor. And value chains have matured, making further specialization more challenging. Meanwhile, the push toward international trade liberalization has stalled. The growth of automation and other labor-saving technologies such as 3D printing may encourage countries to reduce production abroad. Unless trade liberalization is reinforced, value chains are unlikely to expand."[62]

Another factor in the stagnation of global value chains leading up to 2020 was the maturation of the Chinese economy, which shifted as it prospered to focus more on its growing domestic markets. As China climbed up the ladder of comparative advantage, wages in China climbed as well. This rise largely eliminated China's labor cost advantage in the global economy, which had been a magnet for foreign direct investment, and inspired a shift of some production by Western investors from China to other Asian countries with lower wage rates. Combined with the intensifying tensions over trade between China and the United States, these increased labor costs, foreign worries about forced technology transfer and intellectual property theft, and an increasingly uncertain legal climate for investment, all began to alter China's role since the turn of the century as the manufacturing shop floor of the world.[63] In February 2020, just as the pandemic began to spread, the Gartner consulting firm "found that 33% of global supply chain leaders had either shifted sourcing and manufacturing activities out of China or planned to do so in the next three years."[64]

Still another factor in the recent faltering of global value chains has been the shale energy revolution in the United States, where, before 2020, "a booming shale sector reduced oil imports by one-fourth between 2010 and 2015."[65] Moreover, it must be said, at least some of the stagnation in the spread of global value chains can undoubtedly be traced to the abrupt "about face" by the United States on trade beginning in January 2017. There was the sudden shock then of a new transactional focus by the executive branch of the United States on achieving specific trade outcomes in specific sectors and for specific companies – a sharp contrast to the traditional US focus on assuring that wealth-creating trade outcomes be achieved by having fair and agreed rules for trade in the global marketplace. Out of fear of governmental reprisal, this shock doubtless deterred some US companies from extending their supply chains by investing in additional foreign production.

Then came COVID-19. Global demand suddenly disappeared and, with it, much of the demand for using global value chains. Container shipping declined.[66] Air travel and transport "collapsed."[67] Workers could not get to factories. Supply chains seized up. As a result, protective masks, ventilators, gloves, and other products needed to confront the virus emergency were in short and scattered supply. The reverberating economic impacts of the pandemic "zoomed" through the GVCs to convulse a world full of supplier countries.[68] Throughout the world, countries and firms that were made abruptly aware of the extent of their reliance on imports and of their consequent lack of self-sufficiency, questioned the merits of global value chains. Some began to see extended supply chains as "an apparent Achilles' heel of the global economy."[69]

At the same time, others worried about the consequences if global value chains were broken and abandoned. In the spring of 2020, as international supply chains were stalled and strained as never before by the spread of the novel coronavirus, Richard Baldwin and Eiichi Tomiura observed ominously,

There is a danger of permanent damage to the trade system driven by policy and firms' reactions. The combination of the US' ongoing trade war against all of its trading partners (but especially China) and the supply-chain disruptions that are likely to be caused by COVID-19 could lead to a push to repatriate supply chains. Since ... supply chains were internationalized to improve productivity, their undoing would do the opposite.[70]

In China, trade frictions with the United States and the economic impacts of COVID-19 have combined to alter some of the links for global supply chains. Surveys by the American Chamber of Commerce in China show that 40 percent of US companies have either moved their factories out of China or are considering a move.[71] Foxconn, the leading Taiwanese manufacturer that makes the iPhone and has a major commercial presence in China, anticipates a fragmentation of supply chains "into a China supply chain and several others for the rest of the world."[72] Foxconn chairman Liu Young-way has predicted that, while China will still play a major role in global manufacturing, its "days as the world's factory are done."[73]

In the United States, there has been growing sentiment for putting "America First" by reshoring much of the production that has been outsourced through supply chains. This, however, is not the path to added productivity or economic security. Reshoring is the economic equivalent of restricting imports, and, generally, it has the same effect. Only large and developed countries such as the United States are likely to have the capacity and resources to contemplate reshoring. But even in the United States, a policy of reshoring production will have "drawbacks."[74] Trade "allows production to relocate to where it is most efficient and helps to increase access to more goods at affordable prices."[75] Restricting trade through government interventions that force reshoring will require subsidies and tariffs that will result in higher costs to taxpayers and consumers.[76] Also, just as with domestic reliance on foreign suppliers, increased dependency on domestic production coupled with new barriers to imports will be vulnerable to the same supply disruptions and other damaging shocks, but without the current "back-up" of imported sources of supply.[77]

Shannon K. O'Neill of the Council on Foreign Relations has warned us that,

In the long term, dismantling international supply chains will make U.S. businesses less competitive and will blunt their global technological edge. The benefits of comparative advantage that led buyers and suppliers to look abroad in the first place haven't disappeared. Bringing everything onshore threatens to raise costs and reduce the appeal of U.S. products to the 95 percent of the world's consumers who live outside of U.S. borders. National isolation limits innovation, too; the United States has maintained its technological advantage precisely because of its openness to ideas and people, as well as the global sourcing of parts for production.[78]

Understandably, many manufacturers are worried that the persistence and the unpredictability of COVID-19 may cut them off from critical inputs where they rely on only one or a few distant sources of supply. These concerns have increased as the pandemic has continued. Predictably, their governments share these concerns. However, instead of reshoring production by cutting supply chains, O'Neill rightly advises governments and businesses "to focus on redundancy. Industries should look to make or source components in multiple places and from multiple suppliers. They should be prepared to pay more for backup options and to keep larger inventories on hand ... Businesses and policymakers must work to strengthen supply chains, not shut them down."[79]

Previously, to minimize their costs, many firms have embraced a policy of "just in time" – a concept that reflects "the desire to minimize the gap between when an item was produced or purchased, and when it was sold."[80] Peter S. Goodman of the *New York Times* has explained,

Part of the world's vulnerability to supply chain disruption stems from the excessive embrace of the so-called just-in-time mode of manufacturing: Rather than keep warehouses stocked with needed parts, ensuring that they are on hand come what may, the modern factory uses the web to order parts as the need arises, while relying on global air and shipping networks to deliver them on a timeline synchronized with production.[81]

This "just in time" manufacturing, which relies on far-flung supply chains to provide inputs and boost inventories only when needed and not until needed, is a modern business model inspired by the death of distance. In maximizing efficiencies, this business model maximizes profits, and, in turn, maximizes opportunities for more prosperity, including through the creation and operation of global value chains.

This model works well when international trade goes smoothly. It works less well when trade is subject to shortages, uncertainties, and interruptions, as it has been since the beginning of 2020. It is not designed for a world gripped by disease, a desperate world in which the demand for much that is needed far exceeds the supply. In the new pandemic world, in many domains of production, "just in time" should yield to "just in case." Firms and governments alike should have larger stockpiles of strategic products "just in case" of another emergency such as the COVID-19 pandemic. But this necessary recourse to "just-in-case" in some instances must not consist simply of shoving aside altogether the necessity to improve productivity.

Central to economic growth and economic security is increased productivity – making more with less, in part through an international division of labor. Nobel Prize–winning economist Paul Krugman has famously said, "Productivity isn't everything, but in the long run it is almost everything. A country's ability to improve its standard of living over time depends almost entirely on its ability to raise its output per worker."[82] This widespread economic view is reflected in the UN Sustainable Development Goals. SDG Goal 8 is to "[p]romote sustained, inclusive and sustainable economic growth, full and productive employment and decent work for all."[83] One of the targets for attaining this goal is to "[a]chieve higher levels of economic productivity, through diversification, technological upgrading and innovation, including through a focus on high-value added and labour-intensive sectors."[84]

The decade that followed the global financial crisis and that preceded the pandemic "witnessed a broad-based decline in productivity growth."[85] Economists still debate why this happened, with the possible culprits ranging from a decline in technological progress and a decline in the incorporation of new technologies in production processes to a decline in demand.[86] A retreat from global value chains in the wake of the COVID-19 pandemic would not help reverse this trend. Instead, turning inward by cutting the links in supply chains "would choke off an important channel for international technology transmission ... and discourage foreign investment that is often related to" more productive processes of production.[87] Openness to trade, including through international supply chains, helps make domestic economies more productive.[88]

In August 2020, a study conducted by the McKinsey Global Institute concluded that up to 26 percent of the exports of global goods – worth $4.6 trillion – could shift to new countries in the next five years.[89] The analysts who did the study predicted that, on average, companies participating in GVCs can expect a disruption lasting more than a month to hit them every 3.7 years, with, "[o]n average, losses equal to almost 45 percent" of one year's profits every decade.[90] Moreover, the McKinsey study identified 180 products made through value chains for which one country accounts for 70 percent or more of exports, "creating the potential for bottlenecks," especially during a global crisis such as a pandemic.[91] Concentration of product sources is highest in mobile and communications equipment, common in textiles and apparel, and also prevalent in the sector that has drawn the most attention during the pandemic – medicine and medical supplies.

THE LINK BETWEEN TRADE AND HEALTH

As the COVID-19 pandemic continues worldwide, one front on which the battle for human health is being waged is international trade.[92] Domestic policymakers are confronting life-and-death decisions about how to deploy limited resources of vaccines and other medical goods urgently needed throughout the world to combat the pandemic. Amid tense domestic political pressures, tariffs and other restrictions on medical trade have persisted and proliferated. As a global response, the goal of strengthening the links between trade and health in support of global well-being should be at the top of the trade agenda.[93]

Shortly after her election in February 2021, the new director-general of the WTO, Dr. Ngozi Okonjo-Iweala, said her top priority was to ensure that the WTO did more to address the pandemic, including by eliminating tariffs and speeding up efforts to lift export restrictions that were slowing trade in medicines and medical supplies.[94] On the new COVID-19 vaccines, she warned, "The nature of the pandemic and the mutation of many variants makes this such that no one country can feel safe until every country has taken precautions to vaccinate its population."[95]

Yet, it is not the director-general who sets the agenda for the WTO. The 164 members of the WTO do that. The director-general can continue to play an important role through a combination of exhortatory public statements and behind-the-scenes persuasion. But only if WTO members place medical trade at the top of their agenda will it be there; and, as the pandemic continued in 2021, while there was considerable talk by WTO members about freeing medical trade from tariff and other trade restrictions, there was, unfortunately, no action. Worse, the restrictions on medical trade increased. Failure by the members of the WTO to take affirmative actions to free trade in medical goods will only undermine progress toward ending the pandemic.

Goal 3 of the United Nations Sustainable Development Goals for 2030 is to "ensure healthy lives and promote well-being for all at all ages," including by combating communicable diseases and by providing access to affordable essential medicines and vaccines.[96] International trade is indispensable to meeting this global goal. As the WTO, the WHO, and the World Intellectual Property Organization (WIPO) have jointly explained, "International trade is vital for access to medicines and other medical technologies, markedly so for smaller and less-resourced countries."[97] Trade, they have said, is vital to achieving this goal because "[t]rade stimulates competition, which, in turn, reduces prices and offers a wider range of suppliers, improving security and predictability of supply. Trade policy settings – such as tariffs on medicines, pharmaceutical ingredients and medical technologies – therefore directly affect the accessibility of such products."[98]

More than that, the WTO, WHO, and WIPO have emphasized,

Trade policy and the economics of global production systems are also key factors in strategic plans to build domestic production capacity in medical products. Non-discriminatory domestic regulations founded on sound health principles are also import-ant for a stable supply of quality health products. Access to foreign trade opportunities can create economies of scale to support the costs and uncertainties of medical research and product development processes.[99]

These opportunities will be missed – and the pandemic will be longer and deadlier – if freeing trade in medical goods is not a main priority of the WTO-based multilateral trading system.

THE COMPOSITION OF WORLD MEDICAL TRADE

Although international trade has always been important to ensuring health and to combating communicable disease, it has become even more important during the COVID-19 pandemic. According to the WTO, WHO, and WIPO, "[T]he vast majority of countries are net importers of all categories of health technolo-gies, including those needed to address COVID-19."[100] World imports of medical products totaled about $1.01 trillion in 2019.[101] Of these imports, most – about $597 billion – are linked to the pandemic.[102] These products essential to fighting COVID-19 include medicines, medical supplies, medical equipment and technology, and personal protective products (PPP) such as face masks, sanitizer, and hand soaps. Of these imports, 56 percent are medicines.[103]

Medical trade is concentrated. "The top 10 exporters (of medical products) account for almost three-quarters of world exports."[104] Developed countries "have dominated trade in health-related products."[105] Germany, the United States, and Switzerland combined supply 35 percent of the medical products in the world."[106] Medical imports are similarly concentrated. The top ten import-ers of medical products account for 65 percent of all imports.[107] The United States, Germany, China, and Belgium represent 40 percent of all medical imports.[108] With its vast affluent market, the United States is the single largest global importer of medical products, with 19 percent.[109]

China is, however, the world's largest exporter of medical equipment – including several medical devices that have proven crucial to combating COVID-19.[110] Much noticed in the United States during the pandemic has been the fact that – even with the contentious trade conflicts between the United States and China – imports of medical equipment into the United States have remained significant. According to China's Foreign Ministry, between March 2020 and March 2021, Chinese exports to the United States included more than 43 *billion* medical masks.[111]

China was a major global supplier of medical masks, other face shields, protective garments, gloves, and goggles before the pandemic, and it has remained so during the pandemic.[112] Chad Bown of the Peterson Institute for International Economics has noted that, "[A]s the coronavirus spread in China, the rest of the world feared being cut off from critical Chinese supplies just when they would be needed the most." But that did not happen. Although there were some disputed reports of Chinese export restraints, for the most part, China scaled up its production of key medical goods and exported them widely.[113]

One of the most important categories of medical goods is medicines, and the situation with medicines is more complex than with most other medical goods. The chemical or other substance that produces the intended beneficial effect in a drug is called the "active pharmaceutical ingredient." Some drugs have multiple active ingredients. At one time, most pharmaceutical companies created the API, made the tablet or capsule, and packaged the final medical product. With the modern death of distance, however, major pharmaceutical firms in developed countries began to specialize in the value-added portions of the drug production process by "pursuing potentially lucrative, blockbuster patents rather than producing lower-margin bulk pharmaceuticals that are no longer covered by patents."[114] They started outsourcing much of the lower end pharma work in the production of both generic drugs and APIs to factories in developing countries.

About 90 percent of the drugs taken by Americans are generic drugs for which the patents have expired.[115] It is not profitable economically to produce many of these drugs in the United States or in the European Union. Similarly, outsourcing the production of APIs makes sense because most APIs are commodity products that are substitutable irrespective of where they originate. They are also largely tradable; they do not have to be made near to where they are consumed. All drugs contain APIs. Thus, for its huge domestic market, the largest in the world, "The United States sources 80 percent of its APIs from overseas, and a substantial portion of U.S. generic drug imports come either directly from China or from third countries like India that use APIs sourced from China."[116] Sourcing in these developing countries offers distinct cost advantages in labor, energy, water, and other factors of production that lower prices for US pharmaceutical companies and, thus, for US medical consumers.

This shift in the low-end production of pharmaceuticals went largely unnoticed until the arrival of COVID-19. Since then, it has drawn much media attention, especially in the United States. The Center for Disease Research and Policy at the University of Minnesota has listed 156 acute critical drugs often used in the United States – "the drugs without which patients would die in hours."[117] The center's director and a coauthor have explained,

All these drugs are generic; most are now made overseas; and many of them, or their active pharmaceutical ingredients, are manufactured in China or India. A pandemic that idles Asian factories or shuts down shipping routes thus threatens the already strained supply of these drugs to Western hospitals, and it doesn't matter how good a modern hospital is if the bottles and vials on the crash cart are empty.[118]

Specializing as a source of low-end manufacture for such products on global pharmaceutical value chains, China has become the second largest exporter of drugs and biologics to the United States, accounting for 13.4 percent of US imports of those products in 2018.[119] In particular, China has become a key supplier to the United States of APIs and generic medicines for which the patents have expired. China is the world's leading supplier of APIs, accounting for 16 percent of world exports in 2019.[120] Otherwise, though, China is not yet a major source of medical products. Leaving aside APIs and other inputs, in 2019, China accounted for only 1 percent of world exports of *final* medical products.[121] On the other hand, with its growth, China has become the world's second-largest drug market, after the United States.[122] Thus, China is not only a source of low-end supply; increasingly, China also represents a major potential new market for US and European medical exports.

Many Chinese pharmaceutical products are drugs that American companies simply found unprofitable to produce.[123] Notably, Chinese medical exports to the United States are often generic equivalents and raw materials for older medical products that are still used by many Americans. For example, China is the principal source for the United States "of the chemical and raw materials for popular blood pressure medicines and several older antibiotics that are no longer manufactured in the U.S., such as doxycycline and penicillin."[124] China is also "the only maker of key ingredients in a class of decades-old antibiotics known as cephalosporins, which treat a range of bacterial infections, including pneumonia."[125] About 70 percent of the acetaminophen used in the United States is made in China.[126]

Like China, India is one of the world's leading suppliers of drugs. India, in particular, is the world's leading supplier of generic drugs, including 40 percent of the generic drugs consumed by Americans.[127] India imports about 70 percent of the APIs it uses in manufacturing drugs from China.[128] Because of the sizeable extent of India's dependence on these Chinese imports, and because of its need to avoid supply chain disruptions, the Indian government has, since the start of the pandemic, established new incentives to encourage the domestic manufacture of key starting materials and active ingredients that the Indians currently source from China.[129]

Chinese and Indian firms do not monopolize the global marketplace for these and other medical products, however. China ranked only seventh among the top ten exporters of all medical products in 2019, with just 5 percent of world exports; India ranked much lower.[130] The global statistics on API sourcing and production as a part of medical trade are sketchy; but, according to the US Food and Drug Administration, of about 2,000 manufacturing facilities in the world producing API, 13 percent are in China; 18 percent are in India; 26 percent are in the European Union; and 28 percent are in the United States. For those APIs that the World Health Organization has identified as "essential medicines," 21 percent of the manufacturing facilities are in the United States; 15 percent are in China; and the rest are spread among India, Canada, and the European Union. The FDA reports that in 2019, there were 510 API facilities in the United States, and that 221 of them were supplying "essential medicines."[131] Most of the value in medical products is still added in the United States and in Europe.

TARIFFS ON MEDICINES AND OTHER MEDICAL GOODS

Our experience with COVID-19 has demonstrated that we do not yet have free trade in medicines and other medical goods. As with other traded goods, the principal tool used to limit medical trade has been import taxes imposed at the border in the form of taxes. Tariffs increase the prices of medicines and other medical products, and, despite some cuts in the years leading up to the pandemic, tariffs on some medical products remain high. For all medical products, the average "bound" tariff – the average tariff ceiling that is pledged by a country in its WTO concessions – is 26 percent.[132] Almost one-third of WTO members have an average bound tariff on medical goods of more than 50 percent.[133] The average "applied" tariff on medical products – the tariff currently in use – is, however, considerably lower, at 4.8 percent.[134] In the United States, the applied average tariff on medical goods is 0.9 percent.[135] But the gap between the bound and the applied tariffs leaves ample legal room for increasing tariffs on these products without violating WTO rules.

Generally, among international trade negotiators, a tariff of 15 percent or higher is consider a "tariff peak."[136] Some members of the WTO apply tariffs soaring as high as 65 percent on some of these essential products.[137] The average tariffs on the protective supplies used to combat COVID-19 are as high as 27 percent in some countries.[138] The average applied tariff on hand soap is 17 percent.[139] Surprisingly, only nine WTO members allow a health product as basic as soap to enter duty-free.[140] As trade economist Simon Evenett of the University of St. Gallen has mused, "At a time when the frequent washing of hands is recommended by the World Health Organization, policies that increase the cost of soap are particularly difficult to rationalize."[141]

These tariffs on medical products have a protectionist effect; but they are not always imposed for the purpose of protecting domestic industries. Instead, many of them are intended to raise tax revenue, especially in poorer countries. Yet these revenue-raising measures are counterproductive for these countries because tariffs increase the prices of medical products. They are taxes on consumption that undermine health care by increasing the prices of essential medicines and medical supplies, which are often paid by the public health services in these countries. The harmful health effects of these tariffs became apparent to all in the early stages of the pandemic when both consumers and governments scrambled for unprecedented amounts of medical and protective equipment such as masks, respirators, gloves, goggles, garments, and ventilators, as well as numerous hygienic and disinfectant products.[142] International trade in personal protective equipment doubled in the space of only a few months.[143] But much of the trade in medical products was burdened by tariffs.

The shortages of medicines and other medical goods that occurred immediately following the COVID-19 outbreak were not wholly unanticipated. In part to prevent such shortages, in the decades leading up to the pandemic, intermittent efforts were made to free up trade in medical products. Those efforts can be traced back to the Uruguay Round and 1994, when a subset of WTO members concluded the Agreement on Trade in Pharmaceutical Products – the "Pharma Agreement."[144] The parties to this WTO sectoral agreement are Canada; the European Union and its twenty-seven member states; Japan; Macao, China; Norway; Switzerland; the United Kingdom; and the United States. The Pharma Agreement has eliminated tariffs and other duties and charges on a long list of pharmaceutical products and on the ingredients and other substances used to produce them, permanently binding them at duty-free levels.[145] Although only about a quarter of WTO members are currently parties to this agreement, they have eliminated duties on all covered products on a most-favored-nation basis, which means that they have ended the duties on those products in their trade with all other WTO members, and not just with the countries that have signed the agreement.

The Pharma Agreement was updated in 1996, 1998, 2007, and 2010. Even so, it has not kept up with the growth and the diversity of the global trade in pharmaceuticals. The parties to the agreement represent about two-thirds of all pharmaceutical trade, but, since the conclusion of the Uruguay round, other WTO members have entered the pharma market without also signing the Pharma Agreement. As a percentage of the burgeoning trade in pharmaceuticals, the coverage of the Pharma Agreement has shrunk. In 1994, the agreement accounted for about 90 percent of the world trade in the covered products. At present, it accounts for only about 66 percent of that trade. Furthermore, the Pharma Agreement deals only with the tariffs on international trade in medicines and in what goes into making them. It does not address the tariffs on the growing trade in other medical goods.

Thus, tariff-free trade in medical goods other than medicines remains mostly an aspiration for the WTO. To their credit, four WTO members – Macao, China; Hong Kong, China; Singapore; and Iceland – have eliminated all duties on all medical products.[146] The other 160 WTO members have not. While most of the world continues to struggle during the pandemic to secure essential medicines and other medical goods at affordable prices, most WTO members continue to apply tariffs that limit international trade in those products.

Tariffs rarely make sense, and these border taxes on imports of life-saving goods may make the least sense of all because "they increase cost early in the value chain," and, by increasing upstream cost, "their impact on price may be magnified" over and above the amount of the tariffs.[147] Eliminating the tariffs on medicines and other medical products would reduce their costs and the likelihood of shortages. It would, as a result, help end the COVID-19 pandemic and otherwise enhance overall global health. Furthermore, as Anabel Gonzalez, a former Costa Rican trade minister who is now deputy director general of the WTO, has observed, "Eliminating such protectionist measures could also lower the cost of inputs like active ingredients and other chemical products, encouraging domestic investment and production."[148] As she has said, with respect to medical products, "the fact that tariffs exist at all is puzzling in light of the importance of ensuring access to affordable medicines for poor people."[149]

PANDEMIC EXPORT RESTRICTIONS ON MEDICAL GOODS

With the sudden outbreak of the pandemic, trade in essential medical products experienced, simultaneously, demand shock, supply shock, and disruptions of global transport and supply chains. Faced with the immediacy of domestic shortages in medical goods due to "just in time" business practices and less than ample emergency stockpiles, the first frantic response of some countries to the pandemic was to restrict and otherwise distort trade in medical goods. India banned exports of respiratory masks,[150] twenty-six pharmaceutical ingredients, and some of the products made by them.[151] The European Union announced emergency export restrictions on hospital supplies needed to fight the pandemic.[152] German authorities halted delivery of 240,000 medical masks to a Swiss buyer.[153]

At the same time, an executive order by President Trump in the United States in August 2020 required federal agencies in need of "essential drugs" and other medical supplies to "Buy American."[154] In addition, the US federal government contracted with the company that made the first drug licensed for the treatment of COVID-19 – remdesivir – to provide the bulk of its production, at least temporarily, exclusively to Americans.[155] A proliferation of contractual obligations to provide vaccines first to the United States and to other wealthier countries amounted to indirect and de facto export restrictions. As 2020 continued, pandemic protectionism infected more and more countries.[156] By the end of the year, ninety-two governments had taken a total of 215 direct measures restricting exports of medicines and medical supplies.[157] A bewildered Simon Evenett lamented from Switzerland, "Now, beggar-thy-neighbour becomes sicken-thy-neighbor."[158]

Like tariffs, these other restrictive trade measures prevent the limited quantities of drugs and medical supplies from going to where they are most needed to conduct effective coordinated global combat against the global virus, especially in the poorest countries where the outbreak may ultimately be the worst.[159] It is understandable that national leaders will want to secure medicines, medical supplies, and medical care for their own citizens. And yet, once again, on what moral basis do we favor people here over people there? What is more, ultimately, these leaders will not help their citizens by restricting trade in medicines and other medical products. Restrictions on exports of medical goods will have the economic effect of limiting their production, and thus their overall supply, because such measures will limit potential markets and thus reduce the incentive to increase the production of those goods. Measures restricting trade in medicines and medical supplies are self-defeating and "hurt all countries, particularly the more fragile."[160]

Poorer countries, which must import much of the medical goods they need to fight COVID-19, will be hurt first, and maybe the most, from the higher prices resulting from such measures. For them, the consequence "could be deadly."[161] Little understood, though, by many people in the developed world, is that wealthier countries, usually those imposing the restrictions, will likewise be harmed. Not only will domestic production be constrained, World Bank economists Aaditya Mattoo and Michele Ruta have explained that, also, medical prices will "be higher than they need be," and that medical supplies will "be distributed neither efficiently nor equitably."[162] Nigerians and Indonesians, Bolivians and Indians will suffer; but so too will Canadians and Australians, Europeans and Americans.

Further, there is, equally, the timeless but too-often ignored objection to recurring attempts at self-sufficiency. No one country, not even the wealthiest, will be able to make and to assure for itself all the vast variety of essential medicines and medical supplies it needs. Martin Wolf has reminded us that the case with medical export restrictions is much the same as with trade restrictions in general during the pandemic:

Remember that the problem (in the pandemic is) not with trade, but rather with a lack of supply. Export restrictions merely reallocate the shortages, by shifting them on to countries with the least capacity. A natural response to this experience is for every country to try to be self-sufficient in every product that might turn out to be relevant ... Yet businesses would then lose economies of scale, as global markets fragmented. Their capacity to invest in innovation would be reduced. Only the largest and most advanced economies could plausibly seek self-sufficiency in such a wide range of technologies. For all others, this would be a dead end.[163]

In general, WTO rules prohibit export restrictions. Significantly, export taxes are not forbidden by WTO rules (although they are not an option for the United States because they are barred by the US Constitution).[164] But, otherwise, "prohibitions or restrictions other than duties, taxes or other charges, whether made effective through quotas ... export licenses or other measures ... on the exportation or sale for export of any product" are inconsistent with WTO obligations.[165] This obligation, however, does not apply to "[e]xport prohibitions or restrictions temporarily applied to prevent or relieve critical shortages of foodstuffs or other products essential to the exporting" WTO member.[166]

All export restrictions, even when they are applied temporarily because of critical shortages of essential products, must, under WTO rules, be made transparent through publication so that all WTO members can become familiar with them.[167] Also, they must not be discriminatory.[168] Importantly, an export restriction, even if it is not eligible for the carve-out for temporary measures relating to critical shortages, will be excused from the general WTO ban on such measures if it is necessary to protect public health or necessary to secure compliance with laws or regulations that are not inconsistent with WTO obligations, so long as it is not applied "in a manner which would constitute arbitrary or unjustifiable discrimination between countries where the same conditions prevail, or a disguised restriction on international trade."[169] All of these legal terms are, of course, the topics of much trade debate, and are subject to clarification in WTO settlement of international trade disputes.[170]

All this said about the current WTO rules, the fact that many of the export restrictions imposed on medical goods during the pandemic are probably legal under WTO law does not, as Wolf has said, "make them wise."[171] Jennifer Hillman, a leading American trade scholar and former member of the WTO Appellate Body, has explained that

such actions clearly work to the detriment of the world's ability to distribute ... scarce medical resources to where they are needed most with the minimal amount of red tape. When one country imposes an export ban, others tend to follow, resulting in higher prices and pockets of scarcity outside of the silos created by the bans. Moreover, given the number of components that must cross borders in today's global supply chain manufacturing system, export bans may disrupt supply chains and delay the production of critical medical supplies or devices.[172]

More still, export restrictions on medical goods cause "disproportionate harm to developing nations that cannot otherwise compete in bidding wars."[173]

The threat of harm everywhere from medical export restrictions has intensified as the pandemic has persisted. Most visibly, this threat can be seen in the turn toward restrictions on the export of COVID-19 vaccines as the world's handful of vaccine suppliers ramp up to unprecedented levels of production. In March 2020, one major vaccine producer, the European Union, unveiled emergency rules that gave it broad powers to curb vaccine exports temporarily. This EU action seemed likely to cut exports to the United Kingdom and other countries to ease European supply shortages.[174] At the same time, India cut back on its vaccine exports as virus cases surged at home. Like the European action, the Indian action threatened to undermine vaccination in other countries.[175] Depending on how they are structured and applied, actions of this kind may be legal under WTO rules, but they are nevertheless bad policy.

THE NEW RULES NEEDED ON TRADE AND HEALTH

In the new pandemic world, instead of imposing tariffs on and restricting exports of medicines and other medical goods, countries should be freeing up both exports and imports of those goods. G20 trade ministers have urged countries to limit trade-restrictive measures taken to promote public health to those that are "targeted, proportionate, transparent and temporary."[176] This does not go nearly far enough. At the top of the "to-do" list of new rules needed in this new world by the WTO is the pressing necessity for rules that will eliminate all existing tariffs and other trade restrictions on medicines and other medical goods, and that will provide new guidelines and disciplines that will encourage WTO members to refrain from enacting additional restrictions.

With the lives of their citizens at stake, it is exceedingly difficult for politicians to resist the temptation to yield to medical nationalism. Yet, although restrictive national measures limiting medical trade may be politically appealing, and although – depending on how they are applied and for how long they are applied – they may be legal under WTO rules, the reality is, such measures prevent medicines and other essential medical supplies from going to where they are most needed to conduct effective and coordinated global combat against the global virus, especially in the poorest countries where the outbreak may ultimately be the worst. There may be sky-high stacks of protective masks in London but virtually none in Liberia. There may be plentiful supplies of a drug helpful in treating the virus in San Francisco but not nearly enough in South Sudan.

Some of the WTO members that depend heavily on medical imports have sought to encourage multilateral actions to write new rules to free up trade in medicines and other medical goods. Looking outward instead of inward, New Zealand and Singapore committed in March 2020 to continue to keep their own medical supply chains open. Canada, Australia, Chile, Brunei, and Myanmar soon made similar commitments. In April 2020, New Zealand and Singapore entered into a bilateral agreement to eliminate tariffs, refrain from export restrictions, negotiate removal of nontariff barriers, and further trade facilitation for a long list of medical products. These conveners invited other countries to join them in the agreement.[177] In March 2021, New Zealand also pressed the leaders of the twenty-one APEC (Asia-Pacific Economic Cooperation) countries to agree to the free movement of medical supplies.[178]

Encouragingly, in November 2020, thirteen WTO members working together on WTO reform, called the "Ottawa Group," announced that they had joined forces to urge all WTO members to suspend tariffs on medical equipment, refrain from export restrictions on essential medical goods, implement trade-facilitating measures in customs and services, and improve transparency in medical trade.[179] The Ottawa Group includes Australia, Brazil, Canada, Chile, the European Union, Japan, Kenya, the Republic of Korea, Mexico, New Zealand, Norway, Singapore, and Switzerland. The professed aim of these WTO members is to enhance global cooperation on the nexus of trade and health, strengthen global health supply chains, and agree on new WTO rules to facilitate trade in essential medical goods by the end of 2021.[180]

Notably absent from the Ottawa Group thus far has been the United States. The political momentum of the United States under President Trump was not toward medical multilateralism but, rather, was toward achieving more medical self-sufficiency. Trump's successor, President Biden, seems more inclined than his predecessor toward medical multilateralism – but only after all Americans are vaccinated and have been assured of access to the medicines and medical supplies they need. Biden seems more inclined than Trump to join other countries to take meaningful multilateral actions on the links between trade and health. At this writing, though, his primary focus remains on getting Americans fully vaccinated in a fraught domestic political context in which a refusal to get vaccinated has somehow become, for tens of millions of Americans, an assertion of their individual freedom.[181]

In its initiative on the nexus of trade and health, the Ottawa Group has pledged to "make best endeavours to temporarily remove or reduce tariffs on goods that are considered essential to fighting COVID-19 pandemic, as far as possible, taking into account national circumstances. Members may choose the method of implementation of such a temporary tariff removal or reduction, which could take the form of emergency duty relief programs."[182] The group has suggested that "the indicative list of COVID-19 related goods, established by the WCO and WHO could be helpful in the determination of the product scope."[183] Although commendable, this proposal is not nearly as ambitious as it must be during this time of a global health emergency.

WTO members should eliminate all tariffs on medicines and other medical goods. Practically speaking, this could be done in part by expanding both the membership and the scope of the Pharma Agreement. All WTO members should become parties to the Pharma Agreement, making it fully multilateral. And the scope of coverage of the agreement should be expanded to cover trade in all medicines and, also, trade in all other medical goods. One enormously beneficial way in which the United States could begin to show global leadership once again on trade liberalization would be to cooperate with the Ottawa Group in reducing all worldwide medical tariffs to zero.

Needed also are new WTO disciplines on medical export restrictions. The Ottawa Group recommends that WTO members "review and promptly eliminate unnecessary existing restrictions on exports of essential medical goods necessary to combat the Covid-19 pandemic" and "exercise restraint in the imposition of any new export restrictions, including export taxes, on essential medical goods and on any prospective vaccine or vaccine materials."[184] In pursuing these recommendations, WTO members should consider whether any medical export restrictions can ever be necessary and, if so, under precisely what circumstances. They should consider also whether it is sufficient simply to exercise restraint in imposing new export restrictions on medicines and other medical goods when global health would be best served by refraining from imposing such restrictions altogether.

The Ottawa Group rightly advises that, in taking such steps, WTO members should

ensure that any measures deemed necessary to prevent or relieve critical shortages are implemented in a manner that is targeted, transparent, proportionate and temporary, and consistent with WTO obligations; gives particular consideration to the interest of the least developed and developing countries, many of which have scarce manufacturing capacities and are highly dependent on imports, in order to avoid a negative impact of such measures on their access to essential medical goods; and ensures that any trade measures, including export restrictions, do not disrupt the provision of humanitarian shipments of essential medical goods, nor the work of the COVAX facility in distributing vaccines.[185]

Helpfully, the former deputy director-general of the WTO, Ambassador Alan Wolff, has advised that export controls on medical products should be "subject to an agreed code of conduct" providing that "countries imposing export restrictions should first consider their impact on other countries before imposing the controls"; "where feasible, prior notice should be given"; "an opportunity to consult should be offered"; and "immediate international review of export restrictions should be provided for."[186] As he has said, "When export controls are being considered, both countries and businesses should recognize that they would pay a high price in terms of future participation in the world economy were they to become unreliable suppliers."[187]

Erasing tariffs and export restrictions on trade in medicines and other medical goods should be just the start in new WTO rulemaking on medical trade. In the new pandemic world in which moving essential medicines and other medical goods quickly across borders is critical to fighting COVID-19 – and will be equally critical to fighting variants of COVID-19 as well as any other pandemics yet to come – still more must be done also to remove the red tape at the border that impedes the flow of trade. As the Ottawa Group suggests, cooperation is needed among WTO members to share in the "best practices" of "digital customs procedures, and services such as freight, logistics, distribution and transport, which have proven an effective tool for members to facilitate the frictionless movement of essential medical goods across borders."[188]

In 2013, in one of their few real negotiating successes since the creation of the WTO, the members of the WTO concluded an agreement on trade facilitation in Bali, Indonesia.[189] Still being implemented, the Trade Facilitation Agreement cuts a lot of needless red tape at the border while modernizing trade and making it much more digital. Facilitating trade speeds trade and increases the flow of trade. Building on this agreement, WTO members should zero in on further facilitating trade in medicines and in other medical goods. As one example, China and the European Union have each created "green lanes" in their customs procedures to speed the inspection and release of medical goods.[190] This innovation should be emulated everywhere. Other worthy ideas for new WTO rules include: promoting transparency in all national measures taken to fight the virus; waiving all "buy local" requirements for medical goods; eliminating all the nontariff barriers that hinder trade in medicines and medical equipment; adopting international standards to help ensure the safety and the quality of imported medical goods; and giving the go-ahead to targeted subsidies for producing the new medicines urgently needed to stop COVID-19.

All these new rules relating to trade in medicines and other medical products should be combined into a WTO medical trade agreement. Ideally, such an agreement would be fully multilateral, including all 164 WTO members. If that is not at first achievable, then such an agreement could initially include some but not all WTO members, and WTO members could build toward making it fully multilateral over time. The key to the success of such a new "trade and health" agreement would be making it enforceable in WTO dispute settlement. As with other WTO agreements, WTO members would be free to choose not to comply with an obligation in such a medical trade agreement, but choosing not to comply would invite, as a "last resort," application of economic sanctions in the form of a withdrawal of previously granted trade concessions by any WTO members harmed by that decision.[191]

The answer to the challenge of the pandemic is not to break the links in global medical supply chains and attempt to replace them with an exclusive reliance on national production. As Shannon K. O'Neil and others have recommended, the links in supply chains should be strengthened by adding strategic redundancies through more geographically dispersed production facilities and by stockpiling emergency reserves of essential products. In the structure of supply chains, "just in time" should yield to "just in case." During global health emergencies such as COVID-19, the flow of trade in medical and other essential goods must continue. For medical goods and for other essential products, supply chains linked to single sources or to only a few sources on the far side of the world should be diversified to include more sources of supply from reliable and perhaps not so distant locations. Likewise, for those same essential products, local inventories should be increased "just in case" of a crisis. These two changes will increase consumer prices to some extent, but, in trade off, importantly, they will also help secure more ample domestic supplies during times when they are most needed.

Many of these needed changes in medical supply management will not have to be mandated by governments; they will likely occur naturally as an outcome of altered market forces in the wake of the pandemic. Thus, governmental interventions should be kept to the bare minimum required to assure a sufficiency of supplies. With some products, however, targeted governmental actions may be needed to provide incentives for private companies to diversify their supply sources and increase their inventories. Again, and as others have suggested, governments should, in addition, supplement private inventories by increasing strategic public stockpiles of critical medicines and medical products as well as other essential products.[192] As one example, in the United States, two former commissioners for the FDA have advised that maintenance of sufficient diagnostic capacity for testing during a crisis should be part of such a national stockpile.[193]

Former WTO Director-General Pascal Lamy has suggested that the "pre-Covid balance between efficiency and resilience will have to tilt to the side of resilience."[194] In the new pandemic world, to some extent, this must happen.

Indeed, in numerous instances, this is already happening, and it is driven to a great extent by market forces. But self-sufficiency in all that may be desperately needed during a health crisis, remains impossible and undesirable for all countries. Moreover, "The quest for resilience comes with risks of its own."[195] There is abundant reason for governmental actions to help prevent future disruptions in supply chains, but there is no reason whatsoever for governmental actions that cut the links of supply chains. Doing so would only deny people everywhere the many and undeniable advantages of the international division of labor.[196]

Without question, medical supply chains must be made more resilient. But restricting medical trade will not enhance resilience; it will undermine it, locally and globally. To help end the pandemic, and to help end it sooner, global medical trade must be liberalized. The WTO should be the agent and the architect of this liberalization. The 164 members of the WTO must take immediate affirmative actions in the global fight against COVID-19. To the covered agreements in the WTO treaty must be added a medical trade agreement that frees trade worldwide in medicines and other medical goods.

THE ANTIDOTE TO VACCINE NATIONALISM

The world has rightly celebrated the unprecedented speed with which vaccines for COVID-19, the novel coronavirus, have been discovered and brought to the global marketplace, a life-saving testament both to free private enterprise and public/private cooperation.[197] The first new vaccines for the virus became available in limited amounts toward the end of 2020.[198] Production and distribution ramped up in the first months of 2021, almost entirely in the wealthier countries where the new vaccines were first developed. When those vaccines finally become widely available worldwide, millions of lives can be saved, and the loss of $375 billion to the global economy every month can be prevented.[199]

Yet, at this writing, the world remains far from reaching that goal. In mid-April 2021, the World Health Organization reported that wealthier countries had obtained more than 87 percent of the more than 700 million doses of COVID-19 vaccines distributed worldwide, while poorer countries had received only 0.2 percent. In wealthier countries, about one in four people had received a vaccine; in poorer countries, only one in 500 people had been vaccinated.[200] As some places in the United States found it necessary to pay skeptical and misinformed Trump voters and other Americans to take the vaccine, human beings elsewhere in the world searched desperately for doses that were not there.[201]

While billions of people worldwide await their doses of the new vaccines, the gap between the supply of COVID-19 vaccines and the urgent demand for them has led many anxious countries to court "the tragedy of vaccine nationalism."[202] With potentially lethal global consequences, the handful of countries that have produced vaccines in record time have given the limited vaccine doses to their own citizens first, whatever their level of infection risk, while leaving people in other countries, especially poorer countries, without potentially life-saving inoculations. Scientists tell us that vaccinating the most vulnerable people everywhere first and leaving the least vulnerable to last – wherever they may be – is by far the best way to end the pandemic. Yet these countries have given priority to immediate universal *national* vaccination of their own citizens instead of to scientifically targeted *national and international* vaccination. This vaccine nationalism will prolong the pandemic while causing more deaths worldwide.

Wherever we may live, giving preference to vaccinating our fellow nationals who are the least at risk of COVID-19 infection over people from other countries who are the most at risk, is not only morally wrong but also contrary to our own national self-interest. To provide the most protection to the health and jobs of people from anywhere, the emerging COVID-19 vaccines must be distributed in ways that will save the most lives everywhere. They must not be deployed in ways that will hasten the turn away from multilateralism and toward an ever more insular nationalism. Vaccine nationalism saves fewer lives, and it pulls countries even farther apart at a time when the world must unite to be able to end the global emergency of the COVID-19 pandemic.

Vaccine nationalism is a more virulent variation of economic nationalism. However, although the rationale of vaccine nationalism is much the same as that of economic nationalism, the objectives of these two versions of national-istic bias are different. Economic nationalism is a self-defeating effort to save livelihoods. Vaccine nationalism is a self-defeating effort to save lives. These two superficially appealing notions are self-defeating because both have the unintended effect of undermining their stated objectives. Economic nationalism can cost livelihoods. Worse, vaccine nationalism can cost lives as well as livelihoods. For this reason, vaccine nationalism is potentially the more danger-ous of these two errant "isms."

The antidote to vaccine nationalism is vaccine multilateralism. In striking contrast to most of what has been happening during the pandemic, a much more effective international cooperative effort should be working to distribute the vaccine first to wherever it is needed most, without consideration of national wealth or power. Furthermore, this global effort should get the vaccine to all who need it, wherever they may be. In keeping with the common pledge made by all the members of the United Nations in the Sustainable Development Goals, this multilateral effort must make certain that "no one will be left behind," and it must "endeavour to reach the furthest behind first."[203] The goal is to end the pandemic, and this goal cannot be achieved if a vaccine is not available to everyone sooner rather than later, including – and especially – those in the poorer countries of the world that are least prepared to protect their citizens against the pandemic. Without considerably more multilateral cooperation on access to new vaccines, the "whack-a-mole" resurgence of COVID-19 in its ever evolving variations in country after country, cannot be prevented, and the pandemic cannot be stopped. Instead, the devastating health and economic suffering caused by the pandemic will persist and indeed increase worldwide.

Discovering an effective vaccine "is only the first step" toward ending the pandemic.[204] As many millions learned when vaccine rollouts began, this initial step toward vaccination is necessarily followed by an extraordinarily complicated process of production and distribution within and between countries worldwide. This task simply cannot be undertaken successfully by any one country on its own, no matter how large or powerful that one country may be, and no matter whether it happens to be home to the enterprise or enterprises that succeeded first in developing an effective vaccine. The novel coronavirus knows no national borders. Attacking us everywhere, it must be attacked by us everywhere through unprecedented cooperative multilateral action, or it will keep returning in its new variations from continuing contacts with other parts of the world. It is simply unrealistic to think that *all* international contacts can be prevented.

Noble attempts are being made worldwide to ensure sufficient multilateralism. As the threat of vaccine nationalism became apparent in the first months following the COVID-19 outbreak, the World Health Organization (WHO), GAVI (the nongovernmental global vaccine alliance), and the Coalition for Epidemic Preparedness Innovations (CEPI) formed the COVID-19 Vaccine Global Access Facility as an intended vehicle for multilateral cooperation in battling the pandemic.[205] COVAX planned to purchase vaccines in bulk and then distribute two billion doses equitably around the world.[206] The aim was to provide enough vaccine doses for 20 percent of the people in the developing world by the end of 2021, including all the frontline health care workers and the most vulnerable.[207]

At last count, 185 countries are participating in COVAX.[208] But, throughout much of 2020, some of the largest countries in the world refrained from participating, which threatened to undermine this vital multilateral effort. Canada, the European Union, India, Japan, and the United Kingdom are taking part. The Russian Federation is not. After months of hesitation, China announced in October 2020 that it, too, will participate.[209] American health scientists recommended to President Trump that the United States enlist in COVAX.[210] He decided not to join.[211] The Trump administration explained that it did not want its own national endeavors against the pandemic to be "constrained by multilateral organizations influenced by the corrupt World Health Organization and China."[212] In October 2020, President Trump also began the formal process of withdrawing the United States from the WHO.[213]

Instead of acting together with others multilaterally to find an effective vaccine, the United States, under President Trump, chose to go it alone. When the Trump administration was asked about its global responsibilities, it replied that it "would focus on bilateral efforts with international partners and that it would consider supplying vaccines to other countries after Americans are immunized."[214] In effect, this "America First" policy gives priority for vaccines to low-risk Americans over the high-risk health care workers and other vulnerable people in the rest of the world. The Trump administration effectively forfeited the role of global leader that the United States has played in past pandemics. This retreat from global responsibility sparked global concerns that COVAX "could falter without official US support and leadership."[215]

For its part, China was dealing with the aftermath of its own early failure to confront and contain the pandemic, which began in Wuhan and spread quickly after initial denials, delays, and obfuscation by the Chinese government.[216] In early 2021, China continued to resist WHO efforts to trace the source of COVID-19.[217] As the virus spread from China and infected the world, unfavorable views of China in some other countries reached record highs.[218] Chinese President Xi Jinping promised to donate $2 billion to fight the pandemic.[219] He also promised that a vaccine produced in China would be treated as "a global public good" and, indeed, sent Chinese-made vaccines to more than twenty countries in an exercise in "vaccine diplomacy."[220] The Chinese decision to enlist in COVAX and share its own vaccines truly may have been inspired by a conviction that a vaccine should be a global public good (although, unfortunately, Chinese-made vaccines, as the Chinese government eventually acknowledged, did not seem to be working as well as had been hoped).[221] It may also be that China's decision to join COVAX was, in part, a geopolitical move intended to repair China's damaged global reputation. At the same time, China shared its vaccines with developing countries that were the sites for Chinese vaccine trials. Whatever China's motive for joining COVAX and sharing its vaccines, these actions boosted the multilateral effort.

The United States was not alone in succumbing to vaccine nationalism. The European Union, Japan, the United Kingdom, and the United States contracted to buy at least 3.7 billion doses of potential COVID-19 vaccines from drug companies, including options for buying additional doses. Canada prepurchased 300 million vaccine doses for a population of 38 million – nearly eight doses per person.[222] China and India said they would steer much of their vaccine production first to their own citizens. Despite its apparent success in curbing the spread of the virus in China by mid-2020, the rollout of vaccines by the Chinese government to its massive population proceeded slowly in 2021 and, later in the year, China confronted a domestic surge of one of the Covid-19 variants.[223] And the demand for vaccine doses soared in India during a raging resurgence of the virus in the spring of 2021.[224] Global health experts advised that these various national arrangements were "likely to tie up nearly all of the immediate global vaccine manufacturing capacity."[225] Those at risk in the poorest countries would get the doses that were left over – if there were any.

It is only natural for the leaders of a country to assume that they have a greater obligation to citizens of their own country than to those of other countries. The ancient teaching of Aristotle still underlies much of our modern politics, instructing us that our fellow citizens in our own "polis" must come first.[226] Thus, the expectation in every country in the world is that priority will be given to shared nationality over shared humanity. For thousands of years, cosmopolitans have contended that all of humanity is one, and that, therefore, every member of the human species should see and treat every other member equally, no matter their national origin or identity.[227] But try telling this to any parent with a child, any patriot with a flag, or any politician with a constituency. Despite the idealistic entreaties of cosmopolitanism, for most people throughout the world, the circle of human concern encompasses those "like us" who are close to home, but it has not yet widened to include everyone in the world.[228]

Many of the COVID-19 vaccines require two doses. Thus, nearly 16 billion doses are needed to vaccinate all the 7.8 billion people in the world. The WHO estimates global capacity for manufacturing COVID-19 vaccines at between two billion and four billion doses by the end of 2021.[229] The Center for Global Development says it is unlikely there will be enough doses of a vaccine for the entirety of the world's population before September 2023.[230] The world's largest vaccine maker – Serum Institute in India – predicts that there will not be enough doses for everyone in the world until, at the earliest, the end of 2024.[231]

Therefore, COVID-19 vaccines will have to be allocated in ways that give priority to some people over others. Despite the heroic efforts in accelerating vaccine production, for some time to come, vaccine demand will exceed supply worldwide. If vaccine nationalism determines who gets doses of a vaccine, when they get them, and how many of them they get, then cosmopolitan idealism will not avail.[232] The person we know who lives next door will loom large. But will that be so for the person we do not know who lives on the far side of the world? In the absence of a sufficiency of cosmopolitanism, in early 2021, the director general of the WHO warned that the world was "on the brink of a catastrophic moral failure."[233]

At issue is a question of fundamental global justice. The right thing to do is to vaccinate first those who are at the highest risk of being infected by the virus, irrespective of where they may live in the world or what their economic circumstances may be. As a matter of justice, the *Lancet* COVID-19 Commission – a global group of health experts created in July 2020 to help speed up fair and enduring global solutions to the pandemic – has stated that "any new vaccine or therapeutic must be developed and implemented with a view to equitable access across and within countries."[234] Ideally, an appeal to justice should suffice, but, here in the real world where most people must struggle daily merely to get by, it rarely does. No matter how they may be portrayed, national policies on international matters are rarely based on what is thought to be just. They are almost always based instead on a country's pragmatic perception of what is in its own self-interest. For this reason, a multilateral antidote to vaccine nationalism will not be found unless and until more countries see that acting multilaterally is in their self-interest. Fortunately, in addition to the moral question of justice, there is the practical reality that the national self-interest is not served by vaccine nationalism.

To use the United States as an example, it may be asked: Once 330 million Americans have been vaccinated, will that not end the spread of the virus in the United States?[235] Most Americans will readily concede that they should help others elsewhere in the world once they have fully helped all Americans. But they may well ask, how can it be in their self-interest to share a vaccine with foreigners before all Americans have been vaccinated? In combating COVID-19, the rallying cry of the advocates of vaccine multilateralism is, "No one is safe until everyone is safe."[236] This is an appealing applause line at global summits, but it may only draw puzzled looks locally. Why is this lofty assertion true?

No one is safe until everyone is safe for several reasons. To begin with, even though the first effective COVID-19 vaccines may have been made in part by companies based in the United States, going it alone risks limiting access to international medical supply chains, which are necessary for obtaining the often rare and exotic inputs into making vaccine products. Vaccine manufacturing is often necessarily a process that involves many sources of supply in many countries. Many of the inputs and other medical products supplied are rare, exotic, and not easily found or made. As Brad Glosserman of the Pacific Forum has observed, "Vaccine supply chains are global ... No country has everything it needs to create, produce and provide drugs."[237]

An example of a product needed in many vaccines but not universally available is a compound called QS-21, which is an "adjuvant" that boosts the body's immune reaction to a vaccine and is derived from the inner bark of the soapbark tree. The soapbark tree is native to central Chile. From there, the compound is shipped to drugmakers worldwide. QS-21 is a rare ingredient that is vital to the vaccine supply chain.[238] What if QS-21 were an essential ingredient for an American-made vaccine? And what if Chile, unable to obtain doses of the vaccine from the United States, cut off all shipments of QS-21 to the United States just as the United States was trying to ramp up vaccine production to vaccinate every American first before sending any leftover doses to other countries? So much, in that hypothetical but definitely possible situation, for the illusion of self-sufficiency.

Next, vaccinating 330 million Americans will take some time. In the vaccine rollout's early days, lines were long and waiting lists were longer of Americans seeking COVID-19 vaccination. Yet, in one poll, only 58 percent of Americans confirmed that they would be willing to take a vaccine as soon as one became available.[239] Amid a maelstrom of misinformation, millions of Americans skipped their needed second doses.[240] And tens of millions more refused to take the vaccines even after they became readily available throughout the United States and months of experience showed that they were highly effective.[241] Irresponsible claims in the United States by Donald Trump and his acolytes that the virus is a "hoax" have taken their toll.[242] This means that the "herd immunity" that the medical community seeks from the virus will take longer to achieve – if it is achieved at all. Moreover, the science remains unclear on how effective the current global assortment of COVID-19 vaccines will be over the long term, and the extent of any potential side effects.[243] In addition, while the United States focuses on vaccinating every American first, including those at lower risk of serious illness, the people most vulnerable to the virus in many other countries do not have access to vaccination. As a result, COVID-19 has continued to rage in recurring surges in India, Brazil, Turkey, Indonesia, Peru, and other countries.

Once Joe Biden became president, the federal government in the United States started taking COVID-19 seriously, and vaccine production and distribution ramped up quickly. But it remains unclear at this writing how long it will take to inoculate every American against the virus. During the indeterminate interim before attainment of "herd immunity," Americans will continue to be exposed to infection. The United States cannot be placed in an isolation ward and kept safely away from the rest of the world. If COVID-19 continues to rage intermittently elsewhere in the world, it will not only claim more lives elsewhere. It will claim more lives in the United States. "It will ... be likely to mutate faster, possibly into strains against which existing vaccines offer no protection."[244] Those new virus strains will reach the United States, and the current COVID-19 vaccines may not provide protections. If the United States does not fully embrace vaccine multilateralism, then the American death count from COVID-19 will continue to rise even higher.

Yet another reason why it is in the self-interest of the United States to act multilaterally instead of unilaterally against COVID-19 is that, according to public health experts, a global "patchwork pattern of vaccination coverage" in which "wealthier countries vaccinate widely while poorer countries remain exposed could prolong border closures and trade and travel disruption while allowing the virus to thrive in many places and remain a global threat."[245] That can reduce demand for US exports and, as we have seen, disrupt supply chains vital to US trade. American growth could slow, more American jobs could be lost, and more American families could plunge over the edge into financial disaster. A global economic study commissioned by the International Chamber of Commerce concluded that, if wealthier countries were fully vaccinated by the middle of 2021 while the people of poorer countries remained unvaccinated, the global economy would suffer losses of more than $9 trillion, and that the advanced economies such as the United States would incur half of these losses – even if they vaccinated their entire populations.[246]

For all these reasons, in combating the COVID-19 pandemic, being open to and engaged with the rest of the world in finding multilateral solutions makes sense for the United States, just as it does for all other countries. Contrary to the prevailing view in the United States, acting multilaterally rather than unilaterally would be putting the self-interest of the American people first. As COVID-19 vaccines were distributed in ever-growing numbers throughout the United States after the inauguration of Joe Biden as president in 2021, eyes elsewhere in the world were focused on the United States in the hope that Americans would realize that a global approach to COVID-19 vaccination is in their own self-interest, and that they would reclaim their global leadership role by enlisting once more in the search for multilateral solutions.

The election of President Biden gave the United States the opportunity to reconsider its Trump-imposed "America First" policy on the distribution of COVID-19 vaccines. It was, however, unclear just how soon and how far Biden would be willing to move away from vaccine nationalism. Like Trump, he promised to vaccinate all Americans first before sharing any doses with the rest of the world.[247] But, encouragingly, on the day after he was inaugurated in January 2021, the United States joined COVAX and announced its intent to remain in the World Health Organization.[248] Soon afterward, President Biden announced the first exports of shots by the United States – "loan" shipments of four million doses of the AstraZeneca vaccine (then unlicensed in the United States) to neighboring Canada and Mexico.[249] In addition, the United States, Australia, Japan, and India pledged to work together to produce at least one billion doses of COVID-19 for the developing countries of the Indo-Pacific region by the end of 2022.[250]

A dramatic turn away from vaccine nationalism by the United States occurred in April 2021. As COVID-19 caused a torrent of death tolls in India that could not even be accurately counted, and as the crematoriums there were running out of space during a humanitarian crisis of epic proportions, Biden responded to pleas for American assistance by promising to send as many as 60 million doses of one of the vaccines in its national stockpile to India, subject to it being certified as safe.[251] He also promised to send the Indians some of the medical supplies and raw materials they desperately needed. In addition, he promised an additional $4 billion to international vaccine efforts and pledged to ask the Congress for billions more.[252] But, however laudable, these US actions were not nearly enough. With two doses to a person, 60 million doses would inoculate only 30 million Indians out of a population of about 1.4 billion. Also, throughout the waiting world, as the WHO reported, only two-tenths of 1 percent of the shots given worldwide had been administered in low-income countries.[253] According to UNICEF, 130 countries with a combined population of 2.5 billion people had "yet to administer a single dose."[254] The sheer shock of these shameful numbers made it clear that these belated American actions to help other people in other countries battle the pandemic would succeed only if they presaged multilateral actions on a much larger scale. Although less than needed, President Biden's vaccine initiatives gave cause for growing worldwide optimism that the United States would, with Trump defeated, become a positive force in multilateral endeavors to fight the COVID-19 pandemic. Fully committed participation by the United States in these efforts was essential to making multilateralism the antidote to vaccine nationalism.

THE LINK BETWEEN TRADE AND FOOD

The link between trade and food is implicit in the aims of the first two of the seventeen United Nations Sustainable Development Goals. Goal 1 is to "[e]nd poverty in all its forms everywhere."[255] Goal 2 is to "[e]nd hunger, achieve food security and improved nutrition and promote sustainable agriculture."[256] Poverty cannot be ended without trade, and food security to end hunger cannot be secured without trade. As with the fifteen other SDGs, the aim is to achieve these first two goals by 2030. In 2015, when all these ambitious global goals were agreed by 193 countries, accomplishing them within fifteen years seemed possible. At the end of 2019, despite frustrating global foot-dragging, it still seemed possible. But now, in the new pandemic world, the prospect for reaching these two global goals appears to be fast receding farther and farther into the future.

In poverty, as on numerous other fronts of human endeavor, COVID-19 jeopardizes decades of incremental progress. In 1990, 36 percent of the people in the world lived below the World Bank's global extreme poverty line of $1.90 in income a day – 1.9 billion people. By 2016, largely because of economic advances in China, India, and elsewhere in South Asia, 10 percent of the world's population lived in extreme poverty – 734 million people.[257] During the intervening years, due mainly to the rapidly growing participation of many developing countries in the global economy, more than one billion people worldwide had been lifted out of poverty. In no small part, this historic accomplishment can be traced to the new opportunities created by freer trade in more open economies. As the economists for the WTO and the World Bank have explained this link, "[T]here is no doubt that the integration of global markets through trade openness has made a critical contribution to poverty reduction ... Without the growing participation of developing countries in international trade, and sustained efforts to lower barriers to the integration of markets, it is hard to see how this reduction could have been achieved."[258]

In 2020, for the first time since 1998, global poverty rates increased. Eight million Americans slipped into poverty in 2020.[259] Globally, the World Bank estimated that the economic fallout from the coronavirus pandemic could push as many as 150 million people into extreme poverty by the end of 2021.[260] This sharp setback toward meeting Goal 1 of the SDGs is largely because the COVID-19 crisis has had "a disproportionate impact on the poor, through job loss, loss of remittance, rising prices, and disruptions in services such as education and health care."[261] Worldwide, those who live either in or on the edge of extreme poverty "often live in fragile and remote areas" that are much harder to reach with economic growth and other forms of poverty alleviation.[262] Most of them are also part of the "informal economy," working and eating from day to day in lifelong drudgery.[263] As a result, the World Bank's economists lamented, "without intensified action, the global poverty goals will not be met" by 2030.[264]

Poverty leads to hunger, and hunger can only be ended with an adequate supply of nutritious food. During the pandemic, more poverty has meant more hunger as jobless people everywhere have struggled to feed themselves and their families. In 2019, 690 million people – about 8.9 percent of the world's population – were undernourished.[265] Since 2014, this number has been "slowly rising."[266] The world was not on pace to end hunger by 2030 even before the arrival of COVID-19. Amid the pandemic, this crisis became a catastrophe. In April 2020, David Beasley, the executive director of the World Food Programme (and a former governor of South Carolina), said the world faced the prospect of widespread famine "of biblical proportions ... [W]e are talking about extreme conditions, emergency status – people marching to the brink of starvation. If we don't get food to people, people will die."[267]

The United Nations Committee on World Food Security forecast that more people would die of malnutrition and its related diseases than from the pandemic itself.[268] To avert such a tragedy, the WFP launched its largest emergency food aid relief program ever.[269] The initial goal for foreign assistance was $6.7 billion. The billions of dollars sought for assistance by global food relief agencies increased as 2020 continued. Yet, despite the desperation in Beasley's dire warning, as the sums needed for humanitarian relief grew, some wealthier countries were slow to offer sufficient emergency food assistance to poorer countries where people were starving.[270] (The United States gave about $3.66 billion of the approximately $8.47 billion in total contributions to the WFP in 2021.)[271]

Children in Yemen, Uganda, Afghanistan, South Sudan, and other places plagued by "conflict, covid, and climate" faced starvation.[272] Even in a country as wealthy as the United States, according to the US Census Bureau, 26 million adults faced hunger.[273] All told, the WFP anticipated an 82 percent increase in the number of those worldwide who were "acutely food-insecure" in 2020.[274] Worse was expected for 2021.[275] Unfortunately, at this rate, "The world is not on track to achieve Zero Hunger by 2030."[276] Indeed, if current trends persist, by then, the number of people "affected by hunger" will exceed 840 million.[277]

Given this surge in hunger, it is not surprising that, in addition to a turn toward a would-be self-sufficiency in trade in medicines and other medical products, COVID-19 has also provoked a push toward more self-sufficiency in trade in food. Worried about not having enough food to meet their domestic needs, and hopeful of insulating their population from costly food price increases, countries throughout the world have been tempted during the pandemic to limit or halt their food exports. As Kym Anderson has remarked, "Since food is the most basic of human needs, it is not surprising that food security is a sensitive policy concern, particularly in countries that are somewhat dependent on food imports and that have experienced interruptions in import supplies," as happened to many countries in the past.[278]

Food self-sufficiency should not be confused with autarky. Countries that are self-sufficient in food routinely engage in international trade. And many countries are, in fact, already "approximately self-sufficient" in food if self-sufficiency is measured by calorie intake or by the volume or value of the food they produce.[279] These countries can satisfy the food needs of their population solely from their own domestic production.[280] This, however, is not the same as saying that these countries have food security. Food self-sufficiency and food security are not the same thing. As the prominent Canadian political economist Jennifer Clapp has explained, "food self-sufficiency within a country does not guarantee food security."[281] Food self-sufficiency is a concept focused exclusively on whether food is available; it is focused only on supply. In contrast, as defined by the United Nations Food and Agriculture Organization, food security exists when the supply of food is available, accessible, nutritious, and stable.[282] Achieving the UN global goals of ending hunger and of ensuring human health depends not on achieving food self-sufficiency, but rather on achieving food security.

The emphasis must be on the broader concept of food security because a metric of food self-sufficiency that measures only calorie intake does not account for the variety or the nutrition of the food that is consumed. Thus, it cannot qualify as a measure of food security.[283] As Clapp has illustrated, "[S]ome countries that are more than self-sufficient in food can still have high levels of hunger and malnutrition among their population. Countries in this situation may produce more than enough of some food crops, but too little of others that are required for a healthy diet."[284] What is more, although some self-sufficient countries "have little difficulty in ensuring that their populations have access to an adequate and nutritious diet," high levels of poverty in other countries may hinder the food access required for food security.[285] In addition, some countries have become less "food self-sufficient" and more dependent on imported food in recent years, such as Japan and many of the countries in sub-Saharan Africa.[286] Sixty-six countries, too, have limited water, cropland, and fertile soil, and so cannot increase their level of self-sufficiency.[287] International trade in food has increased enormously in recent decades, in no small part to meet the needs of those countries.[288]

All this said, the temptation to restrict food exports is exceedingly difficult to resist in developing countries where the cost of food consumes more than half the income of most people.[289] This temptation has increased as the global food price index has risen during the supply chain and other disruptions of the pandemic to its highest level in a decade.[290] Soon after the new coronavirus ventured out of Wuhan, Vietnam stopped exporting rice; India paused rice exports because of labor shortages and logistical difficulties; and Kazakhstan and Russia imposed restrictions on exports of grains and other staples.[291] Others quickly followed with their own restrictions. Wisely, and in contrast, major food producers accounting for nearly two-thirds of world food exports pledged in April 2020 to keep food supply chains open and refrain from imposing food export restrictions.[292] In a joint statement, leaders of the WTO, FAO, and WHO urged governments to ensure that any trade-related measures they took in response to the COVID-19 crisis did not disrupt food supply chains.[293] Reflecting the essential nature of food, agricultural trade proved more resilient than overall trade as the pandemic proceeded.[294] Even so, by August 2020, thirty-one countries had reported implementing a total of forty-nine export controls of food and agricultural products since the beginning of 2020.[295]

These export restrictions have harmed hungry people in some of the poorest countries in the world. For example, "disproportionately affected" by export restrictions imposed by their neighbors have been poor countries in Central Asia, "including Uzbekistan, Kyrgyzstan, Tajikistan, and Afghanistan. Mongolia, Azerbaijan, and Georgia have also been hit."[296] Elsewhere, in North Africa and the Middle East, "fragile states such as Libya and Sudan have been affected, along with Egypt, Jordan, Tunisia, Turkey, and Yemen – a country on the brink of famine."[297] Poorer countries in sub-Saharan Africa "have been affected, too, with the measures having a disproportionate impact on Burundi, Djibouti, Kenya, Rwanda, and Malawi."[298] Like the novel coronavirus, the harm done by food export restrictions is contagious.

The FAO projects that global food demand in 2050 will be at least 60 percent more than global demand in 2006.[299] It predicts that, "[w]ithout adaptation to climate change, it will not be possible to achieve food security for all and eradicate hunger, malnutrition and poverty."[300] For now, though, there is no overall shortage of food in the world. There is plenty of food available in the world – for those who can afford it and otherwise have access to it. During the pandemic, the "difficulties in ensuring food availability have related more to logistical challenges in ensuring smooth functioning of food supply chains as governments impose health-related restrictions reaching beyond the food sector."[301] At the same time, it is worth recalling the landmark research of economist Amartya Sen on the causes of famine. Sen, the first Indian and first Asian to win the Nobel Prize in economics, demonstrated that stopping hunger is not simply a matter of food availability; it is also a matter of providing access to food.[302] What is more, preventing hunger also depends on how food is utilized and on how stable the delivery systems for providing food are in any given place. In other words, it depends on food security – a concept much influenced by Sen's landmark work.

Today, most of the people in the world live in cities. But one thing has not changed since the time when most of the world's population was rural and worked from before dawn until after sunset on small farms in a struggle for subsistence. As ever in agriculture, the challenge is getting food from where it is grown to where it is needed. Farm-to-market roads are still needed, but so too are international food supply chains. Whatever the merits of the metrics of food self-sufficiency, and whatever the localists may think about the virtues of "buying local," most of the people in the world must buy at least some of their food from somewhere else to be able to eat a variety of food and eat nutritiously. International trade in food is indispensable to this necessary task toward achieving food security.

The last time hunger and the fear of hunger led to a turn toward more food self-sufficiency was during the global financial crisis. During that crisis, many countries used trade measures to try to shield their consumers from higher food prices.[303] These countries saw foreign farm trade as a "threat to food security."[304] Between 2008 and 2011, governments worldwide imposed eighty-five new export restrictions on food products. These "export restrictions exacerbated world price volatility by reducing world supplies and increasing world demand. They encouraged others to follow suit by banning exports or by panic buying in importing countries."[305] World food prices increased 13 percent on average. Prices for staples such as rice, wheat, and corn (maize) rose the most. The price of wheat increased 29 percent.[306] The price of rice increased 45 percent.[307]

There was risk of a repeat of this retreat from food trade upon the arrival of COVID-19. In the frantic months that followed the coronavirus outbreak in Wuhan, a much smaller share of "globally traded calories" was affected by restrictive trade measures aimed at achieving self-sufficiency than in the previous period.[308] Yet the harm was considerable, and the combined weight of the food trade restrictions that were applied during the COVID-19 pandemic only added to the mutual and cumulative pressures for protectionism in trade in goods of all kinds. As the coronavirus surged again and again in many places in 2021, there was more and more talk of imposing restrictions on food trade.

Food export restrictions may help keep the prices of a food product grown in the exporting country lower in that country; however, those restrictions can also drive up prices in other countries that depend on imports of that product.[309] The risk is that such export restrictions will "exacerbate world price volatility by shorting world supplies. That encourages other countries to follow suit by banning exports in their country or by panic buying in importing countries."[310] This risk is especially high for basic food commodities such as wheat and rice, which are often the subject of such trade restraints.[311] Furthermore, when countries restrict their food exports to try to protect their domestic markets from international price fluctuations, it often backfires. As a result of the restriction, "the price volatility faced by other countries is amplified" and "[t]hat reaction ... prompts more countries to follow suit."[312]

As so often happens, trade restrictions lead to tit-for-tat retaliatory trade restrictions, and food prices begin to spiral out of control. Ironically, as Anderson has explained, "when both food-exporting and food-importing countries so respond, each group undermines the other's attempts to stabilize its domestic markets."[313] The more countries involved, the worse this situation becomes. The more vital the products involved are to the human diet, the more risk is posed to food security. Thus, what seems to make sense to one country acting alone, makes little sense when other countries respond by acting in the same way. This tit-for-tat phenomenon applies in food trade as it does with restrictions in all other trade.

Prohibiting food imports would promote food self-sufficiency – but at the cost of food security. Domestic farm prices would increase. Those domestic price increases would encourage more domestic farm production. But those same domestic price increases would discourage domestic food consumption and would, therefore, diminish food security.[314] Ultimately, banning food exports produces the same result. Initially, export restrictions may hold down prices on some food products for domestic consumers. But, as local export restrictions are matched by retaliatory foreign export restrictions, food prices rise, and food security is jeopardized. Those who imposed the restrictions create the exact opposite of what they intended, and they must then confront the political wrath of those who can no longer afford to buy food, most often the poorer people in the poorer countries.

Anderson, like most other agricultural trade economists worldwide, has concluded that, "[I]t is clear that broadening to regional, national, international and ultimately inter-continental and global trade multiplies the gains from production specialization and market exchange, and reduces the extent of food insecurity, malnutrition and risk of famine."[315] In particular, he observes that "[o]pening up to trade would be especially beneficial to food security for two categories of countries: those that are restricting food imports and where the majority of the poor and under-nourished are net buyers of food, and those where the majority of the poor and under-nourished are net sellers of food and their governments are restricting food exports."[316]

In the new pandemic world, the WTO rules should be changed to help free both exports and imports of food from the remaining barriers to food trade as a prerequisite to achieving food security and thereby helping to accomplish the UN Sustainable Development Goals. A good start would be to keep the world from turning inward on food trade. WTO members should begin by agreeing on new rules that repeal all the food export restrictions that have been imposed during the pandemic and that prohibit imposing any more. The fact that these new rules have not yet been written is only one of the many signs of the existential crisis of the World Trade Organization.

3

Links to the Pre-pandemic World

THE EXISTENTIAL CRISIS OF THE WTO

When the coronavirus outbreak occurred in Wuhan, China, near the end of 2019, the World Trade Organization was already in existential crisis. It had been for some time. In the quarter century since its formal establishment as an international institution in 1995, a concatenation of circumstances had left the multilateral trading system largely paralyzed. It languished amid the grumblings of growing global discord when COVID-19 arrived. To be sure, the WTO trade dispute settlement continued, albeit in a truncated and increasingly ineffective form because of the successful assault by the protection-minded Trump administration in the United States on the continued functioning of the system's court of final appeal, the WTO Appellate Body. Trade monitoring continued as usual. Trade reports were still published. But the central task of the trading system – necessary trade rulemaking in timely and relevant response to the ever-changing needs of an ever-changing global economy – was mired in impasse as the WTO trade negotiations that had not already collapsed mostly crawled to nowhere.

The slow suicide of the Doha Development Round; the emerging role of developing countries; the divide over "special and differential treatment" for developing countries; the multiplication of bilateral and regional agreements outside the WTO framework; the historic resurgence of China as a global economic power; the apprehensive US reaction to China's rise; the US retreat from rule-based multilateralism in trade under a unilateralist and protectionist president; and the worldwide surge in managed and manipulated trade as part of an intensifying economic nationalism in the United States and elsewhere, had all combined to call into question the centrality and the very survival of the WTO. The arrival of COVID-19 only worsened these preexisting conditions that had long been leading to this existential crisis.

For five decades, trade multilateralism worked. In the half century that followed the end of the Second World War, the gradual freeing of trade through trade liberalization in what began as the GATT before eventually evolving into the WTO, was accomplished in a series of eight multilateral "rounds" of trade negotiations. At first, these negotiating rounds centered exclusively on cutting tariffs. Later, they expanded to include reducing the mounting number of nontariff barriers to trade. By the conclusion of the eighth and final GATT negotiating round, the Uruguay round, more than a dozen international trade agreements, including the original one still called the GATT, had become part of the legal framework of the multilateral trading system. It was the multilateral agreement reached at the end of the Uruguay round in 1994 that linked all these international trade agreements together and, in 1995, after decades spent trying, at last transformed the ad hoc architecture of the GATT into the international institution named the World Trade Organization.

Each of these successive trade negotiating rounds was conducted in what is described in trade parlance as a "single undertaking." That is, in these global negotiations, nothing was agreed by anyone until everything was agreed by everyone. No country could obtain the benefit of any of the new rules lowering tariffs and other trade barriers unless it agreed to be bound by all the new rules negotiated in the round. Thus, the negotiating countries could not pick and choose among the trade commitments they wished to make.

Another significant characteristic of this traditional approach to trade negotiations is that any one of the negotiating countries has what is tantamount to a veto over approval of the entire agreement. A consensus of all the negotiating countries is required for approval, and any one of them can block approval by refusing to join in a consensus in support of it. Hence, one country, however small, and however peripheral to most of world trade, can prevent the rest of the world from moving ahead toward more trade liberalization.

Not surprisingly, this requirement of universal agreement often caused GATT trade negotiations to go on for years before reaching a conclusion. Not without reason was the GATT sometimes described as the "General Agreement to Talk and Talk." As a practical matter, though, throughout most of the GATT years, the leading developed countries – the United States, the European Union, Japan, Canada, and a few others – benefited by having the cumulative economic clout to impose their shared consensus on the other members of the trading system, mostly the developing countries. The developing countries could not get along in trade unless they went along in accepting the outcomes of trade negotiations in which they often barely participated and had little sway.

Many of those who helped craft the Uruguay round trade agreements to establish the WTO assumed in 1995 that, given the increasing complexities of world trade, and given the ever-accelerating pace of change in the global economy, the Uruguay round would be the last of the lengthy multilateral rounds of trade negotiations. Instead, they expected the WTO to become a forum and a framework for an unending series of singular negotiations on individual issues and sectors in trade. They anticipated that new negotiations would occur as new needs arose, and as new groups of WTO members sought to write new rules to meet those needs. They thought these future negotiations on new rules would frequently begin by including only those countries most interested in a new topic and would build later into fully multilateral agreements including all countries. After all, this had happened previously with the GATT codes on standards, subsidies, dumping, and more, that had not become fully multilateral accords until they were incorporated into the WTO treaty with the conclusion of the Uruguay round.[1]

For a brief time, what these founders of the WTO had anticipated seemed likely to happen. The best example of the early success of this approach is the Information Technology Agreement concluded in Singapore in 1996. The ITA is not the product of a single undertaking. Rather, the ITA is what is called, in the often tongue-twisting vernacular of public international law, a "plurilateral" agreement. It is an agreement among some but not all WTO members. At the outset, the ITA was signed by only twenty-nine WTO members. Since then, the number of participants has grown to eighty-one countries, which together represent 97 percent of world trade in IT products. International trade in IT products accounts for about 10 percent of all global merchandise exports. The ITA has eliminated tariffs on $1.6 trillion in trade.[2]

Many advocates of freer trade hoped to use this same approach to free trade in other sectors and deal with other emerging trade issues. But then terrorists attacked the Twin Towers in the United States on 9/11 in 2001. Terrorism found fertile ground in the arid absence of economic opportunity in much of the developing world. In part to pursue economic development as a counter to terrorism, the members of the WTO launched the Doha Development Round in Doha, Qatar, in November 2001. The Doha Development Agenda for the new round was framed to address many of the world's trade issues at the time – agriculture, manufacturing, services, and the broader issues of development. Yet, fatefully, WTO members chose, mostly out of habit, to frame the Doha round, like all the previous rounds, as a single undertaking. The vision for a new approach to WTO rulemaking that had motivated many trade advocates in 1995 abruptly disappeared at the end of 2001.

More than anything else, this decision doomed the Doha Development Round to failure. Although it started with much fanfare, the Doha round ultimately became the longest international trade negotiations in the history of the world. Year after year the negotiations dragged on. Hopes for success were dashed in conference after conference. The consensus needed for success was endlessly elusive. The developing countries thought the "development" round was intended to secure more trade concessions for them from developed countries without their having to make any additional concessions of their own. In contrast, the developed countries saw "development" as necessarily requiring more open markets in the developing countries. Too, as the years passed, and as the global economy changed, the Doha round seemed less and less relevant to increasing numbers in the trading world because many of the newer trade issues that arose in the twenty-first century were not subjects of the negotiations. Digital trade, for example, was growing exponentially in the new century, but it was not on the Doha Development Agenda.

There were some noteworthy successes along the way. An innovative multi-lateral agreement to cut much of the red tape that hindered trade at the world's borders – the Trade Facilitation Agreement – was concluded in Bali in 2013 and entered into force in 2017.[3] An updated plurilateral agreement on rules for making government purchases entered into force in 2014.[4] During the ministerial conference in Nairobi in 2015, the ITA was expanded to eliminate the tariffs on 201 additional information and communications technology (ICT) products.[5] Also in Nairobi that same year, WTO members concluded a long-sought multilateral agreement to eliminate agricultural export subsidies.[6] Yet, despite these two successes at the Nairobi conference, it was, in retrospect, there where the Doha Development Round finally collapsed. Not only could the WTO members not reach consensus on the substance of the trade issues before them, they could not even agree on how to proceed afterward. In painful fact, the round was over. The headline to the lead editorial in the *Financial Times* the day after the Nairobi conference concluded read, "The Doha Round Finally Dies a Merciful Death."[7]

The stakes were high for the entire world in the Doha Development Round. One estimate is that reaching a global deal to end the remaining barriers to trade would add $11 trillion to the global economy and pull 160 million people out of poverty by 2030.[8] According to trade economists at the Peterson Institute for International Economics, as part of these total global gains from increased trade, "the potential gains from future policy liberalization could be as large as roughly $540 billion for the United States by the year 2025. This figure translates to an additional increase of $1,670 in GDP per capita and $4,400 in GDP per household ... respectively."[9] These potential gains would seem to be sufficient motives for forging a consensus on a global deal.

But these stakes were evidently not high enough to overcome the hurdles that faced the Doha round trade negotiators. They were assailed on all sides by unforeseen impediments. Negotiations that began while prosperity was, in many places, on the rise, stumbled on amid the morass of a financial crisis and its aftermath. Military conflicts, as they tend to do, pulled countries even farther apart. The passions of power politics tainted the talks. Yet, in the end, what caused the demise of the Doha round was a shortage of global political will combined with the conflation of the profound structural and geopolitical changes in the ever-evolving multilateral trading system.

One of these changes was the growing weight of the developing countries within the trading system. Ten of the original twenty-three "Contracting Parties" to the GATT were developing countries, although they had little combined economic clout at the time. By the 1960s, most of the "Contracting

Parties" were developing countries. In the Uruguay round, for the first time, developing countries played a major role in the negotiated outcome. Yet, still, a handful of developed countries, notably the United States and the European Union, directed much of the result. It was only when the WTO was established in the wake of the Uruguay round that developing countries began to have a say in the councils of the trading system commensurate with their growing share of the world economy.

By the end of 1994, 128 countries were part of the trading system. Since then, thirty-six additional countries have joined the WTO, almost all of them developing countries. The global economic role of developing countries has likewise grown. On the eve of the COVID-19 outbreak, developing countries accounted for about 44 percent of all world merchandise trade.[10] Since 2017, the exports of developing countries have represented almost half of all global exports. The largest fifteen developing countries – often characterized as the "emerging economies" – accounted for about three-fourths of those developing country exports.[11]

Yet another change that has held up the progress of multilateral trade negotiations has been the long tradition of granting developing countries "special and differential treatment" in fulfilling their WTO obligations. The United States and some other developed countries have long believed that this special treatment has been used by developing countries to excuse them from opening their domestic markets in full compliance with WTO rules. The developing countries contend in turn that, despite decades of repeated promises, they have never gotten the full benefit of the "special and differential treatment" to which they think they are entitled. Economists point out that this separate category of treatment has done little to help the developing countries achieve development, which depends on having freer trade and other aspects of more open markets. The increasing clout of the developing countries in world trade has only fueled the continuing divide over this issue in the WTO.[12]

Frustrated with their failure to make multilateral progress in the Doha Development Round, many countries – especially developed countries – turned away from the WTO and toward other less comprehensive trade solutions. The impasse in the Doha round stimulated a proliferation of free trade and other regional trade agreements. Perhaps the most well known of these new trade agreements were the CPTPP – the Comprehensive and Progressive Trans-Pacific Partnership among eleven Pacific Rim countries (the twelfth, the United States, having opted out in January 2017, the day after the inauguration of President Trump), and the CETA – the Comprehensive and Economic Trade Agreement between Canada and the European Union. But there were many more. By 2020, 303 regional trade agreements were in force worldwide.[13]

Involving fewer countries and thus fewer competing concerns, RTAs are easier to conclude than multilateral agreements. Positively, they can be proving grounds for new trade approaches that can later be made fully multilateral. Also, they can lower tariffs and other trade barriers among the countries that are parties to them. But, negatively, in a bilateral or regional negotiation between a large country and one or more smaller countries, the large country will often have the leverage to take unfair advantage of the smaller ones at the negotiating table. In multilateral negotiations, the smaller countries, buttressed by their sheer numbers, have more leverage. In addition, by definition, a decision to give freer trade to one trading partner and not another, which is the result of an RTA, creates more trade discrimination. Moreover, although an RTA can create trade, it can also divert it. Lastly, and not least, the shift in recent years from an emphasis on multilateral to regional trade approaches has gradually called into question the continued centrality of the WTO system to world trade.

THE RISE OF CHINA AND THE WTO

By far the most profound change in the multilateral trading system that occurred between the creation of the WTO and the arrival of the COVID-19 pandemic, was the historic rise of China as a force in world trade. A thousand years earlier, Chinese junks had plied the open seas, a dominant force in world trade. Now, China's long-awaited economic resurrection posed profound challenges for the rules-based global trading system. Up until China became a member in 2001, the World Trade Organization was not truly a *world* trade organization *without* China. Two decades into the twenty-first century, the question on many minds was whether it could continue to be a world trade organization *with* China.

For the first thirty years following its revolution in 1949, China largely locked itself away from the rest of the world in a failed experiment in mostly political isolation and economic self-sufficiency. Tens of millions of the Chinese people perished in the wrenching transformation in the aftermath of the communist revolution – in the chaotic collectivization, the autarkic "Great Leap Forward," and the nihilistic "Cultural Revolution."[14] Then, in 1979, with the pragmatic "reform and opening up" by Deng Xiaoping following the death of Mao Zedong, China began to move pragmatically away from total state control and edged toward a semblance of a freer market. It was then when China began to make its great strides toward becoming a part of the modern economy. "As the state gave way to the market, private enterprise and trade flourished, growth quickened, and incomes soared."[15]

The violent suppression of the brave calls for democracy in Tiananmen Square in 1989 was a devastating message for all who had hoped that freer markets would in time be accompanied by freer politics in China. However, in the aftermath, the market opening continued. Because of this opening, the world was soon reminded of the size and vast potential of China. From 1979 to 2017, China's real GDP grew at an average annual rate of 9.5 percent.[16] In 1995, when the WTO was established, China accounted for only 3 percent of global trade in merchandise.[17] In 2019, China ranked first in the

world with 13.2 percent of merchandise exports; the United States was second
at 8.7 percent. That same year, the United States ranked first in the world with
13.4 percent of merchandise imports; China was second at 10.8 percent.[18] The
World Bank hailed China's growth as "the fastest sustained expansion by a
major economy in history."[19]

International trade played a significant role in this historic generation of
growth. In 1995, at the birth of the WTO, China accounted for $280.9 billion
and 3 percent of all world trade. In 2018, China accounted for $4.6 trillion and
12.4 percent of world trade.[20] Joining the WTO and enjoying the benefits of
multilateral WTO trade concessions and WTO rules against trade discrimination, contributed much to China's rapid trade ascent. Because China was a
WTO member, Chinese exports faced much lower tariffs worldwide, and
China's trading partners were prohibited from singling out Chinese exports
for trade discrimination. When the COVID-19 pandemic began, China had
become the world's second largest economy and the world's second largest
trader of goods and services, after the United States.[21]

The United States strongly supported China's entry into the WTO in
2001 after almost fifteen years of laborious multilateral negotiations. The hope
of many Americans and others was that, despite the earlier events in Tiananmen
Square, in becoming more open economically, China would also gradually
become more open politically. Few thought that China would become a democracy, much less one that resembled the United States. But many Americans,
and many others around the world, did hope that China would, in the process
of this opening, become a collaborative and productive partner with the United
States and other countries in shared global governance, as part of an overall
liberal international order. For the most part, however, the hopes for a gradual
political "opening up" in China were dashed as China continued to grow
economically and evolve politically.

The Chinese economy grew exponentially after the turn of the century once
China joined the WTO, powered for the most part by exports. Meanwhile, in
the United States, average income growth stagnated, and manufacturing job
losses increased, especially in the politically pivotal Midwestern industrial
heartland. Americans – along with many others in the world – grew ever more
frustrated by the slow pace of Chinese compliance with many WTO obligations
and by the sheer absence of Chinese compliance with others. Along with
China's other trading partners, the United States became more and more vocal
in its commercial complaints about arbitrary and discriminatory Chinese trade
practices.

Under the leadership of new President Xi Jinping in 2013, the Chinese
government turned away, other than rhetorically, from Deng's "reform and
opening up," and tilted once again toward tighter state control of the Chinese
economy.[22] While continuing to promise additional market-oriented reforms
(and occasionally even keeping those promises – as with the financial sector),
the Chinese government under Xi ramped up control of the Chinese private

sector and relied heavily on subsidies to state-owned enterprises and on debt-laden, make-work infrastructure projects to sustain economic growth.[23] As a longtime foreign correspondent in Asia, Michael Schuman, put it, Xi rejected "decades of tried-and-true policy by reasserting the power of the Communist Party within the economy and redirecting Chinese business inward."[24]

The turn inward was especially evident in Xi's new approach to developing new technologies. The "Made in China 2025" plan for rapid state-led advancement of China's manufacturing sector through strategic investments in robotics, artificial intelligence, electric cars, new synthetic materials, next-generation information technology, aerospace engineering, emerging biomedicines, and other cutting-edge high-tech industries seemed designed to discriminate against US and other foreign goods and services.[25] In the eyes of the United States and other Chinese trading partners, elements of this plan appeared to entail massive governmental subsidies, encourage forced technology transfers, and endanger foreign intellectual property rights – all in violation of China's legal obligations under WTO trade rules.[26]

This turning away from freer trade and freer markets and toward a more protectionist and state-directed industrial policy under Xi Jinping may serve what President Xi sees as his own political interest in solidifying his personal control of the fate of the Chinese people, but it is inconsistent with China's long-term economic interests. Little realized by many in the West (or, for that matter, by many in China) is the fact that China's private sector accounts for more than 60 percent of China's GDP. Furthermore, the private sector, not the state, has been the main driver of China's economic growth, accounting for 70 percent of China's innovation, 80 percent of its urban employment, and 90 percent of its new jobs. All this in China has been aided and abetted by the opening of parts of the Chinese economy in fulfillment of China's WTO obligations. Thus, the Chinese turn away from private enterprise and from free markets under Xi, dictated by the political desire of Xi and his followers in the Chinese Communist Party to reassert the uncontested state control of one-party rule in the short term, could, ironically, threaten that control in the long term by shrinking the economic future of the Chinese people.[27]

The pandemic offered Xi and the Chinese government an opportunity (and an excuse) to shift direction and include the long-promised market reforms in China's recovery plans, but, sadly, this opportunity was missed. Outside observers saw instead a "demonstration of mistrust in markets" in the Chinese government and "a doubling down on state-managed solutions, not real reforms."[28] After an initial plummet following the sudden shock of the outbreak in Wuhan and the national shutdown that followed, the Chinese economy climbed back to its pre-pandemic growth rates by the end of 2020.[29] And it came back sooner than the economies of the United States and China's other trading partners. But, in 2021, China's growth slowed as it struggled with virus variants, economic fallout from the virus, and the emerging consequences of its mountainous debt.

Amid the pandemic, US–China trade tensions further intensified. With the rise of China, the trade links between the two countries had become considerable. Economically, the two were coupled, joined to a great extent in economic interdependence. Billions of dollars in two-way trade between the two countries crossed the Pacific Ocean every day. Billions more were spent by each country in the other on foreign direct investment. Yet their economic grievances were equally considerable. Many Americans believed the rise of China had been at the expense of American workers. They thought more trade with China meant fewer jobs in the United States, especially in manufacturing. The United States was still the most prosperous country on the planet. It still had the world's largest economy (at least for the moment). But many Americans were increasingly anxious about the rise of China. The US economy continued to grow up until the pandemic, but it was growing slowly, and China seemed to be catching up.

For its part, China complained often about what it saw as the excessive and arbitrary use by the United States of antidumping and other trade defenses that limited Chinese exports to the United States in ways the Chinese thought often violated US WTO obligations. Also, although China had been growing rapidly, the Chinese still felt the pain of a "century of humiliation" at the hands of Western powers between the unequal Treaty of Nanjing imposed on the Chinese by the British following the Chinese defeat in the first Opium War in 1842 and the 1949 communist revolution. Although the United States was not a principal culprit in the egregious Western exploitation of the Chinese people throughout the nineteenth century, this lingering Chinese pain nevertheless factored into the complex equations of US–China relations and the effects of those bilateral relations on the multilateral trading system. Over time, it became ever more difficult to disentangle all that the members of the WTO were trying to achieve multilaterally from the twisted bilateral knots of the US–China trade relationship.

When Donald Trump was inaugurated as president of the United States in January 2017, US trade policy changed overnight. For seventy years, the bipartisan trade policy of the United States had been to seek freer trade through agreed trade rules and to uphold those rules through the rule of law in the multilateral trading system. The leaders of both major American political parties believed that Americans would prosper the most by establishing and upholding the international rule of law in trade. The general success of this policy was reflected in the enormous economic gains made by the United States during those decades as a participant and leader in the rule-based multilateral trading system and in other aspects of the liberal international order.

The new policy of the Trump administration was, instead, captured in the new president's old slogan, "America First," borrowed from the American isolationists of the 1930s. President Trump and his trade advisers did not seek freer trade; they sought instead insulation from trade, especially for the steel and other aging smokestack industries in the Midwest that face tough foreign competition (and play an outsized role in American politics). Trump and his administration saw compliance with the rule of international law as optional, not obligatory.[30] And they believed that the United States could best serve its interests in the world by going it alone with the clout (and sometimes the club) of American economic leverage than by working together with its allies and other countries in various arenas of international cooperation, including the often tedious deliberations of trade multilateralism in the WTO.

President Trump did not value deliberation, least of all international deliberation, and he seemed little interested in trade rules. As a self-described dealmaker, he was primarily interested in trade transactions. This was a complete reversal for the United States. Since the Second World War, under both political parties, the United States had emphasized the negotiation of internationally agreed rules to free and maximize trade. Under President Trump, as Robert Z. Lawrence of the Harvard University Kennedy School of Government has expressed, there was "a dangerous shift from an economic system based on rules toward an economic system based on deals."[31] The new focus was on trade outcomes for individual products, sectors, and even companies that were favored by the Trump administration. The president's decided tendency was to try to dictate those outcomes through ad hoc dealmaking that intervened in the buy-and-sell workings of supply and demand in the marketplace.

This Trump policy was not constructed for freeing trade; it was made for managing trade. A managed trade policy assumes that decisions made by governments are better than decisions made by markets. But this is not the case. As Lawrence has explained, in words that would make Smith and Ricardo, not to mention Milton Friedman and Friedrich von Hayek, nod in agreement, "The basis for the U.S. economic system is private enterprise, because the government has neither the knowledge nor the incentives to make business decisions that in the long run will achieve economic efficiency and growth."[32] However well intentioned, the picking of "winners" and "losers" in the marketplace by governmental bureaucrats does not work. The "spontaneous order" of price signals in a market-based commercial society is a much better guide to achieving prosperity than the predetermined plan of any government.[33]

This trumpeted new American policy of managing trade instead of freeing it created much consternation, but it secured few results. Under President Trump, the United States engaged in some trade negotiations, mostly bilateral and mostly outside the WTO. The North American Free Trade Agreement (NAFTA) with Canada and Mexico was rebranded the United States-Mexico-Canada Agreement (USMCA) and was marginally revised, mostly in ways that made it less of a free trade agreement.[34] Some new wrinkles were added to the US trade agreement with South Korea.[35] A minor deal with Japan "was so limited that it required no congressional approval."[36] President Trump told several other countries he wanted new trade deals with them, but his administration never got around to negotiating seriously with any of them. Despite all his tweeting about the supposed outrages of current trade agreements, dealmaker Trump and his trade advisers and negotiators were less than successful in concluding new trade agreements for the United States.

The new Trump trade approach, however, soon had a significant impact on American trade relations with China. After months of threats, in 2018, through an avalanche of steep tariffs imposed unilaterally on imports of Chinese steel, aluminum, and numerous other products, the United States began waging a "trade war" against China. Ultimately, the United States imposed tariffs on $370 billion of imports from China.[37] Many of these unilateral tariffs were applied by the United States in violation of WTO rules. Under the WTO treaty, national measures falling within the scope of the treaty must first be taken to WTO dispute settlement and found to be inconsistent with treaty obligations before tariffs or other retaliatory actions can be taken against them.[38] The United States frequently skipped this mandatory first step and acted wholly on its own, in violation of international trade law. In response, China retaliated in a tit-for-tat exchange of higher barriers to their two-way trade. In retaliating, China also skipped engaging in WTO dispute settlement, arguably committing its own WTO violations. At the same time, China also filed cases in the WTO challenging the US tariff actions. Soon, the rhetoric of both countries ratcheted up, with the most incendiary salvos coming from the White House.

"Trade wars are good, and easy to win," proclaimed President Trump as he intensified the commercial conflict between the two countries.[39] But this is – in the tell-tale Trumpian phrase – an "alternative fact." As international economists Sherman Robinson and Karen Thierfelder have explained, the genuine fact is,

Starting a bilateral trade war is a bad idea. While there are potential gains from imposing tariffs and exploiting market power in world markets, the inevitable retaliation largely erodes or reverses the potential gains. Global markets are disrupted, and countries adjust trade patterns to deal with the high levels of protection in the warring countries. These adjustments are costly and inefficient. The warring countries both lose.[40]

Thus, predictably, both the United States and China suffered economically from the higher trade barriers they each erected in their escalating "trade war." Like all tariffs, the additional tariffs imposed by the two countries were paid by importers (*not*, despite President Trump's repeated protestations, by the countries in which the goods originated), and these added costs were generally passed along to final purchasers in the form of higher prices. The US losses largely related to the higher retail prices paid for imported products by US consumers and the higher input prices paid for manufacturing components in American-made products by US businesses. In contrast, while Chinese consumers also paid higher retail and input prices, the Chinese losses from the trade conflict were largely from lost exports. The higher US tariffs on Chinese products reduced US imports of those products by 25 percent.[41]

By most accounts, the United States suffered the most. In September 2019, Moody Analytics found that the "trade war" with China had already cost the

US economy nearly 300,000 jobs and an estimated 0.3 percent of real GDP.[42] A report that same year by Bloomberg Economics estimated that the conflict would cost the US economy $316 billion by the end of 2020.[43] Perhaps most telling about the bottom-line cost to individual Americans from the back-and-forth with China over trade was that the cost to each American household of the tariffs was *$831 per year*.[44] As with all forms of protectionism, this cost is a hidden tax of which most Americans are not even aware.

Many other countries also suffered from the indirect economic fallout of the increasingly acrimonious commercial confrontation between the two leading trading countries in the world. The diversion of imports by each country from the other to third countries was of some short-term benefit to Mexico, Brazil, Vietnam, and a few other exporters. Yet, overall, the costs to other countries were enormous. The International Monetary Fund predicted in late 2019 that the US–China confrontation would cause the loss of $700 billion for the global economy by 2020.[45]

The arrival of the pandemic only made the global economic situation more precarious. Added to the impacts of the punitive tariffs in US–China trade were the port closings, shipping delays, and other economic impacts of the pandemic on trade. Meanwhile, the WTO was effectively sidelined as all eyes focused on the trade showdown between its two largest members. Making matters worse, it became harder with each passing month to separate the commercial concerns of the two countries from their growing overall geopolitical competition. Many people in both countries feared (and, sadly, a few hoped) that the US–China "trade war" would morph into a second "Cold War."

On January 15, 2020, after months of intermittent negotiations, marked by the blustery tactics of the US president and the impervious intransigence of the Chinese negotiators, the two disputing countries signed what was touted by the United States as a "phase one" trade deal. The interim deal cut some of the new US tariffs on Chinese goods in return mostly for Chinese promises to buy an additional $200 billion in US energy, agricultural, and manufactured goods over and above what it had bought in 2017 – an increase of 55 percent.[46] From the outset, the extent of the Chinese shopping list in "phase one" was widely viewed as unrealistic economically.[47] Further, "phase one" was transactional and not structural; it did nothing to address most of the basic structural concerns of the United States and numerous other Chinese trading partners about the broad discrimination embedded in much of the Chinese economy and industrial policy.

Moreover, the "phase one" promises made by China to buy $200 billion in products from US producers were, implicitly, promises *not* to buy those products from producers in other WTO member countries. Discriminatory trade diversion loomed in violation of WTO trade rules. After all, as one example, the Chinese economy can only absorb so many soybeans. Thus, a purchase of soybeans by China from the United States may in fact be a purchase that would otherwise be from Brazil in a market free from government interference. In such a free market, a purchasing decision would be based on price and quality, not on the nationality of the producer selling the product. Implicitly, this central part of the "phase one" deal was a promise by China to depart from market-based outcomes and from the basic WTO rules of nondiscrimination in trade in order to accommodate the demands of the United States. It was managed trade at its worst.[48]

There was a certain irony in the spectacle of the United States, which is supposedly motivated by its concerns about the Chinese managing their trade, beseeching China to engage in more managed trade by employing governmental intervention to steer individual trade transactions to American producers. Appalled, American economist Gary Hufbauer of the Peterson Institute for International Economics, with decades of high-level experience in international trade, declared,

[T]he only way for China to reach its commitments is to resort to Soviet-style managed trade – in other words, China promises to import a certain dollar or physical volume of detailed goods and services, regardless of market prices or demand conditions. That's the way the old Soviet Union conducted trade with its satellites for 40 years. Likewise, chapter 6 of the China deal contains a secret annex of product-by-product commitments, right out of the handbook of a planned economy. Instead of principally relying on explicit reductions in Chinese tariffs and nontariff barriers to boost US exports – only a few such reductions can be found in the agreement – quantitative targets are inscribed in the text. The targets are ambitious, and it remains to be seen how and whether China can fulfill them.[49]

Under President Trump, the United States was not only engaging in managed trade on many fronts; paradoxically, it was demanding more of it by China when supposedly it is China's penchant for managing trade as part of its state-controlled economy that concerns the United States the most in the trade relations between the two countries. Then, within a few weeks of its signing, the pandemic began, and the planned implementation of the "phase one" deal was overwhelmed. Whatever their intentions, there was no way the Chinese could keep their lofty promises to the United States while their economy was crashing from COVID-19 during the hard first months of 2020. In the midst of the pandemic, achieving some elements of the "phase one" agreement was, as one economist put it, "just clearly impossible."[50] The hopes for the success of the "phase one" deal deflated.[51] China fell far behind in keeping its promises for purchases from the United States. In 2020, the first full year of the agreement, China's purchases of covered products in the deal reached only 58 percent of the target.[52] Along the way, all talk ceased of a promised "phase two" deal to which disputes over the most important of the structural trade issues that separated the two countries had been deferred.

If the goal of the Trump administration was to open the Chinese market, and not just to apply tariffs, then, as Simon Lester of the Cato Institute has summed it up, "we went backwards" during the Trump years.[53] When Joe Biden was inaugurated president of the United States in January 2021, $360 billion in unilateral US tariffs imposed on Chinese imports by President Trump remained in place. These tariffs diminished trade between the two countries and limited growth of both their economies. Some urged the new president to remove these tariffs because they were illegal under international law and because they hurt the American economy.[54] Others urged him to keep them and use them as leverage to obtain further Chinese trade concessions.[55] Ambassador Katherine Tai, a seasoned US negotiator newly appointed by Biden as his trade representative, said in her first interview after taking office that the United States was not ready to lift the tariffs. In defending this position, she asked, "No negotiator walks away from leverage, right?"[56]

Precisely how the United States would be able to exact meaningful concessions from China on its major structural economic concerns, with or without the Trump tariffs, remained unclear. After four chaotic years of Trump trade tactics, China seemed even more committed to a statist industrial policy that in many respects evaded or violated WTO rules. President Trump and his trade advisers and negotiators had done little to alter discriminatory Chinese industrial policies. In dealing with China, what was clear from the beginning of the Biden administration was that, unlike President Trump, President Biden preferred not to "go it alone" but rather to work in concert with like-minded US trading partners to secure structural concessions and otherwise curb China's unfair trade practices.[57] His initial actions seemed to confirm this different approach.[58] Overall, Biden appeared more committed to American adherence to the international rule of law than Trump.[59] This, though, was an exceedingly low bar. And the extent to which the new president would make it a point to work within the constraints of WTO rules in challenging Chinese trade practices was less than clear.

Meantime, despite their commercial and other increasingly tense confrontations, the United States and China remained joined at the proverbial hip economically. Among many other implications, this meant that severing the commercial ties between the two countries would have a considerable cost, not only for China but also for the United States. In a study for the US–China Business Council released several days before President Biden was inaugurated, Oxford Econometrics reported that US exports to China support 1.2 million American jobs and that Chinese multinational companies directly employ 197,000 Americans. The study concluded that a significant decoupling of the economies of the two countries in 2021 could, by 2025, shrink the GDP of the United States by $1.6 trillion, resulting in 320,000 fewer US jobs.[60]

THE RETURN OF ECONOMIC NATIONALISM

The unilateralist tactics employed by the United States against China – tactics often outside the legal framework of the WTO treaty – were only the most headline-grabbing example of the retreat of the United States under Donald

Trump from its previous seventy years of strong bipartisan support for multilateralism in trade. In addition to the unilateral tariffs levied against imports from China, the newly protectionist United States applied a series of unilateral tariffs on products imported from its closest neighbors, long-standing allies, and other trading partners, often on specious grounds of supposedly ensuring "national security."[61] Unilateral US tariffs on imports of steel and aluminum were sometimes accompanied by unseemly actions in trade diplomacy that bordered on bullying.[62] Acting outside the WTO and in flagrant disregard of WTO rules, the United States under President Trump made little effort to act together with US allies and other trading partners on their shared trade concerns. Preferring to act alone, the Trump administration increasingly stood alone in world trade.

The US retreat from multilateralism in trade did not, however, originate with President Trump; it was many years in the making. During the discordant and disappointing years since the launch of the Doha round in 2001, US frustration with multilateralism grew due to the snail's pace of the multilateral negotiations. Unable to get much of anything done through negotiation in the WTO, more and more, the United States and other developed countries turned toward negotiation of bilateral and regional trade agreements outside the WTO. Admittedly, trade solutions were limited in FTAs because the agreements were not fully global. But at least solutions were achievable. Then, with the inauguration of President Trump in January 2017, the slow retreat of the United States from multilateralism suddenly hastened into a solitary sprint away from the very idea of international cooperation, in trade and in much else.

Unlike Adam Smith and Smith's centuries of followers, Donald Trump does not see trade as a "win-win" proposition for all who engage in it. Rather, he sees trade solely as "win-lose," and he is ever emphatic in alleging that the United States has been a "loser" in trade. He thinks that Americans have been "losers" in trade because of how they have been victimized in the trade deals they have made in decades of building the multilateral trading system.[63] In his view, US trade negotiators have repeatedly sacrificed US economic interests to those of other countries, and other countries have taken advantage of US weakness at the negotiating table to take further advantage and impose even more economic pain on Americans.

Thus, not surprisingly, much of his animus against internationalism of all kinds has been directed against the WTO. Trump's critique of the WTO has voiced a visceral economic nationalism and is mostly free of facts, but it is nonetheless appetizing fodder for domestic political consumption at a time when Americans are all too eager to point the finger of political blame for their current misfortunes anywhere but at themselves. Uneasy with the constraints on arbitrary national actions imposed by a treaty full of international trade rules – many of them rules the United States had largely written and had insisted on during the Uruguay round – Trump has denounced the WTO treaty of 1994 as "the single worst trade deal ever made."[64]

During Trump's four years as president, the WTO became his convenient scapegoat for all the fabricated sins of a cosmopolitan "globalism" he sees as justifying a return by the United States to an economic nationalism that he mistakenly believes was the original source of American economic success. Trump and other economic nationalists have an inaccurate view of American economic history. They believe that the high protective tariffs of the nineteenth century made the explosive American economic growth of that century possible, laying the foundation for the continued growth in the century and more since.

In stark contrast, most economic historians view the high tariffs of the United States of that time as self-imposed limits on that national growth.[65] Douglas Irwin attributes the early growth of the United States mainly to openness "in terms of ideas, capital and the movement of people."[66] Ryan Young and Iain Murray of the Competitive Enterprise Institute point out that,

If one controls for population growth and capital accumulation, there was no evidence that tariffs contributed to any productivity boost, which is essential for economic growth. Were it not for America's westward expansion mostly canceling out the market-shrinking effects of these high tariffs, the U.S. economy would have suffered greatly. Even so, the opportunity costs of the move to protectionism were enormous ... Had markets been truly open and free in the 19th century, growth may well have been even faster than it was.[67]

A businessman, Donald Trump assumes that, to be able to grow, governments, like businesses, must create a surplus through exchanges in the marketplace. This assumption, of course, ignores the oft-forgotten facts that governments are not businesses, and that they do not exist to make a profit. In addition, it overlooks the fact that trade transactions in international commerce are mostly made by individuals, not by governments. But, setting these inconvenient facts aside, and based on this belief, Trump and his trade advisers and negotiators also derided the WTO because, during its membership in the organization, the United States had not erased its merchandise trade deficit. (Trump mostly ignored services trade in his lamentations about trade deficits, even though the United States routinely runs a surplus in trade in services, which constitute more than four-fifths of the American economy.) Trump focused especially on bilateral trade deficits with China and other US trading partners. More than that, he focused frequently also on bilateral deficits in trade in specific individual products, such as, for instance, auto parts and automobiles.

In this, Trump resembles the British mercantilists of the eighteenth century whose economic theories were refuted by Adam Smith. His economic nationalism is a modern version of mercantilism supplemented and afflicted by the incendiary passions of *Sturm und Drang*, blood-and-soil national fervor. Much like Trump, the British mercantilists measured their wealth by their success in hoarding gold and silver, and, like him, they believed the accumulation of such wealth depended on encouraging exports and limiting imports. Smith explained that "the wealth of nations" is measured, not by gold and silver, but rather by economic production. He explained, too, that a country's economic production is maximized through the division of labor that is called "trade." The resurrection of economic nationalism in the twenty-first century is evidence that we have not yet learned all that Smith tried to teach us.

As for trade deficits, economists tell us they have little to do with the individual microeconomic transactions in international trade. Gary Hufbauer and Lucy Lu have explained that,

[M]acroeconomic forces largely determine a country's global trade deficit or surplus. The key forces are domestic levels both of private savings and investment and of government deficits. Added together, these levels give net national savings (or, when negative, net national borrowing), which determine the size of the national trade surplus or deficit. What this mean is that the United States is bound to run an overall trade deficit with the rest of the world when combined US savings of the household, business, and government sectors are negative, as they have been for some years. To finance the trade deficit, the United States is obliged to borrow or attract investment from the rest of the world, making a global US trade deficit inevitable. At best, trade agreements exert a second-order impact, possibly changing the size of the global trade deficit, which is determined by underlying forces.[68]

In the case of the United States, as James McBride and Andrew Chatzky of the Council on Foreign Relations have written, the exchange rate of the dollar is a factor in the size of the trade deficit, because "a stronger dollar makes foreign products cheaper for American consumers while making U.S. exports more expensive for foreign buyers."[69] With imports cheaper, consumers buy more of them; with exports more expensive, foreign buyers buy fewer of them. As a result, the US trade deficit increases. Also, in contradiction of the obsession of economic nationalists with what they claim are the harms of trade deficits, "A growing U.S. economy often leads to a larger deficit, since consumers have more income to buy more goods from abroad."[70] Now comes the COVID-19 pandemic to further complicate this economic equation. Because of the extraordinary extent of the fiscal stimulus that has been spent on countering the pandemic, the imbalance in the United States between the savings and investment rates is more atilt in the new pandemic world. This is because "more government spending, if it leads to a larger federal budget deficit, reduces the national savings and raises the trade deficit."[71] And the US federal budget deficit has soared during the pandemic.

From an economic point of view, focusing on an *overall* trade deficit is bad enough as a would-be nationalistic solution for a country's economic ills; focusing on a *bilateral* trade deficit is even worse. A singular emphasis on diminishing a bilateral trade deficit with one country – such as, for instance, the US bilateral goods trade deficit with China – usually leads only to the diversion of trade to another country. It does not reduce the overall trade deficit. Nor does it add jobs. Despite the nonstop rhetoric to the contrary for four years from the Trump White House, there is no correlation between trade deficits and overall employment.[72] Indeed, to the contrary, higher trade deficits seem to accompany strong economies. In a strong economy, more domestic consumers are prosperous, they buy more imports, the gap widens between imports and exports, and the trade deficit goes up. Those who are still not fully persuaded that the economic nationalists are aiming at the wrong target may wish to ponder the fact that, during all the prolonged economic anguish of the Great Depression, the United States had a trade surplus. With the collapse in US domestic consumer demand, Americans could not afford to buy imports.

In any event, even by his own standards, Trump failed as president on trade. In his campaign in 2016, he promised to eliminate the US trade deficit.[73] However, during the four years of his term, the US trade deficit climbed to its highest level since 2008, the beginning of the global financial crisis. In 2016, the year before Trump became president, the combined US goods and services trade deficit was $481 billion. When he left office four years later, the US trade deficit in goods alone was $916 billion.[74] Much of this added gap could be traced to the fact that his 2017 tax cuts gave consumers more money to use to pay for imports and his erratic trade measures harmed US exports. Yet, using the reasoning employed by Donald Trump, while he was president, the United States remained a "loser" from trade.

Burdened by the false premises of economic nationalism and ignoring the abundance of solid empirical evidence of the huge economic gains derived for many decades by the United States from its participation in the GATT and in the WTO, President Trump spent much of his time on Twitter belittling the rules-driven multilateral trading system. He asserted that the WTO "has actually been a disaster for us" in the United States.[75] Distorting the facts – and also inventing a few – he denounced and diminished the independent and impartial WTO dispute settlement system, which he saw as rigged against the United States.[76] He dismantled the WTO Appellate Body – at least for the remainder of his presidential term – by refusing to join with other WTO members in the required consensus to appoint new jurists to replace those whose terms had ended.[77] Having decided to pull the United States out of other multilateral endeavors and institutions, more than once, he went so far as to threaten to pull the United States out of the WTO.[78]

With the Americans threatening to withdraw from the WTO, it made little sense for other WTO members to look to them to help lead the WTO. Yet the shape of the world economy is still such that a multilateral trade agreement cannot be concluded without both the support and the leadership of the United States. The support of the United States is needed to form the required legal consensus for a global agreement. More than that, the active leadership of the United States is indispensable to helping build that consensus through the prolonged, unavoidable, and mutually debilitating torture of complex global trade negotiations. Yet, with American trade energies directed mainly outside the WTO, American influence was often minimized (and was sometimes missing altogether) at the negotiating tables of the WTO during the Trump administration. Without the influence of an affirmative American voice, WTO negotiations mostly lingered in limbo.

Regrettably, while Trump was president, and in the first months after Biden became president, few in public life in the United States seemed willing to offer a full-throated defense of the liberal market-based internationalism that had done so much to help create, perpetuate, and disseminate American and global prosperity. Although less obviously protectionist than the Trump administration, the Biden administration seemed at the outset to have "largely dispensed with the idea of free trade as a goal in and of itself."[79] Pointedly, when she was asked in her Senate confirmation hearing whether the goal of a trade agreement should be the elimination of tariffs and other trade barriers, Ambassador Tai did not say "Yes." Instead, she said such matters would have to be considered on a case-by-case basis. Her appointment was confirmed by a vote of 98–0.[80]

The American advocates of freer trade and international cooperation were not able to make much headway from outside the day-to-day of the political fray in influencing what happened within it. They wrote, but they were not read. They spoke, but they were not heard. Immured in the muddy political mire of the pandemic, the American free traders and internationalists shared at least this much with the American advocates of economic nationalism and isolationism: They agreed that the United States was not what it used to be, and, as insurrectionists stained the steps of the US Capitol with the vilest venom of Trumpism, and as the aftermath of that insurrection led only to further dissimulation and recrimination, they wondered if it could ever be what it should be again.

With the retreat by the United States from its traditional bipartisan commitment to free trade and the international rule of law, an increasingly inward view found a foothold in other countries, especially in those with a mercantilist taint and an authoritarian bent. The fear of change that tends always to engender a reactionary apprehension of the foreign "other" found its way into the economic considerations of more and more of the 164 WTO members. This proliferating fear abetted a growing abundance of homegrown iterations, in many languages, of the familiar politician's phrase "I'm for free trade, but" – which is always a tell for protectionism. Whatever the protestation may be to the contrary, the "but" in the phrase is always a prelude to a profession of ostensibly reluctant devotion to some form of economic nationalism.

There were reassuring exceptions. In November 2020, fifteen Asia-Pacific countries, including China, signed a Regional Comprehensive Economic Partnership covering about one-third of global GDP. In contrast to the CPTPP, the RCEP is largely a tariff-cutting deal. It is limited in scope and does not address services, intellectual property, labor, environment, subsidies, and other less straightforward trade issues. Its most important reform may be the uniform "rules of origin" it establishes that will lower internal tariffs in the region's supply chains. Its main message may be that the other countries in the world that remain willing to enter into new trade agreements will not wait for the United States; they will go ahead and negotiate and conclude new trade agreements without the Americans.[81]

Also certainly reassuring was the successful conclusion of the African Continental Free Trade Area (AfCFTA), which aspires to the integration of Africa over time into a single market. Delayed by the COVID-19 pandemic, which caused significant disruptions in African trade, and plunged the continent into its first recession in twenty-five years,[82] the AfCFTA launched anew in January 2021, "with a focus first on easing trade for small and medium-sized enterprises, which account for 90 percent of the jobs created on the continent."[83] AfCFTA constitutes the largest free trade area in the world as measured by the number of people within it. It connects 1.3 billion people in fifty-five countries with a combined GDP of $3.4 trillion,[84] and has the potential for increasing intra-African trade by more than 50 percent.[85] It "has the potential to transform Africa."[86]

Yet even these exceptions are also indications of WTO members turning away from the WTO to find trade solutions. It can be hoped that these new agreements are simply setting the stage regionally for more multilateral actions later; but they may only add to the potential ascendancy of rival regional trading blocs that will ultimately prove to be obstacles rather than avenues to global free trade. Amid all that was occurring with trade during the pandemic, it was small wonder that many everywhere were asking whether the World Trade Organization, created by and devoted to economic multilateralism, could remain relevant, or even continue to exist. There was growing doubt everywhere that the world would, by 2030, be able to achieve one of the targets of Goal 17 of the Sustainable Development Goals, which is to "[p]romote a universal, rule-based, open, non-discriminatory and equitable multilateral trading system under the World Trade Organization."[87]

4

Links to the Trade Inheritance

THE BASIC RULES

As demonstrated only too well in the long death march of the Doha Development Round, the World Trade Organization is a member-driven institution. The WTO is often criticized by those who do not understand the rules for failing to act against some alleged trade abuse. This lack of understanding has become part of the rhetoric of American protectionists, who have faulted the WTO for having "done nothing" to stop China's trade misdeeds.[1] The fact is, unlike some other international institutions, the WTO has no legal authority whatsoever to act on its own. The WTO can only act when its 164 member countries decide to act. Moreover, traditionally, it usually acts only when all its members decide to act together by consensus, which is never easily achieved.

In every part of the world, the members of the WTO frequently pretend that "the WTO" is some foreign Leviathan that has imposed inconvenient constraints and requirements on their freedom to act or is otherwise responsible for the challenges they face in trade. This is done entirely for domestic political convenience. Because all countries do it, no country talks about it. Politically, it is always preferable to point the finger of blame somewhere else when taking a necessary but currently unpopular public action or when explaining a failure to act.

In truth, the WTO is really nothing more nor less than all the members of the WTO acting in concert as something they choose to call "the WTO." The trade rules that are made and upheld, the judgments about the meanings of the rules that are enforced in trade dispute settlement, and the progress that is made (or not made) in negotiations on new and improved rules, are each and all the result of collective decisions made by the members of the WTO. Pretending the WTO is something other than solely member-driven, only serves the purposes of those who want to claim it is something else, of those who want to pretend for their own purposes that it is some vast imperious conspiracy of globalists against the continued freedom of sovereign states. In domestic politics, this shared worldwide pretense about the WTO consigns it to the realm of the minatory "other."

Nothing in the trade rules requires a WTO member to make a single trade commitment – what is known in the common trade vernacular as a "concession." Yet, in more than seven decades of multilateral trade negotiations, the countries that belong to the rule-based WTO trading system have made thousands upon thousands of concessions and have received as many in return. These trade concessions are included in a *schedule of concessions* for each country, which is incorporated into the WTO treaty and is enforceable in WTO dispute settlement.[2] These schedules detail the kind of treatment a WTO member has promised to provide to the goods and services of other WTO members, including tariff cuts and other forms of trade liberalization. None of these tariff and other trade concessions has been imposed by the WTO. They have all been made voluntarily by sovereign states in exchange for grants of commensurate concessions by other sovereign states.[3]

With respect to the tariff cuts, agreed reductions are *bound* in the WTO members' schedules of concessions; that is, the cuts are legally binding and tariffs cannot exceed the ceiling of the bound rates. *Bound* tariffs are the maximum that WTO members can apply to the products of other WTO members without violating their WTO obligations. Bound tariffs must be distinguished from *applied* tariffs, which are the tariffs that are actually applied to imported products. Applied tariffs are either equal to or less than the bound tariff rate. On average, applied tariffs are about half the rate of bound tariffs for agricultural goods and about one-third the rate for manufactured goods.[4] In trade jargon, the difference between the two rates is called "overhang," and the focus of trade negotiations is often on reducing the overhang by reducing the bound tariff rates.

Central to all trade links are the two fundamental rules of nondiscrimination at the core of the multilateral trading system. One rule is the obligation of WTO members to provide most-favored-nation treatment. The other is their obligation to provide national treatment. These are the two rules that make the world of trade turn. There are thousands of pages of other rules in the WTO treaty and in its accompanying schedules of concessions. There are thousands more pages in the WTO rulings clarifying the meanings of all the rules. But discussions and disputes in the WTO often center on the meaning and application of these two basic rules.

Dating back nearly a thousand years to commercial innovations by the Baltic traders of the Hanseatic League, the *most-favored-nation treatment* rule – the MFN rule – is widely misstated and is even more widely misunderstood. Most-favored-nation treatment is mistakenly thought by many to mean that in reducing a tariff or another trade barrier, one country will give the products of another country treatment *more favorable* than it gives to those of all other countries. In fact, this foundational rule of the trading system means exactly the opposite. MFN treatment means giving to the products of every other country the *same* trade treatment that is given to the like products of the *most favored* of all other countries. The WTO rule requiring MFN treatment forbids discrimination between and among the like traded products of other WTO members.[5]

This core trade principle is enshrined as a general obligation of all WTO members in the goods and services agreements in the WTO treaty. Thus, whenever a concession on trade in a good or a service is made by one WTO member to another, that same concession on that same good or service must be made immediately and unconditionally to every other WTO member. Through the operation of this MFN rule, the mutual reciprocity of trade concessions is "multilateralized," meaning that all WTO members (and the entire multilateral trading system) benefit from each and every trade concession.

By means of this automatic legal mechanism, the reduction of trade barriers since the signing of the GATT in the wake of the Second World War has been achieved globally, and the gains from trade have thus been maximized again and again for all members of the system through successive rounds of multilateral trade negotiations. It was hoped that the Doha round would do the same; for, through the working of the MFN rule, a multilateral agreement has vastly more potential to lower trade barriers and, thus, to increase trade and prosperity, than does any single or series of bilateral or regional agreements between just two or a few countries.

The other core rule of nondiscrimination is the rule requiring *national treatment*. The national treatment rule forbids discrimination in favor of local over foreign producers of like imported products. For protectionists, "buying local" is always a tempting policy tool. Universally, "buying local" is always politically appealing. Witness, in the United States, the unfortunate early executive order and the subsequent legislation proposed by President Biden requiring that US government purchasers "Buy American," a protectionist policy much the same as that of former President Trump.[6] This is a pander in search of a problem. As it is, "97% of the federal government's procurements by value go to U.S. firms," and only 1 percent of federal procurement contracts are with foreign firms.[7]

But, more broadly, favoring local over like foreign products in either public or private purchases has highly harmful economic effects for those that engage in such discrimination. Viewed narrowly, and in the near term, discriminating in favor of local or domestic producers of like products may seem to create jobs, but, overall, and over the long term, it costs jobs in the domestic economy. It "destroys more jobs than it creates. By one estimate America would gain 300,000 jobs if it got rid of its local-content rules" in public purchases.[8] It would gain many more if it eliminated discrimination against foreign products altogether.

Whether it is done publicly or privately, discriminating in favor of domestic products over like imported products is short-sighted and self-defeating economically. It denies consumers the benefits of more choices and lower prices. In addition, it denies domestic producers the benefits that come from foreign inputs and foreign competition. Thus, ironically, the ability of those who make the favored national products to compete in a free marketplace is undermined – which in turn undermines the competitiveness of the national economy. Of course, local discrimination against imports from another country also tends to increase discrimination against local exports to that country. Not surprisingly, the fine nuances of the national treatment rule are topics of numerous trade disputes.[9]

These two basic WTO rules are what lawyers call *negative* obligations. They are obligations *not* to discriminate. Most trade rules are negative obligations such as these. Few are *affirmative* obligations. Few commit WTO members to take any specific actions. One of the relatively few affirmative obligations in WTO trade rules is the obligation of *transparency* – the obligation to publish all measures that affect trade.[10] In other words, WTO rules are mostly "don'ts," not "dos." Consequently, much room remains domestically for WTO members to craft their own domestic policies in a broad terrain of "policy space." WTO rules apply to domestic measures – laws, regulations, and the like – that affect trade. This is the case even if those measures are applied behind the border and not at the border. But this leaves WTO members ample space for the employment of domestic policy discretion – so long as they keep the commitments they have made in their schedules of concessions and do not discriminate in violation of the rules requiring most-favored-nation and national treatment.

Some of the new links needed in WTO trade rules should be old links by now. The current trade inheritance of the WTO – the issues left over from the failure of the Doha Development Round – are a combination of interrelated issues that have long proven intractable in multilateral trade negotiations. One is agricultural trade. A second is manufacturing trade. A third is services trade. Generally, developed countries are seeking additional market access for their manufactured goods and services in developing countries, and developing countries are, in turn, seeking additional market access, especially for their agricultural goods, in developed countries. In the fourteen years of the Doha round, the two sides of the persistent "North–South" divide were unable to find common ground on these interlinked issues. Since the demise of the Doha round in Nairobi in 2015, virtually no progress has been made. Much else has been at stake in these unsuccessful negotiations, but the utter inability of countries at different stages of development to agree on new trade rules in a compromise on these competing concerns is at the heart of the existential crisis of the WTO. A global "grand bargain" on these key long-standing issues is much needed to help accomplish Goal 8 of the UN Sustainable Development Goals, which is to "promote sustained, inclusive and sustainable economic growth, full and productive employment and decent work for all."[11] But such a bargain seems more distant than ever before as the world turns more sharply inward in the wake of the COVID-19 pandemic.

FOOD AND AGRICULTURAL TRADE

Because of the profound political sensitivities about food worldwide, in part due to memories of wartime food shortages, during the half century following the end of the Second World War agriculture was effectively excluded from the then GATT-based multilateral trading system. Technically, trade rules applied to agricultural goods in the same way they applied to all other goods. But practically, they did not. The successive rounds of trade negotiations under the GATT accomplished significant reductions in manufacturing protectionism in developed countries. They did virtually nothing to reduce agricultural protectionism. Agricultural tariffs were often astronomical and tantamount to import bans. Agricultural production and export subsidies abounded. Import quotas and other nontariff forms of agricultural trade protection accumulated. Despite the letter of the trade rules, agricultural trade was frequently the very antithesis of free trade.

One of the accomplishments of the Uruguay round was bringing agricultural trade for the first time fully within the ambit of the multilateral trading system. New rules on agricultural trade cut export subsidies, increased market access for imports, and cut domestic production subsidies.[12] (The least developed countries were not required to make these reduction commitments.)[13] These new rules required nontariff barriers to agricultural trade such as import quotas and import bans to be converted into tariffs.

In truth, in their application, these new rules "involved only very modest liberalization" in industrial countries and even less in developing countries."[14] However, this so-called process of "tariffication" made these trade restrictions transparent. Now that these restrictions were all in the transparent guise of tariffs, which could be measured and compared, the hope was that these tariffs would be cut in future negotiations, and, accordingly, cutting agricultural tariffs became a central goal of the Doha Development Round.[15]

The WTO rules on agricultural trade concluded in the Uruguay round have been beneficial to the farmers and ranchers of the United States, a country blessed with an abundance of fertile land and possessed of highly advanced farm technologies. Since 1995, US farmers and ranchers have, overall, increased the value of their exports of agricultural products by 61 percent in inflation-adjusted terms.[16] This impressive growth "was largely due to the increase in the value of high-value food products like fruit, vegetables, meat, dairy, and packaged foods."[17] During that same time, the number of countries to which the United States exported more than $1 billion annually of farm products nearly doubled – from twenty-six in 1995 to forty-eight in 2018.[18] The volume of US exports of such bulk agricultural commodities as grain, oilseeds, and cotton grew by 17 percent during the same period. The total value of these exports, however, did not grow during that period because prices per ton fell 40–50 percent between 2012 and the arrival of COVID-19.[19] All this helps explain why the US agricultural sector is so desirous of more market access abroad.

Agricultural protectionism is of special concern to developing countries, which often enjoy a comparative advantage in agricultural production. For decades, they have been denied the benefits of this comparative advantage because of the use by some developed countries of tariffs and nontariff barriers to agricultural imports, and because of the grants by those countries of agricultural production subsidies that distort trade in domestic and world agricultural markets. Despite the tariff cuts and other agricultural changes that were gradually made and implemented, developing countries have complained often that they did not get the full benefit of the bargain they made with the wealthier countries in the Uruguay round.

At the same time, where developed countries have a comparative advantage, they seek more market access for their agricultural products in developing countries. The United States, for one, has a comparative advantage in production of numerous farm products. Because the gap between the bound and the applied tariff rates for the most politically sensitive agricultural products is so high in some developing countries, cuts in bound tariff rates will often not suffice to achieve added market access. Two of many examples are India and Indonesia, where tariffs and other trade barriers insulate hundreds of millions of small farmers from foreign competition.[20] All in all, the failure of WTO members to follow up on the initial agricultural trade reforms of the Uruguay round with sizeable additional reductions in agricultural tariffs and other agricultural trade restrictions in the Doha round, has added greatly to the current trade tensions between developed and developing countries.

In agricultural trade, as Kym Anderson has explained,

There is overwhelming conceptual and empirical support for the claim that opening to trade can raise the level and growth of national income. That in turn can provide the wherewithal to reduce poverty, hunger and under-nutrition, and also boost diet diversity, food quality and food safety, and thereby ultimately boost national and global food security, health and well-being. The economic benefits of openness are proportionately greater, the smaller the economy. Such gains are even greater if accompanied by a freeing up of domestic product, factor and other input markets.[21]

What is more, Anderson adds, "The increased competition that comes from trade opening has been shown to boost both farm productivity growth ... and overall economic growth."[22] Thus, reducing agricultural protectionism makes economic sense for developed and developing countries alike. This explains why correcting and preventing trade restrictions and distortions in world agricultural markets is one of the targets of the Sustainable Development Goals.[23]

Even so, a "strong anti-trade bias persists" in much of the world relating to agriculture.[24] This bias is reflected in part in the relatively high levels of tariffs applied to agricultural goods as compared with those applied to manufactured goods. The average *bound* tariff worldwide has been calculated at 36.5 percent for agricultural goods and 11 percent for manufactured goods.[25] Weighted by imports, MFN *applied* agricultural tariffs average about 14 percent for developed countries and about 21 percent for developing countries.[26] To various extents, these farm tariffs are reduced by regional preferential trade agreements and by unilateral tariff reductions; however, the applied tariffs on numerous farm products with domestic political significance are higher.[27]

Moreover, evidencing their ongoing anxiety about the need to maintain their own domestic food production, the average of the bound tariffs on farm products is higher still in many developing countries: 100 percent in Kenya; 113.1 percent in India; 120 percent in Tanzania; 150 percent in Nigeria; 186 percent in Bangladesh; and 199.1 percent in Lesotho.[28] Meat, poultry, sugar, and dairy products are frequently the subjects of the highest bound tariffs.[29] Eighteen countries have bound tariffs on individual products in excess of 500 percent.[30] By maintaining stratospheric bound tariffs, developing countries maintain also the option of hiking their applied agricultural tariffs significantly without risk of violating their WTO obligations, which they may be inclined to do if the world keeps turning inward.

Agriculture accounts for less than 4 percent of global GDP and less than 10 percent of world trade. Yet policies on food and agriculture "are responsible for more than three-fifths of the global gain foregone because of merchandise trade distortions."[31] Thus, freeing up trade in agriculture would accomplish more globally than freeing up trade in all else. Any "global bargain" in trade must therefore include significant reductions in agricultural protectionism, and that means steep cuts in farm tariffs. By one reckoning during the Doha round, in 2006, "*93 percent* of the global welfare cost of agricultural policies was due to market access barriers and only 2% to export subsidies and 5% to domestic support measures."[32] The same study found that market access barriers are responsible for 89 percent of the reductions in global farm trade caused by trade policies.[33] Little has happened since then to alter those percentages. Without doubt, agriculture is where tariff cuts are needed most in world trade; likewise, without doubt, what is needed most in the reform of agricultural trade is tariff cuts.

However, agricultural trade is also distorted by subsidies, and they must likewise be cut. Government support that fits the WTO definition of a "subsidy" comes in many forms – including direct grants, tax breaks, favorable loans, price supports, and other kinds of financial contributions.[34] These subsidies put the government's thumb on the scales of competition. They distort trade when they distort what would, in the absence of the governmental intervention, be the market outcome from free competition. When domestic producers are given an unfair edge over foreign producers in domestic and global markets through the grant of governmental support, trade is distorted, and the overall production of prosperity is constrained.

In agriculture, subsidies are frequently in the form of governmental support conditioned on the amount of farm production. Although the harmful effects of agricultural subsidies are much less than those caused by agricultural tariffs, such subsidies often undermine the natural workings of comparative advantage and, thus, they do much to impede trade by distorting it. According to the OECD, agricultural subsidies also "have significant and negative effects on the welfare, resilience and food security of consumers and producers, as well as on agricultural sustainability, and also reduce agricultural and food trade volumes."[35] Moreover, "while an objective of many trade and domestic support policies is to increase food production, there is little evidence that they achieve this goal: global agricultural and food production would be higher if distorting support (were) removed."[36]

Manufacturing subsidies with adverse market effects are generally in violation of WTO trade rules.[37] Because agriculture was for so long excluded de facto from the effective operation of trade rules, and because agricultural matters are so politically sensitive, negotiators agreed in the Uruguay round that most of the world's agricultural subsidies would violate trade rules only if they exceeded certain negotiated limits.[38] In setting the limits, they chose a familiar "traffic light" metaphor to label certain "boxes" of subsidies. "Green box" subsidies that cause minimal or no trade distortions are unlimited. These include payments for general services such as pest and disease control, spending on research and development, and spending on environmental programs. "Blue box" subsidies that are trade-distorting but have offsetting aspects that limit the agricultural production associated with the support payments are also unlimited. (The "blue box" was negotiated as a concession to the European Union and its Common Agricultural Policy, which is a key component of the economic glue that unites the EU.)[39]

Most agricultural trade disputes are over the remaining farm subsidies – those in the "amber box." Governmental subsidies in the "amber box" provide support linked to production and prices, and support that exceeds certain agreed "*de minimus*" (minimum) thresholds for outlays that are sufficiently small relative to the value of the output.[40] Such support warrants the amber light of caution because it is highly distortive of trade. In addition to the reductions in farm subsidies they made as part of the Uruguay round agreement, WTO members have made legal commitments to put ceilings on their grants of these distortive forms of support. In WTO argot, a country's ceiling is called its "Aggregate Measure of Support." To the extent that "amber" forms of support exceed these ceilings, they are illegal under the trade rules and are subject to challenge in WTO dispute settlement.[41] Significantly, these ceilings were set in the early 1990s using a base period from the 1980s. Even then, some viewed the ceilings as outdated. And that was more than a quarter of a century ago.

In 2020, the OECD reported that fifty-four countries provided net transfers to their agricultural sectors totaling $619 billion per year.[42] OECD member countries – the most economically advanced – provided $319 billion in farm subsidies.[43] Emerging economies – including China, India, Brazil, Indonesia, Russia, and others – granted agricultural subsidies that totaled $295 billion.[44]

The average rate of support for agricultural support in the United States and other developed countries is more than double the rate in developing countries, despite some reduction in the gap since the turn of the century.[45] The three most prolific providers of agricultural subsidies are the United States, the European Union, and Japan.

More than two-thirds of the total global support is "potentially trade-distorting."[46] As explained by the OECD, in addition to altering market outcomes in agricultural trade, "These support measures have the greatest tendency to retain farmers in uncompetitive and low-income activities, harm the environment, stifle innovation, slow structural and inter-generational change, and weaken resilience."[47] At the same time, these subsidies discourage agricultural production in places where the governments cannot compete with the financial largesse of the governments in the wealthier countries. Unable to match this largesse, African countries have been discouraged from growing such staple crops as cotton, wheat, and sugar. Instead of growing, consuming, and exporting those crops, they import.[48]

Since the turn of the century, there has been a gradual decline of agricultural support based on output in the wealthier OECD countries; support in those countries has shifted more toward forms less distortive of trade. There has, however, been no comparable decline in output-oriented, trade-distortive support in the emerging economies, where levels of subsidies have been increasing. With the coming of the COVID-19 pandemic, and with the consequent apprehension about ready access to food supplies, many countries are even more reluctant to negotiate reductions in their farm support. They worry that such reductions would disrupt domestic stability by challenging the way things are in food production and supply at a time when governments are hard pressed to hold things together.

Here, too, the trade tensions between the United States and China further complicate matters. In retaliation against the unilateral tariffs applied by the United States, China restricted imports of some US agricultural products. US farm sales to China plunged from $19.5 billion in 2017 to only $9 billion in 2018.[49] The "phase one" trade deal with China in early 2020 increased Chinese purchases of US farm exports.[50] But American farmers in politically crucial states in the Midwest "hemorrhaged profits" in bearing the financial burden of lost sales to China.[51] Instead of lifting the illegal tariffs that had led to the retaliation, in 2018, President Trump chose instead to try to relieve this burden – and thereby solve a political problem he had created himself by applying illegal tariffs – by writing the farmers checks for billions of federal tax dollars.[52]

In other words, he gave them subsidies. (In their defense, many of the farmers said they would rather have had free trade in a free market instead of a government handout.) During the next three years, the subsidies from this farm bailout totaled $23 billion.[53] By some calculations, this Trumpian cornucopia of governmental largesse violated WTO rules by pushing the United

States up above the ceiling of $19.1 billion it pledged as a limit on its agricultural subsidies in the Uruguay round.[54] At the least, this outpouring of new farm subsidies invited retaliation from US trading partners and diminished the credibility of US trade negotiators in pursuing the longtime bipartisan American goal of boosting America's highly competitive agricultural exports by reducing farm subsidies worldwide.

Globally, moving away from trade-distorting forms of domestic support would improve global welfare. As economist Jared Greenville has said,

Overall, if current domestic support policies were to be removed or restructured so as not to be market distorting, world trade in all agro-food products would increase ... There would be both an increase in the production of supported commodities in countries which did not provide support and a shift to the production of other commodities in the countries where support was previously provided.[55]

Farmers and ranchers would be better served by domestic support that does not distort trade and that "focuses on the provision of public goods," such as through more general services to the agricultural sector and more spending on research and development.[56]

Another complicating factor is the issue of food stockholding. Inspired by the commodity price spikes and price volatility during the first decade of the century, as a precaution, some countries sought to ensure their food security by establishing and maintaining public reserves of stocks of the basic commodities deemed the most important to their population.[57] These food stocks are intended to be insurance policies against the possibility of food scarcity. Indeed, national food stocks can "buffet the effects of drought and other food shortages."[58] At the same time, though, there is the possibility that these public stocks of agricultural commodities, which were purchased for the purpose of maintaining an emergency domestic food supply, will be "ultimately released on to global markets, distorting international prices and undermining global food security."[59]

The question of food stockholding has become a source of increasing contention in WTO trade talks. India, fearful of food shortages, has been a leading defender of such stockholding.[60] The Indians see the issue as critical to the most vulnerable of the Indian people. The United States, fearful of the trade-distortive effects of agricultural subsidies, has claimed that India has not adequately reported the cost of its stockholding program to the WTO. The US is concerned that stockholding could become a backdoor means of discriminating against American farm exports. Unable to reach a consensus in Bali in 2013 or in Nairobi in 2015, WTO members promised to refrain from formal dispute settlement on the issue while they engaged in negotiations on a permanent solution. Five years later, they had still not found such a solution. Then, as with so much else on the trade agenda, the arrival of COVID-19 pushed attempts at a solution farther into the future.

Also complicating agricultural negotiations are the demands of some developing countries for "special safeguards" that would enable them to restore tariffs in the event of fluctuations in prices or surges in imports in the professed hope of helping poor and vulnerable farmers.[61] A limited mechanism for such protection was included as a compromise in the rules negotiated in the Uruguay round. The use of this mechanism, however, is only available for agricultural products for which other forms of trade barriers were transformed into tariffs in the Uruguay round – only about 20 percent of all the "tariff lines" of agricultural products.[62] The developing countries want to broaden and add to this protective mechanism as part of their price for agreeing to any major changes in agricultural market access. The developed countries are concerned that any such additional protection might be abused, "potentially destabilizing global markets and harming domestic consumers."[63]

New rules in agricultural trade are an indispensable part of any "grand bargain" on global trade. The notable success of the WTO in ending agricultural export subsidies in Nairobi in 2015, is certainly evidence that multilateral solutions on agricultural trade can still be found. This success can be exceeded if global farm concerns are addressed cooperatively and constructively and at the same time as global manufacturing and services concerns. New rules to prevent the protectionist use of export credits, food-exporting state trading enterprises, and food aid are needed to reinforce the Nairobi ban on export subsidies.[64] As urged by the United States and echoed by others, new rules must strengthen the requirements for public reporting of agricultural measures to the WTO.[65] But the principal areas where new rules are needed most in agricultural trade are in tariffs, subsidies, public stockholding, and special safeguards.

Large cuts must be made in agricultural tariffs. New rules must cut agricultural tariffs enough to erase the considerable "overhang" between bound and applied tariffs; for "large reductions in bound rates are needed before it is possible to bring about any improvements in market access."[66] Tariffs can be cut by various means: by employing a negotiated formula; imposing a tariff cap; making different levels of tariff reductions for developed and developing countries; implementing across-the-board percentage reductions; or some other agreed approach. To maximize the economic benefits of such cuts, stricter disciplines must be included to prevent the circumvention of agreed tariff cuts by using outdated "baseline" trade statistics or by allocating the cuts in such a way as to keep tariffs high on favored products. Practically speaking, exemptions will undoubtedly be negotiated for some domestically "sensitive" products and other "special" products. But the more the exemptions, the less the benefits. Only with new WTO rules that accomplish significant tariff cuts will agricultural trade become much freer than it is today.

Large cuts must also be made in agricultural subsidies by developed and developing countries alike. New rules must prohibit new trade-distorting farm subsidies and gradually reduce existing trade-distorting subsidies over time. Qualifications for spending exemptions under the "green box" should be tightened. Spending limits within each category should be reduced substantially for all the other allowed forms of domestic support – the "amber box," the "blue box," and *de minimus* support (the last of which has been increasingly used as a legal dodge around the current support ceilings). The main emphasis of the agricultural negotiations should be on cutting spending on domestic support in the "amber box" of trade-distorting subsidies. In addition, to further reduce trade distortions, additional commodity-specific spending constraints should be applied to support for each individual product. All these reductions in agricultural subsidies should be phased in over time and according to agreed time frames, which could be different for developed and developing countries at different stages of development.

Ideally, there should also be an overall global spending limit for each country encompassing all the permitting categories of trade-distorting domestic support – the "amber box," the "blue box," and *de minimus* support. Economists have demonstrated that this all-inclusive approach that sets an overall ceiling for trade-distorting spending – which has been proposed by the Cairns Group of farm export–minded WTO members – would reduce the total domestic support that any country could provide.[67] The key will be to set the overall spending limit for each country at a level that is much smaller than the sum of the individual limits for each category of permitted spending.[68] If large cuts are made in these ways in agricultural tariffs and agricultural subsidies, then compromises will be easier to reach on new rules for both public stockholding and special safeguards.

TRADE IN MANUFACTURED GOODS

New rules on agricultural trade must be accompanied by new rules on manufacturing trade. As Kym Anderson has stressed, "Expanding non-agricultural market access at the same time as reforming agriculture is essential for a balanced exchange of concessions. With other merchandise included, the trade expansion would be four times greater for both rich and poor countries – and poverty in low-income countries would be reduced considerably more."[69] The negotiating history on manufacturing trade helps justify this assertion. The eight GATT negotiating rounds, concluding with the Uruguay round that established the WTO in 1995, made deep tariff cuts, mostly on manufactured goods. The tariffs of the developed countries that accounted for the vast majority of global GDP at the time averaged 40 percent when the multilateral trading system began under the GATT in 1947 and started the first of those eight rounds.[70] Today, the trade-weighted average tariffs applied on manufactured goods are 3 percent in developed countries and 25 percent in developing countries.[71]

This huge difference in the applied tariff levels is a source of considerable contention in WTO negotiations. Bound tariff rates in developing countries average 38 percent on manufactured goods, and 39 percent of all manufacturing imports into developing countries are of products for which there are no bound rates.[72] The tariff sky is without limit in those countries where tariffs are not bound. As with agricultural tariffs, the developed countries are not concerned about high manufacturing tariffs in the least developed countries, which account for only a small portion of world trade; however, they are greatly concerned about those in the most advanced developing countries, which they see as denying them their comparative advantage in exports of manufactured goods.

At the same time, developing countries are equally opposed to some of the higher tariffs that remain on some manufactured goods in developed countries. To be sure, the average tariff rates in the developed countries are low. But the "average tariff figures mask higher tariffs for many labor intensive or value-added goods that are especially of interest in the developing world."[73] They disguise tariff peaks and tariff escalation, which are often used for protective purposes and often limit exports by developing countries to the United States and other developed countries of the manufactured products they are most adept in making.

A "tariff peak" refers to a country's adoption of a relatively high tariff amid generally low tariff levels to protect politically sensitive products from foreign competition. For the advanced economies, the WTO considers a tariff rate of 15 percent or more a tariff peak.[74] In the United States, tariff peaks are applied to such products as textiles, apparels, footwear, and watches, which have long had influential constituencies in politically pivotal states. For decades, these industries have sought and secured protection from foreign trade from successive members of Congress and presidents from both of the major American political parties.

"Tariff escalation" is the practice of raising tariffs as value is added in making and finishing a product. It exists when there are "[h]igher import duties on semi-processed products than on raw materials, and higher still on finished products. This difference in tariff levels protects domestic processing industries and discourages the development of processing activity in the countries where raw materials originate."[75] Tariff escalation has the effect of locking developing countries into exporting raw materials while maintaining most of the value added to products through processing in developed countries. As a result, developing countries are prevented from climbing higher up the global ladder of economic production. In one common example of tariff escalation, cotton is imported at a low tariff; fabric faces a higher tariff; and a finished shirt is charged the highest tariff.[76]

The benefits of tariff cuts are often erased by the substitution of nontariff trade barriers. For instance, the current trade-weighted average import tariff rate on manufactured goods in the United States – the largest importer and exporter of those goods – is 2 percent. Half of all manufactured goods imported into the United States enter duty free.[77] However, in the United States, as in other developed countries, *nontariff* barriers to trade have often been erected to replace tariffs as tariffs have declined. Indeed, Credit Suisse, a Swiss bank, reported even before the election of Donald Trump that the country that imposes more protectionist trade barriers than any other is the United States.[78] This conclusion is highly debatable. Even so, the United States does have an array of nontariff trade barriers.[79] Furthermore, the frequent transformation of tariffs into nontariff barriers to trade worldwide is beyond debate and is the reason why the issue was placed on the Doha negotiating agenda.

In addition to all the mountains of accumulated trade gains from manufacturing tariff cuts in previous global trade negotiations, there are still enormous trade gains to be achieved through further manufacturing tariff cuts. During the Doha round, economists at the University of Michigan calculated that a 33 percent cut in manufacturing tariffs would result in a net welfare benefit to the whole global economy of $163.4 billion.[80] World Bank calculations at the same time produced similar results.[81] The World Bank study found that, while developed countries such as the United States, the European Union, and Japan would receive most of the benefit from full liberalization of manufacturing trade in terms of dollars, developing countries might achieve larger benefits in proportion to the size of their economies, particularly from trade liberalization in textiles and apparels.[82] It is therefore clear that both developed and developing countries have much to gain from reducing tariffs on manufactured goods.

The agreed goal of WTO members on manufacturing trade as stated in the Doha Declaration at the outset of the Doha round is to "reduce or, as appropriate, eliminate tariffs, including the reduction or elimination of tariff peaks, high tariffs, and tariff escalation, as well as non-tariff barriers, in particular on products of export interest to developing countries."[83] Toward these ends, one agreed aim is binding tariff coverage on all manufactured goods. Most developed countries already have full tariff bindings on all manufactured goods, but most developing countries do not. Another agreed aim is continued and rapid liberalization and convergence to free trade in manufacturing goods. In the Uruguay round, developing countries committed to an average level of cuts, which they later made. They were not legally obligated to apply these tariff reductions across-the-board to all their manufactured products. Now, developed countries seek more liberalization from developing countries on a product-by-product basis. Other aims in the manufacturing negotiations are tariff harmonization across countries and greater uniformity of tariffs across product lines, which would simplify the global process of manufacturing trade.

The goal should be to eliminate tariffs on manufactured goods altogether – zero tariffs. In the Doha round, years before the presidency of Donald Trump, this was precisely what the United States proposed. The European Union likewise proposed significant cuts. Developing countries mostly resisted. Try as they did for nearly fifteen years, WTO members could not find a way to come together to improve worldwide market access for manufactured goods. In the wake of this negotiating failure, in the United States, under President Trump, protectionists seized on the wide gap in tariffs on manufactured goods between developed and developing countries to justify the surge in new,

unilateral US tariffs on imports of manufactured goods. The Trump administration threatened to "mirror" tariffs by imposing the same tariff on imports
from other countries that they impose on like products when they are exported
from the United States.[84]

In arguing that the differing average of tariffs on manufactured goods in the
United States and in the developing countries is not "reciprocal," these embold-
ened American protectionists betray their incomprehension of what "reciprocity" has long meant in international trade. They seek product-by-product
reciprocity. But trade deals are not negotiated product by product; they are
negotiated country by country. What is sought in multilateral trade negotiations is not identical tariffs on all products from everywhere. What is sought is
an overall balance of trade concessions that will benefit every country, including tariff cuts. A trade deal is "reciprocal" if all who make the deal feel that
overall the tariff and other concessions they have made are equaled by the
concessions they have received. This is not the same as every country imposing
the same tariffs on the same products.[85]

Trump's product-by-product "mirror" approach would never work.
Practically, such an approach would eliminate what makes multilateral trade
agreements possible – the ability of countries to make different concessions to
different countries across a range of products, which are all "multilateralized" to
apply to all countries through the operation of most-favored-nation treatment,
and thereby add up to what all consider a "balanced" result. Legally, the "mirror"
approach would be a violation of the rule of MFN treatment, which, as American
trade commentator Daniel Griswold has pointed out, does "not allow the United
States or any other WTO member to target another member with specific duties
that (do) not apply to imports from all other members."[86] What is more, as he has
also noted, "If the US government were to implement President Trump's vision of
tit-for-tat duties aimed at individual trading partners, the most immediate result
would be an increase in thousands of US duties on hundreds of billions of dollars
of US imports," with grievous domestic economic effects.[87]

Global cuts in tariffs on manufactured goods will not be made without the
leadership and the concurrence of the United States, where any such cuts will be
seen through the lens of US anxiety over lost manufacturing jobs. Without an
ease in that anxiety, leadership and concurrence from the United States is not to
be assumed. Much of this anxiety is about imports of Chinese manufactured
goods, which surged after China's entry into the WTO in 2001. In a now
ubiquitous study, David Autor, David Dorn, and Gordon Hanson estimated
that the "China Shock" of import competition with Chinese goods caused
about 2.4 million lost jobs for American workers during the first decade of this
century.[88] They said also that the impact of Chinese competition has cut US
wages and has, moreover, extended to affect other US labor markets, such as
those that supply or serve manufacturing production.[89]

The "China Shock" study is often cited as proof of the need for more trade
protectionism in the United States. It is trotted out as sufficient authority every

time someone wants to make the case for more managed trade through the institution of a mercantilist industrial policy. However, those who rely on "China Shock" as offering an open-and-shut case for protectionism overlook the facts that Autor and his colleagues themselves endorsed freer trade and warned against resort to protectionism, and that he himself conceded that their limited study looked at only one part of the economic picture. It did not, for instance, consider the positive results for the United States of increased manufacturing imports from China. "Our research," Autor conceded, "does not tell you the net societal costs and benefits of trade."[90]

Others since have filled in those blanks.[91] By their count, far fewer US manufacturing job losses can be attributed to the impact of Chinese imports.[92] As Adam Posen of the Peterson Institute for International Economics has summarized this impact,

[T]rends run counter to the oft-told story that American workers suffered gravely after China joined the World Trade Organization. After much debate, economists have agreed on an upper-bound estimate of the number of U.S. manufacturing jobs that were lost as a result of Chinese competition after 1999: two million, at most, out of a workforce of 150 million. In other words, from 2000 to 2015, the China shock was responsible for displacing roughly 130,000 workers a year. That amounts to a sliver of the average churn in the U.S. labor market, where about 60 million job separations typically take place each year . . . [F]or each manufacturing job lost to Chinese competition, there were roughly 150 jobs lost to similar-feeling shocks in other industries.[93]

Similarly, Robert Z. Lawrence has concluded that, at the most, "Actual displacement due to Chinese competition . . . probably accounted for less than one-fifth of (US manufacturing job displacement) in recent years and less than 5 percent of overall displacement in the economy at large."[94] Moreover, he and others have underscored that, as Autor acknowledged, he and his colleagues told only half the story. In addition to job losses in manufacturing because of trade, the offsetting job gains in manufacturing exports and services created by trade should be counted.[95] For example, one study found that, in the United States, because of globalization, between 2001 and 2016, "*net* jobs affected by imports and supported by exports were roughly 1.4 million, or around 88,000 jobs per year."[96] According to the US–China Business Council (of American companies doing business with China), in 2019, US exports to China supported more than 1.1 million American jobs.[97] What is more, imports of manufactured goods from China have raised annual US living standards $250 *per person*.[98]

The Federal Reserve Bank of San Francisco has reported that more than half of every dollar that Americans spend on Chinese imports – about 56 percent – in fact go to American firms and workers – the highest percentage of any country.[99] This is mainly because one-third of all Chinese imports are intermediate goods that are imported from China by American companies for use in their production of finished products. With their lower costs, these imported inputs support millions of US jobs by helping make "Made in America" manufacturing products more competitive in US and world markets. What is more, as Scott Lincicome of the Cato Institute has documented, labor market data show that millions more American "blue collar" jobs in areas of the US workforce other than manufacturing could benefit from imports from China – for example, in transportation, logistics, construction, and maintenance and repair.[100]

Although the broad benefits to US consumers from trade with China are of little consolation to American factory workers who have lost their jobs due to trade competition, those benefits should not be overlooked. Economists report that, even at the height of the "China Shock" in the century's first decade, Chinese imports had significant "pro-competitive" effects on US businesses and provided more than $202 billion in consumer benefits through lower prices.[101] Trade with China increased consumer benefits in the United States by about $400,000 for every US job lost.[102] As Lincicome has summed up the situation in the United States, "[T]he claims of harm from Chinese trade are likely wildly overstated while the substantial economic benefits are usually ignored."[103] And, it may be added, even when the benefits are not ignored, they are usually not believed.

If it is correct, the estimate by Autor and his colleagues that roughly 240,000 US manufacturing jobs were lost annually during the first decade of this century due to competition from Chinese imports, is a lot of lost jobs. Every single job layoff causes personal pain to the laid-off worker and that worker's family. It causes pain to that worker's community. Lost jobs can lead to lost lives. All that can be done to help those who have lost their jobs must be done. Yet, in the United States, in an economy of nearly 150 million jobs, about 75,000 workers are laid off or fired *every day*.[104] Even if Autor and his colleagues are right about the extent of the Chinese impact on US manufacturing jobs during those years, their much-mentioned study explains only a very small part of the job losses resulting from the job churn in America's market-based economy.

Moreover, it does not explain why, in the two decades leading up to the COVID-19 pandemic, real, inflation-adjusted manufacturing in the United States grew by almost 40 percent as the annual value added to the US economy by US factories reached a record of $2.4 trillion.[105] This happened even as some jobs were lost, partly due to trade, but mostly due to increased productivity from the adoption of automation and other new technologies. In the first decade after China joined the WTO in 2001, in the immediacy of the "China Shock," about 87 percent of the job displacement in manufacturing in the United States was because of increased productivity due to the introduction of new technologies and other production efficiencies. Only about 13 percent of the job losses were because of trade.[106] And these job losses were due to *all* foreign trade, not solely to trade with China. With these increases in manufacturing productivity leading up to the pandemic, US manufacturing jobs were declining; US manufacturing was not.

The economic disruptions caused by COVID-19 have caused declines in global manufacturing production, which was already declining due to the tariff and other trade restrictions caused by the trade conflict between the United States and China.[107] Eliminating the remaining barriers to trade in manufactured goods will help revive manufacturing in the United States and elsewhere. Far from harming American manufacturing, trade – including trade with China – has helped, by making it more productive. Griswold offers this explanatory insight: "Access to expanding global markets allows U.S. manufacturers to enjoy economies of scale, reducing their per-unit production costs and enhancing their competitiveness. The additional revenue can be reinvested in research and development, leading to new products and expanding market share. This is why U.S. jobs in trade-oriented industries typically pay 18% more than non-trade-connected jobs."[108]

In advice made still more relevant now that manufacturing has been assailed by the pandemic, economists from the Peterson Institute for International Economics have stressed that "policymakers should pay special attention to displaced workers," in manufacturing and otherwise.[109] However, they have also underscored that the costs for displaced workers are "much smaller than gains from expanded trade," and that "*permanent* gains from liberalization and technology advances far outweigh *temporary* adjustment costs."[110] To assist displaced workers, they urge, not protection from foreign trade, but "sharply improved adjustment programs ... to compensate those who lost from deeper integration and from newer technology." They caution that, "Adjustment costs should not be used as a reason to say 'no' to liberalization or new technology."[111]

The Bureau of Labor Statistics predicts the loss of an additional nearly 450,000 manufacturing jobs in the United States by the end of this decade.[112] Moreover, in the new pandemic world, more than half of US companies say they are increasingly open to investing in automation to survive the changing market conditions brought on by COVID-19.[113] On the assembly lines and in the warehouses, people are increasingly being replaced by robots. Daron Acemoglu of MIT and Pascual Restrepo of Boston University have calculated that each new robot added to the workforce means the loss of between 3 and 5.6 jobs in the local commuting area, and that for each new robot added per 1,000 workers, wages in the surrounding area will fall between one-fourth and one-half of one percent.[114] The impact of trade on manufacturing jobs is minor when compared to that of automation.

In response to these alarming projections, we have, so far, only educated guesses about how Americans (and other humans) might be educated and trained for jobs with a future.[115] For all the loud anguish in America about lost jobs and looming economic precarity, no US policy has yet been enacted to help workers make this job transition. In his American Jobs Plan unveiled during his first hundred days in office, in the spring of 2021, President Biden proposed spending $100 billion on training, retraining, transitional assistance for dislocated workers of all kinds, and other innovative workforce development programs.[116] If successful, the added safety net of these proposed new workforce programs in the United States could do much to help temper domestic opposition to free trade among workers in trade- and technology challenged industries, just as – to some extent – similar programs seem to have done in the European Union. At this writing, the Congress has yet to enact this proposal.

The national interest of the United States continues to lie in eliminating the remaining tariff and other barriers to manufacturing trade in the United States and worldwide. This is equally in the interest of the rest of the world. Yet the nostalgic angst about preserving jobs in past ways of manufacturing is likely to complicate future WTO manufacturing negotiations further, because, even if the United States returns to its previous advocacy of freer trade in manufacturing, Americans are not alone in fearing the continued loss of manufacturing jobs. These fears are found in other developed countries and, also, in developing countries that are still striving to establish a manufacturing base.

Notably, in a revival of the false panacea of the "import substitution" of industrial policy in the 1960s and 1970s, some developing countries have resurrected their bogus argument of decades ago that denying them the right to protect their "infant" and other domestic industries with tariffs and other barriers to foreign trade, amounts to kicking away the ladder of economic development.[117] Ironically, these developing countries have been joined in this posture by some thinkers in the United States who seek to recast economic nationalism as "national developmentalism."[118] Yet, irrespective of what protectionism is called or how it is cloaked, there can be no concealing the fact that an economic policy that turns inward and away from the world is doomed to fail. Those who embrace it will not be kicked off the ladder. They will fall off.

TRADE IN SERVICES

If the twentieth century was about the shift in jobs from agriculture to manufacturing, then the twenty-first century is about the shift in jobs from manufacturing to services.[119] Our great-grandparents told us about plowing long furrows on farms. We will tell our great-grandchildren about monotonous tasks on long assembly lines in factories. The transition to a services economy began first in developed countries, which have now been largely transformed by it. The OECD estimates that services account for about 75 percent of GDP; 80 percent of employment; and two-thirds of the inflows of foreign direct investment in the United States and other advanced economies.[120] The shift "from farm to factories to urban offices" is happening now in developing countries, many of which already have sizeable service economies.[121] Developing countries' share of world trade in services has grown rapidly in recent years, especially in the most advanced of the emerging economies, and accounts now for about one-fourth of global services exports and about one-third of global services imports.[122] In all countries, this historic shift is speeding up in an increasingly digital global economy.

Some services are "non-tradable" because they can only be delivered locally. Haircutting is a "non-tradable" service. Lawn mowing is another. But many high value-added services are "tradable" because they can be delivered internationally. Most legal, accounting, financial, logistical, engineering, architectural, travel, transportation, construction, telecommunications, and maintenance and repair services are tradable. Increasingly, these kinds of services are becoming globalized.[123] Because of digitalization, more services are becoming tradable, and are now increasingly being provided internationally through online connections. Think, for instance, of the increases in remote education and remote medical services, both accelerating now in the pandemic world. As the WTO Secretariat has explained, "Thanks to digitalization, the internet and low-cost communications, many services sectors that were once non-tradable – because they had to be delivered face-to-face in a fixed location – have become highly tradable – because they can now be delivered remotely over long distances."[124]

Services are the fastest-growing sector of international trade.[125] While growth in goods trade has slowed as the world has turned inward, growth in services trade has sharply increased. Although services exports currently comprise only one-fifth of international trade, they have grown at three times the rate of goods exports in the past decade.[126] What is more, "the line between manufacturing and services ... is becoming ... blurred across many industries."[127] Nearly one-third of the gross value of goods is the services (banking, insurance, transportation, and the like) that go into making and delivering them.[128] According to the OECD, "accounting for the value added by services in the production of goods shows that the services sector contributes over 50% of total exports in the United States, the United Kingdom, France, Germany and Italy and nearly one-third in China."[129]

But services trade, like goods trade, is constrained by trade restrictions. Worldwide, barriers to trade in services are equivalent to tariffs of between 30 and 50 percent, which impedes the economic growth of those countries whose services providers have a comparative advantage when trading their services.[130] The United States is one of the countries with comparative advantages in numerous sectors of services trade. The United States is also a country that – although many Americans do not realize it – is primarily a services economy. In 2018, services accounted for 78.8 percent of US GDP and for 81.9 percent of US jobs.[131] Services also accounted that same year for $827 billion in US exports – about one-third of all US exports of goods and services and about 14 percent of all global services exports.[132]

President Trump largely ignored trade in services as he dwelt almost entirely on manufacturing jobs and on his atavistic notion that the American economy remained in the 1950s.[133] In his first months in office, President Biden mostly did the same. Despite these bipartisan political preoccupations, here in the twenty-first century, the American economy is likely to become even more dependent on jobs in services. Employment in the services economy – in tourism, travel, restaurants, retail, and other sectors – plunged during the depths of the pandemic.[134] Ordinarily, transportation and travel account for about half of all world trade in commercial services.[135] Yet the fact remains, US employment will continue to be primarily in services. Indeed, the share of US employment in services will likely increase somewhat, including in the health sector that has been so important during the pandemic and will only increase in importance as the American "baby boom" generation continues to age. As the OECD has observed, the economy of the twenty-first century "is characterized by computer-integrated manufacturing, additive manufacturing, automation and advanced analytics of Big Data and the flow of information across the Internet of Things."[136] Given these new economic drivers and the continued automation of both agriculture and manufacturing, "the employment share in services is likely to (continue to) climb until it levels off at around 80–85%."[137]

The United States is the largest trader of services in the world, ranking first in both exports and imports of commercial services.[138] In a global "grand bargain" reducing barriers to trade in agriculture, manufacturing, and services, the United States would gain the most from liberalization of trade in services, with a net welfare benefit of $135 billion.[139] According to the Coalition of Services Industries, eliminating foreign barriers to services trade and digitally enabled trade could increase US exports by as much as $860 billion to $1.4 trillion, creating as many as three million new American jobs.[140]

Services trade, though, is not only of importance to developed countries such as the United States, the European Union, Japan, and Canada. It is also important to developing countries. Services account for 40 percent of the GDP and 70 percent of the employment in major emerging economies, and more and more of these services are on the cutting edge. China and other emerging economies are starting to develop their own comparative advantages in certain sectors of services trade.[141] All the members of the WTO stand to benefit from liberalization of services trade.

Rules on trade in services were agreed for the first time as part of the WTO treaty in 1994, at a time when "less than two percent of the world's population had access to the Internet."[142] These rules are contained in the WTO General Agreement on Trade in Services – the GATS. The GATS was intended as only a start toward fully liberalizing services trade. But these rules have not been changed since 1997, when GATS protocols were adopted on financial services and basic telecommunications services. Even these protocols contained limited liberalization. And both global and plurilateral efforts to add to the initial services commitments in the GATS in the decades since have failed. Trade rules on services are largely still back in 1995.

In the Doha round, the developing countries were reluctant to grant more market access in services because the developed countries were reluctant to limit their use of trade remedies and agricultural subsidies, and to grant more foreign access to their agricultural markets. Faced with this reluctance and with their own unwillingness to make concessions on these other trade concerns, fifty-four WTO members, including the United States, became so frustrated by the glacial progress of the Doha round services negotiations that that they pulled out of those talks and attempted to negotiate a separate "Trade in Services Agreement" on the sidelines of the WTO. It was not clear whether TISA – if agreed – would be legally within or without the WTO legal framework. In the end, these separate talks stalled also when Donald Trump, with his singular focus on manufacturing trade, became president of the United States. Four years later, nothing more had been accomplished to liberalize services trade.

Restrictions on trade in services are sometimes hard to pin down. In part, this is because they are not tariffs, which, if difficult to eliminate, are at least easy to identify because they are transparent. Rather, services trade restrictions are nontariff trade barriers. They are forms of regulation that affect the cross-border movement of products, consumers, and factors of production. Often, these regulations favor domestic over foreign suppliers of services. Air transport, legal services, accounting, and auditing services "tend to be more restrictive on average than other sectors."[143] And, on services, "[o]n average, developing countries tend to have more restrictive trade policies than OECD countries."[144] This is not to say, though, that developed countries have not applied regulatory barriers to services trade. How many of the state bar associations in the United States accept legal credentials from the other American states, much less from foreign countries?

Trade in services is essential to global supply chains, connecting the links of the manufacturing process. With manufactured goods, the linked services are either "embodied" (delivered *within* the final product) or "embedded" (delivered *alongside* the final product). Trade barriers in both embodied and embedded services have been built everywhere in the world, amounting to the equivalent of an invisible tariff on the trade of global services suppliers. Ordinarily, these barriers take the form of such sundry "behind the border" measures as restrictions on foreign entry, restrictions on the movement of people across borders, and regulatory discrimination and a lack of transparency.

WTO rules on trade in services address some of these trade barriers but far from all. The MFN rule forbidding discrimination among different foreign sources of trade, applies automatically to trade in services, just as it does to trade in goods.[145] A major obstacle, however, to reducing barriers to services trade is that, in contrast to WTO rules on trade in goods, where the national treatment rule prohibiting discrimination in favor of local producers and suppliers over foreign producers and suppliers applies automatically, the national treatment rule does not apply automatically to trade in services.[146] National treatment is required for services trade only if the country providing the treatment has made a specific trade concession in its schedule of GATS concessions annexed to the WTO treaty. For services trade, all WTO Members have made some concessions. But no WTO member has made concessions for anything approaching all the trade in all its services sectors. In many sectors of services trade, countries remain free to discriminate in favor of domestic suppliers over foreign suppliers of like traded services.

To strengthen trade links through services, WTO negotiators should begin by reconsidering the efficacy of this approach for liberalization of services trade. After all, this differing treatment of goods and services under the national treatment rule has no logical justification. It exists only because, without an acceptance of this differing treatment, no consensus could have been reached in the Uruguay round negotiations back in 1994 to include *any* rules governing trade in services in the WTO treaty. More than a quarter of a century later, given the growing importance of services trade to developed and developing countries alike, this distinction should be eliminated.

The WTO rules on services trade should be revised to increase current obligations to provide national treatment. WTO members should no longer be permitted to discriminate in services trade unless they "*opt in*" to an obligation of nondiscrimination in a particular sector of services trade. Instead, the rules should oblige them *not* to discriminate in a services sector unless they have been granted an "*opt out*" from national treatment. This approach has been taken in the negotiations on a "Trade in Services Agreement" that were put on hold during the Trump administration, and it should be central to WTO services negotiations.[147]

In addition, new rules are needed to encourage regulatory cooperation on services. Another reason why services negotiations have failed so far is because countries are unwilling to risk opening their markets to more trade in services without the domestic presence of two prerequisites that are needed to make market opening in services trade more successful. One is the domestic capacity for regulation, which can be remedied in part by more technical assistance by developed countries to developing countries. The other is a "framework for international regulatory cooperation."[148] Services trade negotiations have long centered on securing more market access. Services negotiations should focus equally on domestic regulatory reform, which is a key to market access. Because each services sector is unique, regulatory cooperation will necessarily have to be sector by sector. Prudential standards in financial services, for example, present their own unique challenges. Negotiating aims for regulation must include more harmonization – creating one same shared international standard – and more mutual recognition – the mutual acceptance of differing national standards that fulfill the same regulatory purposes.[149]

New rules on trade must also acknowledge the reality of the digital economy and be shaped to advance it. The WTO General Agreement on Trade in Services "predates the digital revolution."[150] There were no smartphones in 1995. The Internet was a novelty and considerably less than a household word. Now, "[d]igitalized commerce relies very heavily on services ... The smallest enterprises can today aspire to serve markets worldwide. At the same time, large multinational firms have also relied increasingly on the Internet to do business, coordinate physically disperse operations and exchange information."[151] New WTO rules on services trade can address some aspects of the new digital economy, but new rules on services trade will not succeed nearly to the extent they should unless they are accompanied by WTO rules on digital trade.

5

Links to the New Commercial Economy

Necessary to global economic recovery in the new pandemic world is a new focus in the WTO on negotiating rules to cover dimensions of global commerce in the twenty-first century that are largely not addressed by twentieth-century trade rules. This is one of the awaiting tasks of trading countries in international cooperation. There is need for new and better rules in a wide array of areas of contemporary commerce. Without these new and better rules, the WTO will be rendered less and less relevant to world trade. Foremost on the list of the commercial areas much in need of WTO rules are four topics: digital trade, intellectual property rights, cross-border competition, and facilitating foreign direct investment.

RULES FOR DIGITAL TRADE

The most significant new dimension of international trade in the twenty-first century is that so much of it is now digital.[1] In the twentieth century, trade was largely comprised of exchanges of physical goods. Late in the century, trade in goods was increasingly accompanied by trade in services. Today, trade links are increasingly digital, relating to both goods and services. Trade now "is increasingly defined by flows of data and information."[2] The McKinsey Global Institute reports that, since 1990, the global economy is 10 percent larger than it would have been without those data and information flows, which amounts to an increased global economic output equivalent to $7.8 trillion.[3] Moreover, "Data flows account for $2.8 trillion of this effect, *exerting a larger impact on growth than traditional goods flows.*"[4]

The surge in global flows of data and information has fundamentally altered the ways the world economy works. The revolutionary impacts of these digital flows on trade are, of course, most apparent in the information and communications technology sector. But those impacts extend far beyond the ICT sector to include manufacturing, agriculture, mining, finance, insurance, and more. Digital flows of data and information enable the logistics of global supply chains. They provide the technical basis for the cost efficiencies of cloud computing. They facilitate 3D printing and further development of machine learning through heightened artificial intelligence. Digital flows further the "smart manufacturing" that uses data to add value to products (as with the computerized global positioning systems in automobiles). They also make it possible to link household and other basic mechanical systems to the Internet to enable the sending and receiving of data in the "Internet of Things." All these new, cutting-edge technologies are possible only because of flows of digital data.

Digital trade has become ubiquitous. The McKinsey Global Institute also reports that "virtually every type of cross-border transaction now has a digital component."[5] About 12 percent of all goods traded internationally are purchased online.[6] About half of global trade in services is digital.[7] International exchanges of virtual goods via the Internet are now commonplace.[8] Sensors, software, and other add-on "digital wrappers" speed goods shipments and encourage the mutual trust needed for international transactions.[9] Container ships still sail. Cargo planes still fly. Trucks still cross borders. But digitalization is altering how all of this takes place, and, in doing so, it is adding both volume and value to international trade.

What is more, digitalization is not only changing *how* we trade.[10] It is also changing *who* trades. One major impact of these digital changes is that international trade is no longer the province principally of multinational corporations. Going digital makes it easy to connect with anyone anywhere with only a few clicks on a handheld device. In the digital economy, "artisans, entrepreneurs, app developers, freelancers, small businesses, and even individuals can participate directly on digital platforms with global reach."[11] This diversifying and "democratizing" impact on participation in trade is widespread. Not all these firms and people are located in New York or Silicon Valley. Many of them – including many women and members of other disadvantaged and marginal groups – are in developing countries. In the most recent count, 361 million people worldwide participate in e-commerce.[12]

One aim of Goal 9 of the UN Sustainable Development Goals is to "foster innovation."[13] Toward this end, the shift to a digital economy has increased economic growth by spurring improved efficiencies and technological innovations worldwide. In many economic sectors, these efficiencies and innovations have increased productivity, which is the key to generating economic growth.[14] The swift spread of the digital economy "is making itself felt in the ways knowledge, skills and expertise can be sourced from around the world, and in the ways in which production can be integrated, 24 hours a day, across time zones and borders."[15] Perhaps most significantly, the innovations of digitalization are "also rapidly spreading the very factors of production – technology, information, and ideas – that make economic advances possible."[16] According to the WTO, these digital "technological innovations have significantly reduced trade costs and transformed the way we communicate, consume, produce and trade."[17]

Digital trade is, of course, important to developed countries, but the shift to a digital economy is especially important to developing countries, which continue to suffer "within and across countries" from a "digital divide."[18] Of the people in the world without internet access, 90 percent are in developing countries;[19] 88 percent of North Americans; 85 percent of Japanese; and 84 percent of Europeans have internet access. In the Middle East and North Africa, 65 percent of the people can get online to connect with the wider world; 63 percent of Latin Americans and 54 percent of Chinese do. But only 34 percent of Indians; 33 percent of the inhabitants of the small Pacific island states; and 25 percent of sub-Saharan Africans can do so.[20] Most of the people in these developing countries remain outside the productive engine of the digital economy. New rules for digital trade must be accompanied by new measures that expand internet access in those countries and in all the world.

If applied along with such measures, new rules that lower the barriers to digital trade can be of disproportionate benefit to developing countries. As the WTO has pointed out, "Many trade costs such as logistics and transactions costs or cumbersome customs procedures ... are much higher in developing countries."[21] Thus, developing countries will benefit proportionately the most by the digitalization of these trade procedures. The WTO predicts that developing countries' share of world trade will increase from 46 percent in 2015 to 51 percent by 2030. But, if developing countries "catch up on the adoption of digital technologies," their share of global trade in 2030 will be 57 percent.[22] If, however, developing countries are left behind in the digital economy by the digital divide, then they will be marginalized in the global economy of the future.

Essential to framing the trade rules required to help secure more innovation by supporting and speeding the shift to a digital economy, is understanding the role of data in this historic shift. The source of the many innovations flowing from the digital economy is the free flow of data and "[u]nderpinning digital trade is the movement of data."[23] The European Political Strategy Centre – the in-house think tank of the European Union – has explained that, "Data is rapidly becoming **the lifeblood of the global economy**. It represents a new type of **economic asset**. Those who know how to use it have a decisive competitive advantage in this interconnected world, through raising performance, offering more user-centric products and services, fostering innovation – often leaving decades-old competitors behind."[24] Or, as Richard Waters of the *Financial Times* has put it, pithily, "In the digital world, data is destiny."[25]

Being able to move data across borders is indispensable to digital trade. The free movement of data has become still more indispensable as more digital transactions have begun to rely on computer cloud services, which are oblivious to borders. Mark Wu of Harvard Law School, formerly an adviser to the

United States Trade Representative, has explained that, as the digital economy transitions more and more toward the Internet of Things, artificial intelligence, virtual reality, and autonomous vehicles, an even greater economic premium will be placed on the free movement of data.[26] "Beyond this economic impact," the World Economic Forum has added, "the free flow of data is, itself, a significant driver of innovation. It allows the sharing of ideas and information and the dissemination of knowledge as well as collaboration and cross-pollination among individuals and companies."[27]

Necessary also to framing rules for digital trade is comprehending that, in the digital economy, the product is often the data. As is frequently the case with internet transactions, the data collected by the seller about the purchaser may be of more value than the money paid by the purchaser. Dan Ciurak and Maria Ptashkina of the Centre for International Governance Innovation in Canada have observed that, in internet transactions, there is an implicit "barter exchange" of free Internet access for useful data; "in the case of consumer data, firms provide the 'free' service of use of their platforms in implicit exchange for the data such use generates."[28] In making the same point, Joshua Meltzer of the Brookings Institution has noted that, "In a digital economy ... data can be used to produce digital goods and services, and can be a source of information that leads to further action," such as with data collection by a bank before authorizing a money transfer, or data collection by an insurer before assessing and insuring against a risk.[29] The success of myriad such economic actions, including countless actions that affect international trade, depends on the free flow of data.

Adding to the pressing need for new rules on digital trade is the persistence of the COVID-19 pandemic. Even before the pandemic, the trend toward more digital trade seemed likely to continue and accelerate. Now, in the new pandemic world, trade is becoming even more digital as part of the overall global transformation to a digital economy. In the vanished world before the pandemic, 41 percent of interactions with customers by North American companies were digital; in the new pandemic world, 65 percent of customer interactions are digital.[30] In international trade, as in all else, COVID-19 has clearly shown the necessity for better digital capability and better digital connectivity. With the pronounced trend toward online commerce speeding up, David Malpass, president of the World Bank, anticipates that, "Faster advances in digital connectivity ... should get a vital boost from the pandemic, which heightened the value of teleworking capabilities, digital information, and broad connectivity."[31] These advances can be expected to help facilitate more digital trade.

Moreover, in the wake of the pandemic, the importance of intangible assets is increasing. The need for physical assets is decreasing as businesses realize that employees do not need to congregate in expensive office space to be productive. Why pay for all those corporate offices and conference rooms? As Greg Ip of the *Wall Street Journal* has observed, "Value is increasingly derived from digital platforms, software and other intangible investments rather than physical assets and traditional relationships."[32] In this altered commercial landscape, "the future arrives early," and the necessity for quick and effective communications is greater than ever before.[33] The businesses that are the most engaged in the digital economy are likely to lead the way in the economic recovery from the COVID-19 pandemic.

The Carlyle Group, a leading global private equity firm, informs us that the pace of digitalization will accelerate in the new pandemic world, for "[t]echnology-enabled adaptation has opened the door to more sweeping changes in business models and strategies ... (and) tech-enabled digital platforms tend to outperform the broader market."[34] Rana Foroohar of the *Financial Times* predicts that, of the new start-up enterprises that will emerge in the aftermath of the pandemic, "it's a fair bet that many will be highly digital. They are likely to hold a large chunk of value in intangible assets such as research and development, brands, content, data, patents or human capital, rather than in physical assets such as industrial machinery, factories or office space."[35] When these new enterprises engage in international trade, whether of goods or of services, they will be more likely to do so digitally.

Yet there are no specific multilateral rules for digital trade. Digital trade is not even defined in the WTO trade rules. There is, moreover, no one recognized and accepted definition worldwide of digital trade. According to the OECD, however,

there is a growing consensus that it encompasses digitally-enabled transactions of trade in goods and services that can be digitally or physically delivered, and that involve consumers, firms, and governments. That is, while all forms of digital trade are enabled by digital technologies, not all digital trade is digitally delivered. For instance, digital trade also involves digitally enabled but physically delivered trade in goods and services such as the purchase of a book through an on-line marketplace, or booking a stay in an apartment through a matching application.[36]

Although there are no WTO rules written specifically for digital trade, there are WTO rules that apply to certain aspects of digital trade. As Ciuriak and Ptashkina have put it, numerous rules that apply to non-digital trade also apply "by default" to digital trade, even in the absence of specific rules on digital trade.[37] Moreover, "WTO rules are technologically neutral," which means that the mere fact that trade is conducted other than by means of a physical transaction should not change WTO obligations.[38] Yet there are many legal uncertainties about whether existing rules apply, which existing rules apply, and how existing rules apply. To some extent, the WTO Appellate Body has eliminated some of this uncertainty by answering some of the questions about the meanings of existing trade rules when it has been required to do so in WTO dispute settlement.[39] But the fact remains, the WTO rules on goods trade date back to 1947, long before the information revolution, and the WTO rules on services trade date back to 1994, when the Internet was still an obscure novelty and "many of today's digital technologies and applications did not yet exist."[40]

Despite their technological neutrality, basic legal questions remain unanswered about the extent to which current WTO rules are relevant to digital trade. For example, is a product provided online a good or a service? To illustrate this dilemma, as economist Robert Staiger has done, it may be asked, "[I]s a blueprint for use in a 3D printer, when delivered from abroad, a traded good or a traded service?"[41] The answer to this question matters in part because, as we have seen, the national treatment obligation applies automatically to all trade in goods but applies to trade in services only when a WTO member has explicitly agreed to it. Once again, there is no logic in this distinction; it is simply a consequence of a political compromise made during the Uruguay round that made it possible to achieve a consensus on including services within the scope of the trade rules. No consensus could be reached then to apply the national treatment rule automatically to all trade in services; instead, it is applied in services trade only if a specific concession has been made. As a result, if a particular traded product is deemed a service instead of a good, WTO members may be free to discriminate against foreign suppliers. This explains the domestic pressures in many places to define as the delivery of services digital trade that also has aspects of the delivery of goods; doing so enables protectionism.

Mindful of these and other limitations in the existing rules, WTO members have been trying to modernize the trade rules to deal with digital trade since 1998. They approved a temporary moratorium that year on the application of customs duties on electronic transactions (which does not prevent *internal* taxes, fees, or charges on content transmitted electronically). This temporary moratorium has been renewed repeatedly.[42] But they have not yet made this moratorium permanent, and they have accomplished little else since then toward addressing the manifold commercial concerns of what has become an increasingly digital economy. The continued absence of specific rules on digital trade in the WTO trade rulebook is emblematic of the near paralysis of the WTO negotiating function thus far in this century.

The inability of the WTO even to agree to try to negotiate specific rules on digital trade was a major reason for the seeming indifference of so many in the international business community to the demise of the Doha round in Nairobi in 2015. Much that was important to them was not on the Doha agenda. Since then, commercial concerns relating to digital trade have continued to multiply and intensify while acquiring an array of geopolitical dimensions. The rise of digital trade has created digital trade rivalry, which is most evident in the commercial relations between and among the United States, the European Union, and China.

In part, this new dimension of trade rivalry reveals in the new digital realm the profound differences between those in the world who believe in open and closed societies – those who wish to maximize the free choices individuals can make about how to live, what to do, and what to think – and those who do not. Trade is a conduit not only for goods and services, but also for ideas. While trade adds to the choices of what to buy, it also adds to the choices of what to think. With the Internet, it is difficult to allow goods and services to flow digitally without also permitting the digital flow of new ideas. Although authoritarian governments may not want to ban all new goods and services, they do want to bar new ideas. Generally, democratic governments are open to both.

Broadly speaking, the European Union and the United States favor open and market-based approaches to digital trade while China does not. The EU and the United States have agreed on certain principles for cross-border ICT services, including transparency, open networks, network access, and use; no governmental restrictions on cross-border flows of data and information; no discrimination in licensing; and no requirements of local infrastructure or local presence as a condition of delivering services.[43] The two differ, however, on the meaning of some of these principles. Most notably, the EU and the United States differ on the sensitive issue of data privacy, with the EU providing in its General Data Protection Regulation more privacy protections for consumers and other internet users than exist in US law.[44] This difference prevents the two of them from presenting an entirely united front on the need for free flows of data and information in their dealings with China.

For their part, the Chinese profess to believe in "internet sovereignty" – the notion that each country has the sovereign right to control its domestic internet space by limiting the free flow of data and information. As Tim Wu, formerly of Columbia Law School and now on the US National Economic Council, has pointed out, while most countries think the Internet is subject to national laws, "China is unique in its lack of respect for the idea of an open Internet."[45] On this philosophical basis, the Chinese defend their digital "Great Firewall," with which they routinely censor online content and online product delivery throughout China. In China's unopposed and omnipresent one-party state, this digital firewall, coupled with their recent intensifying of overall political surveillance of the Chinese people, discourages unwanted domestic dissent, and it deters the introduction of unsanctioned and unsettling ideas from abroad. Continued popular support for the unchallenged reign of the Chinese Communist Party is thereby solidified, and China is untroubled by the domestic political chaos that has so often afflicted the Chinese people in centuries past.

The "Great Firewall" is also a tool employed for digital protectionism. The digital firewall denies Chinese consumers access to online content and to other goods and services accessible on the Internet from foreign suppliers. This gives an unfair trade advantage to Chinese domestic firms, which are, in effect, subsidized by the Chinese government in both Chinese and foreign markets. Digital protectionism may benefit these Chinese firms now, but this policy is shortsighted; it only *seems* to be in the economic self-interest of China. As with all other forms of economic nationalism, by denying these Chinese firms the benefits of foreign competition, this favoritism in the short term sets them up for failure in the long term. As always, the lack of competition diminishes the likelihood of innovation.

Despite these increasing geopolitical tensions, some of the basic issues relating to digital trade seem conducive to negotiated WTO solutions. Issues ripe for WTO resolution include: making the WTO moratorium on customs duties on digital products permanent; defining digital trade and basic terms for digital trade; authorizing electronic signatures to validate online transactions; authorizing cross-border paperless trading; facilitating additional digital trade through electronic means; providing protections for e-consumers equivalent to those for other consumers; and requiring the establishment of domestic legal and regulatory rules and frameworks for electronic commerce.

Yet, amid "[w]idespread concerns ... about the fracturing of the global economy into walled-off and possibly warring data realms," other digital trade issues appear far from resolution.[46] Foremost among these unresolved issues is the question of the free flow of data, which is central to the debate about digital trade among the United States, the European Union, China, and other members of the WTO. Essential to innovation, the free flow of data is also vulnerable to digital protectionism, as seen in China and elsewhere. As Meltzer has explained,

Government intervention in the free flow of data can reduce the potential of the Internet for international trade. Some of these restrictions are for legitimate reasons such as protecting the privacy of data, Internet Protocol (IP) protection, ensuring cybersecurity or regulatory access to harmful contact such as child pornography. In other cases, restrictions on cross-border data flows are being imposed to provide domestic companies with a competitive advantage by redirecting Internet search or blocking access to foreign sites.[47]

Impediments to the free flow of data in the new digital economy also take the form of data localization requirements. Some governments force companies to use domestic servers to store data locally. They prohibit the transfer of data offshore. Other governments do not bar data transfer but do require that a copy of the data be stored domestically. These governments cite the need for personal data protection and for access to data for law enforcement as justifying these restrictions. Yet these restrictions can also function as the equivalent of domestic content requirements to benefit national firms while discriminating against foreign firms. Such digital protectionism, as Mark Wu has noted, becomes especially costly and discriminatory "as data takes on increasing value with big data services and the growth of artificial intelligences."[48]

In addition, some governments require companies to disclose their software source code for review as a condition of doing business in their territory. They justify this requirement as necessary to prevent the possibility that imported digital technologies will undermine personal privacy or threaten national security. This disclosure requirement can be tantamount to a mandate to turn over proprietary trade secrets. Not surprisingly, foreign companies that are compelled to disclose their source codes are much concerned that their compliance with this requirement could lead to illegal technology transfer and the theft of their intellectual property rights.[49] This is a main concern of European and American companies in China.

Frustrated by their continuing inability to negotiate rules on digital trade within the WTO, the United States, the European Union, and other countries with a stake in the digital economy – developed and developing alike – have ventured outside the WTO legal framework to agree on digital trade rules in regional and other preferential trade agreements. About half of WTO members are now parties to non-WTO agreements that contain rules on digital trade.[50] These other agreements lack the advantages of multilateral agreements, in which a balance of mutual obligations can be secured based on a weighing of all global points of view. These other agreements also can reflect the "take-it-or-leave-it" typical of the approach of larger countries in negotiating with smaller ones. Yet the digital provisions in some of these other agreements offer templates for crafting digital trade rules within the WTO.

Notable are the rules on digital trade in what is now named the Comprehensive and Progressive Agreement for Trans-Pacific Partnership (CPTPP). Although President Trump pulled the United States out of the then Tran-Pacific Partnership in one of his first acts as president, the eleven other countries in the TPP retained the digital trade rules the United States had negotiated in their slightly revised agreement, which they rechristened as the CPTPP. For example, the CPTPP requires participating countries to permit cross-border data flows, and it includes a general restriction on data localization. Exceptions to these requirements are limited to those that achieve legitimate public policy goals. In addition, the CPTPP prohibits forced transfer or disclosure of software source code.[51]

The North American Free Trade Agreement – updated in 2020 and now known in the United States as the United States-Mexico-Canada Agreement (USMCA) – goes beyond the CPTPP in establishing rules for digital trade. The Internet was new and digital trade was new when the NAFTA was concluded in 1994. A new chapter on digital trade in the USMCA is more precise than some of the CPTPP rules in broadening the scope of the protections for digital trade. Exceptions to the free flow of data across borders are limited in the USMCA to those that are "necessary to" achieve legitimate public policy goals. In contrast to the CPTPP, there is no specific exception in the USMCA to the restriction on data localization. Also, unlike the CPTPP, the USMCA clearly covers the financial services sector; there is a provision promoting open government data; and there is a prohibition of forced transfer or disclosure not only of software source code but also of the algorithms that are the basic ingredients of digital commerce and communications.[52]

In January 2019, seventy-six WTO members announced the commencement of "negotiations on trade-related aspects of electronic commerce."[53] Although President Trump's priority was the protection of traditional smokestack industries, his administration helped launch these negotiations on WTO digital trade rules. The Biden administration has continued to participate. The European

Union is also engaged in these digital negotiations. Ten more countries have since joined. These eighty-six countries – which account for 90 percent of all world trade – have said they seek the participation of "as many members as possible"; they have not said whether their goal is a multilateral agreement among all WTO members or only a plurilateral agreement among a subset of WTO members. At this writing, they have said, though, that their common goal is "successful progress" by the time of the twelfth WTO Ministerial Conference in Geneva in late November 2021.

During the pandemic, the usual difficulties of negotiating international trade agreements have been magnified. Virtual negotiations are less conducive to making trade deals than are face-to-face discussions around a negotiating table. What is more, China has not joined in these negotiations. Yet there is hope nevertheless for consensus on at least some of the issues of digital trade. And, once there is a consensus on the easier issues, there will be a basis for building on that consensus to confront the harder ones and perhaps to bring China, at least in part, into the ambit of an initial framework of new WTO digital trade rules.

A start toward an early consensus by these eighty-six WTO members on some of the digital issues can be found in the provisions on digital trade in the CPTPP, the USMCA, the RCEP, and other regional and preferential trade agreements. By one recent count, there are sixty-nine RTAs with either a chapter on electronic commerce or provisions on electronic commerce.[54] In particular, an appealing model for moving forward in the WTO is the Digital Economy Partnership Agreement (DEPA), which was concluded during the midst of the pandemic in June 2020 by Chile, New Zealand, and Singapore.[55] The three parties to DEPA are small countries that know well the economic value of freeing trade and shortening long distances. They are "well-known not just for their openness but for their creativity when it comes to trade."[56]

Appropriately, their conclusion of DEPA was conducted virtually. DEPA adds to some of what is already contained in the CPTPP, the USMCA, and other non-WTO agreements on digital trade. For instance, DEPA is the first trade agreement to deal with digital identities (such as national business numbers), which are an important component of the digital economy.[57] DEPA includes rules on financial technology and artificial intelligence that are not in the CPTPP. And DEPA establishes programs to foster the inclusion of women and Indigenous peoples in the digital economy, which should be mirrored in new WTO rules.[58] But what is most distinctive – and most conducive to emulation – about DEPA, is its unique structure.

Chile, New Zealand, and Singapore have agreed to the DEPA in its entirety. The three countries have, however, structured their agreement to contain a dozen separate subject-specific categories of different matters relating to digital trade. As other countries join, they can choose to make commitments in one, more, or all of these different "modular" categories, and accept different levels of commitments in each of them. WTO members could use this same "modular" approach in negotiating rules for digital trade. This would enable individual members of the WTO to agree to commitments in one or more "modular" categories but not in others. This would also enable WTO members to make different levels of commitments within each "module." This would create within the WTO a set of legal building blocks that could be stacked up in different combinations by different countries while establishing a basic framework for the incremental construction of a global legal architecture to promote digital trade.

It may turn out to be a relatively simple matter to achieve global consensus on some of the most basic issues – such as, say, providing consumer protections against the "spam" of unsolicited messages. Unquestionably, issues such as free data flow, source code disclosure, and data privacy will not be easily resolved. Nor are there any ready answers about how best to climb "the lofty heights of grappling with principles and ethics for regulating complex frontier technologies such as artificial intelligence and digital identity."[59] But a consensus on the right answers in rules for digital trade is more likely to be reached with a flexible negotiating approach that permits WTO members to make some commitments without having to make, at the outset, all of the commitments that may be asked of them. And such a consensus is more likely to be reached as well with a flexible approach that permits WTO members also to agree to different levels of commitments within different categories of digital trade.

With the benefit of such a flexible approach, the eighty-six members of the WTO that have agreed to negotiate rules on "trade-related electronic commerce" may be able to conclude an initial and partial WTO digital trade agreement that could ultimately become fully multilateral and fully responsive to the evolving needs of the new digital economy. In so doing, they could also do much to help ensure the continued relevance of the WTO in world trade.

RULES FOR INTELLECTUAL PROPERTY

The COVID-19 pandemic has brought to the fore once more the debate within the WTO over the balance between exclusive ownership of new knowledge and broad public access to it in the current WTO rules on the trade-related aspects of intellectual property rights. Continuing questions over the extent to which those rules protect the exclusivity of intellectual property rights in COVID-19 vaccines – even during the lethal course of a global health emergency in which global access to those vaccines is urgently needed – underscore how much uncertainty remains about where the line of this balance is in this multilateral trade agreement, and how much doubt still exists about whether that line is in the right place. In addition, according to the WTO Secretariat, "The wide adoption of digital technologies changes the composition of trade in services and goods and redefines intellectual property rights in trade."[60] This new digital dimension further complicates the complexities of intellectual property rights as a trade issue.[61]

An intellectual property right is an exception to free trade. If this exception did not exist, anyone could mix sugar, cola, and carbonated water, put it in a red and silver can, and label and sell it as "Coca Cola." (Or, no doubt for less profit, anyone could claim to be the author of this book). Although an IP right is a restriction on trade, it is also, counterintuitively, a driver of more international trade. A right holder who knows that their right will be upheld in another country is more likely to trade in and with that other country. That right holder is also more likely to have an incentive to create a new invention in the first place.

The primary justification for granting and protecting intellectual property rights is that they are incentives for innovation, which is the main source for long-term economic growth and enhancements in the quality of human life. IP rights spark innovation "by enabling innovators to capture enough of the economic gains from their own innovative activity to justify their taking considerable risks."[62] The new knowledge from innovations inspired by IP rights spills over to inspire other innovations. The protection of IP rights promotes the diffusion, domestically and internationally, of new technologies and new know-how. Historically, the principal factors of economic production have been land, labor, and capital. In the new pandemic world, perhaps an even more significant factor is the creation of knowledge, which adds enormously to "the wealth of nations." Digital and other economic growth in the twenty-first century is increasingly ideas-based and knowledge-intensive. Without intellectual property rights as incentives, there would be less new knowledge and thus less innovation.

Countering this logic is a widespread sentiment in many developing countries and among many advocacy groups that intellectual property should not be private property but should instead be public goods. This is a myopic view. In the short term, undermining private rights in intellectual property may accelerate distribution of goods and services – where the novel knowledge that went into making them already exists. But, in the long term, undermining private IP rights will also undermine innovation, thus preventing the development of new knowledge for new goods and services the world needs. This errant but potent view of the link between private property rights and innovations is perhaps best reflected in the fact that, while the United Nations Sustainable Development Goals aspire to "foster innovation," they make no mention of intellectual property rights.[63]

There have long been objections to the decision to include legal obligations to uphold patents, copyrights, trademarks, trade secrets, industrial designs, and other intellectual property rights in WTO rules when the WTO was established in 1995. International economist Jagdish Bhagwati of Columbia University, one of the leading champions of free trade and the multilateral trading system, has long insisted, "Intellectual property is not a trade issue."[64] He believes,

"[S]uch protection does not belong in the WTO. That institution must be about mutually gainful trade. Intellectual property protection, on the other hand, is for most poor countries a simple tax on their use of such knowledge, constituting therefore an unrequired transfer to the rich, producing countries."[65] Bhagwati, ever thoughtful, is far from alone in voicing this view.

Yet this view overlooks the fact that an ever-growing portion of the value of traded goods and services is in the intellectual property that is embedded and associated with them. Intellectual property is foremost among the intangible assets that is assuming more commercial significance in the pandemic world. Trade rules that did not address and protect intellectual property rights would not reflect the true realities of international trade in the twenty-first century. Furthermore, trade rules that do not keep up now with new developments in intellectual property rights in the digital age will reflect those realities even less. IP protections belong in the WTO, and new rules are needed to help secure those protections.

Generally, the debate over the balance between exclusivity and access in WTO IP rules is characterized as a commercial confrontation between the developed countries, which have a huge economic stake in having their IP rights protected in world trade, and the developing countries, which, despite their recent climb up the economic ladder, still, for the most part, do not. For the developed countries, there are millions of jobs and billions of dollars at risk if IP rights are not upheld worldwide. For many developing countries, in the near term, jobs and dollars are at risk if they enforce IP rights by ridding their economies of the vast illegal proceeds of counterfeiting and piracy. Yet counterfeiting and piracy hurt developing countries as well as developed countries, in part by undermining the growth of their own creative sectors. And compliance with WTO IP rules has helped developing countries enjoy greater inflows of foreign direct investment, technology transfer, and IP-sensitive imports. The common view of this ongoing policy confrontation often overlooks the growing stake that developing countries have in protecting IP rights both now and in the longer term.

Unquestionably, the United States has a huge economic stake in the effective international enforcement of intellectual property rights. Most business investments in the United States since the 1990s have been in intangible assets, which have been valued at $14.5 trillion.[66] In the process, the United States has become a much more knowledge-based economy. IP-intensive industries support at least 45 million American jobs – about 30 percent of all the jobs in the country. They contribute more than $6 trillion to US output – nearly 40 percent of US GDP. These industries also account for 52 percent of US merchandise exports. American industries reliant on the respect of trademarks, copyrights, and patents contributed the most to these totals in jobs and output.[67] But upholding intellectual property rights is not of interest only to the United States and other advanced economies, which have, to date, led the way in knowledge-based enterprise. China now ranks second to the United States.[68] Other developing countries are likewise catching up. The multinational companies most heavily engaged in R&D spending are spreading their offices throughout the world; the global share of R&D spending in developing countries is increasing; and the global share of IP filings from China and other developing countries is rising as well.[69] The evidence shows that, when developing countries protect IP rights, they gain in economic growth.[70] As shown in the Global Innovation Index of the World Economic Forum, countries that uphold IP rights "have more creative outputs ... even at varying levels of development."[71] This is especially so when firms and individuals in developing countries are connected to global value chains.[72] The capacity for creative innovation is by no means limited only to people in the developed world.

From the outset, echoing Bhagwati, many developing countries have been ambivalent about including intellectual property protections in WTO trade rules. On the one hand, the decision makers in developing countries have often understood that their own citizens will not have a sufficient incentive to innovate unless they can profit financially from their creations through the assurance of protection of their IP rights. On the other hand, those same decision makers have often been from countries where counterfeiting of goods and piracy of IP rights are major segments of the domestic economy, sometimes employing millions of people. China is perhaps the best example of this ambivalence; the violation of foreign intellectual property rights is a thriving jobs program in China.

The broad extent of counterfeiting and piracy, and the harmful impact such actions have on the global economy, are not always understood, or appreciated. This is in part because so many countries have an economic stake in the lax upholding of IP rights. The United States has listed thirty-three countries that present significant concerns because they do not adequately or effectively protect and enforce IP rights. Highlighted by the United States are China, India, and Indonesia. The United State Trade Representative estimates that 2.5 percent of imports worldwide – valued at nearly half a trillion dollars – are counterfeit or pirated products.[73]

Among the intellectual property rights protected in WTO rules are patent rights. In general, WTO rules protect these rights by requiring that patents be available for inventions in all areas of technology, and by requiring the protection against unfair commercial use and disclosure of undisclosed test data submitted for obtaining local marketing approval.[74] These legal protections apply to all kinds of inventions. In the new pandemic world, as the WTO, WHO, and WIPO have jointly observed, these WTO intellectual property rules, in place since 1995, have "considerable implications for the application of IP to medical technologies," and, thus, the upholding of these IP rules is even more important now than it was before the advent of COVID-19.[75] Yet, as Stephen Ezell and Nigel Cory of the Information Technology & Innovation Foundation in the United States have emphasized, "A fundamental fault line in the debate over intellectual property pertains to the need to achieve a reasoned balance between access and exclusive rights."[76] This fault line is drawn adroitly in the

WTO rules on the trade-related aspects of intellectual property rights. These trade rules affirm intellectual property rights and establish a minimum level of protection for IP rights in the global conduct of trade. They recognize that "intellectual property rights are private rights," and that WTO rules and disciplines are necessary for "the provision of effective and appropriate means for the enforcement of trade-related intellectual property rights."[77]

Where social and economic welfare is at stake, though, WTO members have sought to strike a balance in these rules between upholding intellectual property rights and fulfilling immediate domestic needs. The rules provide that the protection and enforcement of intellectual property rights should be accomplished "in a manner conducive to social and economic welfare, and to a balance of rights and obligations."[78] In addition, they specify that, "Members may ... adopt measures necessary to protect public health and nutrition, and to promote the public interest in sectors of vital importance to their socioeconomic and technological development, provided that such measures are consistent with the provisions of this Agreement."[79] Also, the rules state that, provided they are consistent with the rules, "Appropriate measures ... may be needed to prevent the abuse of intellectual property rights by right holders or the resort to practices which unreasonably restrain trade or adversely affect the international transfer of technology."[80]

Striking this fine balance must remain the aim in modernizing the WTO by adding new WTO rules on the trade-related aspects of intellectual property rights. The protection of intellectual property rights in WTO rules must be expanded to incorporate new developments since the current rules were written in the early 1990s, before the era of the Internet. For example, as it is, WTO rules incorporate by reference several long-standing international intellectual property conventions, including on patents and copyrights.[81] In legal theory, these preexisting IP conventions have always been binding international law. Previously, though, there was no effective international forum for enforcing these IP conventions. Incorporating them into the WTO rules has had the legal effect of making them fully enforceable for the first time through the trade sanctions of the binding WTO dispute settlement system.

In addition to these conventions, two more treaties, concluded in 1996 by the World Intellectual Property Organization, should be incorporated by reference in WTO rules. Commonly known together as the "Internet Treaties," one of these agreements provides added protections for copyrights in response to advances in information technology, including the protection of IP rights in computer programs and databases.[82] The other agreement updates protections of the rights of performers and producers of phonograms for the digital age.[83] Likewise incorporated by reference into WTO rules should be the Marrakesh Treaty to Facilitate Access to Published Works for Persons Who Are Blind, Visually Impaired or Otherwise Print Disabled, which was adopted in 2013.[84] Incorporating these three treaties into the WTO rules would make them, too, fully enforceable.

Giving more reality to the balance in the TRIPS Agreement by modernizing it, must also include making multilateral many of the advances made in recent years in protecting IP rights in bilateral and regional trade arrangements. Because of the ongoing standoff between the developed and developing countries on extending and modernizing intellectual property protections inside the legal framework of the WTO, those who have sought modernization have gone outside the WTO to make new rules. One example is the added protection for trade secrets in the new NAFTA – the USMCA.[85] Another is the Asian RCEP, which includes, for the first time in any trade agreement, provisions to protect genetic resources, traditional knowledge, and folklore – shared inheritances that have been passed down for generations as the heritage of Indigenous communities, often in developing countries where there are inadequate domestic legal rights.[86]

In addition, much more must be done to encourage the spread of new technologies so that developing countries can do more to improve their social and economic welfare through a just, green transition. The WTO treaty supports technology transfer. WTO rules not only state as an objective that "the protection and enforcement of intellectual property rights should contribute to the promotion of technological innovation." They also say that these IP protections should contribute to "the transfer and dissemination of technology, to the mutual advantage of producers and users of technological knowledge and in a manner conducive to social and economic welfare, and to a balance of rights and obligations."[87]

WTO rules also state that developed countries "*shall* provide incentives to enterprises and institutions in their territories for the purpose of promoting and encouraging technology transfer to least-developed country Members in order to enable them to create a sound and viable technological base."[88] For the past quarter of a century and more, this mandatory obligation to transfer technology to forty-seven countries with per capita incomes of less than $1,000 has largely been honored in the breach. Many developed countries have not even bothered to submit required annual reports of their attempts at compliance with this mandatory obligation. Developed countries should be challenged in WTO dispute settlement if they continue to fail to fulfill this mandatory obligation. Furthermore, new rules must give more concrete reality to this obligation. Moreover, this existing obligation of technology transfer to the least developed countries should be extended to benefit all other developing countries on the condition that they enforce the rights of foreign intellectual property right holders.

Striking the proper balance between IP rights and IP access is always especially emotionally charged on the issue of public health;[89] all the more so during the COVID-19 pandemic. Confronted by vaccine nationalism, and concerned that COVAX may not succeed, many developing countries have felt the need to turn to the WTO to try to realign the current balance. In October 2020, India and South Africa urged all of the members of the WTO to waive protections in the WTO intellectual property rules for patents, copyrights, industrial designs, and undisclosed information (trade secrets) in relation to the "prevention, containment or treatment of COVID-19 ... until widespread vaccination is in place globally, and the majority of the world's population has developed immunity."[90] These two WTO members sought to give all WTO members the complete freedom to refuse to grant or enforce patents and other intellectual property rights relating to COVID-19 vaccines, drugs, diagnostics, and other technologies for the duration of the pandemic.

In requesting a broad waiver of IP rights to COVID-19 vaccines, India and South Africa maintained that "many countries especially developing countries may face institutional and legal difficulties when using flexibilities available" under existing WTO rules.[91] They also noted that a "particular concern for countries with insufficient or no manufacturing capacity" is that the 2017 amendment to the rules that permits countries that produce generic medicines under compulsory license to export all of those medicines to least developed countries that lack manufacturing capabilities themselves will lead to a "lengthy and cumbersome process."[92] They did not offer any further explanation or any evidence to support these assertions.

Later that same month, the European Union, the United Kingdom, the United States, Japan, Switzerland, and other developed countries opposed the waiver request in WTO deliberations.[93] One WTO delegate, from the United Kingdom, described it as "an extreme measure to address an unproven problem."[94] A spokesperson for the European Union explained, "There is no evidence that intellectual property rights are a genuine barrier for accessibility of COVID-19-related medicines and technologies."[95] Pharmaceutical companies were also quick to express their opposition to the proposed waiver of IP rights for the pandemic's duration. They underscored their support for COVAX but warned that allowing their vaccines to be copied in the developing countries through recourse to compulsory licensing "would undermine innovation and raise the risk of unsafe viruses."[96]

The text of the existing WTO IP rules suggests that this request for a COVID-19 vaccine waiver is an unnecessary proposal. For, as they are, the rules providing that WTO members may adopt measures "necessary to public health" and protect intellectual property rights "in a manner conducive to social and economic welfare" appear significantly capacious to include any reasonable health measures a WTO member may take during a time of health emergency such as a pandemic.[97] WTO jurists would be much inclined to uphold such actions where, in the facts of a crisis situation, they seemed justified. Yet doubt remains among many developing countries about the precise reach of these existing WTO rules. They are apprehensive, too, of the legal – and perhaps other negative economic and geopolitical – consequences if they assert their treaty rights without previous systemic clarification.

As Jennifer Hillman has pointed out, ordinarily the "inherent tension between the protection of intellectual property and the need to make and distribute affordable medicines" is "resolved through licensing, which allows a patent holder to permit others to make or trade the protected product – usually at a price and with some supervision from the patent holder to ensure control."[98] But, in public health emergencies, it may be impossible to obtain a license. In such cases, existing WTO rules permit governments to issue "compulsory licenses" to local manufacturers, which authorize them to make patented products or use patented processes even though they do not have the authorization of the patent holders.[99] With a compulsory license, the patent owner still retains the rights over the patent, including the right to be paid compensation for copies of the product made under the license.

Compulsory licensing was a controversial issue for the WTO during the height of the HIV/AIDS crisis at the turn of the century. Countries from sub-Saharan Africa especially could not afford the high-priced HIV/AIDS drugs patented by pharmaceutical companies in developed countries. Having spent vast sums on developing the drugs, the patent holders resisted lowering prices. The global credibility of the pharmaceutical companies, the countries that resisted compulsory licensing, and the WTO itself were all damaged by an extended controversy over whether patent rights should take precedence over providing affordable medicines for people afflicted by a dread and lethal disease.

After years of debate, in the Doha Ministerial Declaration of November 2001, WTO members declared that the existing WTO IP rules do not prevent national measures taken to protect public health by the promotion of access to new medicines and the creation of new medicines.[100] They confirmed that every WTO member "has the right to grant compulsory licenses and the freedom to determine the grounds upon which such licenses are granted."[101] In August 2003, WTO members followed up on their 2001 declaration by adopting a waiver that allows poorer countries that do not have the capacity to make pharmaceutical products – and thus cannot benefit from compulsory licensing – to import cheaper generic drugs from countries where those drugs are patent protected.[102] This waiver was transformed into an amendment to the WTO IP rules in 2017.[103]

Compulsory licensing of medicines is a derogation from the usual workings of market-based capitalism. It is not, however, a derogation from the legal balance struck by the members of the WTO between protecting intellectual property rights and ensuring access to essential medicines. The legal balance in the WTO treaty includes the option of compulsory licensing during health emergencies as well as the enactment of other crisis health measures. IP rights are not absolute. This noted, it is unclear why the countries that have advocated this proposed IP waiver believe a waiver of intellectual property rights for COVID-19 vaccines would accomplish much toward vaccinating the whole of the waiting world.

As one European Commission official said amid the debate over the proposed waiver, "We have not been given a single example where [production] capacity has been restricted because of the protection of patents or other IP rights."[104]

At the heart of the trade debate over COVID-19 vaccines is a fervent belief by many people throughout the world that all medicines should be treated as global public goods. There is little room in such a belief for consideration of any private rights to intellectual property. As one group of United Nations human rights experts has expressed this view, "There is no room for … profitability in decision-making about access to vaccines, essential tests and treatments, and all other medical goods, services and supplies that are at the heart of the right to the highest standard of health for all."[105] How can we speak of profit when human lives are at stake?

Yet this seemingly noble view is shortsighted. Compulsory licensing that subordinates patents and other intellectual property rights to pressing public needs temporarily during a pandemic or some other health emergency is one thing. Eliminating altogether any consideration of "profitability" in policy-making relating to "access to vaccines, essential tests and treatments, and all other medical goods, services and supplies" is quite another. To be sure, there is a superficial moral appeal in such a view. But does this moral appeal hold up in the end if such a supposed "human rights" approach to international trade in medicines and in other medical goods does not result in meeting those urgent public needs?

Given the belief that medicines should be "public goods," there is, in some quarters, literally no support for the application of WTO rules to protect private intellectual property rights in medicines. Any protection of the intellectual property rights in such goods is seen as a violation of human rights and the overall public interest. This widespread conviction, though, does not reflect the practical reality of a disease-ridden world in which many medicines simply would not exist if it were not for the existence of intellectual property rights and the protections they are afforded. The profit motive is by no means the only motive for human invention. But eliminate the profit motive, and much invention will be eliminated as well.

In early May 2021, the profit motive took a body blow when President Biden reversed the policy of the Trump administration and announced that his administration would support a waiver of IP rights for COVID-19 vaccines in the WTO.[106] The developing countries and civil society applauded this surprising move. The pharmaceutical industry denounced it. Surprising some, other developed countries did not all automatically fall into line behind the United States as some of them might have done in years past. Ambassador Tai predicted that negotiations on a waiver would take some time. It was suggested that the goal should be to achieve a consensus on a waiver by the time of the planned WTO Ministerial Conference in late November 2021. There was the widespread expectation that – if such a consensus were reached – the resulting waiver would be more limited in scope than the waiver proposed by India and South Africa, and it would also be limited in duration.[107]

Unknown at this writing are the consequences if a WTO vaccine waiver is ultimately approved. In the United States, following the Biden announcement, vaccine producers seemed as much concerned about the potential loss of their trade secrets as their patents – if not more. At the center of the heated debate in the United States was whether hard-won US trade secrets in the cutting-edge technologies of biological medicines – which are generally protected under the WTO IP rules – would simply be handed over to China, Russia, Iran, and other economic and geopolitical competitors.[108] Global health experts such as Rachel Silverman of the Center for Global Development predicted that the impact of the prospective waiver would be "pretty marginal" in boosting worldwide inoculations, and that it could take years to build factories and begin production in most developing countries.[109] Compulsory licensing has often taken time to show any results; there is every reason to think that a blanket waiver of IP rights would take at least as much time to do so.[110]

In the early aftermath of the Biden decision, unanswered was whether a WTO vaccine waiver, if approved, would, in its ultimate impact on international trade, be mostly a political gesture, a signal of their virtue by a socially and globally minded subset of politicians and activists in the United States and in other developed countries, a welter of well-intended advocates blithely heedless of the possible "real world" consequences of the action they are advocating; or, instead, a crack in the foundation of WTO and other international intellectual property protections worldwide, a crack that might widen to include other medicines and other technological innovations of all kinds, and might diminish the incentives that are so essential to those innovations.

The current existential crisis of the WTO would be further complicated by a repeat of the long and self-defeating delay in resolving the highly contentious dispute between developed and developing countries over the compulsory licensing and generic distribution of HIV/AIDS drugs nearly two decades ago. Such a delay would not be in the interest of the developed countries, the developing countries, the pharmaceutical companies, or the WTO. Most certainly, it would not be in the interest of the victims of COVID-19 or the potential victims, who may confront currently unforeseen variants of COVID-19 that will require the invention of additional new vaccines. A sideshow in the WTO could siphon global energies for what ought to be the main event in this instance – multilateral actions to end the pandemic outside the WTO.

What is more, it is not at all clear that waiving IP rights in COVID-19 vaccines would hasten global vaccination. Although the nearly 100 WTO members and their numerous allies in civil society that have sought a waiver of intellectual property rights over COVID-19 vaccines are clearly well intentioned, their waiver proposal aims at the wrong target. The sad failure to distribute vaccines quickly worldwide is not a problem caused by the existence of intellectual property rights. What the world is experiencing in the COVID-19 pandemic is not an abuse of their rights by vaccine patent holders; it is a shortage of vaccine supply and a searing slowness in vaccine inoculation.

What is needed to speed the spread of COVID-19 vaccines worldwide is not a waiver of IP rights; it is a rapid scaling up of vaccine production and a swift acceleration of vaccine distribution.

Even if they got a waiver, developing countries would find it exceedingly difficult to make COVID-19 vaccines. Few of them have anything approaching the existing capacity to engage in the needed scale of production. Nor do they have ready access to all the raw materials and the other inputs that go into making those vaccines. According to the maker of one new COVID-19 vaccine, making it requires 280 components from eighty-six suppliers in nineteen countries (added evidence, if we need more, of the inescapable interconnectedness of the world).[111] Furthermore, developing countries do not yet have the necessary technical know-how to make the new kinds of biological messenger RNA vaccines and make them safely. Looking beyond the appealing political rhetoric of those advocating a WTO vaccine waiver to the practical reality of vaccine production, the fact is, "manufacturing the Covid-19 vaccines is a complex scientific process that involves securing hard-to-find raw materials and scaling them in a way that has never been done before ... Factories must be built or retrofitted with special, expensive equipment, and employees must have the manufacturing know-how."[112]

Further complicating this reality, the pioneering bioengineered COVID-19 vaccines, as Rachel Silverman has written, "are harder to make than ordinary drugs." As she explains, most drugs are "simple chemical compounds" that can be made "with relative ease." They can be copied; they can be "reverse engineered." In contrast, COVID-19 vaccines "are complex biological products. Observing their contents is insufficient to allow for imitation. Instead, to produce the vaccine, manufacturers need access to the developer's 'soft' IP – the proprietary recipe, cell lines, manufacturing processes and so forth."[113] Drug manufacturers also need the skills and the training to maintain strict controls over production. All this would be unavailable to developing countries even if they secured the waiver they are seeking.

Instead of battling over a waiver of IP rights, the developed and developing countries alike should be cooperating to identify and provide the necessary combination of means and incentives to increase vaccine production and distribution. Freeing trade in the medical goods that provide necessary parts for medical production is part of this; so is encouraging more voluntary licensing agreements. In addition, governments and international institutions should, as Silverman has suggested, "invest to build up the capabilities of potential vaccine manufacturing plants."[114] Much more capacity for production is needed in many more places across the world, for now and for the future; for, alas, this will not be the last pandemic. A global scale-up of the capacity for vaccine production would be a global insurance policy against new variants of COVID-19 and against new zoonotic and other diseases that have yet to darken the human door. It would be cheaper for developed countries to fund such a global build-up for future health crises than it would be for them to confront the shutdowns and the death tolls of a new and possibly even more lethal pandemic when it arrives on their shores.

Furthermore, the developed countries should give special emphasis to transfer of the technical knowledge that is crucial to the success of the COVID-19 vaccines. This transfer of knowledge should start with those vaccines. At a bare minimum, there should be more voluntary agreements by vaccine producers to help make their doses available in the desperate developing world. But more than that, know-how must be shared along with the doses. Furthermore, this sharing of know-how must extend beyond the vaccines. As David M. Fox has observed, in the modern world, technology includes not only machinery and equipment; it includes knowledge and skills, human resource development, and domestic capacity building. Much of all of this happens every day in the normal course of the buy-and-sell of international commerce, but it does not happen automatically, and the developed countries must put incentives in place to help make it happen more often and more widely. At the same time, it is vital to build the capacity in developing countries – especially in the least developed countries – to absorb and benefit from new imported technologies. This requires investments in human capital, human connectivity, better business conditions, and, not least, the rule of law.[115]

The solution to the fair distribution of COVID-19 vaccines is not another prolonged multilateral impasse in the WTO. The solution is multilateral action. In addition to providing substantial financing to add to the global capacity for vaccine production, the focus should be on vaccine distribution through COVAX and through a slew of additional ad hoc distribution deals. It is the slow advance and the uncertain success of COVAX and other multilateral initiatives that have led developing countries to try to waive intellectual property rights in the WTO. Rather than continuing to press for a WTO waiver, the developing countries should redouble their combined efforts to reach solutions through these non-WTO initiatives. And the European Union, the United Kingdom, the United States, Japan, Canada, and other developed countries should do much more to work with them toward that end.

In no event should intellectual property rights become legal obstacles to ensuring access to affordable medicines for everyone in the world during a pandemic that has already killed millions of people worldwide and threatens to kill millions more. But also, in no event should WTO members act in ways that would eliminate the incentives that are necessary to inspire the innovations that make new medicines possible. The right balance in the WTO rules on intellectual property is a balance that provides developing countries with sufficient flexibility to protect intellectual property rights while also promoting access to life-saving medicines. For COVID-19 medicines, there is no proof as yet that this right balance does not currently exist. Maintaining this balance must remain the aim of the WTO, and it must be the aim of every other multilateral endeavor in the fight to end the COVID-19 pandemic.

RULES FOR COMPETITION

In addition to new rules to further digital trade and new rules to strike the best balance between innovation and access when protecting intellectual property rights, one of the keys to ensuring a "rapid and consistent" recovery in the new pandemic world is, according to the OECD, "[r]estoring effective competition."[116] Competition fuels growth. Sustainable growth is essential to recovery. Thus, as part of seeking a green recovery, in crafting responses to the economic downturn caused by COVID-19, policies must be avoided that will limit competition and thereby limit success in addressing "the market failures that arise from this crisis" and "will slow the economic recovery."[117] Because trade and competition are more and more linked, and likely to become even more tightly linked in the new world, rules for competition are needed in the WTO. Such rules can help make certain that global policy responses to the pandemic downturn increase competition, and do not impede it.

Rules for international competition also have obvious implications for trade in medical goods, services, and technologies. Such rules are "relevant to all stages in the process of supplying medical technologies to patients, from their development to their sale and delivery."[118] They can be important in "informing regulatory measures and other relevant policy choices relating to innovation in, and access to, medical technologies."[119] They can encourage cooperation among the regulatory authorities of different countries.[120] They can help counter anticompetitive behavior in the marketplace.[121] They can, for example, help combat the licensing, merger, cartel, bid-rigging, and other anticompetitive practices that often drive up drug prices in much of the world.[122]

Trade law and competition law have evolved separately, but this is not what was intended by those who created the Bretton Woods institutions in the immediate aftermath of the Second World War. As originally envisaged, the 1947 Havana Charter for an International Trade Organization included an entire chapter of rules for competition that would have disciplined restrictive business practices.[123] These proposed ITO rules would have applied to "business practices affecting international trade which restrain competition, limit access to markets or foster monopolistic control whenever such practices have harmful effects on the expansion of production or trade."[124] The ITO failed to obtain the support of the Congress of the United States in part because of the reluctance of the Congress at the time to have sovereign US decisions on competition policy – what Americans call "antitrust" policy – second-guessed by an international institution.[125]

In the nearly three-quarters of a century since, numerous efforts have been made in a number of international institutions, including first in the GATT and now in the WTO, to agree on appropriate rules for competition in a world increasingly characterized by international economic integration. Some useful, nonbinding principles and guidelines have been advanced along the way by the OECD, UNCTAD, the United Nations, and others. Yet, despite these cooperative efforts, little has been accomplished toward international rulemaking. Competition rules have largely remained national while competition itself has become increasingly international.

In 1996, shortly after the establishment of the WTO, a renewed push was made to negotiate competition rules in the WTO, led by the European Union, which has benefited enormously from its own internal international competition rules that have done much to establish a European single market. But the United States remained suspicious of international second-guessing of outcomes in the American marketplace. In addition, most developing countries had not yet enacted their own competition laws, and many of them feared that the adoption of international competition rules would constrain their domestic decisions and herald heightened leverage for large multinational corporations over their smaller domestic firms. With this array of opposition, the proposal to launch WTO negotiations to write competition rules was quashed in Cancun in 2003.[126]

As it is, there are some WTO rules that do relate to certain aspects of competition and contain elements of competition policy. Scattered rules on trade in goods, trade in services, intellectual property rights, state trading enterprises, and government procurement deal with specific forms of restrictive business practices and with other anticompetitive business abuses.[127] Noteworthy, too, as a form of competition policy, is a WTO Reference Paper on Basic Telecommunications Services, a blueprint that sets out "best practices" in regulation for a sector that is central to all international commerce, including especially digital trade.[128] Yet this scant scattering of existing rules falls far short of constituting the comprehensive set of rules on competition sought by the EU and some other WTO members.

Currently, the closest the WTO rulebook comes to a set of rules on competition is its rules on "trade remedies" – its rules permitting retaliatory tariffs against foreign trade practices that distort what would otherwise be fair competition. Under these WTO trade remedy rules, "antidumping" tariffs can be applied when foreign products are "dumped" – when they are sold in the importing country for less than their normal value in their home market.[129] "Countervailing" duties can be applied to imported products to offset the benefits of governmental subsidies that give them an advantage in the marketplace.[130] "Safeguard" duties can be applied – without an allegation of an unfair trade practice – when imports are increasing in quantities and in conditions that cause serious injury to a domestic industry that produces like or competitive products.[131]

The use of such trade defenses has skyrocketed since the creation of the WTO, increasing tariffs worldwide. In part, this is due to an increase in trade-distorting practices, particularly through the wider and more impactful use by developed and developing countries alike of governmental subsidies for domestic production, which are always enticing politically, and are especially favored by all the varied versions of economic nationalists. In part, too, this tide of trade remedies is due to an increased reliance on antidumping measures, which can erode the economic benefits of tariff cuts in trade agreements, and which thus afford added insulation for domestic producers from import competition with foreign producers in domestic markets.

The United States is by far the biggest user of antidumping trade remedies. The reliance of the United States on antidumping measures long preceded the presidency of Donald Trump, but it increased substantially under his administration.[132] At year-end 2019, 388 US antidumping measures were in effect covering imports of 455 products.[133] (India was second with 251 measures in place covering 483 products; Turkey was third; China was fourth; and the European Union was fifth.)[134] Most of these measures restrict trade in minerals, metals, chemicals, wood, paper, machinery, textiles, and clothing, in which there is intense international competition.[135] These antidumping measures are the antithesis of trade liberalization, but, when applied consistently with WTO rules, they are entirely legal actions under the WTO agreement.

Trade rules tell us dumping is to be "condemned" where "it causes or threatens material injury" to a domestic industry or where it "retards the establishment of a domestic industry."[136] The logic that underlies antidumping duties is that a foreign producer should not be allowed to establish a dominant position in the domestic market by undercutting prices, and that by lowering prices below the cost of production now, that foreign producer can crowd out competition and secure leverage in the domestic market that will enable it to raise prices later. In contrast, many economists point to what they perceive as the "absence of any legitimate economic rationale for antidumping" actions.[137] Their reasoning goes: If foreign producers want to sell their products to us at low prices, then why stop them? They maintain that imposing antidumping duties to raise the prices of "dumped" imported goods results in losses to domestic consumers that almost always exceed the gains to protected domestic producers.

Michael Trebilcock, a professor of law and economics at the University of Toronto and a leading scholar on international trade, has summarized the economic argument against the application of antidumping duties. He points out that "international price discrimination yields a low-priced market in the importing country and a high-priced market in the exporting country, which would seem of little or no concern to importing countries that benefit from the lower-priced imports."[138] Furthermore, he notes, "predatory pricing" is "a relatively rare occurrence ... given the certainty of short-run losses and the uncertainty of future monopoly profits in the face of the prospect of future competitive entry."[139] And predatory pricing is rarer still internationally, where the past experience of dumping cases suggests that it is "totally implausible to assume that the foreign exporters could realistically aspire to monopolizing the importing country's market," in particular where the importing market is, as with the United States, a decidedly large market.[140]

Whatever its economic merits, worldwide, antidumping "[i]n many respects ... has become the protectionist remedy of choice."[141] In the United

States, as trade scholar Dan Ikenson has said, the antidumping law "has become a commercial weapon used by U.S. companies against other U.S. companies. Antidumping has become a convenient channel through which domestic firms can saddle their competition (both foreign and domestic) with higher costs and their customers with fewer alternative sources while giving themselves room to raise their own prices, reap higher profits, and reinforce their market power."[142] This weaponizing of antidumping law, as Ikenson has explained, has been accomplished in part by bureaucratic "methodological sleights of hand" that create dumping where it does not exist, and that magnify the margin of dumping where it does exist, thus adding to the lists of anti-dumping measures and the totals of antidumping duties.[143] In a classic case of what economists call "regulatory capture" – where regulatory agencies come to be dominated by the interests or industries they are charged with regulating – the US agencies that administer the antidumping laws often appear to do the bidding of domestic firms and sectors seeking trade protection. Indeed, as Ikenson has demonstrated, there is an abundance of evidence of a "discretionary bias in favor of protectionism" in these agencies.[144]

WTO rules on antidumping procedures – which the United States played a leading role in writing and to which it has agreed – require fair cost comparisons in dumping calculations and, thus, prohibit some of these "methodological sleights of hand." In a long series of rulings, WTO panels and the WTO Appellate Body have repeatedly ruled that the United States has acted inconsistently with some of these procedural obligations in the antidumping rules in the WTO treaty. These correct legal rulings against this favored form of US protectionism are the source of much of the considerable political animus of the protectionist interests in the United States – and of those who serve those interests in the US government – against the WTO and, especially, against WTO jurists.

These bureaucratic practices are beginning to backfire on the United States. Other countries are starting to emulate US evasions of WTO antidumping rules, and, to the extent that the United States gets the wide latitude it seeks from the WTO in applying antidumping measures, other countries will get that same latitude. China is now using "methodological sleights of hand" much like those employed by the United States in antidumping cases.[145] By a wide margin, China remains the biggest target of antidumping measures, many by the United States. At year-end 2019, China, as an exporter, faced 641 antidumping measures covering 1,006 products.[146] But the United States is moving quickly up the target list. It ranked sixth on the list at year-end 2019, when American exports faced seventy-two antidumping measures covering ninety-nine products.[147]

Any consideration of new rules on competition by the WTO should include a submission of the antidumping rules to competition principles so that the benefits of trade concessions are not offset, and the flow of trade is not impeded, by anticompetitive behavior. As Bernard Hoekman and Petros Mavroidis argued as long ago as 2002, "Despite often being regarded as *the* example of a trade policy that is consistent with the objectives of competition law, most economists agree that the purported rationale of antidumping – to combat predatory pricing by foreign firms – is the exception, not the rule ... Instead, antidumping is straightforward protectionism, with the added twist that it can be used strategically by firms to collude."[148] They noted then that, "Introduction of competition criteria into the rules of the game for" the "contingent protection" of antidumping duties "has been proposed by many as a way to reduce its perverse impact on domestic competition."[149] What was true of the protectionism in many antidumping measures in 2002 is truer still today.

Politically, this is a lot to ask; in the United States, strict enforcement of the antidumping laws has universal bipartisan political support, and the bureaucratic manipulation of those laws to serve protectionist interests has equally widespread tacit support. But economically, this is part of all that is needed in resisting economic nationalism and thus assuring that the United States remains a globally competitive economy. The adamant refusal of American politicians in both major parties to negotiate on the application of antidumping measures in the WTO has the effect of perpetuating the domestic damage done by antidumping measures and preventing the United States from securing concessions from other countries in digital trade, intellectual property, services, and other competitive sectors of the American economy that have no need for the rank "crony capitalism" of antidumping protectionism.

New competition rules in the WTO must also provide for competitive neutrality between privately owned and state-owned businesses.[150] The host of state-owned enterprises that are taking ever-larger shares of world trade should not enjoy competitive advantages over their rivals in the private sector, in their home markets or in other markets, simply because they are owned by states. Yet in many cases they do, which is usually due to the distortions in the allocation of resources that often arise out of public ownership and afford advantages in the marketplace. These trade distortions can be caused by privileges and immunities and grants of monopolies given by governments to SOEs. They can also result from government subsidies for SOEs, which are already subject in many respects to disciplines in WTO subsidies rules but require additional rules discipline.[151]

In the United States and in some other developed countries, there is increasing concern about the competitive edge that Chinese governmental ownership provides to Chinese SOEs, which have risen in reach with the rise of China as a world trader. At the turn of the century, Chinese SOEs were barely a factor in world trade. Today, seventy-five of China's more than 150,000 SOEs are listed in the Fortune Global 500, including several ranked near the top, and many others are trading throughout the world.[152] China is far from the only country with state-owned enterprises, but the rise of the desire for international rules to assure "competitive neutrality" between private firms and SOEs has paralleled the rise of China.

The role of Chinese SOEs in the global marketplace would surely be a principal focus of any WTO negotiations on new competition rules. Undoubtedly, there would be pushback from China as well as from other countries where the state occupies much of the national economy. Yet, it is clearly in the long-term interest of all WTO members – including China – that any new WTO competition rules be centered on assuring competitive neutrality between privately owned and publicly owned enterprises. Ultimately, state control over individual companies, like other forms of state-directed economic control, does not lead to international competitiveness, and, therefore, it does not lead to sustainable economic growth.

Some doubt the capacity of the WTO as an international institution to confront the unique challenge of an economy such as that of twenty-first-century China. Mark Wu maintains that "the WTO is struggling to adjust to a rising China" because of "China's distinctive economic structure."[153] Wu may overstate the uniqueness of China's form of state-controlled capitalism coupled with an increasingly coercive authoritarianism; the structural economic differences between China and other state-centered economies are differences more of degree than kind. But the Chinese economic structure, coupled with China's vast size, certainly does present the WTO with a unique challenge. In the face of this challenge, though, the problem is not so much that WTO rules are insufficient to deal with China, as it is that WTO rules have been used insufficiently to deal with China. No formal legal claims have yet been brought against China in WTO dispute settlement on technology transfer and other Chinese obligations relating to some of the trade issues that most concern the United States and China's other trading partners. President Trump chose to take unilateral action rather than bring multilateral cases against China in the WTO that could have been brought and won by the United States and others under existing WTO rules. Given China's generally solid record so far of complying with adverse rulings in WTO dispute settlement, such cases could have produced positive results – and they still could if the Biden administration brought them against China in concert with China's other trading partners.[154]

The answer for the United States and for others aggrieved by China's unfair trade practices is not to abandon the WTO; the answer is to use it. Where existing WTO rules apply to China's errant trade practices, enforce those rules in WTO dispute settlement. Where WTO rules do not yet discipline the unfairness of China's trade practices, negotiate new rules. Multilateral pressure, instead of unilateral pressure, will be much more likely to convince China to agree to make concessions on at least some of the most egregious discriminations against foreign goods and foreign suppliers in its current forms of domestic economic governance. Rules that tighten the disciplines on subsidies, for example, should be part of new WTO rules on competition.

As with digital trade rules, WTO members that seek international competition rules have, in their frustration with the WTO as a negotiating forum, shifted their negotiating emphasis to regional trade agreements. Nearly three-quarters of regional trade agreements contain provisions on various aspects of competition policy.[155] The CPTPP, among eleven countries along the Pacific Rim, has an entire chapter that disciplines the activities of SOEs and designated state monopolies.[156] The successor to NAFTA – the USMCA among the United States, Mexico, and Canada – has chapters on competition policy and state-owned enterprises.[157] These and other provisions in RTAs can on many issues be employed as starting points for WTO competition negotiations.

Most of these RTAs recognize core principles of competition. One of these core principles is transparency – publication and full disclosure of all information on national competition laws and on how they are implemented and enforced. Another is nondiscrimination – treating foreign companies the same as domestic companies. Still another is procedural fairness – what Americans call due process. Yet another is cooperation – technical and other forms of cross-border collaboration to help promote competition. These are all principles on which WTO members are likely to reach consensus. Indeed, even many of the developing countries that have voiced reservations about having WTO competition rules, have nevertheless agreed to these core principles in dozens of RTAs.

At the start, these core principles can form the basis for a WTO framework agreement on competition. This legal framework can begin as a plurilateral agreement among a subset of WTO members desirous of having binding international rules for competition in the WTO. Like some previous WTO agreements, it can then grow over time to add more members and eventually become fully multilateral. As international economic integration continues, this WTO competition agreement can also grow over time to address other global competition concerns in addition to those reflected in the core principles of the framework.

In 2004, Mitsuo Matsushita of Japan, a founding member of the WTO Appellate Body and a leading authority on trade and competition, recommended the negotiation of

> a plurilateral agreement on competition policy within the framework of the WTO with a two-stage implementation. In the first stage, there would be binding rules, which would prohibit such private anti-competitive conduct that directly injures the objectives of the WTO, such as international cartels, import cartels, and export cartels. In the second stage, the WTO should consider the introduction of an international agreement on competition policy which would cover a wider area, including vertical restraints and mergers and acquisitions.[158]

All these years later, this recommendation remains the best option.

In particular, a WTO competition agreement could include a commitment by all WTO members to eliminate "hardcore" cartels, which are "anticompetitive agreements by competitors to fix prices, restrict output, submit collusive tenders, or divide and share markets."[159] Such economically destructive cartels dominated world trade before the Second World War, and today they are still the main target of national competition authorities throughout the world. They wreak enormous economic damage. One study has shown that, on average, cartels raise consumer prices by 48 percent. The worst ones raise consumer prices by as much as 80 percent.[160] By restricting and otherwise distorting trade competition, they devour what would otherwise be the gains from national economic growth. Hardcore cartels are increasingly international and, thus, they increasingly have harmful effects on international trade. WTO rules on competition could reduce these harmful effects by imposing international disciplines on this pernicious form of anticompetitive behavior.

WTO members should also write new rules to deal with the overcapacities in production that distort competition and thus distort trade in such sectors as steel and aluminum.[161] The utter failure to address these overcapacities was a major factor in inspiring Trump's unilateral tariffs on those two key products. WTO rules address "critical shortages of foodstuffs and other products" in situations of short supply.[162] They do not, however, address situations of oversupply. This is in part for historical reasons. Oversupply situations seemed unimaginable to negotiators of trade rules amid the global scarcities in the first years following the Second World War. The new pandemic world is a much different world. In the steel industry, for example, the OECD estimated that, in 2020, the global gap between production and capacity was expected to reach 700 million tons, despite declines in steel production caused by the impacts of COVID-19.[163]

The OECD also reported that, while steel production elsewhere had declined, the production of steel in China reached record volumes in 2020. China is not the only source of overcapacity in the steel and aluminum industries (for steel, Iran, which is not a WTO member, is a source), but China "has been without a doubt the most significant source of overcapacity."[164] The shortcomings of central planning are much on display in the excess of Chinese steelmaking capacity. State-driven instead of market-driven decisions by the central Chinese government have "encouraged undisciplined investments" in steel and aluminum capacity, and "have led to a large gap between China's ability to produce" these products and the demand for them.[165]

As a result, the flood of cheap Chinese steel and aluminum worldwide has led to numerous antidumping and antisubsidies tariffs, and it has contributed to much consternation among China's trading partners about the harmful consequences of overcapacity in production in China and in other countries in steel, aluminum, cement, shipbuilding, and other sectors. Overcapacity is also becoming a concern in the production of new technologies of the digital age, such as liquid crystal displays for smartphones and flat-panel television sets.[166] Antidumping and antisubsidy trade remedies address such concerns only on the margins. These trade remedies also have the counterproductive effect of making downstream producers less competitive because they must pay higher prices for necessary inputs in their production. Such remedies can cost more jobs than they preserve. In the United States, steel, aluminum, and other primary metal manufacturing industries employ several hundred thousand workers while downstream industries dependent on metal inputs employ millions.[167]

The huge extent of overcapacity in steel, aluminum, and other critical sectors of the global economy requires new rules. OECD talks on overcapacity faltered as President Trump and his trade advisers placed more emphasis on unilateral tariffs than on multilateral solutions.[168] The United States, the European Union, and Japan have been working on the sidelines of the WTO on their mutual "concerns with non-market-oriented policies and practices of third countries" (read: China), but the nonmarket actions of the United States in trade have not helped these trilateral talks.[169] Nor have they been aided by the exclusion of other countries from the talks. The European Union has offered a starting point with basic proposals on notification and transparency.[170] These ongoing endeavors should become part of a broader effort by WTO members to write new rules on competition – an effort that, ideally, should include China.

These new rules will not work if other WTO members are not able within the rules to retaliate with countervailing duties against the subsidies resulting from financial contributions granted by state-owned enterprises – such as when an SOE is directed by the government that owns it to provide raw materials or loans to foster the development of key industries. Not subjecting such aid to the WTO disciplines on subsidies constitutes a potentially huge loophole that enables governments to do indirectly through SOEs what they cannot do directly without violating the WTO rules. Therefore, new rules on competition should make it clear that subsidies granted not only by a government but also by any entity that is controlled by a government, are subject to the discipline of countervailing duties under the trade rules even if that entity does not exercise governmental authority. State-owned enterprises should be treated as "public bodies" under the WTO rules.[171]

Conceivably, antidumping rules, subsidies rules, and new rules on overcapacity could all be aligned in concert with new rules in a WTO competition agreement. Also, competition rules in the WTO should likewise account for the impact of the rise of the digital economy on global competition. The digital economy demands that competition be viewed from two contrasting perspectives. As Dan Ciuriak of the Centre for International Governance Innovation in Canada has observed, where trade concerns are ordinarily "focused on government measures that reduced competition, the data-driven economy features market features that reduce competition, such as economies of scope, economies of scale, network externalities in many cases and pervasive information asymmetries."[172] The links between trade and competition are not what they were in 1947, and new trade rules for competition should reflect the realities of the new digital world.

RULES FOR FACILITATING INVESTMENT

As the OECD has explained, "Investment is central to growth and sustainable development. Under the right conditions, international investment can enhance the host economy's productive capacity and growth potential, drive job creation and improvements in living standards, allow the transfer of technology and know-how, and spur domestic investment, including through the creation of local supplier linkages."[173] Skeptics of economic globalization see foreign direct investment as nefarious and exploitative, leading to worker oppression and environmental destruction. To be sure, this is true of some FDI. But, for the most part, the opposite is the case. For the most part, FDI leads to higher wages, better working conditions, and better environmental protections. And, without question, more foreign direct investment will be needed for the world to recover from the COVID-19 pandemic.

Foreign direct investment and international trade are mirror images of the same face of economic growth. There is a tendency to think of the two separately. But FDI and trade are mutually reinforcing. As the WTO Secretariat has explained, "Given that two-thirds of world exports are governed by ... multinational firms, deciding where to invest is simultaneously deciding from where to trade."[174] More trade creates more FDI by making more markets receptive to FDI. Also, more FDI creates more trade by spreading technology; shifting relationships between importers and exporters; enhancing financial relationships; and shaping supply chains.[175] In the new world linked by global value chains, the links between trade and investment have become all the more significant to economic growth. What is more, these links have acquired still more significance in the new pandemic world, where the world-wide spread of new technologies that accompanies foreign direct investment has acquired added urgency.

Because of the pandemic, global foreign direct investment plunged 35 percent in 2020. FDI was almost 20 percent below its lowest level in 2009 after the global financial crisis. In developing countries, the number of new investment projects fell by 42 percent. UNCTAD projected that global flows of FDI would "bottom out in 2021 and recover some lost ground, with an increase of 10 to 15 percent. This would leave FDI some 25 percent below the 2019 level," and it would be followed by "a further increase in 2022 which, at the upper bounds of projections, would bring FDI back to the 2019 level."[176] As UNCTAD acknowledged, though, these projections are "highly uncertain" and depend on a number of factors, including "the pace of economic recovery and the possibility of pandemic relapses."[177]

In these circumstances, countries have sought to provide incentives to spur investment to increase their national production in the health sector and other sectors related to or impacted by the pandemic.[178] The urgent need for more production facilities worldwide for the novel COVID-19 vaccines is just one aspect of a much broader need for more FDI in the health sector and more openness to the delivery of health services by foreign health service suppliers. During the pandemic, countries have also tried to spur investment by maintaining and enhancing the links between their struggling small- and medium-sized enterprises to global value chains.[179] In general, to promote sustainable investment, there is need for more FDI in "resources, manufacturing, and services linked to global supply chains" and in "international infrastructure investment in physical and social essentials such as transport systems, utilities, industrial zones, and health and educational facilities."[180]

The plummet in foreign direct investment during the pandemic has had virtually nothing to do with the absence of multilateral investment rules. But more and better international investment rules could help facilitate more foreign direct investment. Like rules for competition, rules for foreign direct investment have evolved separately from trade rules. For decades, there have been efforts to establish multilateral rules for FDI comparable to the multilateral rules for trade. Thus far, those efforts have failed. Instead, international investment rules are found in nearly 3,000 bilateral investment treaties and hundreds of other treaties containing investment provisions.[181] The investment rules in these treaties sometimes conflict. They also lack the coherence that is largely characteristic of WTO trade rules and would help ease and speed the flow of FDI. On the one hand, the existing investment rules are frequently too weak in countering investment protectionism; while, on the other, they are often too vague in assuring host countries a sufficiency of "policy space" for legitimate regulation.

Just as they did with their call for WTO competition rules, shortly after the establishment of the WTO, the European Union and some other WTO members proposed the negotiation of comprehensive rules dealing with the link between trade and investment in the WTO. But, as with the simultaneous proposal for competition negotiations, the proposal for investment negotiations was rejected. Thus, as it is, there are only limited WTO rules on "trade-related investment measures," which were concluded in 1994 in the Uruguay round.[182] These WTO rules mandate most-favored-nation treatment for FDI.[183] They also prevent quantitative restrictions on FDI.[184] They do not, however, do much more. New WTO rules that address the many connections between trade and investment are much needed. Much needed too are multilateral rules on investment, ideally in the WTO but possibly in some other global framework.

Although there is seemingly no apparent political appetite among the members of the WTO at this time for negotiating more substantive investment rules in the WTO, there is an apparent desire to negotiate new procedural rules that would help facilitate foreign direct investment. In Buenos Aires in 2017, seventy WTO members announced their support for negotiations on a multilateral framework for investment facilitation.[185] In 2019, ninety-eight WTO members announced their intent to try to conclude a multilateral agreement on "investment facilitation for development" by the time of the WTO Ministerial Conference in Geneva in November 2021.[186] In September 2020, 105 WTO members began "structured discussions" as a prelude to securing a consensus of all WTO members to commence formal negotiations.[187] These two-thirds of WTO members have encouraged the rest of the WTO to join in these "structured discussions." Perhaps due to the Trump administration's oft-professed distaste for foreign direct investment by American companies, the United States did not join in these discussions while he was president. It was widely hoped that the Biden administration would.[188]

The proposed WTO agreement on investment facilitation for development is widely viewed as a counterpart to the WTO Trade Facilitation Agreement, which is the only full-fledged multilateral trade agreement concluded by the WTO since its establishment in 1995.[189] The TFA, concluded in Bali in 2013, deals mostly with "the simplification, modernization and harmonization of export and import processes" to prevent delays and eliminate "red tape" in moving goods across borders.[190] The aim with investment facilitation is much the same as with trade facilitation. The stated intent is to "improve the transparency and predictability of investment measures; streamline and speed up administrative procedures and requirements; and enhance international cooperation, information sharing, the exchange of best practices, and relations with relevant stakeholders, including dispute prevention."[191] Thus, the WTO discussions on investment facilitation, like the TFA, are centered on cutting international "red tape" and eliminating bureaucratic overlap.

Because some of the developing countries remain apprehensive about negotiating multilateral rules on investment liberalization in the WTO, the WTO members working on investment facilitation have specifically said that these talks will exclude sensitive substantive issues such as easing market access and assuring investment protection.[192] However, as scholars from the International Institute for Sustainable Development in Canada have observed,

[t]he distinction between investment facilitation on the one hand and market access and protection on the other is blurry at best, so that the distinction would be hard to implement. Indeed, some issues that are already being considered could lead to potential disciplines, such as mandatory time limits for government decisions on the admission of proposed investments, go directly to market access questions and the ability of governments to evaluate proposed investments effectively before making decisions.[193]

In practice, there will be real difficulty in drawing this line. By far the biggest hurdle in making an investment framework agreement is likely to be that of distinguishing between facilitating investment and assisting in market access and investment protection. Finding the right line between the two will be even more of a task at a time when FDI has declined and countries have turned inward – even as many of them are much in need of more foreign direct investment. Likely to make this line-drawing even more delicate is the fact that, while trade facilitation deals solely with what happens in crossing the border, investment facilitation reaches beyond the border to dig deeper into second-guessing domestic decision-making.[194]

Investment facilitation is a broader concept than trade facilitation and not as easily defined. It is sometimes confused with mere investment promotion. The OECD has explained that, while investment promotion is about making a country more enticing as a potential target for FDI, investment facilitation is about making it easier for investors to establish investments and then operate and expand them. For this to happen, there must be a domestic framework for investment that is transparent, predictable, and efficient.[195] UNCTAD suggests, further, that investment facilitation relates to all stages of foreign direct investment, beginning with the pre-establishment phase, continuing through investment installation, and to services provided throughout the lifespan of an investment project.[196]

Perhaps the leading academic advocate of a WTO framework agreement for trade facilitation has been Karl Sauvant of Columbia University. In terms of "concrete measures" to include in such an agreement, he and Matthew Stephenson of the Graduate Institute of International and Development Studies in Geneva have recommended provisions that would facilitate access to business visas; deliver project evaluation assistance for large-scale projects; create early grievance mechanisms to avoid legal disputes; increase the transparency of investment incentives; create databases of lists of local suppliers; require investor statements on corporate social responsibility; and facilitate coordination on investment policy and measures among domestic government agencies and between those agencies and the private sector.[197] Also included in an agreement could be additional provisions on transparency of investment procedures; simplification of administrative procedures and requirements; international coordination and cooperation; and digitalization.[198] For their part, the WTO members discussing the matter have identified an eighty-one-item checklist of issues for further examination and possible inclusion in such a framework agreement.[199]

Sauvant has focused extensively on capacity-building; he has rightly stressed the imperative of providing the necessary assistance to enable the full engagement of developing countries in negotiating and implementing an investment facilitation agreement.[200] As with trade facilitation, investment facilitation is in no small part a matter of providing developing countries – and especially least developed countries – with the assistance they will need to fulfill any new international obligations. Technical assistance will be needed. So too will financial assistance. And, like the TFA, an agreement on investment facilitation should include different categories of obligations that developing countries can choose depending on their stage of development and their access to assistance in compliance.

Although these potential new WTO investment rules will be procedural in nature, they will be part of a framework agreement that, if WTO members wished, could be augmented over time to add substantive obligations. The current rules on trade-related investment measures could be relocated within the new framework, and they could be supplemented with new multilateral commitments on matters that would include ensuring market access and investment protection while also preserving the sovereign space of countries to regulate on the environment and public health and safety. This will be an even more challenging act of line-drawing. Attitudes have been changing in developing countries as they have emerged economically and have become sources as well as hosts for FDI. But, unless and until all developing countries fully realize that more foreign direct investment is in their interest and is essential to their further development, a WTO framework agreement on investment will remain purely procedural. It will not address the substance of the further development that is needed, now more than ever, by developed and developing countries alike.

Not just any development will do, of course. Importantly, the WTO Ministerial Statement in 2017 that initiated the WTO talks on investment facilitation speaks about "investment facilitation *for development*."[201] This anticipated development must be sustainable development that advances a green recovery from the COVID-19 pandemic.[202] The 2017 statement did not mention the Sustainable Development Goals. Nor have WTO members engaged in the discussions on investment facilitation focused on *sustainable* development as opposed simply to development. They should. As the SDGs clearly affirm, development in the new pandemic world must mean sustainable development. It must mean "achieving sustainable development in its three dimensions – economic, social and environmental – in a balanced and inte-grated manner."[203] No longer can any aspect of trade or investment be viewed independently of these three dimensions of sustainable development. The links of trade and investment with sustainable development must be central to all international commercial deliberations. They can no longer be pushed to the periphery or, worse, ignored.

6

Links to Climate Change

THE KALEIDOSCOPE OF SUSTAINABLE DEVELOPMENT

Trade rules are viewed through a kaleidoscope. We see trade rules through the revealing lens of each national action that is taken that falls within the wide legal scope of the rules. We adjust the lens to account for the shape, color, and lineaments of each such action. As we peer through the lens of the kaleidoscope, we ask: Is this action consistent with the rules, or is it not?[1] Now, as Philip Stephens of the *Financial Times* has observed, "Coronavirus has shaken the kaleidoscope."[2] It has done so at a time when the necessity to confront climate change and the need to construct sustainable development have likewise shaken it. Now, through the lens of the kaleidoscope, we can see more clearly the links between trade and much else that matters immensely today and will matter still more tomorrow.

In the new pandemic world, we must see trade, and we must see the global role of trade rules, differently. Trade is more important than ever before as a tool for achieving human flourishing through sustainable development. Trade must help us find our way through the pandemic. Trade must help us make a green recovery from the pandemic. Trade must also help us to accomplish the seventeen UN Sustainable Development Goals even as we struggle with the impacts of the pandemic. As with trade itself, trade rules must likewise be tools for achieving human flourishing through sustainable development. Trade rules must be reimagined in response to what we can see through the kaleidoscope now that it has been shaken. And nothing has shaken the kaleidoscope more than the inescapable fact of the worst threat to sustainable development – man-made climate change.

CLIMATE CHANGE AND A CARBON PRICE

Goal 13 of the UN Sustainable Development Goals is to "take urgent action to combat climate change and its impacts."[3] The expectation is that this goal will be achieved by 2030 by the Conference of Parties (the COP) to the United Nations Framework Convention on Climate Change (the UNFCCC) in implementing the 2015 Paris Agreement on climate change.[4] The climate COP hopes to prevent the worst impacts of global warming between now and the end of this century by holding the increase in the global average temperature to "well below" 2 degrees Celsius (3.6 degrees Fahrenheit) above preindustrial levels and, ideally, by limiting the temperature increase to 1.5 degrees Celsius (2.7 degrees Fahrenheit).[5]

With the brief pause in the rise of global greenhouse gas emissions because of the economic slowdown during the pandemic now over, emissions are again rising steeply.[6] With each passing day, exceeding the temperature limits set out in the Paris Agreement in 2015 seems harder to avoid.[7] The Intergovernmental Panel on Climate Change – the UN panel of the world's leading climate scientists – calculates that global warming is already between 0.8C and 1.2C above preindustrial levels and rising at a pace of about 0.2C per decade.[8] The climate scientists predict that global temperatures are likely to reach the lower limit of 1.5C sometime between 2030 and 2052.[9] There is, however, at least a one-in-four chance that 1.5C will be surpassed as soon as 2024.[10] In 2018, the IPCC warned that, to be able to achieve these temperature goals and thereby to prevent the worst extreme impacts of global warming, global greenhouse gas emissions must drop by about 45 percent from 2010 levels by 2030, and reach net zero by 2050.[11]

So far, we have done much too little to keep the worst from happening. The sum of countries' currently submitted climate mitigation pledges under the Paris Agreement – assuming they are kept – falls far short of the emissions cuts needed to reach the 2C goal, much less the 1.5C goal. According to the UN Environment Programme, even full implementation of current nationally determined contributions (NDCs) – countries' individual climate action pledges – will deliver only one-third of the emissions cuts needed to keep global warming below the 2 degrees Celsius limit. To achieve the 2C goal, countries must triple their promised emissions cuts.[12] To achieve the 1.5C goal, countries must increase their current climate pledges fivefold.[13] Without deeper emissions cuts, this puts the world on a path toward a 3 degrees Celsius increase from preindustrial levels by 2100.[14] In the meantime, only two countries – Morocco and Gambia – are fulfilling their Paris pledges.[15]

As the pandemic continued to reap a lethal toll toward the end of 2020, there were, at last, some encouraging signs that more countries were starting to take more seriously the urgent necessity of emissions cuts. Facing a year-end deadline in the Paris Agreement for improving their climate pledges, more than seventy countries made new pledges for deeper reductions in emissions.[16] South Korea and Japan promised net zero carbon emissions by 2050. The European Union, as part of its "Green Deal," committed to a target of a 55 percent cut in net carbon emissions by 2030 from 1990 levels. The United Kingdom – set to host COP26 in Glasgow in November 2021 – pledged to reduce greenhouse gas emissions from their 1990 levels by at least 68 percent by 2030.[17]

Significantly, China, which had not previously made a long-term commitment to emissions reductions, promised in 2020 that it would become carbon-neutral by 2060 – albeit at the same time as it was ramping up construction of coal-fired power plants in countering the economic doldrums of the pandemic.[18] In 2020, according to the Global Energy Monitor, a San Francisco–based think tank, China commissioned 38.4 gigawatts of new coal-fired power plants – which translates into more than one large coal plant every week. That sum was more than three times the rest of the world.[19] Coal is the dirtiest of fossil fuels; it is the most carbon-intensive fossil fuel we burn. The Chinese government seems to understand that it must ultimately stop using coal to produce energy, but it must also keep churning out economic growth if it hopes to remain in power by meeting the increasing economic expectations of the Chinese people. China is caught in a closing vise between coal and climate.

In 2019, for the first time, China's greenhouse gas emissions exceeded those of all the developed countries in the world combined.[20] With its economic rise, China has become by far the leading producer in the world of GHG emissions, with 28 percent. This is almost double the amount of the second leading emitter, the United States, with 15 percent.[21] The United States, however, remains the world's largest cumulative emitter of greenhouse gases – responsible for 25 percent of historical emissions since 1751, more than twice as much as China.[22] (The European Union and the United Kingdom together account for 22 percent of historical emissions.) Also, the United States is tied with Saudi Arabia at the top of the global chart in per capita emissions while China ranks fifteenth.[23] Clearly, any solution on emissions must involve both China and the United States, in concert with other leading emitters. The climate emergency cannot be ended by only one without the other; nor can it be ended by the rest of the world without them both.

Optimists saw the new and more ambitious climate pledges in late 2020 as evidence that the 2C goal and perhaps even the 1.5C goal in the Paris Agreement might still be achievable. All told, more than 120 countries have announced a zero emissions goal.[24] "If all these countries meet their long-term targets of net zero, then the Paris agreement goals are within reach again," said one climate scientist, Niklas Hohne of Wageningen University in the Netherlands.[25] Hoping for further confirmation of justification for such optimism, eyes worldwide turned to the new administration of President Biden in the United States in the expectation of renewed American leadership in confronting climate change.

Donald Trump withdrew the United States from the Paris climate agreement upon entering the White House in January 2017. He said that "climate change is a hoax invented by and for Chinese" for the purpose of undermining the American economy.[26] He spent much of his time as president ridiculing the climate agreement and rolling back domestic environmental protections. In his presidential campaign in 2020, Biden endorsed unprecedented action against climate change. He said he aimed to reach zero carbon in electricity by 2035 and net zero emissions overall by 2050.[27] His early appointments and proposals as president suggest his seriousness about addressing climate change.[28] In an about-face from his predecessor, he returned the United States to the Paris Agreement, and he wasted little time in attempting to reassert American climate leadership.[29]

In April 2021, on Earth Day, President Biden hosted a virtual climate summit of forty world leaders at which he pledged to cut US greenhouse gas emissions by between 50 and 52 percent below 2005 levels by 2030.[30] This is about twice what President Obama promised previously, before President Trump entered the White House and largely dismantled Obama's climate initiatives.[31] Even so, US emissions had declined during the decade, largely because of the shift from coal to cheaper and less carbon-intensive natural gas made possible by the shale revolution. In 2019, emissions were down 13 percent below 2005 levels. By the end of 2020, due to the economic collapse during the pandemic, they were down 21 percent – although this percentage was expected to decrease as the American economy recovered.[32] Clearly, producing only half the emissions of 2005 by 2030 will require a dramatic reshaping of much of the American economy. Moreover, Biden's pledge at the summit, bold as it was, still had to be translated into legislation and then law, with vertiginous political hurdles ahead in a polarized country. At this writing, his $3.5 trillion spending proposal including significant climate reforms remains before the Congress.[33]

There were other encouraging signs at the Biden climate summit, as other countries also added to their previous promises. Japan, Canada, and the United Kingdom all raised their previous targets. Leading the way, the United Kingdom lifted its previous pledge of emissions cuts to 78 percent by 2030. South Korea and Brazil made new climate promises. A week earlier, in a potentially significant diplomatic turn, the United States and China had agreed, despite all their other differences, to tackle the climate crisis.[34] At the Earth Day summit, in perhaps the first fruits of that cooperation, President Xi promised that China would limit increases in coal consumption until 2025 and would then phase it down between then and 2030.[35] As with Biden's summit pledge, though, the pledge by Xi had yet to be translated into action. All the promises made at the Biden climate summit, while "solemn," were nevertheless nonbinding.[36]

Given the accelerating pace of climate change, the world's ambitious aspirations as expressed in the Paris Agreement can only be achieved if all countries significantly increase their promised reductions in carbon and other greenhouse gas emissions formally within the framework of the Paris climate agreement – and then keep their promises. Such promises are much more likely to be kept if a price is put on the extensive climate harms caused by carbon emissions from the use of fossil fuels. As it is, though, "Fossil fuels are now massively underpriced, reflecting undercharging for production and environmental costs – including for air pollution and global warming."[37] The right price signal is not being sent in the marketplace for the use of fossil fuels because the "externalities" of climate harms are not included in their price. Thus under-priced, fossil fuels continue to have a competitive edge over renewable fuels, even as the price of renewable fuels is rapidly declining. And so, the world resists ending its long carbon addiction.

To level the competition between fossil fuels and renewable fuels and make the needed transition to a decarbonized economy, a price must be put on carbon. Some progress has been made in recent years – but it does not add up to nearly enough. Sixty-four carbon pricing initiatives are "planned or in place globally," but these laudable initiatives cover altogether only 22 percent of global greenhouse gas emissions.[38] Not having to worry about getting reelected, the leaders of China's government launched a national emissions trading system to price carbon in July 2021. By volume, the Chinese carbon market is the largest in the world, including more than 2,000 power plants.[39] Many democratic countries, however, hesitate to take such action because of the political difficulties of selling a carbon tax or another carbon pricing mechanism to their voters.

For all his worthy climate ambition, President Biden did not include a carbon tax or any other carbon pricing scheme in his initial climate-related proposals as president of the United States.[40] He is betting instead mainly on a regulatory Clean Electricity Standard that would set rising emissions reduction targets for the power sector, and on a range of other regulations and government-selected investments that smack in some respects of a state-directed industrial policy. Some of these regulations and subsidies may not work, and, in some instances, they would not be necessary if a price were put on the use of carbon.[41] What is more, those who would regulate to manipulate the market must be mindful of the ever-present prospect of unintended consequences, which often cannot be foreseen by even the most far-sighted of social engineers.

The Sustainable Development Goals do not specifically mention carbon pricing. Nor is there any mention of carbon pricing in the legal text of the Paris Agreement. Pointedly, however, the decision accompanying the Paris Agreement recognizes "the important role of providing incentives for emission reduction activities, including tools such as domestic policies and carbon pricing."[42] Despite Trumpian political posturing to the contrary, the fact is, virtually nothing is required of sovereign countries by the terms of the Paris Agreement, which is a voluntary agreement.[43] It mandates almost nothing apart from some periodic reporting, most of which was already being done before the Paris Agreement.[44] Putting a price on carbon is in no way mandated by the Paris Agreement or by other international law. But climate change cannot be limited to the extent the countries of the world have agreed to limit it if the climate harms caused by fossil fuel emissions are not incorporated into the prices of products. As it is, these costs are not included in the sales prices of the products of carbon emitters, and, thus, there is no disincentive to their continued use of fossil fuels, and there is less incentive to develop and use alternative, renewable forms of energy.[45]

Some worry that putting a price on carbon will also constrain economic growth in the global economy. Instead, carbon pricing is more likely to spur a new and innovative generation of sustainable growth for the global economy. According to the High-Level Commission on Carbon Prices, created at COP-22 in Marrakesh in 2016 and comprised of prominent economists and leading climate and energy specialists worldwide,

[C]limate policies, if well designed and implemented, are consistent with growth, development, and poverty reduction ... While the design of these packages will vary, based on national and social circumstances, a well-designed carbon-pricing system is an indispensable part of a strategy for reducing emissions in an efficient way. Many have argued that the transition to a low-carbon economy is a powerful growth story. In the medium term, it can be a strong driver of discovery, innovation, and investment ... in the shorter term, the necessary investments in sustainable infrastructure could be a key driver of growth ... And in the longer term, any extended attempt at high-carbon development could create an environment hostile to global growth, threatening to undermine future development gains or even reverse past ones.[46]

Basically, there are two ways to put a price on carbon. One way is through the market. The other way is through regulation. Market-based measures create incentives and disincentives. Regulatory measures impose requirements. Market-based measures are more flexible. Regulatory measures may mandate the installing of a particular technology or the meeting of a specific performance standard. By relying on incentives and disincentives, market-based measures leave the ultimate decision to the private producer or consumer. In contrast, regulations are decisions made by government officials. Regulation of market actions is often needed in a mix of both. In the absence of regulation, unrestrained market forces can lead to the concentration of power and the corrosiveness of abuse. If unrestrained, however, governmental regulation can pose a variety of societal and economic risks. The road from unrestrained regulation leads to state-directed economic planning, which is fraught with peril for innovative and sustainable economic growth.

Importantly, in the struggle to cut carbon emissions, there is solid evidence that market-based measures can be more environmentally effective than regulatory measures, and that they can also cost less. The International Monetary Fund affirmed that regulations are "less efficient" than market-based measures in raising the price of carbon.[47] A joint study by researchers from the University of Zurich and the Massachusetts Institute of Technology concluded that regulatory approaches reduce emissions only one-fourth as much as market approaches, and that the costs of regulatory approaches "substantially exceed the cost" of market approaches.[48] Added to this, analysts for the IMF say that carbon pricing through fiscal policies is preferable to regulation for two reasons: it is more environmentally effective, and it can be used to raise significant revenues.[49] These revenues, of course, can be repaid to those who pay for carbon pricing, whether directly or indirectly, through lower income or other taxes.

A carbon tax is the simplest and best market-based approach to carbon pricing. It "is a tax that sets a price on each unit of pollution."[50] Ordinarily, this price is a price per ton of carbon emitted for a sector or for a whole economy. Thus, the pollution from carbon emissions is no longer what economists call an "externality" – it is no longer a cost excluded from the seller's calculation of the price of a product. In paying a carbon tax, the taxpayer incurs an additional cost based on the amount of the carbon pollution produced. This additional cost is "internalized" into – it is added to – the sales price of the product. This, in turn, gives the purchaser a means of factoring fossil fuel use into the buying decision, and gives the taxpayer a financial incentive to reduce carbon pollution by shifting from fossil fuel energy to new energy sources, and by using energy more efficiently. The more the tax, the more the incentive. In the production of energy, a carbon tax "provides a continuous incentive for innovation."[51]

The other market-based approach to carbon pricing is a "cap-and-trade" program. Instead of putting a price in the form of a tax on each unit of carbon pollution, a determination is made upfront about how much total carbon emission will be allowed – the "cap." The "cap" is reduced over time with the idea that overall emissions will thus be reduced over time. Within the "cap," companies buy and sell their rights to produce carbon emissions – the "trade." These rights take the form of tradable emissions certificates that permit certain amounts of carbon emissions based on individual company needs – "allowances." Because the number of these emission "allowances" is limited by the gradually shrinking "cap," there is a resulting scarcity that creates a demand and thus a market for them. Emissions allowances are traded. As the "cap" shrinks, the expectation is that the price of the traded allowances will increase over time and thus provide an incentive for companies to cut their carbon emissions. Firms that are best in holding down their carbon emissions are rewarded by their increased energy efficiency and their profits from emissions trading. Firms that are unsuccessful in holding down their carbon emissions pay higher costs in the form of payments for emissions allowances that permit them to make emissions, and they suffer accordingly because the prices of their products are consequently higher in the marketplace.

Both a carbon tax and a "cap-and-trade" program are market-based approaches to setting a carbon price. Economists say their effects can be mostly the same. But the two approaches to pricing carbon differ in how they work. Carbon taxes impose a uniform price on carbon pollution but allow the amount of pollution to fluctuate. "Cap-and-trade" schemes impose a "cap" on the amount of pollution but allow the carbon price to vary. In addition, carbon taxes are more straightforward – the polluter pays, consistent with the basic international environmental rule in Principle 16 of the Rio Declaration at the Earth Summit in 1992.[52] In comparison – and disconcertingly for many environmentalists – "cap-and-trade" schemes are indirect. They work in part, and counterintuitively, by allowing polluters to buy the right to pollute. Cap-

and-trade measures can also raise questions about environmental justice if they are not linked to measures sufficient to make certain that the poor and minorities are not disadvantaged by the pollution those measures permit.

Whether through a carbon tax, a cap-and-trade system, or some other form of putting a price on carbon, the evidence is: Carbon pricing works. The average annual growth rate of carbon dioxide emissions from fuel combustion has been about 2 percent lower in countries that have adopted a carbon price compared to those that have not.[53] Moreover, "the emissions trajectories of countries with and without carbon prices tend to diverge over time," thus underlining the necessity of carbon pricing for fighting climate change.[54]

The alternative to a market-based approach to pricing carbon is a regulatory approach. Carbon regulation can assume many guises. One regulatory approach is a sectoral approach, which singles out one or more sectors of the economy for regulations intended to induce the transition toward a green economy. In the United States, one example of a long-standing sectoral regulatory approach has been the Corporate Average Fuel Economy (CAFE) standards used for regulating the fuel economy of motor vehicles. Another is the Clean Power Plan for the power plant sector proposed by President Barack Obama in 2015 but never implemented. As compared to a carbon tax, many economists would doubtless say that such sectoral plans are "second-best solutions." Moreover, if the Zurich and MIT study is to be believed, a sectoral plan could, when compared to a carbon tax, accomplish much less environmentally while costing much more economically.

Regulations are in some cases necessary to help place a price on the climate and other environmental harms caused by carbon emissions, but regulations should be supplements to, and not substitutes for, market-based solutions. A mix of both that draws the right line in speeding the shift to a decarbonized economy is needed. A policy that relies exclusively on regulation will produce less climate action because it will forgo use of the transformative power of market-based decisions. A policy that relies exclusively on the market will produce less climate action because it will lack the complementary force that the right mix of regulations can bring to market-based decisions.

In the United States, the National Academies of Sciences, Engineering, and Medicine have advised that, to achieve deep decarbonization, an economy-wide price on carbon is essential as part of an effective strategy.[55] The academy scientists also say that carbon pricing must be accompanied by "a range of complementary interventions" by government in the economy, due to "the existence of other market failures," especially as relate to equity and justice and the shortcomings of reliance on carbon pricing alone in some sectors.[56] One example they cite as needed is federal emissions standards for automobiles.[57] They worry, though, that carbon pricing through a carbon tax could be regressive in that it would fall more heavily on lower income Americans because it would raise prices of gasoline, fuel oil, natural gas, and electricity.[58]

Any potential inequity in the impact of a carbon tax would be diminished if the revenues produced by the tax were remitted in their entirety to American taxpayers on an equal and regular basis by making it "revenue neutral," through per capita dividends or reductions in other taxes. Although some climate activists would prefer to invest at least some of the revenues from a carbon tax in climate programs, returning all the revenues to those who pay the tax would generate much more political support for a carbon tax and thus would make it much more likely that one could be enacted to help advance decarbonization. Taking this approach would be well worth it for climate reasons alone. A study for Resources for the Future concluded that the United States could cut its carbon emissions 54 percent by 2030 if it enacted a carbon tax that started at $40 per ton and increased every year by 5 percent above inflation.[59] This alone would achieve President Biden's goal for US emission cuts by that year, without doing anything else he has proposed. To make even more emissions cuts sooner, the addition of the right combination of targeted regulations could deepen the decline.

Whatever approach is employed by a country when taking climate action – whether it be market, regulatory, or a blend of both – the approach that is chosen should not be impeded from accomplishing climate action by an inflexibility in the rules of the World Trade Organization. As it is, there is a looming collision between the climate COP and the WTO, between the fight against climate change and the fight to save the multilateral trading system. Neither the climate institution nor the trade institution has considered seriously the consequences of the trade restrictions that are likely to be a part of many national measures enacted to address climate change. These measures will fall within the legal scope of the WTO Agreement, and they will surely lead to WTO dispute settlement.

This collision will occur sooner rather than later. In a foreshadowing of what will surely come, one of the last acts of the Trump administration, in December 2020, was the submission in the WTO of a proposal that the failure of a WTO member to adopt, implement, and enforce national laws and regulations that ensure environmental protections "at or above a threshold of minimum standards" be treated as a subsidy subject to countervailing duties.[60] The US submission reasoned that "imposing countervailing measures on subsidies that take the form of weak or unenforced environmental standards would promote stronger environmental standards and enforcement, would encourage the proper internalization of environmental costs into the calculations of production costs, and would correct policies that create transaction-specific market inefficiencies which thereby distort trade."[61] There was a certain irony in such a proposal coming from a president and an administration that had spent four years repealing and otherwise undermining environmental laws and regulations in the United States.[62] Yet there is merit in this proposal – if it is applied to all WTO members, including the United States.[63] This said, achieving consensus on a "threshold of minimum standards" among the 164 WTO members would be no easy task.

Similar proposals linking trade treatment to climate and other environmental protections are emerging and will soon be multiplying. As a key part of the European Green Deal, the European Commission has proposed imposing border adjustment measures on greenhouse-gas-intensive imports from countries that have implemented no or – in the eyes of the EU – insufficient measures for climate mitigation.[64] These proposed EU measures would be the first climate-related trade limits in the world. They raise a number of concerns under current WTO law.[65] Likewise, there are signs that Democrats in the Congress of the United States will offer similar proposals and that the Biden administration may support them.[66] Biden endorsed the idea of border carbon adjustments as a candidate, and, as he began to turn his climate proposals into legislation, his advisers suggested that such trade-restrictive border measures could be included.[67] Canada is also considering a border carbon adjustment mechanism.[68] Other developed countries seem likely to follow suit with similar measures of their own. The result could be an escalating cycle of tariffs and retaliatory tariffs in a "climate trade war" throughout the world.

Ultimately, there will be a showdown over the legality of such measures under the current trade rules – most likely between developed and developing countries – in WTO dispute settlement. As the legal results of such disputes depend to a great extent on the details of each dispute – the nature of the challenged measure, the way in which it is applied, the facts surrounding it – predicting the outcome is difficult. But this much is certain: WTO disputes resulting from such trade-restrictive national climate measures will confront numerous unanswered legal questions in WTO jurisprudence while raising global concerns about a confrontation between the claims of trade and the cause of climate change, which will end up damaging the credibility and impeding the effectiveness of both the international trade and climate regimes.

This is also clear: To minimize the potential harm from such a collision in WTO dispute settlement, the modernization of WTO rules in the pandemic world must further legitimate efforts by WTO Members to adapt to and mitigate the impacts of climate change. High on the list of proposed WTO reforms must therefore be WTO action that will help do the most to address climate change while posing the least risk to the continued success of the multilateral trading system. WTO rules should not present obstacles to genuine climate action; they should be affirmative means for helping achieve it. In the WTO, much of the challenge consists in making the essential tool of carbon pricing available in ways that further climate actions while also allowing international trade to flow and grow.

BORDER CARBON ADJUSTMENTS

Climate solutions that employ market forces send most directly the price signal that is urgently needed in the marketplace to inspire a shift away from carbon-emitting fossil fuels and toward clean renewable forms of energy. Even with the disruptions of the pandemic, even with the reluctance of governments to ramp up their climate actions during a global economic decline, and even with their hesitancy about the potential political repercussions of imposing carbon taxes, many governments around the world are accelerating their climate actions through carbon pricing. The long-term global trend toward addressing climate change includes, in many places, employing carbon pricing as a principal means of cutting emissions through these more ambitious actions.[69] It also includes the enactment of climate actions that affect trade. "Trade-related elements feature prominently in climate contributions under the Paris Agreement," and, according to one assessment of the national climate pledges, "around 45 percent of all climate contributions include a direct reference to trade or trade measures."[70]

Kateryna Holzer of the University of Bern in Switzerland has summarized the commercial and climate concerns that can arise in crafting carbon pricing and pose political obstacles. With respect to commerce, she explains,

The unilateral introduction of carbon constraints creates unequal conditions of competition between domestic and foreign markets. This happens because foreign producers in countries with lax, or no, carbon legislation in place do not pay carbon charges and then go on to sell their products in the market of a country with carbon restrictions and in the markets of other countries tax-free. At the same time, domestic producers are obliged to bear emissions costs and are not compensated for these costs on exportation.[71]

Predictably, there is domestic political pressure to, in the tired but universal phrase, "level the playing field" between the domestic producers that are paying a carbon price and the foreign producers that are not.

With respect to the climate, Holzer has elaborated,

The unfair price competition might force domestic firms to relocate their carbon-intensive production to countries with no emissions constraints and no carbon charges in place, i.e. to 'pollution havens', while domestic consumers increase consumption of cheaper imported carbon-intensive products. Consequently, an emissions reduction by one country with a strict climate policy in place would lead to an increase in emissions in another country with no carbon constraints, in the end making no difference in the fight against climate change.[72]

Through such a net shift in emissions offshore, the emissions-reduction goal of the domestic climate policy measure is defeated.

In common parlance, this is known as "carbon leakage." Such "leakage" may result from either the displacement of exports by the lower priced high-carbon products of other countries or the import from other countries and local consumption of lower priced high-carbon products. Carbon leakage is widely feared by environmentalists. It is equally feared by producers in developed economies whose production results in extensive carbon emissions. Especially, it is feared by "energy-intensive, trade exposed" industries such as cement, steel, pulp and paper, metal casting, aluminum, chemicals, and glass. These manufacturing industries employ energy-intensive production processes, and they compete with foreign products at home and abroad.

Because of the significance of these heavy industries to local economies as employers and sources of growth, they often have substantial local political clout. This local political pressure is often magnified "against a backdrop in which heavy industries in many countries have for a long time been under pressure from more competitive producers, mainly in emerging economies, resulting in declining market shares and losses in employment."[73] In many cases, these industries have long sought trade protection from this increasing foreign competition, some of it legitimate, some not. Now, the global climate crisis threatens to add a new and unnerving dimension to their struggle to maintain and increase market shares, by introducing into the competitiveness equation national measures compelling them to reduce their carbon footprint when their competitors in other countries may not.

Not surprisingly, anxieties arise about a loss of competitiveness when a price is put on carbon here at home but not over there in some other country. Rhetoric rises about "unfair" trade. Indeed, the prices of products produced in countries that put a price on carbon will be higher, while the prices of like products produced in countries that do not put a price on carbon will be less. As a result, the products of those countries that put a price on carbon may be displaced both at home and abroad by cheaper like products from countries that have not done so. Therefore, the producers in countries that choose higher environmental standards as climate action may suffer a loss of competitiveness, both domestically and internationally.

Economists disagree about the reality and true extent of the carbon leakage causing such a decline in competitiveness. Despite the widespread anxieties about the competitive impact of environmental regulation, the OECD tells us that thus far, generally, "more stringent environmental policies ... have had no negative effect on overall productivity growth."[74] According to the World Bank, "Empirical examinations tend to find limited evidence of carbon leakage."[75] Developmental economists for the bank say, "Evidence from developed countries suggests that there are no discernible impacts on productivity and jobs from introducing cost-increasing environmental regulations or pricing schemes."[76] Similarly, the global advocates of a "new climate economy" assure us, "There is substantial evidence suggesting that the direct competitiveness impacts are small for a country which is an early mover in legislating climate policy."[77]

Furthermore, early movers may well benefit from domestic climate measures that encourage increases in technological innovation. Thus, the competitiveness of early movers may not only *not* be harmed by climate regulation; it may be enhanced. Furthermore, even in the heavy carbon-intensive industries that are often the most apprehensive about leaking carbon, "most studies fail to find evidence that" climate actions "have had a significant effect on business competitiveness."[78] Thus, the evidence suggests that, while "carbon leakage" can be a genuine concern in some instances, there may not always be as much of all the varied kinds of "carbon leakage" as feared.[79]

Of course, there has, so far, been only limited carbon pricing; carbon leakage may increase as carbon pricing increases. Furthermore, no politician anywhere in the world will vote knowingly for a national measure that may reduce national competitiveness or that may require their citizens to take noble and self-sacrificing actions locally to reduce carbon emissions while other countries are permitted to be "free riders" that make few or no cuts in their own emissions. In the United States, for example, opponents of President Biden's climate action proposals point as justification for their opposition, to what they perceive as the absence of any significant climate action by China.[80] For this reason, as a practical matter, it is not politically possible today in much of the world to enact national climate actions if these widespread apprehensions about the commercial and climate impacts of carbon leakage are not addressed in such actions. Thus, commercial interests and climate campaigners alike plead for the imposition of trade-restrictive carbon adjustment measures as part of national climate actions and posit them as the price for their political support.

Given this inescapable political reality, domestic actions that establish carbon pricing are likely to include border carbon adjustments intended to help ensure fair competition on the proverbial "level playing field." The choice of the legal instrument for making a border carbon adjustment and the way in which that instrument is applied will affect its legality under WTO rules. In the abstract, an ideal national measure for carbon adjustment can be imagined that could conceivably thread the needle of legality under the current WTO rules. Numerous WTO scholars have opined precisely on the right contortions of such needle-threading.[81] But such measures will not be crafted in impeccable fashion by WTO scholars who may know how to thread the legal needle of the WTO rules. Climate measures featuring border carbon adjustments will be written by politicians in the give-and-take of the domestic political fray and, in the absence of action by the WTO to help facilitate carbon pricing, these measures will therefore be likely to run afoul of those rules.

This likelihood will be increased by the sheer array of forms such measures will take. The human mind is endlessly creative when it comes to influencing international trade. A border carbon adjustment meant to level the field of international competition could well come in any number of shapes and sizes, and it could be affixed with any number of names. It could be a carbon tariff. It could be a requirement that emissions allowances be purchased for imports as one part of, or alongside of, a domestic cap-and-trade program. It could be the free allocation of emissions allowances to domestic industries as an inducement to secure their support for climate action. It could be governmental subsidies or some other type of beneficial state aid to domestic producers. It could be an import quota or an import ban. It could be a labeling requirement, a carbon-intensity standard that is extended to imports, or some other kind of non-fiscal regulation that imposes a trade restriction.

Or it could be a carbon tax.

BORDER TAX ADJUSTMENTS

Not only is a carbon tax the best approach to putting a price on the use of carbon, it is also the best approach to imposing a border carbon adjustment consistently with WTO rules. This is because a carbon tax can be collected at the border without changing the existing trade rules. Since the founding of the multilateral trading system in 1947, a GATT rule has permitted a border tax adjustment equivalent to an internal tax as a charge on imported products; likewise, this rule has also permitted a border tax adjustment as a remission on exported products. The theory underlying this rule is that taxes should be based on where goods are consumed and not on where they are produced. Under this trade rule, only indirect taxes on products – such as sales taxes – may be adjusted at the border, while direct taxes on producers – such as income taxes – may not be.[82] The logic underpinning this distinction is that indirect taxes are passed through to the prices of products while direct taxes have a more complex relationship with prices. Assuming a carbon tax is an indirect tax on a product, it should be adjustable at the border and therefore consistent with this current and long-existing WTO rule.

This is a reasonable assumption, and this is, most likely, the conclusion WTO jurists would reach in WTO dispute settlement. The problem is, in the current absence of such a ruling, it is uncertain under WTO law whether a carbon tax is eligible for a border tax adjustment under this long-standing trade rule. There are two main reasons for this lack of certainty. First, it is not clear whether a carbon tax is a direct tax or an indirect tax. Second, it is not clear whether a carbon tax is a tax on a product. A carbon tax is a tax on a product only if taxes on inputs that are not physically incorporated into the final product can be adjusted on imports at the border.

A carbon tax appears to be an indirect tax. As Ingrid Jegou, a noted Swedish trade economist, has reasoned, "[G]iven that a carbon tax is imposed at the border and 'border taxes' are classified as indirect taxes, it seems logical to classify a carbon tax as an indirect tax."[83] Also, a carbon tax appears to be a tax on a product. The carbon-emitting fuel that is used in making a product but is not present physically in the final product can be viewed under the current trade rules as "an *article* from which the imported product has been manufactured or produced in whole or in part."[84] These are both logical conclusions that would likely be reached by WTO jurists if these legal issues were raised in WTO dispute settlement. But, meanwhile, the uncertainties about the legal status of carbon taxes under the trade rules remain. And these uncertainties are disincentives to the enactment of carbon taxes by WTO members.

These uncertainties can be eliminated now. There is no need to await the outcome of future WTO dispute settlement or to change the trade rules. The members of the WTO can adopt a formal legal interpretation of the existing rule to clarify that a tax on inputs such as fossil fuels that are not physically incorporated into a final product is a tax on a product that can be adjusted at the border under WTO law, and that a carbon tax or any other similar tax on the amount of carbon consumed or emitted in making a product is an indirect tax on a product that is eligible for a border tax adjustment. A decision to adopt such a formal legal interpretation can be taken by a three-fourths majority of WTO members.[85] To date, WTO members have never used their exclusive authority under the WTO treaty to adopt a legal interpretation of the trade rules. The need to address climate change should compel them to use it now. To further carbon pricing, new rules for the new world should include these overdue clarifications of this long-existing rule.

THE CASE FOR A WTO CLIMATE WAIVER

Of course, not all national climate measures will be carbon taxes. In many countries, instead of carbon taxes, other kinds of border measures will be used in attempts to ensure that national climate action does not undermine national competitiveness. Indeed, climate action and competitiveness will in many places be linked in legislation; for the inclusion of these other types of border adjustments will be an unavoidable political requirement for undertaking ambitious domestic climate action. Under WTO rules, national measures are not eligible for environmental exceptions unless they are necessary to protect human, animal, or plant life or health, or relate to the conservation of exhaustible natural resources.[86] To help further the effectiveness of ambitious climate action, the WTO must find a way to accommodate border measures that are mixed measures – measures that are taken for economic as well as climate reasons. The risks to the rules–based WTO trading system from international trade disputes inspired by carbon border adjustment and other climate-related trade restrictions as a part of national climate actions cannot be eliminated without a unique trade solution.[87]

Many other concerns of the world – including many noble global aspirations that are set out in the United Nations Sustainable Development Goals – are prominent and pressing and deserving of much more significant worldwide attention.[88] As with anthropogenic (man-made) climate change, there are other human encroachments pushing up against and past the outer limits of the planetary boundaries of Earth's imperiled ecosystems. But climate change is unique as a matter of public policy in the experience thus far of the world. In a singular surge of nature in response to humanity's reckless ways, climate change threatens the fate of human civilization and the future of the planet, and in a way that transcends all our artificial borders. It threatens, too, our collective ability to address all our other global environmental, economic, and social concerns. Therefore, the right trade constraints on national carbon adjustment measures will be those that address climate change *uniquely*.

It may be objected by some trade purists that making an accommodation in the trade rules for trade-restrictive climate measures would be tantamount to managing international trade. It would not be. This objection does not consider the grave global stakes that are involved. Nor does it allow for the fact that trade is, in dangerous effect, being managed now by omission where there is no price on the use of carbon. Market decisions about energy use globally have long been distorted because the climate costs and the other environmental costs of fossil fuel use have been excluded from the calculation of the market prices of products. Despite all the recent advances in renewable energy, fossil fuels are still the source of more than 80 percent of all the world's energy.[89] Creating a unique trade solution for climate measures will not be managing trade; it will be freeing trade from destructive indirect management by not pricing carbon.

For trade can only occur in a civilization that is not overwhelmed by climate change and other ecological catastrophes. Free trade is not sustainable over time if it does not reflect the true economic realities of the world in which trade takes place. Economic realities are framed within the boundaries of environmental realities. In the twenty-first century, those realities include the harmful costs of our continued reliance on fossil fuels for the energy that drives our economy. Adding shape and flexibility in the trade rules to accommodate ambitious lifesaving and planet-saving climate actions through carbon taxes and other border carbon adjustments is not managing trade. Rather, it is aligning trade to account for the realities of climate change and for the necessities of what we must do to confront it, preferably through market-based solutions that put a price on the emission of carbon from the use of fossil fuels.

The challenge in crafting this accommodation of trade to the realities of climate change is to do it in a way that does the most for climate action while risking the least to the integrity and the continued success of the rules-based trading system. If this reshaping of the WTO trade rules to address climate change is done wrongly – or if it is not done at all – the multilateral trading system will eventually bend and bow to the worldwide impacts of grim climate realities that no one will any longer be able to deny. But, if this task is done rightly, and soon, trade will become an affirmative part of combating climate change, and much will be accomplished toward ending the existential crisis of the WTO.

WTO members have their choice of several options under the trade rules. One option is simply to await the outcome of future WTO dispute settlement. In due course, a collision will occur in a WTO trade dispute between a trade restriction applied by one WTO member as part of a purported national climate measure, and a claim by another WTO member that the trade restriction is inconsistent with obligations under the WTO Agreement. Upsides from such a collision between our goals for trade and our goals for addressing climate change are conceivable. Trade jurists for the WTO could well reach a decision that would draw a soothing legal line between the dictates of trade rules and the demands of climate change that would be widely seen as being right and just.

But the potential downsides of such a collision in WTO dispute settlement are more. Even if the right decision were reached, the outcome of future dispute settlement based on the current state of WTO rules would take at least two years to produce, and likely longer. Also, however optimistic we may be about the prospects of a right result, the outcome of such a trade dispute is utterly unpredictable. Moreover, the acrimony that would surely be sparked by such a trade dispute both before and after any ruling would likely be damaging to both the trade and climate regimes. And, in any event, any such ruling, even if it produced a positive solution, would be limited legally only to the facts relating to the measure examined in that one dispute. It would probably be followed by other WTO jurists in subsequent disputes, but it would not be a rule of general application. Altogether, simply waiting and relying on the outcome of future WTO dispute settlement is considerably less than ideal.

Another option is the adoption by WTO members of a formal legal interpretation akin to the one that should be adopted on border tax adjustments for carbon taxes.[90] In some limited instances, a legal interpretation of an existing rule would suffice. But for most border measures other than border taxes, there are no WTO provisions comparable to that dealing with border tax adjustments that could be as readily clarified by a legal interpretation to help further climate action through national measures that include non-tax border carbon adjustments. In contrast to the logical legal ease of reading border tax adjustments to include carbon taxes, a reliance on a series of legal interpretations that would shoehorn other kinds of border measures into other existing rules could lead to tortured readings of those rules. Instead, amendments in those rules would likely be needed.

Thus, still another option is to amend the existing rules.[91] However, the long frustration of the members of the WTO in trying to assemble the consensus needed to conclude the Doha round strongly suggests that the obstacles at this time to summoning the requisite support for amendments to the existing rules to respond to the urgent necessity of assisting in enabling global action to address climate change, would be insurmountable. Over the course of nearly two decades, the members of the WTO failed to reach a consensus on issues they had all agreed to place on the WTO negotiating agenda. How much longer would it take for them to agree on amending the existing WTO rules to address the "trade and climate change" issues that are not yet on the negotiating agenda? Such an agreement might be structured to require the support of less than a consensus of WTO members, but, even then, reaching it could take many years.

Yet another option, and the best by far, would be to adopt a WTO climate waiver.[92] Because a climate waiver will not change the rules but will only apply them differently in certain carefully defined and limited circumstances to certain specific kinds of measures, a climate waiver is the option available to WTO members that can do the most to help confront climate change while posing the least risk to the rule-based multilateral trading system.[93] The unquestioned legal authority they share under the WTO treaty to adopt waivers is familiar through repeated use to the members of the WTO, and thus more fit for the purpose of beginning to address climate change within the multilateral trading system. The adoption of a climate waiver would build on a long-standing WTO practice under the existing trade rules.

Under the WTO treaty, a waiver of the trade rules can be adopted when there are "exceptional circumstances." Without doubt, the global emergency of climate change is an exceptional circumstance. Most waivers granted in the past have been individual waivers granted to one country, but trade rules also authorize collective waivers to groups of WTO members or to all WTO members. A collective waiver of certain carefully defined WTO obligations for climate measures taken by all WTO members should be approved, ideally, by a consensus of WTO members. If no consensus can be reached at the outset, then a waiver can and should be approved by three-fourths of the members. To adopt a WTO climate waiver, the following must happen: WTO members must, first of all, be persuaded that a multilateral effort to frame a WTO climate waiver is far better for the multilateral trading system than waiting for the approaching legal collision between trade and climate change that will add to all that is already threatening the survival and continued success of the system. Next, the separate silos of trade and climate must bring together negotiators on both topics to discuss the nexus between the two. Then the topic of the relationship between trade and climate change must be put on the WTO negotiating agenda. A group of WTO members must then request a collective waiver of the Multilateral Trade Agreements due to the "exceptional circumstances" created by climate change. Next, a WTO working party must be tasked with framing and proposing such a WTO climate waiver; a draft waiver decision must be prepared by the working party; and the waiver decision must be adopted by the members of the WTO.

To succeed on a scale that will fulfill the higher ambitions urgently needed in climate actions, carbon markets must be linked, nationally and internationally. Linking carbon markets creates more opportunities for more emitters to cut their emissions, which in turn makes emissions cuts more cost-effective and, thus, more extensive. Therefore, in addition to supporting national climate measures, a climate waiver should also encourage carbon pricing by permitting the international linking of carbon markets and the successful operation of "climate clubs" of willing countries that wish to come together to do more to forestall climate change by cutting their emissions beyond the extent of their current commitments under the Paris Agreement. Climate clubs could start with ad hoc alliances of those that wish to adopt a common set of rules cutting across legal jurisdictions that would make deeper emissions cuts in exchange for mutual commercial, technological, and other concessions. What is learned from the practical experience of such climate clubs could then be scaled up and linked up over time, eventually culminating in a global consensus.[94]

A club is only a club if the members enjoy benefits that are not enjoyed by those who are not members of the club. Thus, a climate club would necessarily result in discrimination, likely including discrimination in trade. To prevent the enjoyment of the benefits of being in the climate club by those who have not made the additional climate commitments required for membership in the club, there will need to be penalties. Whether in the form of tariffs, or in some other form, the use of restrictions on trade as penalties is widely seen as indispensable to the success of climate clubs in advancing carbon pricing.[95] As it stands, in their nexus with trade, these creative but discriminatory arrangements aimed at furthering carbon pricing to curb climate change are more than likely inconsistent with the rules of the WTO. The prospect of these inconsistencies must be eliminated by a WTO climate waiver. This kind of trade discrimination must be permitted if trade rules are not to impede progress toward combating climate change.

A WTO climate waiver would be considerably more extensive and would have more far-ranging implications than any previous collective waiver, but such a waiver is warranted in these circumstances where trade action is needed to help secure the success of climate action. Under WTO rules, a waiver would, at the outset, be temporary. But it could later be made permanent. The WTO waiver in 2003 of some WTO intellectual property rules to permit compulsory licensing of certain HIV-AIDS drugs, needed to ensure public health, stated that it would remain in effect until the date when an amendment to the IP rules replacing the provisions of that waiver took effect. This happened with respect to two-thirds of WTO members in January 2017.[96] At the same time, because a waiver would not change WTO rules but would only apply them differently in carefully defined and limited circumstances to certain kinds of measures that relate to climate actions, it would pose less risk to the trading system than amending the current trade rules.

A WTO climate waiver would, for example, avoid the slippery slope of altering the trade rules by declaring that products that are produced by emitting more carbon and those that emit less or no carbon emissions are not "like products." The "most-favored-nation" and national treatment rules of nondiscrimination that are the foundation of the multilateral trading system are legal obligations, not to individual traders, but rather to traded products. These obligations against nondiscrimination between and among traded products can work only if we have some way of identifying which particular products are to be compared when determining whether these obligations are being fulfilled. For this reason, the trade rules have long stated that the comparison must be made between "like products." The concept of the "likeness" of products is at the core of the WTO trading system.

There is no definition of "like" products in the WTO Agreement. Indeed, the jurisprudence indicates that "likeness" means different things in different places in the WTO Agreement. The Appellate Body has famously compared the concept of "likeness" in trade to an "accordion" that "squeezes and stretches" from rule to rule and from agreement to agreement, depending on the intent of WTO members as expressed in each rule and agreement.[97] The traditional GATT and current WTO criteria for identifying whether traded products are "like" or not are: (1) the properties, nature, and quality of the products; (2) the end-uses of the products; (3) consumers' tastes and habits in respect of the products; and (4) tariff classification of the products.[98] These four criteria for determining "likeness" do not specifically take into account *how* products are made; that is, they do not account for the "process and production methods" (the PPMs) of traded products.

The endless permutations of process and production methods in the context of trade law will not be repeated here. Entire books have been written on this one topic.[99] It is sufficient here to explain that PPMs are of two kinds, product related and non-product-related. Product-related PPMs leave physical traces in the end product. Non-product-related PPMs leave no physical traces in the end product. Carbon taxes and other carbon adjustment measures focus on how products are made. They treat products differently based on the amount of carbon and other greenhouse gases emitted during their production. These emissions leave no physical traces in the end product. Such measures are therefore non-product-related PPMs. How WTO judges view non-product-related PPMs in clarifying WTO obligations would thus be pivotal to the outcome of any legal collision between trade and climate change in WTO dispute settlement.

Generally, in WTO dispute settlement, the fact that two products have different PPMs has not kept them from being treated as like products. To be sure, the Appellate Body, in the *EC – Asbestos* dispute, may have cracked open the legal door to distinctions made on the basis of consumers' tastes and habits. Consumers' tastes and habits vary in different places and cultures, and the WTO jurists observed in that dispute that "evidence about the extent to which products can serve the same end-uses, and the extent to which consumers are – or would be – willing to choose one product instead of another to perform those end-uses, is highly relevant in assessing the 'likeness' of those products."[100]

Reinforcing this possibility, the Appellate Body observed in passing in the *Canada – Feed-in Tariffs* dispute that, "What constitutes a competitive relationship between products may require consideration of inputs and processes of production used to produce the product."[101] Therefore, conceivably, if it can be proven to the satisfaction of a WTO panel on the basis of the facts found in a particular dispute that local consumers draw a distinction in their market purchases based on a PPM and that, therefore, the products being compared are not in a competitive relationship, then those products might not be deemed to be "like."

Instead of relying on the legal difficulties of trying to prove such a possible local distinction in consumer preferences, the temptation for climate advocates is simply to assert that products produced with low carbon emissions and products produced with high carbon emissions are *not* "like" products. If this assertion is legally correct, then WTO rules limiting tax amounts and prohibiting trade discrimination do not apply because those rules apply only to "like" products. A WTO ruling to this effect would thus provide a legal permission slip for carbon taxes and other kinds of carbon adjustment measures that restrict or otherwise affect trade.

But such a ruling could also lead to increased trade duties and additional trade discriminations extending far beyond the nexus of trade and climate change. The understandable apprehension of trade advocates is that declaring products to be "unlike" because of their process and production methods – especially when the PPMs are non-product-related – could unleash such a vast cornucopia of ostensibly legitimate trade discrimination that it would undermine the basic principles of nondiscrimination and mutually binding trade concessions that are the core of the WTO–based world trading system. There would be no end to the number and the variety of international disputes emerging from Pandora's trade box.

This fear dates back at least to 1952, when an early GATT panel ruled against a Belgian law that imposed a charge on foreign goods when they came from a country with a system of family allowances that did not live up to Belgian standards.[102] If WTO judges declared that trade products are not like because of the different amounts of carbon emissions released when making them, then where would the discrimination stop? What other environmental, economic, or societal considerations would be permitted for making such distinctions in determinations of "likeness"? Because a WTO climate waiver would deal with the challenge of climate change uniquely and would not change the existing trade rules, it would not directly raise such difficult legal questions; hence the advantage of a WTO climate waiver as a temporary solution that does not change the basic trade rules.

But, of course, the climate crisis is not temporary. Climate change will surely continue for years to come, no matter how successful we are now in mitigating it. Consequently, with the passing of time, and with the incrementally acquired knowledge of experience, WTO members would be likely to decide to make aspects of a WTO climate waiver permanent through agreed changes in the trade rules. In employing the option of a waiver initially on a temporary basis to prevent conflicts between trade rules and national attempts to combat climate change, WTO members would give themselves the opportunity to experiment country by country with new and better ways to confront climate change while also continuing to increase the global gains from trade. With a WTO climate waiver, there is no need to choose trade over climate or climate over trade. Trade goals and climate goals can both be met while furthering the overall global progress of sustainable development.

Such collective waivers have been granted twice before, both in 2003. The first was the "TRIPS Waiver" of certain pharmaceutical intellectual property rights during the HIV/AIDS crisis, which permits poorer countries that do not have the capacity to make pharmaceutical products – and thus cannot benefit from compulsory licensing – to import cheaper generic drugs from countries where those drugs are patented.[103] The second was the "Kimberley Waiver," which clarified that trade actions taken against nonparticipant WTO members to help suppress trade in "conflict" or "blood" diamonds under the Kimberley Process Certification Scheme for Rough Diamonds are justified under the trade rules.[104] Adoption of a collective WTO climate waiver now is equally appropriate. Indeed, as with those two important previous waivers, it is, in these circumstances of climate peril, a matter of global urgency.

THE CONTENT OF A WTO CLIMATE WAIVER

A WTO climate waiver must, at the outset, state the "exceptional circumstances" of the global climate change emergency that justifies a collective waiver of WTO rules. Of course, the "exceptional circumstances" are those presented by the unique global challenge of climate change that creates the unique necessity for realigning trade rules to help confront that challenge. A waiver must also state the specific trade obligations that are to be waived for the application of specific national climate measures. A waiver must specify, too, the date on which the waiver will terminate, which will be the date on which an amendment is adopted by two-thirds of WTO members replacing the provisions of the climate waiver with new and revised rules.[105]

A WTO climate waiver should also state that nothing in the waiver should be construed in WTO dispute settlement as suggesting that all climate-related trade restrictions in national measures would necessarily be inconsistent with WTO rules in the absence of a waiver. A legitimate substantive concern about a WTO climate waiver is that the adoption of such a waiver, if not properly presented, could signal that trade-related climate measures are all illegal in the absence of a waiver, and that this could "narrow down existing flexibility under WTO law."[106] This possible concern should be eliminated in the content of the climate waiver, which should state that nothing in the waiver should be construed in WTO dispute settlement as suggesting that a climate waiver is needed because, without one, all climate-related trade restrictions will necessarily be inconsistent with WTO rules. It should be emphasized, in particular, in the content of the climate waiver that the environmental and other exceptions in the trade rules remain in full force and are available to justify climate actions affecting trade.

A waiver should state also that the adoption of a waiver is not a signal that existing WTO rules cannot already be used to support national climate actions. They can be. Furthermore, a waiver should state that nothing in it should be construed to support disguised trade protection, and that national measures must continue to comply with GATT Article XX and with Article 3.5 of the UNFCCC, which provide, in virtually identical language, that, to be eligible for an exception to what would otherwise be treaty obligations, national measures must not be applied in a manner that would constitute a means of arbitrary or unjustifiable discrimination or a disguised restriction on international trade.[107]

To further carbon pricing and to facilitate the necessary transition to a decarbonized global economy, the core of the content of a WTO climate waiver should be a waiver from the application of WTO rules for trade-restrictive national measures that:

- Discriminate based on the amount of carbon and other greenhouse gases consumed or emitted in making a product;
- Fit the definition of a climate response measure as defined by the climate COP; and
- Do not discriminate in a manner that constitutes a means of arbitrary or unjustifiable discrimination or a disguised restriction on international trade.

A significant result of the adoption of such a waiver would be that national measures with mixed climate and competitiveness motives could be enacted and applied without running afoul of WTO rules. Under the rules, any hint of a protectionist purpose in the architecture of a national measure that restricts trade risks rendering that measure ineligible for the "free pass" of an environmental or other general exception to the application of the rules. Because of the unique urgency of addressing climate change, the rules must be waived for certain agreed measures that restrict trade while taking climate action.

Importantly, the mere fact that one motivation of a trade restriction in a national measure to combat climate change is to protect the domestic and international competitiveness of domestic products should not alone prevent that measure from being eligible for the climate waiver by fitting within the definition of a climate response measure. Putting this another way, national measures that address climate change but also are structured so as to preserve the competitiveness of domestic products should not automatically be excluded from the definition of a climate response measure and thus from the scope of a WTO climate waiver, if they truly address climate change. Certain kinds of discriminatory trade effects should be allowed in what is genuinely a climate adaptation or mitigation measure without disqualifying it from the climate waiver. However, trade discrimination should not be permitted within the definition of a climate response measure if the discrimination is arbitrary or unjustifiable, whether the measure takes climate action or not. In addition, a trade restriction should not fall within the definition of a climate response measure if the restriction is purely a pretext for protectionism, cloaked in a climate disguise and with only the pretense of a climate motive.

To illustrate, a climate measure that imposed a restriction on imported products from one country because of their carbon content but did not impose that same restriction on like imported products with the same carbon content from other countries, would not be eligible for the climate waiver. This would be arbitrary and unjustifiable discrimination. Likewise, a measure that imposed a trade restriction purportedly because of the carbon content of imported products but actually because of a purely protectionist intent, as reflected in the structure of the restrictive measure itself, would likewise be ineligible for the climate waiver. This would be a disguised restriction on trade. As with all disputes under WTO agreements, judgments about the eligibility of specific measures for the climate waiver, when questions arise, would be made on a case-by-case basis.

As Carolyn Deere Birkbeck, Harro van Asselt, and others have suggested, having a common understanding of what is legally permissible in carbon border adjustment mechanisms will hasten ambitious climate action while avoiding international trade disputes.[108] Such an understanding can be provided by a common definition of what is permissible in a WTO climate waiver. With such a waiver in place, any "chilling effect" from the looming presence of WTO constraints on climate measures that also address competitiveness concerns would be lifted, but WTO members would also know the limits to which they could go in such measures in responding to competitiveness concerns. In this way, climate action could be maximized while minimizing trade harm.

WHAT IS A CLIMATE RESPONSE MEASURE?

One obstacle to the effectiveness of such a WTO climate waiver would be the continuing lack of commonly agreed metrics for measuring the amount of carbon or other greenhouse gases consumed or emitted in making a product. At COP25 in Madrid in 2019, there was no resolution, or even progress, in ongoing negotiations to establish common metrics. One source of controversy in these negotiations is about how non-CO_2 emissions such as methane and nitrous oxide are to be uniformly converted into CO_2 equivalents and then reported. The precise way that methane emissions are reported is especially important to agricultural countries, where cattle raising results in emissions of methane. There is also debate over how best to calculate the methane emissions from fossil fuel production. There is a lack of consensus, too, on which among several metrics for measuring overall GHG emissions that have been used by the IPCC should be employed by the COP going forward for the purposes of national climate reports and national climate pledges. For a WTO climate waiver to be workable, the COP must adopt common metrics for measuring greenhouse gas emissions, and these metrics must be used by the WTO for purposes of a climate waiver.

Another obstacle to the adoption of such a WTO climate waiver is the absence of a definition of a climate response measure by the climate COP.[109] Climate rules speak of "response measures," but those rules do not define them.[110] In the climate regime, the discussion of climate "response measures" has generally been limited to the narrow context of the adverse extraterritorial effects of domestic climate policies adopted by developed countries. Although this discussion has continued for many years, it has not yet led to any agreed resolution. The topic of trade has often been a part of this climate discussion; but there has long been a hesitancy among climate negotiators to grapple more broadly with the international legal implications of the connections between national responses to climate change and trade, and especially trade law. Speaking at COP24 in Katowice, Poland, in 2018, UNCTAD senior economic officer Alexey Vikhlyaev summed up this challenge succinctly: "Both trade and climate are central to the 2030 Agenda of the United Nations. But trade has become a taboo subject when talking about climate change. This should not be the case."[111]

Nor can it remain the case much longer. For "[t]he inter-linkages between response measures and the WTO will become more pronounced as parties implement their ... post-2020 nationally determined contributions" under the Paris climate agreement.[112] As this occurs, "Trade disputes are more likely in a world of uncoordinated and conflicting national responses to climate challenges."[113] Foreseeing the coming collision between the international trade and climate change regimes, climate scientists on the Intergovernmental Panel on Climate Change, in their Fifth Assessment Report in 2014, called for "preemptive cooperation" between the trade and climate regimes, noting that "there are numerous and diverse explored opportunities for greater international cooperation in trade-climate interactions. While mutually destructive conflicts between the two systems have thus far been largely avoided, preemptive cooperation could protect against such developments in the future."[114]

Without a definition of a climate response measure, there can be no legal certainty about which national measures can potentially be justified as climate actions. This legal uncertainty may well have a "chilling effect" on the taking of national climate actions. It will surely also contribute to the collision of trade and climate change in contentious international litigation in the WTO. If the COP climate negotiators do not soon provide a definition of a climate response measure, then, for the 164 parties to the COP that are also WTO members, the task of defining which national climate measures are permissible and which are not when those measures restrict trade, will be left to the legal reasoning of trade jurists in WTO dispute settlement. To prevent this from happening, the climate negotiators must break the trade taboo in the climate talks and define what specific kinds of trade restrictions can be justified in national responses to the urgent necessity for climate adaptation and mitigation. Once they have done so, the COP definition of a climate response measure should then be adopted as part of a WTO climate waiver.

The task of defining a "response measure" in ongoing climate negotiations will necessarily require the drawing of a legal line that will include some measures but not others within the definition. The location of this line will be determined by the outcome of a debate between developed and developing countries. Unavoidably, this debate will be driven on both sides by competitiveness concerns as much as by climate concerns. A consensus will be reached on the definition of a "response measure" only if the competitiveness concerns of both sides are sufficiently addressed. In achieving this consensus, a line "in between" must be identified and drawn that will allow the most to be done to mitigate climate change, while doing the least to hinder the continuing endeavour to liberalize trade that is essential to fulfilling the hopes of all those in the world in search of sustainable global prosperity.

As the increasingly ominous reports of the world's climate scientists have underscored, vastly more ambitious climate actions are urgently needed than those that parties to the climate COP have already pledged to take. Current signs of sufficient climate ambition to accomplish the aims of the Paris climate agreement are less than encouraging, especially as countries continue to struggle with the economic impacts of the pandemic. Because of their understandable apprehension about how "green protectionism" could affect their trade and their overall economies, many developing countries may be of the view that the definition of a "response measure" should be limited to measures taken in fulfilment of countries' current voluntary climate pledges – their "nationally determined contributions" under the Paris Agreement. The existing NDCs are, however, supposed to be merely the beginning of what must become much more ambitious national commitments of climate action. To help provide the needed support for more ambitious climate actions, and to prevent thwarting such actions, the national measures included within the definition of a "response measure" should *not* be limited only to those measures relating to current national climate pledges.

In defining a "response measure," most developed countries are likely to seek a broad scope for acceptable measures while most developing countries are likely to seek a narrow scope. Thus, most developed countries will likely prefer a non-exhaustive and open-ended list of permitted measures, while most developing countries will likely prefer an exhaustive and closed list. To do the most to counter climate change, a list of the kinds of measures falling within the definition of a "response measure" must not be exhaustive; it must not be closed. Having a closed list will not account for the fact that the future cannot be foreseen. National measures not yet envisaged may prove in the end to be the most effective kinds of response measures to climate change. A closed list will inhibit legislative and regulatory innovation. It will perpetuate the "chilling effect" that already exists due to legal uncertainty. A model for a non-exhaustive list of climate response measures is the illustrative list of export subsidies in WTO rules.[115]

There should not be one definition of a climate response measure for measures taken by developed countries and another definition for measures taken by developing countries. It is certainly the case that almost all the focus of the climate regime so far has been on the impact on developing countries of response measures taken by developed countries. It is also reasonable to anticipate that, in the near term, most of the response measures containing trade restrictions will be applied by developed countries to imports from developing countries. But the shape of the world is changing for both trade and climate change.

Increasingly, developing countries are not interested only in ensuring access for their products to the markets of developed countries; more and more, they are interested also in maintaining domestic markets for their domestic production in the face of growing competition from the products *of other developing countries.* Some of these other developing countries will have lower climate ambitions and thus their traded products may have lower prices, and therefore a competitive advantage in the marketplace. For these reasons, one of the changes we will see sooner or later in the realms of both trade and climate change, is some developing countries imposing trade restrictions on imports from other developing countries as a feature of their climate response measures. Increasingly, too, developed countries may be imposing trade restrictions on imports from other developed countries as part of climate response measures, as may well happen with the carbon border adjustment mechanism of the European Union or with a similar measure imposed by the United States.

Developing countries rightly fear the temptation in developed countries to engage in "green protectionism" by restricting competing imports from developing countries for purely protectionist reasons while claiming climate change as a pretext. A carefully crafted WTO climate waiver should minimize this likelihood. At the same time, at least initially, the burden of trade restrictions in climate response measures is likely to fall most heavily on the trade of those developing countries that have not yet adopted ambitious climate measures. In exchange for their agreement to a definition of a climate response measure that includes measures that will restrict their trade, developing countries should be offered increased and accelerated climate finance; more and faster transfer of new green technologies; and greatly enhanced financial and technical support for capacity building for mitigating and adapting to climate change. Developed countries should also offer developing countries additional concessions in textiles, agriculture, and other trade sectors that will enable them to maximize their gains from their comparative advantages in those sectors in the global marketplace.

Predictably, it will be argued that the adoption of a WTO climate waiver is not politically possible at this time. Without doubt, this is true. But climate change is accelerating. Despite repeated ritual rounds of earnest promises, international efforts to confront climate change largely are not. The need for a WTO climate waiver to help facilitate carbon pricing is growing more urgent with each passing day. Nothing is politically possible if it is not first politically pursued. WTO reforms to help counter climate change while continuing to help increase world trade will begin to become possible only when we take the first step by advocating them. The time for that first step is now. And this first step should be one of many. The first step toward a WTO climate waiver should be one of numerous steps taken by the WTO to establish and solidify trade links to all the dimensions of sustainable development.

TRADE AND TRANSPORT

Climate-damaging greenhouse gas emissions result not only from the process of producing the manufactured and agricultural goods that are traded internationally. Emissions also result from the international transport of those traded goods. Therefore, more international trade means more use of international transportation as goods travel from the country where they are produced to the country where they are consumed, often with further GHG-emitting intermediate stops for adding value along the way. Adding to these emissions is the augmented use of international transport occasioned by the rise of global value chains due to the fragmentation of production.

Given these emissions, many climate campaigners contend that "products should be sourced as much as possible locally and that labels of food products should include information on the origin of the product."[116] In agricultural trade, a widely endorsed concept among advocates of trade localism is "food miles," which "involves the calculation of CO_2 emissions associated with the transport of food over long distances to arrive at the final consumer."[117] Although intuitively appealing, the concept of "food miles" as a measure of climate-friendly trade is not supported by empirical evidence. Nor is the same sort of metric justified as a gauge for green action for manufacturing trade.

Overall, international transport in trade *lowers* greenhouse gas emissions. Like the concept of comparative advantage, this statement is counterintuitive. But, again like comparative advantage, the fact that it is contrary to what we might expect to be true before empirical examination, does not keep it from being true. Although the real "carbon footprint" of domestic goods versus imported goods is complex, involving many factors (such as the means of transport, the distance, the product life cycle, and the production methods), studies of the "carbon mileage" of traded goods have shown that the effect can be the opposite of what is commonly believed.[118] To cite just one of numerous possible examples, cut roses grown in faraway Kenya and flown to the United Kingdom create fewer emissions than roses shipped to the United Kingdom from the nearby Netherlands.[119]

As economist Rikard Forslid of Stockholm University has shown, transportation of traded products may actually decrease emissions if production is "dirtier" than transportation; and furthermore "the gains from cleaner production can outweigh even very dirty transportation."[120] One study has found that a quarter of all trade flows – 31 percent of global trade by value – lead to reduced emissions compared with the autarky of refraining from trade.[121] Another has concluded that "the benefits of international trade exceed trade's environmental costs due to CO_2 emissions by two orders of magnitude."[122] Still another environmental study by Forslid has demonstrated that "trade and transportation may actually decrease emissions even when there are no gains from cleaner production."[123]

Thus, all in all, and contrary to what is widely assumed, "Trade can lead to less global emissions in spite of the pollution from transportation."[124] As Forslid explains, "The reason is that transportation uses primary production factors, and transportation will therefore crowd out some production in equilibrium. If production is dirtier – in a well-defined sense – than transportation, then global emissions will fall as a result of trade and transportation."[125] Counterintuitive indeed.

All this said, greenhouse gas emissions from trade transport must be reduced, and significantly. Shipping and aviation have been shunted to the side during the past three decades of United Nations climate negotiations. The COP has looked to two specialized agencies of the UN for climate action – for shipping, the International Maritime Organization (the IMO), and for aviation, the International Civil Aviation Organization (the ICAO). Despite years of promises and negotiations, not until recently have either of these two international organizations done much to try to cut greenhouse gas emissions. Now they are doing more – but not nearly enough.

The IMO estimates that 90 percent of global merchandise trade by volume is transported by sea.[126] Emissions from shipping in the six-year period to 2018 (the most recent numbers available) accounted for 2.9 percent of the world's overall carbon emissions.[127] These emissions have been rising due to increased maritime trade. Confronted by climate change and by increasing pressures to address it, the IMO has promised to reduce overall greenhouse gas emissions from ships by 50 percent from 2008 levels by 2050.[128] Toward this end, in November 2020, the 174 member countries of the IMO approved new rules to reduce the carbon intensity of commercial ships. These measures add to already agreed energy efficiency regulations for new vessels. Together, these reforms are intended to reduce the carbon intensity of international shipping by 40 percent by 2030 compared with 2008 levels. To achieve these goals, major investments will be required to modernize maritime fleets and the technology they use. Ships will need to combine new technical and operational approaches to reduce their carbon intensity – the amount of carbon emitted per each unit of energy consumed.

These will be the latest revisions to the International Convention for the Prevention of Pollution from Ships, commonly known as "MARPOL."[129] These new rules were adopted by the Marine Environment Protection Committee in July 2021, and will enter into force on January 1, 2023. Belatedly, the IMO has enlisted in the fight against climate change.

While helpful, these new IMO rules are not enough to do all that must be done to cut emissions from international shipping. For this reason, green groups have opposed them, saying they risk not achieving the climate goals of the Paris Agreement and will allow the shipping sector's share of emissions to keep rising over the next decade and at a time when it should be declining. They point out that reducing the carbon intensity of energy use in shipping will not necessarily result in an actual reduction in shipping emissions. Instead, they explain, the overall amount of carbon emitted could still increase, even while ships became more efficient.[130]

If no action is taken, the IMO itself has projected that shipping emissions will rise by 50 percent by 2050.[131] Cutting carbon intensity alone will not be enough to accomplish the IMO's professed emissions-cutting goal. Additional changes in MARPOL rules must be made to require real emission cuts in addition to the new requirements for reductions in carbon intensity. To make certain these required cuts are made, retaliatory trade restrictions against countries that refuse to make them could be applied. Any such restrictions should be upheld by the WTO, so long as they do not result in arbitrary or unjustifiable discrimination or disguised restrictions on international trade. Still, far better, there should be affirmative multilateral agreement to do all that must be done without further delay to make international shipping compliant with global climate goals.

Like shipping emissions, aviation emissions are an increasingly significant part of overall global greenhouse gas emissions. Before the COVID-19 pandemic, the ICAO predicted that emissions from air travel would triple by 2050.[132] International flights account for 65 percent of the aviation industry's CO_2 emissions and about 1.3 percent of global CO_2 emissions.[133] Most public attention on the emissions costs of international travel since the arrival of COVID-19 has focused on the merits of resuming previous levels of international passenger travel in the new pandemic world. But traded goods are also shipped by air. Air cargo comprises only 1 percent of world trade by volume, but it constitutes 35 percent of world trade by value.[134] Between 1980 and 2020, the average annual global growth in air cargo was 5.3 percent.[135] Air travel and air cargo, of course, both plunged following the onset of the pandemic. But they both can be expected to rise anew in the new pandemic world as vaccinations occur, better health measures are put in place, and the worst of the virus subsides.

Unlike the IMO, the ICAO has not committed to reduce absolute emissions. It has committed only to hold them at 2020 levels. It plans to accomplish this goal through its "Carbon Offsetting and Reduction Scheme for International Aviation," which is commonly called "CORSIA," and which took effect in January 2021. Agreed by 192 countries in 2016, CORSIA is a market-based mechanism designed to "offset" the anticipated rise in international aviation emissions by using lower-carbon fuels and by granting credits for certified emissions reductions in other sectors.[136] For example, in November 2020, ICAO agreed that airlines could use reductions in emissions from deforestation and degradation certified under REDD+, the leading international forest agreement, as eligible credits to offset their emissions under CORSIA.[137]

Like the revised MARPOL rules, CORSIA has been criticized by green groups as insufficient. There is legitimate concern about the quality of the offsets and the criteria that alternative lower carbon fuels must meet. More, there is disappointment that, unless it is extended, CORSIA will cover only 6 percent of projected CO_2 emissions from all international aviation between 2015 and 2050.[138] This is far from enough. Much more ambitious ICAO action is necessary to require not merely holding the current line on aviation emissions but pulling back that line by making real and deep emissions cuts. As with shipping emissions, retaliatory trade restrictions against countries that refuse to make these required cuts should be upheld by the WTO if they are not applied through arbitrary or unjustifiable discrimination or as a disguised restriction on international trade. But here, too, multilateral agreement is much preferred to make international aviation compliant with global climate goals, and also an affirmative agent for achieving global sustainable development.

7

Links to Sustainable Development

Climate change is the gravest threat ever faced by humanity. And putting a price on carbon is indispensable for combating climate change. Yet, according to economists at the World Bank, while "carbon pricing is necessary for an efficient transition toward decarbonization ... carbon pricing alone cannot solve the climate change problem, given the many market failures and behavioral biases that distort economies.[1] Thus, those same economists have contended, to fight climate change, "Policy makers also need to adopt measures such as targeted investment subsidies, performance standards and mandates, or communication campaigns that trigger the required changes in investment patterns, behaviors and technologies – and if carbon pricing is temporarily unavailable, to use those measures as a substitute."[2]

Combating climate change with whatever mix of measures may be needed is not only essential for saving the climate; it is a requirement for saving much else in the Earth's ecosphere, on which all life on the planet depends. More rapid and more ambitious global actions to cut global greenhouse gas emissions could prevent an impending "abrupt" collapse of some of the planet's ecosystems, which, at the current pace of their destruction, may occur within the next few decades – if action is not taken now to prevent it.[3] Scientists define an "abrupt exposure event" as "when more than 20% of all species in an ecosystem are exposed to temperatures beyond their natural range in a single decade."[4] Without significantly accelerated reductions in GHG emissions, tropical forests and tropical ocean ecosystems in particular could be exposed to "potentially catastrophic" temperature increases by 2030, with untold costs for the environment and humanity.[5]

Often overlooked in global discourse is the fact that human actions are not only warming the world; our actions are altering the contours and composition of the natural world in other ominous ways. Climate change is far from the only environmental threat facing our imperiled planet. Although addressing climate change is urgent and long overdue, if we focus *only* on addressing climate change, then the planet will not be saved from ecological destruction. Simultaneously, we must address all else happening on the planet that puts the normal workings of nature at grave and growing risk. For this reason, even amid the upheavals of the COVID-19 pandemic, there have been new "efforts to expand the focus of ... activism from a narrow debate around carbon emissions and fossil fuels towards a wider one around biodiversity and natural capital."[6]

This broader focus is much needed in ensuring global public health in the new pandemic world. Where the threat of new and potentially more dangerous zoonotic pandemics is concerned, the global health experts on the *Lancet* COVID-19 Commission have explained that, "To protect humanity from these zoonotic diseases ... [w]e require new precautions on many fronts: ending deforestation, respecting and protecting conservation areas and endangered species, intensifying the monitoring and surveillance of zoonotic events, and ensuring safe practices in the animal trade, meat production, and markets."[7] In other words, in public health as in all else, the emphasis in all we do must be on the objective of sustainable development. This includes all we may do in writing and rewriting the rules for trade in the pandemic world.

The first paragraph in the preamble on the first page of the Marrakesh Agreement of 1994 that established the World Trade Organization proclaims that "trade and economic endeavour should be conducted with a view to ... allowing for the *optimal use* of the world's resources in accordance with *the objective of sustainable development*, seeking both to protect and preserve the environment and to enhance the means for doing so."[8] This should be done in "in a manner consistent with" the "respective needs and concerns" of WTO members "at different levels of economic development."[9] The WTO Appellate Body has explained that this language in the preamble "gives colour, texture and shading to the rights and obligations of Members under the *WTO Agreement.*"[10]

Thus, the WTO has, from the beginning, been meant to be, not only a forum and a framework for lowering barriers to trade, but, more, an active agent for advancing trade while also achieving global sustainable development. In declaration after declaration, this commitment to sustainable development has consistently been acknowledged by the members of the WTO, beginning with the conclusion of the Uruguay round, and continuing throughout the long duration of the ill-fated Doha round. Unfortunately, to date, in their collective actions, WTO members have done little more than ritually acknowledge this commitment. They have not done much affirmatively to fulfill it.

There has been endless talk since the WTO was established in 1995 about one critical aspect of sustainable development, the inescapable nexus between trade and the environment. When the WTO was established, a WTO Committee on Trade and the Environment was formed and was instructed "to make appropriate recommendations on whether any modifications of the provisions of the multilateral trading system are required, compatible with the open, equitable and non-discriminatory nature of the system."[11] More than a quarter of a century later, we still await those recommendations. Despite long years of deliberations, this critical WTO committee has yet to make a single recommendation that has resulted in a single binding decision by the members of the WTO.[12]

It is long past time for WTO members to give genuine meaning to their commitment to "the objective of sustainable development."[13] Every single one of the 164 members of the WTO agreed to the United Nations Sustainable Development Goals for 2030. In reimagining the trade rules to combat climate change and to achieve the sixteen other SDGs by the end of this decade, their original commitment to protecting the environment and to all the other objectives of sustainable development must remain the objective of the members of the WTO. More important, this commitment must motivate and be made manifest in their actions in modernizing the WTO.

Some WTO members have always taken this commitment seriously. More are doing so now as the imperative of sustainable development becomes clearer throughout the world. Five small countries have taken the lead. In September 2019, Costa Rica, Fiji, Iceland, New Zealand, and Norway launched an initiative aimed at negotiating and establishing a WTO Agreement on Climate Change, Trade and Sustainability (ACCTS).[14] To begin, these five WTO members have centered their initiative on three core proposals: the removal of all tariffs on environmental goods and services; the establishment of concrete obligations to eliminate fossil fuel subsidies; and the development of voluntary guidelines for eco-labeling of traded products.[15] As Christopher Barnard of the market-minded British Conservation Alliance has expressed it, "[T]hese five countries hope to unleash a veritable market of environmentally beneficial goods and services, by tearing down barriers to their global free trade."[16]

These five countries are "punching above their weight" in international trade.[17] One advantage of the multilateral trading system is that smaller countries can have an outsize influence with the right mix of expertise and leadership, which all five of these countries have long enjoyed in the WTO. (The classic example is the vast influence long held by the late Julio Lacarte Muro, one of the founders of the GATT and the first chairman of the WTO Appellate Body – even though he came from the small country of Uruguay.)[18] These five countries have encouraged other WTO members to join in their negotiations on trade links with sustainable development. They have explained that they seek a "living agreement" that, in addition to the three topics with which they have started, will in time tackle more issues relating to the connections among, trade, climate change, and sustainability.

More recently, fifty-three WTO members have joined in what they describe as "structured discussions on trade and environmental sustainability."[19] At their first meeting in March 2021, they discussed a range of "trade and environment" issues: fossil fuel subsidy reform; reforming environmentally harmful subsidies; freeing trade in environmental goods and services; border carbon adjustments; plastics; biodiversity; a circular economy; and more.[20] As noted by the International Institute for Sustainable Development in Canada, "[Q]uestions remain as to what the agenda of the structured discussions will entail, whether this group will seek to launch formal negotiations on any agenda items, and what risk there may be in duplicating work already underway in the WTO bodies or elsewhere."[21]

Still, at long last, the WTO does seem to be truly engaged on the nexus between trade and the environment. Adding encouragement is the apparent attitude on this issue of the Biden administration in the United States. President Biden's trade ambassador, Katherine Tai, underlined the significance of the issue to the new president by choosing the relationship between trade and the environment as the topic for her first speech in her new cabinet role.[22] If the Biden administration does not conflate environmental protection with trade protectionism, and if it does not succumb to the specious notion that trade rules have been structured to undermine environmental protection, then it will be better able, along with other WTO members, to succeed in making trade rules more affirmative tools for increasing environmental protection.

Such success should begin by achieving a consensus among the members of the WTO to amend the content of the general exceptions in the trade rules to provide that national measures taken in compliance with an agreed list of multilateral environmental agreements would not constitute violations of those rules. As UNEP has explained, "Complementing national legislation and bilateral or regional agreements, multilateral environmental agreements form the overarching international legal basis for global efforts to address particular environmental issues. The role of multilateral environmental agreements in achieving sustainable development has long been recognized."[23] In 2012, the United Nations Conference on Sustainable Development in Rio de Janeiro, Brazil – "Rio + 20" – which set the stage for agreement on the SDGs – acknowledged "the significant contributions to sustainable development" made by the MEAs and urged countries to conclude more such agreements.[24] These contributions are less likely to happen if trade rules stand in the way.

Success by the WTO should also include greatly intensified efforts to wring the environmental risks out of global supply chains. Supply chains, as beneficial as they are, are nevertheless "a missing link for sustainability."[25] According to McKinsey & Company, "The typical consumer company's supply chain creates far greater social and environmental costs than its own operations, accounting for more than 80 percent of greenhouse-gas emissions and more than 90 percent of the impact on air, land, water, biodiversity, and geological resources."[26] In a belated awakening to this reality, and also in the face of mounting consumer pressures, many companies and industries throughout the world have begun to reduce these costs by reducing these risks in their supply chains. Increasingly, these private actions are being supplemented – and in some cases mandated – by public actions in the form of national measures. Where they are evenhanded, where they do not discriminate in an arbitrary or unjustifiable way, and where they are not a disguised restriction on international trade, these national measures should be allowed under WTO rules.

Success by the WTO might also borrow from the innovative chapters on environment and sustainable development in the Comprehensive Economic and Trade Agreement between Canada and the European Union – the CETA.[27] The CETA chapter on the environment protects each side's right to regulate on environmental matters; requires each side to enforce its own domestic environmental laws; prevents either side from relaxing its environmental laws to increase trade; promotes trade and investment in environmental goods and services; and encourages the conservation and sustainable management of forests and fisheries.[28] This chapter on trade and sustainable development aspires in part to "promote sustainable development through the enhanced coordination and integration of" the parties' "respective labour, environmental and trade policies and measures" while also improving "enforcement of their respective labour and environmental law and respect for labour and environmental international agreements."[29] These bilateral obligations could become multilateral through adoption by the WTO.

In addition, success by the WTO might build on some of the recent initiatives of the United Nations Conference on Trade and Development (UNCTAD), which has given increasing emphasis in recent years to the relationship between trade and the Sustainable Development Goals.[30] Because it has been, traditionally, a forum mainly for developing countries, the growing engagement of UNCTAD with these issues reflects the growing concern of developing countries about them.[31] UNCTAD has also stressed the necessity of narrowing the $2.5 trillion annual investment gap of developing countries in key sectors of sustainable development – a sum calculated *before* the plunge in foreign direct investment that accompanied the pandemic.[32] Moreover, UNCTAD has continued its decades of highlighting the trade discrimination that is often faced by developing countries, especially in areas such as agriculture and textiles where they have long been denied what should be the benefits of their comparative advantages in trade.

Revision and addition to the current WTO trade rules to do more to help accomplish global sustainable development must be founded in no small part on an awareness of these legitimate concerns of developing countries. It must, therefore, include and be accompanied by more aid for trade; more greening of aid for trade; more trade finance; and more forgiveness of developing countries' debt. As part of a green recovery, developing countries must be provided with aid to help encourage and support their trade in the most sustainable of their exports – such as, for instance, eco-tourism and the ocean-derived commerce of the "blue economy." The International Chamber of Commerce has urged action by the United Nations on the $1.6 trillion shortfall in trade finance – which burdens most heavily the small and medium-sized enterprises that represent about 95 percent of the world's companies and 60 percent of private sector jobs – including millions of companies and jobs in the developing countries.[33]

In May 2020, the IMF and the World Bank called on the wealthiest countries to suspend debt payments by the poorest seventy-six countries if they were asked to do so during the pandemic.[34] Assailed by both the novel coronavirus and climate change, the debt of developing countries exploded during the pandemic. In April 2021, the United Nations calculated that the economic collapse jeopardized nearly $600 billion in debt service payments by seventy-two low- and middle-income countries during the next five years.[35] Yet, despite numerous proposals and increasingly distraught pleas, the wealthier countries stopped short of taking definitive global actions on their own and through the international financial institutions to provide significant debt relief.[36] In the absence of financial relief, considerably less can be achieved for the developing countries through new trade rules.[37]

Success in supporting sustainable development through trade might come sooner if WTO members embrace the same "modular" structure that Chile, New Zealand, and Singapore have adopted in the DEPA – their Digital Economy Partnership Agreement – in which countries can pick and choose which commitments and which commitment levels they wish to accept at any given time. Similarly, WTO negotiators should draw from the innovative provisions relating to sustainability that already exist in regional and other bilateral and regional trade agreements outside the WTO. Lastly, the WTO negotiations should be informed at every turn by the seventeen Sustainable Development Goals and by the 169 targets for achieving those goals; for these goals and targets are based on an understanding of the hard reality of what is happening to us and all that surrounds us on a planet we have put increasingly at risk.

BIODIVERSITY ON OUR IMPERILED PLANET

Human civilization evolved during an era of climate and ecological stability. Now the survival of our civilization is challenged by climate and ecological instability. Much of that instability can be traced to ever-accumulating amounts of carbon dioxide and other greenhouse gases in the Earth's atmosphere. Much of it, too, can be attributed to the loss of biological diversity on the land surface of the planet and in the oceans that cover most of it. There is one overwhelming source of this planetary instability. It is humanity. As the Scottish anthropologist and essayist Esther Woolfson has written, "*Homo sapiens* is the most invasive species there has ever been."[38]

It is not that we humans are any worse than we have been in the past. It is simply that today we are capable of doing so much more damage than we have done in the past. Renowned environmental economist Sir Partha Dasgupta of Cambridge University, in a seminal account of the economics of biodiversity, has explained, "At their core, the problems we face today are no different from those our ancestors faced: how to find a balance between what we take from the biosphere and what we leave behind for our descendants. But while our distant ancestors were incapable of affecting the earth system as a whole, we are not only able to do that, we are doing it."[39] We have been aware for some time that one human hand is poised above the nuclear trigger, but only lately have we become aware that the other human hand hovers over a biological trigger that could also destroy human civilization.

Evidence of our guilt is all around us. Every year, WWF – formerly the World Wildlife Fund – releases a "Living Planet Report" on the current state of the natural world. WWF reported in 2020 that,

Since the industrial revolution, human activities have increasingly destroyed and degraded forests, grasslands, wetlands and other important ecosystems, threatening human well-being. Seventy-five percent of the Earth's ice-free land surface has already been significantly altered, most of the oceans are polluted, and more than 85% of the area of wetlands has been lost. This destruction of ecosystems has led to 1 million species (500,000 animals and plants and 500,000 insects) being threatened with extinction.[40]

In what has been identified as the sixth mass extinction in the geological history of the Earth, species are now becoming extinct at a rate about 1,000 times higher than before humans came to dominate the planet.[41] Unknowingly, species that have graced Creation for millions of years await their imminent demise. They each have their own sad story of a slow attrition toward oblivion. In one such story, on the grassy savannah of Kenya, the last two northern white rhinos on Earth grazed "in a strange existential twilight."[42] They were both female.

Perhaps most alarming of all the disquieting news in this annual report was that the numbers of mammals, birds, fish, amphibians, and reptiles collapsed by an average of 68 percent globally between 1970 and 2016 – more than two thirds in less than fifty years.[43] When the level of toxins in surface water skyrocketed because of climate change and killed more than 300 elephants in Botswana in late 2020, it was just one more in a long series of human-induced outrages against our fellow creatures.[44] And these are not the only denizens of Earth threatened by the acceleration of climate change and the prospect of ecological collapse. Scientists tell us that the number of insects in the world has declined by 25 percent since 1990.[45] Why should we care? Biologist Edward O. Wilson, the world's leading expert on ants, has said that, if humanity were to disappear, the Earth would "regenerate back to the rich state of equilibrium that existed 10,000 years ago," but "if insects were to vanish, the environment would collapse into chaos."[46]

The WWF findings echo those of a global assessment of biodiversity and ecosystem services by hundreds of experts in dozens of countries for the United

Nations in 2019, which concluded that "[t]he rate of global change in nature during the past 50 years is unprecedented in human history."[47] In those fifty years, "the human population has doubled, the global economy has grown nearly 4-fold, and global trade has grown 10-fold, together driving up the demands for energy and materials" and increasing and intensifying the human impact on the planet.[48] Since the early 1990s, our global stock of natural capital has declined by nearly 40 percent.[49] As lamented by the Global Environment Facility, an international organization serving 183 countries, "The human population, though representing only 0.01% of all living things by weight, has already caused the loss of 83%, by biomass, of all wild mammals and half of the biomass of all plants, along with severely reducing the genetic diversity that underpins all life."[50]

In 2020, as COVID-19 upended human life across the planet, the scientific advisers to the UN warned that, unless there are significant changes in how we humans treat the planet, COVID-19 will be followed by more lethal pandemics.[51] Instead of dealing with zoonotic pandemics only after they emerge, they recommended preventing such pandemics by addressing their root causes in the ever-expanding human encroachment on the environment.[52] In particular, they noted that vaccines and therapies for viruses often depend "on access to the diversity of organisms, molecules and genes found in nature."[53] They calculated that preventing pandemics would be 100 times cheaper than responding to them after they have already begun.[54]

According to these scientists, among the other human causes of this planetary ecological crisis, "The recent exponential rise in consumption and trade, driven by demand in developed countries and emerging economies, as well as by demographic pressure, has led to a series of emerging diseases that originate mainly in biodiverse developing countries, driven by global consumption patterns."[55] They advised that confronting this cause to prevent pandemics will require "transformative change to reduce the types of consumption, globalized agricultural expansion and trade that have led to pandemics (e.g. consumption of palm oil, exotic wood, products requiring mine extraction, transport infrastructures, meat and other products of globalized livestock production)."[56]

Nature is an end unto itself. The planet's biodiversity and its ecosystems have an intrinsic value separate and apart from their uses to humanity. Philosophers debate the exact sources of such value.[57] But all who recognize that nature is something more than merely an instrumental means to the material ends of humanity, agree that nature has a purpose beyond whatever purpose we may choose to attribute to it. They all acknowledge that, as the American environmental historian Donald Worster has expressed it, we humans must approach nature with "a measure of humility and restraint," and we must not see it as only "raw material for whatever man may imagine."[58]

Now, with the acceleration of anthropogenic climate change, and with the ominous threats of ecological collapse, "nature rebels."[59] Sir Robert Watson, the British chemist who led the assessment for the United Nations, insists, "[I]t is not too late to make a difference, but only if we start now at every level from local to global."[60] The key, he and other experts say, is linking international cooperation to local action.[61] Yet, even in the midst of nature's rebellion, many people throughout the world still ask: Why should we not use nature as we choose? Why, indeed, should we refrain from harming nature?[62] Is it because we humans have the right to a healthy ecosystem? Is it because there are rights that reside within the ecosystem? Or are these both compelling reasons for preserving and protecting the natural world?[63]

For millennia, our species has perceived nature almost entirely through the prism of our own self-centered perspective. Yet we are but a blink in time and a blurred bypass on the vast highways of the universe. Creation is far larger than we are, and it is necessary for us to look upon nature separate and apart from our role in it. One visionary thinker who took the exact opposite of a human-centered perspective of nature was the nineteenth–century American transcen-dentalist and naturalist Henry David Thoreau, who saw, long before others did, that, "The earth I tread on is not a dead, inert mass; it is a body, has a spirit, is organic and fluid to the influence of the spirit . . . What we call wildness is a civilization other than our own."[64]

Nature also is of vast instrumental value to humanity. Biodiversity and ecosystems are valuable to people for the economic and myriad other support services they provide for human endeavor in all its forms. We depend on a vast array of "ecosystem services." Yet, in an increasingly urban civilization in which many city-dwellers rarely give much thought to their countless links to nature, there is a tendency to minimize the value to us of "natural capital" – "the stock of renewable and non-renewable natural resources (e.g. plants, animals, air, water, soils, minerals) that combine to provide benefits to people."[65] We wear clothing – but we do not ponder cotton. We turn on the water tap – but we do not dwell on the reservoir. We gaze endlessly at the smartphone – but we are unaware of the rare elements that go into making it.

Business thinker Geoffrey Heal has identified one splendid example of how we tend to overlook natural capital – aspirin. As he notes, no other drug exceeds the common aspirin as a painkiller and anti-inflammatory agent. Yet, few of us who routinely take aspirin know that "nature invented aspirin," and that "[i]t occurs naturally, in the bark of willow trees."[66] In the nineteenth century, Bayer, the German pharmaceutical company, discovered how to syn-thesize the chemical in willow bark that combats pain and fever. However, as Heal recounts, "Greek authors mentioned this as far back as 500 BC."[67] What is more, "It's not just humans who know" about the healing properties of this natural remedy; "gorillas in the wild medicate themselves with willow bark when they are sick, too."[68]

Who knew? Which is, of course, precisely the point.

Natural capital, in all its manifestations, is big business. The far-sighted Swiss reinsurance firm Swiss Re found in a 2020 study that 55 percent of global GDP – equal to $41.7 trillion – depends on high-functioning biodiversity and ecosystem services.[69] Also, the same Swiss Re study showed that a fifth of the countries in the world are at risk of the collapse of their ecosystems from biodiversity loss and the destruction of wildlife and their habitats.[70] South Africa, Australia, India, Turkey, Mexico, Italy, China, Saudi Arabia, and more all have fragile ecosystems.[71] In July 2021, the World Bank reported that "by a conservative estimate a collapse in select services such as wild pollination, provisions of food from marine fisheries and timber from native forests, could result in a significant decline in global GDP: $2.7 trillion in 2030."[72] The bank predicted that the relative impacts of this collapse would be "most pronounced in low-income and lower-middle-income countries, where drops in 2030 GDP may be more than 10 percent."[73]

The economic costs of widespread ecological collapses would vastly exceed those of COVID-19. The overall costs to the planet would be incalculable.

Yet, despite these unprecedented stakes, humanity is "underestimating the challenges of avoiding a ghastly future," and is, as a result, doing not nearly enough to prevent it.[74] The world's countries have failed to meet even one of the twenty Aichi Biodiversity Targets – the global targets they set in Japan in 2010 for reducing the destruction of species and life-sustaining ecosystems by 2020.[75] The Aichi targets are largely paralleled in the targets of the United Nations Sustainable Development Goals, including Goal 2 (food security and nutrition); Goal 6 (clean water); Goal 12 (sustainable production and consumption); Goal 13 (climate change); Goal 14 (life below water); and Goal 15 (life on land). "Biodiversity underpins 14 of the 17 Sustainable Development Goals."[76] Thus, continued failure to achieve the Aichi targets by addressing "the underlying drivers that influence the direct pressures on biodiversity" is also failure to accomplish the Sustainable Development Goals.[77] According to the global scientific advisers to the United Nations, continued failure could significantly undermine the attainment of 80 percent of the SDG targets by 2030 that are "related to poverty, hunger, health, water, cities, climate, oceans and land."[78]

To remedy this failure, the 196 countries that are parties to the United Nations Convention on Biological Diversity are engaged in negotiations on a "Paris-style" agreement on biodiversity that they hope to conclude at their next global summit meeting in Kunming, China, in April and May of 2022; a conference delayed three times by the COVID-19 pandemic.[79] The current biodiversity convention was concluded at the Earth Summit in Rio de Janeiro, Brazil, in 1992, and it is long overdue for an update. There is no biodiversity agreement comparable to the Paris climate agreement. The biodiversity negotiators seek one that will provide a legal framework for biodiversity action resembling the legal framework for climate action in the Paris Agreement.[80]

The aim of these negotiations is "a world living in harmony with nature" by 2050.[81] Toward this end, one target is no net losses of freshwater, marine, and terrestrial ecosystems by 2030 and increases in those ecosystems of 20 percent by 2050.[82] Also sought are reductions in the percentage of species threatened with extinction; maintenance and enhancement of genetic diversity; improved nutrition, increased access to safe and drinkable water, better resilience to natural disasters, climate mitigation, and other benefits from ecosystem services; and the fair and equitable sharing of all these benefits.[83] These steps are intended to "contribute to the implementation of the 2030 Agenda for Sustainable Development."[84]

The United States is the only member of the United Nations that has not ratified the biodiversity convention (due to long-standing specious fears of a loss of national sovereignty, especially in the US Senate). The United States usually attends the biodiversity meetings as an observer, but the fact that it has still not ratified the convention means that it cannot participate in the decision-making. This reduces the ability of the United States to show leadership on this urgent global issue at a time when American leadership is much needed.[85] The new president of the United States, Joe Biden, can be expected to be supportive of this global attempt to live "in harmony with nature by 2050." In an executive order signed one week after he was sworn in as president, Biden set an ambitious conservation goal of conserving 30 percent of the lands and waters of the United States by 2030.[86] But no American president has had the temerity to send the biodiversity convention to the Senate and ask for its ratification since President Bill Clinton in 1993, and even if President Biden did so, as in the past, it is hard to see how the US Senate would be able to muster the constitutionally required two-thirds vote to ratify this essential international agreement.

Although the links between both biodiversity loss and ecosystem destruction on the one hand, and international trade on the other, are many and various, the multilateral trading system has barely begun to address those links in achievement of its express goal in the WTO treaty of fulfilling the objective of sustainable development. There is much to do in reimagining the trade rules to serve this objective – particularly on the links between trade and the environmental pillar of sustainable development. Two topics on which WTO members have been trying for some time to address the links between trade and the environment through negotiations, are freeing trade in environmental goods and disciplining subsidies on fisheries. A third topic on which they are just beginning to consider those links is fossil fuel subsidies. These are three of the right places for the members of the multilateral trading system to begin in modernizing the WTO to maximize trade's contribution to sustainable development.

TRADE IN ENVIRONMENTAL GOODS AND SERVICES

Goal 9 of the Sustainable Development Goals is to "[b]uild resilient infrastructure, promote inclusive and sustainable industrialization and foster innovation."[87] One way of achieving this goal is by speeding the spread of the flow of new green goods throughout the world. These green goods can be helpful tools for confronting the many perils to the planet. They are especially needed in developing countries, which do not always have access to the advanced technologies of the developed countries. The global distribution of these environmental goods can best be accomplished through international trade. The lower the prices of these goods, the more will be sold, and the greater the volume will be in the trade in them. The border taxes we call tariffs add to the prices of goods and thus limit sales. Thus, abolishing tariffs on environmental goods will help achieve Goal 9.[88]

Negotiations to free trade in environmental goods began soon after the turn of the century as part of the negotiations on trade and the environment in the Doha Development Round. All WTO members agreed in Doha in 2001 to negotiate multilaterally on "the reduction or, as appropriate, elimination of tariff and non-tariff barriers to environmental goods and services."[89] For more than a decade, these multilateral negotiations were unsuccessful. Then, at the annual World Economic Forum in Davos in January 2014, a group of fourteen WTO members announced their intent to negotiate a plurilateral agreement in pursuit of global free trade in environmental goods. Formal negotiations were launched at the WTO later that year. Eventually, forty-six members of the WTO participated in these plurilateral negotiations, representing nearly 90 percent of global trade in environmental goods, which totals more than $1 trillion and has been growing rapidly.[90]

The Obama administration in the United States was late in giving priority to this issue, but it did ultimately push hard for a deal. Even so, the negotiations collapsed in December 2016, when trade negotiators failed to find common ground on which goods would be covered by the proposed agreement. The United States was on a political deadline, trying to conclude an eleventh-hour "trade and environment" agreement to help advance climate action in the last weeks before Donald Trump was inaugurated as president. China, which had appeared a hesitant party to the talks all along, made new requests at the last minute that others could not accept.

Everyone involved promised at the time that they would conclude an agreement in 2017. But the new Trump administration in the United States, bent on denying climate change and repealing domestic regulations protecting the environment, and more inclined to raise tariffs rather than lower them, displayed scant interest in continuing with the environmental goods talks. The environmental goods negotiations stalled in 2017 and have remained frozen ever since. After two decades, there is still no WTO agreement on environmental goods.

Because these are plurilateral negotiations, a consensus of all 164 WTO members is not needed to conclude an agreement. The aim of the subset of WTO members that has been engaged in the negotiations on environmental goods has been to get coverage of environmental goods sufficient to constitute a "critical mass" of all the trade in such goods. Although there is no WTO rule defining such a "critical mass" of trade, the general rule of thumb in past trade negotiations has pegged a "critical mass" at 90 percent. This percentage minimizes the "free riders" among WTO members when the tariff cuts in a plurilateral agreement are extended on a "most-favored-nation" basis to benefit all WTO members, including those who have not yet signed the agreement. Negotiating countries are confident at this point that they have that "critical mass" of 90 percent coverage of the trade in environmental goods.

The highest hurdle to a WTO environmental goods agreement is reaching a consensus on which goods are in fact environmental goods. All are agreed on including wind turbines, solar panels, and the like. But, beyond this, an absence of agreement on the scope of what more should be included within the meaning of "environmental goods," has impeded success from the outset. In their long effort to reach agreement, the trade negotiators have not tried to define environmental goods; they have only tried to list them. The negotiations began with a list of fifty-four products previously agreed by the APEC countries of the Asia-Pacific region.[91] The OECD has a broader list.[92] The environmental groups have even broader lists. So does the business community. Some interest groups have proffered lists that contain seemingly everything, including (literally) the kitchen sink.[93] The Chinese want the covered list to include bicycles, which they claim are environmental goods. This request has been resisted by the European Union and the United States, which have imposed antidumping duties on imports of Chinese-made bicycles and see no need for such imports to be duty-free.[94]

Looking beyond the question of which products will be on the list for duty-free treatment, an underlying obstacle to reaching an agreement is that there is a difference in the goals of the United States and the European Union on the one hand and China on the other. The United States and the European Union want to free trade in environmental goods. China wants to secure more and freer market access abroad for Chinese exports of environmental goods. These are not the same goals. As Maureen Hinman, a former US trade negotiator on this issue, has written insightfully, this difference makes for a "mismatch" in goals that heeds a successful outcome to the negotiations.[95]

China's approach to the environmental goods negotiations might best be described as green mercantilism. China leads the world in the export of environmental technology (such as, for example, solar panels), but China badly trails the developed countries, including the United States and the European Union, in "enforcing its own environmental rules and implementing environmental technologies."[96] In other words, China produces environmental goods; but it does not use them much domestically. Consequently, as Hinman explains, China's domestic market for non-energy related environmental technologies is much smaller than it should be, given the size of the Chinese economy. Compared to the markets of the developed countries, the Chinese market is consuming a much smaller portion of these advanced environmental goods. Thus, China has less domestic demand to import these green goods, and the

Chinese government is able to focus on limiting foreign competition by maintaining tariffs on some of the most significant of China's domestic production of them.[97]

Another hurdle to reaching an agreement is the expressed hope of the negotiators that it will become a "living agreement" that can expand and evolve over time.[98] The joint statement in Davos in 2014 of the countries that began the plurilateral negotiations speaks of concluding "a future-oriented agreement able to address other issues in the sector and to respond to green growth and sustainable development."[99] One key to the success of such an open-ended agreement will be agreeing on a timely means of applying duty-free treatment to new environmental goods as they as they are produced. This, of course, relates to the debate over the appropriate definition of the scope of coverage of the proposed agreement. In a comparable situation, it took WTO negotiators nearly twenty years to agree on adding new IT goods to the list of goods for duty-free treatment in the WTO Information Technology Agreement – even though information technology was revolutionized several times over during the interim.[100] A repeat of this long impasse would render a WTO agreement on environmental goods increasingly irrelevant as changes in technology continued.

Generally, developing countries have either seemed indifferent to a WTO environmental goods agreement or have actively resisted it. The indifference of developing countries seems to be driven by the fact that, as Mark Wu has observed, "very few developing countries have much at stake in terms of exports," and also by the likelihood that they can achieve their objectives "through free riding."[101] Their resistance seems to be motivated by their apprehension of being overwhelmed by a flood of imports of environmental goods. This is ironic; for the principal beneficiaries of an environmental goods agreement will be developing countries. Of course, developed countries will profit by selling more environmental goods in developing countries. But developing countries can gain even more than developed countries by virtue of having ready access to these goods in their pursuit of sustainable development.

As the United States Chamber of Commerce has put it, "The business of providing sustainability solutions has reached its present scale thanks to growing international demand and expectations of considerable growth potential. Trade policies can play an important role in enabling (the) private sector to mobilize its resources and creativity to deliver innovations where they are most needed and where they can have the biggest environmental payoff." Scientific evidence must be used, and special and differential treatment must be afforded to least developed countries. But urgently needed innovations can be delivered more easily to developing countries if tariffs on environmental goods are eliminated.

Whatever the final list may be, the goods covered by an environmental goods agreement will include "important environment-related products ... that can help achieve environmental and climate-protective goals, such as generating clean and renewable energy, improving energy and resource efficiency, controlling air pollution, managing waste, treating waste water, monitoring the quality of the environment, and combatting noise pollution."[102] Tariffs on some environmental goods are as high as 35 percent.[103] Abolishing tariffs would lower the prices of environmental goods and thereby hasten their spread worldwide. This can only be of benefit to developing countries at a time when so many of them are sorely lacking in much of what they need to help further their development and help make it sustainable.

One frequent objection to the current approach of trying to structure the environmental goods agreement as a "living agreement" is that, based on the experience of other, more limited exercises in identifying and classifying environmental standards, it is unrealistic to think that a "living list" of environmental goods eligible for duty-free treatment can be maintained. Some who favor freeing trade in environmental goods advocate instead an approach that employs existing environmental standards, and, where such standards do not exist, establishes "objective criteria for including goods that would allow future additions. That is, if there is no standard for automobile fuel that would give preference to ethanol blends or other clean fuels, then those fuels should not be listed. But there should be certainty that, if and when a fuel standard is created that meets certain criteria, then fuels will be covered by the EGS regime."[104]

Another oft-heard objection to a sectoral agreement that would end tariffs on environmental goods is that environmental goods should not be singled out for special treatment, and that all tariffs on all goods should be eliminated. Tim Worstall of *Forbes* has wondered what makes environmental goods special. He asked, while applauding the collapse of the environmental goods negotiations in 2016, "Why not all goods? ... How about we just go with the idea that more trade makes us all richer and so we'll not have tariffs at all?"[105] This is the right goal, and the ultimate goal. But this view ignores the urgency of our climate and our ecological situation, which is what makes environmental goods special, and what makes their rapid spread worldwide essential. Those who express this attitude also commit the always tempting mistake of making the perfect the enemy of the good. By this reasoning, no trade agreement in history should ever have been concluded.

A more legitimate objection is that an agreement to free trade in environmental goods should also free trade in environmental services. This was the original intent of WTO members as voiced in the Doha Declaration. This should likewise be their intent now. For, increasingly, environmental goods and environmental services are integrated. Indeed, in trade, services are increasingly embedded in goods. Because goods and services are increasingly intertwined, and because their delivery is therefore often integrated, their trade treatment should likewise often be integrated. One example is with wind power plants: Freeing trade in environmental goods will boost international shipments of the makings of wind power plants, while freeing trade in environmental services will lift the current obstacles to providing the international services that are often needed to maintain those plants.[106]

This said, again, the perfect should never be allowed to become the enemy of the good in international trade negotiations. If that were the practice, no trade agreement would ever be acceptable; for they are all imperfect. Thus, the conclusion of a WTO environmental goods agreement should not be conditioned on the simultaneous conclusion of an agreement that would free trade in the delivery of environmental services. Instead, an environmental goods agreement should serve as a foundation for the negotiation of an expanded agreement that would later include environmental services.

With Donald Trump no longer in the White House, global hopes for renewed leadership by the United States in concluding such an agreement were heightened in April 2021 when ninety members of Congress in President Biden's own party urged him to resume the long deadlocked WTO negotiations. They advised him that restarting these negotiations "represents a significant opportunity to help countries across the world access high-quality affordable environmental goods while also levelling the playing field for American manufacturers and supporting green jobs."[107] It is unclear, though, at this writing, whether the Biden administration will exercise leadership on this issue, which would seem to fit nicely within the new president's focus on fighting climate change. It is equally unclear whether China and other WTO members will be willing to join in the compromises needed to reach a consensus.

FISHERIES AND FISHERIES SUBSIDIES

Goal 14 of the Sustainable Development Goals is to "conserve and sustainably use the oceans, seas and marine resources for sustainable development."[108] The United Nations has been laboring to conclude a new oceans agreement under the United Nations Convention on the Law of the Sea, which would center on "the conservation and sustainable use of marine biological diversity of areas beyond national jurisdiction."[109] The greatest impact on ocean biodiversity is caused by fishing for food.[110] Scientists advising the UN have said that, "To protect biodiversity, and to support people's livelihoods and the emerging 'blue economy,' there is a clear need to rebuild fisheries, improve the management of fishing fleets, and to improve the management and planning of all marine activities in an integrated manner, applying the ecological approach."[111] Curtailing governmental subsidies for fisheries must be part of that integrated ecological approach.[112]

Like the prolonged negotiations on environmental goods, WTO negotiations on fisheries subsidies also began two decades ago during the Doha round. Like other production subsidies, fisheries subsidies are covered by existing WTO subsidies rules. WTO members have, however, concluded that fisheries subsidies require special treatment in the form of additional disciplines. As part of the

Doha Development Agenda, they have endeavored since 2001 to "clarify and improve WTO discipline on fisheries subsidies, taking into account the importance of this sector to developing countries."[113] WTO members have now labored diligently through eighteen rounds of negotiations on fisheries subsidies without achieving success.

These negotiations were given renewed impetus in 2015, when all the members of the United Nations (including all members of the WTO) agreed in Target 14.6 under Goal 14 of the Sustainable Development Goals to "prohibit certain forms of fisheries subsidies which contribute to overcapacity and overfishing, eliminate subsidies that contribute to illegal, unreported, and unregulated fishing and refrain from introducing new such subsidies, recognizing that appropriate and effective special and differential treatment for developing and least developed countries should be an integral part of the World Trade Organization fisheries subsidies negotiation."[114] Because of the urgency of stopping the depletion of the world's fish stocks, the United Nations agreed to meet this target, not (as with most other SDGs) by 2030, but by 2020. Despite this added incentive, WTO members failed to conclude a WTO agreement on fisheries subsidies at the 11th Ministerial Conference in Buenos Aires, Argentina, in 2017. They pledged then to conclude an agreement by the next ministerial conference, which, after delays due to the pandemic, was to be held in Geneva in late November of 2021.

Throughout these many years of negotiations, the United States has always been fully engaged. According to the initial American proposal submitted in concert with a number of allied countries to the WTO in 2005, "[T]he United States believes that a broad prohibition addressing all elements that contribute most directly to overcapacity and overfishing would be the most effective way to fulfill our mandate."[115] In contrast to some other ongoing WTO efforts, the Trump administration voiced support for the fisheries talks, stating that it continued "to support stronger disciplines and greater transparency in the WTO with respect to fisheries subsidies."[116] Thus, the United States continued to take part in the fisheries negotiations in the run-up to and following the November 2020 presidential election.

The state of global fisheries is a major concern everywhere. Worldwide, three billion people depend on fish and fish products for up to 15 percent of their daily protein and nutrition.[117] Many of them live in the poorest and least developed countries. Moreover, at least 140 million people depend on fisheries for their livelihood.[118] The demand for fish has been growing with the increasing numbers of a growing – and increasingly prosperous – global population. We now eat more fish than ever before, an average of 20 kilograms – 44 pounds – per person every year.[119] We eat more fish than beef.[120]

Meanwhile, the global fish catch has been declining.[121] According to the Food and Agricultural Organization of the United Nations, fish stocks that are within biologically sustainable levels fell from 90 percent in 1974 to 65.8 in 2017.[122] Underfished stocks accounted for only 6.2 percent.[123] In its

2020 annual report on the status of fisheries and aquaculture, the FAO said that, although there have been some improvements in sustainable fisheries practices, the statistics indicate that the United Nations target of ending over-fishing of marine fisheries by 2030 will not be achieved.[124] The authors of a study released in the Proceedings of the National Academy of Sciences examined 4,713 fisheries worldwide, accounting for 78 percent of the world's catch. They found that only a third of these fisheries are in good biological condition. Yet, offering hope for change, these scientists also concluded that – if applied globally – modern fishery management plans can make nearly every fishery in the world healthy by 2050.[125]

In this grim ecological context, almost 38 percent of all the fish caught or farmed in the world is traded, with a total export value of $164 billion.[126] The impact of COVID-19 has, of course, "negatively impacted" fish trade.[127] By far the major producer and exporter of fish and fish products is China, with 14 percent.[128] China has ranked first since 2002.[129] Norway is second, and Vietnam is third.[130] The United States accounts for 4 percent of global fish exports.[131] The United States and the European Union lead in global fish imports, with China third.[132] Developing countries account for 49 percent of global fish imports.[133] Trade in fish is of significance in every part of the world.

This trade is driven in part by subsidies. As explained by Elizabeth Wilson of the Pew Charitable Trusts,

Fisheries subsidies are one of the key drivers behind this decline in fish stocks. Governments pay ... each year in damaging types of fisheries subsidies, primarily to industrial fishers, to offset costs such as fuel, gear, and vessel construction. Although not all subsidies are harmful, many encourage fishing beyond sustainable biological limits by helping vessels go farther and fish for longer periods and with greater capacity than they would without this assistance. Today, in part driven by fisheries subsidies, global fishing capacity—the total capability of the world's fleets—is estimated at 250 percent of the level that would bring in the maximum sustainable catch.[134]

Most countries, regardless of their stage of development, subsidize their fisheries.[135] Although "overfishing is one of the greatest threats to ocean health ... for decades many governments have paid subsidies to their fishing fleets, helping them fish beyond levels that are biologically sustainable."[136] In 2018, fisheries subsidies totaled $35.4 billion worldwide. Of these total subsidies, 22 percent were for fuel subsidies, which permit fishing trawlers, largely from the wealthier countries, to range farther into the global commons of the high seas. China granted 21 percent of total global fisheries subsidies; the European Union 11 percent; the United States 10 percent; and South Korea 9 percent.[137] The global total of fisheries subsidies is between 30 and 40 percent of the landed value generated by wild fisheries worldwide.[138]

The Global Ocean Commission has estimated that 60 percent of global fisheries subsidies directly encourage "unsustainable, destructive and even illegal fishing practices."[139] The Commission said in 2016 that high seas fishing fuel subsidies should be capped immediately and then phased out over five years, and suggested that the money saved should be put into a dedicated "Blue Fund" to achieve the Sustainable Development Goal of saving the ocean.[140] This reform is still more imperative now when, according to the OECD, "All aspects of fish supply chains are strongly affected by the COVID-19 pandemic, with jobs, incomes and food security at risk."[141]

Fearful of lost markets, many developing countries have resisted new disciplines of fisheries subsidies, even though about two-thirds of the subsidies are provided by developed countries.[142] Oft-cited are the perceived risks from losing their subsidies for more than 30 million small-scale fishers in the world, who, it is maintained, may be unable to continue to make a living without state aid.[143] An express target of the SDGs is to "[p]rovide access for small-scale artisanal fishers to marine resources and markets."[144]

Yet, most of the subsidies go to large fishers through fuel and other support to huge corporate fishing fleets. These subsidies "support large-scale fishing operations, which discriminate against smaller ones and ultimately undermine food security and livelihoods in poorer coastal communities."[145] By far the largest distant-water fishing fleet is that of China, which, according to the Overseas Development Institute, numbers close to 17,000 vessels. In contrast, the distant-water fishing fleet of the United States totals fewer than 300 vessels.[146] As Ian Urbina has observed, "Most Chinese ships are so large that they scoop up as many fish in a week as a local boat might catch in a year."[147] Not surprisingly, China has resisted additional disciplines on fisheries subsidies. Moreover, 2020 case studies commissioned by the International Institute for Sustainable Development in Canada show that new WTO trade disciplines on fisheries subsidies "could help local fishers while increasing global cash."[148] These studies indicate that, in addition to improving fishery sustainability, "reforming harmful fisheries subsidies could lead to higher yields for local fishers, which could help provide more stable jobs, raise fishers' incomes, reduce poverty, and improve food security in local communities."[149]

One of the missed opportunities for the United States in international trade in recent years has been its withdrawal under President Trump from the proposed Trans-Pacific Partnership in January 2017. In addition to other trade reforms and liberalization, what has since been renamed the Comprehensive and Progressive Agreement for Trans-Pacific Partnership among the remaining eleven Pacific Rim countries "contains the first disciplines on fisheries subsidies in any free trade agreement."[150] These countries have recognized in the innovative provisions of the CPTPP that "the implementation of a fisheries management system that is designed to prevent overfishing and overcapacity and to promote the recovery of overfished stocks must include the control, reduction and eventual elimination of all subsidies that contribute to overfishing and overcapacity."[151]

As one leading advocate of trade and sustainable development, Ricardo Melendez-Ortiz, has observed, the impact of this obligation in the CPTPP could demonstrate that fisheries subsidies can be disciplined by a "select group of countries, and, in part for that reason," should serve "as inspiration for the so-far unsuccessful multilateral talks."[152] Generally, the trade rules frown on subsidies where they have distortive effects on trade.[153] Fisheries subsidies have distortive effects on trade, and they also have harmful effects on the environment. This is also true of some other governmental subsidies that must be addressed in modernizing the global rules for trade.

Following a meeting of government ministers and heads of national delegations in July 2021, negotiators spoke optimistically about being able to reach consensus on an agreement by the time of the planned year-end ministerial conference in Geneva. Terms of a draft text were yet to be finalized. The draft proposed three categories of prohibited subsidies: those that affect overfished stocks; lead to overcapacity and overfishing; or support illegal, unreported, and unregulated (IUU) fishing.[154] At this writing, one roadblock to a consensus "is whether and how to grant exceptions to allow certain countries to continue using subsidies."[155] The African, Caribbean, and Pacific countries want to excuse all developing countries except for the five biggest fishing countries from having to comply with new subsidies disciplines. The United States and the European Union seek a much narrower exemption. The EU has complicated negotiations by proposing that countries be permitted to maintain subsidies for fuel or fish price support if they can demonstrate that they have sustainability programs in place to replenish declining fish stocks. The APC countries have protested that this proposal would allow the EU to continue with its extensive fisheries subsidies while requiring developing countries that cannot afford such sustainability programs to take an ax to their subsidies.[156]

Having agreed on new disciplines on fisheries subsidies, WTO members should then go on to address in more detail the equally urgent issue of the worldwide increase in illegal, unreported, and unregulated fishing. As the United Nations has reported in its annual assessment of progress toward achieving the UN Sustainable Development Goals, "Illegal, unreported and unregulated fishing threatens the social, economic and environmental sustainability of global fisheries: it also hinders countries' ability to manage their fisheries effectively."[157] Global losses from IUU fishing are estimated at between $10 billion and $23.5 billion each year, meaning that "overall, as many as one in three fish entering international trade could come from IUU fishing."[158]

One target of Goal 14 of the SDGs is to "end illegal, unreported and unregulated fishing" by 2020. That deadline having passed, the need for collective action is all the more urgent. Attempts by individual countries to address the issue with unilateral actions that include trade restrictions can risk violations of WTO rules. Required is multilateral action. By February 2020, sixty-six countries had become parties to the Agreement on Port State Measures, the first binding international agreement that specifically targets IUU fishing. It establishes "a minimum set of standard measures for Parties to apply when foreign vessels seek entry into their ports or while they are in their ports."[159] More such action is necessary to impose effective disciplines and sanctions on IUU fishing. Without question, these disciplines and sanctions would be respected by the WTO, so long as they are not applied in a manner that would constitute arbitrary or unjustifiable discrimination or a disguised restriction on international trade.[160]

In the United States, the Biden administration has made securing new disciplines on fisheries subsidies a high priority on its trade agenda. In her first speech as United States Trade Representative, Ambassador Katherine Tai stressed the necessity of "addressing overfishing that is destroying the marine ecosystem."[161] She said,

We have ... started to address fisheries and our oceans in our trade agreements, whether through disciplines on the massive subsidies that promote overfishing, or through provisions that address the millions of tons of plastic and other forms of pollution that are destroying the marine environment. But again, we will only truly address the global scale of the problem through global rules. This is why the fisheries negotiations at the WTO are so critical.

In Geneva, those negotiations continued.

FOSSIL FUEL SUBSIDIES AND SUSTAINABLE ENERGY

Fossil fuel emissions are not only causing climate change. By causing climate change, they are also doing much to cause the loss of species and the devastation of ecosystems; for climate change is a major driver of the biodiversity crisis.[162] Indeed, climate change is making species losses and ecological threats even worse. According to scientists advising the United Nations, the extreme weather events, fires, floods, and droughts that can be traced back to climate change "have contributed to widespread impacts in many aspects of biodiversity," and "the effects are accelerating in marine, terrestrial and freshwater ecosystems and are already impacting agriculture, aquaculture, fisheries and nature's contributions to people."[163]

In December 2020, the United Nations reported that, to limit global warming to 1.5 degrees Celsius above preindustrial levels, the world must decrease fossil fuel production by about 6 percent per year between 2020 and 2030.[164] And yet, amid the pandemic, "countries are instead planning and projecting an average increase of 2%, which by 2030 would result in more than double the production consistent with the 1.5C limit."[165] Despite the desire of many people throughout the world for a green recovery from the pandemic, "[t]o date, governments have committed far more COVID-19 funds to fossil fuels than to clean energy."[166] Worst of all, at a time of crisis when humanity urgently needs to end its worldwide addiction to fossil fuels as a source of energy, governments are continuing, perversely, to *subsidize* the production and consumption of fossil fuels. Instead of helping liberate people from their dependency on fossil fuels, these governments are literally *paying people to use them.*

Here we face another aspect of the challenge of carbon pricing."[167] As it is, "[f]ossil fuels are now massively underpriced, reflecting undercharging for production and environmental costs – including for air pollution and global warming."[168] According to the International Monetary Fund, incentivizing the energy efficiencies and the increased use of renewable energies needed for a "deep decarbonization of human activity ... will require carbon-intensive energy to become much more expensive relative to both low-carbon energy and other goods and services than it is today."[169] Fossil fuel subsidies are the opposite of carbon pricing. Rather than putting a price on carbon that incorporates all its environmental and social costs into the price of a product, fossil fuel subsidies help perpetuate the underpricing of fossil fuels, which, in turn, prolongs their harmful use.

Estimates of the global total of fossil fuel subsidies vary with varying valuation methods, lists of countries, and definitions of what constitutes a "subsidy."[170] The International Energy Agency estimates the annual total of global fossil fuel consumption subsidies at $300 billion.[171] The OECD reports that fossil fuel production and consumption subsidies in its forty-three member countries total between $150 million and $250 billion annually.[172] The International Monetary Fund says that global production and consumption subsidies for fossil fuels combined add up to $333 billion every year.[173] When the "negative externalities" from the emission of fossil fuels, such as the health costs due to air pollution, are included in the reckoning, the IMF calculates that annual global energy subsidies total $5.3 trillion.[174] Total global GDP was about $84.5 trillion in 2020.[175]

Eliminating fossil fuel subsidies could cut global carbon dioxide emissions by between 1 and 4 percent by 2030,[176] and by between 6 and 8 percent by 2050.[177] In addition, according to a small group of non-G20 countries (and WTO members) acting together since 2010 as the Friends of Fossil Fuel Subsidy Reform, "**reforming fossil fuel subsidies can also release funds on a national level for other development priorities** such as health, environment, education, renewable energy or infrastructure. Furthermore, fossil fuel subsidy reform would have a **significant positive impact on public health**" by reducing deaths caused by air pollution from emissions of fossil fuels."[178]

Toward these ends, one of the targets for ensuring "sustainable consumption and production patterns" under Goal 12 of the Sustainable Development Goals is to "[r]ationalize inefficient fossil-fuel subsidies that encourage wasteful consumption by removing market distortions."[179] In testimony to the political sensitivities of fossil fuel consumption subsidies especially, this target is to be pursued "in accordance with national circumstances" while "taking into account the specific needs and conditions of developing countries and minimizing the possible adverse impacts on their development in a manner that protects the poor and the affected communities."[180]

WTO rules on subsidies already apply to fossil fuel subsidies.[181] These existing rules, however, do not include any specific trade disciplines on fossil fuel subsidies. Nor have such subsidies ever been challenged in WTO dispute settlement. Strikingly, to date, all the challenges to energy subsidies in the WTO have been to subsidies for renewable energy.[182] Subsidies for solar and wind energy have run afoul of WTO rules where they have included domestic content requirements, which discriminate in favor of domestic over imported inputs into green energy products. Domestic content requirements distort trade while denying domestic producers and consumers alike the benefits of the competition, the lower prices, and the broader choices of the more effective energy and environmental alternatives offered by being open to foreign trade and foreign direct investment.[183]

Why have there been no legal actions to date in the WTO against fossil fuel subsidies? There are several reasons. One is the reluctance of WTO members to risk exposing their own fossil fuel subsidies to legal scrutiny in retaliatory challenges by other members. Another is the hesitancy of small countries that produce no fossil fuel products to file a legal complaint against large countries that do, for fear of retaliatory litigation in other sectors of trade. Still another reason is the fact that, under the current trade rules, subsidies are inconsistent with the rules if they have harmful trade effects but not if they have harmful environmental effects. It is much easier to demonstrate harmful environmental effects from fossil fuel subsidies than to prove harmful trade effects.

Against this backdrop, there have been increasing calls to single out fossil fuel subsidies in WTO rules because of their adverse environmental effects. These calls produced a groundbreaking initiative at the 11th WTO Ministerial Conference in Buenos Aires in December 2017 that could help attain the SDG target. Twelve of the 164 members of the WTO issued a declaration there expressing their desire to add specific disciplines to the existing WTO subsidies rules to rationalize and phase out "inefficient" fossil fuel subsidies.[184] Their initiative is "aimed at achieving ambitious and effective disciplines on inefficient fossil fuel subsidies that encourage wasteful consumption."[185] This WTO ministerial declaration was the first time, in dealing with fossil fuel subsidies, that WTO members asserted that there is "a link with trade."[186] These dozen members have since embarked on a diplomatic campaign to enlist the remaining 152 WTO members in proposed negotiations on how the trade rules should be amended to help meet the SDG target.

The whole membership of the WTO has yet to place this issue on the WTO negotiating agenda. Adding it to the agenda will be hard. The forces in favor of fossil fuel subsidies are powerful. Also, once it is on the agenda, reaching a consensus on how best to deal with fossil fuel subsidies in the trade rules will be even harder. The dimensions of the issue are many, and the ramifications of addressing it will be many as well. All the same, it is imperative that the WTO begin to negotiate new and specific disciplines on fossil fuel subsidies, and it is imperative also that those WTO negotiations proceed quickly to global success.

The world can ill afford for any multilateral WTO negotiations on fossil fuel subsidies to last for the two decades that the WTO negotiations on environmental goods and fisheries subsidies have, so maddeningly, plodded on without success.

At the outset of WTO negotiations on fossil fuel subsidies, preliminary decisions will be required. To begin, an answer will be needed to the central question: What is a fossil fuel subsidy? There must be an agreed definition. The estimates made by different international institutions of the annual amounts of fossil fuel subsidies globally range from hundreds of billions of dollars to trillions of dollars annually because the definitions used by these institutions vary widely. Should, for example, both production and consumption subsidies be included in the definition? Or should one form of subsidy be included but not the other? In addition, once there is agreement on a definition of a fossil fuel subsidy, there must be an agreement on how to tally the costs of such subsidies. Should only the direct costs be included in this sum, or should the extra health costs and the other negative externalities resulting from the burning of subsidized fossil fuels be included as well?

To be answered also in such negotiations must be: What is an "inefficient" fossil fuel subsidy? Setting aside for the moment the suspicion that the pressures of domestic politics played a major role in the choice of phrasing in this target of the UN Sustainable Development Goals and in the language of the 2017 WTO ministerial declaration, the simple fact that the word "inefficient" modifies the term "fossil fuel subsidies" nevertheless presumes that some fossil fuel subsidies are efficient while others are not. Is this so, or is this simply an example of temporizing to attain a consensus? Can any fossil fuel subsidy ever truly be efficient, given the devastating climatic consequences of such subsidies? And, if this is so, where then should the legal line be drawn between "efficient" and "inefficient" fossil fuel subsidies?

Furthermore, once decisions are made defining these terms for WTO purposes, how then should fossil fuel subsidies be measured? As with the calculation of greenhouse gas emissions, what metrics should be used? Something that can be measured can be counted and compared. But something that cannot be measured cannot be counted and compared, and thus cannot be disciplined. The answer to this critical question is, of course, inextricably related to the answers agreed to the questions about the definition of fossil fuel subsidies, and the line between efficient and inefficient fossil fuel subsidies. To provide more effective disciplines for fossil fuel subsidies under WTO rules, there must be one agreed means of measuring them.

At a minimum, this crucial process of ensuring accurate measurement will require prompt and full international transparency for all such subsidies – including timely notification of their subsidies to the WTO.[187] WTO rules already require members to notify the WTO of all their subsidies annually.[188] However, WTO members frequently do not notify the WTO of their subsidies, and, when they do deign to notify them, they often fail to do so on time. In recent years, most fossil fuel subsidies have not been notified to the WTO.[189] WTO rules should be revised to mandate immediate disclosure of all fossil fuel subsidies, and WTO members should be subject to the potential loss of some of their trade benefits under the WTO treaty if they do not comply with this mandate.[190]

Once these preliminary questions have been answered, what new WTO disciplines are needed for fossil fuel subsidies? Under the current rules, subsidies are prohibited if they are contingent "upon export performance" or "upon the use of domestic over imported goods."[191] These prohibited subsidies are automatically illegal under the WTO trade rules. Other "actionable" subsidies are illegal under those rules only if they are "specific" to "certain enterprises"[192] and if they have certain "adverse effects."[193] Prohibited subsidies are presumed to be "specific" and to have "adverse effects." Fossil fuel subsidies are often general and not specific. Moreover, the harmful environmental effects of such subsidies are not included within the current scope of "adverse effects." These obstacles to imposing new disciplines on fossil fuel subsidies should be eliminated by revising trade rules to include fossil fuel subsidies within the WTO definition of prohibited subsidies.

Goal 7 of the Sustainable Development Goals is to "[e]nsure access to affordable, reliable, sustainable and modern energy for all."[194] Amartya Sen has rightly reminded us that sufficient energy is "essential for conquering poverty," and that, "[i]n thinking about expanding human freedom today and sustaining it into the future, we have to take fuller note of the need for greater energy use for a larger number of deprived people in the world."[195] Nearly 600 million people in Africa – about 70 percent of the population of the continent – do not have access to electricity.[196] In our zeal to shed the shackles of fossil fuels, and in our zest for the transition to clean energy, we must remain mindful that fossil fuels still provide about 80 percent of the energy consumed in the world and still present the most immediate opportunity for access to energy for those who do not have it.[197]

At the same time, Goal 13 of the SDGs is to "[t]ake urgent action to combat climate change and its impacts."[198] The achievement of this goal demands nothing less than a revolution in the energy we use and in how we use it. It requires decarbonization. And it requires decarbonization sooner rather than later. Yet it is one thing to tell someone in a wealthy country who is long accustomed to being able to turn a light switch on and off that they must switch from one source of energy to another. It is quite another to tell someone in a poor country who has never had a light switch that they must refrain from using the cheapest and most accessible energy source available to them – fossil fuels – to turn on their lights for the first time, and that, instead, they must wait patiently in the dark until renewable energy is available and affordable.

Achieving both these global goals necessitates a transition, and, in pursuit of both these goals, fossil fuel subsidies are pernicious. *Production* subsidies for fossil fuels are clearly pernicious because they distort the allocation of limited resources in global energy markets by artificially lowering fossil fuel prices and by discouraging needed investments in renewable sources of energy. In seeming contrast, *consumption* subsidies for fossil fuels are widely seen as less pernicious because they are thought to help provide access to energy for poorer people at more affordable prices. However, the facts about such subsidies tell quite a different story. Because wealthier households buy larger amounts of energy, "they capture most of the benefits" of fossil fuel consumption subsidies. Poorer households benefit much less.[199]

To be precise, the IMF has concluded that, worldwide, the poorest 40 percent of the people receive only 7.4 percent of gasoline subsidy benefits, while the wealthiest 40 percent receive 83.2 percent. Likewise, for liquefied petroleum gas subsidies, only 12.7 percent of the benefits go to the poorest 40 percent of the people, while 73.9 percent go to the wealthiest 40 percent.[200] According to the IMF, the much larger share of benefits from price subsidies going to high-income households further reinforces "existing income inequalities."[201] Moreover, "untargeted fossil fuel subsidies are at best an inefficient and unjust tool for improving energy access. At their worst, they can have a negative impact on energy access."[202] To some extent, these consumption subsidies do help the poor, but there are many other ways to help the poor without encouraging them to use fossil fuels. The simplest way would be through targeted cash transfers to the poor that would not be tied to fossil fuel use.[203]

Even so, as a practical matter, it makes political sense to make a distinction between production subsidies and consumption subsidies in new trade rules. The transition to clean energy must be eased for the poorest among us, including those in developing countries without ready and reliable access to energy. No doubt with this in mind, in their declaration of their desire to negotiate new disciplines on fossil fuel subsidies, the dozen WTO members declared in Buenos Aires in 2017, "We recognise that reform needs to take fully into account the specific needs and conditions of developing countries and minimize the possible adverse impacts on their development in a manner that protects the poor and the affected communities."[204]

One logical means of minimizing the transitional effects for the developing countries would be, as these dozen members of the WTO have suggested, to phase out their fossil fuel subsidies, including especially their consumption subsidies, over time. Here distinctions could be made between countries based on their different stages of development. Another means of minimizing the transitional effects would be to provide the developing countries with technical assistance and capacity building "on how to identify, measure, and evaluate fossil fuel or wider energy subsidies" and, also, on how best to go about phasing them out.[205] Developing countries – especially the least developed ones – cannot be expected to undertake such changes without such assistance.

Over time, new disciplines on fossil fuel subsidies could give rise to a WTO sustainable energy trade agreement. Although there is more international trade in oil than in anything else, there are "no energy-specific rules or commitments in the WTO."[206] Moreover, as Rafael Leal-Arcas has observed, "[T]he GATT/ WTO has historically not preoccupied itself with energy trade."[207] This must change. New trade rules in a sustainable energy trade agreement could do much to help achieve both Goal 7 and Goal 13 of the SDGs if they promoted mutual recognition and harmonization of clean energy standards and technical regulations, assuring the timely transition to clean energy; encouraged the transfer of new green technologies from wealthier to poorer countries; lowered barriers to trade in energy services; and set out "best practices" on emissions and sustainability for such carbon-intensive and import-sensitive industrial sectors as glass, cement, paper, aluminum, and steel.

As part of a sustainable energy trade agreement, too, the trade rules on subsidies should be aligned with sustainable development. Despite the rapid declines in the prices of renewable energies, governmental intervention in the form of subsidies is still needed on a transitional basis to help steer energy users and producers more quickly toward clean energy. To accomplish this, lapsed WTO rules that originally permitted certain environmental subsidies should be restored, updated, and widened in scope.[208] Legal room must be created by the WTO for governmental measures that advance the green transition in energy and in other modern manufacturing.

In so doing, though, we should be ever mindful of the admonition of Adam Smith about the potential harms of governmental subsidies. In 1776, in *The Wealth of Nations*, Smith singled out for criticism the "bounties" that subsidized Scottish white herring fisheries in their competition with the Dutch. He saw those "bounties" to the Scottish fishing industry as a waste of money, with an added opportunity cost in the form of forgone and therefore lost economic opportunities elsewhere. Smith noted that one "bounty to the white herring fishing industry is a tonnage bounty; and is proportioned to the burden of the ship, and not to her diligence or success in the fishery." And what was the result of paying this subsidy based on the size of the ship instead of the size of the catch? Lamented Smith, "(I)t has, I am afraid, been too common for vessels to fit out for the sole purpose of catching, not the fish, but the bounty."[209]

With Smith's admonition in mind, in the realignment of the WTO rules on subsidies to advance sustainable development, we should be wary of permitting too much governmental direction of the decisions of the marketplace. Although governmental subsidies are needed in some instances to further and speed carbon pricing, the basic truth of his admonition remains. Thus, the green subsidies that are needed should not target individual companies or individual technologies. They should, instead, be "winner-neutral" green subsidies that target sustainable outcomes that have been identified as agreed goals for the green transition.[210] In this way, carbon pricing and, as a result, decarbonization, can be accelerated while minimizing the societal costs and inefficiencies that would otherwise result from subsidies that are not targeted to particular outcomes. These are the kinds of governmental subsidies that should be exempted as environmental subsidies in revised and modernized WTO rules.[211]

Subsidies to speed the shift away from our stubborn reliance on carbon are commonly characterized as a key component of a green industrial policy. Yet, as with any industrial policy, there is an ever-present danger of descent into a self-defeating protectionism. Many ask, why not encourage domestic production by favoring it? Domestic content requirements – which condition the grant of subsidies "upon the use of domestic over imported goods" – are always tempting politically.[212] However, they are prohibited under WTO rules, and they should not be permitted in green subsidies. Such requirements not only increase costs, raise domestic demand even when domestic goods are of less quality than imported goods, and insulate domestic firms from fair foreign competition,[213] they are also environmentally counterproductive. As Robert Howse of New York University has pointed out, "[H]owever politically useful in gaining support for clean energy, domestic content requirements and other discriminatory measures actually undermine environmental objectives by shifting production to higher-cost jurisdictions, and therefore making clean energy, or clean energy technologies, more expensive than they need to be."[214]

In addition, WTO members should clarify and change other WTO rules on subsidies to advance the green transition. They should make it clear that subsidies are eligible for the affirmative defenses in the general exceptions to obligations relating to trade in goods and, thus, are permissible when they are environmental or health measures that are not applied in a manner that constitutes arbitrary or unjustifiable discrimination or a disguised restriction on international trade.[215] Furthermore, WTO members should revise the current rules to make subsidies of all kinds illegal not only if they have adverse economic effects, but also if they have adverse environmental effects.

Central to sustainable development is the essential shift away from fossil fuels and toward a zero-carbon economy. Trade rules must hasten this shift. They can do so in part by providing the first planks in a legal framework for global energy governance. Although energy is the "oxygen" of the global economy,[216] there is to date no overarching framework for global energy governance in international economic law. As Rafael Leal-Arcas and Andre Filis have lamented, "'[G)]obal energy governance' today is a theoretical concept that does not exist in actuality ... [T]he currently fragmented and multi-layered global energy governance is not conducive to energy security that is truly global ... (and) fails to address global energy security needs."[217]

The conclusion of a sustainable energy trade agreement by members of the WTO could begin to remedy this omission in international law and governance. Energy standards and regulations could be harmonized. Nontariff trade barriers could be reduced. Initiatives could be undertaken to transfer more green energy technologies to developing countries and to assist them in other ways in making the green transition. International cooperation on energy-related trade issues within the WTO could be increased and institutionalized. Likewise, cooperation between the WTO and other international institutions on energy issues could be enhanced.

At the outset, a WTO sustainable energy agreement could be a plurilateral agreement among a subset of WTO members willing to adopt new commitments on the use of green energy. As with other previous plurilateral WTO agreements, it could then gradually evolve into a fully multilateral agreement as part of the WTO treaty. Countries could assume obligations when they are ready to do so, and the initial obligations could expand along with the gradual expansion of the membership of the new agreement.[218] Instead of continuing to acquiesce to a world filled with a perverse panoply of fossil fuel subsidies, the WTO could become an affirmative force for advancing sustainable energy through the construction of new and much-needed trade links.

8

Links to Ecology and a Circular Economy

LINKS TO ECOLOGY

Animal Life and Wildlife Trade

In December 2020, a Chinese national was arrested in Malaysia and extradited to the United States to face charges of orchestrating an illegal international criminal smuggling ring that shipped more than 1,500 endangered sea turtles from the United States to China. Five species of turtles – all listed as endangered – were taken illegally from the marshes of Florida, the Gulf Coast, and other American wetlands. Many of them "were bound with duct tape, stuffed into socks and shipped in mislabeled packages." Upon arrival in China, they were sold in the pet black market for as much as $20,000 each. The most colorful fetched the highest prices. The smugglers conducted their sophisticated operation mostly on social media. Payments to the poachers were made through PayPal.[1]

History may be written by the victors, but it can be rewritten to acknowledge the victims. An historical revision is underway now to acknowledge the truth of the shameful treatment through the centuries in the United States and in many other places in the world of enslaved Blacks, Indigenous peoples, oppressed women, and untold other victims of the saddest sins of our species. For too long, we have been mostly blind to the fact that a cruel barbarism has often accompanied the heralded rise to civilization. We look back on those who preceded us and realize belatedly that they had "moral blind spots" that kept most of them from seeing the unspeakable truth of their transgressions.[2] We ask: What are our moral blind spots? What are our own transgressions that are largely unseen by most of us but will appall our successors in centuries to come? Or, as commentator Nicholas Kristof has put it, "We live in a time of felled statues of men of the past. In the future, what will topple our statues?"[3]

Our statues will be toppled by our treatment of animals. Like the rest of nature, animals have intrinsic value. And, like we do with the rest of nature, we humans routinely abuse animals. If the circle of human concern is not yet wide enough to include all human animals, it is not surprising that it is also not wide enough to include other animals. Some visionaries have long hoped that this narrow circle of human concern will eventually widen to include all humanity and all the rest of the living world. In 1871, in *The Descent of Man*, Charles Darwin contended that moral values are evolutionary, that they develop "over time from a narrow focus on the self to an eventual concern for the entire web of life."[4] On one bright future day, Darwin believed, all other living creatures will be brought within the circle of human concern and will be linked with us at last, in Donald Worster's apt phrase, "through empathy as well as biology."[5]

We are not nearly there yet, not for other humans, and certainly not for other animals. This is one reason why it has been suggested that a goal addressing animal concerns should be added as the eighteenth goal to the existing seventeen Sustainable Development Goals.[6] Ingrid J. Vieeren-Hankers of Radboud University in the Netherlands argues that we have "neglected animal considerations in our discussions on sustainable development."[7] In echoing Darwin, she maintains that

the definition of sustainable development must be broadened to include the interest of the individual animal. The best way to do so is an 18th SDG on animal health, welfare and rights. In this manner, it becomes explicit that attention for the individual animal is an integral aspect of sustainable development. It also underscores that animal concerns are not only instrumental for human wellbeing but are a sustainable development goal in their own right, on equal footing with the other 17 goals.

As Vieeren-Hankers acknowledges, her views are consistent with those of the advocates of the "One Health" scientific movement, which sees the health and welfare of humans, ecosystems, and individual animals as one.[8] One Health emphasizes these links, and stresses that they have caused, and will cause again, the transmission of zoonotic diseases from animals to humans.[9] Emphasized in this integrated concept of health is that the "[c]omplex interactions among human, animal, and environmental health" must be treated as a whole, and that the "competing demands for high-quality natural resources that foster human and animal health" must be balanced "while not exhausting, polluting, or contaminating the environment."[10] Significantly, One Health does not exclude animals from the health equation.

Although there is no specific SDG on animals, they are not ignored in the SDGs. In the political declaration that accompanies the Sustainable Development Goals , the signatories say, "We envisage a world ... in which humanity lives in harmony with nature and in which wildlife and other living species are protected."[11] With this aim in mind, among the specific targets for halting biodiversity loss under Goal 15 are, importantly, two relating to illegal trade in turtles and in thousands of other wildlife species. One of these targets is to "[t]ake urgent action to end poaching and trafficking of protected species of flora and fauna and address both demand and supply of illegal wildlife products."[12] The other is to "enhance global support" toward those ends, "including by increasing the capacity of local communities to pursue sustainable livelihood opportunities."[13] The human plunder of the natural abundance of animal species worldwide through illegal wildlife trade is one of the most significant ways in which trade is linked to ecology.

Experts on biodiversity tell us that, "About 24 percent of all wild terrestrial vertebrate species are traded globally."[14] *Legal* international wildlife trade in these species has multiplied fivefold since 2006 and was estimated at $107 billion for 2019.[15] *Illegal* wildlife trade is estimated at between $7 billion and $23 billion annually.[16] This makes "wildlife crime one of the world's most lucrative illegal businesses."[17] In fact, "illegal trade in wildlife is the fourth largest illegal global trade, behind only narcotics, counterfeiting, and human trafficking."[18] Stewart Patrick of the Council on Foreign Relations has pointed out that, "While transnational criminals do not disclose quarterly reports, law enforcement officials and economists estimate" that the "total economic damage" of wildlife crime "is astronomical."[19] The World Bank estimates that illicit trafficking in animals, fish, and timber costs the global economy between $1 trillion and $2 trillion every year if lost ecosystem services such as carbon sequestration and genetic resources are included.[20]

Yet only a small fraction of the money spent annually on combating all these international crimes is spent on fighting illegal wildlife trade. The World Bank has found that about $260 million a year is spent by international donors to combat illegal wildlife trade in sixty-seven Asian and African countries, while the United States alone spends $30 billion a year in its "war on drugs."[21] This sum is a pittance when compared to the vast resources we are devoting to other global international lawbreaking. It is also a tiny amount when compared to the sheer size of the global industry that trades in wildlife, legally and illegally. In China alone – where the government is beginning, albeit belatedly, to crack down on illegal wildlife trade – wildlife farming is a $20 billion industry employing about 15 million people.[22] And, for its part, the United States is one of the foremost global importers of wildlife, "including for the massive exotic pet industry."[23]

Illegal wildlife trade not only threatens the nearly 6,000 animal species that are the targets of it – including, in addition to mammals, "reptiles, corals, birds, and fish."[24] Because it is not subject to the usual sanitary controls imposed by law, such illicit trade also greatly increases the potential exposure of humans to zoonotic diseases such as COVID-19 that leap from animals to humans. The animals are not to blame for this. We are. Our heedless destruction of our natural surroundings has made many of the animals that are most likely to be reservoirs – hosts – for harmful pathogens more vulnerable to human exploitation, and our "insatiable demand for consumption, status, and traditional medicine" has fueled the explosion in illegal wildlife trade.[25]

At present, "[t]here is no global agreement on wildlife crime," nor is there "any universally agreed definition of wildlife crime."[26] The best tool currently available in international law for fighting illegal wildlife trade is the 1973 Convention on Trade in Endangered Species of Wild Fauna and Flora – commonly known as "CITES."[27] As former CITES Secretary-General John Scanlon has noted, CITES "has done much of the heavy lifting in responding to the surge in wildlife crime."[28] By default, CITES has become the first stop for those seeking action against illegal wildlife trade, and it has worked closely with other international agencies and institutions in trying to combat that trade, including the World Trade Organization.[29]

However, as Scanlon has explained, CITES has a limited jurisdiction. Although CITES covers international trade, it does not cover domestic trade or poaching. Also, CITES applies only to those animals and plants that have been listed as threatened or endangered – currently about 36,000 species.[30] It does not apply to the eight million other known animal and plant species. (Millions more are thought to be still unknown.) In addition, although the countries that are parties to CITES are obliged by it to penalize trade that does not comply with the convention, CITES does not require that they criminalize illegal wildlife trade. As Scanlon has put it, "CITES is not a crime-related convention."[31]

In addition to CITES, noteworthy also is the World Organization for Animal Health, commonly known as the "OIE," the acronym for the original French name of the body – *Office International des Epizooties*,[32] which was formed in 1928 in part to establish rules for safe animal trade. To ensure food safety and animal welfare, the OIE strives to "safeguard world trade by publishing health standards for international trade in animals and animal products," which must be based on both science and ethics, and "to provide a better guarantee of food of animal origin and to promote animal welfare through a science-based approach."[33] Originally, the OIE focused solely on international efforts to prevent the spread of disease in farm animals, but its remit has since been expanded to include animal welfare and greater human respect for animals.[34] In 2017, the OIE recommended that "animal welfare should be an integral part of the broader goal of sustainable development, given its capacity to contribute to socio-economic development."[35]

Toward these ends, OIE works in concert with the Codex Alimentarius Commission – a joint agency of the FAO and the WHO that sets global food standards, guidelines, and codes of practice – to protect consumer health and promote fair practices in international food trade.[36] The Food and Agriculture Organization has also incorporated animal welfare into its portfolio of work, and has recognized the links between and among animal welfare and food safety, food security, poverty reduction, and economic development. In the view of the FAO, "concern for animal welfare … has to be considered alongside with environmental sustainability and secure access to food."[37] Other international treaties and institutions also address aspects of animal conservation and welfare, but none of them deal directly with illegal wildlife trade.

To remedy this omission, Scanlon has called for negotiation of an international agreement on wildlife crime that would establish a "comprehensive legally binding regime for tackling wildlife crime, within the framework of international criminal law rather than trade law."[38] He has suggested housing this new agreement in the United Nations Convention against Transnational Organized Crime of 2000 (also known as the Palermo Convention), which has already been done for such other serious crimes as human trafficking.[39] As he envisages it, "Such an agreement should oblige countries to prohibit the import of any wildlife, supported by criminal sanctions, unless the importer can prove it was legally obtained."[40] It could define wildlife crime and coordinate international efforts to deal with it. Moreover, "It could apply to CITES-listed species as well as species that are being illegally exploited by transnational organized criminals but are not yet listed under CITES."[41] An international agreement on wildlife crime could do much to help eliminate the scourge of illegal wildlife trade.

The WTO has an important supportive role to play in international endeavors to ensure animal protection and animal welfare. To a considerable extent, WTO rules are already crafted to fulfill this role. For example, WTO members have the right to take sanitary and phytosanitary measures to protect animal health, provided that such measures are applied "only to the extent necessary" to accomplish that purpose; are "based on scientific principles"; are not "maintained without sufficient scientific evidence"; do not result in arbitrary or unjustifiable discrimination; and are not disguised restrictions on international trade.[42]

To help facilitate safe trade, the WTO rules encourage the harmonization of SPS measures "on as wide a basis as possible," and generally provide that WTO members "shall base" their SPS measures "on international standards, guidelines or recommendations where they exist."[43] When they do so, those measures are "presumed to be consistent" with WTO rules.[44] WTO members can maintain SPS measures that result in a higher level of protection than would be achieved by measures based on the relevant international standards if there is a "scientific justification" or if they determine that a higher level of protection is appropriate.[45] These WTO rules make specific reference to the IOE and the Codex Alimentarius Commission as "relevant international organizations" that serve as science-based sources for standards, guidelines, and recommendations on SPS measures.[46]

Likewise, WTO rules on technical regulations, which address technical barriers to trade, can also affect animal welfare. Under these rules, the "legitimate objectives" of technical regulations specifically include the protection of animal health.[47] Such technical regulations cannot discriminate between and among foreign providers of like products or in favor of domestic or foreign providers of like products.[48] Nor can they create or intend to create "unnecessary obstacles to trade."[49] Also, they cannot be "more restrictive than necessary to fulfil a legitimate objective."[50] Like the WTO SPS rules, the WTO rules on technical regulations encourage the use of relevant international standards but permit countries to use other standards when the international standards "would be an ineffective or inappropriate means for the fulfilment of the legitimate objectives pursued."[51]

WTO rules also provide a general exception to what would otherwise be WTO obligations for measures "necessary to protect human, animal or plant life or health," so long as those measures "are not applied in a manner which would constitute a means of arbitrary or unjustifiable discrimination between countries where the same conditions prevail, or a disguised restriction on international trade."[52] This exception has proven effective in protecting animal welfare during the WTO's first decades. WTO jurists have ruled in favor of trade-restrictive national measures protecting sea turtles,[53] seals,[54] and dolphins.[55] The legal outcomes of these and other WTO trade disputes have long since established that trade concerns do not automatically trump environmental concerns in the WTO.

This general exception would certainly apply to measures taken to combat illegal wildlife trade. Even so, more could be done through WTO rules to combat illegal wildlife trade and to advance human awareness of the links between us and other animals. The WTO should certainly cooperate with other relevant international institutions in supporting global negotiations on an international agreement on wildlife crime. But more, as a complement to a new global agreement that would address *illegal* wildlife trade, WTO members should negotiate a trade agreement on animal protection and welfare that would extend the scope of the current trade rules to do more to ensure the respectful treatment of animals in wildlife trade that is *legal.*

Consistently with the current WTO rules, in May 2020, the OIE urged that countries "introduce no COVID-19-related sanitary measures unless and until these have been shown necessary to protect human or animal health, are scientifically justified by a risk analysis, and are fully in line with relevant International Standards."[56] The COVID-19 pandemic provides a compelling reason for WTO members to revisit the current rules to strengthen them in ways that will help limit the spread of the next zoonotic pandemic. As much as illegal wildlife trade threatens us with the prospect of dread and new diseases, legal wildlife trade, which is vastly larger, can do so even more. Yet, all too often, our border protections are porous to the health threats from legal wildlife trade.[57]

One of the best ways to strengthen the safeguards against the spread of disease is by giving much more importance to animal protection and welfare in the trade rules. This could be done in a new WTO agreement on the trade-related aspects of animal protection and welfare. In such an agreement, the current trade rules should be extended to include added attention to production, transportation, and other trade-related dimensions of animal protection and welfare that have often been overlooked in trade deliberations. The OIE defines "animal welfare" as "freedom from hunger, malnutrition and thirst;

freedom from fear and distress; freedom from heat stress or physical discomfort; freedom from pain, injury and diseases; and freedom to express normal patterns of behaviour."[58] Adding to the legal significance already accorded in WTO rules to OIE standards, this definition should be the touchstone for a new WTO accord.

A multilateral agreement on the trade-related aspects of animal protection and welfare could draw from and improve on pioneering provisions in the increasing number of bilateral and regional agreements that have dealt with wildlife trade and other animal issues. These might include the public participation and consultation procedures, and the environmental trade capacity building provisions, in the CAFTA-DR among the United States, Costa Rica, El Salvador, Guatemala, Honduras, Nicaragua, and the Dominican Republic; the biodiversity conservation, forest governance, and endangered species provisions in the US–Peru Trade Promotion Agreement; the provisions on environmental cooperation in the CPTPP among eleven countries along the Pacific Rim; and the provisions on illegal wildlife trade and species conservation in the USMCA among the United States, Mexico, and Canada.[59]

This new WTO agreement on the trade-related aspects of animal protection and welfare should be founded on an explicit recognition that animals are sentient beings; that they can perceive and feel the world around them; and that they each possess intrinsic value. Rene Descartes, the seventeenth-century French rationalist philosopher, famously saw animals as merely biological machines.[60] Today we know better. Today we know that animals are individual beings with unique characteristics all their own. The truth of nonhuman animal sentience has been increasingly demonstrated and acknowledged by scientists.[61] It has been gaining currency in national laws.[62] It is not yet expressed widely in international law.[63]

If we conclude a multilateral trade agreement that professes our kinship with other animals; if it affirms that animals have as much right as we do to coexist with us on our common planetary home; if it prevents the exploitation and abuse of animals in trade; and if it is one part of a broader commitment to animal protection and welfare through international law and the international rule of law, then perhaps future generations will be less inclined to topple our statues.

The Nexus of Natural Resources

Land, forests, water, minerals, energy, manufactures, food – there is a connecting nexus among the Earth's natural resources and the uses we derive from them. Each links with another. All link with all. The links of all are broadly and increasingly burdened by the cross-cutting and "compounding effects of multiple and interacting drivers" such as population growth, urbanization, technological change, and the cumulative weight of seemingly insatiable human resource demand and consumption.[64] Goals 14 and 15 of the Sustainable

Development Goals seek to ease these burdens on our natural resources of water and land, respectively. These goals can be achieved only through insistence on more sustainable links to the part of this nexus that is trade.

One of the worst threats to the nexus of our natural resources is deforestation – the permanent conversion of forest area to other land uses. Forests cover about 30 percent of the land area of the Earth, and they contain 80 percent of the planet's land animals and plants.[65] Yet forests are falling worldwide as more woodlands are cleared to make room for more crops and more livestock, as mining and drilling increase, and as growing cities extend their inexorable reach into the green reserves of nature. The destruction of forests is fed by the voracious demand of consumers in developed countries for the natural resources of developing countries. We are, quite literally, consuming the world's forests. About 10 percent of the forested areas of the world has already been lost to deforestation.[66] The extent of the ongoing losses of tropical forests has been the equivalent of thirty football fields per minute.[67] In addition to losses in biodiversity and other ecological harms, tropical deforestation accounts for about 20 percent of annual global greenhouse gas emissions.[68]

Three decades of international cooperation have been devoted to stopping the reckless and relentless destruction of forests. A set of aspirational "Forest Principles" was adopted at the UN Earth Summit in Rio de Janeiro in 1992.[69] In curbing carbon emissions from forests to fight climate change, the main focus since has been on an international mechanism now commonly known as REDD +, which addresses the "Reduction of Emissions from Deforestation and Forest Degradation." REDD was first discussed as a global framework for reducing forest emissions and degradation under the UNFCCC at COP11 in 2005. It was expanded into REDD+ at COP13 in 2007, with the "plus" referring to the sustainable management of forests and the conservation and enhancement of forest carbon stocks. [70] In furtherance of these forest ambitions, in 2014, a large group of national governments, subnational governments, companies, Indigenous peoples, and NGOs agreed to the New York Declaration on Forests, with a goal of cutting forest loss in half by 2020 and ending it by 2030.[71]

Goal 15 of the SDGs aspired, by 2020, to accomplish "the sustainable management of all types of forests, halt deforestation, restore degraded forests and substantially increase afforestation and reforestation globally."[72] In the three decades following the 1992 Earth Summit, up until the arrival of the COVID-19 pandemic, although an alarming amount of deforestation continued, the rate of forest loss decreased.[73] After the adoption of the SDGs in 2015, progress occurred in many places, but the UN fell short of meeting its ambitious deadline of stopping deforestation by 2020.

Then came the COVID-19 pandemic. One of the grimmer results of the pandemic is a belated realization of one of the direst and deadliest consequences for humanity of deforestation and other forms of land-use change. With deforestation, more forest edges "arise as humans build roads or clear forests for timber production and agriculture."[74] Novel viruses emerge from these forest edges when animal carriers of zoonotic diseases lose their habitat due to these human encroachments and are brought into closer contact with humans. New viruses then jump from animals to humans. Biologists and epidemiologists advise us that "a major effort to retain intact forest cover would have a large return on investment even if its only benefit was to reduce virus emergence events."[75] Otherwise, there will be a long succession of new and potentially more dangerous pandemics stretching out into the future.

Unquestionably, stopping deforestation could help prevent pandemics.[76] Yet, during the COVID-19 pandemic, deforestation has increased as "forests have been razed at alarming rates across Asia, Africa and Latin America," adding to the risks of COVID-19 infection in some of the world's most populous countries.[77] The World Resources Institute has reported that, despite the decline in economic activity due to the pandemic, the loss of primary old-growth tropical forests – critical as sinks for carbon and sources for biodiversity – increased by 12 percent between 2019 and 2020.[78] Reasons for these forest losses are many amid the pandemic's unprecedented disruptions – slackened law enforcement, relaxed government management, government policy changes, migration from cities to rural areas, and more logging by the poor to secure more cash for health care.[79] All told, worldwide, monitored forest loss alerts during the pandemic have increased from the previous dozen years by 77 percent.[80]

This sharp increase in deforestation during the pandemic is also adding to global carbon dioxide emissions. In addition to protecting us against pandemics, forests are also carbon sinks. They soak up and store carbon in trees. When trees are felled, carbon is released. "Cutting and burning trees adds as much pollution to the atmosphere as all the cars and trucks in the world combined."[81] And the higher global temperatures caused in no small part by deforestation, are creating negative feedback; they are reducing the value of forests as carbon sinks by limiting photosynthesis and thus making the lives and the heights of trees shorter.[82]

Vital to reducing global carbon emissions is the largest rainforest in the world – the Amazon River Basin. Long a carbon sink for the entire planet, the Amazon soaks up 5 percent of all global carbon emissions annually.[83] Today it absorbs about a third less carbon than it did a decade ago.[84] During the past fifty years, the Amazon has lost about 17 percent of its size.[85] In 2020, as the virus raged, destruction in the Amazon surged 21 percent, deforesting an area the size of Israel.[86] At that rate, the Amazon rainforest will become less and less useful as a carbon sink offsetting carbon emissions, and it will "reach a tipping point in 10 to 20 years, after which it will enter a sustained death spiral as it dries out and turns into a savanna."[87]

Does international trade contribute to deforestation?

One major cause of deforestation is the clearing of forests for the permanent conversion of lands for commercial agriculture – soybeans and cattle in Latin America; palm oil in Southeast Asia; tropical fruits in Central America; cotton in India; and cocoa and sugar in West Africa. Notably, there has been a concentration of deforestation in the tropical areas in Africa, Asia, and South America.[88] This process of land conversion has contributed during the past quarter of a century to a global explosion in agricultural trade. Agricultural exports have doubled in volume and tripled in value since 1995, and account now for more than $1.8 trillion in global exports.[89]

When additional trade affects local agricultural prices, it also affects deforestation rates. When trade liberalization lowers local agricultural prices, deforestation decreases; when freer trade lifts local agricultural prices, deforestation increases.[90] Additional international trade can also have the effect of shifting deforestation into "ecologically sensitive locations."[91] Those countries with a comparative advantage in agricultural production are likely to be the most affected. They will be lured by trade to specialize in agricultural production and thus will engage in agricultural expansion, often in the wrong places ecologically. This has proven to be the case especially for countries in the tropics such as Brazil and Indonesia.

Another main cause of deforestation is timber extraction. International trade gives countries with a comparative advantage in natural resources an incentive to increase resource extraction, such as by felling trees for timber. But here the evidence of the effects of trade on deforestation is ambiguous. On the one hand, higher prices for timber extraction resulting from increased international trade may lead to more deforestation. On the other hand, "high prices of timber" resulting from more trade "might actually lead to increases in forest plantations" because of additional forest investments.[92] Thus, trade can lead to cutting trees, and it can also lead to planting them.

The destruction of forests because of trade is not inevitable. With both agriculture and timber extraction, a combination of conservation and sustainable forest management can help offset any negative effects from additional international trade. Damage to forests from increased trade can be reduced by sound policies that keep forestlands inaccessible and by "conservation efforts in accessible forest areas, stronger institutions and long term sustainability policies."[93] To save the forests, the relationship between trade and deforestation suggests that "trade liberalization efforts should be accompanied by policies to direct agricultural land expansion away from forests and sensitive habitat regions."[94] This relationship also suggests that agricultural and timber trade concessions in trade agreements should be contingent on making "the allocation of the gains from trade ... sensitive to the size of the remaining (forest) stock."[95]

The WTO must do much more to link agricultural trade and "trade in forest products to sustainability in the forest sector."[96] Additional trade in both agricultural and timber products must be conditioned in WTO trade rules on sustainable forest management. As Christian Mersmann explained in a report to the UN Food and Agriculture Organization as long ago as 2004, "Forest governance and trade are linked in two ways: policies and institutions determine and influence patterns of trade, and the scale and dynamics of trade can influence the nature and quality of forest governance and thus sustainable forest management."[97] The bountiful benefits of trade in timber and in agricultural products can be secured without sacrificing the sustainability of the forests of the world.

In the European Union, a new forest strategy was announced in 2020 as part of the far-reaching EU Green Deal.[98] The new strategy centers on measures to support deforestation–free value chains and to protect and restore forests. It looks especially at the effects of land use, land-use change, and forestry in a global context. Under this new strategy, measures taken must be compliant with climate change and biodiversity regulations, and, importantly, must account for the impact of EU consumption patterns on forests in other countries.[99] The EU forestry strategy can serve as a model for new WTO rules that establish forest management conditions to further increases in timber and agricultural trade. These new trade rules could be part of a new WTO plurilateral or – ideally – multilateral legal framework for the promotion of trade in sustainable timber and agricultural products.

One way in which WTO members have tried to curb deforestation is by imposing restrictions on trade in timber in violation of national laws, which "can lead to degraded forest ecosystems and loss of biodiversity, impede economic development, challenge local governance, and contribute to crime and corruption."[100] According to INTERPOL, illegal logging accounts for between 50 and 90 percent of all the forest activities in regions with large tropical forests, "such as the Amazon and areas in Central Africa and Southeast Asia."[101] Globally, annual trade in illegally harvested timber is between $51 billion and $151 billion.[102] In addition, illegal logging reduces the prices of legal timber by between 7 and 16 percent.[103] Annual revenue losses for the countries that are the sources of illegal timber total $5 billion.[104]

In the United States, the Lacey Act makes it illegal to import illegal timber and place it in the US market.[105] In the European Union, the Forest Law Enforcement, Governance and Trade (FLEGT) Action Plan and the EU Timber Regulation do the same in the EU market while also requiring that European operators implement a system of "due diligence" to minimize the risk of illegal timber imports.[106] In Australia, the Illegal Logging Prohibition Act takes the same approach as the EU Timber Regulation.[107] More such national laws are much needed. These laws should include not only restrictions on imports of illegally harvested timber but also restrictions on imports of agricultural products grown on illegally deforested lands. Such a national measure should be considered consistent with current WTO rules so long as it is not applied in an arbitrary or unjustifiable manner and not structured as a disguised protection for the timber products of the domestic industry of the country enacting the law.

Other ways in which WTO members have tried to reduce deforestation have included market-based measures such as forest certification schemes, chain of custody verifications, and eco-labeling. The most widespread of these approaches is forest certification by the Forest Stewardship Council, an independent, international nongovernmental organization that certifies that wood is from managed forests that meet an established set of criteria. About 440 million hectares – about 1.09 billion acres – have been certified by the FSC. This area comprises about 10.7 percent of all global forests and accounts for 29.6 percent of industrial roundwood production.[108] Unless there is arbitrary or unjustifiable discrimination or disguised protectionism, these measures are likewise consistent with existing WTO rules.

The question of the link between deforestation and trade caused controversy in 2020 and 2021 during consideration by the European Union of approval of a long-awaited trade agreement between the EU and the South American countries comprising the MERCOSUR trade bloc, including Brazil. The deforestation in Brazil's Amazon rainforests climbed to a twelve-year high in 2020, and the EU refused to ratify the new trade deal unless Brazil committed to do more to save the Amazonian forests. Under President Jair Bolsonaro, Brazil has removed numerous environmental protections in the Amazon.[109] At President Biden's climate summit in April 2021, the Brazilian president pledged to end illegal deforestation in Brazil by 2030 if outside help with financing is provided, but there was widespread skepticism about the sincerity of this pledge.[110] Without such protections, additional forest clearance could result from the increased trade inspired by the new trade agreement with the EU. The territories of Indigenous people are the most at risk.[111] The EU-MERCOSUR trade agreement should become a tool to help protect the forests. It could then become an additional model for the WTO in dealing with the nexus of forests and trade.

Other models are in other bilateral and regional trade agreements. In particular, there is the Forest Annex of the United States–Peru Trade Promotion Agreement, which contains provisions for Peru to reduce illegal logging through law enforcement and monitoring.[112] The United States has provided financial and technical assistance to Peru to meet these goals. In other bilateral agreements, the United States has provided direct financial aid to countries to address illegal logging. For example, a bilateral agreement with Indonesia contains a Working Group on Combating Illegal Logging and Associated Trade, which promotes the legal trade of timber products.[113] Drawing on these and other examples of how trade agreements can be used for the prevention of deforestation, new multilateral WTO rules should be negotiated to help protect the world's forests.

In the nexus of natural resources, more sustainable links are needed equally in the mining of minerals and metals, especially as they relate to renewable energy and other new high technologies. These extractive industries must also become much more sustainable; as the European Commission has summarized the current situation, "[T]he economic importance of critical minerals and metals is influenced by their irreplaceable role in emerging technologies. These include new high-tech applications in information and communication technology, automotive and aerospace engineering, electrical equipment manufacturing, optical technologies and in the metallurgical and chemical industries."[114]

With these links, all is not as may be assumed by some advocates of a green recovery, in no small part because of what is happening in global energy markets. As innovation has worked its usual economic magic, the prices of renewable forms of energy have plunged. According to Bloomberg New Energy Finance, "Innovation and scale have driven down the costs of renewable energy ... and at the same time the technology keeps getting better."[115] The cost of solar panels has fallen 89 percent in the past decade.[116] Solar energy and wind energy are expected to comprise 56 percent of electricity generation worldwide by 2050.[117] By 2025, solar energy and wind energy "are on track to be cheaper than running existing coal and gas."[118]

This is all good news for the green transition. But, as *Wall Street Journal* columnist Joseph C. Sternberg has written, "[R]enewables won't so much free the world of strategic flash points as create new ones around rare-earth minerals, those dirty-to-mine, found-in-only-a-few-places-on-earth metals whose use is indispensable to green tech."[119] Equally, the same can be said of lithium, cobalt, graphite, and the other essential metal and mineral ingredients of a green economy. As economists for the OECD have observed, "Almost all consumer goods today contain raw materials from the mining sector; for example, a mobile phone can contain 50 different minerals and metals."[120] Lithium-ion batteries will be required for energy storage to sustain wind energy when the wind does not blow and solar energy when the sun does not shine.[121] The number of electric vehicles is expected to rise from five million today to 125 million by 2030, but these new cars will use four times the minerals used in cars driven by fossil fuels.[122]

The World Bank has noted this irony, explaining that, "A low-carbon future will be very mineral intensive because clean energy technologies need more materials than fossil-fuel-based electricity generation technologies."[123] Economists for the bank project increases in the production of minerals such as lithium, cobalt, and graphite of nearly 500 percent by 2050.[124] Countries such as China and the United States have abundant resources of many of these minerals. But no one country is self-sufficient in every mineral and metal; many of them must be imported. Paradoxically, along with this increased trade to facilitate a green industrial future – much of it flowing from developing to developed countries – will come significantly increased pressures on the Earth's threatened natural resources.

While consumer demands have exploded in recent decades for minerals and metals, the quest for these essential raw materials has, simultaneously, ranged farther and wider than ever before. In some instances, increased extraction has outpaced the discovery of new and accessible deposits of resources. In others, declines in high-quality resources have led to the extraction of larger amounts of resources of lower grades. These and other factors have combined to intensify the impact of resource extraction on the environment.[125] They have also led to ever-growing piles of mining waste, toxic and radioactive dust emissions from that waste, proliferating water pollution, and the destruction of ancient Indigenous historical sites.[126] Most often, these harms fall most heavily on the poorest and most powerless among us.

As with agricultural and forest products, the international trade in mining products should be conditioned on sustainable practices in their production. In 2019, in concert with the UN Sustainable Development Goals, the World Bank launched the Climate-Smart Mining Initiative, which features a public/private fund that supports "the sustainable extraction and processing of minerals and metals used in clean energy technologies, such as wind, solar power, and batteries for energy storage and electric vehicles. It focuses on helping resource-rich developing countries benefit from the increasing demand for minerals and metals, while ensuring the mining sector is managed in a way that minimizes the environmental and climate footprint."[127] Support for this and similar initiatives, and for recycling, reuse, and sustainable supply chains, should be conditions for increased mineral and metal extraction for international trade under new WTO trade rules.

Competition for natural resources – through trade and other less redeeming means – is nothing new. In the Bronze Age, trade with the Greek city-state of Mycenae provided pharaonic Egypt "with supplies of precious cobalt, which was used as a dark blue dye in its glassmaking industry."[128] Today, millennia later, cobalt is eagerly sought in a worldwide "mad scramble" as "a mineral essential to the rechargeable lithium-ion batteries that power smartphones, laptops and electric vehicles,"[129] so much so that it is often dug by hand in places such as the Congo, where an estimated 100,000 cobalt miners "use hand tools to dig hundreds of feet underground with little oversight and few safety measures."[130] These manual laborers "include children, who labor in harsh and dangerous conditions."[131]

The lives of these children and other modern cobalt miners are, perhaps, not so very different from those of the untold thousands of Egyptians who built the Great Pyramids 5,000 years ago. On the other end of the global supply chain for cobalt are a multinational corporation publicly pledged to sustainable practices and a teenager in a wealthy country with eyes glued to a smartphone. Clearly, mining practices must not only be sustainable; they must also be humane. Thus, national measures that condition trade in mining products on being humane, on being consistent with basic labor and other human rights, must be upheld by the WTO.

As with trade in medical supplies and trade in food, the advent of COVID-19 has accentuated long-existing concerns about restrictions on exports of minerals and metals. Exports of these natural resources have been increasingly constrained by export taxes, export bans, export quotas, export licensing schemes, minimum export prices, administered pricing, and "captive mining" rules that bar mine owners from trading internationally. Export taxes on a wide range of critical minerals and metals are increasingly prevalent, with China,

Vietnam, Argentina, and the Russian Federation prominent in relying on them. Often these export restrictions are not reported to the WTO.[132]

These export restrictions on minerals and metals have much the same consequences as those on medical supplies and food. Generally, they turn domestic producers toward the domestic market, driving down domestic prices, but ultimately driving down domestic production and, ironically, making the domestic economy worse off. At the same time, this version of "beggar-thy-neighbor" trade policy reduces global welfare by damaging the economies of other countries, which, in turn, invariably respond by imposing retaliatory trade barriers of their own which, in the end, makes everyone worse off.[133] Sometimes these export restrictions are defended as essential tools of national industrial policy, but, as is usually the case with talk of industrial policy, this is mostly just a euphemism for protectionism in trade, which is the opposite of what is needed to improve national welfare. Sometimes also these export restrictions are said to be necessary to protect the environment by conserving exhaustible natural resources. Where this is truly the case, WTO rules permit such restrictions.[134] But, in general, studies suggest that the conservation of such resources may not occur if the restricted mining products are "sold in domestic markets to expanding downstream industries."[135]

It will be recalled that "prohibitions or restrictions other than duties, taxes or other charges, whether made effective through quotas ... export licenses or other measures ... on the exportation or sale for export of any product" are inconsistent with WTO obligations.[136] This does not apply to "[e]xport prohibitions or restrictions temporarily applied to prevent or relieve critical shortages of foodstuffs or other products essential to the exporting" WTO member.[137] But all export restrictions, even when they are applied because of critical shortages, must be transparent and nondiscriminatory.[138] Any export restriction, even if unrelated to critical shortages, will be excused if it is "necessary to protect human, animal or plant life or health," or "essential to the acquisition or distribution of products in general or local short supply," and if it is not applied "in a manner which would constitute arbitrary or unjustifiable discrimination between countries where the same conditions prevail, or a disguised restriction on international trade."[139]

It will be recalled also that export taxes are not forbidden by WTO rules. This explains why so many export restrictions, including those on minerals and metals, are in the form of taxes. This also largely explains why, in trade disputes over its export restrictions on bauxite, fluorspar, and other raw materials, and on rare earth elements, China has twice been found in WTO dispute settlement to have violated its WTO obligations.[140] Most of these restrictions were export taxes. China had agreed upon becoming a member of the WTO not to impose export restrictions on a list of minerals and metals. All the minerals and metals at issue in the two disputes were on that list. However, except for the United States, which has a constitutional ban on export taxes, all other WTO members are free to tax exports as they choose under the current WTO rules.

At a minimum, WTO rules must be changed to make certain that sanctions can be applied on the traded products of countries that do not notify the WTO of their export restrictions. More broadly, the trade rules must be changed to prohibit taxes on exports, except for those that are "temporarily applied to prevent or relieve critical shortages of foodstuffs or other products essential to the exporting" WTO member.[141] Given the likely reluctance of many countries to relinquish their existing right to impose export taxes, this prohibition can probably only be secured as part of a comprehensive WTO agreement on the trade-related aspects of the mining of minerals and metals. Such a trade agreement could include negotiated guidelines on the environmental, labor, and other standards for "best practices" that should be employed in the industry, and assurances that production in accordance with those "best practices" would not be subject to export restrictions.

Land Use, Water, and Sustainable Agriculture

Land is the home of vast biodiversity. Land is the source of countless human ecological services. Land is a "provider of food, fodder, fibre and forest products."[142] Not least, land is where we live. Yet, throughout the world, there is an accelerating degradation of land, ranging from declines in biodiversity to destructions in ecosystems to disruptions in ecosystem services. Currently, the "degradation of the Earth's land surface through human activities is negatively impacting the well-being of at least 3.2 billion people, pushing the planet towards a sixth mass species extinction, and costing more than 10 percent of the annual gross product in loss of biodiversity and ecosystem services."[143]

This is why Goal 15 of the UN Sustainable Development Goals aspires to "protect, restore and promote sustainable use of terrestrial ecosystems" in part by halting and reversing land degradation.[144] Even before the adoption of the SDGs in 2015, the members of the United Nations pledged in 2012 at the "Rio +20" summit in Rio de Janeiro, Brazil (held twenty years after the original Earth Summit), to "strive to achieve a land-degradation neutral world in the context of sustainable development."[145] According to the scientists advising the United Nations, though, "[c]ontinuing on the current track," it will be "difficult to achieve" this globally agreed target.[146] Their "[a]ssessments based on satellite data show that land degradation hotspots cover about 29 per cent of global land area."[147]

Any endeavor to reduce land degradation must begin with its links to agriculture. Humanity has been occupying ever larger reaches of land for agriculture for the past 8,000 years.[148] Today, half of the Earth's habitable land is used for agriculture.[149] Combining pasture land with land for animal feed crops, livestock accounts for 77 percent of global agricultural land.[150] Given these facts, it is not surprising that "[a]gricultural and food production are ... responsible for most of the changes of land, including forests and other types of ecosystems," or that "human-induced land degradation remains a fundamental environmental problem affecting food security, livelihoods and lives of the people on this planet."[151]

Further complicating matters in the new pandemic world are the links between land use and agriculture and the global spread of the pandemic. "Agricultural intensification, often combined with production of domesticated animals in more intensive settings ... creates ideal conditions for disease organisms to thrive, evolve, and make the jump to human hosts."[152] For this reason, "Over 30% of emerging infectious diseases are linked to land use change, including the conversion of land for agriculture and livestock production."[153] Land clearing to produce more food also produces the potential for more zoonotic pandemics as humans and animals are brought in closer proximity. Thus, improving land use worldwide will improve public health.

Far too much global land is used for livestock. Growing global demand for protein, especially in developing countries, has vastly increased global demand for meat, which has in turn vastly increased the amount of land used for raising cattle, pigs, chickens, and other animals to help feed us.

Although 77 percent of global agricultural land is devoted to livestock, this land produces less than 20 percent of the world's food calories.[154] And the ways these animals are treated on the "factory farms" on this land are often appalling.[155] About 70 billion land animals are raised and slaughtered to fill our food plates each year.[156] These numbers would be reduced significantly and much less land would be needed for growing livestock if we ate less meat and if our climate plans included supporting new technologies for plant-based meat and cultivated meat grown directly from animal cells.[157] Trade can help spread these new technologies worldwide.

According to UNEP, "By 2050, the world needs to produce at least 50 per cent more food to feed the projected global population of 10 billion people."[158] With global food production expected to rise significantly to feed a growing global population, the conversion of still more extensive tracts of land to agriculture worldwide can also be expected.[159] Human hunger will push food production farther and farther into what will no longer be forests and plant and animal habitats. With this prospect before us, the only way to feed the people of the world while also preventing widespread ecological devastation is for agriculture to become more sustainable.

Sustainable agriculture can feed us today without starving our children and our grandchildren. Toward this end, throughout the world, we must "find new food systems, adapted to local ecological conditions and causing much less ecological damage."[160] The land ethic of ecologist Aldo Leopold teaches us that the land is a community to which we belong, which "changes the role of *Homo sapiens* from conqueror of the land-community to plain member and citizen of it."[161] Proceeding from this insight, we must treat agricultural land in a way that harmonizes the uses of humanity with the necessities of nature. Thus, a sustainable approach to agriculture must include "promoting sustainable soil management, the rehabilitation and restoration of degraded habitats, promoting research on crop efficiency and resilience, support and promotion of organic agriculture and agro-forestry, encouraging agricultural diversification, and improved watershed management."[162]

Agriculture is the world's largest industry, and, as it is, the pressures of food production weigh heavily on the planet – more heavily with each passing day.[163] Moreover, these pressures have impacts that extend far beyond food production through the links of agriculture to the breadth of the Earth's natural resources and the scope of the world's climate and other ecological challenges. When these pressures are eased, "[w]hen agricultural operations are sustainably managed, they can preserve and restore critical habitats, help protect watersheds, and improve soil health and water quality."[164] They can feed each and every one of us today and tomorrow.

A central requirement of sustainable agriculture is sustainable water use. Of the habitable land in the world, 1 percent is covered by lakes and rivers that, along with underground aquifers, provide us with freshwater.[165] About 70 percent of freshwater use worldwide is for agriculture.[166] Global water withdrawals are forecast to increase by 15 percent by 2050 to help sustain all of those ten billion people who will hunger and thirst by then.[167] Amid reports of floods in Jakarta, water shortages in Cape Town, and droughts in Australia, Chile, Madagascar, the Middle East, and the western United States, there are well-founded fears of impending and multiplying water crises around the world.

In 2020, business leaders involved with the World Economic Forum ranked the prospect of water crises as a top global risk.[168] They did so while knowing that "some 1.1 billion people worldwide lack access to water, and a total of 2.7 billion people find water scarce for at least one month of the year," and that "[i]nadequate sanitation is also a problem for 2.4 billion people," who are therefore "exposed to diseases, such as cholera and typhoid fever, and other water-borne illnesses."[169] The risk of water scarcity and water pollution threatens to add to these already alarming numbers. Much of this global risk can be traced back to the use of water in agriculture.

Because of this risk, Goal 6 of the UN Sustainable Development Goals is to "[e]nsure availability and sustainable management of water and sanitation for all."[170] Already missed is the ambitious SDG target of protecting and restoring the water-related ecosystems of "wetlands, rivers, aquifers and lakes" by 2020, which remains imperative.[171] Given the inescapable link between water and agriculture, the ultimate achievement of this global goal cannot be separated from the achievement of Goal 2 of the SDGs, which is to "[e]nd hunger, achieve food security and improve nutrition and promote sustainable agriculture."[172] Nor can either of these goals be accomplished without due consideration of the links between both of them and trade, and without changes in the trade rules to ensure water quantity and quality and to further sustainable agriculture.

Feeding the world depends on having enough quality water to drink and to grow food. World trade rules must help, and not hinder, all the local "bottom up" efforts throughout the world to prevent water scarcity and improve water security. As it is, WTO rules on technical regulations support water labeling as one form of eco-labeling. Such labeling can inform consumers of the impacts of producing traded goods on water scarcity and water security.[173] In addition, WTO subsidies rules should be revised to make illegal any production that creates water scarcity or damages water security. This should be part of a broader reform to discipline governmental subsidies that cause environmental harms. Moreover, beyond the WTO, there should be negotiations on global rules that will uphold the right to water while setting global standards for water pricing.[174]

Feeding the world also increasingly depends on international trade. Most food is still grown and consumed domestically. "Just under one-quarter of all food produced for human consumption is traded on international markets."[175] The percentage of food that is imported for consumption has, however, been rising in recent decades through deeper integration of the world's food markets. Because of rapid population growth and heightened demands for greater food variety as the size of the middle classes expands in developing economies, "[m]ost developing countries have become increasingly reliant on imports to meet domestic demand, a trend that will be likely to continue to 2050."[176]

Eighty percent of the people in the world live in food deficit countries[177] that must import food to feed all their populations.[178] As UNEP has pointed out, "Global food supply has become dependent on the growing trade in a small number of crops grown in a few 'breadbasket' regions with increasing specialization," and "[t]his had led to lower food prices with food-deficit countries benefiting from these food imports."[179] Thus, international trade "links countries with a food deficit with countries with a food surplus and raises consumption possibilities through specialization according to comparative advantage."[180]

Trade can support sustainable agriculture. To be sure, when not done sustainably, agricultural trade can and does contribute to climate and other environmental harms. It can have damaging direct effects, such as increased pollution or the degradation of natural resources; and it can have destructive indirect effects, such as the displacement of farmers onto marginal lands "leading to deforestation and soil erosion."[181] But studies show that agricultural trade can also help the environment. "[F]ree trade may lead to more effective environmental management, promote more efficient production, reduce energy use and improve access to new technologies."[182] For example, freeing trade can alleviate the impact of climate change on agricultural production.[183] Moreover, it can contribute to the transfer of renewable energy products and other new technologies that can improve agricultural production while reducing resulting environmental harms.[184]

Especially, freeing trade from the trade distortions caused by agricultural subsidies can also free the environment from other equally damaging distortions. Not only do the trade distortions caused by agricultural subsidies make no economic sense. Their adverse impacts are not limited to agriculture. In addition to distorting farm trade, agricultural subsidies "lead to massive health costs, in terms of malnutrition and obesity, as well as vast environmental externalities – deforestation, ecosystem loss, fertilizer runoff, eutrophication."[185] The nexus of natural resources is revealed all too clearly in the breadth of the deleterious effects of agricultural subsidies.

In agricultural trade, the path to more sustainability is through the openness of freer trade. It is through more transparency and more market access. It is through an end to tariffs and an elimination of trade-distorting subsidies. As with manufactured goods, it is through adding environmental harms to the adverse effects that can make a subsidy illegal under WTO rules. It is through sanitary and phytosanitary measures and technical regulations that establish higher domestic and international standards for the use of chemicals and pesticides, and for limiting nutrient runoff from agricultural fields. It is through more mutual recognition of standards and more international regulatory cooperation. Not least, the path to more sustainability in agricultural trade is through recasting WTO agricultural negotiations to center on sustainability.

Trade can also support sustainable use of freshwater in agriculture; for it can "foster transparent and open markets to absorb the impact of domestic water risks and to allow food to be produced where it is economically efficient and environmentally sustainable to do so."[186] Champions of "food localism" – of eating locally grown instead of imported food – often fail to discern the link between water use and agriculture. Thus, they also fail to see the link between water use and agricultural trade. So, they are blind to the fact that openness to trade leads to using less water in agriculture, not more. The evidence indicates that an *increase* of 1 percent in openness to trade leads to a *decrease* of 5.21 percent in agricultural water withdrawals, primarily because engagement in international trade leads farmers "to produce more with less water, such as through the adoption of technology."[187] Overall, "[i]nternational trade ... reduces global water use by 5%."[188]

Broadly speaking, to achieve sustainability and water security, water-scarce countries should import water-intensive products and export products for which less water is consumed in production. Sustainability is enhanced when countries with scarce water resources import water-intensive crops from somewhere else, which preserves local water supplies for other uses. In contrast, sustainability is diminished when water-scarce countries grow and export water-intensive crops, which drains local water supplies.[189] International trade can help make the most sustainable approaches to agriculture profitable by providing more access to markets in countries that would otherwise have to engage in unsustainable agricultural practices to obtain some of their staple foods. Why try to grow wheat in a desert when you can import it more cheaply and without the drain on local water supplies?

Skeptics of trade often wrongly assume that increasing trade has the effect of decreasing water supply and thus water security because of the "virtual water" in traded products. Virtual water is not actual liquid water; rather, it is the quantity of water used in producing a traded good. This amount of water is embedded in traded goods, mostly in agricultural goods but also in manufactured goods. About one-fourth of water use "is exported as virtual water," resulting, in effect, in the transfer of water from the country in which the traded product is produced to the importing country.[190] The misapprehension of those who work for water security is that trade thereby necessarily makes water supplies less secure.

Laboring under this mistaken assumption, some water activists have called for altering WTO rules to allow discrimination in trade between goods based on the amounts of virtual water embedded in them. They perceive developing countries as prejudiced by the present structure of trade in virtual water, and they see this rule change as necessary to safeguard their water supplies and water security.[191] But there is no need to make such a change in the trade rules. Trade in virtual water does not deplete water. It saves water.[192] In fact, estimates are that the current trade in virtual water results in average savings of 22 percent of the world's water.[193] Any WTO decision to reduce trade between developed and developing countries because of the amount of virtual water in traded products would be "a perfect formula for global impoverishment."[194]

Poverty is perpetuated in part by food waste, mostly in developed countries. "Approximately one-third of the food produced for human consumption is wasted or lost annually, at a financial cost of US$750 billion to US$1 trillion ... This wasted food could feed over 2 billion people."[195] As the WWF has observed, "In a multiplier effect, when food loss and waste occurs along the supply chain, all the land, water, energy, seeds, fertiliser, labour, capital and other resources that went into its production also go to waste."[196] Food waste and loss also contribute to climate change, accounting for at least 6 percent of global greenhouse gas emissions – three times that from aviation.[197] If food waste were a country, it would be the third largest emitter of greenhouse gases.[198] One of the targets of Goal 12 of the Sustainable Development Goals is to "halve per capita food waste at the retail and consumer levels and reduce food losses along production and supply chains, including post-harvest losses" by 2030. Making supply chains more sustainable can help us reach this target. But this target cannot be attained simply by altering trade practices and finessing trade rules. It can be met only if we begin to look at agricultural production and consumption in an entirely new way.

It can be met only if we start to see the economy as circular.

LINKS TO A CIRCULAR ECONOMY

Sustainable Consumption and Production

The concept of a "circular economy" emerged from the thinking of American industrial ecologist Robert Ayres in the 1990s.[199] Ayres, a polymath who was originally trained as a physicist, maintains that the ideal state of an industrial system resembles nature in that it supports a complete internal cycle of materials *with no loss*. From this initial insight has been extrapolated the notion that the ideal economic system should be like the ideal industrial system. It should be self-perpetuating and self-regenerating. It should be "circular."

Most of global growth is "linear" growth in which "virgin resources are extracted, traded and processed into goods, which are then used and discarded as waste or emissions."[200] The line of the "linear" economy, which proceeds straight from extraction to production to consumption, to a growing global heap of relentless disposal, should be transformed into a circle. In this circle, the full life cycle of every product should be accounted for, and the focus should be on eliminating waste and ending the unnecessary use and exhaustion of resources. "In contrast to the 'take-make-waste' linear model, a circular economy is regenerative by design; it aims to gradually decouple growth from the consumption of finite resources."[201] The idea of a "circular economy" is a systemic approach to development in which the central concern is sustainable development.

In 2002, proceeding from Ayres' insight, American architect William McDonough and German chemist Michael Braungart proposed an economic design model that posited "cradle-to-cradle" instead of "cradle-to-grave" thinking.[202] They emphasized the need to manufacture products with the aim of returning biological materials to the environment and recycling all other materials in a continuous process they described as "upcycling."[203] Since then, the idea of a circular economy has "evolved into a broad-based approach to make resource use more sustainable throughout the product lifecycle"[204] and to maintain resources "at their highest value possible."[205] The concept has slowly spread worldwide, and it has been increasingly embraced by various international institutions.[206]

In 2018, when pondering whether the concept of a circular economy had become "the new normal," UNCTAD explained,

A circular economy entails markets that give incentives to reusing products, rather than scrapping them and then extracting new resources. In such an economy, all forms of waste, such as clothes, scrap metal and obsolete electronics, are returned to the economy or used more efficiently. This can provide a way to not only protect the environment, but use natural resources more wisely, develop new sectors, create jobs and develop new capabilities.[207]

Today, the concept of a circular economy is still evolving, in part through the process of implementing its incorporation into the Sustainable Development Goals.[208] Goal 12 of the SDGs is to "ensure sustainable consumption and production patterns."[209] To accomplish this goal, the first target is to implement the "10-Year Framework of Programmes on Sustainable Consumption Patterns," which was adopted at the "Rio+20" summit in Rio de Janeiro in 2012, reaffirming the view first advanced by the United Nations in 2002 that "fundamental changes in the ways societies produce and consume are indispensable for achieving global sustainable development."[210]

Targets of this ambitious global goal also include the sustainable management and efficient use of natural resources; halving per capita food waste; environmentally sound management of chemicals and their wastes throughout their life cycle; the substantial reduction of waste generations through prevention, reduction, recycling and reuse; sustainable public procurement practices; and support for scientific and technological capacity-building for developing countries to help them attain these and other related ends.[211]

Still far from being achieved, this goal and these targets have come none too soon. The burden we impose on the Earth now exceeds the Earth's rate of regeneration. In the past sixty years, humanity's "ecological footprint," a measure of the impact of our production and consumption on the planet, has increased by 173 percent and today exceeds Earth's biocapacity by 56 percent.[212] As the WWF has observed, we are "living off 1.56 Earths."[213] According to the United Nations, if, as expected, global population rises to ten billion people by 2050, resources equivalent to three Earths will be needed to maintain our current lifestyle.[214]

Most of the resources we currently consume are simply wasted. More than 100 billion tons of the Earth's resources are consumed by the global economy every year, and more than 60 percent of those resources "ends up as waste or greenhouse gas emissions."[215] There are numerous dimensions to this never-ending flow of human-created waste. Three tons of material extraction are required to produce one ton of goods.[216] Only 8.6 percent of the world economy is circular.[217] Some poorer countries do a much better job than richer countries of being circular, in part because of the traditional circular practices of many Indigenous peoples.[218] But the otherwise ubiquitous human habit is to use something and then throw it away – without really knowing where it goes.

In our still predominantly linear economy, there remain high levels of extraction, low levels of end-of-use processing and recycling, and rising levels of buildup in noncircular long-term buildings, infrastructure, and capital equipment in which materials become embedded and are unavailable for circular use.[219] As Karsten Steinfatt of the WTO Secretariat has explained, this is in part because "it is generally more cost-effective to produce goods from virgin resources and then to use and discard them, than to keep goods, components and materials in use at their highest utility at any time."[220] What seems cheaper in the short term, however, is often not cheaper in the long term.

The pattern of human consumption is not even. People in the wealthiest countries consume ten times as much as people in the poorest countries.[221] One consequence of this disparity in consumption is additional greenhouse gas emissions. According to UNEP, "The emissions of the richest 1 per cent of the global population account for more than twice the combined share of the poorest 50 per cent."[222] The wealthiest countries also stand out in the sheer amount of their waste. With just 4 percent of the world's population, the United States produces 12 percent of global municipal waste. This is equivalent to 234 pounds of waste per person per year. And only 35 percent of this waste is recycled. In contrast, although China and India together have 36 percent of the global population, they account for just 27 percent of global municipal waste.[223]

There is much to be gained economically everywhere from altering the current patterns of human consumption by shifting from a linear to a circular economy. As David McGinty of the World Resources Institute has observed, creating a circular economy in just five economic sectors – cement, aluminum, steel, plastics, and food – "could cut CO_2 emissions by 3.7 billion tons in 2050, equivalent to eliminating current emissions for all forms of transport."[224] The worldwide economic benefits of implementing circular strategies have been estimated at $700 billion per year by 2050.[225] With respect to just one sector, the World Economic Forum has estimated that "a circular battery value chain" for producing and recycling storage batteries for electric cars and other new technologies could account for 30 percent of the emissions cuts required in the transport and power sectors to meet the targets in the Paris climate agreement; provide access to electricity to 600 million people who currently have none; and also "create 10 million safe and sustainable jobs."[226]

Modernization of the WTO trade rules can help us achieve these economic benefits. Intermittently, the WTO has participated on the periphery in the gathering global debate about the merits of a circular economy. WTO members have, however, not yet sought to revise the trade rules to make them more circular. WTO rules do not generally pose obstacles to measures that promote a circular economy. But, as Steinfatt has written,

[P]ast trade policies have often been designed with a linear 'take-make-discard', instead of a circular model in mind. They have paid little, if any, attention to the optimum management of resources throughout their life cycle. As a result, many trade policies and measures inadvertently hinder and reduce the competitiveness of the activities and functions that are at the core of a circular economy.[227]

She cites, as an example, metal recycling. Trade in metallic waste and scrap is often subject to export restrictions. Such restrictions "tend to lower the prices of metal scrap in the restricting country, creating a disincentive for collecting it."[228] Also, government subsidies for metal production "may also affect the competitiveness of metal scrap and processing," thus causing a shift from manufacturing to primary resource production, which uses raw material inputs more intensively.[229] An end to metals trade barriers and distortions "would promote the expansion of the global supply chains needed to create a more efficient circular economy in metals," which "would result in sizeable environmental benefits."[230]

All and all, as Steinfatt rightly contends,

opening and facilitating trade in goods, components, materials and services related to key circular economy activities (such as reuse, repair, refurbishment, remanufacturing and recycling) would help to ensure that these activities happen in the best possible locations in terms of cost, quality, skills and other location-specific advantages.

Moreover, open trade would give companies involved in circular economic activities improved access to a larger supply of recovered goods, components and materials for circulation.[231]

Where necessary, trade barriers should be eliminated to fulfill these purposes. Furthermore, the WTO should ensure that trade rules promote circularity and sustainability in the trade in domestically prohibited goods, secondhand or refurbished goods, and remanufactured goods, all of which have significant environmental implications.[232]

The value of a circular economy has been acknowledged in WTO dispute settlement. In a trade dispute over Brazil's waste management policy for used and retreaded automobile tires, WTO jurists recognized the importance of protecting public health and the environment against the accumulation of waste.[233] The legal door is therefore wide open in WTO jurisprudence for WTO members to seek ways through additional rulemaking to encourage circular practices in such areas as sustainable supply chains, sustainable investment, and sustainable public procurement. The place to start could be with the urgent global issue of plastics pollution.

Trade Solutions to Plastics Pollution

The concept of a circular economy has gradually been gaining more currency within the World Trade Organization. Amid all else that was happening in the world, there was little notice in November 2020 of a WTO session in Geneva that may open a new front in reconciling trade with the environment. In a meeting convened by China and Fiji, a small group of interested members of the WTO launched an "open-ended informal dialogue" on the trade-related aspects of plastics pollution.[234] Such dialogues in the WTO can eventually end up as formal trade negotiations, and the impetus for negotiations on trade in plastic waste within the WTO seems to be increasing even as the wider world strives to grapple with this pressing issue of sustainable development.

These informal WTO talks were held just days after the release by Oceana, the world's largest ocean conservation organization, of evidence that nearly 1,800 marine animals from forty different species – 88 percent of them endangered or threatened with extinction – swallowed or became entangled in plastic bags, plastic wrappers, and other plastic waste in US waters in the past decade. Among these at-risk species are Florida manatees, Hawaiian seals, and all six species of American sea turtle.[235] And these discussions occurred just weeks after the release of a new scientific study showing that the United States is the world's largest source of plastic waste, releasing about 42 million metric tons into the global environment in 2016 (the most recent data available). The then twenty-eight member states of the European Union (including the soon-to-depart United Kingdom) ranked second that year. Third was India.[236]

Made from fossil fuels, plastic is a ubiquitous part of the global carbon economy.[237] Since 1950, about 6.3 billion tons of plastic waste has been created worldwide, and 91 percent of it has never been recycled.[238] Two-thirds of all the plastic ever produced has been released into the environment, where it "has remained and continues polluting."[239] By one reckoning, 2.5 percent of global greenhouse gas emissions are from the production and incineration of plastics.[240] We humans produce more than 300 million tons of plastic every year, and about half of it is single use – it is used just once and then thrown away.[241] This tsunami of plastic has caused untold harm to the earth's ecosystems and all that live in them and depend on them, and it will continue to do so "for at least several hundred years."[242]

Plastic waste ranges from ordinary plastic grocery bags and plastic food wrappers to tiny plastic fibers no larger than sesame seeds that are called "microplastics," many of which are created when larger pieces of plastic debris degrade in the water.[243] These microplastics are especially harmful when ingested by birds and aquatic life, and nowadays they are everywhere. In 2018, plastic debris was found 36,000 feet deep in the Pacific Ocean in the Mariana Trench, the deepest point on Earth.[244] In 2020, scientists announced they had discovered microplastics in snow from near the summit of Mount Everest, the highest point on Earth.[245]

The Earth's marine environment suffers especially from plastics pollution. Every year, more than eleven million metric tons of plastic is dumped into the ocean.[246] This is the equivalent of dumping one garbage truck of plastic into the ocean every minute.[247] According to a study for the Pew Charitable Trusts, "the flow of plastic into the ocean is projected to nearly triple by 2040. Without considerable action to address plastic pollution, 50 kg of plastic will enter the ocean for every metre of shoreline."[248] One of the unexpected byproducts of the COVID-19 pandemic is that surgical masks and other plastic-containing "personal protective equipment" are polluting the waters off the coasts of California.[249] An estimated 129 billion plastic-containing masks and 65 billion plastic-containing gloves have been used globally each month during the pandemic, and "a significant portion of them end up in the world's oceans."[250]

For decades, richer countries have exported much of their plastic waste (along with much of their other waste) to poorer countries. As Helena Varkkey of the University of Malaya in Malaysia has explained, developed countries have often found it cheaper "to ship containers of plastic waste halfway around the world to be 'recycled' in developing countries than to deal with the trash themselves."[251] Thus, "out of sight and out of mind," and increased plastic consumption by the wealthier in the world continues apace.[252] Although there are some legitimate plastic importing and recycling companies in developing countries, there are also numerous environmentally reckless firms that, instead of recycling imported plastic waste, either burn it or dump it in landfills. Burning it pollutes the air. Dumping it in landfills ultimately passes it into the water. Plastic consumption in richer countries is transformed into an accumulation of plastics pollution in poorer countries.

China imported about half of the world's traded plastic waste until the Chinese decided enough was enough and banned imports of most of it in 2018.[253] This action has "left municipalities and waste companies from Australia to the U.S. scrambling for alternatives."[254] And it has led to a marked shift of these exports away from China to Malaysia, Indonesia, Thailand, and the Philippines, where there has increasingly been a backlash.[255] These and other Southeast Asian countries say they do not want to become a dumping ground for the trash of the rest of the world, and, in some instances, they have even sent plastic waste back to where it came from.[256] Because of this backlash, exporters of plastic waste have begun to look elsewhere, including to Africa, which, already littered by plastic waste, has been on the forefront globally in the enactment of a rapidly growing number of recent bans on single-use plastic bags and other single-use plastics.[257]

Until now, the WTO has remained on the sidelines in this intensifying North–South trade-related dispute while most of the international action has been in multilateral environmental forums and the United Nations. One such arena has been the 1988 Basel Convention on the Control of Transboundary Movements of Hazardous Wastes and Their Disposal. Amendments took effect on January 1, 2021 that include plastic waste within the coverage of the convention for the first time and allow international shipments of most plastic waste only with the prior written consent of the importing country and any countries through which it passes in transit.[258]

Although the United States has signed the Basel Convention, it is not one of the 187 countries that have ratified it and agreed to these amendments. Even so, American imports and exports of plastics recyclables will be affected. The Basel Convention prohibits trade in the products covered by the convention between countries that have ratified the convention and those that have not – unless a non-ratifying country has agreed separately to abide by the requirements of the convention. For this reason, the United States may agree separately to these requirements even if it continues to refrain from ratifying the Basel Convention.[259]

Action could also be taken under the Stockholm Convention on Persistent Organic Pollutants of 2001, which bans or severely limits the production and the use of chemicals that threaten human and environmental health. Amendments to the Stockholm Convention could be made to address particular aspects of plastics pollution, such as the toxicity of certain chemicals that are found in some plastics. The United States has not yet signed the Stockholm Convention, but, given that 184 countries are parties to it,[260] for practical commercial reasons, American businesses "have largely eliminated production of the chemicals the treaty regulates."[261]

All that has been done or announced so far to limit and clean up plastic waste worldwide will, however, reduce such waste in volume by only 7 percent.[262] Moreover, the Basel Convention, the Stockholm Convention, and other relevant international agreements may prove to be insufficient to the imposing global task of attacking plastic waste. For these reasons, momentum has been building for negotiating a global treaty on plastics pollution. More than two-thirds of the members of the United Nations have said they are open to negotiation of a UN plastics agreement, which might resemble the Paris climate agreement or the Montreal Protocol on ozone layer depletion.[263]

Meeting virtually in late February 2021, the United Nations Environment Assembly (UNEA-5), which is headquartered in Kenya, resolved to push ahead with the aim of starting negotiations on a global plastics agreement at what was hoped to be an in-person meeting in early 2022.[264] Negotiators sought to build both governmental and business support for such a UN agreement. Under President Trump, the United States did not express much concern about plastics pollution and was adamantly opposed to a United Nations plastics treaty. With Joe Biden as president, the United States has made it clear that it will now be fully engaged, as part of its broader plan for confronting climate change and other environmental and ecological concerns, in "addressing marine plastics litter and microplastics."[265]

It is unclear at this early date what might end up in a UN agreement on plastics pollution, which would likely take the form of a framework for facilitating current and future cooperative international action relating to the full life cycle of plastics.[266] Worldwide scientific work is already underway "to explore barriers to and options for combating marine plastic litter and microplastics from all sources, especially land-based."[267] At a minimum, there would likely be provisions on transparency, metrics, monitoring and reporting, coordination, and technical and financial support for developing countries – all necessary to an effective foundation for curbing worldwide plastic waste. Such an agreement might also include provisions for national plastics management plans and common sustainability criteria that could be linked to plastics and plastics-related trade.[268]

As the Environmental Investigation Agency, an international NGO, has speculated, conceivably, a United Nations agreement could also go beyond the scope of the Basel Convention and the Stockholm Convention in preventing plastics pollution by having more legal teeth. A global plastics agreement could include provisions that would "ban certain single-use plastic products, and [put] restrictions on new plastic production (particularly those that are hard to recycle or used in single-use applications) and toxic additives."[269] Treaty obligations under a United Nations plastics agreement would undoubtedly be recognized as relevant public international law by WTO jurists when WTO members sought to justify any trade restrictions that resulted from compliance with that agreement. The WTO general exceptions for environmental measures would be available and apply.

These negotiations in the United Nations should be complemented by negotiations in the WTO. WTO rules do not prevent national action against plastics pollution. As with other national measures of similar concern, in general, import and export bans and other quantitative trade restrictions are permitted under the trade rules to achieve environmental, health, and safety objectives so long as they are not applied in a manner that would constitute "a means of arbitrary or unjustifiable discrimination between countries where the same conditions prevail," and are not "a disguised restriction on international trade."[270] (This long-standing legal exception to free trade in the trade rules undoubtedly explains why no other WTO member has challenged China's ban on imports of plastic waste; China would surely prevail in WTO dispute settlement.)

Likewise, although the issue has not yet come up in WTO dispute settlement, national actions restricting or otherwise affecting trade that may be taken pursuant to international obligations in the Basel Convention or in the Stockholm Convention, are likely to be entitled to this same exception in the trade rules. WTO jurists are authorized to uphold only the trade obligations in the WTO treaty.[271] They do not have the jurisdiction to uphold obligations in other public international law. But, since the start of the WTO in 1995, they have routinely taken other public international law into account when upholding WTO law, most notably when defenses are raised to what would otherwise be inconsistencies with WTO obligations.[272]

However, WTO rules do not currently include affirmative actions against plastics pollution, and this is what is sought by the countries that have started the new "open-ended informal dialogue" in the WTO. They wish to "explore how improved trade cooperation, within the rules and mechanisms of the WTO, could contribute to domestic, regional, and global efforts to reduce plastics pollution and transition to a more circular and environmentally sustainable global plastics economy."[273] Potentially, this exploration could have profound implications for the modernization of WTO rules.

As with the push for a UN agreement on plastics pollution, it is not clear at this time what WTO members may see as the role of trade rules in finding a solution to this grave environmental crisis. But, clearly, the need for trade rules is becoming more apparent. At last count, WTO members have notified the trade organization of 128 plastics-related trade measures, about 80 percent of them by developing countries.[274] These proliferating measures include import bans and other import restrictions on plastic waste and various forms of support for domestic plastics industries, including tariffs and governmental subsidies. No longer can this pressing international issue remain on the periphery of the rules-based multilateral trading system.

Goal 14 of the Sustainable Development Goals is conserving and sustainably using the oceans, seas, and marine resources for sustainable development.[275] One target of this global goal, for 2025, is preventing and significantly reducing marine pollution of all kinds, including marine debris.[276] Trade law scholar Carolyn Deere Birkbeck of the Graduate Institute of International and Development Studies in Geneva has rightly pointed out that, "At a time of uncertainty about the WTO's role and relevance, action on plastic pollution at the WTO could help build confidence in the multilateral trading system's ability to deliver on its core objective of sustainable development."[277]

There is much WTO members could do to complement and supplement any UN negotiations on plastics pollution. As Birkbeck has noted, in addition to such vital basics as transparency and notification, the subjects of possible WTO negotiations could include mutual recognition and harmonization of new environmental standards for plastics production; standardized eco-labeling requirements for plastics products; public procurement policies that reduce reliance on single-use plastics; specific disciplines on subsidies for plastics production and trade; abolition of trade restrictions on plastics substitutes; and carve outs from the current WTO subsidies rules for tax incentives that encourage recycling and spur more environmentally friendly innovations in plastics production.[278]

Precisely what should fill the framework of a WTO plastics agreement need not and should not be spelled out at the outset. The details should be determined through negotiations on this new "trade and environment" front. Most needed now is a strong show of political will throughout the entirety of the membership of the WTO to build on what the new "open-ended informal dialogue" has begun. The positive engagement of the Biden administration on this issue in the WTO would do much to help. The short-term goal is, at this writing, expected to be approval of a formal negotiating initiative on plastics pollution at the 12th WTO ministerial conference in Geneva in late November 2021.

If the delegates to the WTO from the United States and other WTO member countries need a reminder of the urgency of dealing with plastics pollution, they need only step outside the back door of the Italianate villa in Geneva that serves as the headquarters of the WTO, where the runoff from Swiss rain is adding unrelentingly to the accumulation of pellets of microplastics in Lac Leman, the storied lake of Geneva.[279]

9

Links to Cooperation, Equity, and Inclusion

LINKS TO COOPERATION

In the new pandemic world, human optimism and human pessimism are both fully on display. Speaking for the optimists, American geographer Jared Diamond, who worries about societal suicides causing global "collapse," is nevertheless optimistic about our current plight.[1] He maintains that

a best-case outcome of our current crisis would be for it to create, at last, a widespread sense of world identity: to make all peoples recognize that we now face the common enemy of global problems that can be solved only by a united global effort ... [I]f the world joins to solve the current visible Covid-19 crisis against heavy odds, our current pandemic might thus represent the beginning, not of a dismal era of chronic worldwide danger, but of a bright era of worldwide co-operation.[2]

In reply, speaking for the pessimists, British philosopher John Gray insists, "The belief that this crisis can be solved by an unprecedented outbreak of international cooperation is magical thinking in its purest form."[3]

Our duty of optimism compels us to make optimistic thinking about international cooperation not magical but logical. Goal 17 of the United Nations Sustainable Development Goals is to "strengthen the means of implementation and revitalize the global partnership for sustainable development."[4] The achievement of this global goal is essential to the achievement of all the rest. Only through the global partnerships of international cooperation can we produce the global public goods that must be produced for the use of all of humanity if we are to attain global sustainable development. Among these needed global public goods are international institutions for international cooperation, including the World Trade Organization.

To create the links required to accomplish this central global goal in the new pandemic world, there must be enhanced international cooperation at every level of global governance, including significantly more cooperation in rule-driven multilateral institutions. Countries must turn outward, not inward, by making more links with other countries, and by using and expanding those links to confront their common concerns. They must understand that sharing their sovereignty through international cooperation is not ceding sovereignty; it is an exercise of sovereignty that is the only way for sovereign countries to confront shared concerns that extend beyond their borders and will otherwise be beyond their reach for resolution.[5] They must comprehend that, like the pandemic, global challenges such as climate change, ecological collapse, and the multitude of other manifestations of planetary and human peril that we must somehow face, can only be faced successfully if we come together and if we face them together.[6] They must realize that international cooperation is a logical imperative, including in international trade.

The ways in which WTO members can strengthen trade links by making new rules for a new world are already known. Ideally, they can conclude multilateral agreements. Alternatively, they can make plurilateral agreements among some WTO members that can evolve over time into multilateral agreements that will bind all WTO members. Potentially, they can create other arrangements within the WTO legal framework that affect individual industrial sectors or address individual issues, such as with a WTO climate waiver. The procedures exist for implementing the substance of a new approach to trade that will make trade a more affirmative means of achieving global sustainable development. The rules also exist – and can be improved – for upholding both the procedures and the substance of the trade rules through a renewed multilateral commitment to the rule of law in trade by means of WTO dispute settlement. What does not yet exist is the sufficiency of global political will that is needed to accomplish these goals through more international cooperation.

Impassioned entreaties for international cooperation have been made for millennia. As classicist Josiah Ober has observed, the Athenian statesmen who governed the ancient Athenian Empire in and surrounding the Aegean Sea assumed that, so long as the island states and the other city-states in the empire were "net gainers from the existence of the empire ... [t]hey would realize that their collective interests were better served by cooperation ... than by defection."[7] In due course, though, the Athenians learned that the logic of cooperation does not always prevail, especially when lofty calls for cooperation are accompanied by incidents of exploitation.

In the twenty-five centuries since, there have been countless similar calls for cooperation among countries to accomplish shared goals, up to and including the calls today for more international cooperation within the WTO. Some of these calls have been sullied by motives of exploitation, others not. Some have been heeded, others not. Some have led to success through cooperation, others not. Throughout history, the calls for international cooperation that have led to success have been successful because they have occurred in a receptive context.

For a call for cooperation *among* countries to be successful, there must be trust *within* countries. Democratic leaders usually want to be reelected, and even despotic leaders must respond to popular discontent, at least to some extent, if they wish to remain in power. What some are free to protest with their votes, others can find the courage to voice with their protests, as we have seen with multiplying popular protests throughout the world. As evidenced in the global protests for action on climate change, for example, less and less are people – and particularly young people – content with the prevarications and procrastinations of those who would deign to lead them. And, more and more, even those in the darkest corners of the world who possess political power but have not been elected by the people, are finding that they must at least seem to assuage widespread popular concerns.

In the United States, the members of Congress will hesitate to agree to new trade agreements if their constituents believe those agreements will deplete American employment, however in error that popular belief might be. And in China, despite the increasing public surveillance and extensive and intensifying suppression of popular dissent under the regime of President Xi Jinping, the communist leaders are nevertheless more likely to agree to make international environmental commitments because of popular protests against rampant air and water pollution.[8] Some governments seek popular support; others seek merely popular acquiescence. All governments have more latitude to cooperate with other governments if they have the trust of their people.

In addition, for international cooperation to succeed, there must be trust *between* countries. To be willing to make – and keep – binding commitments through international agreements, countries must believe that the other countries that participate in those agreements will in turn be willing to be bound by the commensurate commitments they make, and that they will work with other countries to uphold all of their mutual obligations. The ancient Athenians knew nothing of modern game theory, but today we recognize the quandary of a country contemplating whether to cooperate with other countries as an instance of the Prisoner's Dilemma, in which defection creates a bigger payoff than cooperation but all are worse off if all defect.[9] As Robert Axelrod has suggested, what makes international cooperation more likely in this circumstance is the prospect that the countries involved will meet again. International cooperation is built on the *reiteration* of cooperation, on the realization that countries will need to meet in need of cooperation again and again. As he has written, the chances of them cooperating are enhanced if they know that decisions they make today will influence the choices that are made by others tomorrow, and if the stakes that demand cooperation are high.[10]

Furthermore, for international cooperation to succeed, there must be a shared sense of mutual self-interest. But this sense of self-interest must be of a particular kind. It must be an enlightened self-interest that peers beyond the narrow concerns of the here and now and takes a broader and longer view. It must be an expression of what the nineteenth–century French political thinker Alexis de Tocqueville called, in his classic work *Democracy in America*, "the principle of interest rightly understood."[11] This principle espoused in his timeless book is wholly consonant with the contemporary principle of sustainable development, that of "development that meets the needs of the present without compromising the ability of future generations to meet their own needs."[12] This enlightened view of self-interest must be shared by all countries if there is to be success through international cooperation.

Lastly, for international cooperation to succeed, there must be sufficient motivation for countries to pursue their mutual self-interest through more – and through more effective – cooperation. In the new pandemic world, there surely are motivations aplenty for cooperation: the COVID-19 pandemic itself (plus the ominous prospect of more and perhaps worse pandemic threats still to come); the sheer ubiquity of the manifold consequences of man-made climate change; the alarming loss of biodiversity; the imminence of other interrelated ecological threats; the emergence of artificial intelligence; the existential questions arising from the sequencing of the human genetic code; the continued proliferation of nuclear weapons; the danger of cyber warfare; and the emerging geopolitical competition for control of outer space, among more. On this long list, and linked to much else that is on it, are the commercial and noncommercial considerations relating to international trade.

Certainly, these circumstances exist with the call for more international cooperation in securing the many links of trade. Yet, always there are imposing obstacles to international cooperation of any kind, and today the obstacles to more international cooperation on trade are imposing indeed. Notable among them are the obstacles that impede trust within countries and between countries and that stand in the way of the shared perception of a mutual self-interest and the shared motivation to pursue it. These are the obstacles posed by questions about the equity of trade, the inclusiveness of trade, and the ability of countries to govern trade in ways that will promote equity and inclusiveness while also increasing trade. Cooperation on trade links through multilateral action will be possible only if it is accompanied by domestic actions that make multilateralism politically possible, and by international actions that acknowledge the centrality of the worldwide questions about whether trade is both equitable and inclusive.

Failure to answer these questions about equity and inclusion in trade will be fatal to summoning the political will needed to fulfill the international aspirations for further trade liberalization. Answering them with restrictive national measures solely intended to provide insulating trade protection will likewise be fatal; for that answer will foreclose the further economic gains that can be made by freeing more trade. Without the right answers to these deeply divisive questions, politicians throughout the world will be able to support new trade agreements only at great political risk, making the negotiation and conclusion of such new agreements much less likely. As the global economy struggles to recover in the new pandemic world, trade liberalization and trade reassurance must necessarily go hand in hand.

If these questions about the equity and inclusiveness of trade are answered, then the world can cooperate anew on trade; multilateral action to strengthen trade links can occur. But if they are not answered, and answered persuasively, then the existential crisis of the WTO will not be overcome, and the links of trade will continue to fray until, at last, they tear apart, leaving an unraveled commercial chaos of "might makes right," and dashing the hopes of people everywhere for human flourishing amid a sustainable global prosperity.

LINKS TO EQUITY

Goal 10 of the UN Sustainable Development Goals is to "reduce inequality *within* and *among* countries."[13] Targets for accomplishing this global goal by 2030 include progressively achieving and sustaining "income growth of the bottom 40 percent of the population at a rate higher than the national average";[14] empowering and promoting "the social, economic and political inclusion of all, irrespective of age, sex, disability, race, ethnicity, origin, religion or economic or other status";[15] ensuring "equal opportunity and reducing inequalities of outcome, including by eliminating discriminatory laws, policies and practices";[16] adopting "fiscal, wage, and social protection policies"; and "progressively" achieving "greater equality."[17] The SDGs do not, however, tell us how to attain these targets to achieve this global goal. Nor do they mention the role international trade should play in its accomplishment.

In reporting on progress made toward achieving Goal 10 before the arrival of the pandemic, the United Nations stated that, while progress had been made in the previous decade in reducing inequality *within* some countries, especially in eastern and southeastern Asia, global data about inequality within many countries was insufficient to draw conclusions, while "in all countries with data, the bottom 40 percent of the population received less than 25 percent of the overall income, while the richest 10 percent received at least 20 percent of the total income."[18]

The pledge of the United Nations in the Sustainable Development Goals is that "no one will be left behind."[19] Yet, in reporting on inequality *within* countries during the pandemic, the United Nations explained that the poorest people in the world

are falling behind in relative numbers. The latest estimates show that in some countries, as much as 25 per cent of the population live on less than half the median income. On average, 13 per cent of people experience (this level of) relative low income across the 104 countries with available data, although considerable differences are observed among regions. In countries in Latin America and the Caribbean, almost one in five people live on less than half their national median income, on average, although some progress has been made in many countries since 2010. Around 9 per cent of people live on less than half the national median in countries in Central and Southern Asia, the lowest level among all regions.[20]

Thus, the year-to-year data collected and assembled by the United Nations demonstrates that, *within* countries, "[i]nequality was bad" in the years leading up to 2020; and, now that the novel coronavirus has arrived, spread, surged, and surged again, "the COVID-19 pandemic is making it worse."[21] This increasing inequality has many dimensions. Two in particular stand out. Amid the dire precarity of the new pandemic world, "workers are receiving a smaller portion of the output they helped produce."[22] And, ominously, "[r]-acial and economic inequalities may deepen unless they're addressed forcefully."[23]

International trade, of course, exists precisely because of the inequality of resources *among* countries. Different countries have different natural resources. They also have unequal allocations of natural resources. It is from this natural situation of an unequal distribution of what economists call "factor endowments" that international trade results. And it is from their singular mix of factor endowments that countries derive their comparative advantages in making specific products that can be traded. As David Ricardo taught, confronted with these inequalities, and capitalizing on these comparative advantages, countries tend to specialize in making one product rather than another and trading that product internationally for what they cannot produce domestically as relatively efficiently. This international specialization adds to the overall economic wealth of the world.[24]

By establishing and upholding rules that support this specialization, the WTO–based multilateral trading system has done much to increase trade and reduce what would otherwise be the effects of this natural inequality *among* the countries that belong to the system. Increasing the volume of trade through trade liberalization under the auspices of the WTO has increased the gains from trade. In turn, the gains from trade have given many developing countries the wherewithal to reduce their domestic economic disparities where their governments have sought to do so, and participation in trade enabled lower income people and other marginal groups in those countries to benefit from trade, by engaging in it directly and by profiting from it indirectly.

To be sure, vast income gaps remain between developed and developing countries. There can be no mistaking the huge differences in the average levels of income between Boston and Bangladesh, and between Nice and Nairobi. But, up until the economic shock of the COVID-19 pandemic, trade and other forms of globalization had narrowed those gaps.[25] Optimistically, expectantly, Michael Spence wrote of this income narrowing as "the next convergence."[26] Now, such hopefulness is faced with the pandemic. Whether, in the new pandemic world, there will be a further economic convergence between the richer and the poorer countries, will depend to a great extent on when and how the global economy fully recovers.

There has, however, been no such economic convergence *within* countries leading up to or during the pandemic. The gap between rich and poor within the United States, China, and many other countries was growing wider in the years that preceded the pandemic, and, since it began, that gap has grown wider still. While billions of other people have suffered economically because of the ravages of COVID-19, "[b]illionaires as a class have added about $1 trillion to their net worth since the pandemic began."[27] (In fact, about one-fifth of that sum went to just two people – Americans Jeff Bezos and Elon Musk.)[28] The financial markets have soared while the real economy has struggled. Even many of those who, quite rightly, advise us that our goal should be equal opportunities and not equal outcomes, are nevertheless shocked by the extent of the inequality in today's world, and appalled by how much that inequality has increased during the global struggle with the novel coronavirus. They worry that the extent of inequality will, in time, undermine the legitimacy of national and international institutions. At the least, it provides fodder for those who would achieve their ignoble ends by transforming disgruntled masses into destructive mobs.

Economists Matthew Klein and Michael Pettis posit that it is the extent of the inequality within countries that causes trade conflicts between and among countries. For them, a "trade war" is not so much a conflict between and among countries as it is an extension of the tension created by income inequality within countries. They see "trade wars" as "class wars."[29] "Rising inequality," they contend, "has produced gluts of manufactured goods, job loss, and rising indebtedness. It is an economic and financial perversion of what global integration was supposed to achieve."[30] As Pettis has summed up their thesis,

Our argument is fairly straightforward: trade cost and trade conflict in the modern era don't reflect differences in the cost of production; what they reflect is a difference in savings imbalances, primarily driven by the distortions in the distribution of income. We argue that the reason we have trade wars is because we have persistent imbalances, and the reason we have persistent trade imbalances is because around the world, income is distributed in such a way that workers and middle class households cannot consume enough of what they produce.[31]

In other words, these people are working less for themselves and more for others.

To date, the WTO has not seen as part of its portfolio the taking of direct action to help diminish the income and other economic inequalities *within* countries. WTO rules focus on making the economic pie larger. They do not address how that pie should be divided up domestically. The pie slicing is left to the domestic decisions of the individual WTO members. And yet, as Oisin Suttle of Queen's University, Belfast, Ireland, has rightly observed, "after we have done all we can through cooperation to enlarge the collective economic pie, we will always and necessarily face questions of how that pie is to be divided, given the many competing claims" for the gains from trade.[32] Some fundamental questions cannot be escaped: Who gets how much of the pie? And who slices it?

As Suttle recollects, the eighteenth–century Scottish philosopher David Hume, a close friend of Adam Smith, in his *A Treatise of Human Nature* of 1740, described the circumstances of justice as being twofold: having enough that all can have enough, but not so much that all have everything they desire; and simultaneously acknowledging the claims of others that they, too, should have enough. Hume saw justice as a human artifice, as a necessary convention arising from the natural combination of human self-regard and resource scarcity. He saw laws and governments as instruments created for resolving these competing claims.[33] Hume also believed that, as trade and other relations were expanded with other countries, the boundaries of justice would likewise expand; they would "grow larger, in proportion to the largeness of men's views, and the force of their mutual connections."[34] Nearly three centuries later, this Enlightenment description of justice still seems apt, and Hume's high hopes for the expansion of the boundaries of justice still seem visionary.

Free trade accords reality to this account of justice. As Frank J. Garcia of Boston College Law School has maintained, the structuring of trade rules to enable the pursuit of comparative advantage is consistent with the pursuit of justice. From a utilitarian perspective, it maximizes welfare through the efficiency gains of trade. From a libertarian perspective, it expands individual liberty by expanding economic liberty. Furthermore, from an egalitarian perspective, as Garcia has explained,

By allowing the principle of comparative advantage to operate, free trade moves the trading system in the direction of operating to the benefit of the least advantaged, by affording them the benefit of welfare increases through specialization. Moreover, in a contingent sense, since free trade can lead to welfare growth, it is a precondition to a more just distribution of wealth and an improved standard of living for the least advantaged.[35]

In illustration, the economic burdens of trade restrictions in the form of tariffs fall disproportionately on those with lower incomes, while the benefits of the lower prices that result from eliminating tariffs accrue disproportionately to the poor. Free trade not only produces more overall wealth. Free trade is just.

But are not there other, more direct actions that can, and should, be taken affirmatively by the WTO to induce WTO members to reduce their own internal inequalities? Should not WTO members be required by the trade rules to reduce their own inequalities and provide a certain level of social benefits as conditions for receiving the economic benefits of trade concessions from other WTO members? Are not there goals other than economic efficiency that should be embraced more explicitly in WTO trade rules? In answer, Rafael Leal-Arcas has asserted, "[T]rade makes every country richer. But it is not for the WTO to decide who individually (as citizens) gets how much from the benefits of trade. That is for national governments to decide based on national taxation."[36]

This is the traditional and prevailing view; however, as Leal-Arcas would undoubtedly agree, this view does not address Hume's account of justice. To cite, for instance, the same example of taxation, no small amount of the domestic frustration with the impact of international trade can be traced back to the refusal of national governments to tax more of the income of their wealthiest citizens and use it to provide more social spending that would, among other individual and societal benefits, help assuage any losses caused by trade. The United States has been one such recalcitrant, up until the advent of the Biden administration, but it has been far from the only one.

Wherever it has occurred, this domestic refusal to tax more of the income of the wealthy has done much to skew the distribution of the domestic gains from trade up toward the top of the economic ladder, with unjust results. And yet, does anyone anywhere in the world truly wish to anoint the WTO to determine the rates of income taxation within their country? The WTO has no such power. Nor should it. Different means that do not intrude on the sovereignty of nation-states must be used by the WTO to help achieve the global goal of reducing inequality within countries. These different means of reducing inequality should center on helping more people participate in trade and on helping more of them share more equitably in the great gains from trade. There will be more equity if, within countries, there is more social inclusion.

LINKS TO INCLUSION

Links to the concept of social inclusion are found throughout the UN Sustainable Development Goals, with their promises that "no one will be left behind," and that, in fulfilling the seventeen global goals, the countries of the United Nations "will endeavour to reach the furthest behind first."[37] Goal 16 of the SDGs is to "promote peaceful and inclusive societies for sustainable development, provide access to justice for all and build effective, accountable and inclusive institutions at all levels."[38] Goal 4 seeks "inclusive" education.[39] Goal 8 aspires to "inclusive" economic growth.[40] Goal 9 aims to "promote inclusive and sustainable industrialization."[41] And, again, one of the targets of Goal 10 for reducing inequality within and among countries, is to "empower and promote the social, economic and political inclusion of all, irrespective of age, sex, disability, race, ethnicity, origin, religion or other economic or social status."[42]

As the COVID-19 pandemic began to spread in early 2020, the United Nations lamented, in its annual report on the progress made to date toward accomplishing the aims for justice in SDG Goal 16, that "[c]onflict, insecurity, weak institutions and limited access to justice remain threats to sustainable development." It warned that "[t]he COVID-19 pandemic threatens to amplify and exploit fragilities across the globe."[43] The reality of this global threat has become only too real in what many millions of people worldwide have suffered since. In 2021, the United Nations reported that "the crisis has created major disruptions in government functioning and has tested, weakened and sometimes even shattered countries' systems of rights and protection."[44] Just how more social inclusion can be forged at a time when the novel coronavirus has fostered vastly more social exclusion, is a central and growing concern of those around the world who continue to work for the fulfillment of the Sustainable Development Goals.

The overarching goal of the SDGs is human flourishing through human development. How we pursue this goal is shaped by how we perceive it. Here the most persuasive approach is that advocated by Amartya Sen, who sees "development as freedom."[45] As Sen views it, "human freedom" is "the pre-eminent objective of development," and the "expansion of freedom" is rightly seen "both as the primary end and as the primary means of development."[46] He contends that, "Development consists of the removal of various types of unfreedoms that leave people with little choice and little opportunity of exercising their reasoned agency."[47] For him, human freedom is an individual act of choice made through an exercise of human reason. Therefore, it follows that development should "be seen ... as a process of expanding the real freedoms that people enjoy" to make individual, personal choices.[48]

Consequently, for Sen, the appropriate measure of whether human freedom is being expanded is "the expansion of the 'capabilities' of persons to lead the kind of lives they value – and have reason to value."[49] His is thus a "capabilities" approach. With this approach, a reference only to the latest growth in the Gross Domestic Product omits much that is necessary to gauge whether freedom is in fact being expanded. American philosopher Martha Nussbaum, the other originator of this approach to assessing human development, contends that "the key question to ask, when comparing societies and assessing them for their basic decency or justice, is, 'What is each person able to do and to be?' In other words, the approach takes *each person as an end*, asking not just about the total or average well-being but about the opportunities available to each person."[50] Again, "It is *focused on choice or freedom*."[51]

The "capabilities" approach is thus a departure to some extent from the original needs-based formulation of "sustainable development" in the seminal Brundtland Report of 1987. To be sure, needs must be identified and met. But human development is not solely about meeting basic needs for food, water, and shelter. As Sen argues, we must "integrate the idea of sustainability with the perspective of freedom, so that we see human beings not merely as creatures who have needs but primarily as people whose freedoms really matter."[52] As part of this integration, he adds, "Sustainable development in the form of freedom can take note of political and social liberties as well as the fulfillment of economic and material needs."[53]

William Easterly, who has, like Sen, delved deeply into the sources of development, contends, "[P]overty is really about a shortage of rights ... [T]he cause of poverty is the absence of political and economic rights, the absence of a free political and economic system that would find the technical solution to the poor's problems."[54] Part of being free is being able to choose your leaders. This is one essential factor when measuring the extent to which individuals are free to make their own choices. Genuine democracy generates more human capabilities and thus more freedom.

Use of the "capabilities" approach requires seeing numerous developmental topics through this perspective of freedom as choosing. For example, because poverty prevents the exercise and acquisition of capabilities and thus precludes many individual choices, "poverty must be seen as the deprivation of basic capabilities rather than merely as lowness of incomes."[55] Similarly, the motives for market access and market participation must be viewed as more than merely commercial; for, as Sen points out, "the more immediate case for the freedom of market transaction lies in the basic importance of that freedom itself. We have good reasons to buy and sell, to exchange, and to seek lives that can flourish on the basis of transactions. To deny that freedom in general would be in itself a major failing of society."[56] The freedom to engage in trade must therefore be seen as a human right. Likewise, "the need to go beyond market rules" to embrace an ethic of protecting the natural environment must be acknowledged as sustaining and enhancing human capabilities.[57] Because the economy is contained within the environment, the environment must always be a part of developmental calculations.

The "capabilities" approach has enormous implications for sustainable development. Through the prism of his perspective of "development as freedom," Sen eyes development as "fundamentally an empowering process" that must always be about the agency of individual human beings.[58] From this premise, he reasons that,

If the importance of human lives lies not merely in our living standard and need-fulfillment, but also in the freedom we enjoy, then the idea of sustainable development has to be correspondingly formulated. There is cogency in thinking not just about sustaining the fulfillment of our needs, but more broadly about sustaining – or extending – our freedom (including the freedom to meet our needs). Thus recharacterized, *sustainable freedom* can be broadened ... to encompass the preservation, and when possible expansion, of the substantive freedoms and capabilities of people today 'without compromising the ability of future generations' to have similar – or more – freedom.[59]

This concept of "sustainable freedom" is the core of the "capabilities" approach, and it is the implicit philosophical foundation for the UN Sustainable Development Goals, which range considerably beyond conventional economic considerations. This approach has also been used for the past two decades as the philosophical underpinning for the annual Human Development Report of the United Nations Development Program, which relies on a broad measure of development called the Human Development Index.[60] The Human Development Index measures not only traditional economic criteria such as GDP, but also the health of a people, their level of educational attainment, and their standard of living. In general, when calculating the HDI, health is measured by life expectancy at birth; education is measured by the expected years of schooling for children of school-entering age and the mean of years of schooling for adults aged twenty-five years or more; and the standard of living is measured by per capita gross national income.[61]

International trade is an integral part of this approach. As the UNDP has pointed out, "Trade touches all aspects of human development."[62] The two "are interlinked."[63] These links, however, "are not automatic";[64] they depend on much else. The links between trade and human development depend on the circumstances of individual countries; on their factor endowments (land, labor, and capital); their geography (whether coastal or landlocked); and their local climate.[65] They depend, too, on the stages of development in individual countries; the oversight of their natural resources; the mobility of their people; and much more.[66] Not least, the quality and durability of these links depend on the willingness of countries to engage in trade, and on their success in creating and sustaining a just society in which individuals can be free to choose their own destiny, so that the gains from trade can be shared equitably.

With respect to trade, it is this broad view of development, one that sees development as sustainable development, and one that sees development as "an empowering process" for securing "sustainable freedom" for individual human beings, which is embedded in the preamble of the WTO Agreement, and which must be the guide for the members of the WTO in seeking development. This broad view of development includes the various traditional measurements of economic advance, but it also encompasses much more of all that furthers the full flourishing of individual human freedom. In this more expansive view of what development means, an empowering and sustainable freedom will not be attained by billions of individual people in the world unless their eyes and their lives are opened to the instructive challenges and the boundless opportunities of the wider world – including those created by international trade. For individual human beings everywhere, trade can be, and must be, a means for achieving and furthering human freedom.[67]

If human development is a matter of removing the "unfreedoms" that limit individual human choices, and if trade is a means for achieving freedom by removing those limits, then the task of WTO members, domestically and multilaterally, is eliminating the "unfreedoms" that are barriers to trade and to a broader and fairer access to the gains from trade. As it is, many millions of people throughout the world lack access to trade because outdated trade rules impede or inhibit it; and many more millions of people, living in developed and developing countries alike, are, in effect, denied access to their fair share of the gains from trade in part because they lack the "capabilities" they need to secure it. This lack of access stokes the opposition to trade and blocks the additional trade liberalization that could produce more trade gains for everyone.

In the United States and throughout the world, the domestic actions needed to ensure that all will be capable of making the most of the gains from trade, have often been missing. For example, in the United States, much too little has been done in the past generation to help retrain, reemploy, and make more resilient the jobless workers and the hollowed communities that have been – through no fault of their own – cast adrift and often abandoned in the wake of the relentless and disruptive advances of technology and globalization. The economic anxieties of those worldwide who have been unable to transition from the jobs of the past to the jobs of the future, have done much to create and inflate the wide populist reaction against globalization. In the United States and elsewhere, accompanying status anxieties and cultural anxieties have fanned the populist flames.

All these overlapping anxieties have provided the brittle kindling for the sham adventurers and glib opportunists who have sought political power and maintained it by fanning the flames of division with their demagoguery. In particular, the widespread failure to ease their economic anxieties is what has most led to a misplaced opposition to freer trade by many people around the world who fear rather than welcome the openness of trade, and who, gripped by their fearfulness, invite unwittingly the further shrinking of their own economic future. The fact that some other developed countries have more extensive social safety nets than exist in the United States helps explain why this anxious opposition to freer trade has been most highly charged among so many wary Americans.

In the new pandemic world, instead of taking actions to protect people from fair competition by shielding them from trade, governments should be taking actions to help provide people with additional capabilities that will better prepare them for engaging in trade and confronting the effects of trade. In contemplating a green recovery, much thought must be given to helping the workers in the fossil fuel industries and in the other senescent sectors of the old economy to make the transition to the new, green economy of the new pandemic world. Some national decision makers are committed to the dark deceits of protectionism. They pretend that this transition can be prevented. Others are blinded by the bright rays of idealism. They cannot see that this transition will be a hard one for many who are not prepared for it, and who do not yet have the technical skills and the other capabilities they need to prosper from it. What is required of decision makers everywhere, is a strategy for a green recovery and a just transition that will both support trade and enhance human capabilities while preserving the dignity of people who are trying their best to find their way to the future.

Although freer trade benefits the entire economy over the long term, and although it creates more jobs than it costs over the long term, there can be no denying that in the short term it can cause some workers to lose their jobs. These workers need help in making this necessary transition. They need help in supporting themselves and their families, in acquiring new skills, and in finding new jobs that will pay them as much or more than the jobs they lost. Sufficient help of this kind is often not forthcoming. In the United States, for example, a long-standing federal trade adjustment assistance program has also been long-standing in its multitudinous inadequacies.[68] A failure of funding has been accompanied by a failure of imagination.

One obstacle to providing sufficient help is that those who are conscientious about the proper use of taxpayer dollars worry about the cumulative costs of providing such assistance. Reassurance is offered by Gary Hufbauer and Zhijao (Lucy) Lu of the Peterson Institute for International Economics. Their research shows that the private costs incurred by displaced workers – including those who are displaced for reasons other than trade, such as innovation and automation – are "much smaller than gains from expanded trade." Moreover, the *"permanent* gains from liberalization and technology advances far outweigh *temporary* adjustment costs." To help displaced workers, they have urged, not trade protection, but, instead, "sharply improved adjustment programs ... to compensate those who lost from deeper integration and from newer technology." These trade economists have stressed that, "Adjustment costs should not be used as a reason to say 'no' to liberalization or new technology."[69]

Charged with recommending ways to implement the SDGs, the United States Network of the United Nations Sustainable Development Solutions Network has proposed a plan to reach zero carbon emissions in the United States by 2050.[70] Their plan centers on job creation and a just transition to a carbon-free economy. They recommend $389 billion annually between 2020 and 2050 in new spending on the green energy transition.[71] They calculate that "total direct plus indirect job creation generated in the U.S. by this large-scale expansion in energy supply expenditures will amount to an average of about 946,000 direct jobs and 860,000 indirect jobs per year between 2020–2050. This totals to 1.8 million direct and indirect jobs." They "also estimate that, as an average between 2020–2050, an additional 1.4 million induced jobs will be generated by these investments. This brings the total of direct, indirect and induced jobs generated by net energy supply investments to 3.2 million jobs."[72]

At the same time, the US Network estimates that, during this transition, the oil, natural gas, and coal industries dependent on use of fossil fuels will lose an average of 30,500 jobs annually between 2021 and 2030, and an average of 34,200 jobs annually between 2031 and 2050.[73] For these displaced workers, they recommend that the Congress of the United States enact a "just transition program" that would include pension guarantees, employment guarantees in the clean-energy and public sectors, wage insurance, retraining support, and relocation support.[74] They also recommend that Congress provide transitional assistance for fossil fuel–dependent communities, which are mostly located in the states of Kentucky, Montana, Pennsylvania, West Virginia, and Wyoming.[75] Many of these ideas are reflected in the Biden administration's American Jobs Plan, which, at this writing, awaits Congressional action.[76]

In addition to all else that must be done to help improve human capabilities through domestic actions, such transitional assistance is essential. But why stop with helping only those Americans who will be dislocated by the clean energy transition? Why not also help those whose jobs are lost because of automation and other new technologies? And why not also help the (many fewer) workers whose jobs are lost because of competition from foreign trade? As Robert Z. Lawrence has suggested (and as former President Barack Obama proposed but could not get enacted), there is need for a comprehensive adjustment program in the United States that provides universal assistance to all displaced workers and does not distinguish between displaced workers based on why they were displaced.[77]

What is more, and over and above all that must be done domestically in the United States and elsewhere to increase equity and inclusion in trade, there are ways in which WTO rules and practices should be altered multilaterally to make trade a more affirmative part of achieving these important Sustainable Development Goals. These needed changes could be implemented in trade rules and practices without intruding excessively in the sovereign decisions of WTO members about how they choose to govern their domestic economies. With these changes, the WTO would become a more active agent for domestic equity and inclusion without dictating the precise terms for achieving those goals.

One of these needed changes in WTO rules would address the link between *trade and labor*. A leading concern of those workers in the United States and other developed countries who seek tariffs and other devices of trade protectionism, is their impression that the products they make are routinely competing at home and abroad with foreign products that are made under oppressive labor conditions in developing countries. At the same time, developing countries are quick to counter these criticisms as often inaccurate, and are apprehensive of losing the benefit of the lower labor costs they see as among their comparative advantages. To secure popular support for further trade liberalization in developed and developing countries alike, WTO members must find their way to a consensus on this issue of the relationship between trade and labor.

They should start by fully embracing in the trade rules the labor-related targets under Goal 8 of the Sustainable Development Goals, which, it will be recalled, is to "promote sustained, inclusive and sustainable economic growth, full and productive employment and decent work for all."[78] One target under this goal is to "take immediate and effective measures to eradicate forced labour, end modern slavery and human trafficking, and secure the prohibition and elimination of the worst forms of child labour, including recruitment and use of child soldiers, and by 2025 end child labour in all its forms."[79] Another target under Goal 8, for 2030, is to "protect labour rights and promote safe and secure working environments for all workers, including migrant workers, in particular women migrants, and those in precarious employment."[80] All the members of the United Nations – including all the members of the WTO – have agreed on these targets to meet this global goal. These targets should be the immediate focus of the WTO in addressing the link between trade and labor.

With these targets in mind, some politicians and some trade law scholars have suggested that, to increase social inclusion, WTO rules should be revised to permit the imposition of tariffs and other trade restrictions in response to what they call "social dumping." One of these scholars, Gregory Shaffer of the University of California, Irvine, has submitted that, "The real underlying concern should be social dumping of products—that is, products produced under exploitative labor conditions—that sell for less than domestically produced products, and that thus lead to concerns over wage suppression and reductions of labor protections in the 'North.' These policies can undermine the domestic social contract and trigger political contestation against trade."[81] As Shaffer acknowledges, if too broad, measures on "social dumping" could undermine the legitimate comparative advantages of developing countries that are afforded by their lower wage costs; yet, as he says, if "social dumping" is not addressed, then unfair trade advantages will result where the governments of developing countries do not prevent exploitation of labor.

"Social dumping" measures should restrict trade where exploitative labor conditions – whether in developing or developed countries – are inconsistent with the SDGs and are in violation of the core labor standards that have been established in international law by the International Labour Organization of the United Nations. The ILO core labor standards are comprised of four fundamental, universal, and indivisible human rights: freedom from forced labor; freedom from child labor; freedom from discrimination at work; and freedom to form and join a union and to bargain collectively. These core labor standards are set out in the eight main ILO conventions.[82] The 1998 Declaration on Fundamental Principles and Rights at Work of the ILO makes it clear that these universal rights apply to all people in all states – regardless of that state's stage of economic development – and are binding on all members of the ILO. These core labor standards are also regarded as human rights by the United Nations, and they are incorporated into other international law. They are the minimum enabling rights that people require to be able to defend and improve their rights and their conditions at work; to work in freedom and dignity; and to attain the capabilities of human development.[83] As such, they are instrumental to achieving the fundamental goal of sustainable freedom.

"Social dumping" measures should not, however, restrict trade simply to deny developing countries their comparative advantages in producing goods while paying their workers lower wages than are paid in wealthier, developed countries. As Shaffer has said, such measures should be applied in response to violations of labor rights, and "not undercut developing countries' comparative advantage in producing goods with lower skilled labor in reflection of differences in productivity."[84] A model for how the members of the WTO might proceed in permitting measures against "social dumping" is the labor chapter in the CPTPP, which requires compliance with the core labor standards and allows trade sanctions or monetary compensation if a party to the agreement violates its core labor obligations.[85] This plurilateral approach to linking trade and labor by the countries along the Pacific Rim should be made multilateral by the WTO.

It is one thing to expect *developing countries* to uphold core labor standards to which they have agreed in global treaties. It is quite another to perpetuate the extent of their continued exclusion from enjoyment of the full benefits that should be theirs from participating in global trade. For too long, the mind of the "North" has been too dismissive about the immiseration of the "South." The solipsism of the "haves" has often blinded them to the human entitlements of the "have-nots." Despite the heights of the hopes expressed in the aspirations of such global endeavors as the UN Sustainable Development Goals, the drive for human progress has, as historian Priya Satia has said, often prolonged the "exclusion of 'others' from that narrative."[86] For all those who have been so long excluded, lofty rhetoric has not been reflected in lowly reality.

In the nineteenth century, even so "enlightened" a "Northerner" as John Stuart Mill evidently saw no contradiction in being both an ardent apostle of human freedom and a loyal employee for many years of that consummate agent of British imperialism, the British East India Company. Mill wrote expressively about freedom but dismissively about the British colonies. While pondering "the principles of political economy," he mused,

These (outlying possessions of ours) are hard to look upon as countries ... but more properly as outlying agricultural or manufacturing estates belonging to a larger community. Our West Indian colonies, for example, cannot be regarded as countries with a productive capital of their own ... (but are rather) the place where England finds it convenient to carry on the production of sugar, coffee and a few other tropical commodities.[87]

Although developed countries tend to minimize the lingering legacies of their past colonialism, developing countries still see evidence of this dismissiveness in the inequities of the modern world.

In the twenty-first century, WTO members must eliminate the vestiges of this dismissiveness in trade. Toward this end, one of the specific targets of Goal 10 of the UN Sustainable Development Goals, which is to reduce inequality within and among countries, is to "implement the principle of *special and differential treatment for developing countries*, in particular least developed countries, in accordance with the World Trade Organization agreements."[88] Implicit in this trade target is the assumption that achieving it will reduce inequality. A total of 183 rules in the WTO agreement give developing countries special trade rights, which include more time to implement their trade obligations, preferential tariffs schemes, and technical support from the developed countries. Long in place in the WTO–based trading system, this "special and differential treatment" is supposed to help the poorest WTO members develop economically while also enabling them to fulfill their WTO trade obligations as much and as soon as they can. Developed and developing countries have long been at odds in the WTO over the nature, extent, and consequences of this different level of trade expectation for developing countries.

Because equity is advanced by inclusion, because inclusion is most successful when trade gains are maximized, and because trade gains are maximized when countries are open to trade, the equitable treatment of developing countries is the greatest when developing countries meet their WTO obligation to be open to trade sooner rather than later. Yet, for more than seven decades, "special and differential treatment" has largely had the effect of postponing more openness in developing countries, and thus has had the effect also of postponing their ability to enjoy the fullest extent of the economic benefits from the gains of trade. The basic flaw in the current approach to "special and differential treatment" by the WTO is that it is founded on seeking exemptions from WTO trade obligations instead of on enabling developing countries to meet those obligations, and thus integrate those countries more quickly and more fully into the multilateral trading system and the overall global economy.[89]

The laudable intent of those who seek special and differential treatment for the developing countries in trade is "to support the marginalized and to make them less unequal."[90] This special treatment is a form of "affirmative action" for narrowing the development gap.[91] Yet there is little evidence that special and differential treatment serves this intent. The available evidence strongly suggests, instead, that this intent has been undermined by how, over the years, special and differential treatment has been conceived and implemented.[92] Trade economist Ernesto Ornelas has concluded from his research that, "if anything, the design of SDT policies seems to be biased *against* the interests of developing countries."[93] The denial of their comparative advantages in agriculture and textiles by developed countries in tacit exchange for their special and differential treatment, together with the opportunity costs resulting from their continued maintenance of high trade barriers, have, quite simply, prevented the developing countries from developing as much as they could have developed, had they opened up more and sooner to trade.

Giving the developing countries the same kind and extent of "special and differential treatment" they have gotten in the past is simply a way of continuing to dismiss them. It perpetuates their second-class status in the world economy. Therefore, in meeting this global target of the SDGs, a new approach to providing "special and differential treatment" is needed in the WTO. Unlike the current approach, this new approach should make distinctions between the stages of development of different developing countries, and between different cases, products, and sectors. Moreover, it should focus on inclusion and not exclusion; it "should enable rather than exempt."[94] It should bring developing countries more completely within the WTO trading system and not continue to exclude them from the full range of its benefits. Above all, it should center on improving human capabilities for securing more sustainable freedom. It should proceed from the premise that the people of developing countries will have more sustainable freedom if they have more access to all that they need and should be able to obtain from world trade to help facilitate their individual development.

Thus, the question that should be asked by the other members of the WTO when a developing country member seeks "special and differential treatment" should be: Will the treatment requested add to the human capabilities and the sustainable freedom of the individual people of this WTO member? To answer this question, requests for "special and differential treatment" will need to be evaluated case by case and in accordance with guidelines agreed by the members of the WTO. These guidelines could be based in part on the Human Development Index. In any one case, the inquiry should center on whether the result of granting the request for special treatment would be only to excuse the requesting country from a trade obligation or, instead, to enable it to comply with that obligation better and completely over time.[95] "Special and differential treatment" must not be a means merely of excusing developing countries from their WTO obligations; it must be a means of empowering the countries that receive it to take the actions necessary in order to enable their citizens to achieve more personal prosperity as a part of a full human flourishing.[96]

In both developing and developed countries, to increase inclusion in trade, the WTO must help *micro, small,* and *medium-sized enterprises* – MSMEs – engage in more trade and benefit more from it. Larger companies usually have the expertise and other internal resources to participate in international trade. Smaller companies often do not. MSMEs – companies with fewer than 250 employees – represent 95 percent of businesses worldwide and almost two-thirds of global employment.[97] Yet, as the WTO has acknowledged, "MSMEs lag behind large firms when it comes to international trade and they are the most vulnerable during times of crisis." The COVID-19 pandemic has certainly demonstrated the truth of their vulnerability. MSME participation in international trade "is typically weak," and it is even weaker in the new pandemic world.[98]

One of the targets of Goal 8 of the Sustainable Development Goals, on jobs and growth, is to "encourage the formalization and growth of micro-, small-and medium-sized enterprises, including through access to financial services."[99] With this target in mind, more than half of the members of the WTO are taking part in an effort launched at the WTO Ministerial Conference in Buenos Aires in 2017 to establish a formal work program to facilitate more participation by MSMEs in international trade.[100] Their objective is not to discriminate between companies based on their size. Nor is it to negotiate new trade rules. Rather, it is to identify and pursue means of increasing the role of MSMEs in world trade without the need of new rules.

As it is, "Fixed market entry costs, such as access to information about foreign distribution networks, border regulations and standards, are the main barriers hindering" the participation of MSMEs in trade.[101] In addition, "recent evidence suggests that all trading costs, including those that increase with the size of shipments, impede (MSME) participation in trade more than that of larger firms."[102] The WTO members working on this topic have identified access to information, access to trade finance, access to the Internet, trade costs, trade facilitation, good regulatory practice, technical assistance, and capacity building as the main factors affecting whether MSMEs can engage successfully in international trade.[103] Proposals for enhancing access for

MSMEs on all of these fronts as part of a formal work program were to be made at the WTO Ministerial Conference in Geneva in late November 2021.

Yet another way in which the WTO can help increase social inclusion to achieve the Sustainable Development Goals is by achieving *gender equity*. In developing countries, 36 percent of MSMEs are partly or entirely owned by women.[104] Yet only one in five companies that export is owned by a woman.[105] Moreover, according to the International Trade Centre, 99 percent of trade and 99 percent of purchase contracts, whether from governments or companies, are controlled by men.[106] As Linda Scott has written, "International trade is a male monopoly."[107] This gender gap in trade and in the overall economy is harmful to women and men alike, and it is harmful also to all our hopes for global economic progress and prosperity. How can we hope to progress if we handcuff half of humanity? The World Economic Forum has reported that there is a "strong correlation between a country's gender gap and its economic performance ... [C]ountries that want to remain competitive and inclusive will need to make gender equality a critical part of their nation's human capital improvement."[108] A recent study found that if women played a role equal in labor markets to that of men, then the global GDP in 2025 would be higher by 26 percent.[109]

Women are on the frontlines in the fight against COVID-19, which has only worsened the gender gap.[110] The pandemic has "had disproportionate effects on women and their economic status."[111] It "threatens to roll back gains in women's economic opportunities, widening gender gaps that persist despite 30 years of progress."[112] Women are more likely to work in jobs in economic sectors – such as tourism, retail, and hospitality – that are necessarily face-to-face and cannot be done remotely through online work. In developing countries, women are also more likely to be employed in the more tenuous work of the informal economy, with poor working conditions and no benefits. The pandemic has put women at greater risk of losing their jobs, and girls and younger women have been "forced to drop out of school and work to supplement household income," which is causing declines in their skills and thus their human capabilities within the labor force.[113] Making matters worse, women are generally more vulnerable than men to the negative impacts of climate change.[114]

Goal 5 of the UN Sustainable Development Goals is to "achieve gender equality and empower all women and girls."[115] The aim for 2030 is to "end all forms of discrimination against all women and girls everywhere."[116] The SDGs do not mention gender equity in trade specifically, but one significant way of achieving gender equity is by advancing it in trade. Toward this end, along with the MSME initiative that was launched in Buenos Aires in 2017, 118 WTO members issued there a Joint Declaration on Trade and Women's Economic Empowerment.[117] In this declaration, they announced their joint intention to make trade and development policies more gender responsive and to work together "to remove barriers for women's economic empowerment and increase their participation in trade."[118] More than two-thirds of all the members of the WTO, since joined by others, "have realized they can no longer afford to treat trade in isolation from its gender-related human rights impacts."[119]

"Gender equality is gradually emerging as a policy norm in trade agreements. Out of 292 FTAs currently in force, almost 75 have at least one gender-explicit provision."[120] In 2016, Chile and Uruguay included gender measures in their free trade agreement.[121] In 2017, Canada and Chile added a stand-alone gender chapter to their FTA.[122] The CPTPP has a provision on "Women and Economic Growth."[123] The USMCA, which replaced NAFTA, recognizes "the goal of eliminating discrimination in employment and occupation," and supports "the goal of promoting equality in the workplace."[124] These provisions on gender equity in these FTAs are, however, largely exhortatory. They "contain few nationally specific goals and measures, and are not covered by dispute settlement mechanisms."[125] Furthermore, they are usually couched in language that extols gender equity for socioeconomic reasons; they do not speak of gender equity as a matter of human rights.

By contributing to the enormous explosion in international trade since 1945, the WTO–based multilateral trading system "has contributed to lifting millions out of poverty – among them, many women. But so far, trade policy design has not paid specific attention to the situation of women."[126] The follow-up to the Buenos Aires Declaration of 2017 is a chance to change this. Thus far, though, the efforts by the trading system to align trade with gender equity have focused mostly on gathering facts, making reports, perceiving trade through a "gender lens," and cooperating on raising the commercial consciousness about the role of women in trade and about the need to include more women in trade.

Although these efforts are helpful, they do not go to the heart of the issue of gender inequity. Maria Panezi of the University of New Brunswick insists, quite rightly, that much more must be done. She contends that, in seeking gender equity in trade,

national implementation strategies cannot be limited to the establishment of committees, data collection, cooperation activities and consultations. A partial response to gender and trade concerns will not bridge the current large gap between men and women in international trade. In the national context, countries implementing these agreements must move beyond the language of cooperation and determine the next steps, such as loan facilitation, educational programs and other policies that will lower entry barriers for women.[127]

With respect to women, there is need to shift the orientation of the multilateral trading system more toward human rights and the human capabilities that lead to human flourishing.

Perhaps most marginalized in international trade are the *Indigenous peoples* of the world, with a population of 476 million in more than ninety countries. Culturally distinct and often clustered in their own communities worldwide,

Indigenous peoples comprise about 6 percent of the global population and about 15 percent of the extreme poor.[128] As John Borrows of the University of Victoria in Canada has put it, bluntly but accurately, "As for many marginalized people, globalization has not done many favors for Indigenous peoples. Nation-states have stolen their lands, labor and resources while international law has broadly sanctioned these thefts."[129] Economically, they have often been abandoned. Legally, they have often been "invisible."[130] They have benefited little from international trade and have often been overlooked in the contemplation of global economic integration.

Now, in the new pandemic world, Indigenous peoples are suffering still more. Already burdened by "a long history of devastation from epidemics brought by colonizers," they are enduring even more devastation caused by COVID-19.[131] One measure of their global exclusion is the shocking extent of their exposure to the ravages of contagious disease. In disproportionate numbers, they fall into the most vulnerable health categories; fall outside any formal systems for social protection; and fall prey to the precarity of the informal economy – all of which speeds the deadly spread of the novel coronavirus in Indigenous communities.[132] In the United States, the infection rate of the Navajo Nation has been ten times higher than that of the general population of their state of Arizona.[133]

The Sustainable Development Goals are meant to begin to right these wrongs. As the United Nations has underscored, the SDGs refer "to indigenous people six times" – three times in the political declaration; once in a target of Goal 2 for ending hunger; once in a target of Goal 4 for education; and once in plans for implementation that call for the participation of Indigenous peoples.[134] Indeed, all seventeen of the SDGs arguably relate to Indigenous peoples. Accomplishment of the SDGs will reduce their social and economic exclusion and begin to realize the vision of the United Nations Declaration on the Rights of Indigenous Peoples of 2007.[135] But perhaps the surest way of achieving the inclusion of Indigenous peoples is by integrating them more extensively into the flow of commerce, including international trade.

"[I]nternational trade and investment agreements have traditionally excluded Indigenous thought and practices and physically restricted any representations by Indigenous peoples."[136] But, slowly, the world has been awakening to the rightful demands of Indigenous peoples for inclusion in the mainstream of the global economy. An affirmation in the preamble to the CPTPP of "the importance of promoting ... Indigenous rights" was the first reference in any trade agreement to Indigenous rights.[137] Since then, largely at the instance of Canada, the rights of Indigenous peoples have been acknowledged in the USMCA.[138] Confirmed in the agreement is that the parties to the USMCA can take measures they deem necessary to protect Indigenous peoples as long as any discrimination in those measures is not arbitrary or unjustifiable and does not constitute a disguised restriction on international trade in goods, services, or investment.[139]

This can be a start for WTO members in framing a multilateral approach to making more room for Indigenous peoples within the WTO trading system. A declaration by WTO members – similar to the one on the economic empowerment of women – could be the beginning for the WTO in simultaneously seeking the economic empowerment of Indigenous peoples. More Indigenous peoples must be linked to trade. More Indigenous peoples must be permitted to participate by right in the global governance of trade. And ways must be crafted, too, for the multilateral trading system to benefit from all that Indigenous peoples have to offer in reimagining trade for the new pandemic world, including on the nexus between trade and the environment. In remaking trade rules to do more to further sustainable development, the WTO can learn much from the devotion of Indigenous peoples to a circular economy of "wealth creation without exploitation."[140]

Not least – never least – are the many millions of people throughout the world who suffer from discrimination because of their race. Sadly, in the new pandemic world, the *racial discrimination* of the old world still afflicts and diminishes humanity everywhere. Unknown to the ancients, the concept of race is a relatively recent invention. So too is the notion of superiority and inferiority based on race. As Europeans ventured out to new shores and new worlds during the Age of Discovery, they encountered, frequently for the first time, people who looked, thought, and acted differently than they did. As with their other discoveries, the Europeans wondered how they should characterize and categorize these other people from other far and foreign places.

Thus, in the eighteenth and nineteenth centuries, a pseudoscience that passed for science, demarcated the differences among people by their color, in an artificial hierarchy that placed "white over black."[141] Slaveholders, slave traders, and all the others who benefited directly or indirectly from the existence of slavery, used this pseudoscience to rationalize to others – and to themselves – the indelible shame of presuming to "own" other human beings, steal their labor, and keep them in chains.[142] Even David Hume – so otherwise advanced as a thinker for the eighteenth century, and an ardent opponent of slavery – was not immune to this racist pseudoscience; he believed Blacks "to be naturally inferior to whites."[143] Like some other Enlightenment thinkers, he fell short in his own thinking of the full implications of his revolutionary right reasoning.

Those implications have been more fully understood since then. Science has long since rejected racial stereotyping, and slavery has long since been declared illegal under international law. Article 4 of the United Nations Declaration on Human Rights of 1948 states that "no one should be held in slavery or servitude, slavery in all its forms should be abolished."[144] Slavery is the very antithesis of freedom, and opposition to slavery is an indispensable element of human morality. For this reason, the WTO rules support restrictions on trade relating to products of prison labor, and WTO jurists would surely declare that trade restrictions on products made with other forms of forced labor are "necessary to protect public morals."[145]

And it may become necessary for them to do so; for one of the worst of the sins of contemporary human society is that, despite all, slavery still exists. More than 40 million people – about 70 percent of them women and girls – may be living in some form of modern slavery today, whether forced labor, forced marriage, or some other type of de facto bondage.[146] Illegal human trafficking – especially of women and children – is one manifestation of this global obscenity. The legacy of slavery also lingers, of course, in the multitude of daily indignities imposed by the abomination of racial discrimination that mocks the very thought of the current existence of global justice.[147] As Frantz Fanon wrote in *The Wretched of the Earth*, "[W]hat parcels out the world is to begin with the fact of belonging to or not belonging to a given race."[148]

The very concept of race is a stain on modern civilization. Until we can, at long last, see past the superficiality of skin color to the common identity and the common kinship of all humanity, there can be no achieving the full measure of justice in the world. Without a human development that includes the realization that we are, each and all, one and the same, and that our individual lives are the individual expressions of the shared aspirations of one unique and striving species on one irreplaceable planet, there can be no true and lasting attainment of our shared global goals for sustainable development. In centuries past, international trade facilitated the bonds of slavery. In this century, and in the centuries to come, international trade must be enlisted in the cause of removing the remaining shackles of racial discrimination and forging instead the freeing links of one humanity.

Anne Case and Angus Deaton have written eloquently about the sad "deaths of despair" among many white working-class Americans who have sought the American Dream but have found only futility in this deracinating season of globalization.[149] Uprooted, alienated, distrustful, shorn of hope, bereft of belonging, forlorn in facing an unforeseeable future in which they fear they will have no part, many white Americans are dying from drink, drugs, and suicide.[150] Their lives have lost meaning. But these white Americans are not the only Americans who have lost meaning amid a dark despair. Black Americans also confront meaningless. So too do other Americans. And Americans are far from alone among a grieving humanity in suffering the deaths of despair, which are happening throughout the world, and are more numerous now because of the COVID-19 pandemic.

Everywhere in the world, people who have lost their way are searching for meaning in their lives during a disruptive time that has brought both unprecedented bounty and unparalleled upheaval to many millions. Truths that seemed eternal seem no longer quite so true. Received certitudes seem no longer quite so certain. More open societies bring with them not only new goods and services but also new ideas. They bring with them new ways of seeing, new ways of thinking, new ways of believing. More open societies mean more possibilities for finding and exercising freedom, but they also bring with them the open-endedness of freedom, the awestricken personal responsibility of freedom. Being able to decide for yourself in a free and open society means also *having* to decide for yourself. In the exercise of their freedom, many people everywhere are trying to decide – what is freedom *for* ?

It is not for the World Trade Organization to answer this question. It is not for any institution of human governance to do so. In the fullness of human flourishing, this question can only be answered by each of us as individuals. Each of us alone must find our own purpose; each of us alone must determine what our freedom is for. The governmental institutions we create, from the nearest to us to the global in reach, cannot impart meaning to our lives. At best, they can only establish and maintain the conditions in which each of us can find our own chosen meaning. If they do not free and enable us to discern our own meaning for ourselves, or, worse, if they attempt to impose some dictated meaning upon us, then they are not the forms of governance we need.

And what of international trade? Life's meaning will not be found in things. There is more to life than the material. There is more to inclusion than trade. Yet trade can be an instrument for an inclusion that can provide us with life's fundamentals of food, water, clothing, shelter, health, and a clean and safe environment; and it can thus afford each of us with more latitude in our own individual quests for meaning. Trade can also help provide each of us with yet another of the fundamentals of a life in which inclusion can be accomplished and individual meaning can be found – peace. Often forgotten is why the multilateral trading system was created in the first place. It was created in the aftermath of the Second World War to help prevent a third world war. It was created to help secure and ensure world peace.[151] So far, it has succeeded.

The success of the WTO as an agent of world peace must continue in the new pandemic world. The Sustainable Development Goals envisage education for the "promotion of a culture of peace and non-violence."[152] Trade, which abhors violence, can foster peace. But more, trade, which communicates so many new ideas, must also help communicate the idea of justice. Even more, trade, while fostering peace, must also help achieve justice; for all those who have been called to a life of service by an abiding commitment to civil and human rights, understand that there is much more to peace than the avoidance of war. They remember what the dreamer Martin Luther King, Jr., the greatest American since Abraham Lincoln, wrote in the immediate aftermath of the memorable struggle against racial segregation in the Montgomery, Alabama bus boycott of 1957: "True peace is not merely the absence of tension; it is the presence of justice ... Injustice anywhere is a threat to justice everywhere."[153]

Conclusion

Lasting Links

The COVID-19 pandemic is a plague upon us. It is also an opportunity for us. It is an opportunity to begin anew with a just transition to a carbon-free world of human flourishing through sustainable development. Essential to that transition are the global partnerships envisaged in Goal 17 of the United Nations Sustainable Development Goals.[1] The links of those partnerships must be forged at every level of global action and governance. They must be built up from the bottom up, beginning at the creative "grass roots" of the world, in innovative partnerships between local and regional governments; between individuals, civic and business organizations, and governments; and among the members of civil society outside of governments. They must be shaped through the learning by doing of a multitudinous variety of people and groups coming together and working together toward common ends throughout the world.[2] At the same time, other worldwide partnerships are needed to help achieve Goal 17. These are the global international institutions where – as with so much of sustainable development – solutions for global concerns can only be found if they are innovated and implemented through cooperative international action. The World Trade Organization is one of the international institutions that has been created to constitute one of these needed global links, one of these necessary global partnerships.

To achieve our global goals for sustainable development, the frayed links of the WTO must be repaired and restored by making the WTO the forum for forging links that it was originally intended to be. Through multilateral cooperation, the WTO must be brought into the twenty-first century with the new and revised trade rules required to fit the new shape of the world in this century. WTO trade rules must be improved to include additional – and long overdue – liberalization in trade in agriculture, manufacturing, and services. They must be updated to address more comprehensively and effectively digital trade, intellectual property, competition, sustainable foreign direct investment, and other aspects of the modern commercial economy. In addition, through freer trade in medical goods and services, and though numerous other reforms, WTO rules must be revised to respond to the lasting changes wrought in the world by the pervasive impacts of the COVID-19 pandemic.

WTO rules must also be rewritten in many places to account for the links between trade and climate change and between trade and the other dimensions of sustainable development. They must support a global green recovery from the COVID-19 pandemic. They must facilitate carbon pricing and help advance other ambitious climate action through a WTO climate waiver. They must help protect our planet against other ecological perils. Toward these ends, WTO rules must free trade in environmental goods and services and must discipline subsidies for fisheries and fossil fuels. They must help preserve biodiversity, protect animal health and welfare, and stop illegal wildlife trade. They must help stop deforestation and help promote sustainability in the mining of minerals and metals. And they must promote sustainability in land use, water use, and agriculture.

All these changes in WTO trade rules must be accompanied by a combination of domestic and international actions that will help magnify international cooperation by achieving equity and inclusion through trade and by helping advance the assurance of justice worldwide. The bountiful benefits of trade will continue, and they will grow, only if all people everywhere are able to share in those benefits. The WTO will overcome its existential crisis, it will survive and add to its previous successes, only with global agreement on new trade rules for a new world, a world in which the fraying links of trade are made anew into lasting links, links that will serve all of humanity for many years to come.

The logic of international cooperation is there. It has always been there. It is there now more than ever before. But how, amid such painful impacts from a pandemic; amid such polarization; amid such widespread political paralysis; and amid such soothing temptations to escape from the demanding responsibilities of freedom into the clutches of an authoritarianism in which difficult personal decisions need no longer be made; will we be able at last to summon the shared political will to cooperate across borders in forging these lasting links?

Not long before he died in 1790, in his final revision of *The Theory of Moral Sentiments*, his too often ignored companion and complement to his far more famous book, *The Wealth of Nations*, Adam Smith added a passage he had written decades earlier that we today would call a "thought experiment." He wrote, "Let us suppose that the great empire of China, with all its myriads of inhabitants, was suddenly swallowed up by an earthquake, and let us consider how a man of humanity in Europe, who had no sort of connection with that part of the world, would be affected upon receiving intelligence of the dreadful calamity."[3] Smith surmised that this European man would express humane sentiments and then go on about his business "as if no such accident had happened." For, he added, "[i]f he was to lose his little finger tomorrow, he would not sleep to-night; but, provided he never saw them, he will snore with the most profound security over the ruin of a hundred millions of his brethren, and the destruction of that immense multitude seems plainly an object less interesting to him than this paltry misfortune of his own."[4]

Then Smith asked, "To prevent, therefore, this paltry misfortune to himself, would a man of humanity be willing to sacrifice the lives of a hundred millions of his brethren, provided he had never seen them?"[5] Or, to put this timeless question in contemporary terms, to enable us to watch videos on our smartphones, would we, good humanitarians though we claim to be, be willing to sacrifice the lives of our brethren in poor countries who struggle to scrape a meager living by digging the precious metals that are essential to making the batteries in those smartphones, provided we had never seen those people?

In variations of this thought experiment, this same question has been posed through the years by Hume, Diderot, Chateaubriand, Balzac, Dostoevsky, and others.[6] What if we could benefit from the deaths of faraway people we have never seen without anyone ever knowing we had done so? Would we do so? Should their deaths matter to us if distance or time make them invisible to us and, thus, render to their sad fates only a dim reality, and reduce them to abstractions, statistics, mere phantom reports, devoid of the tangible verity of flesh and blood?

Smith understood that "we are always so much more deeply affected by whatever concerns ourselves than by whatever concerns other men."[7] If this is so, then how, in our new pandemic world, can we summon the expanded moral sentiments and the enlightened understanding of our self-interest to take the broader and longer view? How can we come to comprehend that an earthquake in China is something that concerns those of us on the other side of the world? And how can we come to realize that, as best we can, we must shield future generations from the aftermath of today's "earthquakes" of so many kinds that impact sustainable development?

Earthquakes occur in China. The bodies of virus victims pile up in public parks in India. Small Pacific Island states sink into the rising sea. Older people sit all alone, waiting for the virus to take them. Children everywhere will have a smaller future because of our failure to look beyond the here and now; so will their children – if we do not act. Morality dictates that we should see our species as one and our world as one – and act together. Yet empathy too often depends on proximity. Distance and time diminish our moral view. We do not truly see that person in desperate need on the far side of the planet; we do not really grasp that their pain should pain us, and that their fate will surely shadow our own. And we do not truly see that person who is not yet born and who will live long after we have left; we do not fully comprehend the sustainability concept of "intergenerational equity." All the religions of the world, all the ethical systems of the world, all the professed ideals of the world, teach us that morality should be enough, but it is not. Given our inherent and inescapable human nature, given the dictates of our DNA, it is not.[8]

What, then, if not morality, must be the source of the global political will we seek? In the new pandemic world of the twenty-first century, what should be done as a matter of morality, will be done – as Tocqueville foresaw nearly two centuries ago – only if it is seen as a matter of mutual self-interest. To make new rules for the new world – to make the links that must be made, in trade, and in health, climate, biodiversity, cybersecurity, nuclear security, and so much else of what should be mutual global concern – all the countries of the world, and all those who would aspire to lead them, must learn to look beyond the here and now in perceiving their national self-interest. So too must all those who live in all those countries. For, if we do not, today will be less than it could be, and tomorrow will be less still. All that we cherish will be at risk.

Throughout human history, there has been a never-ending struggle over how best to see self-interest. Is it just me and mine, or is it also them? Is it just today, or is it also tomorrow? At this crucial turning point in the brief history of our singular species, the only hope for our ultimate survival is in the embrace of an enlightened self-interest, the common clasp of a rational self-interest that is not limited to the narrow demands of the near term but extends in space and time to take the broader and longer view.[9] For each of us, our self-interest is a shared interest. For all of us, this shared interest must motivate more cooperative action at every level of human interaction, including the interactions among nation states. This is a prerequisite to trade action, climate action, and all the other global actions necessary for the achievement of human flourishing from sustainable development.

We have acted together before. Recall the revolutionary moment in 1945 when we made the new architecture of the postwar world. We can act together again. But, in the new pandemic world, we must do so on a scale we have never done before. We can act together on this unprecedented scale only if we are willing to see beyond the here and now to all that must be done for humanity, and for the planet humanity calls home. Trade links are essential, but trade links are not the only links that tie us together. Trade is but a part of the larger task of human connection. One to another, we are all linked. We are linked to all that surrounds us, all that nourishes us, and all that mystifies us on this planet and in the vast wonderment of the beckoning spaces beyond. Linked as we all are, we "canst not stir a flower without troubling of a star."[10] How, then, can we think that what happens to us will not affect others, and that what happens to others will not affect us? How, then, can we take anything other than a broader and longer view of our self-interest?

If we take the broader and longer view, then we can, in this new pandemic world, make all the trade and other links we need, and, in this making, we can lay the foundations for yet another new world to come. Our perception of our self-interest can continue to evolve. Our links through trade can help forge other human connections. Our habits of cooperation can become ingrained. Our circle of concern can grow to be worldwide. Our potential for achievement can be lifted far above our current imagining. And, with time, and through the links we can forge with time, perhaps we can come to see at last that our true self-interest lies in allegiance to a morality in which we are no longer invisible to each other, no matter who or where we may be; a universal morality in which we are each vital to each other simply because we are each linked in living and in sharing the common gift of the ever-striving and ever-aspiring spirit of humanity. Through trade, and beyond trade, those are, above all else, the lasting links we must seek.

Notes

INTRODUCTION

1 World Health Organization, "Origins of the SARS-CoV-2 Virus" (March 30, 2021), at www.who.int/health-topics/coronavirus/origins-of-the-virus.

2 Amy Qin, "China Raises Coronavirus Death Toll by 50% in Wuhan," *New York Times* (April 17, 2020).

3 www.who.int/news-room/detail/30-01-2020-statement-on-the-second-meeting-of-the-international-health-regulations-(2005)-emergency-committee-regarding-the-outbreak-of-novel-coronavirus-(2019-ncov).

4 *See generally* the classic account in William H. McNeill, *Plagues and People* (New York: Anchor, 1976).

5 Ferris Jabr, "How Humanity Unleashed a Flood of Zoonotic Diseases," *New York Times* (June 17, 2020).

6 www.who.int/dg/speeches/detail/who-director-general-s-opening-remarks-at-the-media-briefing-on-covid-19—11-march-2020.

7 Don Babwin and Paul J. Weble, "Rural Areas Seeing Viruses Spike, Too," *Associated Press* (June 27, 2020).

8 "Covid-19 Is Yet to Do Its Worst," *Economist* (July 4, 2020).

9 "COVID-19 Dashboard by the Center for Systems Science and Engineering (CSSE), Johns Hopkins University, at https://coronavirus.jhu.edu/map.html.

10 Ibid.

11 Ibid.

12 The official number is 2,996 deaths of citizens from seventy-eight countries. *See* "September 11 Attacks," at www.history.com/topics/21st-century/9-11-attacks.

13 Bank of International Settlements, "A Global Sudden Stop: BIS Annual Economic Report" (June 30, 2020), 1.

14 Centers for Disease Control and Prevention, "Social Distancing," at www.cdc.gov/coronavirus/2019-ncov/prevent-getting-sick/social-distancing.html.

15 Simon Romero, Manny Fernandez, and Marc Santana, "'We May Be Surprised Again': An Unpredictable Pandemic Takes a Terrible Toll," *New York Times* (September 21, 2020).

16 Pragyan Deb, Davide Furceri, Jonathan D. Ostry, and Nour Tawk, "How the Great Lockdown Saved Lives," International Monetary Fund (June 2, 2020), at https://blogs.imf.org/2020/06/02/how-the-great-lockdown-saved-lives.

17 Rebecca Elliott and Christopher M. Mathews, "This Is What It Looks Like When a Texas Oil Boom Busts," *Wall Street Journal* (July 11, 2020).

18 "The Pandemic's Next Stage: The New Normal," *Economist* (July 4, 2020).

19 "*Lancet* COVID-19 Commission Statement on the Occasion of the 75th Session of the UN General Assembly" (September 14, 2020), 2, at https://doi.org/10.1016/S0140-6736(20)31927-9.

20 Committee for Coordination of Statistical Activities, "How COVID-19 Is Changing the World: A Statistical Perspective," at 8.

21 "UN Launches COVID-19 Plan That Could Defeat the Virus and Build a Better World," *UN News* (March 31, 2020), at https://news.un.org/en/story/2020/03/1060702.

22 WHO, "Covid-19 Virus Variants – How Concerned Should We Be?" at www.who.int/emergencies/diseases/novel-coronavirus-2019/media-resources/science-in-5/episode-20—covid-19—variants-vaccines?gclid=CjoKCQiAorSABhDlARIsAJtjf CcNtT4bPUuEMvzyL4prOsUVM_hhbgUb6OTGNPgQdK6BLJ2EoA572a4aA mI9EALw_wcB.

23 Elliot Hansen, "Lancet Study Finds 40 Percent of U.S. COVID-19 Deaths Could Have Been Avoided," Slate (February 11, 2021), at https://slate.com/news-and-politics/2021/02/lancet-study-40-percent-u-s-covid-19-coronavirus-deaths-avoidable-unnecessary.html; *see* Steffie Woolhandler et al., "Public policy and health and health in the Trump era," *The Lancet*, Vol. 397, No. 10275 (February 20, 2021), 705–753, at www.thelancet.com/journals/lancet/article/PIIS0140-6736(20)32545-9/fulltext. Those who conducted the study reached this conclusion by comparing the US health outcomes from COVID-19 with the weighted averages of the other G-7 countries.

24 Katherine T. Wu, "One in 1,000 African Americans Has Been Killed Because of the Coronavirus," *New York Times* (September 30, 2020).

25 Minouche Shafik, "Redesigning Society after Covid-19," *Financial Times* (July 10, 2020).

26 OECD, "Global Economic Outlook 2020: Facing the Jobs Crisis" (July 7, 2020), at http://oecd.org/employment-outlook.

27 Ibid.

28 Douglas A. Irwin, "The Pandemic Adds Momentum to the Deglobalization Trend," Peterson Institute for International Economics (April 23, 2020), at www.piie.com/blogs/realtime-economic-issues-watch/pandemic-adds-momentum-deglobalization-trend.

29 Ibid.

30 OECD Economic Outlook, Volume 20, Number 1 (June 2020).

31 Committee for Coordination of Statistical Activities (CCSA), "How COVID-19 Is Changing the World: A Statistical Perspective" (UNCTAD, 2020), 20 (a joint effort by several dozen international institutions).

32 Ibid.

33 Stephanie Nebehay, "Pandemic Slashes Worldwide Income from Work," *Reuters* (September 23, 2020).
34 OECD, "Global Economic Outlook 2020: Facing the Jobs Crisis."
35 CCSA, "How Covid-19 Is Changing the World: A Statistical Perspective."
36 Sergei Klebnikov, "IMF Slashes Global GDP Forecasts, Warning of an Economic Crisis 'Like No Other'" *Forbes* (June 24, 2020).
37 Ibid. at xiii.
38 World Bank, "The Global Economic Outlook during the COVID-19 Pandemic: A Changed World" (Washington, DC: World Bank Group, June 2020), xv.
39 Ibid.
40 Ibid. at 13–20.
41 OECD, "Coronavirus: Living with Uncertainty," OECD Interim Economic Assessment (September 16, 2020), 1.
42 "U.S. Added Nearly 5 Million Jobs in June," *New York Times* (July 2, 2020).
43 Delphine Strauss, "Hidden Unemployment Threatens Recovery across Developed World," *Financial Times* (October 8, 2020).
44 Ruth Simon, "Covid-19's Toll on U.S. Business? 200,000 Extra Closures in Pandemic's First Year," *Wall Street Journal* (April 17, 2021).
45 David M. Cutler and Lawrence H. Summers, "The Covid-19 Pandemic and the $16 Trillion Virus," *JAMA, Journal of the American Medical Association*, Vol. 324, No. 15 (October 12, 2020), 1495–1596, at 1496.
46 Jeff Stein, "Coronavirus Fallout Will Haunt U.S. Economy for Years, Costing It $8 Trillion through 2030, CBO Says," *Washington Post* (June 1, 2020).
47 Ibid.
48 Siobhan O'Grady, "Economic Havoc Leaves World's Most Vulnerable in More Precarious Straits, *Washington Post*, July 6, 2020). *See also* Andrew Hill, "Pandemic and Economic Downturn 'Hitting Women Hardest,'" *Financial Times* (July 6, 2020); Jeffrey Gettleman, "Coronavirus Crisis Shatters India's Big Dreams," *New York Times* (September 5, 2020); Kejal Vyas and Vibhuti Agarwal, "Covid-19 Pandemic Ravages World's Largest Developing Economies," *Wall Street Journal* (September 4, 2020).
49 "Inequality Stings as Virus Cases Rise," *Economist* (July 11, 2020).
50 Ibid. *See also* Jonathan Wheatley, "Covid-19 Curbs 'Not Worth Pain' for Low-Income Countries," *Financial Times* (September 7, 2020).
51 Mandar Oak and Peter Mayer, "India's Lockdown Locks Out the Poor," *East Asia Forum* (June 20, 2020), at www.eastasiaforum.erg/2020/06/20/indias-lockdown-locks-out-the-poor.
52 Helen Coster, "In Sign of the Times, Ayn Rand Institute Approved for PPP loan," *Reuters* (July 6, 2020).
53 Alexandra Villegas, Anthony Faoila, and Leslie Wroughton, "Many Countries Facing 'Debt Tsunami,'" *Washington Post* (January 11, 1021).
54 Sebastian Mallaby, "The Age of Magic Money: Can Endless Spending Prevent Economic Calamity?" *Foreign Affairs* (July/August 2020), 65.
55 Eric Martin, "IMF Sees Developing Nations Needing $2.5 Trillion for Virus," *Bloomberg* (March 27, 2020.
56 Avantika Chilkoti and Gabriele Steinhauser, "Covid's Next Economic Crisis: Developing-Nation Debt," *Wall Street Journal* (July 26, 2020).

57 Alexandra Villegas, Anthony Faoila, and Leslie Wroughton, "Many Countries Facing 'Debt Tsunami.'"

58 Jonathan E. Hillman, *The Emperor's New Road: China and the Project of the Century* (New Haven, CT: Yale University Press, 2020).

59 Ibid. The reference here is to a study by The Johns Hopkins School of Advanced International Studies.

60 World Bank, "Global Economic Prospects" (Washington, DC: World Bank Group, January 2021), 5–6, at www.worldbank.org/en/publication/global-economic-prospects.

61 Yuka Hayashi, "Covid-19 Aftermath Could Spell a 'Lost Decade" for Global Economy, World Banks Says," *Wall Street Journal* (January 5, 2020).

62 Tom Braithwaite, "Forget the 'Beginning of the End,' Covid Is a Permawar," *Financial Times* (January 22, 2021).

63 Jonathan Cheng, "China Growth Numbers Betray Waning Momentum," *Wall Street Journal* (April 16, 2021).

64 Ibid.

65 Ibid.

66 Ibid.

67 Orange Wang, "China's Economy Shakes Off Coronavirus 'Hiccups,' but Outlook Clouded by Beijing's Stimulus Plans," *South China Morning Post* (April 16, 2021), at www.scmp.com/economy/china-economy/article/3129857/chinas-economy-surges-back-pre-coronavirus-levels-outlook.

68 US Bureau of Labor Statistics, "The Employment Situation – March 2021" (March 5, 2021), at www.bls.gov/news.release/pdf/empsit.pdf.

69 Rakesh Kochhar and Jesse Bennett, "U.S. Labor Market Inches Back from the COVID-19 Shock, but Recovery Is Far from Complete," Pew Research Center (April 14, 2021), at www.pewresearch.org/fact-tank/2021/04/14/u-s-labor-market-inches-back-from-the-covid-19-shock-but-recovery-is-far-from-complete/#:~:text=Adjusting%20the%20unemployment%20rate%20for,of%206.6%25%20as%20officially%20reported.

70 Kate Sullivan, "Biden Signs Historic $1.9 Trillion Covid-19 Relief Law," *CNN* (March 11, 2021), at www.cnn.com/2021/03/11/politics/biden-sign-covid-bill/index.html.

71 Matthew Fox, "'Flood Gates Are About to Open': Bank of America Just Boosted Its Forecast for 2021 US GDP Growth for 3 Reasons," *Business Insider* (February 22, 2021), at www.businessinsider.com/us-economy-outlook-bofa-boost-gdp-growth-forecast-2021-stimulus-2021-2.

72 Dion Rabouin, "Goldman Sachs Predicts U.S. Economy Will Growth 8% This Year," *Axios* (March 15, 2021), at www.axios.com/goldman-sachs-us-economy-grow-8-per-cent-2021-eb7e1d84-b6fa-483a-9e19-37a7faddadco.html.

73 Morgan Stanley Research, "2021 US Economic Outlook: Resilient, and Self-Sustaining" (November 15, 2020), at https://advisor.morganstanley.com/scott.altemose/documents/field/s/sc/scott-a–altemose/2021%20MS%20US%20Economic%20Outlook.pdf.

74 International Monetary Fund, "World Economic Outlook, April 2021: Managing Divergent Recoveries (March 23, 2021), at www.imf.org/en/Publications/WEO/Issues/2021/03/23/world-economic-outlook-april-2021.

75 Ibid.

76 Ibid.

77 Karan Deep Singh and Hari Kumar, "Covid-19 Pushes India's Middle Class toward Poverty," *New York Times* (April 16, 2021)

78 World Bank, "Brazil: Overview," at www.worldbank.org/en/country/brazil/overview.

79 Ona Gaur, "The Ganges Is Returning the Dead. It Does Not Lie," *New York Times* (June 19, 2021).

80 "The Other Crisis: Can Covid Help Flatten the Climate Curve?" *Economist* (May 21, 2020).

81 Brad Plumer and Nadia Popovich, "Emissions Are Surging Back as Countries and States Reopen," *New York Times* (June 17, 2020).

82 Johan Rockstrom, "Why We Need to Declare a Global Climate Emergency Now," *Financial Times* (July 27, 2020).

83 UNEP, "Emissions Gap Report 2020" (Nairobi: United Nations Environment Programme, December 2020), xv.

84 Brad Plumer and Nadia Popovich, "Emissions Are Surging Back as Countries and States Reopen."

85 "Analysis: What Impact Will the Coronavirus Pandemic Have on Atmospheric CO_2?" *Carbon Brief*, at www.carbonbrief.org/analysis-what-impact-will-the-coronavirus-pandemic-have-on-atmospheric-co2.

86 Leslie Hook, "Last Year Was Joint Hottest on Record," *Financial Times* (January 9, 2021).

87 International Energy Agency, "Global Energy Review 2021" (April 20, 2021).

88 Christopher Flavelle, "Climate Change Could Cut World Economy by \$23 Trillion in 2050, Insurance Giant Warns," *New York Times* (April 23, 2021).

89 United Nations, "World on the Verge of Climate 'Abyss,' as Temperature Rise Continues: UN Chief," *UN News* (April 19, 2021).

90 "Climate Change 2021: The Physical Science Basis: Summary for Policymakers," Contribution of Working Group I to the Sixth Assessment Report of the Intergovernmental Panel on Climate Change(August 2021), A3, 10.

91 David Lee, "Worst US wildfires on Record Ravage the West Coast," *Financial Times* (September 11, 2020).

92 Jack Guy, "Nearly Three Billion Animals Killed or Displaced by Australia's fires," *CNN* (July 28, 2020), citing report by WWF (World Wildlife Fund).

93 "Flooding in India Kills Score of Animals, Including Endangered Rhinos," *New York Times* (July 25, 2020).

94 Kevin Spear, "Probe: Gopher Tortoise Deaths Unreported," *Orlando Sentinel* (April 25, 2021).

95 Robin Naidoo and Brendan Fisher, "Reset Sustainable Development Goals for a pandemic world," *Nature*, Vol. 583, No. 7815 (July 6, 2020), 198–201, at 199.

96 Yinon M. Bar-On, Rob Phillips, and Ron Milo, "The Biomass Distribution on Earth," *Proceedings of the National Academy of Sciences*, Vol. 115, No. 25 (June 19, 2018), 6506-6511, at www.pnas.org/content/115/25/6506.

97 Carl Zimmer, "Birds Are Vanishing from North America," *New York Times* (September 19, 2019). See Kenneth V. Rosenberg et al., "Decline of the North American Avifauna," *Science*, Vol. 366, No. 6461 (October 4, 2019), 120–124.

98 Ibid.
99 "70% of All Birds on Earth Are Farmed Poultry," Food Security Center (May 18, 2020), at www.foodsecuritycenter.org/seventy-percent-of-birds-are-farmed-poultry.
100 "Are the 2019–20 Locust Swarms Linked to Climate Change?" *Carbon Brief*, at www .carbonbrief.org/qa-are-the-2019-20-locust-swarms-linked-to-climate-change.
101 World Bank, "Global Economic Prospects," at 9.
102 David J. Lynch, "Pandemic Aftershocks Overwhelm Global Supply Chains," *Washington Post* (January 24, 2021).
103 WTO, "World Trade Primed for Strong but Uneven Recovery after COVID-19 Pandemic Shock" (March 31, 2021), at www.wto.org/english/news_e/pres21_e/ pr876_e.htm.
104 WTO, "Trade Shows Signs of Rebound from COVID-19, Recovery Still Uncertain" (October 6, 2020), at www.wto.org/english/news_e/pres20_e/pr862_e .htm.
105 Ibid.
106 Cathleen D. Cimon-Isaacs, Rachel F. Feher, and Ian F. Fergusson, "World Trade Organization: Overview and Future Direction," *Congressional Research Service*, R45417 (August 21, 2020), at https://crsreports.congress.gov/product/details?prod code=R45417.
107 Here I am mindful of the sage advice of Timothy Garton Ash in Timothy Garton Ash, "Hearts Don't Beat Faster for 'the Rule-Based International Order,'" *Financial Times* (September 12, 2020).
108 For a lengthier discussion of the centrality of the rule of law in trade, *see* James Bacchus, *The Willing World* (Cambridge: Cambridge University Press, 2018), at 62–75.
109 Editorial, "The Case for Liberal Trade Remains as Robust as Ever," *Financial Times* (December 31, 2020).
110 *See* James Bacchus, "Might Unmakes Right: The American Assault on the Rule of Law in World Trade," Centre for International Governance Innovation, CIGI Papers No. 173 (May 2018), at www.cigionline.org/publications/might-unmakes-right-american-assault-rule-law-world-trade.
111 Bryce Baschuk, "Does the WTO Matter Anymore?" *Bloomberg* (September 16, 2020).

CHAPTER I

1 OECD, "Global Economic Outlook: Facing the Jobs Crisis."
2 Caitlin McFall, "UN Says the World Cannot Return to 'Previous Normal' after Coronavirus," *Fox News* (June 26, 2020).
3 Here I pay homage to the phrase of Stefan Zweig in another context, the title of his classic memoir, *The World of Yesterday* (Lincoln: University of Nebraska Press, 1964) [1943].
4 Caitlin McFall, "UN Says the World Cannot Return to 'Previous Normal' after Coronavirus."
5 Ferris Jabr, "How Humanity Unleashed a Flood of New Diseases."
6 Editorial, "Free Money," *Economist* (July 25, 2020).

7 International Monetary Fund, "Fiscal Monitor: Policies for the Recovery" (October 2020), at www.imf.org/en/Publications/FM/Issues/2020/09/30/october-2020-fiscal-monitor.

8 Kimberly Amadeo, "US Debt by President by Dollar and Percentage," *The Balance* (November 5, 2020), at www.thebalance.com/us-debt-by-president-by-dollar-and-percent-3306296.

9 Jim Tankersley and Michael Crowley, "Biden Outlines $1.9 Trillion Spending Package to Combat Virus and Downturn," *New York Times* (January 14, 2021).

10 Ruchir Sharma, "The Rescues Ruining Capitalism," *Wall Street Journal* (July 24, 2020).

11 Principle 3, Rio Declaration on Environment and Development (1992).

12 Ruchir Sharma, "The Rescues Ruining Capitalism."

13 Martin Wolf, "How Covid-19 Will Change the World," *Financial Times* (June 16, 2020).

14 "2019 Annual Edelman Trust Barometer – Global Report" (December 2019).

15 David Brooks, "Two Cheers for Liberalism! (Or Maybe One and a Half)," *New York Times* (July 10, 2020).

16 Karen Kornbluh, Arienne Goldstein, and Eli Weiner, "New Study by Digital New Deal Finds Engagement with Deceptive Outlets Higher on Facebook Today Than Run-Up to 2016 Election," German Marshall Fund (October 12, 2020), at www.gmfus.org/blogs/2020/10/12/new-study-finds-engagement-deceptive-outlets-higher-facebook-today.

17 Seema Yasmin and Craig Spencer, "'But I Saw It on Facebook': Hoaxes Are Making Doctors' Lives Harder," *New York Times* (August 30, 2020), referencing a report of Avaaz, a nonprofit advocacy organization that tracks false information.

18 George F. Will, "Trump's Kinship with His Critics," *Washington Post* (January 17, 2021).

19 *See* Stephen R. C. Hicks, *Explaining Postmodernism: Skepticism and Socialism from Rousseau to Foucault*, expanded edition (Roscoe, IL: Ockham's Razor Publishing, 2018) [2004].

20 Adam Garfinkle, "The Darkening Mind," *American Purpose* (December 7, 2020), at www.americanpurpose.com/articles/the-darkening-mind.

21 George F. Will, "Trump's Kinship with His Critics."

22 Martin Wolf, "Covid Exposes Society's Dysfunctions," *Financial Times* (July 15, 2020).

23 *See, e.g.*, Tom Nichols, *The Death of Experience: The Campaign against Established Knowledge and Why It Matters* (Oxford: Oxford University Press, 2017).

24 Ibid. at 2.

25 David Brooks, "Two Cheers for Liberalism! (Or Maybe One and a Half)," *New York Times* (July 9, 2020).

26 For examples, *see* Mark Honigsbaum, *The Pandemic Century: One Hundred Years of Panic, Hysteria, and Hubris* (New York: W. W. Norton, 2019).

27 Charles M. Blow, "Conservatives Try to Lock in Power," *New York Times* (September 21, 2020).

28 Joby Warrick, "Across the Globe, Extremist Violence Has Emerged as a Side Effect to the Virus," *Washington Post* (July 12, 2020).

29 Douglas A. Irwin, "The Pandemic Adds Momentum to the Deglobalization Trend," Peterson Institute for International Economics (April 23, 2020), at www.piie.com/blogs/realtime-economic-issues-watch/pandemic-adds-momentum-deglobalization-trend.

30 William Davies, *Nervous States: How Feeling Took Over the World* (London: Jonathan Cape, 2018).

31 Douglas A. Irwin, "The Pandemic Adds Momentum to the Deglobalization Trend."

32 Kenneth Rapoza, "The Post-Coronavirus World May Be the End of Globalization," *Forbes* (April 3, 2020). At www.forbes.com/sites/kenrapoza/2020/04/03/the-post-coronavirus-world-may-be-the-end-of-globalization.

33 Robert D. Kaplan, "Coronavirus Ushers in the Globalization We Were Afraid Of," *Bloomberg* (March 20, 2020), at www.bloomberg.com/opinion/articles/2020-03-20/coronavirus -ushers-in-the-globalization-we-were-afraid-of.

34 John Gray, "Why This Crisis Is a Turning Point in History," *New Statesman* (April 2020), at www.newstatesman.com/america/2020/04/why-crisis-turning-point-history.

35 *See*, for example, John Gray, *Heresies: Against Progress and Other Illusions* (London: Granta Books, 2004).

36 This, of course, is the credo and the phrase of the late Sir Karl Popper, the great champion of freedom and of open societies.

37 Adam Smith, *The Wealth of Nations* (New York: The Modern Library, 1994) [1776], 19.

38 David Ricardo, *The Principles of Political Economy and Taxation* (London: Everyman's Library, 1974) [1817].

39 For elaboration, *see* the discussions in James Bacchus, *The Willing World*, at 24–25; and in James Bacchus, *Trade and Freedom* (London: Cameron May, 2004), 174–183.

40 John Stuart Mill, *Principles of Political Economy* (London: Longmans, 1909), 580ff [1848]; for more, *see* my previous discussions of Mill's three perceived gains from trade in James Bacchus, *The Willing World*, 82–84, and in James Bacchus, *Trade and Freedom*, 168–170.

41 WTO Agreement on Safeguards.

42 I have made this same point elsewhere. *See* James Bacchus, *The Willing World*, at 81, and James Bacchus, *Trade and Freedom*. For this formulation of freedom, *see* the writings of Sir Karl Popper, especially Karl R. Popper, *The Open Society and Its Enemies, Volume I: The Spell of Plato* (Princeton, NJ: Princeton University Press, 1971) [1945], 173.

43 For more on the connection between trade and freedom, *see* James Bacchus, *Trade and Freedom*.

44 Article 3.2, WTO Dispute Settlement Understanding.

45 Michael Spence, *The Next Convergence: The Future of Economic Growth in a Multispeed World* (New York: Farrar, Straus and Giroux, 2011), 28–29.

46 Angus Maddison, *The World Economy: A Millennial Perspective* (Paris: Organization for Economic Co-operation and Development, 2001), 125.

47 Mario Larch, Jose-Antonio Monteiro, Roberta Piermartini, and Yoto Yotov, "Trade Effects of WTO: They're Real and They're Spectacular," *Vox* (November 20, 2019), at https://voxeu.org/article/trade-effects-wto; Mario Larch, Jose-Antonio Monteiro, Roberta Piermartini, and Yoto Yotov, "On the Effect of GATT/WTO

Membership on Trade: They Are Positive and Large after All," CESifo Working Paper No. 7721 (2019).

48 Kym Anderson, "Contributions of the GATT/WTO to Global Economic Welfare," *Journal of Economic Surveys*, Vol. 30, No. 1 (2016), 56–92, at 56.

49 Ibid. at 57.

50 Roberto Azevedo, "The WTO at 25: A Message from the Director-General" (January 1, 2020), at https://wto.org/english/news_e/news20_e/dgra_01jan20_e .htm.

51 "Trade and America Jobs: The Impact of Trade on U.S. and State-Level Employment: 2019 Update," prepared by Trade Partnership Worldwide for Business Roundtable (March 2019), 2.

52 Gary Clyde Hufbauer and Zhiyao (Lucy) Lu, "The Payoff to America from Globalization: A Fresh Look with a Focus on Costs to Workers," Peterson Institute for International Economics Policy Brief 17–16 (May 2017), 1. These numbers are in 2016 dollars and reflect a household consisting of 2.64 persons.

53 Ibid.

54 Gabriel Felbermayr, Mario Larch, Yoto V. Yotov, and Erdal Yalcin, "The World Trade Organization at 25: Assessing the Economic Value of the Rules Based Global Trading System," Bertelsmann Stiftung (November 2019), 33.

55 Ibid. at 30–31.

56 Global Agenda Councils on Trade and FDI and on Competitiveness, "The Case for Trade and Competitiveness" (Geneva: World Economic Forum, 2015). I was among those who prepared this report.

57 Commission on Growth and Development, "The Growth Report: Strategies for Sustained Growth and Inclusive Development" (Washington, DC: World Bank, 2008), 21.

58 Ibid.

59 David Furceri, Swarnali A. Hannan, Jonathan David Ostry, and Andrew K. Rose, "Macroeconomic Consequences of Tariffs," International Monetary Fund, Working Paper No. 19/9 (January 15, 2019), at www.imf.org/en/Publications/ WP/Issues/2019/01/15/Macroeconomic-Consequences-of-Tariffs-46469.

60 Global Agenda Councils on Trade and FDI and on Competitiveness, "The Case for Trade and Competitiveness," 5.

61 On the "human capabilities" approach to human development, *see* the works of Amartya Sen and Martha C. Nussbaum, including Amartya Sen, *Development as Freedom* (New York: Random House, 1999) and Martha C. Nussbaum, *Creating Capabilities: The Human Development Approach* (Cambridge, MA: Harvard University Press, 2011). *See also* Enrica Chiappero-Martinelli, Siddiqur Osmani, and Mozaffar, eds., *The Cambridge Handbook of the Capability Approach* (Cambridge: Cambridge University Press, 2021).

62 James Bacchus, *The Willing World*, 84–90.

63 OECD, "Towards a More Open Trading System and Job-Rich Growth" (2012), at 2.

64 Eric Hoffer, *The Ordeal of Change* (New York: Harper and Row, 1952).

65 Michael Spence, *The Next Convergence*, 67.

66 Ibid.

67 Quoting his speech to the Commonwealth Club of San Francisco in Edmund Fawcett, *Liberalism: The Life of an Idea* (Princeton, NJ: Princeton University Press, 2014), 270.

68 "How Steel Is Made," American Iron and Steel Institute, at www.steel.org/steel-technology/steel-production.

69 Editorial, "How Are These Steel Tariffs Working?" *Wall Street Journal* (March 18, 2019).

70 Commission on Growth and Development, "The Growth Report: Strategies for Sustained Growth and Inclusive Development" (Washington, DC: World Bank, 2008), 8.

71 Ibid.

72 Michael Spence, *The Next Convergence*, 68.

73 Ibid. at 66.

74 On comparative advantage, *see* Robert M. Stern, *Comparative Advantage, Growth, and the Gains from Globalization: A Festschrift in Honor of Alan V. Deardorff* (Hackensack, NJ: World Scientific, 2011).

75 Michael Spence, *The Next Convergence*, 67.

76 IPBES, "IPBES Workshop on Biodiversity and Pandemics: Executive Summary," Intergovernmental Platform on Biodiversity and Ecosystem Services (October 2020), 5.

77 *See generally* Warren A. Andiman, *Animal Viruses and Humans, a Narrow Divide: How Lethal Viruses Spill Over and Threaten Us* (Philadelphia: Dry, Paul Books, 2018).

78 IPBES, "IPBES Workshop on Biodiversity and Pandemics," at 5.

79 Sahir Doshi and Nicole Gentile, "When Confronting a Pandemic, We Must Save Nature to Save Ourselves," Center for American Progress (April 20, 2020), 4.

80 Kate Ng, "Coronavirus: Humanity's 'Intrusion' into Nature Led to Pandemic, Scientist Says," *Independent* (April 25, 2020).

81 Thomas L. Friedman, "How We Broke the World," *New York Times* (May 23, 2020).

82 Ferris Jahr, "How Humanity Unleashed a Flood of New Diseases."

83 Ibid.

84 Ibid.

85 Josef Settele, Sandra Diaz, Eduardio Brondizio, and Peter Daszak, "Covid-19 Stimulus Measures Must Save Lives, Protect Livelihoods, and Safeguard Nature to Reduce the Risk of Future Pandemics," Intergovernmental Science-Policy Platform on Biodiversity and Ecosystem Services (April 25, 2020), at https://ipbes.net/covid19stimulus.

86 William H. McNeill, *Plagues and Peoples* (New York: Anchor Books, 1998) [1976].

87 Mark Honigsbaum, *The Pandemic Century: One Hundred Years of Panic, Hysteria, and Hubris* (New York: W. W. Norton & Company, 2019).

88 Megan Siebert, "Systems Thinking and How It Can Help Build a Sustainable World: A Beginning Conversation," *The Solutions Journal*, Vol. 9, No. 3 (July 2018), at www.thesolutionshournal.com/articles/systems-thinking-can-help-build-sustainable-world.

89 David Crow, "The Next Virus Pandemic Is Not Far Away," *Financial Times* (August 6, 2020).

90 Ferris Jahr, "How Humanity Unleashed a Flood of New Diseases."

91 For further discussion of the notion of the economy and environment as one, *see* James Bacchus, *The Willing World*, at 46–49.

92 *See, e.g.*, Peter Jacques, *Sustainability: The Basics* (London: Routledge Press, 2015); Jeremy L. Caradonna, *Sustainability: A History* (London: Oxford University Press, 2014); Leslie Paul Thiele, *Sustainability* (Cambridge: Polity Press, 2013); Ulrich Grober, *Sustainability: A Cultural History* (Totnes: Green Books, 2012); and Paul Warde, *The Invention of Sustainability: Nature and Destiny, c. 1500–1870* (Cambridge: Cambridge University Press, 2018).

93 Megan Siebert, "Systems Thinking and How It Can Build a Sustainable World: A Beginning Conversation."

94 Ibid.

95 *Our Common Future: Report of the United Nations Commission on Environment and Development* (Oxford: Oxford University Press, 1987).

96 Ibid.

97 Ibid.

98 United Nations, "Transforming Our World: The 2030 Agenda for Sustainable Development."

99 Ibid. at para. 55.

100 An asterisk to this goal adds: "Acknowledging that the United Nations Framework Convention on Climate Change is the primary international, intergovernmental forum for negotiating the global response to climate change."

101 United Nations, "Transforming Our World," at para. 41.

102 Ibid. at paras. 7–9.

103 Ibid. at para. 27.

104 "Voluntary National Reviews," at https://sustainabledevelopment.un.org/hlpf/2020#vnrs.

105 United Nations, "The Sustainable Development Goals Report" (July 2020), 2.

106 Ibid.

107 Ibid.

108 Vicky McKeever, "Pandemic Has Delayed Sustainable Development Goals by Decades, Says Former Unilever CEO," *CNBC* (April 12, 2021), at www.cnbc.com/2021/04/12/paul-polman-pandemic-delayed-sustainable-development-goals-by-decades.html.

109 United Nations, "The Sustainable Development Goals Report" (July 2020), 2.

110 Erna Solberg and Nana Addo Dankwa Akufo-Addo, "Why We Cannot Lose Sight of the Sustainable Development Goals during Coronavirus," World Economic Forum (April 23, 2020), at www.weforum.org/agenda/2020/04/coronavirus-pandemic-effect-sdg-un-progress.

111 Robin Naidoo and Brendan Fisher, "Reset Sustainable Development Goals for a Pandemic World."

112 "GSDR 2019: Global Sustainable Development Report 2019: The Future Is Now: Science for Achieving Sustainable Development" (United Nations, 2019).

113 Jeffrey D. Sachs, Guido Schmidt-Traub, Mariana Mazzucato, Dirk Messner, Nebojsa Nakicenovic, and John Rockstrom, "Six Transformations to Achieve the Sustainable Development Goals," *Nature Sustainability*, Vol. 2 (September 2019), 805–814.

114 "Transformations to Achieve the Sustainable Development Goals: Report Prepared by the World in 2050 Initiative," International Institute for Applied Systems Analysis (IIASA) (Laxenburg: IIASA, July 2018).

115 Robin Naidoo and Brendan Fisher, "Reset Sustainable Development Goals for a Pandemic World." *See also* editorial, "Time to Revise the Sustainable Development Goals," *Nature*, Vol. 583, No. 7816 (July 16, 2020), 331–332.

116 Ibid.

117 Ruchir Sharma, "The Rescues Ruining Capitalism."

118 "Daily CO2," at www.co2.earth/daily-co2.

119 Andre Freedman and Chris Mooney, "Earth's Carbon Dioxide Levels Hit Record High, Despite Coronavirus-Related Emissions Drop," *Washington Post* (June 4, 2020), citing recordings by the Scripps Institution of Oceanography.

120 Ibid.

121 Joseph E. Stiglitz, "Are We Overreacting on Climate Change?" *New York Times* (August 9, 2020).

122 http://400.350.org.

123 Laura Millan Lombrana, "Global Temperatures Already 1.2C above Pre-industrial Levels," *Bloomberg* (December 2, 2020), citing estimates by the World Meteorological Organization.

124 "World of Change: Global Temperatures," at www.earthobservatory.nasa.gov.

125 Climate Action Tracker, at www.climateactiontracker.org/global/temperatures.

126 IPCC, "Climate Change 2014: Impacts, Adaptation, and Vulnerability: Part A: Global and Sectoral Aspects," Working Group II Contribution to the Fifth Assessment Report of the Intergovernmental Panel on Climate Change (Cambridge: Cambridge University Press, 2014).

127 IPCC, "Climate Change 201: Synthesis Report. Contributions of Working Groups I, II and III to the Fifth Assessment Report of the Intergovernmental Panel on Climate Change (Geneva: IPCC, 2015), 8.

128 Ibid. at 17.

129 Ibid. at 16.

130 Marianne Fay, Stephane Hallegatte, Adrien Vogt-Schilb, Julie Rozenberg, Ulf Narloch, and Tom Kerr, "Decarbonizing Development: Three Steps to a Zero-Carbon Future" (Washington, DC: World Bank Group, 2015), 1, at https://openknowledge.worldbank.org/handle/10986/21842.

131 BP Statistical Review of World Energy, "Energy Consumption by Source, World," at https://ourworldindata.org/energy.

132 For more detail about the structure of the Paris Agreement, *see* James Bacchus, *The Willing World*, at 134–143.

133 Paris Decision 1/CP. 21.

134 "Synthesis Report on the Aggregate Effect of the Intended Nationally Determined Contributions," Conference of Parties, United Nations Framework Convention on Climate Change (October 30, 2015), FCCC/CP/20157.

135 "Cut Global Emissions by 7.6 Percent Every Year for Next Decade to Meet 1.5C Paris Target – UN Report," at https://.unenvironment.org/news-and-stories/press-release/cut-global-emissions-76-percent-every-year-next-decade-meet-15degc.

136 Ibid.

137 Ibid. *See* United Nations Environment Programme, "Emissions Gap Report 2019 (UNEP: Nairobi, November 2019).

138 Intergovernmental Panel on Climate Change, "Global Warming of 1.5C" (October 2018). This report was written and edited by ninety-one scientists from forty countries who analyzed more than 6,000 scientific studies.

139 Ibid. at 11.

140 Ibid. at 6.

141 Ibid. at 7.

142 Alan Buis, "The Atmosphere: Getting a Handle on Carbon Dioxide," NASA's Jet Propulsion Laboratory (October 9, 2019).

143 Casey Ivanovich, "Six Takeaways from the New Climate Report" (October 8, 2018), at http://blogs.edf.org/climate411/2018/10/18/six-takeaways-from-the-new-climate-report.

144 Ibid.

145 Intergovernmental Panel on Climate Change, "Global Warming of 1.5C," at 14. *See* Coral Davenport, "Major Climate Report Describes a Strong Risk of Crisis as Early as 2040," *New York Times* (October 7, 2018); and Jonathan Watts, "We Have 12 Years to Limit Climate Change Catastrophe," *Guardian* (October 8, 2018).

146 Article 4.9, Paris Agreement, FCCC/CP/2015/L.9 (December 12, 2015).

147 Carbon Brief, "COP25: Key Outcomes Agreed at the UN Climate Talks in Madrid" (December 15, 2019), at www.carbonbrief.org/cop25-key-outcomes-agreed-at-the-UN-climate-talks-in-madrid.

148 "COP26 Postponed," UN Climate Press Release (April 1, 2020), at https://unfccc .int/news/cop26-postponed.

149 Andrew Scott and Anna Locke, "How to Build Back Greener in the Covid-19 Recovery" (May 11, 2020), at www.odi.org/blogs/16943-how-build-back-greener-covid-19-recovery.

150 Jenessa Duncombe, "'Now Is the Time' for Green Recovery, Scientists Say," at https://eos.org/articles/now-is-the-time-for-green-recovery-scientists-say.

151 Fiona Harvey, "World Health Leaders Urge Green Recovery from Coronavirus," *Guardian* (May 26, 2020).

152 Akshat Rathi and Thomas Seal, "Companies Worth $2 Trillion Are Calling for a Green Recovery," *Bloomberg* (May 18, 2020).

153 OECD, "Building Back Better: A Sustainable Resilient Recovery after COVID-19" (June 5, 2020), at https://read.oecd-ilibrary.org/view/?ref=133_133639-s08q2ridhf& title=Building-back-better-A-sustainable-resilient-recovery-after-COVID-19.

154 Ibid.

155 Eleanor Russell and Martin Parker, "How the Black Death Made the Rich Richer," *BBC* (July 1, 2020), at https://bbc.com/worklife/article/20200701-how-the-black-death-made-the-rich-richer.

156 Marina Andrijevic, Carl-Friedrich Schleussner, Matthew J. Gidden, David L. McCollum, and Joeri Rogelj, "COVID-19 Recovery Funds Dwarf Clean Energy Investment Needs," *Science* , Vol. 370, No. 6514 (October 16, 2020), 298–300, at https://science.sciencemag.org/content/370/6514/298tab-pdf.

157 Piers M. Forster et al., "Current and Future Global Climate Impacts Resulting from COVID-19," *Nature Climate Change* (August 6, 2020), at www.nature,com/art icles/s41558-020-0883-0#citeas.

158 The Global Commission on the Economy and Climate, "Unlocking the Inclusive Growth Story of the 21st Century: Accelerating Climate Action in Urgent Times" (2018), at www.newclimateeconomy.report.

159 Ibid.
160 International Monetary Fund, "Mitigating Climate Change – Growth-and-Distribution-Friendly Strategies," World Economic Outlook, chapter 3 (October 7, 2020), 93.
161 Ibid. at 91.
162 Ibid. at 92.
163 "IEA: 'Green' Coronavirus Recovery Would Keep Global Emissions below 2019 Peak," *Carbon Brief* (June 18, 2020), at www.carbonbrief.org/iea-green-corona virus-recovery-would-keep-global-emissions-below-2019-peak.
164 Fiona Harvey, "We Now Have the Proof: Greening the Economy Doesn't Come at the Price of Prosperity," *Guardian* (May 22, 2020).
165 Cameron Hepburn, Brian O'Callaghan, Nicholas Stern, Joseph Stiglitz, and Dimitri Zenghelis, "Will COVID-19 Fiscal Recovery Packages Accelerate or Retard Progress on Climate Change?" *Oxford Review of Economic Policy*, Vol. 36, No. Supplement 1 (2020), S359–S381, S360, at https://academic.oup.com/oxrep/article/36/Supplement_1/S359/5832003.
166 Ibid.
167 Ibid. at 13.
168 *See* Emmanuel Krieke, *Scorched Earth: Environmental Warfare as a Crime* (Princeton, NJ: Princeton University Press, 2021).
169 John Larsen, Emily Wimberger, Ben King, and Trevor Houser, "A Just Green Recovery," Rhodium Group (June 29, 2020), at https://rhg.com/research/a-just-green-recovery.
170 Ibid.
171 Ibid.
172 Fiona Harvey, "We Now Have the Proof: Greening the Economy Doesn't Come at the Price of Prosperity."
173 Ibid.
174 Hepburn et al., "Will COVID-19 Fiscal Recovery Packages Accelerate or Retard Progress on Climate Change?" at 8.
175 Ivetta Gerasimchuk and Indira Urazova, "G20 Recovery Packages Benefit Fossil Fuels More Than Clean Energy" (July 15, 2020), at https://iisd.org/articles/tracker-recovery-packages-benefit-fossil-fuels.
176 Ibid.
177 www.bloomberg.com/features/2020-green-stimulus-energy-future/?sref=Oz9Q3OZU#toaster.
178 Greenness of Stimulus Index, at www.vivideconomics.com.
179 Green Stimulus Index, 3, at www.vivideconomics.com/casestudy/greenness-for-stimulus-index.
180 Ibid.
181 Ibid.
182 Nadja Popovich, Livia Albeck-Ripka, and Kendra Pierre-Louis, "The Trump Administration Is Reversing 100 Environmental Rules. Here's the Full List," *New York Times* (July 15, 2020).
183 Richard C. Paddock and Mukhita Suhartono, "Indonesia's Stimulus Plan Draws Fire from Environmentalists and Unions," *New York Times* (October 3, 2020); Richard C. Paddock, "Indonesia's Parliament Approves Jobs Bill, Despite Labor and Environmental Provisions," *New York Times* (October 6, 2020).

184 Lauri Myllyvirta and Yedan Li, "Analysis: China's Covid Stimulus Plans for Fossil Fuels Three Times Larger Than Low-Carbon," Carbon Brief (September 29, 2020).

185 Oxford University Economic Recovery Project, Executive Summary, "Are We Building Back Better? Evidence from 2020 and Pathways for Inclusive Green Recovery Spending" (March 2020), 2, 7, at www.unep.org/resources/publication/are-we-building-back-better-evidence-2020-and-pathways-inclusive-green.

186 Ibid. at 12.

187 Sarah Kaplan and Dino Grandoni, "Raft of Climate Action Measures in Relief Deal Won Bipartisan Backing," *Washington Post* (December 22, 2020); Coral Davenport, "Climate Change Legislation Included in Coronavirus Relief Deal," *New York Times* (December 22, 2020).

188 Frank Jordans, "World Leaders Cheer US Return to Climate Fight under Biden," *Associated Press* (January 21, 2021), at https://apnews.com/article/joe-biden-climate-climate-change-paris-emmanuel-macron-2451e1abc0e486b3055b639878b5181c.

189 Lisa Friedman, "With John Kerry Pick, Biden Selects a 'Climate Envoy' with Stature," *New York Times* (November 23, 2020).

190 Dmitris Mavrokefalidis, "Boris Johnson and Joe Biden Discuss Green Recovery in First Call after Inauguration," *Energy Live News* (January 25, 2021), at www.energylivenews.com/2021/01/25/boris-johnson-and-joe-biden-discuss-green-recovery-in-first-call-after-inauguration.

191 Scott Waldman, "Biden Says Infrastructure Is the Pillar of His Climate Plan," *Scientific American* (April 8, 2021), at www.scientificamerican.com/article/biden-says-infrastructure-is-the-pillar-of-his-climate-plan.

192 Heather Long, "What's in the $1.2 Trillion Senate Infrastructure Package," *Washington Post* (August 10, 2021); Jonathan Wiseman, "House Democrats Say They Won't Back Budget Vote Until Infrastructure Bill Passes," *New York Times* (August 13, 2021).

193 Green Stimulus Index, at 3.

194 Pilita Clark, "This Recovery Will Be Greener Than the Last," *Financial Times* (June 7, 2020).

195 Ibid.

196 Green Stimulus Index, at 3.

CHAPTER 2

1 Douglas A. Irwin, *Against the Tide: An Intellectual History of Free Trade* (Princeton, NJ: Princeton University Press, 1996), 14.

2 Alfred Zimmern, *The Greek Commonwealth: Politics and Economics in Fifth-Century Athens* (Oxford: Oxford University Press, 1969)[1911], 67.

3 Douglas A. Irwin, *Against the Tide*, at 14.

4 Plato, *The Republic* (London: Penguin Books, 1987) [1955] (translated by Desmond Lee), part two, book two, 119.

5 Ibid.

6 Aristotle, *Politics*, Loeb Classical Library (Cambridge, MA: Harvard University Press, 1932), 561–563.

7 *See generally* M.I. Finley, *The Ancient Economy* (Berkeley: University of California Press, 1999) [1973].

8 For more on ancient Athens and trade, *see* James Bacchus, *The Willing World*, at 83–84, 347–348.

9 For a classic contemporary account, see Joachim Joesten, "Hitler's Fiasco in the Ukraine," *Foreign Affairs* (January 1943), at www.foreignaffairs.com/articles/ukraine/ukraine-1943-01-01/hitlers-fiasco-ukraine.

10 M. I. Finley, *The Ancient Economy*, at 144–147.

11 *See* "Thoreau's Pencil: Sharpening Our Understanding of World Trade," in James Bacchus, *Trade and Freedom*, 347–360.

12 For a full and eloquent illustration of this point, *see* Virginia Postrel, *The Future and Its Enemies: The Growing Conflict over Creativity, Enterprise, and Progress* (New York: Simon & Schuster, 1998).

13 Esteban Ortiz-Ospina and Diane Beltekian, "Trade and Globalization," *Our World in Data* (October 2018), at https://ourworldindata.org/trade-and-globalization.

14 WTO, "Report of the TPRB from the Director-General on Trade-Related Developments," WT/TPR/OV/W/14 (July 10, 2020), 8.

15 Douglas A. Irwin, "The Pandemic Adds Momentum to the Deglobalization Trend."

16 WTO, "Report of the TPRB from the Director-General on Trade-Related Developments," at 2.

17 Ibid.

18 Ibid.

19 www.wto.org/english/news_e/news19_e/dgra_12dec19_e.htm.

20 Global Trade Alert, "Going It Alone? Trade Policy after Three Years of Populism" (London: CEPR Press, 2019), 6.

21 Ibid.

22 Ibid.

23 Ibid.

24 Ibid. at 22.

25 "The Myth of Localism," *Yale Global Online*, at https://yaleglobal.yale.edu/content/myth-localism.

26 E. F. Schumacher, *Small Is Beautiful: Economics as If People Mattered* (London: Blond and Briggs, 1973).

27 Robert D. Atkinson and Michael Lind, "National Developmentalism: From Forgotten Tradition to New Consensus," *American Affairs*, Vol. III, No. 2 (Summer 2019), 165–191, at https://americanaffairsjournal.org/2019/05/national-developmentalism-from-forgotten-tradition-to-new-consensus.

28 *See* the discussion on the link between trade and freedom in Chapter 1.

29 Steven Horwitz, "Economic Localism Is No Better than Economic Nationalism," Foundation for Economic Education (November 27, 2016), at https://fee.org/articles/economic-localism-is-no-better-than-economic-nationalism.

30 *See* Louis D. Rubin, ed., *I'll Take My Stand: The South and the Agrarian Tradition* (New York: Harper Torchbooks, 1962). *See also* the longer discussion of this topic in James Bacchus, *Trade and Freedom*, at 199–203.

31 *See, e.g.*, Wendell Berry, *The Art of the Commonplace: The Agrarian Essays of Wendell Berry* (Berkeley, CA: Counterpoint, 2002).

32 George Scialabba, "Back to the Land: Wendell Berry in the Path of Modernity," *The Baffler*, No. 49 (January 2020), at https://thebaffler.com/salvos/back-to-the-land-scialabba.

33 Voltaire, *Candide, Zadig and Selected Stories* (New York: Penguin Books, 1981) [1759], 101.

34 Steven Horwitz, "Economic Localism Is No Better than Economic Nationalism," Foundation for Economic Education (November 27, 2016), at https://fee.org/art icles/economic-localism-is-no-better-than-economic-nationalism.

35 Douglas A. Irwin, *Clashing over Commerce: A History of US Trade Policy* (Chicago: University of Chicago Press, 2017), 394–400.

36 Daniel W. Drezner, *The System Worked: How the World Stopped Another Great Depression* (Oxford: Oxford University Press, 2014).

37 Douglas A. Irwin, "The Truth about Trade: What Critics Get Wrong about the Global Economy," *Foreign Affairs* (July/August 2016), 89. See WTO, "WTO Report 2017" (Geneva: World Trade Organization, 2017), 9.

38 Michael J. Hicks and Sribant Devaraj, "The Myth and the Reality of Manufacturing" (Muncie, IN: Center for Business and Economic Research, Ball State University, June 2015), at https://conexus.cyberdata.org/files/MfgReality.pdf.

39 Elhanan Helpman, "Globalization and Wage Inequality," National Bureau of Economic Research, Paper Number w229944 (December 2, 2016), 39.

40 Elhanan Helpman, *Globalization and Inequality* (Cambridge, MA: Harvard University Press, 2018), 170.

41 *See* Eric Hoffer, *The Ordeal of Change* (New York: Harper & Row, 1952).

42 *See* James Bacchus, *The Willing World*, at 190–191, 207–208, 227–228.

43 World Bank, Overview, "World Development Report 2020: Trading for Development in the Age of Global Value Chains" (Washington, DC: World Bank Group, 2020).

44 Richard Baldwin, *The Great Convergence: Information Technology and the New Globalization* (Cambridge, MA: Harvard University Press, 2016).

45 *See* Marc Levinson, *Outside the Box: How Globalization Changed from Moving Stuff to Spreading Ideas* (Princeton, NJ: Princeton University Press, 2020).

46 OECD, "Trade Policy Implications of Global Value Chains" (February 2020), 1.

47 Richard Baldwin, *The Great Convergence*, at 5, 131.

48 World Bank, "World Development Report 2020," at 1.

49 Richard Baldwin, *The Great Convergence*.

50 Ibid. at 150.

51 World Bank, "World Development Report 2020," at xiii, 67.

52 Stephanie Barrientos and Charlotte Pallangyo, "Global Value Chain Policy Series: Gender," World Economic Forum (September 2018), at www.weforum.org/white papers/global-value-chain-policy-series-gender.

53 World Bank, "World Development Report 2020," at 79.

54 Ibid.

55 Ibid. at 80.

56 Karl R. Popper, *The Open Society and Its Enemies*, Volume I, at 173.

57 Sebastien Miroudot, Rainer Lanz, and Alexandros Ragoussis, "Trade in Intermediate Goods and Services," OECD Trade Policy Working Papers No. 93 (2009), 2.

58 Ibid. at 48.

59 World Bank, "World Development Report 2020," at 2.

60 Ibid. at xi.

61 Ibid. at 19.

62 Ibid. at xi.

63 Kevin Sieff, "Mexico Tries to Wrest U.S. Firms from China as Supply Chains Shift," *Washington Post* (August 16, 2020).

64 Ibid; for details, *see* Gartner, Inc., "Weathering the Storm: Supply Chain Resilience in an Age of Disruption" (June 24, 2020).

65 World Bank, "World Development Report 2020," at 19.

66 WTO, "World Statistical Report 2020," at 27.

67 Ibid. at 28.

68 Christopher Findlay, Fukunari Kimura, and Shandre Thangavelu, "COVID-19 and the 'Zoom' to New Global Value Chains," East Asia Forum (April 5, 2020), at www.eastasiaforum.org/2020/04/05/covid-19-and-the-zoom-to-new-global-value-chains.

69 Jacob M. Schlesinger, "How the Coronavirus Will Reshape World Trade," *Wall Street Journal* (June 19, 2020).

70 Richard Baldwin and Eichi Tomiura, "Thinking Ahead about the Trade Impact of COVID-19," in Richard Baldwin and Beatrice Weder di Mauro, *Economics in the Time of COVID-19*, Centre for Economic Policy Research (London: CEPR Press, 2020), 58.

71 Kathryn Halle, "The Great Uncoupling: One Supply Chain for China, One for Everyone Else," *Financial Times* (October 6, 2020).

72 Ibid.

73 Chris Nuttall, "Foxconn Calls Time on Chinese Era," *Financial Times* (August 12, 2020).

74 WTO, "World Trade Report 2020: Government Policies to Promote Innovation in the Digital Age" (2020), 121.

75 Ibid.

76 Ibid.

77 Anna Stellinger, Ingrid Berglund, and Henrik Isakson, "How Trade Can Fight the Pandemic and Contribute to Global Health," in Richard Baldwin and Simon J. Evenett, eds., *COVID-19 and Trade Policy: Why Turning Inward Won't Work* (London: Centre for Economic Policy Research, 2020), 21–30.

78 Shannon K. O'Neil, "How to Pandemic-Proof Globalization: Redundancy, Not Reshoring, Is the Key to Supply Chain Security," *Foreign Affairs* (April 1, 2020).

79 Ibid.

80 Richard N. Haass, "Supply Chains and Demand," Council on Foreign Relations (December 10, 2020), at www.cfr.org/article/supply-chains-and-demand.

81 Peter S. Goodman, "A Global Outbreak Is Fueling the Backlash to Globalization," *New York Times* (March 5, 2020).

82 Paul Krugman, *The Age of Diminished Expectations: US Economic Policy in the 1990s*, (Cambridge, MA: MIT Press, 1990), 11.

83 Goal 8, "Transforming Our World."

84 Target 8.3, "Transforming Our World."

85 World Bank, "Global Productivity: Trends, Drivers, and Policies" (Washington, DC: World Bank Group, 2020), i.3.

86 Ibid.

87 Ibid at i.9.

88 Ibid. at 50.

89 McKinsey Global Institute, "Risk, Resilience, and Rebalancing in Global Value Chains" (August 6, 2020),

90 Ibid.

91 Ibid.

92 *See* James Bacchus, "Trade Is Good for Your Health: Freeing Trade in Medicines and Other Medical Goods during and beyond the COVID-19 Emergency," Cato Institute, Policy Analysis No. 918 (June 30, 2021), at www.cato.org/policy-analysis/trade-good-health-freeing-trade-medicines-other-medical-goods-during-beyond-covid.

93 For more on this topic, *see* James Bacchus, "Trade Is Good for Your Health: Freeing Trade in Medicines and Other Medical Goods during and beyond the COVID-19 Emergency," Cato Institute, Policy Analysis No. 918 (June 30, 2021).

94 Andrea Shalai, "WTO Chief Ngozi Okonjo-Iweala on Vaccine Nationalism: 'No One Is Safe Until Everyone Is Safe," World Economic Forum (February 16, 2021), at www.weforum.org/agenda/2021/02/world-trade-organisation-head-vaccine-nationalism-covid-19.

95 Jonathan Josephs, "New WTO Boss Warns against Vaccine Nationalism," *BBC News* (February 16, 2021), at www.bbc.com/news/business-56079088.

96 Goal 3, "Transforming Our World." *See* Targets 3.3 and 3.b under Goal 3.

97 WTO, WIPO, WHO, "Promoting Access to Medical Technologies and Innovation: Intersections between Public Health, Intellectual Property and Trade," Second Edition (2020), 21.

98 Ibid.

99 Ibid.

100 Ibid. at 8.

101 WTO, "Trade in Medical Goods in the Context of Tackling Covid-19," Information Note (April 3, 2020), 2.

102 Ibid.

103 Ibid. at 3.

104 Ibid. at 4.

105 WTO, WIPO, WHO, "Promoting Access to Medical Technologies and Innovation," at 21.

106 WTO, "Trade in Medical Goods in the Context of Tackling Covid-19," at 4.

107 Ibid. at 3 (Table 1).

108 Ibid.

109 Ibid.

110 Andreas Fuchs et al., "China Sent Masks, Gloves and Gowns to Many U.S. States. Here's Who Benefited," *Washington Post*, January 29, 2021, www.washingtonpost.com/politics/2021/01/29/china-sent-masks-gloves-gowns-many-us-states-heres-who-benefited.

111 Yang Jinghao, "Despite Trade War, China Remains Top U.S. Medical Product Provider," *CGTN News*, March 20, 2021, https://news.cgtn.com/news/2021-03-20/Despite-trade-war-China-remains-top-U-S-medical-product-provider-YMzodMvLuo/index.html.

112 Chad P. Bown, "COVID-19: China's Exports of Medical Supplies Provide a Ray of Hope," Peterson Institute for International Economics, March 26, 2020, www.piie .com/blogs/trade-and-investment-policy-watch/COVID-19-chinas-exports-medical-supplies-provide-ray-hope.

113 Brown, "COVID-19: China's Exports of Medical Supplies Provide a Ray of Hope."

114 Chuin-Wei Yap, "Pandemic Lays Bare U.S. Reliance on China for Drugs," *Wall Street Journal* (August 5, 2020).

115 Denise Roland and Jared S. Hopkins, "FDA Cites Shortage of One Drug, Exposing Supply-Line Worry," *Wall Street Journal* (February 28, 2020).

116 "Growing U.S. Reliance on China's Biotech and Pharmaceutical Products," 2019 Report to Congress of the U.S.–China Economic and Security Review Commission, Section 3 (March 2020), 250.

117 Michael T. Osterholm and Mark Olshaker, "Chronicle of a Pandemic Foretold: Learning from the COVID-19 Failure – Before the Next Outbreak Arrives," *Foreign Affairs* (July/August 2020), 10, 13.

118 Ibid.

119 Karen M. Sutter, Andres B. Schwarzenberg, and Michael D. Sutherland, "COVID-19: China Supply Chains and Broader Trade Issues," Congressional Research Service, R46304 (April 6, 2020), 19

120 Denise Roland and Jared S. Hopkins, "FDA Cites Shortage of One Drug, Exposing Supply-Line Worry," WTO, "World Statistical Report 2020," at 57.

121 Ibid.

122 Preetika Rana and Denise Roland, "Drugmakers Gain More Access to China, but at a Price," *Wall Street Journal* (November 27, 2018).

123 Chuin-Wei Yap, "Pandemic Lays Bare U.S. Reliance on China for Drugs."

124 Denise Roland and Jared S. Hopkins, "FDA Cites Shortage of One Drug, Exposing Supply-Line Worry."

125 Ibid.

126 Chuin-Wei Yap, "Pandemic Lays Bare U.S. Reliance on China for Drugs."

127 Karen M. Sutter, Andres B. Schwarzenberg, and Michael D. Sutherland, "COVID-19: China Supply Chains and Broader Trade Issues," at 20.

128 Yanzhong Huang, "The Coronavirus Outbreak Could Disrupt the U.S. Drug Supply," Council on Foreign Relations (March 5, 2020), at www.cfr.org/in-brief/ coronavirus-disrupt-us-drug-supply-shortages-fda; *see also* Kritika Krishnakumar, "Active Pharmaceutical Ingredients Business in India Gains as Pharma Firms Diversify Raw Material Sourcing from China," *Indian Wire* (July 31, 2020).

129 "India's Incentives for Domestic API Production Could Cut Supply Risk: Fitch," *Economic Times* (August 10, 2020), at https://health.economictimes.indiatimes .com/news/pharma/indias-incentives-for-domestic-api-production-could-cut-supply-risk-fitch/77459098.

130 WTO, "Trade in Medical Goods in the Context of Tackling Covid-19," at 4.

131 For an excellent in-depth analysis of this issue and its implications for managed trade, *see* Scott Lincicome, "The Government's Plan to Turn Kodak into a Pharmaceutical Company Sure Seems *Underdeveloped*," Cato (July 29, 2020), at www.cato.org/blog/governments-plan-turn-kodak-pharmaceutical-company-seems-underdeveloped.

132 WTO, ITC, and UNCTAD, "World Tariff Profiles 2020," at 225–226.
133 Ibid. at 226.
134 WTO, "Trade in Medical Goods in the Context of Tackling Covid-19," at 6.
135 Ibid.
136 www.wto.org/english/thewto_e/glossary_e/tariff_peaks_e.htm.
137 Ibid. at 1.
138 WTO, "Trade in Medical Goods in the Context of Tackling Covid-19,"at 1.
139 Ibid.
140 Simon J. Evenett, "Tackling Coronavirus: The Trade Policy Dimension," *Global Trade Alert* (March 11, 2020), 4.
141 Ibid.
142 European Union, "Trade in Healthcare Products: Concept Paper," June 11, 2020, p. 2.
143 World Trade Organization, "DDG Wolff Calls for New Initiatives to Cut Tariffs on Medical Supplies and Equipment," November 12, 2020, www.wto.org/english/news_e/news20_e/ddgaw_12nov20_e.htm.
144 World Trade Organization, "The WTO's Pharma Agreement," www.wto.org/english/tratop_e/pharma_ag_e/pharma_agreement_e.htm.
145 "Trade in Medical Goods in the Context of Tackling COVID-19," p. 7.
146 Ibid. p. 6.
147 *Promoting Access to Medical Technologies and Innovation*, p. 21.
148 Anabel Gonzalez, "A Memo to Trade Ministers on How Trade Policy Can Help Fight COVID-19," Peterson Institute for International Economics, March 23, 2020, www.piie.com/blogs/trade-and-investment-policy-watch/memo-trade-minis ters-how-trade-policy-can-help-fight-covid19.
149 Matthias Helble and Benjamin Shepherd, "Trade in Health Products: Reducing Trade Barriers for Better Health," Asian Development Bank Institute, Working Paper no. 643 January 6, 2017.
150 "Coronavirus Outbreak: India Bans Exports of All Kind of Respiratory Masks; Toll Due to Virus Tops 200 in China," *First Post* (February 1, 2020).
151 Simon J. Evenett, "Tackling Coronavirus: The Trade Policy Dimension," *Global Trade Alert* (March 11, 2020), 3.
152 Chad P. Bown, "EU Limits on Medical Gear Exports Put Poor Countries and Europeans at Risk," Peterson Institute for International Economics (March 19, 2020), at www.piie.com/blogs/trade-and-investment-policy-watch/eu-limits-med ical-gear-exports-put-poor-countries-and-europeans-at-risk.
153 Simon J. Evenett, "Tackling Coronavirus: The Trade Policy Dimension," at 3.
154 David Lim, "Trump Signs 'Buy American' Executive Order for Essential Drugs," *Politico* (August 6, 2020).
155 Maria Cheng, "Health Experts Slam US Deal for Large Supply of the Only Drug Licensed So Far to Treat COVID-19," Associated Press (July 1, 2020).
156 Simon J. Evenett, "Tackling Coronavirus: The Trade Policy Dimension," at 3.
157 Global Trade Alert at www.globaltradealert.org .
158 Ibid. at 2.
159 James Bacchus, "Governments Should Rely More on the WTO in the Fight against the Coronavirus," Cato (April 3, 2020).
160 Aaditya Mattoo and Michele Ruta, "Don't Close Borders against Coronavirus," *Financial Times* (March 13, 2020).

161 Ibid.

162 Ibid.

163 Martin Wolf, "The Dangerous War on Supply Chains," *Financial Times* (June 23, 2020).

164 Article I, Section 10, Clause 2, United States Constitution. *See* Boris I. Bittker and Brannon P. Denning, "The Import-Export Clause," *Mississippi Law Journal*, Vol. 68 (1998), 521–564. Some WTO members, including China, have accepted limits on their right to impose export taxes as part of their accession agreements to membership in the WTO.

165 Article XI (1), General Agreement on Tariffs and Trade.

166 Article XI (2) (a), General Agreement on Tariffs and Trade.

167 Article X, General Agreement on Tariffs and Trade.

168 Article XIII, General Agreement on Tariffs and Trade.

169 Article XX, General Agreement on Tariffs and Trade.

170 For a more extensive legal analysis, *see* James Bacchus, "Trade Is Good for Your Health," 7–8.

171 Wolf, "The Dangerous War on Supply Chains."

172 Jennifer A. Hillman, "Six Proactive Steps in a Smart Trade Approach to Fighting COVID-19," Think Global Health, March 20, 2020, www.thinkglobalhealth.org/article/six-proactive-steps-smart-trade-approach-fighting-COVID-19.

173 Richard Baldwin and Simon Evenett, "COVID-19 and Trade Policy: Why Turning Inward Won't Work," *VoxEU*, April 29, 2020, https://voxeu.org/article/new-ebook-COVID-19-and-trade-policy-why-turning-inward-wont-work.

174 Matina Stevis-Gridneff, "E.U. Will Curb Covid Vaccine Exports for 6 Weeks," *New York Times*, March 28, 2021, www.nytimes.com/2021/03/23/world/europe/eu-curbs-vaccine-exports.html.

175 Jeffrey Gettelman, Emily Schmail, and Mujib Mashal, "India Cuts Back on Vaccine Exports as Infections Surge at Home," *New York Times*, March 25, 2021, www.nytimes.com/2021/03/25/world/asia/india-covid-vaccine-astrazeneca.html.

176 https://g20.org/en/media/Documents/G20_Trade%20&%20Investment_Ministerial_Statement_EN.pdf.

177 World Trade Organization, "DDG Wolf: Policy Coordination Needed to Address Pandemic Challenges," April 20, 2020, www.wto.org/english/news_e/news20_e/ddgaw_20apr20_e.htm.

178 Jamie Smyth, "New Zealand to Push for Deal on Medical Supply Chains at Apec," *Financial Times*, March 30, 2021, www.ft.com/content/4de31f86-540f-4280-ab37-166428539eb2.

179 Communication from Australia, Brazil, Canada, Chile, the European Union, Japan, Republic of Korea, Mexico, New Zealand, Norway, Singapore, and Switzerland, "COVID-19 and Beyond: Trade and Health," WT/GC/223, November 24, 2020.

180 Terence P. Stewart, "The Ottawa Group's November 23 Communication and Draft Elements of a 'Trade and Health' Initiative," *Current Thoughts on Trade* (blog), Washington International Trade Association, November 27, 2020, www.wita.org/blogs/the-ottawa-trade-health-initiative.

181 Anthony Dworkin, "Americans before Allies: Biden's Limited Multilateralism," European Council on Foreign Relations (June 9, 2021), at https://ecfr.eu/articles/americans-before-allies-bidens-limited-multilateralism.

182 Terence P. Stewart, "The Ottawa Group's November 23 Communication and Draft Elements of a 'Trade and Health' Initiative."

183 Ibid.

184 Ibid.

185 Ibid.

186 WTO, "DDG Wolff Calls for New Initiatives to Cut Tariffs on Medical Supplies and Equipment."

187 Ibid.

188 Communication from Australia, Brazil, Canada, Chile, the European Union, Japan, Republic of Korea, Mexico, New Zealand, Norway, Singapore, and Switzerland, "COVID-19 and Beyond: Trade and Health."

189 WTO, Trade Facilitation Agreement, WT/L/940, November 27, 2014.

190 Anabel Gonzalez, "A Memo to Trade Ministers on How Trade Policy Can Help Fight COVID-19."

191 WTO, Dispute Settlement Understanding, Articles 3.7 and 22.2.

192 *See* Anshu Siripurapu, "The State of U.S. Strategic Stockpiles," Council on Foreign Relations (June 15, 2020), at www.cfr.org/backgrounder/state-us-strategic-stockpiles.

193 Scott Gottlieb and Mark McClellan, "Covid Shows the Need for a Diagnostic Stockpile," *Wall Street Journal* (July 26, 2020).

194 Jacob M. Schlesinger, "How the Coronavirus Will Reshape World Trade."

195 Editorial, "Building Resilience Should Not Lead to Trade Barriers," *Financial Times* (June 12, 2020).

196 Ibid.

197 *See* James Bacchus, "The Antidote to Vaccine Nationalism," Centre for International Governance Innovation (December 21, 2020), at www.cigionline .org/articles/antidote-vaccine-nationalism.

198 Donato Paolo Mancini, Guy Chazan, and Joe Miller, "International Rollout of Covid-19 Vaccine on Track for Next Month," *Financial Times* (November 29, 2020).

199 World Health Organization, "Why We Need COVAX," at www.who.int/initia tives/act-accelerator/covax.

200 Alice Tidey, "'No way to sugarcoat this': World leaders need to boost COVID-19 job distribution, WHO says," *EuroNews* (April 21, 2021), at euronews.com/2021/10/21/no-way-to-sugarcoat-this-world-leaders-need-to-boost-covid-10-iab-distribution-who-says.

201 Bryan Pietsch, "West Virginia Will Give $100 Savings Bonds to People 16 to 35 Who Get Vaccinated," *New York Times* (April 26, 2021).

202 Thomas J. Bollyky and Chad P. Bown, "The Tragedy of Vaccine Nationalism: Only Cooperation Can End the Pandemic," *Foreign Affairs* (July 27, 2020).

203 Introduction, "Transforming Our World."

204 Thomas J. Bollyky and Chad P. Bown, "The Tragedy of Vaccine Nationalism."

205 WHO, "172 Countries and Multiple Candidate Vaccines Engaged in COVID-19 Vaccine Global Access Facility" (August 24, 2020), at www.who.int/news/item/24-08-2020-172-countries-and-multiple-candidate-vaccines-engaged-in-covid-19-vac cine-global-access-facility.

206 Ibid.

207 Ibid.

208 European Commission, "EU Increases Its Contribution to €500 Million to Secure COVID-19 Vaccines for Low and Middle-Income Countries" (November 12, 2020), at https://ec.europa.eu/commission/presscorner/detail/en/ip_20_2075.

209 Huizhong Wu, "China Joins COVAX Coronavirus Vaccine Alliance," *Associated Press* (October 9, 2020), at https://apnews.com/article/virus-outbreak-xi-jinping-taiwan-china-archive-aae1708207d3510a434d35aec994d4d1.

210 National Academies of Sciences, Engineering, and Medicine, "A Framework for Equitable Allocation of Vaccine for the Novel Coronavirus," at www.nationalacademies.org/our-work/a-framework-for-equitable-allocation-of-vaccine-for-the-novel-coronavirus.

211 Huizhong Wu, "China Joins COVAX Coronavirus Vaccine Alliance."

212 Scott Neuman, "U.S. Won't Join WHO-Led Coronavirus Vaccine Effort, White House Says," *National Public Radio* (September 2, 2020), at www.npr.org/sections/coronavirus-live-updates/2020/09/02/908711419/u-s-wont-join-who-led-coronavirus-vaccine-effort-white-house-says.

213 Katie Rogers and Apoorva Mandavilli, "Trump Administration Signals Formal Withdrawal from W.H.O.," *New York Times* (October 22, 2020).

214 Saeed Shah and Drew Hinshaw, "China Joins Covax Global Initiative to Provide Covid-19 Vaccines to Poor Countries," *Wall Street Journal* (October 10, 2020).

215 Tom McCarthy, "The Race for a Vaccine: How Trump's 'America First' Approach Hinders the Global Search," *Guardian* (May 12, 2020), at www.theguardian.com/world/2020/may/12/the-race-for-a-vaccine-how-trumps-america-first-approach-slows-the-global-search.

216 "China Delayed Releasing Coronavirus Info, Frustrating WHO," *Associated Press* (June 3, 2020), at https://apnews.com/article/3c061794970661042b18d5aeaaed9fae.

217 Javier C. Hernandez, "Two Members of W.H.O. Team on Trail of Virus Are Denied Entry to China," *New York Times* (January 13, 2021).

218 Laura Silver, Kat Devlin, and Christine Huang, "Unfavorable Views of China Reach Historic Highs in Many Countries," Pew Charitable Trusts (October 6, 2020), at www.pewresearch.org/global/2020/10/06/unfavorable-views-of-china-reach-historic-highs-in-many-countries.

219 Andrew Jacobs, Michael D. Shear, and Edward Wong, "U.S.–China Feud Over Coronavirus Erupts at World Health Assembly," *New York Times* (May 18, 2020), at www.nytimes.com/2020/05/18/health/coronavirus-who-china-trump.htm.

220 Sarah Wheaton, "Chinese Vaccine Would Be 'Global Public Good,' Xi Says," *Politico* (May 18, 2020), at www.politico.com/news/2020/05/18/chinese-vaccine-would-be-global-public-good-xi-says-265039.

221 "Chinese Official Says Local Vaccines 'Don't Have High Protection Rates'," *BBC News* (April 12, 2021), at www.bbc.com/news/world-asia-china-56713663.

222 David Moscrop, "Canada Is Trying to Secure Millions of Covid-19 Vaccine Doses. It Should Share," *Washington Post* (October 15, 2020), at www.washingtonpost.com/opinions/2020/10/15/canada-vaccine-nationalism.

223 Jane Li, "China's Covid-19 Success Is Slowing Down Its Vaccine Rollout," *Quartz* (March 10, 2021), at https://qz.com/1981186/chinas-covid-19-success-is-slowing-its-vaccine-rollout; Roxanne Liu and Ryan Woo, "China Reports Most New COVID-19 Cases since January amid Delta Surge," *Reuters* (August 4, 2021).

224 Jessie Yeung, "India Is Spiraling Deeper into Covid-19 Crisis. Here's What You Ned to Know," *CNN* (April 27, 2021), at www.cnn.com/2021/04/26/india/india-covid-second-wave-explainer-intl-hnk-dst/index.html.

225 Saeed Shah, "In Race to Secure Covid-19 Vaccines, World's Poorest Countries Lag Behind," *Wall Street Journal* (September 1, 2020), at www.wsj.com/articles/in-race-to-secure-covid-19-vaccines-worlds-poorest-countries-lag-behind-11598998776.

226 *See* Aristotle, *The Politics* (London: Penguin Books, 1992)[335–323 B.C.], 56–61.

227 *See* Martha C. Nussbaum, *The Cosmopolitan Tradition: A Noble but Flawed Ideal* (Cambridge, MA: Harvard University Press, 2019).

228 For my view on the appropriate circle of human concern, *see* "Lecky's Circle: Thoughts from the Frontier of International Law," in James Bacchus, *Trade and Freedom* (London: Cameron May, 2004), 475–511. *See* this essay also at www .researchgate.net/publication/315354444_Lecky%27s_circle_thoughts_from_the_ frontier_of_international_law_I.

229 Saeed Shah, "In Race to Secure Covid-19 Vaccines, World's Poorest Countries Lag Behind."

230 Paul Hannon, "Covid-19 Vaccine Deployment Would Give Global Economy a Lift Next Year," *Wall Street Journal* (October 5, 2020), at www.wsj.com/articles/ covid-19-vaccine-deployment-would-give-global-economy-a-lift-next-year-11601820001.

231 Stephanie Findlay and Anna Gross, "Not Enough COVID Vaccine for All until 2024, Says Biggest Producer," *Financial Times* (September 15, 2020), at www.ft .com/content/a832d5d7-4a7f-42cc-850d-8757f19c3b6b.

232 Kiran Stacey, "First Doses of Vaccine Must Be Strictly Rationed, Say Report," *Financial Times* (October 3, 2020), at www.ft.com/content/fc5f3fa6-5a71-4903- 83f0-efed19349500.

233 Editorial, "On the Brink of a Catastrophic Moral Failure," *Washington Post* (January 25, 2021).

234 "Lancet COVID-19 Commission Statement on the Occasion of the 75th Session of the UN General Assembly" (September 14, 2020), 2, at https://doi.org/10.1016/ S0140-6736(20)31927-9.

235 I am grateful to Daniel Ikenson, my friend and former colleague at the Cato Institute, for helping me frame this question.

236 GAVI, "Why Is No One Safe until Everyone Is Safe during a Pandemic?" (August 17, 2020), at https://gavi.org/vaccineswork/why-no-one-safe-until-everyone-safe-during-pandemic.

237 Ibid.

238 Brendan Borrell, "The Tree That Could Help Stop the Pandemic," *The Atlantic* (October 21, 2020), at www.theatlantic.com/science/archive/2020/10/single-tree-species-may-hold-key-coronavirus-vaccine/61672.

239 Ed Silverman, "STAT-Harris Poll: The Share of Americans Interested in Getting Covid-19 Vaccine as Soon as Possible Is Dropping," *Stat News* (October 19, 2020), at www.statnews.com/pharmalot/2020/10/19/covid19-coronavirus-pan demic-vaccine-racial-disparities.

240 Rebecca Robbins, "Millions Are Skipping Their Second Doses of Covid Vaccines," *New York Times* (April 25, 2021).

241 Apoorva Mandavilli, "The Delta Variant Is the Symptom of a Bigger Threat: Vaccine Refusal," *New York Times* (July 25, 2021).

242 Lauren Egan, "Trump Calls Coronavirus Democrats' 'New Hoax,'" *NBC News* (February 28, 2020), at www.nbcnews.com/politics/donald-trump/trump-calls-cor onavirus- democrats-new-hoax-n114572.

243 Susanne H. Hodgson, Kushal Mansatta, Garyt Mallett, Victoria Harris, Katherine R. W. Emary, and Andrew J. Pollard, "What Defines an Efficacious COVID-19 Vaccine? A Review of the Challenges Assessing the Clinical Efficacy of Vaccines against SARS-CoV-2," *The Lancet: Infectious Diseases* (October 27, 2020), at www.thelancet.com/journals/laninf/article/PIIS1473-3099(20)30773-8/fulltext.

244 David Pilling, "Unequal Vaccine Access Will Return to Haunt," *Financial Times* (January 22, 2021).

245 Saeed Shah, "In Race to Secure Covid-19 Vaccines, World's Poorest Countries Lag Behind."

246 Peter S. Goodman, "If Poor Countries Go Unvaccinated, a Study Says, Rich Ones Will Pay," *New York Times* (January 23, 2021).

247 "Biden Says Americans Will Be First to Get Vaccines; Any Surplus to Be Shared," *Reuters* (March 10, 2021), at www.reuters.com/article/us-health-coronavirus-biden-surplus/biden-says-americans-will-be-first-to-get-vaccines-any-surplus-to-be-shared-idUSKBN2B22OY.

248 Donato Paolo Mancini, "US Joins International Effort to Ensure Global Access to Vaccine," *Financial Times* (January 22, 2021).

249 Zeke Miller, Christopher Sherman, and Rob Gillies, "Biden Plans to Send COVID Doses to Mexico, Canada," *Associated Press* (March 18, 2021), at https://apnews .com/article/biden-plans-to-send-astrazeneca-vaccine-canada-mexico-5776131b02e3350e5613aa2aaeac8ee7.

250 "'Quad' Countries Pledge Cooperation on COVID, Climate and Security," *Reuters* (March 12, 2021), at www.reuters.com/article/usa-asia-statement/quad-countries-pledge-cooperation-on-covid-climate-and-security-idUSKBN2B42AS.

251 Sabrina Siddique and Jessica Donati, "U.S. to Share AstroZeneca Covid-19 Vaccine Doses with World," *Wall Street Journal* (April 27, 2021); "US Joins Global Efforts to Help India Fight Coronavirus Surge," *Financial Times* (April 27, 2021).

252 Sheryl Gay Stolberg, "As Virus Rages Abroad, Biden Promises to Ship Millions of Vaccine Doses," *New York Times* (April 27, 2021).

253 "Coronavirus (COVID-19) Vaccinations," Our World in Data, at https:// ourworldindata.org/covid-vaccinations.

254 Jason Beaubien, "You Think the U.S. Has Vaccine Issues? 130 Countries Haven't Even Started Vaccinating," *NPR* (February 14, 2021), at www.npr.org/sections/ goatsandsoda/2021/02/14/966418960/you-think-the-u-s-has-vaccine-issues-130-countries-havent-even-started-vaccinati.

255 Goal 1, "Transforming Our World."

256 Goal 2, "Transforming Our World."

257 World Bank, "Poverty At-a-Glance," at www.worldbank.org/en/topic/poverty/ overview.

258 World Bank and WTO, "The Role of Trade in Ending Poverty" (Geneva: WTO, 2015), 7.

259 Jason de Parle, "8 Million Have Slipped into Poverty since May as Federal Aid Has Dried Up," *New York Times* (October 16, 2020).

260 World Bank, "Poverty and Shared Prosperity 2020: Reversals of Fortune" (Washington, DC: World Bank Group, October 2020). *See also* "Coronavirus May Push 150 Million People into Extreme Poverty: World Bank," *Reuters* (October 7, 2020)

261 World Bank, "Poverty-At-a-Glance." *See also* Maria Abi-Habib, "Millions Had Risen Out of Poverty. Coronavirus Is Pulling Them Back.," *New York Times* (April 30, 2020).

262 Ibid.

263 Paul Collier, "Pandemic Threatens African Economic Success," *Financial Times* (August 9, 2020).

264 World Bank, "Poverty At-a-Glance."

265 FAO, IFAD, UNICEF, WFP, and WHO, "The State of Food Security and Nutrition in the World 2020: Transforming Food Systems for Affordable Healthy Diets" (Rome: FAO, 2020), viii, at https://doi.org/10.4060/ca9692en.

266 Ibid.

267 Fiona Harvey, "Coronavirus Pandemic 'Will Cause Famine of Biblical Proportions,'" *Guardian* (April 21, 2020).

268 Lyric Hughes Hale, "Food Inflation Threatens Lives and Economic Recovery," *Financial Times* (September 8, 2020).

269 "UN Issues $6.7 Million Appeal to Protect Millions of Lives and Stem the Spread of Coronavirus in Fragile Countries," UNHCR (May 7, 2020).

270 Ann Hollingsworth, "The Global Humanitarian Response Plan for Covid-19 Is Massively Underfunded" (June 9, 2020), at www.refugeesinternational.org/reports/2020/6/9/the-global-humanitarian-response-plan-is-massively-underfunded.

271 World Food Programme, "Contributions to WFP in 2020," as of January 17, 2021, at www.wfp.org/funding/2020.

272 Siobhan O'Grady, "A Hunger Crisis That Worsened Last Year Is Set to Grow More Dire," *Washington Post* (January 10, 2021).

273 Ibid.

274 WTO, "Covid-19 and Agriculture: A Story of Resilience" (August 26, 2020), 2.

275 Siobhan O'Grady, "A Hunger Crisis That Worsened Last Year Is Set to Grow More Dire."

276 FAO et al., "The State of Food Security and Nutrition in the World 2020," at xvi.

277 Ibid.

278 Kym Anderson, *Finishing Global Farm Trade Reform: Implications for Developing Countries* (Adelaide: University of Adelaide Press, 2017), 6.

279 Jennifer Clapp, "Food Self-Sufficiency and International Trade: A False Dichotomy?" (Rome: FAO, 2016), 4.

280 Ibid.

281 Jennifer Clapp, "Food Self-Sufficiency: Making Sense of It, and When It Makes Sense," *Food Policy*, Vol. 66 (2017), 88–96, 89.

282 FAO, "An Introduction to the Basic Concepts of Food Security" (Rome: FAO, 2008), at www.fao.org/docrep/013/a19363/a19363e00.pdf.

283 Widely used is a self-sufficiency ratio ("SSR") that calculates food production as a ratio of available supply. The SSR can be measured in either calories or in volume or value of food produced by a country. It is typically based on specific commodities. However, "The FAO recommends caution in applying the SSR concept to the

overall food situation in a country, because it may mask instances where a country produces one food commodity in abundance while needing to rely on imports for other food commodities." Jennifer Clapp, "Food Self-Sufficiency: Making Sense of It, and When It Makes Sense," at 89.

284 Ibid. at 89–90.

285 Ibid. at 90.

286 Jennifer Clapp, "Food Self-Sufficiency and International Trade: A False Dichotomy," at 4.

287 Ibid. at 5.

288 Ibid.

289 "Anticipating and Avoiding Global Food Price Crises," Council on Foreign Relations (March 14, 2016).

290 "How the Rising Cost of Food Is Sweeping around the World," *Bloomberg Opinion* (July 13, 2021).

291 Adam Behsudi, "Trade in a Post Coronavirus World, *Politico Morning Trade* (March 27, 2020).

292 "U.S., EU, and Other WTO Countries Pledge to Keep Food Channels Open," *Reuters* (April 23, 2020).

293 WTO, "Agency Chiefs Issue Joint Call to Keep Food Trade Flowing in Response to COVID-19"(March 31, 2020), at www.wto.org/english/news_e/news20_e/igo_26mar20_e.htm.

294 Jennifer Doherty, "WTO Ties Growing Hunger to Hardship, Not Supply Chain," *Law 360* (August 27, 2020).

295 "Export Curbs on Food," Global Trade Alert (August 7, 2020).

296 Jonathan Hepburn, David Laborde, Marie Parent, and Carin Smaller, "Could Food Export Restrictions Worsen a Looming Food Crisis?" International Institute for Sustainable Development and International Food Policy Research Institute (2020), 1.

297 Ibid.

298 Ibid.

299 FAO, "The State of Food and Agriculture: Climate Change, Agriculture and Food Security" (Rome: Food and Agriculture Organization, 2016), xi.

300 Ibid.

301 Jonathan Hepburn, David Labarde, Marie Parent, and Carin Smaller, "COVID-19 and Food Export Restrictions: Comparing Today's Situation to the 2007/08 Price Hikes," International Institute for Sustainable Development (2020).

302 Amartya Sen, *Poverty and Famines: An Essay on Entitlement and Deprivation* (Oxford: Oxford University Press, 1983); *see also* Jean Dreze and Amartya Sen, *Hunger and Public Action* (Oxford: Clarendon Press, 1991).

303 *See* "Lessons from the World Food Crisis of 2006–2008," in FAO, "The State of Food Insecurity in the World 2011" (Rome: FAO, 2011), 21–31.

304 Jennifer Clapp, "Food Security and International Trade" (Rome: Food and Agriculture Organization, 2015), 2.

305 Will J. Martin and Joseph W. Glauber, "Trade Policy and Food Security," in Richard Baldwin and Simon J. Evenett, eds., *COVID-19 and Trade Policy*, 89–102, 95.

306 Will Martin and Kym Andersen, "Export Restrictions and Price Insulation during Commodity Price Booms," Policy Research Paper 5645 (Washington, DC: World Bank, May 2011), 10.

307 Paolo E. Giordani, Nadia Rocha, and Michele Ruta, "Food Prices and the Multiplier Effect of Trade Policy," *Journal of International Economics*, Vol. 101 (July 2016), 102–122.
308 Jonathan Hepburn et al., "COVID-19 and Food Export Restrictions."
309 OECD, "The Role of Food and Agricultural Trade in Ensuring Domestic Food Availability," in OECD, "Global Food Security: Challenges for the Food and Agricultural System" (Paris: OECD, 2013).
310 Kym Anderson, *Finishing Global Farm Trade Reform*, at 95.
311 OECD, "The Role of Food and Agricultural Trade in Ensuring Domestic Food Availability."
312 Kym Anderson, *Finishing Global Farm Trade Reform*, at 20.
313 Ibid.
314 Ibid. at 6–7.
315 Ibid. at 8.
316 Ibid.

CHAPTER 3

1 Here I should perhaps acknowledge my own engagement in these events, including as one of the six original cosponsors of the implementing legislation for the Uruguay Round trade agreements while a member of the United States House of Representatives. I shared in these hopes at the time. A year later, I was appointed by consensus of the members of the WTO as one of the seven founding members of the WTO Appellate Body.
2 WTO, "Information Technology Agreement – An Explanation," at https://wto.org/english/tratop_e/enftec_e/itaintro_e.htm.
3 WTO Agreement on Trade Facilitation, at www.wto.org/english/docs_e/tfa-nov14_e.htm.
4 WTO, "Revised WTO Agreement on Government Procurement Enters into force" (April 7, 2014), at www.wto.org/english/news_e/news14_e/gpro_07apr14_e.htm.
5 WTO, "Information Technology Agreement," at www.wto.org/english/tratop_e/inftec_e.htm.
6 WTO, "Agriculture Negotiations," at www.wto.org/english/tratop_e/agric_e/negoti_eNEW.htm.
7 Editorial, "The Doha Round Finally Dies a Merciful Death," *Financial Times* (December 21, 2015).
8 Kym Anderson, "Trade Assessment Paper: Benefits and Costs of the Trade Targets for the post-2015 Development Agenda," Copenhagen Consensus Center (October 10, 2014), at www.copenhagenconsensus.com/publication/post-2015-consensus-trade-assessment-anderson.
9 Gary Clyde Hufbauer and Zhiyao (Lucy) Lu, "The Payoff to America from Globalization," at 1. These numbers are in 2016 dollars and reflect a household consisting of 2.64 persons.
10 UNCTAD, "2019 Handbook of Statistics" (Geneva: UNCTAD, 2019), 16.
11 Anabel Gonzalez, "Bridging the Divide between Developed and Developing Countries in WTO Negotiations," Peterson Institute for International Economics

(March 12, 2019), at www.piie.com/blogs/trade-investment-policy-watch/bridging-divide-between-developed-developing-countries-in-WTO-negotiations.

12 For more on this topic, *see* James Bacchus and Inu Manak, *The Development Dimension: Special and Differential Treatment in Trade* (London: Routledge Press, 2021).

13 www.wto.org/english/tratop_e/region_e/region_e.htm.

14 *See* the magisterial "The People's Trilogy" by historian Frank DiKotter; in chronological order: *The Tragedy of the Chinese Revolution, 1945–1957* (London: Bloomsbury, 2013); *Mao's Great Famine: The History of China's Most Devastating Catastrophe, 1958–1962* (London: Bloomsbury, 2010); *The Cultural Revolution: A People's History, 1962–1976* (London: Bloomsbury, 2016).

15 Michael Schulman, "The Undoing of China's Miracle," *The Atlantic* (January 11, 2021).

16 Wayne M. Morrison, "China's Economic Rise: History, Trends, Challenges, and Implications for the United States," Congressional Research Service, RL33534 (June 25, 2019).

17 Center for Strategic and International Studies, "Is China the World's Top Trader?" at https://chinapower.csis.org/trade-partner.

18 WTO, "World Statistical Review 2020," at 82.

19 World Bank, "China Overview" (March 28, 2017), at www.worldbank.org/en/country/china/overview.

20 https://chinapower.csis.org/trade-partner.

21 WTO, "World Trade Statistical Review 2020," at 15.

22 *See* Nicholas Lardy, *The State Strikes Back: The End of Economic Reform in China* (Washington, DC: Peterson Institute for International Economics (January 2019).

23 Lingling Wei, "China's Xi Ramps Up Control of Private Sector. 'We Have No Choice but to Follow the Party,'" *Wall Street Journal* (December 11, 2020).

24 Michael Schuman, "The Undoing of China's Miracle."

25 For an overview of American business concerns, *see* U.S. Chamber of Commerce, "Made in China 2025: Global Ambitions Built on Local Protections" (2017), at www.uschamber.com/report/made-china-2025-global-ambitions-built-local-protections-0.

26 James McBride and Andrew Chatzky, "Is 'Made in China 2025' a Threat to Global Trade?" Council on Foreign Relations (May 13, 2019), at www.cfr.org/backgrounder/made-china-2025-threat-global-trade.

27 Rainer Zitelman, "State Capitalism? No, the Private Sector Was and Is the Main Driver of China's Economic Growth," *Forbes* (September 30, 2019), at www.forbes.com/sites/rainerzitelmann/2019/09/30/state-capitalism-no-the-private-sector-was-and-is-the-main-driver-of-chinas-economic-growth.

28 Kevin Rudd and Daniel Rosen, "China Backslides on Economic Reform," *Wall Street Journal* (September 23, 2020).

29 Jonathan Cheng, "China Is the Only Major Economy to Report Economic Growth for 2020," *Wall Street Journal* (January 18, 2021).

30 *See* James Bacchus, "Might Unmakes Right: The American Assault on the Rule of Law in World Trade," Center for International Governance Innovation, CIGI Papers No. 173 (May 2018), at www.cigionline.org/publications/might-unmakes-right-american-assault-rule-law-world-trade.

31 Robert Z. Lawrence, "Trump's Carrier Deal Is Not a Victory for US Manufacturing," *Fortune* (December 5, 2016).

32 Ibid.

33 This phrase and this insight must, of course, be attributed to the Austrian economist Friedrich A. Hayek. *See* Friedrich A. Hayek, "The Results of Human Action but Not of Human Design," in Hayek, *Studies in Philosophy: Politics and Economics* (London: Routledge and Kegan Paul, 1967), 96–105.

34 Daniel J. Ikenson, "USMCA: A Marginal NAFTA Upgrade at a High Cost," Cato Institute (April 10, 2019), at www.cato.org/commentary/usmca-marginal-nafta-upgrade-high-cost.

35 Simon Lester, Inu Manak, and Kyounghwa Kim, "Trump's First Trade Deal: The Slightly Revised Korea-U.S. Trade Agreement," Cato Institute, Free Trade Bulletin No. 73 (June 13, 2019), at www.cato.org/free-trade-bulletin/trumps-first-trade-deal-slightly-revised-korea-us-free-trade-agreement.

36 Adam S. Posen, "The Price of Nostalgia," *Foreign Affairs* (May/June 2021), at www.foreignaffairs.com/articles/united-states/2021-04-20/america-price-nostalgia.

37 For the details, *see* Chad P. Bown and Melina Kolb, "Trump's Trade War Timeline: An Up-to-Date Guide," Peterson Institute for International Economics (August 6, 2020), at www.piie.com/blogs/trade-investment-policy-watch/trump-trade-war-china-data-guide.

38 Article 23.1, WTO Dispute Settlement Understanding; *see* Appellate Body Report, *US – Continued Suspension*, ABR/WT/DS230 (2008), para. 373.

39 Ryan Hass and Abraham Denmark, "More Pain Than Gain: How the US-China Trade War Hurt America," Brookings Institution (August 7, 2020), at www/brookings.edu/blog/order-from-chaos/2020/08/07/more-pain-than-gain-how-the-uschina-trade-war-hurt-america.

40 Sherman Robinson and Karen Thierfelder, "US-China Trade War: Both Countries Lose, World Markets Adjust, Others Gain," Peterson Institute for International Economics, Policy Brief 19–17 (Washington: PIIE, November 2019), 5, at www.piie.com/publications/policy-briefs/us-china-trade-war-both-countries-lose-world-markets-adjust-others-gain.

41 Alessandro Nicita, "Trade and Trade Diversion Effects of United States Tariffs on China," UNCTAD Research Paper No. 37 (Geneva: UNCTAD, November 2019), 14, at https://unctad.org/webflyer/trade-and-trade-diversion-effects-united-states-tariffs-china.

42 Ryan Hass and Abraham Denmark, "More Pain Than Gain."

43 Shawn Donnan and Reade Pickert, "Trump's China Buying Spree Unlikely to Cover Trade War's Costs," *Bloomberg* (December 18, 2019).

44 Mary Amiti, Stephen J. Redding, and David E. Weinstein, "New China Tariffs Increase Costs to U.S. Households," Liberty Street Economics (May 23, 2019), at https://libertystreeteconomic.newyorkfed.org/2019/05/new-china-tariffs-increase-costs-to-us-households.html. These authors are from the New York Federal Reserve, Princeton University, and Columbia University, respectively.

45 Greg Robb, "Trade Was Could Cost Global Economy $700 by 2020, New IMF Chief Says," *Market Watch* (October 9, 2019), at www.marketwatch.com/story/trade-war-could-cost-global-economy-700-billion-by-2020-new-imf-chief-says-2019-10-08; *see* International Monetary Fund, "World Economic Outlook, October 2019:

Global Manufacturing Downturn, Rising Trade Barriers" (Washington, DC: IMF, October 2019), at www.imf.org/en/Publications/WEO/Issues/2019/10/01/world-eco nomic-outlook-octorber-2019.

46 "What's in the U.S.-China Phase 1 Trade Deal," *Reuters* (January 15, 2020).

47 Gary Clyde Hufbauer, "Managed Trade: Centerpiece of the US-China Phase One Deal," Peterson Institute for International Economics (January 16, 2020), at www .piie.com/blogs/trade-and-investment-policy-watch/managed-trade-centerpiece-us-china-phase-one-deal; *see also* Geoffrey Gertz, "'Phase One' China Trade Deal Tests the Limits of US Power," Brookings Institution (March 11, 2020), www .brookings.edu/opinions/phase-one-china-trade-deal-tests-the-limits-of-us-power.

48 Joshua P. Meltzer and Neena Shenai, "Why the Purchase Commitments in the US-China Trade Deal Should Not Be Replicated, Ever," Brookings Institution (February 4, 2020).

49 Gary Clyde Hufbauer, "Managed Trade: Centerpiece of the US-China Phase One Deal."

50 David Dollar and Anna Newby, "How Is COVID-19 Affecting Trade?" Brookings Institution (August 10, 2020), at www.brookings.edu/podcast-episode/how-is-covid-19-affecting-us-trade.

51 Chad P. Bown, "US-China Phase One Tracker: China's Purchase of US Goods," Peterson Institute for International Economics (January 21, 2021), at www.piie .com/research/piie-charts/us-china-phase-one-tracker-chinas-purchases-us-goods.

52 Ibid.

53 Simon Lester, "The Trump/Lighthizer Legacy on Trade," *International Economic Law and Policy Blog* (January 20, 2021), at https://worldtradelaw.typepad.com.

54 James Bacchus, "Democrats and Trade 2021: A Pro-Trade Policy for the Democratic Party," Cato Institute, Policy Analysis No. 900 (August 11, 2020), at www.cato.org/publications/policy-analysis/democrats-trade-2021-pro-trade-policy-democratic-party.

55 Bob Davis, "Trade Chief Lighthizer Urges Biden to Keep Tariffs on China," *Wall Street Journal* (January 11, 2021).

56 Bob Davis and Yuka Hayashi, "New Trade Representative Says U.S. Isn't Ready to Lift China Tariffs," *Wall Street Journal* (March 28, 2021).

57 Bob Davis and Lingling Wei, "Biden Plans to Build a Grand Alliance to Counter China. It Won't Be Easy," *Wall Street Journal* (January 6, 2021).

58 Thomas Franck, "U.S.-China Trade Relations Remain Strained as Biden Team Takes Tough Stance Similar to Trump," *CNBC* (March 20, 2021), at www.cnbc .com/2021/03/20/us-china-trade-relations-strained-biden-team-keeps-trumps-tough-stance.html.

59 Jose E. Alvarez, "Biden's International Law Restoration," *International Law and Politics*, Volume 53 (March 2021), 523–586, at www.nyujilp.org/wp-content/uploads/2021/04/NYI205.pdf.

60 David Lawder, "U.S.-China Trade War Has Cost Up to 245,000 U.S. Jobs: Business Group Study," *Reuters* (January 14, 2021).

61 Scott Lincicome, "Manufactured Crisis: 'Deindustrialization,' Free Markets, and National Security," Cato Institute, Policy Analysis No. 907 (January 27, 2021), at www.cato.org/publications/policy-analysis/manufactured-crisis-deindustrialization-free-markets-national-security.

62 *See*, among numerous examples, Ana Swanson, "Trump Says U.S. Will Impose Metal Tariffs on Brazil and Argentina," *New York Times* (December 2, 2019).

63 Kevin Freking, "Trump Has Long Seen Previous US Trade Agreements as Losers," *Associated Press* (May 11, 2019), at https://apnews.com/8340b62c950e4e8494 793623c629d72c.

64 "Trump Threatens to Pull US Out of World Trade Organization," *BBC News* (August 31, 2018), at www.bbc.com/new/world-us-canada-45364150.

65 *See* Douglas A. Irwin, *Clashing Over Commerce: A History of U.S. Trade Policy* (Chicago: University of Chicago Press, 2017), 193–202, 253–258.

66 Douglas A. Irwin, "Tariffs and Growth in Late Nineteenth Century America," *The World Economy*, Vol. 24, No. 1 (January 2001), at www.dartmouth.edu/~dirwin/docs/Growth.pdf.

67 Ryan Young and Iain Murray, "Traders of the Lost Ark: Rediscovering a Moral and Economic Case for Free Trade," Competitive Enterprise Institute (August 15, 2018), 35–36.

68 Gary Clyde Hufbauer and Zhiyao (Lucy) Lu, "Macroeconomic Forces Underlying Trade Deficits," Peterson Institute for International Economics (March 31, 2016), at www.piie.com/blogs/trade-investment-policy-watch/macroeconomic-forces-underlying-trade-deficits.

69 James McBride and Andrew Chatzky, "The Size of the U.S. Trade Deficit: Does It Matter?" Council on Foreign Relations (March 8, 2019), at www.cfr.org/back grounder/us-trade-deficit-how-much-does-it-matter.

70 Ibid.

71 Ibid.

72 Derek Scissors, "The Trade Deficit Does Not Cost Us Jobs," American Enterprise Institute (March 16, 2015), at www.aei.org/foreign-and-defense-policy/the-trade-deficit-does-not-cost-us-jobs.

73 Desmond Lachman, "Donald Trump's Broken Trade Promises," *The Bulwark* (February 26, 2020), at www.aei.org/articles/donald-trumps-broken-trade-promises.

74 Doug Palmer, "America's Trade Gap Soared under Trump, Final Figures Show," *Politico* (February 5, 2021).

75 Peter S. Goodman, "Trump Just Pushed the World Trade Organization toward Irrelevance," *New York Times* (March 23, 2018).

76 Claude Barfield, "President Trump's Persistent Falsehoods about the World Trade Organization," American Enterprise Institute (April 20, 2020), at www.aei.org/economics/president-trumps-persistent-falsehoods-about-the-world-trade-organization.

77 Chad P. Bown, "Why Did Trump End the WTO's Appellate Body? Tariffs," Peterson Institute for International Economics (March 4, 2020), at www.piie.com/blogs/trade-and-investment-policy-watch/why-did-trump-end-wtos-appellate-body-tariffs.

78 James Politi, "Donald Trump Threatens to Pull US Out of the WTO," *Financial Times* (August 30, 2018).

79 Ana Swanson, "In Washington, 'Free Trade' Is No Longer Gospel," *New York Times* (March 17, 2021).

80 Ibid.

81 Jon Emont and Alastair Gale, "Asia-Pacific Countries May Sign Major Trade Pact in Test for Biden," *Wall Street Journal* (November 15, 2020); Keith Bradsher and Ana Swanson, "China-Led Trade Pact Is Signed, in Challenge to U.S.," *New York Times* (November 15, 2020); Jeffrey Goldfarb, "Breaking Views – Subpar Asian Trade Deal Shines in Splintered World," *Reuters* (November 15, 2020).

82 WTO, "Strengthening Africa's Capacity to Trade" (March 2021), 2, at www.wto.org/english/res_e/publications_e/strengthening_africa2021_e.htm.

83 Gyude Moore and Bogolo Kenewendo, "Meet the World's Largest Free Trade Area," *Foreign Policy* (November 13, 2020), at https://foreignpolicy.com/2020/11/13/afcfta-free-trade-africa-economics.

84 World Bank, "The African Continental Free Trade Area" (July 27, 2020), at https://worldbank.org/en/topic/trade/publication/the-african-continental-free-trade-area.

85 United Nations Economic Commission for Africa, "African Continental Free Trade Area – Questions & Answers," www.uneca.org/publications/african-continental-free-trade-area-questions-answers.

86 "What Is the African Continental Free Trade Area?" *Economist* (January 26, 2021).

87 Goal 17.10, "Transforming Our World."

CHAPTER 4

1 Curtis Ellis, "It's Time to Exit Relics of Globalism Like the WTO," *American Greatness* (May 13, 2020), at https://amgreatness.com/2020/05/13/its-time-to-exit-relics-of-globalism-like-the-wto/#.Xr2VTvS9FR8.twitter.

2 Article II, General Agreement on Tariffs and Trade.

3 *See* Peter Van den Bossche and Werner Zdouc, *The Law and Policy of the World Trade Organization: Text, Cases and Materials*, fourth edition (Cambridge: Cambridge University Press, 2017), 436–440.

4 Jean-Christophe Bureau, Houssein Guimbard, and Sebastian Jean, "Agricultural Trade Liberalisation in the 21st Century: Has It Done the Business?" *Journal of Agricultural Economics*, Vol. 70, No. 1 (2019), 3–25, 7–8. These numbers from 2013 did not change significantly between then and the onset of the pandemic.

5 Article I, General Agreement on Tariffs and Trade; Article II, General Agreement on Trade in Services.

6 Yuka Hayashi, "Biden Signs Buy American Order for Government Procurement," *Wall Street Journal* (January 25, 2021).

7 U.S. Chamber of Commerce, "Q&A on 'Buy American' Policies" (January 25, 2021), at www.uschamber.com/issue-brief/qa-buy-american-policies.

8 "The Folly of Buying Local: Buy American Is an Economic-Policy Mistake," *Economist* (January 28, 2021).

9 Article III, General Agreement on Tariffs and Trade.

10 Article X, General Agreement on Tariffs and Trade.

11 Goal 8, "Transforming Our World."

12 WTO Agreement on Agriculture.

13 Article 15.2, WTO Agreement on Agriculture.

14 Kym Anderson, *Finishing Global Farm Trade Reform*, at 38.

15 For a thoughtful view of agricultural trade, *see* Fiona Smith, *Agriculture and the WTO: Towards a New Theory of International Agricultural Trade Regulation* (Cheltenham: Edward Elgar, 2009).

16 Anita Regmi, "Reforming the WTO Agreement on Agriculture," Congressional Research Service, R46456 (July 20, 2020), 2.

17 Ibid.

18 Ibid. at 2.

19 Ibid.

20 Jean-Christophe Bureau et al., "Agricultural Trade Liberalisation in the 21st Century," at 11.

21 Kym Anderson, *Finishing Global Farm Trade Reform*, at xiii.

22 Ibid. at 8

23 Target 2.b, "Transforming Our World."

24 Kym Anderson, *Finishing Global Farm Trade Reform*, at xiv.

25 Jean-Christophe Bureau, Houssein Guimbard, and Sebastian Jean, "Agricultural Trade Liberalisation in the 21st Century," at 7. These numbers are from 2013. Overall, changes in agricultural tariffs were insignificant in the years between 2013 and the beginning of the pandemic. Hence their citation in this article, which was published in 2019.

26 Kym Anderson, *Finishing Global Farm Trade Reform*, at 62.

27 UNCTAD, "Key Statistics and Trends in Trade Policy 2018" (Geneva: UNCTAD, 2018), 8.

28 WTO, "World Tariff Profiles 2020" (Geneva: WTO, 2020), 14–19.

29 P. Gibson, J. Waino, D. Whitley, and M. Bohman, "Profiles of Tariffs in Global Agricultural Markets," Agricultural Economic Report Number 796 (Washington, DC: USDA Economic Research Service, 2001).

30 WTO, "Tariff Implementation Issues – Communication from the United States," JOB/AG/141 (July 25, 2018).

31 Kym Anderson, *Finishing Global Farm Trade Reform*, at 68.

32 Ibid. at 68–69, citing K. Anderson, M. Kurzweil, and E. Valenzuela, "The Relative Importance of Global Agricultural Subsidies and Market Access," *World Trade Review*, Vol. 5, No. 3 (November 2006), 357–376 (emphasis added).

33 Ibid. at 69.

34 Article 1, WTO Agreement on Subsidies and Countervailing Measures.

35 OECD, "Agricultural Trade," at www.oecd.org/agriculture/topics/agricultural-trade.

36 Ibid.

37 Article 6, WTO Agreement on Subsidies and Countervailing Measures.

38 Article 6 and Article 7, WTO Agreement on Agriculture.

39 Ibid.

40 Article III (a)(ii), WTO Agreement on Agriculture.

41 Article 6 and 7, WTO Agreement on Agriculture.

42 These numbers represent an annual average for 2017–2019. OECD, "Agricultural Policy Monitoring and Evaluation 2020" (Paris: OECD, 2020), 19, at www.oecd.org/publications/agricultural-policy-monitoring-and-evaluation-22217371.htm.

43 Ibid. at 94.

44 Ibid. at 97.

45 Chuck Abbott, "World Farm Subsidies Hit $2 Billion a Day," *Successful Farming* (June 30, 2020), at www.agriculture.com/news/business/world-farm-subsidies-hit-2-billion-a-day.

46 OECD, "Agriculture Policy Monitoring and Evaluation 2020," at 20.

47 Ibid.

48 World Bank, "Africa Can Help Feed Africa: Removing Barriers to Regional Trade in Food Staples" (Washington, DC: World Bank Group, 2012).

49 Ryan McCrimmon, "'Here's Your Check': Trump's Massive Bailout to Farmers Will Be Hard to Pull Back," *Politico* (July 14, 2020).

50 "USTR and USDA Release Report on Agricultural Trade between the United States and China," Office of the United State Trade Representative (October 23, 2020), at https://ustr.gov/about-us/policy-offices/press-office/press-releases/2020/october/ustr-and-usda-release-report-agricultural-trade-between-united-states-and-china.

51 Ibid.

52 Simon Lester, "Trump Spends Billions in Taxpayer Dollars to Fix a Problem He Created: Taypayer Subsidies Thrown at U.S. Agriculture Are a Huge Waste," Cato Institute (July 24, 2018), at www.cato.org/publications/commentary/trump-spends-billions-taxpayer-dollars-fix-problem-he-created-taxpayer.

53 Ryan McCrimmon, "Here's Your Check."

54 Mike Dorning, "Trump Farm Bailouts Raise Risks of Reprisals from Trade Partners," *Bloomberg* (June 18, 2020). *See* "U.S. Farm Support: Compliance with WTO Commitments," Congressional Research Service, R45940 (October 4, 2019).

55 Jared Greenville, "Domestic Support to Agriculture and Trade: Implications for Multilateral Reform" (Geneva: International Center for Trade and Sustainable Development, March 2017), 22; *see also* Jonathan Hepburn and Christophe Bellman, "Negotiating Global Rules on Agricultural Domestic Support: Options for the World Trade Organization's Buenos Aires Conference" (Geneva: International Center for Trade and Sustainable Development (April, 2017).

56 Jared Greenville, "Domestic Support to Agriculture and Trade," at 28.

57 Annex 2, Paragraph 3, WTO Agreement on Agriculture.

58 Kym Anderson, *Finishing Global Farm Trade Reform*, at 95.

59 Ibid.

60 "India Asks WTO Members to Constructively Engage for Permanent Solution to Food Stockholding," *Economic Times* (July 27, 2020).

61 Article 5, WTO Agreement on Agriculture.

62 WTO, "Market Access: Special Agricultural Safeguards (SSGs)," at www.wto.org/English/tratop_e/agric_e/negs_bkgmd11_ssg_e.htm.

63 Kym Anderson, *Finishing Global Farm Trade Reform*, at 94.

64 Ibid. at 85.

65 WTO, "Notification of Select Domestic Support Variables in the WTO," submission by the United States, JOB/AG/181 (February 19, 2020).

66 Kym Anderson, *Finishing Global Farm Trade Reform*, at 71.

67 WTO, "Revised Draft Modalities for Agriculture," TN/AG/W/4/Rev. 4 (December 6, 2008).

68 Kym Anderson, *Finishing Global Farm Trade Reform*, at 71.

69 Ibid. at 81.

70 Douglas A. Irwin, "The GATT in Historical Perspective," *AEA Papers and Proceedings* (May 1995), 323–328, 326.

71 WTO, "Tariffs: Comprehensive tariff data," at www.wto.org/English/tratop_e/tariffs_e/tariff_data_e.htm.

72 Ibid.

73 CRS, "The World Trade Organization: The Non-market Access (NAMA) Negotiations," at 1.

74 WTO, "tariff peaks," at www.wto.org/english/thewto_e/glossary_e/tariff_peaks_e.htm.

75 WTO, "Tariff Escalation," at www.wto.org/english/thewto_e/glossary_e/tariff_peaks_e.htm.

76 CRS, "The World Trade Organization: The Non-agricultural Market Access (NAMA) Negotiations," Congressional Research Service, RL33634 (September 11, 2011).

77 United States Trade Representative, "Industrial Tariffs," at https://ustr.gov/issue-areas/industry-manufacturing/industrial-tariffs.

78 Lucinda Shen, "The Country That Imposes the Most Restrictions on Trade Might Surprise You," *Business Insider* (September 2015), at www.businessinsider.com/the-us-is-the-most-protectionist-nation-2015-9.

79 Scott Lincicome, "Unfettered Free Trade? If Only...," Cato Institute (November 17, 2016), at www.cato.org/blog/unfettered-free-trade-only.

80 Drusilla K. Brown et al., "Computational Analysis of Multilateral Trade Liberalization in the Uruguay Round and Doha Development Round."

81 Kym Anderson, Will Martin and Dominique van der Mensbrugghe, "Doha Merchandise Trade Reform: What's At Stake for Developing Countries," World Bank Policy Research Paper (February 2006), at https://elibrary.worldbank.org/doi/10.1093/wber/lhj009.

82 Ibid.

83 Paragraph 16, Doha Declaration.

84 Daniel Griswold, "Mirror, Mirror, on the Wall: The Danger of Imposing 'Reciprocal' Tariff Rates," Mercatus Center (2019), 1.

85 Phil Levy, "Reciprocity And Trade Deals – Are Other Countries Taking Advantage?" *Forbes* (January 29, 2019).

86 Daniel Griswold, "Mirror, Mirror, on the Wall," at 5.

87 Ibid. at 10.

88 David H. Autor, David Dorn, and Gordon H. Hanson, "The China Syndrome: Local Labor Market Effects of Import Competition in the United States," National Bureau of Economic Research, Working Paper 18054 (2012).

89 Ibid.

90 "Shock Horror: Economists Argue about the Impact of Chinese Imports on America," *Economist* (May 11, 2017).

91 For the best summary and overall analysis, *see* Scott Lincicome, "Testing the 'China Shock': Was Normalizing Trade with China a Mistake?" Cato Institute, Policy Analysis Number 895 (July 8, 2020).

92 Lorenzo Caliendo, Maximiliano A, Dvorkin, and Fernando Parro, "Trade and Labor Market Dynamics: General Equilibrium Analysis of the China Trade Shock," Federal Reserve Bank of St. Louis, Working Paper No. 24886 (February 21, 2019); Bradford DeLong, "NAFTA and Other Trade Deals Have Not Gutted American Manufacturing – Period," *Vox* (January 24, 2017).

93 Adam S. Posen, "The Price of Nostalgia," *Foreign Affairs* (May/June 2021), at www.foreignaffairs.com/articles/united-states/2021-04-20/america-price-nostalgia.

94 Robert Z. Lawrence, "Adjustment Challenges for US Workers," in C. Fred Bergsten, Gary Clyde Hufbauer, and Sean Miner, eds., *Bridging the Pacific: Toward Free Trade and Investment between China and the United States* (Washington, DC: Peterson Institute for International Economics, 2014), 85–108, 99.

95 Robert C. Feenstra and Akira Sasahara, "The 'China Shock,' Exports and U.S. Employment: A Global Input-Output Analysis," National Bureau of Economic Research, Working Paper No. 24022 (November 2017).

96 Gary Clyde Hufbauer and Zhiyao (Lucy) Lu, "The Payoff to America from Globalization: A Fresh Look with a Focus on Costs to Workers," Peterson Institute for International Economics, Policy Brief 17–16 (May 2017), 2, 14, 21, 25.

97 US-China Business Council, "2019 State Export Report: Goods and Services Exports by US States to China Over the Past Decade" (July 2019), at www .uschina.org/reports/2019-state-export-report.

98 Robert Z. Lawrence, "Adjustment Challenges for U.S. Workers," at 85.

99 Galina Hale, Bart Hobijn, Fernando Nechio, and Doris Wilson, "How Much Do We Spend on Imports?" Federal Reserve Bank of San Francisco, FRBSF Newsletter (January 8, 2019), at www.frbsf.org/econimc-research/publications/economic-letter/2019/january/how-much-do-we-spend-on-imports/amp.

100 Scott Lincicome, "Testing the 'China Shock,'" at 3.

101 Xavier Jaravel and Erick Jager, "What Are the Price Effects of Trade? Evidence from the US and Implications for Quantitative Trade Models," Feds Working Paper No. 2019-068 (September 9, 2020), at https://papers.ssrn.com/so13/papers .cfm?abstract_id=3473054.

102 Ibid.

103 Scott Lincicome, "Testing the 'China Shock,'" at 8.

104 Paul Krugman, "Publicity Stunts Aren't Policy," *New York Times* (April 10, 2017).

105 Daniel Griswold, "Globalization Isn't Killing Factory Jobs. Trade Is Actually Why Manufacturing Is Up 40%," *Los Angeles Times* (August 1, 2016).

106 Stephen J. Hicks and Srikant Devaraj, "The Myth and Reality of Manufacturing in America," Conexus Indiana and Ball State University Center for Business and Economic Research (June 2015 and April 2017), at https://conexus.cberdata.org/ files/MfgReality.pdf.

107 CCSA, "How COVID-19 Is Changing the World," at 26.

108 Daniel Griswold, "Globalization Isn't Killing Manufacturing Jobs. Trade Is Actually Why Manufacturing Is Up 40%."

109 Gary Clyde Hufbauer and Zhiyao (Lucy) Lu, "The Payoff to America from Globalization," at 21.

110 Ibid.

111 Ibid.

112 Bureau of Labor Statistics, Department of Labor, "Employment Projections – 2019–2029" (September 1, 2020).

113 "Companies Planning to Increase Automation Investments Due to COVID-19, Honeywell Study Shows" (July 8, 2020), at www.honeywell.com/en-us/news room/pressreleases/2020/07/companies-planning-to-increase-investment-due-to-covid19-honeywell-study-shows.

114 Gary Clyde Hyfbauer and Zhiyao (Lucy) Lu, "The Payoff to America from Globalization," at 21.

115 *See, e.g.*, from the Obama Administration, Executive Office of the President, "Artificial Intelligence, Automation, and the Economy" (December 2016), 18–19.

116 The White House, "FACT SHEET: The American Jobs Plan (March 31, 2021), at www.whitehouse.gov/briefing-room/statements-releases/2021/03/31/fact-sheet-the-american-jobs-plan.

117 *See, e.g.*, Ha-Joon Chang, *Kicking Away the Ladder: Development Strategy in Historical Perspective* (London: Anthem Press, 2003); and Dani Rodrik, *Straight Talk on Trade: Ideas for a Sane World Economy* (Princeton, NJ: Princeton University Press, 2018).

118 Robert D. Atkinson and Michael Lind, "National Developmentalism: From Forgotten Tradition to New Consensus."

119 *See* James Bacchus, "After Covid, Services Are Where the Trade Action Is," *Wall Street Journal* (March 22, 2021).

120 Hildegunn K. Nordas and Dorothee Rouzet, "The Impact of Services Trade Restrictiveness on Trade Flows," OECD Trade Policy Papers No. 178 (Paris: OECD, 2015), 6, at www.oecd-ilibrary.org/trade/the-impact-of-services-trade-restrictiveness-on-trade-flows_5js6ds9b6kjb-en.

121 WTO, "World Trade Report 2019: The Future of Services Trade," (2019), 15, at www.wto.org/english/res_e/publications_e/wtr19_e.htm.

122 Ibid. at 4.

123 Ibid. at 14.

124 Ibid.

125 Ibid.

126 Ibid.

127 Ibid. at 16.

128 OECD/WTO, "Trade Value Added Data Base," https://oecd.org/trade/valueadded.

129 Sebastian Miroudot, Dorothee Rouzet, and Francesca Spinelli, "Trade Policy Implications of Global Value Chains," Organization for Economic Co-operation and Development, OECD Trade Policy Papers No. 161 (December 24, 2013), at http://dx.doi.org/10.1787/5k3tpt2tozs1-en.

130 Christine LaGarde, "Creating a Better Global Trade System," *IMF Blog* (May 29, 2018), at https://blogs.imf.org/2018/05/29/creating-a-better-global-trade-system; Lionel Fontagne, Amelie Guillin, Christina Mitartonna, "Estimations of Tariff Equivalents for the Services Sectors," *Centre D'Etudes Prospectives et D'Informations Internationalles*, No. 2011 (December 24, 2011).

131 US International Trade Commission, "Recent Trends in U.S. Services Trade: 2020 Annual Report," Publication 5094 (July 2020), 13, at www.usitc.gov/publications/industry_econ_analysis_332/2020/recent_trends_us_services_trade_2020_annual_report.htm. At the time of writing, these were the most current statistics available.

132 US Bureau of Economic Analysis, "Trade in Goods and Services," at www.bea.gov/international/index.htm.

133 Neil Irwin, "Most Americans Produce Services, Not Stuff. Trump Ignores That in Talking about Trade," *New York Times* (March 16, 2018).

134 CCSA, "How COVID-19 Is Changing the World," 18–23.

135 OECD, "Services Trade Policies and the Global Economy" (June 8, 2017), 17, at www.oecd.org/publications/services-trade-policies-and-the-global-economy-97892 64275232-en.htm.

136 Ibid. at 13.

137 Ibid. at 17.

138 Rachel F. Feher, "U.S. Trade in Services: Trade and Policy Issues," Congressional Research Service, R43291 (January 22, 2020), 9.

139 Drusilla K. Brown et al., "Computational Analysis of Multilateral Trade Liberalization in the Uruguay Round and Doha Development Round."

140 Coalition of Services Industries, "Services Trade Means U.S. Economic Growth," at https://uscsi.org/policy-issues.

141 Ibid.; *see* Daniel Pruzin, "OECD Cites Widespread Barriers, Opportunities in Global Services Trade," *Inside US Trade* (March 7, 2014); and *see also* OECD, "Services Trade Policies and the Global Economy" (Paris: OECD, 2017).

142 ICTSD/WEF, "Rethinking Services in a Changing World: Synthesis of the Policy Options," International Center for Trade and Sustainable Development and World Economic Forum, E15 Initiative (Geneva: ICTSD and WEF, 2016), 2. *See also* Pierre Sauve, "To Fuse or Not to Fuse? Assessing the Case for Convergent Disciplines on Goods and Services Trade," International Center for Trade and Sustainable Development and World Economic Forum, E15 Expert Group on Services (Geneva: ICTSD and WEF, 2015).

143 OECD, "Services Trade Policies and the Global Economy," at 39.

144 Ibid. at 40.

145 Article II, General Agreement on Trade in Services.

146 Article XVII, General Agreement on Trade in Services.

147 In contrast to the "positive list" approach in current WTO services rules, in which concessions on national treatment are made only if they are listed, the negotiations conducted on the sidelines of the WTO on the proposed "Trade in Services Agreement" have been conducted on a "negative list" approach, requiring each participant to provide national treatment for all services and services suppliers of other participants, subject to any agreed reservations in its schedule of concessions. *See* Amy Porges and Alice Enders, "Data Moving across Borders: The Future of Digital Trade Policy," International Center for Trade and Sustainable Development and World Economic Forum E15 Initiative (Geneva: ICTSD and WEF, April 2016), 11.

148 ICTSD/WEF, "Rethinking Services in a Changing World," at 19.

149 Aaditya Mattoo, "Services Trade and Regulatory Cooperation," E15 Initiative (Geneva: ICTSD and WEF, July 2015), 7–10.

150 ICTSD/WEF, "Rethinking Services in a Changing World," at 8.

151 Ibid. at 15.

CHAPTER 5

1 For a lengthier analysis of digital trade and my proposals for addressing it in the WTO, *see* James Bacchus, "The Digital Decide: How to Agree on WTO Rules for Digital Trade," Centre for International Governance Innovation, Special Report (August 2021).

2 McKinsey Global Institute, "Digital Globalization: The New Era of Global Flows" (March 2016), 1.

3 Ibid. These number are for 2016.

4 Ibid. (emphasis added)

5 McKinsey Global Institute, "Digital Globalization," at 30.

6 Ibid. at 7.

7 Ibid.

8 Ibid.

9 Ibid.

10 Daniel Griswold, "The Dynamic Gains from Free Digital Trade for the U.S. Economy," testimony before the U.S. Congress Joint Economic Committee (September 12, 2017).

11 McKinsey Global Institute, "Digital Globalization," at 7.

12 Ibid. at 8. These numbers are as of 2016; the total is, undoubtedly, larger now.

13 Goal 9, "Transforming Our World."

14 World Bank, "World Development Report 2016: Digital Dividends" (Washington, DC: World Bank Group, 2016), 105–130, at www.worldbank.org/en/publication/wdr2016.

15 Ibid. at 19.

16 Ibid.

17 WTO, "World Trade Report 2018: The Future of World Trade: How Digital Technologies Are Transforming Global Commerce" (Geneva: WTO, 2018), 6, at www.wto.org/english/res_e/publications_e/wtr18_e.htm.

18 Mark Wu, "Digital Trade-Related Provisions in Regional Trade Agreements: Existing Models and Lessons for the Multilateral Trading System," Inter-American Development Bank and International Centre for Trade and Sustainable Development, RTA Exchange, Overview Paper (November 2017), 1.

19 Joshua P. Meltzer, "The Internet and International Data Flows in the Global Economy," E15 Initiative, World Economic Forum and International Centre for Trade and Sustainable Development (May 27, 2016).

20 Richard Webb, "The Greatest Network the World Has Ever Seen: The Global Internet Map," *New Scientist* (October 23, 2019). These are 2017 numbers.

21 WTO, "World Trade Report 2018," at 9.

22 Ibid. at 11.

23 OECD, "The Impact of Digitalization on Trade," at www.oecd.org/trade/topics/digital-trade.

24 European Political Strategy Centre, "Enter the Data Economy: EU Policies for a Thriving Data Ecosystem," *EPSC Strategic Notes*, No. 21 (January 11, 2017), 1 (emphasis in original), at https://euagenda.eu/publications/enter-the-data-economy-eu-policies-for-a-thriving-data-ecosystem.

25 Richard Waters, "They're Watching You," *Financial Times* (October 24, 2020).

26 Mark Wu, "Digital Trade-Related Provisions in Regional Trade Agreements," at 23.

27 Robert Pepper, John Garrity, and Connie LaSalle, "1.2 Cross-Border Data Flows, Digital Innovation, and Economic Growth," World Economic Forum (2016), at www.reports,weforum.org/global-information-technology-report-2016/1-2-cross-border-data-flows-digital-innovation-and-economic-growth.

28	Dan Ciuriak and Maria Ptashkina, "The Digital Transformation and the Transformation of International Trade," Inter-American Development Bank and International Centre for Trade and Sustainable Development, RTA Exchange Issues Paper (January 2018), vi.

29	Joshua P. Meltzer, "Governing Digital Trade," *World Trade Review*, Vol. 18, No. S1 (2019), s23–s48, s29.

30	David Ignatius, "After Covid-19, It Will Be a Different World," *Washington Post* (October 9, 2020).

31	World Bank, "Global Economic Outlook" (June 2020), at xiv.

32	Greg Ip, "Pandemic Hastens Shift to Asset-Light Economy," *Wall Street Journal* (October 8, 2020).

33	Jason Thomas, "When the Future Arrives Early," *Carlyle Group Global Insights* (September 16, 2020), at www.carlyle.com/global-insights/when-the-future-arrives-early-thomas.

34	Ibid. at 14, 16.

35	Rana Foroohar, "Covid Recovery Will Stem from Digital Business," *Financial Times* (October 4, 2020).

36	OECD, "The Impact of Digitalization on Trade."

37	Dan Ciuriak and Maria Ptashkina, "The Digital Transformation and the Transformation of International Trade," at 1.

38	Dan Ciuriak, "The WTO in the Digital Age," Centre for International Governance Innovation (May 4, 2020), at www.cigionline.org/articles/wto-digital-age.

39	*See* Appellate Body Report, *China – Measures Affecting Trading Rights and Distribution Services for Certain Publications and Audiovisual Entertainment Products*, WT/DS363/AB/R (2009), para. 196.; *see also* Panel Report, *United States – Measures Affecting the Cross-Border Supply of Gambling and Betting Services*, WT/DS285/R (2004).

40	Mark Wu, "Digital Trade-Related Provisions in Regional Trade Agreements," at 2.

41	WTO, "World Trade Report 2018," at 150.

42	WTO Work Programme on Electronic Commerce, Ministerial Decision of 13 December 2017, WT/MIN(17)/65, December 18, 2017.

43	European Commission, "European Union-United States Trade Principles for Information and Communication Technology Services" (2011), at www.trade.ec.europa.eu/doclib/docs/2011/april/tradoc_147780.pdf.

44	*See* EU General Data Protection Regulations, L119/1, 679, Article 45 (April 27, 2016).

45	Shannon Tiezzi, "China's 'Sovereign Internet,'" *The Diplomat* (June 24, 2014), at http://thediplomat.com/2014/06/china-sovereign-internet.

46	Dan Ciuriak, "World Trade Organization 2.0: Reforming Multilateral Trade Rules for the Digital Age," Centre for International Governance Innovation (July 11, 2019), 3, at www.cigionline.org/publications/world-trade-organization-20-reforming-multilateral-trade-rules-digital-age.

47	Joshua P. Meltzer, "A New Digital Trade Agenda," E15 Initiative, E15 Expert Group on the Digital Economy Overview Paper (Geneva: World Economic Forum and International Centre for Trade and Sustainable Development, August 2015), 4.

48	Mark Wu, "Digital Trade-Related Provisions in Regional Trade Agreements," at 24.

49 Ibid. at 25.
50 Ibid.
51 Chapter 14, Comprehensive and Progressive Agreement for Trans-Pacific Partnership.
52 Chapter 19, United States-Mexico-Canada Agreement.
53 "Joint Statement on Electronic Commerce," WT/L/1056 (January 25, 2019).
54 Mark Wu, "Digital Trade-Related Provisions in Regional Trade Agreements," at 6.
55 *See* Digital Economy Partnership Agreement, at www.mfat.govt.nz/assets/FTAs-agreed-not-signed/DEPA/DEPA-Chile-New-Zealand-Singapore-21-Jan-2020-for-release.pdf.
56 Stephanie Honey, "Digging DEPA: The Digital Economy Partnership Agreement," *Trade Works* (June 16, 2020), at www.tradeworks.org.nz/digging-depa-the-digital-economy-partnership-agreement.
57 Module 7, DEPA.
58 Module 11, DEPA.
59 Stephanie Honey, "Digging DEPA."
60 WTO, "World Trade Report 2018," at 5.
61 *See* James Bacchus, "TRIPS-Past to TRIPS-Plus: Upholding the Balance between Exclusivity and Access on Trade-Related Intellectual Property," Centre for International Governance Innovation, CIGI Papers No. 254 (June 2021) .
62 Stephen Ezell and Nigel Cory, "The Way Forward for Intellectual Property Internationally," Information Technology & Innovation Foundation (April 2019), at 6.
63 Goal 9, "Transforming Our World: The 2030 Agenda for Sustainable Development," A/RES70/1 (September 25–27, 2015).
64 Jagdish Bhagwati, "Keep Free Trade Free," *Wired* (September 22, 2008), at www.wired.com/2008/09/sl-bhagwati.
65 Jagdish Bhagwati, letter to the editor, *Financial Times* (February 14, 2001).
66 Kevin A. Hassett and Robert J. Shapiro, "What Ideas Are Worth: The Value of Intellectual Capital And Intangible Assets in the American Economy" (Sonecon LLC, 2011), iv. These are 2011 numbers.
67 US Department of Commerce, "Intellectual Property and the U.S. Economy: 2016 Update" (2016), 1. These are 2016 numbers.
68 James Manyika et al., "Global Flows in a Digital Age," McKinsey Global Institute (April 2014), at www.mckinsey.com/business-functions/strategy-and-corporate-finance/our-insights/global-flows-in-a-digital-age.
69 Stephen Ezell and Nigel Cory, "The Way Forward for Intellectual Property Internationally," at 4.
70 Ricardo Cavazos Cepeda, Douglas C. Lippoldt, and Jonathan Senft, "Policy Complements to the Strengthening of IPRs in Developing Countries," Working Paper (Paris: OECD, 2010), at http://dx.doi.org/10.1787/5km7fmwz85d4-en.
71 Stephen Ezell and Nigel Cory, "The Way Forward for Intellectual Property Internationally," at 9.
72 OECD, "The Links between Global Value Chains and Global Innovation Networks" (Paris: OECD, 2017), at https://doi.org/10.1787/76d78fbb-en.
73 USTR, "2020 Special 301 Report" (April 2020).
74 Section 5, WTO Agreement on Trade-Related Aspects of Intellectual Property Rights.

75 WTO, WIPO, WHO, "Promoting Access to Medical Technologies and Innovation," at 64.

76 Stephen Ezell and Nigel Cory, "The Way Forward for Intellectual Property Internationally," at 18.

77 Preamble, WTO Agreement on Trade-Related Intellectual Property Rights.

78 Article 7, WTO Agreement on Trade-Related Aspects of Intellectual Property Rights.

79 Article 8.1, WTO Agreement on Trade-Related Aspects of Intellectual Property Rights.

80 Article 8.2, WTO Agreement on Trade-Related Aspects of Intellectual Property Rights.

81 Footnote 1, Article 1.3, WTO Agreement on Trade-Related Aspects of Intellectual Property Rights.

82 WIPO Copyright Treaty (December 20, 1996), S. Treaty Doc. No. 105-17 (1997); 2186 U.N.T.S. 121, 36 I.L.M. 65 (1997), at www.wipo.int/treaties/en/ip/wct.

83 WIPO Performances and Phonograms Treaty (December 20, 1996), S. Treaty Doc. No. 105-17 (1997), 2186 U.N.T.S. 203, 36 I.L.M. 76 (1997), www.wipo.int/treaties/en/ip/wppt.

84 Marrakesh Treaty to Facilitate Access to Published Works for Persons Who Are Blind, Visually Impaired or Otherwise Print Disabled (June 27, 2013), at www.wipo.int/treaties/en/ip/marrakesh.

85 Article 20.69-20.77, United States-Mexico-Canada Agreement, at https://ustr.gov/trade-agreements/free-trade-agreements/united-states-mexico-canada-agreement/agreement-between.

86 Chapter 11, Section G, Regional Comprehensive Economic Partnership, at https://rcepsec.org/legal-text.

87 Article 7, WTO Agreement on Trade-Related Aspects of Intellectual Property Rights.

88 Article 66.2, WTO Agreement on Trade-Related Aspects of Intellectual Property Rights (emphasis added).

89 *See* James Bacchus, "An Unnecessary Proposal: A WTO Waiver of Intellectual Property Rights for COVID-19 Vaccines," Cato Free Trade Bulletin Number 78 (December 16, 2020), at www.cato.org/publications/free-trade-bulletin/unnecessary-proposal-wto-waiver-intellectual-property-rights-covid.

90 Communication from India and South Africa, "Waiver from Certain Provisions of the TRIPS Agreement for the Prevention, Containment and Treatment of COVID-19," IP/C/W/669 (October 2, 2020), paragraphs 12 and 13.

91 "Declaration on the TRIPS Agreement and Public Health," at paragraph 10.

92 Communication from India and South Africa, "Waiver from Certain Provisions of the TRIPS Agreement for the Prevention, Containment and Treatment of COVID-19," at paragraph 10.

93 Helen Collis, "WTO Members Reject IP Rules Waiver for Coronavirus Technologies," *Politico Pro Trade* (October 16, 2020).

94 UK Statement to the TRIPS Council (October 14, 2020), at www.gov.uk/government/news/uk-statement-to-the-trips-council-item-15?source=email.

95 Helen Collis, "WTO Members Reject IP Rules Waiver for Coronavirus Technologies."

96 Saeed Shah, "Developing Countries to Push to Limit Protections for Covid-19 Vaccines," *Wall Street Journal* (September 17, 2020).

97 Articles 7 and 8, WTO Agreement on Trade-Related Aspects of Intellectual Property Rights.

98 Jennifer Hillman, "Drugs and Vaccines Are Coming – But to Whom?" Council on Foreign Relations (May 19, 2020), at www.foreignaffairs.com/articles/world/2020-05-19/drugs-and-vaccines-are-coming-whom.

99 William Alan Reinsch, "Compulsory Licensing: A Cure for Distributing the Cure?" Center for Strategic & International Studies (May 8, 2020), at www.csis.org/analysis/compulsory-licensing-cure-distributing-cure.

100 "Declaration on the TRIPS Agreement and Public Health," WT/MIN(01)/DEC/2 (November 20, 2001), paragraph 6.

101 Ibid. at paragraph 5(b).

102 "Implementation of Paragraph 6 of the Doha Declaration on the TRIPS Agreement and Public Health," WT/L/540 and Corr. 1 (September 1, 2003).

103 Article 31bis, WTO Agreement on Trade-Related Intellectual Property Rights.

104 Sam Fleming and Jim Brunsden, "Macron Plays Down Biden Waiver Plan," *Financial Times* (May 8, 2021).

105 "Statement by UN Human Rights Experts: Universal Access to Vaccines Is Essential for Prevention and Containment of COVID-19 around the World" (November 9, 2020), at https://reliefweb.int/report/world-statement-un-human-rights-experts-universal-access-vaccines-essential-prevention-and.

106 Yuka Hayashi and Jared S. Hopkins, "U.S. Backs Waiver of Intellectual Property Protection for Covid-19 Vaccines," *Wall Street Journal* (May 6, 2021).

107 Dan Diamond, Tyler Pager, and Jeff Stein, "Biden Commits to Waiving Vaccine Patents, Driving Wedge with Pharmaceutical Companies," *Washington Post* (May 6, 2021).

108 Jenny Leonard, Eric Martin, and Viktoria Dendrinou, "U.S. Vaccine Patent Surprise Roils Pharma as WTO Debate Heats Up," *Bloomberg* (May 5, 2021), at www.bloomberg.com/news/articles/2021-05-05/u-s-to-back-waiver-of-vaccine-ip-protections-at-wto-tai-says.

109 Tyler Pager, Dan Diamond, and Jeff Stein, "'It's Pretty Marginal': Experts Say Biden's Vaccine Waiver Unlikely to Boost Supply Quickly," *Washington Post* (May 6, 2021).

110 *See generally* Jerome H. Reichman, "Compulsory Licensing of Patented Pharmaceutical Inventions: Evaluating the Options," *Journal of Law and Medical Ethics*, Vol. 37, No. 2 (Summer 2009, 247–263, at www.ncbi.nlm.nih.gov/pmc/articles/PMC2893582.

111 Sheryl Gay Stolberg, Thomas Kaplan, and Rebecca Robins, "Pressure Mounts to Lift Patent Protections on Coronavirus Vaccines," *New York Times* (May 4, 2021).

112 Yuka Hayashi and Jared S. Hopkins, "U.S. Backs Waiver of Intellectual Property Protection for Covid-19 Vaccines."

113 Rachel Silverman, "Waiving Vaccine Patents Won't Help Inoculate Poorer Nations," *Washington Post* (March 15, 2021).

114 Ibid.

115 David M. Fox, "Technology Transfer and the TRIPS Agreement: Are Developed Countries Meetings Their End of the Bargain?" *Hastings Science and Technology Law Journal*, Vol. 10, No. 1 (Winter 2019), 1–38, 4.

116 OECD, "OECD Competition Policy Responses to COVID-19" (April 27, 2020).
117 Ibid.
118 WTO, WIPO, and WHO, "Promoting Access to Medical Technologies and Innovation," at 21.
119 Ibid. at 96.
120 Ibid.
121 Ibid.
122 Ibid.
123 Chapter V, Articles 46–54, "Final Act of the United Nations Conference on Trade and Development: Havana Charter for an International Trade Organization" (April 1948), at www.wto.org/english/docs_e/legal_e/prewto_legal_e.htm.
124 Julian Grollier and Karen Somasundaram, "Trade and Competition Policy: Has Past WTO Work Stood the Test of Time?" CUTS International (2017), 9.
125 Ibid.
126 Ibid.
127 *See, e.g.*, Article XVII, General Agreement on Tariffs and Trade; Articles 8 and 9, General Agreement on Trade in Services; and Article 8.2 and Article 40, Agreement on Trade-Related Aspects of Intellectual Property Rights.
128 "Telecommunications Services: Reference Paper" (April 24, 1996), at www.wto .org/english/tratop_e/serv_e/tel23_e.htm.
129 Part I, WTO Agreement on Implementation of Article VI of the General Agreement on Tariffs and Trade 1994.
130 Parts I, II, and III, WTO Agreement on Subsidies and Countervailing Measures.
131 Article 2, WTO Agreement on Safeguards.
132 "Fair Trade or Protectionism? Trade Enforcement Measures Taken by the United States," Federation of German Industries (BDI) (March 11, 2020), at https://english.bdi.eu/article/news/fair-trade-or-protectionism-trade-enforcement-measures-taken-by-the-united-states.
133 WTO, ITC, UNCTAD, "World Trade Profiles 2020," at 202.
134 Ibid.
135 Ibid. at 205.
136 Article VI.1, General Agreement on Tariffs and Trade.
137 Daniel J. Ikenson, "Antidumping 101: Everything You Need to Know about the Steel Industry's Favorite Protectionist Bludgeon," Cato Institute (April 27, 2017), at www.cato.org/blog/anti-trade-barbarians-gate.
138 Michael Trebilcock, *Advanced Introduction to International Trade Law* (Cheltenham: Edward Elgar, 2015), 71.
139 Ibid.
140 Ibid.
141 Ibid. at 61.
142 Daniel Ikenson, "Tariffs by Fiat: The Widening Chasm between U.S. Antidumping Policy and the Rule of Law," Cato Institute, Policy Analysis No. 896 (July 16, 2020), 14, at www.cato.org/publications/policy-analysis/tariffs-fiat-widening-chasm-between-us-antidumping-policy-rule-law.
143 Ibid. at 5.
144 Ibid. at 7.
145 Simon Lester and Huan Zhu, "The Spread of Anti-Dumping Abuse," Cato Institute (August 5, 2020), at www.cato.org/blog/spread-anti-dumping-abuse.

146 WTO, ITC, UNCTAD, "World Trade Profiles 2020," at 201.

147 Ibid. at 203.

148 Petros C. Mavroidis, "Economic Development, Competition Policy and the WTO," *Journal of World Trade*, Vol. 37, No. 1 (2003), 1–27, 17.

149 Ibid.

150 *See* Antonio Capobianco and Hans Christiansen, "Competitive Neutrality and State-Owned Enterprises: Challenges and Policy Options," OECD Corporate Governance Working Papers No. 1 (Paris: OECD, 2011); "OECD Guidelines on Corporate Governance of State-Owned Enterprises" (Paris: OECD, 2015), at www .oecd.org/guidelines-corporate-governance-SOEs.htm.

151 WTO Agreement on Subsidies and Countervailing Measures.

152 See www.fortune.com/global500; *see also* Karen Jingrong Lin, Xiaoyan Lu, Junsheng Zhang, and Ying Zheng, "State-Owned Enterprises in China: A Review of 40 Years of Research and Practice," *China Journal of Accounting Research*, Vol. 13 (2020), 31–55, at https://doi.org/10.1016/j.cjar.2019.12.001.

153 Mark Wu, "The 'China, Inc.' Challenge to Global Trade Governance," *Harvard International Law Review*, Vol. 57, No. 2 (Spring 2016), 261–324, 269.

154 For a detailed outline of a proposed case that could be brought against China under existing WTO rules, *see* James Bacchus, Simon Lester, and Huan Zhu, "Disciplining China's Trade Practices at the WTO: How WTO Complaints Can Help Make China More Market-Oriented," Cato Institute, Policy Analysis No. 856 (November 15, 2018), at www.cato.org/policy-analysis/disciplining-chinas-trade-practices-wto-how-wto-complaints-can-help-make-china-more.

155 Robert D. Anderson and Anna Caroline Muller, "Competition Law/Policy and the Multilateral Trading System: A Possible Agenda for the Future," E15 Initiative (Geneva: ICTSD and WEF, 2015), at 8.

156 Chapter 17, Comprehensive and Progressive Agreement for Trans-Progressive Partnership.

157 Chapters 21 and 22, United States-Mexico-Canada Agreement.

158 Mitsuo Matsushita, "Basic Principles of the WTO and the Role of Competition Policy, 3 *Washington University Global Studies Law Review* (2004), 363–385, 381–382.

159 OECD, "Hardcore Cartels 2000" (Paris: OECD, 2000), 6.

160 Vinod Dhall, "Act Decisively against Cartels," *Financial Express* (September 26, 2020).

161 *See* "Subsidies and Overcapacity: Recent Developments at the G20 and the WTO" (August 29, 2017), at www.dentons.com/en/insights/alerts/2017/august/29/subsid ies-and-overcapacity-recent-developments-at-the-g20-and-the-wto.

162 Article XI:2(a), General Agreement on Tariffs and Trade.

163 "OECD Steel Committee: Global Steelmaking Overcapacity Returns after Four Years," *Eurometal* (October 1, 2020), at https://eurometal.net/oecd-steel-commit tee-global-steelmaking-overcapacity-returns-after-four-years.

164 Raj Bhala and Nathan Deuckjoo (D. J.) Kim, "The WTO's Under-Capacity to Deal with Global Over-Capacity," *Asian Journal of WTO & International Health Law and Policy*, Vol. 14, No. 1 (2019), 1–32, 4.

165 Daniel R. Pearson, "Global Steel Overcapacity: Trade Remedy 'Cure' Is Worse Than the 'Disease'," Cato Institute, Free Trade Bulletin No. 66 (April 11, 2016), 1, at www.cato.org/publications/free-trade-bulletin/global-steel-overcap acity-trade-remedy-cure-worse-disease.

166 Raj Bhala and Nathan Deuckjoo (D.J.) Kim, "The WTO's Under-Capacity to Deal with Over-Capacity," at 14–15.

167 Daniel R. Pearson, "Global Steel Overcapacity," at 2.

168 OECD, "Steelmaking Capacity," at www.oecd.org/industry/steelcapacity.htm.

169 USTR, "Joint Statement on Trilateral Meeting of the Trade Ministers of the United States, Japan, and the European Union" September 25, 2018), at https://ustr.gov/about-us/policy-offices/press-office/press-releases/2018/septembeer/jopint-statement-trilateral.

170 "Rules Negotiations-Transparency," WTO Doc. TN/RL/W/260 (July 16, 2015).

171 *See* Dukgeun Ahn, "Why Reform Is Needed: WTO 'Public Body' Jurisprudence," Global Policy, Vol. 12, No. S3 (April 28, 2021), 61–70, at https://onlinelibrary.wiley.com/doi/10.1111/1758-5899.12929.

172 Dan Ciuriak, "Word Trade Organization 2.0," at 6.

173 Ana Novik and Alexandre de Crombrugghe, "Towards an International Framework for Investment Facilitation," OECD Investment Insights (April 2018), 1.

174 WTO, "World Trade Report 2013: Factors Shaping the Future of World Trade," 138, at www.wto.org/english/res_e/publications_e/wtr13_e.htm.

175 Ibid. at 135, 141. *See* James Bacchus, *The Willing World*, at 110–111.

176 UNCTAD, "World Investment Report 2021: Investing in Sustainable Recovery," x–xi, at https://unctad.org/system/files/official-document/wir2021_en.pdf.

177 Ibid.

178 UNCTAD, "World Investment Report 2020: International Production Beyond the Pandemic," at https://unctad.org/webflyer/world-investment-report-2020, 90.

179 Ibid.

180 UNCTAD, "World Investment Report 2021: Investing in Sustainable Recovery," at 159.

181 https://investmentpolicy.unctad.org/international-investment-agreements/by-economy.

182 WTO Agreement on Trade-Related Investment Measures.

183 Article 2, WTO Agreement on Trade-Related Investment Measures.

184 Ibid.

185 "Joint Ministerial Statement on Investment Facilitation for Development," WT/MIN(17)/59 (December 13, 2017).

186 "Joint Ministerial Statement on Investment Facilitation for Development," WT/L/1072/Rev.1 (November 22, 2019).

187 WTO, "Structured Discussion on Investment Facilitation for Development Move into Negotiating Mode" (September 25, 2020), at www.wto.org/english/news_e/news20_e/infac_25sep20_e.htm.

188 Terence P. Stewart, "Biden Administration Should Join the Joint Statement Initiatives That It Is Not Presently Party To," *Current Thoughts on Trade* (March 9, 2021), at www.wita.org/blogs/biden-should-joint-initiatives.

189 WTO Agreement on Trade Facilitation, "Annex to the Protocol Amending the Marrakesh Agreement Establishing the World Trade Organization," WT/L/940 (November 28, 2014).

190 WTO, "Trade facilitation," at www.wto.org/english/tratop_e/tradfa_e.htm.

191 Paragraph 4, "Joint Ministerial Statement on Investment Facilitation for Development," WT/MIM(17)/59 (December 13, 2017).

192 Sofia Balino and Nathalie Bernaconi-Osterwalder, "Investment Facilitation at the WTO: An Attempt to Bring a Controversial Issue into an Organization in Crisis," International Institute for Sustainable Development (June 27, 2019).

193 Ibid.

194 Ibid.

195 Ana Novik and Alexandre de Crombrugghe, "Towards an International Framework for Investment Facilitation," at 3.

196 UNCTAD, "World Investment Report 2016: Investor Nationality: Policy Challenges," 117, at https://unctad.org/webflyer/world-investment-report-2016.

197 Karl P. Sauvant and Matthew Stephenson, "Concrete Measures for a Framework on Investment Facilitation for Development: Report," Expert Workshop on Opportunities and Challenges of Establishing an International Framework on Investment Facilitation for Development in the WTO held at the WTO (December 12, 2019).

198 Karl P. Sauvant, Mathew Stephenson, Khalil Hamdani, and Yardenne Kagan, "An Inventory of Concrete Measures to Facilitate the Flow of Sustainable FDI: What? Why? How?" (Geneva: International Trade Centre, November 2020).

199 Sofia Balino and Nathalie Bernasconi-Osterwalder, "Investment Facilitation at the WTO."

200 Karl P. Sauvant, "Enabling the Full Participation of Developing Countries in Negotiating an Investment Facilitation Framework for Development," Columbia FDI Perspectives, Number 275 (April 6, 2020).

201 Emphasis added.

202 Karl P. Sauvant, Axel Berger, Ahmad Ghouri, Tomoko Ishikawa, and Matthew Stephenson, "Towards G20 Guiding Principles on Investment Facilitation for Sustainable Development," G20 Insights (February 6, 2020), at www.g20-insights.org/policy_briefs/towards-g20-guiding-principles-on-investment-facilitation-for-sustainable-development.

203 Introduction, "Transforming Our World."

CHAPTER 6

1 I owe this metaphor to my dear friend and late colleague on the WTO Appellate Body, Justice Florentino "Toy" Feliciano.

2 Philip Stephens, "The Path from Covid to a New Social Contract," *Financial Times* (July 24, 2020).

3 Goal 13, "Transforming Our World."

4 Paris Agreement, FCCC/CP/2015/L.9.

5 Article 2.1(a), Paris Agreement.

6 International Energy Agency, "Global Energy Review 2021" (April 20, 2021).

7 Richard Betts, "Guest Post: Global Warming Edges Closer to Paris Agreement 1.5C Limit," *Carbon Brief* (July 9, 2020), at www.carbonbrief.org/guest-post-global-warming-edges-closer-to-paris-agreement-1-5c-limit.

8 IPCC, "Special Report: Global Warming of 1.5C: Framing and Context," Intergovernmental Panel on Climate Change (October 2018), 51.

9 IPCC, "Global Warming of 1.5C: Summary for Policymakers," Intergovernmental Panel on Climate Change (October 2018), 6.

10 Chelsea Harvey, "Worrisome Signs Emerge for 1.5-Degree-C Climate Target," *Scientific American* (July 10, 2020).

11 IPCC, "Global Warming of 1.5C," at 14. *See* Coral Davenport, "Major Climate Report Describes a Strong Risk of Crisis as Early as 2040," *New York Times* (October 7, 2018).

12 UNEP, "Emissions Gap Report 2020" (Nairobi: United Nations Environment Programme, December 2020), xxi.

13 Ibid.

14 Ibid.

15 Walter Russell Read, "Climate Finance May Foul the Economy," *Wall Street Journal* (December 8, 2020).

16 Leslie Hook, "Climate Change: 'The Paris Goals Are within Reach,'" *Financial Times* (December 12, 2020).

17 Ibid.

18 Somini Sengupta, "China, in Nudge to U.S., Makes a New Promise to Tackle Global Warming," *New York Times* (December 13, 2020).

19 Dimitris Mavrokefalidis, "China 'Built over Three Times as Much Coal Plant Capacity as the Rest of the World in 2020'." *Energy Live News* (February 4, 2021), at www.energylivenews.com/2021/02/04/china-built-over-three-times-as-much-coal-plant-capacity-as-the-rest-of-the-world-in-2020.

20 Kate Larsen, Hannah Pitt, Mikhail Grant, and Trevor Houser, "China's Greenhouse Gas Emissions Exceeded the Developed World for the First Time in 2019," Rhodium Group (May 6, 2021), at https://rhg.com/research/chinas-emissions-surpass-developed-countries.

21 Jean Chemnick and Benjamin Storrow, "China Says It Will Stop Releasing CO_2 within 40 Years," *Scientific American* (September 23, 2020), at www.scientificamerican.com/article/china-says-it-will-stop-releasing-co2-within-40-years.

22 Hannah Ritchie, "Who Has Contributed Most to Global CO_2 Emissions?" at https://ourworldindata.org/contributed-most-global-co2.

23 "Wealthy Nations Lead Per-Capita Emissions," *Statistica* (March 1, 2021), at www.statista.com/chart/24306/carbon-emissions-per-capita-by-country.

24 Leslie Hook, "Climate Change: 'The Paris Goals Are within Reach.'"

25 Ibid.

26 Edward Wong, "Trump Has Called Climate Change a Chinese Hoax. Beijing Says It Is Anything But," *New York Times* (November 18, 2016).

27 Derek Brower, "Biden Gambles on Placing Climate Change at Heart of US Energy Policy," *Financial Times* (August 17, 2020).

28 Zack Colman and Ben Lefebvre, "Biden Pitching a Much Vaster Climate Plan Than Obama Ever Attempted," *Politico* (January 27, 2021).

29 Elian Peltier and Somini Sengupta, "U.S. Formally Rejoins the Paris Climate Accord," *New York Times* (February 19, 2021).

30 Lisa Friedman, Somini Sengupta, and Coral Davenport, "Biden, Calling for Action, Commits U.S. to Halving Its Climate Emissions, *New York Times* (April 23, 2021).

31 Ibid.

32 Andrew Restuccia and Timothy Puko, "At Earth Day Climate Summit, Biden Pushes for Sharp Cut to Greenhouse-Gas Emissions," *Wall Street Journal* (April 23, 2021).

33 Richard Cowan and Susan Cornwell, "U.S. Senate Pivots to $3.5 Trillion Bill, Key to Biden's Agenda," *Reuters* (August 10, 2021).

34 Hyung-Jim Kim, "US, China Agree to Cooperate on Climate Crisis with Urgency," *Associated Press* (April 18, 2021), at https://apnews.com/article/joe-biden-climate-shanghai-climate-change-john-kerry-905125d79b6c31940b8747df86c2a87a.

35 Lisa Friedman, Somini Sengupta, and Coral Davenport, "Biden, Calling for Action, Commits U.S. to Halving Its Climate Emissions."

36 Walter Russell Mead, "A Liberalish New World Order," *Wall Street Journal* (April 27, 2021).

37 IMF, "Mitigating Climate Change – Growth-and-Distribution-Friendly Strategies," at 87.

38 Editorial, "The Merits of a Global Carbon Offset Market," *Financial Times* (December 7, 2020).

39 "China's Carbon Trading Scheme Makes Debut with 4.1 Mln T in Turnover," *Reuters* (July 20, 2021).

40 Myles McCormick, "Carbon Price Missing from Biden's Climate Overhaul," *Financial Times* (April 26, 2021).

41 Eric Roston and Leslie Kaufman, "Experts Tell Biden: Your Climate Goals Require a Carbon Price," *Bloomberg* (February 4, 2021); Editorial, "Biden's Climate Plan Is a Risky Bet for the Planet," *Washington Post* (April 14, 2021).

42 Paragraph 137, Paris Decision 1/CP.21.

43 Deb Reichmann and Aya Batrawy, "Trump Slams Global Climate Agreement Biden Intends to Rejoin," *Associated Press* (November 22, 2020), at https://apnews.com/article/joe-biden-donald-trump-climate-climate-change-saudi-arabia-5e425ce92e26d34561d629331461289d.

44 United Nations Framework Convention on Climate Change, "The Paris Agreement," at https://unfccc.int/process-and-meetings/the-paris-agreement/the-paris-agreement.

45 Economists speak of these climate and other environmental costs as "externalities" and argue that they must be "internalized" through carbon pricing. For more on this topic, *see* James Bacchus, *The Willing World*, 221–227.

46 Carbon Pricing Leadership Coalition, "Report of the High-Level Commission on Carbon Prices" (Washington, DC: World Bank, May 29, 2017), 8.

47 IMF, "Mitigating Climate Change – Growth-and-Distribution-Friendly Strategies," at 87.

48 Sebastian Rausch and Valerie J. Karplus, "Markets versus Regulation: The Efficiency and Distributional Impacts of U.S. Climate Policy Proposals," Report No. 263, MIT Joint Program on the Science and Policy of Global Change (May 2014). This 2014 study modeled how a United States cap-and-trade policy would compare to a variety of regulatory options, including a federal renewable portfolio standard, a clean energy standard, and fuel economy standards.

49 IMF Staff Discussion Note, "After Paris: Fiscal, Macroeconomic, and Financial Implications of Climate Change" (January 2016), 15–16.

50 "Market Mechanisms: Understanding the Options," Center for Climate and Energy Solutions (April 2015), 3.

51 Ibid.

52 Principle 16, Rio Declaration on Environment and Development, A/CONF. 151/26 (vol. I) (June 14, 1992).

53 Rohan Best, Paul J. Burke, and Frank Jotzo, "Carbon Pricing Efficacy: Cross-Country Evidence," *Environmental and Resource Economics*, Vol. 77 (2020), 69–94.

54 Ibid.

55 National Academies of Sciences, Engineering and Medicine, "Accelerating Decarbonization of the U.S. Energy System" (February 2021), at www.nap.edu/catalog/25932/accelerating-decarbonization-of-the-us-energy-system.

56 Ibid. at 138.

57 Ibid.

58 Ibid.

59 Marc Hafstead, "Emissions Projections for the Climate Leadership Council Carbon Dividends Plan: 2021," Resources for the Future, Issue Brief 21-01 (April 2021).

60 Draft Ministerial Decision, "Advancing Sustainability Goals through Trade Rules to Level the Playing Field," WT/GC/W/814 (December 17, 2020).

61 Ibid.

62 Samantha Gross, "What Is the Trump Administration's Record on the Environment?" Brookings Institution (August 4, 2020), at www.brookings.edu/policy2020/votervital/what-is-the-trump-administrations-track-record-on-the-environment.

63 Terence P. Stewart, "U.S. Proposed Draft Ministerial Decision – Making Weak or Unenforced Environmental Standards Potentially Countervailable" (December 26, 2020), at https://currentthoughtsontrade.com/2020/12/26/u-s-proposed-draft-ministerial-decision-making-weak-or-unenforced-environmental-standards-poten tially-countervailable.

64 Bernice Lee and Scott Vaughan, "Is a Clash Coming When Trade and Climate Meet at the Border?" SDG Knowledge Hub, International Institute for Sustainable Development (November 25, 2020), at https://sdg.iisd.org/commentary/guest-art icles/is-a-clash-coming-when-trade-and-climate-meet-at-the-border.

65 For my analysis of these WTO legal issues, *see* James Bacchus, "Legal Issues with the European Carbon Border Adjustment Mechanism," Cato Briefing Paper Number 125 (August 9, 2021), at www.cato.org/briefing-paper/legal-issues-euro pean-carbon-border-adjustment-mechanism; *see also* James Bacchus, "When Two Global Agendas Collide: How the EU's Climate Change Mechanism Could Fall Afoul of International Trade Rules," World Economic Forum (July 7, 2021), at www.weforum.org/agenda/2021/07/how-the-eus-carbon-border-adjustment-mech anism-could-fall-afoul-of-wto-regulation.

66 For more on the Democratic proposal, *see* James Bacchus, "Striking a Balance on Climate Change and Global Trade," *The Hill* (July 19, 2021), at https://thehill .com/opinion/energy-environment/563680-striking-a-balance-on-climate-change-and-global-trade.

67 Ari Natter, Jennifer A. Dlouhy, and David Westin, "Biden Exploring Border Adjustment Tax to Fight Climate Change," *Bloomberg Green* (April 23, 2021), at www.bloomberg.com/news/articles/2021-04-23/biden-exploring-border-adjustment-tax-to-fight-climate-change.

68 Kait Bolongaro, "Canada Says It's Open to Carbon Tariffs Amid Global Climate Push," *Bloomberg* (February 12, 2021), at www.bloomberg.com/news/articles/2021-02-12/canada-says-it-s-open-to-carbon-tariffs-amid-global-climate-push.

69 Ibid. at 6.

70 Clara Brandi, "Trade Elements in Countries' Climate Contributions under the Paris Agreement," International Centre for Trade and Sustainable Development (Geneva: ISTSD, 2017), vii; *see also* Rana Elkahwagy, Vandana Gyanchandani & Dario Piselli, "UNFCCC Nationally Determined Contributions: Climate Change and Trade" (2017) Centre for Trade and Economic Integration Working Paper 2017-02 (Trade Lab).

71 Kateryna Holzer, *Carbon-Related Border Adjustment and WTO Law* (Cheltenham: Edward Elgar, 2014), 2.

72 Ibid. at 42–43.

73 Ingrid Jegou, "Competitiveness and Climate Policies: Is There a Case for Restrictive Unilateral Trade Measures?" International Centre for Trade and Sustainable Development (Geneva: ICTSD, December 2009), 6.

74 "Environmental Policies Don't Have to Hurt Productivity," *OECD Observer* No. 301 Q4 (2014), 9.

75 World Bank, "Carbon Leakage: Theory, Evidence and Policy Design," Technical Note 11 (October 2015), at 24.

76 World Bank, "Decarbonizing Development" (Washington, DC: World Bank Group, 2015), 17.

77 "Better Growth, Better Climate: The New Climate Economy Report," The Global Commission on the Economy and the Climate"(2014), 187, citing Bassi, S. and Zenghelis, D., "Burden or Opportunity? How UK Emissions Reduction Policies Affect the Competitiveness of Business," Policy Paper, Grantham Growth Research Institute on Climate Change and the Environment, London School of Economics (2014).

78 Ibid. at 187, citing the same study.

79 U.S. Congressional Budget Office, "Border Adjustments for Economywide Policies That Impose a Price on Greenhouse Gas Emissions" (Washington: CBO, December 2013). *See* the text of page 9 and the empirical studies listed in footnote 9.

80 Lisa Friedman, Somini Sengupta, and Coral Davenport, "Biden, Calling for Action, Commits U.S. to Halving Its Climate Emissions," *New York Times* (April 23, 2021).

81 *See, e.g.*, these excellent studies on various aspects of carbon adjustment by leading WTO authorities: Patrick Low and Gabrielle Marceau, "The Interface between the Trade and Climate Change Regimes: Scoping the Issues," Staff Working Paper ERSD-2011-1 (Geneva: World Trade Organization, 2011); Jennifer Hillman, "Changing Climate for Carbon Taxes: Who's Afraid of the WTO?" Climate & Energy Papers Series 2013 (Washington, DC: German Marshall Fund, July 2013); Joost Pauwelyn, "Carbon Leakage Measures and Border Tax Adjustments under WTO Law," in Geert Van Calster and Denise Prevost, eds., *Research Handbook on Environment, Health and the WTO* (Edward Elgar, 2012), 448; Maria Panezi, "When CO_2 Goes to Geneva: Taxing Carbon Across Borders – Without Violating WTO Obligations," CIGI Papers No. 83 (Waterloo: Centre for International Governance Innovation, November 2015); and Joel Trachtman, "WTO Law Constraints on Border Tax Adjustment and Tax Credit Mechanisms to Reduce the Competitive Effects of Carbon Taxes," RFF DP 16-03 (Washington, DC: Resources for the Future, January 2016).

82 Article II(2)(a), General Agreement on Tariffs and Trade.

83 Ingrid Jegou, "Competitiveness and Climate Policies: Is There a Case for Restrictive Unilateral Trade Measures?" at 9.

84 Article II:2(a), General Agreement on Tariffs and Trade.

85 Article IX:2(a), WTO Agreement.

86 Article XX, General Agreement on Tariffs and Trade.

87 *See* James Bacchus, "The Case for a WTO Climate Waiver," Centre for International Governance Innovation, Special Report (November 2, 2017), at www.cigionline.org/publications/case-wto-climate-waiver.

88 *See* United Nations, "Transforming Our World: The 2030 Agenda for Sustainable Development" (2015).

89 McKinsey & Company, "Global Energy Perspective 2021" (January 2021).

90 Article IX:2(a), WTO Agreement.

91 Article X, WTO Agreement.

92 Article IX:3, WTO Agreement.

93 Previously, I have explained this point at length in James Bacchus, "The Case for a WTO Climate Waiver," and, in particular as it relates to the notion of "like products" in James Bacchus, *The Willing World*, 239–243.

94 For more on climate clubs, *see* James Bacchus, *The Willing World*, 248–253.

95 William D. Nordhaus, "A New Solution: The Climate Club," *New York Review of Books* (June 4, 2015).

96 WTO General Council, Implementation of Paragraph 6 of the Doha Declaration on the TRIPS Agreement and Public Health, Decision of 30 August 2003, WTO Doc. WT/L/540, 2 September 2003. An amendment to the TRIPS Agreement entered into force in January 2017 for two-thirds of WTO members, replacing this waiver for those members.

97 Appellate Body Report, *Japan – Taxes on Alcoholic Beverages*, WT/DS11/AB/R (1996), 114.

98 *See* Appellate Body Report, *European Communities – Measures Affecting Asbestos and Asbestos Containing Products*, WT/DS135/AB/R (2001) (*EC – Asbestos*), paras. 90–122, and especially para. 101.

99 The papers and books written on this topic are too many to cite. One excellent overview of this critical issue is Christiane R. Conrad, *Processes and Production Methods (PPMs) in WTO Law: Interfacing Trade and Social Goals* (Cambridge: Cambridge University Press, 2011).

100 *EC – Asbestos*, para. 117.

101 Appellate Body Report, *Canada – Feed-in Tariffs Program*, WT/DS426/AB/R (2013), para. 5.63

102 GATT Panel Report, *Belgian Family Allowances*, G/32, BISD 1S, 59 (1952).

103 "Implementation of Paragraph 6 of the Doha Declaration on the TRIPS Agreement and Public Health," WT/L/540 and Corr. 1 (September 1, 2003).

104 General Council, Waiver Concerning Kimberley Process Certification Scheme for Rough Diamonds, Decision of 15 May 2003, WTO Doc. WT/L/518 (May 27, 2003).

105 *See* James Bacchus, "The Content of a WTO Climate Waiver," Centre for International Governance Innovation, CIGI Papers No. 204 (December 4, 2018), at www.cigionline.org/publications/content-wto-climate-waiver.

106 Kasturi Das, Harro van Asselt, Susanne Droege, and Michael Mehling, "Making the International Trade System Work for Climate Change: Assessing the Options" (London: Climate Strategies, July 2018), 8.

107 Article XX, General Agreement on Tariffs and Trade; Article 3.5, United Nations Framework Convention on Climate Change.

108 Carolyn Deere Birkbeck et al., "Governance to Support a Global Green Deal: 11 Ways to Align Global Economic Institutions with Climate Action in the Next 12–36 months," *Future of Climate Cooperation* (December 2020), at www/bsg.ox .ac.uk/research/research-projects/future-climate-cooperation.

109 *See* James Bacchus, "What Is a Climate Response Measure? Breaking the Trade Taboo in Confronting Climate Change," Centre for International Governance Innovation, CIGI Papers No. 220 (July 9, 2019), at www.cigionline.org/publica tions/what-climate-response-measure-breaking-trade-taboo-confronting-climate-change.

110 Articles 4.8 and 4.10, United Nations Framework Convention on Climate Change; Preamble and Article 4.15, Paris Agreement.

111 UNCTAD, "Tackling Trade in Trying Times" (December 19, 2018), at https:// unctad.org/en/pages/newsdetails.aspx?OriginalVersionID=1996.

112 Peter Govindsamy, "Economic Development and Climate Protection: Coloring, Texturing and Shading of Response Measures in Sustainable Development," *Chinese Journal of Urban and Environmental Studies*, Vol. 2, No. 2 (2015), 1–32, 5.

113 Ibid.

114 IPCC, Fifth Assessment Report, Working Group 3, IPCC WG III AR5 (December 13, 2013), chapter 13, "International Cooperation: Agreements and Instruments."

115 Annex 1, WTO Agreement on Subsidies and Countervailing Measures.

116 WTO, "The Impact of Trade Opening on Climate Change," at www.wto.org/ english/tratop_e/envir_e/climate_impact_e.htm.

117 Ibid.

118 Rikard Forslid, "Trade Transportation and the Environment," *VoxEU* (April 3, 2020), at https://voxeu.org/article/trade-transportation-and-environment.

119 Adrian Williams, "Comparative Study of Cut Roses for the British Market Produced in Kenya and the Netherlands," Précis Report for World Flowers, National Resources Institute, Cranfield University (February 12, 2007), at www .fairflowers.de/fileadmin/flp.de/Redaktion/Dokumente/Studien/Comparative_ Study_of_Cut_Roses_Feb_2007.pdf.

120 Rikard Forslid, "Trade Transportation and the Environment," *VoxEU* (April 3, 2020), at https://voxeu.org/article/trade-transportation-and-environment.

121 Anca D. Cristea, David Hummels, Laura Puzzello, and Misak G. Avetisyan, "Trade and the Greenhouse Gas Emissions from International Freight Transport," *Journal of Environmental Economics and Management*, Vol. 65, No. 1 (2013) 153–73, at www.nber.org/papers/w17117.

122 Joseph S. Shapiro, "Trade Costs, CO_2, and the Environment," *American Economic Journal: Economic Policy*, Vol. 8, No. 4 (2016), 220–254, 220, at https://pubs.aeaweb.org/doi/pdfplus/10.1257/pol.20150168.

123 Rikard Forslid, "Trade, Transportation and the Environment," CEPR Discussion Paper 14228 (2019), at https://cepr.org/active/publications/discussion_papers/dp .php?dpno=14228.

124 Ibid.

125 Ibid.

126 Jessica Green, "Why Do We Need New Rules on Shipping Emissions? Well, 90 Percent of Global Trade Depends on Ships," *Washington Post* (April 17,

2018), at www.washingtonpost.com/news/monkey-cage/wp/2018/04/17/why-do-we-need-new-rules-on-shipping-emissions-well-90-of-global-trade-depends-on-ships.

127 Jonathan Saul, "UN Approves Extra Steps to Curb Shipping Emissions," *Reuters* (November 17, 2020), at www.reuters.com/article/us-shipping-environment-imo/un-approves-extra-steps-to-curb-shipping-emissions-idUSKBN27X2JC.

128 Ibid.

129 International Convention for the Prevention of Pollution from Ships (MARPOL), 1340 U.N.T.S. 61; 12 I.L.M. 1319 (1973).

130 Fiona Harvey, "Campaigners Criticise Global Deal on Carbon Emissions from Shipping," *Guardian* (October 23, 2020), at www.theguardian.com/environment/2020/oct/23/green-groups-condemn-proposals-to-cut-shipping-emissions.

131 "Emissions Projected to Rise 50 Percent by 2050 in IMO Fourth GHG Study," *Maritime Executive* (August 5, 2020), at www.maritime-executive.com/article/emissions-projected-to-rise-50-percent-by-2050-in-imo-fourth-ghg-study.

132 ICAO, "Trends in Emissions that affect Climate Change," at www.icao.int/environmental-protection/Pages/ClimateChange_Trends.aspx.

133 Ibid.

134 Environmental Energy and Study Institute, "Fact Sheet: The Growth in Greenhouse Gas Emissions from Commercial Aviation" (October 17, 2019), at www.eesi.org/papers/view/fact-sheet-the-growth-in-greenhouse-gas-emissions-from-commercial-aviation#6.

135 Ibid.

136 Carbon Brief, "Corsia: The UN's Plan to 'Offset' Growth in Aviation Emissions" (February 4, 2019), at www.carbonbrief.org/corsia-un-plan-to-offset-growth-in-aviation-emissions-after-2020.

137 Environmental Defense Fund, "Forest Credits Approved for Airlines' Compliance with ICAO Carbon Market" (November 20, 2020), at www.edf.org/media/forest-credits-approved-airlines-compliance-icao-carbon-market.

138 Brandon Graver, "COVID-19's Big Impact on ICAO's CORSIA Baseline," International Council on Clean Transportation (May 26, 2020), at https://theicct.org/blog/staff/covid-19-impact-icao-corsia-baseline.

CHAPTER 7

1 Marianne Fay, Stephane Hallegatte, Adrien Vogt-Schilb, Julie Rozenberg, Ulf Narloch, and Tom Kerr, "Decarbonizing Development: Three Steps to a Zero-Carbon Future" (Washington, DC: World Bank Group, 2015), 2–3.

2 Ibid.

3 Christopher H. Trisos, Cory Merow, and Alex L. Pigot, "The Projected Timing of Abrupt Ecological Disruptions from Climate Change," *Nature* 580 (April 8, 2020), 496–501, at www.nature.co/articles/s41586-020-2189-9.

4 Carbon Brief, "Deep Emissions Cuts This Decade Could Prevent 'Abrupt Ecological Collapse,'" at https://carbonbrief.org/deep-emissions-cuts-this-decade-could-prevent-abrupt-ecological-collapse.

5 Ibid.

6 Gillian Tett, "Why We Need to Put a Number on Our Natural Resources," *Financial Times* (September 26, 2020).

7 "*Lancet* COVID-19 Commission Statement on the Occasion of the 75th Session of the UN General Assembly," at 4.

8 Preamble, Marrakesh Agreement Establishing the World Trade Organization.

9 Ibid.

10 Appellate Body Report, *United States – Import Prohibition of Certain Shrimp and Shrimp Products*, WT/DS58/AB/R (1998), para. 155.

11 Preamble, WTO Agreement.

12 To date, the closest the Committee on Trade and Environment has come to any such decision had been to make recommendations to the General Council of the WTO on what items should be on the committee's agenda.

13 Paragraph 51, Doha Declaration.

14 "Agreement on Climate Change, Trade and Sustainability (ACCTS) negotiations," at https://mfat.govt.nz/en/trade/free-trade-agreement/climate/agreement-on-climate-change-trade-and-sustainability-accts-negotiations.

15 Ronald Steenblik and Susanne Droege, "Time to ACCTS? Five Countries Announce New Initiative on Trade and Climate Change," International Institute for Sustainable Development (September 25, 2019), at www.iisd.org/articles/time-accts-five-countries-announce-new-initiative-trade-and-climate-change.

16 Christopher Barnard, "Opening Up Post-COVID-19 Free Trade to Save the Planet," *The Hill* (September 1, 2020).

17 Harro van Asselt, "Small Countries Punching above Their Weight: The New Initiative for an Agreement on Climate Change, Trade and Sustainability (ACCTS)," *Climate Diplomacy* (October 10, 2019).

18 *See* "The Silver Fox," in James Bacchus, *Trade and Freedom*, 89–98.

19 International Institute for Sustainable Development, "Trade and Environment Structured Discussions among WTO Member Group Get Underway" (March 10, 2021), at http://iisd.org/commentary/policy-briefs/trade-and-environment-structured-negotiations.

20 Ibid.

21 Ibid.

22 "Remarks from Ambassador Katherine Tai on Trade Policy, the Environment and Climate Change" (April 15, 2021), at https://ustr.gov/about-us/policy-offices/press-office/press-releases/2021/april/remarks-ambassador-katherine-tai-trade-policy-environment-and-climate-change.

23 UNEP, "Role of Multilateral Environmental Agreements (MEAs) in Achieving the Sustainable Development Goals (SDGs)" (2016), 8.

24 Paragraph 89, "The Future We Want," outcome document of the United Nations Conference on Sustainable Development, Rio de Janeiro, Brazil (June 20–22, 2012).

25 Anne-Titia Bove and Steven Swartz , "Starting at the Source: Sustainability in Supply Chains," McKinsey & Company (November 11, 2016), at www.mckinsey.com/business-functions/sustainability/our-insights/starting-at-the-source-sustainability-in-supply-chains.

26 Ibid.

27 Comprehensive Economic and Trade Agreement between Canada, of the One Part and the European Union and Its Member States, of the Other Part, O.J. (L 11) 23

(October 30, 2016) (hereinafter CETA), at https://ec.europa.eu/trade/policy/in-focus/ceta/ceta-chapter-by-chapter.

28   Article 24, CETA.

29   Article 22(2)(a) and (c), CETA.

30   UNCTAD, "Trade and the Sustainable Development Goals (SDGs), at https://unctad.org/topic/trade-analysis/trade-and-SDGs.

31   I owe this thought to a generous anonymous peer reviewer.

32   UNCTAD, "Developing Countries Face $2.5 Trillion Annual Investment Gap in Key Investment Sectors, UNCTAD report estimates" (June 24, 2014), at https://unctad.org/press-material/developing-countries-face-25-trillion-annual-investment-gap-key-sustainable.

33   International Chamber of Commerce, "ICC Calls for UN Action to Address Trade Finance Gap" (May 22, 2017), at https://iccwbo.org/media-wall/news-speeches/icc-calls-un-action-address-trade-finance-gap.

34   Michael Fahy, "World Bank and IMF Call for Debt Relief to Help Poorer Countries Fight Coronavirus" *The National News* (March 25, 2020), at www.thenationalnews.com/business/economy/world-bank-and-imf-call-for-debt-relief-to-help-poorer-countries-fight-coronavirus-1.997443.

35   Andrea Shalal, "New U.N. Study Shows 72 Nations and $598 Billion in Debt Payments at Risk through 2025," *Reuters* (April 1, 2021), at www.reuters.com/article/us-un-debt/new-un-study-shows-72-nations-and-598-billion-in-debt-payments-at-risk-through-2025-idUSKBN2BO612.

36   Somini Gentupta, "How Debt and Climate Change Pose 'Systemic Risk' to World Economy," *New York Times* (April 7, 2021).

37   Thanks are due also to the same anonymous peer reviewer for inspiring these observations.

38   Esther Woolfson, *Between Light and Storm: How We Live with Other Species* (London: Granta Books, 2020), 167.

39   Quoted in Martin Wolf, "Humanity Is a Cuckoo in the Planetary Nest," *Financial Times* (March 9, 2021); see "Final Report: The Economics of Biodiversity: The Dasgupta Review," HM Treasury (February 2, 2021) [updated April 23, 2021], at www.gov.uk/government/publications/final-report-the-economics-of-biodiversity-the-dasgupta-review.

40   WWF, "Living Planet Report 2020: Bending the Curve of Biodiversity Loss" (Gland, Switzerland: WWF, 2020), 12.

41   Patrick Greenfield, "All Eyes on China: What to Look for at the UN Biodiversity Summit," Guardian (September 29, 2020).

42   Sam Anderson, "The Last Two Northern White Rhinos on Earth," *New York Times* (January 10, 2021).

43   WWF, "Living Planet Report 2020," at 16.

44   Brian Benza, "Botswana Says Toxins in Water Killed Hundreds of Elephants," *Reuters* (September 21, 2020), at www.reuters.com/article/us-bostwana-elephants/botswana-says-toxins-in-water-killed-hundreds-of-elephants.

45   Harry Cockburn, "Biodiversity Crisis: Insect Numbers Collapse by 25 Per Cent around the World since 1990," *Independent* (April 24, 2020), at www.independent.co.uk/environment/insects-numbers-collapse-biodiversity-crisis-extinction-pollination-climate-change-a9482416.html.

46 Elizabeth Kolbert, "Where Have All the Insects Gone?" *National Geographic* (April 23, 2020), at www.nationalgeographic.com/magazine/2020/05/where-have-all-the-insects-gone-feature.

47 IPBES, "Summary for Policymakers of the Global Assessment Report on Biodiversity and Ecosystem Services of the Intergovernmental Science-Policy Platform on Biodiversity and Ecosystem Services" (May 6, 2019), 3.

48 Ibid. at 4.

49 WWF, "Living Planet Report 2020," at 7.

50 Global Environment Facility, "The Complexities and Imperatives of Building Back Better," white paper on a GEF COVID-19 Response Strategy, GEF/C.59/Inf.14 (November 17, 2020), at www.thegef.org/sites/default/files/council-meeting-docu ments/EN_GEF_C.59_Inf.14_White%20Paper%20on%20a%20GEF%20COVID-19%20Response%20Strategy.pdf.

51 Jane Dalton, "Halt the Climate and Nature-Loss Crises to Prevent More Pandemics, Scientists Tell World Leaders," *Independent* (October 29, 2020).

52 IPBES, "IPBES Workshop on Biodiversity and Pandemics: Executive Summary," at 7.

53 Ibid.

54 Ibid. at 6; *see also* Matthew Green, "Protect Nature or Face Deadlier Pandemics Than COVID-19, Scientists Warn," *Reuters* (October 29, 2020).

55 IPBES, "IPBES Workshop on Biodiversity and Pandemics: Executive Summary," at 5.

56 Ibid. at 8.

57 *See, e.g.*, Leena Vikka, *The Intrinsic Value of Nature* (Amsterdam: Rodopi Press, 1997).

58 Donald Worster, "The Intrinsic Value of Nature," *Environmental Review*, Vol. 4, No. 1 (1980), 43–49, 45, 46.

59 Ibid. at 46.

60 IPBES, "Nature's Dangerous Decline: 'Unprecedented' Species Extinction Rates 'Accelerating'" (May 9, 2019), at www.ipbes.net/news/Media-Release-Global-Assessment.

61 IPBES, "Summary for Policymakers," at 7. *See also* Brad Plumer, "Humans Are Speeding Extinction and Altering the Natural World at an 'Unprecedented' Pace," *New York Times* (May 6, 2019).

62 Ibid.

63 *See* Roderick Frazier Nash, *The Rights of Nature: A History of Environmental Ethics* (Madison: University of Wisconsin Press, 1989), 9–10.

64 Henry David Thoreau, *The Writings of Henry Thoreau* (Boston: Bradford Torrey, 1906), Vol. 3, No. 165, and Vol. 11, 450.

65 Bruno Vander Velde, "What on Earth Is 'Natural Capital'?" Conservational International (July 13, 2016), at www.conservation.org/blog/what-on-earth-is-nat ural-capital?gclid=CjwKCAiAnvj9BRA4EiwAuUMDf6700Eys5Tc_cG1Zcp6xbd5 pStsynRrJWT9lWxYUNiZB5x9Cg2f8cxoCCRkQAvD_BwE.

66 Geoffrey Heal, *Endangered Economies: How the Neglect of Nature Threatens Our Prosperity* (New York: Columbia University Press, 2017), 129.

67 Ibid.

68 Ibid.

69 Press Release, "A Fifth of Countries Worldwide at Risk from Ecosystem Collapse as Biodiversity Declines, Reveals Pioneering Swiss Re Index," Swiss Re (September 23, 2020).

70 Damian Carrington, "Fifth of Countries at Risk of Ecosystem Collapse, Analysis Finds," *Guardian* (October 12, 2020).

71 Press Release, "A Fifth of Companies Worldwide at Risk from Ecosystem Collapse as Biodiversity Declines, Reveals Pioneering Swiss Re Index," at www.swissre.com/media/news-releases/nr-20200923-biodiversity-and-ecosystems-services.html.

72 World Bank, "The Economic Case for Nature: A Global Earth-Economy Model to Assess Development Policy Pathways" (Washington, DC: World Bank, 2021), at vi.

73 Ibid.

74 Corey J. A. Bradshaw et al., "Underestimating the Challenges of Avoiding a Ghastly Future," *Frontiers in Conservation Science*, Vol. 1 (January 13, 2021), at www.frontiersin.org/articles/10.3389/fcosc.2020.615419/full.

75 Patrick Greenfield, "World Fails to Meet a Single Target to Stop Destruction of Nature – UN Report," *Guardian* (September 15, 2020).

76 "A Place for Nature at the High-Level Political Forum," International Institute for Sustainable Development (July 9, 2020), at https://sdg.iisd.org/commentary/guest-articles/a-place-for-nature-at-the-high-level-political-forum.

77 United Nations Environment Programme and Convention on Biological Diversity, "Global Biodiversity Outlook 5: Summary for Policymakers" (September 2020), 3.

78 "A Place for Nature at the High-Level Political Forum."

79 Kanupriya Kapoor and Kate Abnett, "UN Biodiversity Summit to Be Delayed for Third Time – Sources," *Reuters* (July 28, 2021).

80 Ibid.

81 Convention on Biological Diversity, "Zero Draft of the Post-2020 Global Biodiversity Framework," CBD/WG2020/23 (January 6, 2020), II.A.9.

82 Ibid. at II.B.10.

83 Ibid.

84 Ibid. at I.B.4.

85 William J. Snape III, "Joining the Convention on Biological Diversity: A Legal and Scientific Overview of Why the United States Must Wake Up," *Sustainable Development Law & Policy* (Spring 2010), 6–16, 44–47.

86 Erik Stokstad, "Protect Species? Curb Warming? Save Money? Biden's Big Conservation Goals Mean Trade-Offs," *Science* (February 2, 2021), at www.sciencemag.org/news/2021/02/protect-species-curb-warming-save-money-biden-s-big-conservation-goal-means-trade-offs.

87 Goal 9, "Transforming Our World."

88 For a more extensive analysis of the issue of environmental goods and services, *see* James Bacchus and Inu Manak, "Free Trade in Environmental Goods Will Increase Access to Green Tech," Cato Institute, Free Trade Bulletin Number 80 (June 8, 2021).

89 Paragraph 31(iii), Doha Declaration.

90 WTO, "Environmental Goods Agreement (EGA)," at www.wto.org/english/tratop_e/envir_e/ega_arc_e.htm.

91 APEC, "The APEC List of Environmental Goods," APEC Secretariat (November 2012), at https://apec.org/Publications/2012/11/The-APEC-List-of-Environmental-Goods.

92 OECD Joint Working Party on Trade and Environment, "The Stringency of Environmental Regulations and Trade in Environmental Goods (November 19, 2014), Annex 1, 51.

93 This was the suggestion of the National Association of Manufacturers in the United States. *See* Matt Roessing, "Greed Is (an Environmental) Good" (June 27, 2014, at https://roessinglawblog.com/2014/06/27/greed-is-an-environmental-good.

94 "Environmental Goods Agreement – Why Talks Faltered," *Borderlex* (December 6, 2016), at www.borderlex.eu/2016/12/06/environmental-goods-agreement-talks-faltered.

95 Maureen Hinman, "Green Goods Market Access Is Key to Biden's Build Back Better Agenda" (March 11, 2021), at www.wita.org/blogs/green-goods-market-access.

96 Ibid.

97 Ibid.

98 *See* James Bacchus, "Good News for Green Goods," World Economic Forum (February 3, 2014).

99 "Joint Statement regarding Trade in Environmental Goods" (January 24, 2014), at https://kr.usembassy.gov/p_econ_012414b.

100 WTO, "Information Technology Agreement," at www.wto.org/english/tratop_e/inftec_e.htm.

101 Mark Wu, "Why Developing Countries Won't Negotiate: The Case of the WTO Environmental Goods Agreement," *Trade, Law & Development*, Vol. 6, No. 1 (2014), 93–176, 94.

102 WTO, "Environmental Goods Agreement (EGA)," at www.wto.org/english/tratop_e/envir_e/ega_e.htm.

103 For more details, *see* James Bacchus, "Ending Tariffs on Green Goods Will Show Free Trade Can Fight Climate Change," *Guardian* (August 12, 2014).

104 Aaron Cosbey, Soledad Aguilar, Melanie Ashton, and Stefano Porte, "Environmental Goods and Services Negotiations at the WTO: Lessons from the Multilateral Environmental Agreements and Ecolabels for Breaking the Impasse," International Institute for Sustainable Development (March 2010), 57.

105 Tim Worstall, "How Excellent, WTO Talks on Environmental Goods Agreement Collapses," *Forbes* (December 4, 2016), at https://forbes.com/sites/timworstall/2016/12/04/how-excellent-wto-talks-on-environmental-goods-agreement-collapse.

106 *See*, in part for a slightly different view, Bernhard Potter, "TTIP in Green: Free Trade for Ostensibly Eco-Goods," *Green European Journal* (June 24, 2016).

107 "We Can Do Right by the Planet and the Economy," American Leadership Initiative, at www.american-leadership.org/issues/we-can-do-right-by-the-planet-and-the-economy.

108 Goal 14, "Transforming Our World."

109 "Draft Text of an Agreement under the United Nations Convention on the Law of the Sea on the Conservation and Sustainable Use of Marine Biological Diversity of Areas beyond National Jurisdiction," A/CONF.232/2019/6 (May 17, 2019).

110 WWF, "Living Planet Report 2020," at 70.

111 Un, "Global Biodiversity Outlook 5," at 156.

112 *See* James Bacchus and Inu Manak, "The Fate of the WTO and Global Trade Hangs on Fish," *Foreign Policy* (May 5, 2020), at https://foreignpolicy.com/2020/05/05/wto-global-trade-fisheries-fishing-subsidies.

113 Ministerial Declaration, Ministerial Conference, Fourth Session, Doha, Qatar, November 9–14, 2001, WT/MIN(01)DEC/1.

114 Target 14.6, "Transforming Our World."

115 "Paper from Brazil, Chile, Colombia, Ecuador, Iceland, New Zealand, Pakistan, Peru and the United States to the Negotiating Group on Rules, Fisheries Subsidies," TN/RL/W/196 November 22, 2005).

116 USTR, "2017 Trade Policy Agenda and 2016 Annual Report" (March 2017), 5.

117 U. Rashid Sumaila, "Trade Policy Options for Sustainable Oceans and Fisheries," at 6. *See generally* "Fish to 2030: Prospects for Fisheries and Aquaculture," World Bank Report 83177-GLB (Washington, DC: World Bank, 2013), at https://openknowledge.worldbank.org/handle/10986/17579.

118 Ibid.

119 "Ocean Fishing: All the Fish in the Sea," *Economist* (May 27, 2017).

120 Editorial, "The Marine World: Deep Trouble," *Economist* (May 27, 2017).

121 U. Rashid Sumaila, "Trade Policy Options for Sustainable Oceans and Fisheries," at 10.

122 FAO, "The State of World Fisheries and Aquaculture 2020: Sustainability in Action" (2020), 13.

123 Ibid.

124 Ibid.

125 Christopher Costello et al., "Global Fishery Prospects under Contrasting Management Regimes," Proceedings of the National Academy of Sciences (March 29, 2016).; *see also* Editorial, "How to Save the World's Fisheries," *Washington Post* (March 29, 2016).

126 FAO, "The State of World Fisheries and Aquaculture 2020," at 16.

127 Ibid. at 18.

128 Ibid. at 17.

129 Ibid. at 18.

130 Ibid. at 17.

131 Ibid.

132 Ibid.

133 Ibid. at 18.

134 Elizabeth Wilson, "Fishing Subsidies Are Speeding the Decline of Ocean Health" (July 19, 2018), at www.pewtrusts.org/en/research-and-analysis/article/2018/07/19/fishing-subsidies-are-speeding-the-decline-of-ocean-health.

135 Basak Bayramoglu, Brian Copeland, Marco Fuguzza, and Jean-Francois Jacques, "Trade and Negotiations on Fisheries Subsidies" (October 21, 2019), at https://voxeu.org/article/trade-and-negotiations-fisheries-subsidies.

136 Isabel Jarrett, "Fisheries Subsidies Reform Could Reduce Overfishing and Illegal Fishing Case Studies Find," Pew Charitable Trusts (July 22, 2020), at www.pewtrusts.org/en/research-and-analysis/articles/2020/07/22/fisheries-subsidies-reform-could-reduce-overfishing-and-illegal-fishing-case-studies-find.

137 U. Rashid Sumaila et al., "A Global Dataset on Subsidies to the Fisheries Sector," *Marine Policy*, Vol. 109 (November 19, 2019), 103695–104706.

138 U. Rashid Sumaila, "Trade Policy Options for Sustainable Oceans and Fisheries," at 6.

139 Global Ocean Commission, "The Future of Our Ocean: Next Steps and Priorities. Report 2016," 7, 23.

140 Ibid.

141 OECD, "Fisheries, Aquaculture and COVID-19: Issues and Policy Responses" (June 4, 2020), 1.

142 U. Rashid Sumaila, "Trade Policy Options for Sustainable Oceans and Fisheries," at 13.

143 FAO, "Small-Scale Fisheries," at www.fao.org/fishery/fishcode-stf/activities/ssf/en.

144 Target 14.b, "Transforming Our World."

145 Bryce Baschuk, "A Once-Promising Global Deal to Prevent Overfishing Runs Aground," *Bloomberg* (December 9, 2020).

146 Ian Urbina, "How China's Expanding Fishing Fleet Is Depleting the World's Oceans," Yale Environment 360 (August 17, 2020), at https://e360.yale.edu/fea tures/how-chinas-expanding-fishing-fleet-is-depleting-worlds-oceans.

147 Ibid.

148 Isabel Jarrett, "Fisheries Subsidies Reform Could Reduce Overfishing and Illegal Fishing Case Studies Find."

149 Ibid.

150 Ricardo Melendez-Ortiz, "Additionality, Innovation and Systemic Implications of Environment, Fisheries and Labour in TPP: A Preliminary Review," (March 2016) (unpublished paper in possession of the author), 3.

151 Article 20.16 (5), Comprehensive and Progressive Agreement for Trans-Pacific Partnership.

152 Ricardo Melendez-Ortiz, "Additionality, Innovation and System Implications of Environment, Fisheries and Labour in TPP: A Preliminary Review," at 4.

153 *See* Article 3 and Article 6, WTO Agreement on Subsidies and Countervailing Measures.

154 Fermin Koop, "WTO Inches Closer to Agreement on Harmful Fishing Subsidies," *China Dialogue Ocean* (July 27, 2021), at https://chinadialogueocean.net/18033-wto-inches-closer-to-agreement-on-harmful-fishing-subsidies.

155 Sarah Anne Aarup, "EU Aims to Slice Up Global Fish Rules in Its Favor," *Politico* (August 3, 2021).

156 Ibid.

157 United Nations, "The Sustainable Development Goals Report 2020," 53, at https://unstats.un.org/sdgs/report/2020.

158 Gilles Hosch, "Trade Measures to Combat IUU Fishing: Comparative Analysis of Unilateral and Multilateral Approaches," International Centre for Trade and Sustainable Development (2016), 3.

159 FAO, "Agreement on Port State Measures (PSMS): Background," at www.fao.org/port-state-measures/background/en.

160 For more on IUU fishing, *see* James Bacchus, *The Willing World*, at 326–328.

161 "Remarks from Ambassador Katherine Tai on Trade Policy, the Environment and Climate Change" (April 15, 2021), at https://ustr.gov/about-us/policy-offices/press-office/press-releases/2021/april/remarks-ambassador-katherine-tai-trade-policy-environment-and-climate-change.

162 Sabrina Shankman, Georgina Custin, and John H. Cushman, Jr., "Humanity Faces a Biodiversity Crisis. Climate Change Makes It Worse," *Climate Change News* (May 6, 2019), at https://insideclimatenews.org/news/05052019/climate-change-biodiversity-united-nations-species-extinction-agriculture-food-forests.

163 IPBES, "Summary for Policymakers of the Global Assessment Report on Biodiversity and Ecosystem Services of the Intergovernmental Science-Policy Platform on Biodiversity and Ecosystem Services," at B2.

164 United Nations Environment Programme and Stockholm Environment Institute, "The Production Gap: 2020 Report."

165 Ibid. at 2.

166 Ibid.

167 IMF, "Mitigating Climate Change – Growth- and Distribution-Friendly Strategies," World Economic Outlook (October 2020), 87.

168 Ibid.

169 Ibid.

170 For an excellent overview, *see* Cleo Verkuijl, Harro Van Asselt, Tom Moerenhout, Liesbeth Casier, and Peter Wooders, "Tackling Fossil Fuel Subsidies Through International Trade Agreements: Taking Stock, Looking Forward," *Virginia Journal of International Law*, Vol. 58 (2019), 309–368, 316–317.

171 International Energy Agency, "World Energy Outlook 2018" (2018), 55. These are 2017 numbers.

172 OECD, "OECD Companion to the Inventory of Support Measures for Fossil Fuels 2018" (2018), 3. These are 2017 numbers.

173 David Coady, Ian Parry, Louis Sears, and Baoping Shang, "How Large Are Global Energy Subsidies?" International Monetary Fund, Working Paper No. 15/2015 (2015), 17. These are 2015 numbers.

174 Ibid.

175 "Global Gross Domestic Product (GDP) at Current Prices from 1985 to 2026," Statista, at www.statista.com/statistics/268750/global-gross-domestic-product-gdp.

176 Jessica Jewell et al., "Limited Emissions Reductions from Fossil Fuel Subsidy Removal Expected in Energy Exporting Countries," *Nature*, Vol. 554 (February 8, 2018), 229–230, at www.nature.com/articles/nature25467.

177 Valeria Jane Schwanitz, Franziska Piontek, Christoph Bertram, and Gunnar Luderer, "Long-Term Climate Policy Implications of Phasing Out Fossil Fuel Subsidies," *Energy Policy*, Vol. 67 (April 2014), 882–894, at www.sciencedirect.com/science/article/abs/pii/S0301421513012597.

178 Submission by Switzerland, Costa Rica, Finland, New Zealand and Sweden, supported by Monaco, "Talanoa Dialogue – How Do We Get There? Fossil Fuel Subsidy Reform," (emphasis in original) at http://fffsr.org/statements. The countries are Costa Rica, Denmark, Ethiopia, Finland, New Zealand, Norway, Sweden, Switzerland, and Uruguay.

179 Target 12.c, "Transforming Our World."

180 Ibid.

181 WTO Agreement on Subsidies and Countervailing Measures.

182 *See generally* Joanna I. Lewis, "The Rise of Renewable Energy Protectionism: Emerging Trade Conflicts and Implications for Low Carbon Development," *Global Environmental Politics*, Vol. 14, No. 4 (November 2014), 10–35.

183 See Gary Clyde Hufbauer et al., "Local Content Requirements: A Global Problem," in *Policy Analyses in International Economics* (Washington, DC: Peterson Institute of International Economics, 2013).

184 "Fossil Fuel Subsidies Reform Ministerial Statement," WT/MIN(17)/54 (December 12, 2017). The statement was made by Chile, Costa Rica, Iceland, Liechtenstein, Mexico, Moldova, New Zealand, Norway, Samoa, Switzerland, the Separate Customs Territory of Taiwan, Penghu, Kinmen and Matsu, and Uruguay.

185 Ibid.

186 Ronald Steenblik, Jehan Sauvage, and Christina Timiliotis, "Fossil Fuel Subsidies and the Global Trade Regime," in Jakob Skovgaard and Harro van Asselt, eds., *The Politics of Fossil Fuel Subsidies and Their Reform* (Cambridge: Cambridge University Press, 2018), 121–139, 132.

187 Article 25, WTO Agreement on Subsidies and Countervailing Measures. There are widespread concerns among WTO members about the failure of many WTO members to comply with the notification obligations in Article 25.

188 Article 25.1, WTO Agreement on Subsidies and Countervailing Measures.

189 Cleo Verkuijl et al., "Tackling Fossil Fuel Subsidies through International Trade Agreements," at 357.

190 *See* my previous advocacy with others of this reform in James Bacchus, "Global Rules for Mutually Supportive and Reinforcing Trade and Climate Regimes," E15 Initiative (Geneva: World Economic Forum and International Centre for Trade and Sustainable Development, 2016) and in James Bacchus, "Triggering the Trade Transition: The G20's Role in Reconciling Rules for Trade and Climate Change" (Geneva: World Economic Forum and International Centre for Trade and Sustainable Development, February 2018).

191 Article 3, WTO Agreement on Subsidies and Countervailing Measures.

192 Article 2, WTO Agreement on Subsidies and Countervailing Measures.

193 Article 5, WTO Agreement on Subsidies and Countervailing Measures.

194 Goal 7, "Transforming Our World."

195 Ibid.

196 These estimates by the International Finance Corporation were for 2012. Hari Manoharan and Madhavan Nampoothiri, "Using Trade Policy to Address Renewable Energy Access Challenges in Africa," *BioRes* Vol. 8, No. 5 (June 2014), 16.

197 Hannah Richie and Max Roser, "Fossil Fuels," at https://ourworldindata.org/fossil-fuels.

198 Goal 13, "Transforming Our World."

199 Anna Zinecker, "How Fossil Fuel Subsidy Reform Could Get Us on Target towards Universal Energy Access," International Institute for Sustainable Development (July 30, 2018).

200 David Coady, Valentini Flamini, and Louis Sears, "The Unequal Benefits of Fuel Subsidies Revisited: Evidence for Developing Countries," International Monetary Fund, WP/15/250 (November 25, 2015).

201 Ibid. at 1.

202 Anna Zinecker, "How Fossil Fuel Subsidy Reform Could Get Us on Target towards Universal Energy Access."

203 Ibid. at 15.

204 "Fossil Fuel Subsidies Reform Ministerial Statement."

205 Cleo Verkuijl et al., "Tackling Fossil Fuel Subsidies through International Trade Agreements," at 355.

206 Ricardo Melendez-Ortiz, "Enabling the Energy Transition and Scale-Up of Clean Energy Technologies: Options for the Global Trade System," E15 Initiative, E15 Expert Group on Clean Energy Technologies and the Trade System, Policy Options Paper (Geneva: World Economic Forum and International Centre for Trade and Sustainable Development, January 2016), 5.

207 Rafael Leal-Arcas, *Solutions for Sustainability: How the International Trade, Energy and Climate Change Regimes Can Help*, European Yearbook of International Economic Law (Cham: Springer, 2019), 66.

208 Article 8, WTO Agreement on Subsidies and Countervailing Measures.

209 Adam Smith, *The Wealth of Nations*, book four, chapter 5 [1776].

210 Michael Trebilcock and James S. F. Wilson, "Policy Analysis: The Perils of Picking Technological Winners in Renewable Energy Policy," *Energy Probe* (February 28, 2010).

211 For more on this distinction, *see* James Bacchus, *The Willing World*, at 262–264; *see also* Michael Trebilcock and James S. F. Wilson, "Policy Analysis: The Perils of Picking Technological Winners in Renewable Energy Policy," *Energy Probe* (February 28, 2010).

212 Article 3.1(b), WTO Agreement on Subsidies and Countervailing Measures.

213 Gary Hufbauer, Jeffrey Schott, Cathleen Cimino-Isaacs, Martin Vieiro, and Erika Wanda, *Local Content Requirements: A Global Problem*, Peterson Institute for International Economics (September 2013), at www.piie.com/bookstore/local-content-requirements-global-problem.

214 Robert Howse, "Securing Policy Space for Clean Energy Under the SCM Agreement: Alternative Approaches," E15 Initiative, E15 Expert Group on Clean Energy Technologies and the Trade System (Geneva: World Economic Forum and International Centre for Trade and Sustainable Development, December 2013), 1.

215 *See* Felicity Deane, *Emissions Trading and WTO Law: A Global Analysis* (Cheltenham: Edward Elgar, 2015), 171–173.

216 Peter Voser, foreword, "Energy for Economic Growth" (Geneva: World Economic Forum, 2012), 2.

217 Rafael Leal-Arcas and Andre Filis, "The Fragmented Governance of the Global Energy Economy," *Journal of World Energy Law & Business* (July 19, 2013), 2, 4.

218 For a longer discussion of my thoughts on the possible contents of a WTO sustainable energy trade agreement, *see* James Bacchus, *The Willing World*, at 257–270.

CHAPTER 8

1 Clare Fieseler, "Chinese National Detained in $2.2 Million Global Turtle Smuggling Scheme," *Washington Post* (December 12, 2020).

2 Nicholas Kristof, "The Mistakes That Will Haunt Our Legacy," *New York Times* (July 11, 2020).

3 Ibid.

4 This is Donald Worster's summary of Darwin's view, in Donald Worster, "The Intrinsic Value of Nature," at 47.

5 Ibid.; *see* Charles Darwin, *The Origin of Species and The Descent of Man* (New York: Modern Library, 1936), 493 [1859 and 1871]; Charles Darwin, *Life and*

Letters of Charles Darwin (New York: D. Appleton and Company 1887), Vol. I, 368, Vol. II, 378–380.

6 Ingrid J. Visseren-Hamakers, "The 18th Sustainable Development Goal," *Earth System Governance*, at www.doi.org/10.1016/j.esg.2020.100047.

7 Ibid.

8 Michael P. Murtaugh, Clifford J. Steer, Srinand Sreevatsan, Ned Patterson, Shaun Kennedy, and P. Sriramarao, "The Science behind One Health: At the Interface of Humans, Animals, and the Environment," *Annals of the New York Academy of Sciences*, Vol. 1395, No. 1 (May 5, 2017), at https://nyaspubs.onlinelibrary.wiley .com/doi/abs/10.1111/nyas.13355.

9 Ibid.

10 Ibid.

11 Paragraph 9, "Transforming Our World."

12 Target 15.7, "Transforming Our World."

13 Target 15.c, "Transforming Our World."

14 IPBES, "IPBES Workshop on Biodiversity and Pandemics: Executive Summary," at 7.

15 Ibid.

16 Ibid.

17 Tanya Rosen, "The Evolving War on Illegal Wildlife Trade," International Institute for Sustainable Development (October 2020), 2.

18 Earth Negotiations Bulletin, "Summary of the Sixteenth Meeting of the Conference of Parties to the Convention on International Trade in Endangered Species of Wild Fauna and Flora" (March 3–14, 2013), at https://enb.iisd.org/vol21/enb2183e .html.

19 Stewart M. Patrick, "To Prevent Pandemics and Protect Biodiversity, Combat Wildlife Crime," *World Politics Review* (January 25, 2021), at www .worldpoliticsreview.com/articles/29374/to-prevent-pandemics-and-protect-bio diversity-combat-wildlife-crime.

20 Benoit Blarel, "The Real Costs of Illegal Logging, Fishing and Wildlife Trade: $1 Trillion–$2 Trillion Per Year," World Bank Blogs (October 29, 2019), at https:// blogs.worldbank.org/voices/real-costs-illegal-logging-fishing-and-wildlife-trade-1- trillion-2-trillion-year.

21 *See* https://enb.iisd.org/vol21/enb2183e.html.

22 Andrew O. Dobson et al., "Ecology and Economics for Pandemic Prevention," *Science*, Vol. 369, No. 6502 (July 24, 2020), 379–381, 379, at https://science .sciencemag.org/content/369/6502/379.

23 Ibid.

24 United Nations Office on Drugs and Crime, "World Wildlife Crime Report: Trafficking in Protected Species" (Vienna: UNODC, 2020), 9, at www.unodc.org/ unodc/en/data-and-analysis/wildlife.html.

25 Tanya Rosen, "The Evolving War on Illegal Wildlife Trade," at 2.

26 John E. Scanlon, "Do We Need a Wildlife Crime Convention?" The Planetary Press (February 2019), at www.theplanetarypress.com/2019/02/do-we-need-a-wildlife- crime-convention.

27 Convention on International Trade in Endangered Species of Wild Fauna and Flora, 27 U.S.T. 1087, 993 U.N.T.S. 243, 12 I.L.M. 1085 (1973).

28 John E. Scanlon, "Do We Need a Wildlife Crime Convention?"
29 *See* CITES and the WTO, "CITES and the WTO: Enhancing Cooperation for Sustainable Development" (Geneva: CITES and WTO, 2015).
30 Ibid.
31 Ibid.
32 *See* www.oie.int.
33 Ibid.
34 Ibid.
35 OIE, "Fourth OIE Global Conference on Animal Welfare: Recommendations," Guadalajara, Mexico (December 6–8, 2016).
36 *See* www.fao.org/fao-who-codexalimentarius/en.
37 FAO, "Gateway to Farm Welfare," at www.fao.org/ag/againfo/themes/animal-welfare/aw-awhome/en/?no_cache=1.
38 John E. Scanlon, "Do We Need a Wildlife Crime Convention?"
39 John E. Scanlon, "The Imperative of Ending Wildlife Crime," International Institute for Sustainable Development (March 24, 2020), at https://sdg.iisd.org/commentary/guest-articles/the-imperative-of-ending-wildlife-crime.
40 Ibid.
41 John E. Scanlon, "Do We Need a Wildlife Crime Convention?"
42 Articles 2.1, 2.2, and 2.3, WTO Agreement on the Application of Sanitary and Phytosanitary Measures.
43 Article 3.1, WTO Agreement on the Application of Sanitary and Phytosanitary Measures.
44 Article 3.2, WTO Agreement on the Application of Sanitary and Phytosanitary Measures.
45 Article 3.3, WTO Agreement on the Application of Sanitary and Phytosanitary Measures.
46 Article 3.4, WTO Agreement on the Application of Sanitary and Phytosanitary Measures.
47 Article 2.2, WTO Agreement on Technical Barriers to Trade.
48 Article 2.1, WTO Agreement on Technical Barriers to Trade.
49 Article 2.2, WTO Agreement on Technical Barriers to Trade.
50 Ibid.
51 Article 2.4, WTO Agreement on Technical Barriers to Trade.
52 Article XX(b), General Agreement on Tariffs and Trade.
53 Appellate Body Report, *United States – Import Prohibition of Certain Shrimp and Shrimp Products*, AB/R, WT/DS58 (1998).
54 Appellate Body Report, *European Communities – Measures Prohibiting the Importation and Marketing of Seal Products*, AB/R, WT/DS400 and WT/DS/401 (2014).
55 Appellate Body Report, *United States – Measures concerning the Importation, Marketing and Sale of Tuna and Tuna Products – Recourse to Article 21.5 of the DSU*, AB/R, WT/DS381 (2015).
56 OIE, "OIE Considerations on the Application of Sanitary Measures for International Trade Related to Covid-19" (May 26, 2020), at www.oie.int/Home/eng/docs/pdf/COV-19.
57 Jonathan Kolby, "To Prevent the Next Pandemic, It's the Legal Wildlife Trade We Should Worry About," *National Geographic* (May 7, 2020), at www

.nationalgeographic.com/animals/2020/05/to-prevent-next-pandemic-focus-on-legal-wildlife-trade.

58 OIC, "What Is Animal Welfare?" at www.oie.int/en/animal-welfare/animal-wel fare-at-a-glance.

59 *See*, for an overview, Andrew Lurie, "Protecting Animals in International Trade: A Study of the Recent Success at the WTO and in Free Trade Agreements," *American University International Law Review*, Vol. 30, No. 3 (2015), 432–487.

60 Rene Descartes, "Animals as Machines," at https://webs.wofford.edu/williamsnm/ back%20up%20jan%204/hum%20101/animals%20are%20machines%20descartes.pdf; *see also* Peter Harrison, "Descartes on Animals," *The Philosophical Quarterly*, Vol. 42, No. 167 (April 1992), 219–227.

61 *See* "The Cambridge Declaration on Consciousness" (July 7, 2012), at https://en.wikipedia.org/wiki/Animal_consciousness#Cambridge_Declaration_on_ Consciousness.

62 Ross Kelly, "Recognition of Animal Sentience on the Rise," VIN News Service (May 14, 2020), at https://news.vin.com/default.aspx?pid=210&Id=9639465.

63 *See* Charlotte E. Blattner, "The Recognition of Animal Sentience by the Law," *Journal of Animal Ethics*, Vol. 9, No. 2 (Fall 2019), 121–136; *see also* Grace Hudson, "Animal Sentience Within the Law – An International Perspective" (June 2019), at www.alaw.org.uk/2019/06/animal-sentience-within-the-law-an-inter national-perspective-by-grace-hudson.

64 UNEP, "Healthy Planet Healthy People," Global Environment Outlook 6 (Cambridge: Cambridge University Press, 2019), 4.

65 Christina Nunez, "Deforestation Explained," *National Geographic* (February 7, 2019), at www.nationalgeographic.com/environment/global-warming/deforest ation/#close.

66 FAO, "The State of the World's Forests 2020: Forests, Biodiversity and People" (Rome: FAO and UNEP, 2020), 13, at www.fao.org/3/ca8642en/CA8642EN.pdf.

67 Matt McGrath, "Deforestation: Tropical Tree Losses Persist at High Levels," *BBC News* (April 25, 2019), at www.bbc.com/news/science-environment-48037913.

68 Gregory P. Asner, "Measuring Carbon Emissions from Tropical Deforestation: An Overview," Environmental Defense Fund (2019), at https://edf.org/sites/default/files/ 10333_Measuring_Carbon_Emissions_from_Tropical_Deforestation–An_Overview .pdf.

69 Report of the UN Conference on Environment and Development, Rio de Janeiro, June 3–14, 1992, Annex III: Non-legally Binding Authoritative Statement of Principles for a Global Consensus on the Management, Conservation and Sustainable Development of all Types of Forests, UN Doc. A/CONF.151.26 (Vol. III), August 14, 1992 (commonly, the "Forest Principles").

70 Anja Eikermann, *Forests in International Law: Is There Really a Need for an International Forest Convention?* (London: Springer, 2015), 63–66.

71 Goal 1, New York Declaration on Forests (September 2014), section 1, at www.un.org/climatechange/summit/wp-content/upload/sites/2/2014/07/New-York-Declaration-on-Forests-Action-Statement-and-Action-Plan.pdf.

72 Target 15.1, "Transforming Our World."

73 FAO, "State of the World's Forests 2020," at xvi.

74 Andrew B. Dobson et al., "Ecology and Economics for Pandemic Prevention," at 379.

75 Ibid.

76 Editorial, "Stopping Deforestation Can Prevent Pandemics," *Scientific American* (June 2020), at www.scientificamerican.com/article/stopping-deforestation-can-pre vent-pandemics1.

77 Anna Gross, Andrea Schipani, Stefania Palma, and Stephanie Findlay, "Global Deforestation Accelerates during Pandemic," *Financial Times* (August 9, 2020).

78 Henry Fountain, "Tropical Forest Destruction Accelerated in 2020," *New York Times* (March 31, 2021).

79 Global Environment Facility, "The Complexities of Building Back Better," at 22.

80 Ibid.

81 Ibid.

82 Damian Carrington, "Climate Crisis Making World's Forests Shorter and Younger, Study Finds," *Guardian* (May 28, 2020).

83 Anna Jean Kaiser, "AP Explains: Role of the Amazon in Global Climate Change," *Associated Press* (August 27, 2019).

84 Robert McSweeney, "Amazon Rainforest Is Taking Up a Third Less Carbon Than a Decade Ago," *Plants and Forests* (March 18, 2015), at www.carbonbrief.org/ amazon-rainforest-is-taking-up-a-third-less-carbon-than-a-decade-ago.

85 "The Amazon Is Approaching an Irreversible Tipping Point," *Economist* (August 1, 2019).

86 "Amazon Biome Hurtles toward Death Spiral as Deforestation Jumps in 2020," *Reuters* (January 28, 2021).

87 Ibid.

88 European Union, "How Can International Trade Contribute to Sustainable Forestry and the Preservation of the World's Forests through the Green Deal?" Policy Department for External Relations, Directorate General for External Policies of the Union, PE 603.513 (October 2020), v.

89 Joseph W. Glauber, "The Current State of Agricultural Trade and the World Trade Organization," Statement before the Senate Finance Committee (July 29, 2020), at www.ifpri.org/news-release/current-state-agricultural-trade-and-world-trade-organ ization; *see* WTO, "World Statistical Review 2019."

90 Juan Robalino and Luis Diego Herrera, "Trade and Deforestation: What Have We Found?" WTO Report (2010), at www.wto.org/english/res_e/publications_e/ wtr10_robalino_herrera_e.htm.

91 Ryan Abman and Clark Lundberg, "Does Free Trade Increase Deforestation? The Effects of Regional Trade Agreements," *Journal of the Association of Environmental and Resource Economics*, Vol. 7, No. 1 (2020), 35–72, at www .journals.uchicago.edu/doi/abs/10.1086/705787?journalCode=jaere.

92 Brad Harstad, "Trade and Trees: How Trade Agreements Can Motivate Conservation Instead of Depletion," CESifo Working Paper Series 9567 (September 2020), at https://ideas.repec.org/p/ces/ceswps/_8569.html.

93 Juan Robalino and Luis Diego Herrera, "Trade and Deforestation: What Have We Found?"

94 Ryan Abman and Clark Lundberg, "Does Free Trade Increase Deforestation?" at 35.

95 Brad Harstad, "Trade and Trees."

96 Christian Mersmann, "Links between Trade and Sustainable Forest Management: An Overview," United Nations Food and Agriculture Organization (2004), 10, at www.fao.org/3/y5918e/y5918e02.htm.

97 Ibid. at 6.

98 European Environment Agency, "A New EU Forest Strategy," at www.eea.europa .eu/policy-documents/the-eu-forest-strategy-com.

99 Ibid.

100 Congressional Research Service, "International Illegal Logging: Background and Issues," IF11114 (February 26, 2019), at www.hsdl.org/?abstract&did=822444.

101 Ibid.

102 Ibid.

103 Ibid.

104 Kenneth E. Wallen, "Global Timber Trafficking Harms Forests and Costs Billions of Dollars – Here's How to Curb It," *The Conversation* (April 24, 2018), at https:// theconversation.com/global-timber-trafficking-harms-forests-and-costs-billions-of-dollars-heres-how-to-curb-it-93115.

105 16 U.S.C. sections 3371–3378, [USC02] 16 USC 3371: Definitions (house.gov).

106 EU FLEGT Facility, "Evaluation of the EU FLEGT Action Plan," at EU FLEGT Action Plan evaluation | FLEGT (efi.int); Regulation (EU) No. 995/2010 of the European Parliament and of the Council of 20 October 2010 laying out the obligations of operators who place timber and timber products on the market, at EUR-Lex - 32010R0995 - EN - EUR-Lex (europa.eu).

107 Illegal Logging Prohibition Act 2012, No. 166, 2012.

108 "Global Forest Atlas: Forest Certification," Yale School of the Environment, at https://globalforestatlas.yale.edu/conservation/forest-certification.

109 Anthony Boadle, "Brazil Pledge on Amazon Needed to Save EU-Mercosur Trade Deal – EU Diplomat," *Reuters* (December 7, 2020), at www.reuters.com/article/eu-mercosur-brazil/brazil-pledge-on-amazon-needed-to-save-eu-mercosur-trade-deal-eu-diplomat-idUSKBN28H1SP.

110 Louse Boyle, "Bolsanaro Points Finger at Developed Nations for Historic Fossil-Fuel Use in White House Summit Speech," *Independent* (April 23, 2021), at www .independent.co.uk/climate-change/news/bolsonaro-brazil-biden-climate-summit-b1835864.html.

111 Paulo Barreto, "Brazil Must Reverse Deforestation Trends before EU Finalizes Mercosur Trade Deal," *Climate Change News* (January 12, 2020), at www .climatechangenews.com/2020/12/01/brazil-must-reverse-deforestation-trends-eu-finalises-mercosur-trade-deal.

112 Annex 18.3.4, United States-Peru Trade Promotion Agreement (February 1, 2009), at https://ustr.gov/trade-agreements/free-trade-agreements/peru-tpa/final-text.

113 Congressional Research Service, "International Illegal Logging: Background and Issues" (February 26, 2019).

114 European Commission, "Report on Critical Raw Materials for the EU: Non-critical Raw Materials Profiles," (May 2014), 39–46, at http://ec.europa.eu/enter prise/policies/raw-materials/critical/index_en.htm.

115 Bloomberg New Energy Finance, "New Energy Outlook 2020."

116 Ibid.

117 Ibid.

118 Ibid.

119 Joseph C. Sternberg, "The 'New Map' Review: Tapping the Unthinkable," *Wall Street Journal* (September 29, 2020).
120 OECD, "Trade in Raw Materials" (February 2019), 1.
121 Rochelle Toplensky, "Green Energy Will Need More Storage Space," *Wall Street Journal* (December 30, 2020).
122 Francis R. Fannon, "The Green Revolution's Inconvenient Truth about Mining," *Financial Times* (March 17, 2020).
123 World Bank, "Minerals for Climate Action: The Mineral Intensity of the Clean Energy Transition" (2020), 11, at http://pubdocs.worldbank.org/en/961711588875536384/Minerals-for-Climate-Action-The-Mineral-Intensity-of-the-Clean-Energy-Transition.pdf.
124 Ibid.
125 UNEP, "Healthy Planet Healthy People," at 92.
126 Ibid. at 220; Livia Albeck-Ripka, "Mining Firm Plans to Destroy Indigenous Australian Sites, Despite Outcry," *New York Times* (June 11, 2020).
127 World Bank, "New World Bank Fund to Support Climate-Smart Mining for Energy Transition" (May 1, 2019), at www.worldbank.org/en/news/press-release/2019/05/01/new-world-bank-fund-to-support-climate-smart-mining-for-energy-transition.
128 Toby Wilkinson, *The Rise and Fall of Ancient Egypt* (New York: Random House, 2010), 245.
129 Todd C. Frankel, "The Cobalt Pipeline," *Washington Post* (September 30, 2016).
130 Ibid.
131 Ibid.
132 For a comprehensive analysis of this issue, *see* Ilaria Espa, *Export Restrictions on Critical Minerals and Metals: Testing the Adequacies of WTO Disciplines* (Cambridge: Cambridge University Press, 2015).
133 Ibid. at 103–110, 119–123.
134 *See* Appellate Body Report, *United States – Import Prohibition of Certain Shrimp and Shrimp Products*, WT/DS58, AB/R (1998).
135 Ilaria Espa, *Export Restrictions on Critical Minerals and Metals*, at 103–110, 119–123.
136 Article XI (1), General Agreement on Tariffs and Trade.
137 Article XI (2) (a), General Agreement on Tariffs and Trade.
138 Article X, General Agreement on Tariffs and Trade.
139 Article XX(b) and Article XX(j), General Agreement on Tariffs and Trade.
140 *See* Appellate Body Report, *China – Measures Related to the Exportation of Various Raw Materials*, WT/DS394, AB/R (2012); Appellate Body Report, *China – Measures Related to the Exportation of Rare Earths, Tungsten, and Molydenum*, WT/DS341, AB/R (2014).
141 Article XI, General Agreement on Tariffs and Trade.
142 UNEP, "Healthy Planet Healthy People," at 204.
143 IPBES, "The Assessment Report on Land Degradation and Restoration" (2018), xx.
144 Goal 15, "Transforming Our World."
145 Paragraph 206, "The Future We Want," Outcome Document of the United Nations Conference on Sustainable Development, Rio de Janeiro, Brazil, June

20–22, 2012, A/RES/66/288, at https://sustainabledevelopment.un.org/futurewew ant.html.

146 UNEP, "Healthy Planet Healthy People," at 203.
147 Ibid.
148 UNEP, "Healthy Planet Healthy People," at 160.
149 Hannah Ritchie, "Half of the World's Habitable Land Is Used for Agriculture," *Our World in Data* (November 11, 2019), at https://ourworldindata.org/global-land-for-agriculture.
150 Ibid.
151 UNEP, "Healthy Planet Healthy People," at 202.
152 Global Environment Facility, "The Complexities and Imperatives of Building Back Better," at 10.
153 Global Environment Facility, "The Complexities and Imperatives of Building Back Better," at 20.
154 Hannah Ritchie, "How Much of the World's Land Would We Need in Order to Feed the Global Population with the Average Diet of a Given Country?" *Our World In Data* (October 3, 2017), at https://ourworldindata.org/agricultural-land-by-global-diets.
155 Humane Society of the United States, "Improving the Lives of Farm Animals," at www.humanesociety.org/all-our-fights/protect-farm-animals.
156 Ezra Klein, "Let's Launch a Moonshot for Meatless Meat," *New York Times* (May 3, 2021).
157 Ibid.
158 UNEP, "Health Planet Healthy People," at 202.
159 UNEP, "Healthy Planet Healthy People," at 148.
160 Jeffrey D. Sachs, *The Age of Sustainable Development* (New York: Columbia University Press, 2015), 207.
161 Aldo Leopold, *A Sand County Almanac with Essays on Conservation from Round River* (New York: Ballantine Books, 1970), 240 [1949].
162 UNEP and CBD," Global Biodiversity Outlook 5," United Nations Environment Programme and Convention on Biological Diversity (2020), at 64.
163 WWF, "Sustainable Agriculture: Overview," at www.worldwildlife.org/industries/sustainable-agriculture.
164 Ibid.
165 Hannah Ritchie, "Half of the World's Habitable Land Is Used for Agriculture."
166 Tariq Khokhar, "Chart: Globally, 70% of Freshwater Is Used for Agriculture," *World Bank Blog* (March 22, 2017), at https://blogs.worldbank.org/opendata/chart-globally-70-freshwater-used-agriculture#:~:text=In%20most%20regions%20of%20the,freshwater%20is%20used%20for%20agriculture.
167 Ibid.
168 World Economic Forum, "Global Risks Report 2020," (2020), at www.weforum.org/reports/the-global-risks-report-2020.
169 WWF, "Water Scarcity: Overview," at www.worldwildlife.org/threats/water-scarcity.
170 Goal 6, "Transforming Our World."
171 Target 6.6, "Transforming Our World."
172 Goal 2, "Transforming Our World."

173 Annex 1.1, WTO Agreement on Technical Barriers to Trade.
174 For more on these water issues and my proposals, see James Bacchus, *The Willing World*, at 330–337.
175 UNEP, "Healthy Planet Healthy People," at 218.
176 Ibid., at 219.
177 Ibid. at 218.
178 Ibid.
179 UNEP, "Healthy Planet Healthy People," at 219.
180 Charlotte Janssens et al., "Global Hunger and Climate Change Adaptation through International Trade," *Nature Climate Change*, Vol. 10 (2020), 829–835, 829, at www.nature.com/articles/s41558-020-0847-4#:~:text=Discussion,64% 25%20under%20open%20trade%20scenarios.
181 Jeremiás Máté Balogh and Attila Jámbor, "The Environmental Impacts of Agricultural Trade: A Systematic Literature Review," *Sustainability*, Vol. 12 (February 5, 2020), 1152–1167, 1153 at www.doi:10.3390/su12031152; *see also* OECD, "Trade and the Environment: How Are Trade and Environmental Sustainability Compatible?" (2019), at www.oecd.org/trade/topics/trade-and-the-environment.
182 Ibid.
183 Charlotte Janssens et al., "Global Hunger and Climate Change Adaptation through International Trade," at 829.
184 Jeremiás Máté Balogh and Attila Jámbor, "The Environmental Impacts of Agricultural Trade: A Systematic Literature Review," at 1160.
185 Letter, "Put Nature at the Heart of Climate Solutions," *Financial Times* (February 19, 2020).
186 OECD, "Water and Agriculture," policy brief (November 19, 2018), at https://issuu.com/oecd.publishing/docs/water_and_agriculture.
187 Qian Dang and Megan Konar, "Trade Openness and Domestic Water Use," *Water Resources Research*, Vol. 55 (December 14, 2017), 4–18, at https://doi.org/10.1002/2017WR021102.
188 Mike Muller and Christophe Bellman, "Trade and Water: How Might Trade Policy Contribute to Sustainable Water Management?" (Geneva: International Centre for Trade and Sustainable Development, October 2016), 1.
189 Jeremiás Máté Balogh and Attila Jámbor, "The Environmental Impacts of Agricultural Trade," at 160.
190 Jenny Kehl, "The Hidden Global Trade in Water," *Yale Global* (February 13, 2013), citing a UNESCO study done in 2003, at https://yaleglobal.yale.edu/content/hidden-global-trade-water, citing a UNESCO study done in 2003 at the IHE Delft Institute for Water Education, www.un-ihe.org/institute.
191 Erik Gawel and Kristina Bernsen, "What Is Wrong with Virtual Water Trading? On the Limitations of the Virtual Water Concept," *Environment and Planning C: Government and Policy*, Vol. 31, No. 1 (January 2013), 168–181, at www.researchgate.net/publication/260452604_What_is_Wrong_with_Virtual_Water_Trading_On_the_Limitations_of_the_Virtual_Water_Concept.
192 A. K. Chapagain, A. Y. Hoekstra, and H. H. G. Savenjie, "Water Saving through International Trade of Agricultural Products," *Hydrology and Earth System Sciences*, Vol. 10 (2006), 455–468. *See also* UNEP, "Healthy Planet Healthy People," at 257.

193 Alexandre Le Vernoy and Patrick Messerlin, "Water and the WTO: Don't Kill the Messenger" (January 10, 2001), prepared for a workshop on "Accounting for Water Scarcity and Pollution in the Rules of International Trade," Amsterdam, The Netherlands, November 25–26, 2010, 5.

194 Erik Gawel and Kristina Bernsen, "What Is Wrong with Virtual Water Trading?" at 172.

195 UNEP, "Healthy Planet Healthy People," at 4.

196 WWF, "Living Planet Report 2020," at 62.

197 Ibid.

198 FAO, "Food Wastage Footprint," at www.fao.org/nr/sustainability/food-loss-and-waste/en.

199 Among his many books, *see, e.g.,* Robert Ayres, *Turning Point: The End of the Growth Paradigm* (Milton Park: Earthscan, 1996).

200 Karsten Steinfatt, "Trade Policies for a Circular Economy: What Can We Learn from the WTO Experience?" WTO Staff Working Paper ERSD-2020-10 (June 23, 2020), 3.

201 "The Circular Economy in Detail," Ellen MacArthur Foundation, at www .ellenmacarthurfoundation.org/explore/the-circular-economy-in-detail.

202 William McDonough and Michael Braungart, *Cradle to Cradle: Remaking the Way We Make Things* (San Francisco: North Point Press, 2002).

203 Ibid.

204 Karsten Steinfatt, "Trade Policies for a Circular Economy," at 3.

205 Felix Preston and Johanna Lehne, "A Wider Circle? The Circular Economy in Developing Countries," *Chatham House Briefing* (December 5, 2017), at www .chathamhouse.org/2017/12/wider-circle-circular-economy-developing-countries.

206 Karsten Steinfatt, "Trade Policies for a Circular Economy," at 3.

207 UNCTAD, "Circular Economy: The New Normal?" Policy Brief Number 61 (June 5, 2018), 1, at https://unctad.org/search?keys=Circular+Economy%3A+The+New +Normal%3F%22.

208 M. M. Alonso-Almeida and J. M. Rodriguez-Anton, "Circular Supply Chain and Business Model in Apparel Industry: An Exploratory Approach," Ulas Akkucuk, ed., *The Circular Economy and Its Implications on Sustainability and the Green Supply Chain* (Hershey, PA: IGI Global, 2019); 66–83, 69.

209 Goal 12, "Transforming Our World."

210 Target 12.1, "Transforming Our World"; *see* https://sustainabledevelopment.un .org/index.php?page=view&type=400&nr=1444&menu=35.

211 Targets 12.2, 12.3, 12.4, 12.5, 12.7, and 12.b, "Transforming Our World."

212 "WWF Living Planet Report 2020," at 56.

213 Ibid.

214 United Nations, "Sustainable Production and Consumption," at www.un.org/ sustainabledevelopment/en/sustainable-consumption-production.

215 David McGinty, "How to Build a Circular Economy," World Resources Institute (August 5, 2020), at https://wri.org/blog/2020/08/how-to-circular-economy; *see also* "The Circularity Gap 2020," at www.circularity-gap.world/2020.

216 "The Circularity Gap 2020," at 15.

217 Ibid. at 8.

218 UNCTAD, "Circular Economy: The New Normal?" at 3; Felix Preston and Johanna Lehne, "A Wider Circle? The Circular Economy in Developing Countries."

219 Ibid. at 15.

220 Karsten Steinfatt, "Trade Policies for a Circular Economy," at 3.

221 UNEP, "Global Material Flows and Resource Productivity: Assessment Report for the UNEP International Resource Panel" (Nairobi: United Nations Environment Programme, 2016), 17; UNEP, "Healthy Planet Healthy People," 76–77.

222 UNEP, "Emissions Gap Report 2020," at xxv.

223 Niall Smith, "US Tops List of Countries Fuelling the Waste Crisis: Waste Generation and Recycling Indices," Verisk Maplecroft (July 2, 2019), at www .maplecroft.com/insights/analysis/us-tops-list-of-countries-fuelling-the-mounting-waste-crisis.

224 David McGinty, "How to Build a Circular Economy;" *see also* "Completing the Circle: How the Circular Economy Tackles Climate Change," Material Economics and the Ellen MacArthur Foundation (September 26, 2019), at www .ellenmacarthurfoundation.org/assets/downloads/Completing_The_Picture_How_ The_Circular_Economy-_Tackles_Climate_Change_V3_26_September.pdf.

225 "Completing the Circle," at 44.

226 World Economic Forum, "A Vision for a Sustainable Battery Value Chain in 2030: Unlocking the Full Potential to Power Sustainable Development and Climate Change Mitigation" (September 2019), at 5.

227 Karsten Steinfatt, "Trade Policies for a Circular Economy," at 7.

228 Ibid.

229 Ibid. at 8.

230 Ibid.

231 Ibid.

232 Ibid. at 9, 13.

233 Appellate Body Report, *Brazil – Measures Affecting Imports of Retreaded Tyres*, AB/R, WT/DS332 (2007).

234 "WTO Members Launch 'Open-Ended Informal Dialogue' to Promote Sustainable Plastics Economy," International Institute for Sustainable Development (November 18, 2020), at https://sdg.iisd.org/commentary/policy-briefs/wto-members-launch-open-ended-informal-dialogue-to-promote-sustainable-plastics-economy.

235 "Choked, Strangled, Drowned: The Plastics Crisis Unfolding in Our Oceans," Oceana Report (November 2020), at https://usa.oceana.org/publications/reports/ choked-strangled-drowned-plastics-crisis-unfolding-our-oceans.

236 Kara Lavender Law, Natalie Starr, Theodore R. Siegler, Jenna R. Jambeck, Nicholas J. Mallos, and George H. Leonard, "The United States' Contribution of Plastic Waste to Land and Ocean," *Science Advances*, Vol. 6, No. 44 (October 30, 2020), at https://usa.oceana.org/publications/reports/choked-strangled-drowned-plastics-crisis-unfolding-our-oceans.

237 Center for International Environmental Law, "Fossil Fuels and Plastics," at www .ciel.org/issue/fossil-fuels-plastic.

238 Joe Brock, "The Plastics Pandemic," *Reuters* (October 5, 2020), at www.reuters .com/investigates/special-report/health-coronavirus-plastic-recycling.

239 Joe Zhang and Sofia Balino, "Coherent Global Trade Policy Frameworks Needed for Circular Economy for Plastics," International Institute for Sustainable Development (December 16, 2020), at http://sdg.iisd.org/commentary/policy-

briefs/coherent-global-trade-policy-frameworks-needed-for-circular-economy-for-plastics.

240 Ibid.

241 Plastic Oceans, "The Facts Are Overwhelming," a https://plasticoceans.org/the-facts.

242 Ibid.

243 National Ocean Service, "What Are Microplastics?" at https://oceanservice.noaa.gov/facts/microplastics.html.

244 Sarah Gibbens, "Plastic Bag Found at the Bottom of the World's Deepest Ocean Trench," *National Geographic* (July 3, 2019), at www.nationalgeographic.org/article/plastic-bag-found-bottom-worlds-deepest-ocean-trench.

245 Damian Carrington, "Microplastic Pollution Found Near Summit of Mount Everest," *Guardian* (November 20, 2020).

246 Winne W. Y. Lau et al., "Evaluating Scenarios toward Zero Plastic Pollution," *Science*, Vol. 369, No. 6510 (September 18, 2020, 1455–1461, at https://science.sciencemag.org/content/369/6510/1455.

247 Green Cities, "Fact Sheet: Plastics in the Ocean," at www.earthday.org/fact-sheet-plastics-in-the-ocean.

248 Simon Reddy and Winnie Lau, "Breaking the Plastic Wave: Top Findings for Preventing Plastic Pollution," Pew Charitable Trusts (July 23, 2020), at www.pewtrusts.org/en/research-and-analysis/articles/2020/07/23/breaking-the-plastic-wave-top-findings.

249 Scott Wilson, "Along California Coast, PPE Becomes New Source of Plastic Pollution," *Washington Post* (December 21, 2020).

250 Joana C. Prata, Ana L. P. Silva, Tony R. Walker, Armando C. Duarte, and Teresa Rocha-Santos, "COVID-19 Pandemic Repercussions on the Use and Management of Plastics," *Environmental Science & Technology*, Vol. 54, No. 13 (June 12, 2020), 7760–7765, at https://pubs.acs.org/doi/abs/10.1021/acs.est.0c02178#.

251 Helena Varkkey, "By Exporting Trash, Rich Countries Put Their Waste Out of Sight and Out of Mind," *CNN Opinion* (July 29, 2019), at www.cnn.com/2019/07/29/opinions/by-exporting-trash-rich-countries-put-their-waste-out-of-sight-and-out-of-mind-varkkey/index.html.

252 Ibid.

253 Amy L. Brooks, Shunli Wang, and Jenna R. Jambeck, "The Chinese Import Ban and Its Impact on Global Plastic Waste Trade," *Science Advances*, Vol. 4, No. 6 (June 20, 2018), at https://advances.sciencemag.org/content/4/6/eaat0131.

254 Cheryl Katz, "Piling Up: How China's Ban on Importing Waste Has Stalled Global Recycling," *Yale Environment*, 360 (March 7, 2019), at https://e360.yale.edu/features/piling-up-how-chinas-ban-on-importing-waste-has-stalled-global-recycling.

255 Laura Parker, "China's Ban on Trash Imports Shifts Waste Crisis to Southeast Asia," *National Geographic* (November 16, 2018), at www.nationalgeographic.com/environment/2018/11/china-ban-plastic-trash-imports-shifts-waste-crisis-southeast-asia-malaysia.

256 Hillary Leung, "Southeast Asia Doesn't Want to Be the World's Dumping Ground. Here's How Some Countries Are Pushing Back," *Time* (June 3, 2019), at www.time.com/5598032/southeast-asia-plastic-waste-malaysia-philippines/.

257 *See, e.g.*, Greenpeace Africa, "34 Plastic Bans in Africa: A Reality Check," at www .greenpeace.org/africa/en/blogs/11156/34-plastic-bans-in-africa.

258 United States Environmental Protection Agency, "New International Requirements for the Export and Import of Plastic Recyclables and Waste," at www.epa.gov/ hwgenerators/new-international-requirements-export-and-import-plastic-recycl ables-and-waste.

259 Ibid.

260 UNEP, "Stockholm Convention: Status of Ratification," at www.pops.int/ Countries/StatusofRatifications/PartiesandSignatoires/tabid/4500/Default.aspx.

261 Anastasia Telesetsky, "Why Stop at Plastic Bags and Straws? The Case for a Global Treaty Banning Most Single-Use Plastics," *The Conversation* (February 7, 2019), at https://theconversation.com/why-stop-at-plastic-bags-and-straws-the-case-for-a-global-treaty-banning-most-single-use-plastics-109857.

262 Karen McVeigh, "Global Treaty to Tackle Plastic Pollution Gains Steam without US and UK," *Guardian* (November 16, 2020).

263 Ibid.

264 Steve Toloken, "UN Environment Body Pushes Ahead on Plastics Treaty," *Plastics News* (February 23, 2021), at www.plasticsnews.com/news/un-environment-body-pushes-ahead-plastics-treaty.

265 Ibid.

266 Environmental Investigation Agency, "A Legally Binding Agreement on Plastics Pollution – FAQs."

267 Ibid.

268 Nordic Council of Ministers, "Possible Elements of a New Global Agreement to Prevent Plastic Pollution" (2020), at www.nordicreport2020.com.

269 Ibid.

270 Article XX, General Agreement on Tariffs and Trade.

271 Article 3, WTO Understanding on Rules and Procedures Governing the Settlement of Disputes.

272 *See, e.g.*, Appellate Body Report, *United States – Import Prohibition of Certain Shrimp and Shrimp Products*, AB/R, WT/DS58 (1998); *see also* James Bacchus, "Not in Clinical Isolation," in Gabrielle Marceau, ed., *A History of Law and Lawyers in the GATT/WTO: The Development of the Rule of Law in the Multilateral Trading System* (Cambridge: Cambridge University Press, 2015), 507–516.

273 "WTO Members Launch 'Open-Ended Informal Dialogue' to Promote Sustainable Plastics Economy."

274 Ibid.

275 Goal 14, "Transforming Our World."

276 Target 14.1, "Transforming Our World." "WTO Members Launch 'Open-Ended Informal Dialogue' to Promote Sustainable Plastics Economy."

277 Carolyn Deere Birkbeck, "Policy Brief – Strengthening International Cooperation to Tackle Plastic Pollution: Options for the WTO," *Plastic Politics* (January 9, 2020), at www.plasticpolitics.solutions/research-1/2020/1/9/policy-brief-strengthening-international-cooperation-to-tackle-plastic-pollution-options-for-the-wto.

278 Ibid.

279 Florian Faure, Colin Demars, Olivier Wieser, Manuel Kunz, and Luiz Felippe de Alencastro, "Plastic Pollution in Swiss Surface Waters: Nature and Concentrations, Interactions with Pollutants," *Environmental Chemistry*, Vol. 12, No. 5 (January 2015), at www.researchgate.net/publication/283028984_Plastic_pollution_in_Swiss_surface_waters_Nature_and_concentrations_interaction_with_pollutants.

CHAPTER 9

1 Jared Diamond, *Collapse: How Societies Choose to Fail or Succeed* (New York: Penguin Books, 2006).
2 Jared Diamond, "Lessons from a Pandemic," *Financial Times* (May 28, 2020).
3 John Gray, "Why This Crisis Is a Turning Point in History," *New Statesman* (April 2020), at www.newstatesman.com/america/2020/0/why-crisis-turning-point-history.
4 Goal 17, "Transforming Our World."
5 For an excellent analysis of the "sovereignty" issue, *see* Stewart Patrick, *The Sovereignty Wars: Reconciling America with the World* (Washington, DC: Council on Foreign Relations and Brookings Institution Press, 2018).
6 For a lucid explanation of the logic of international cooperation, *see* Scott Barrett, *Why Cooperate? The Incentive to Supply Global Public Goods* (Oxford: Oxford University Press, 2007).
7 Josiah Ober, *The Rise and Fall of Classical Greece* (Princeton, NJ: Princeton University Press, 2015), 203.
8 Klaus Muhlhahn, "Can Environmental Activism Succeed in China? On the Aftereffects of the 'Economic Miracle,'" *Lit Hub* (January 28, 2019), at https://lithub.com/can-environmental-activism-succeed-in-china.
9 *See* James Bacchus, *The Willing World*, at 98–99.
10 Robert Axelrod, *The Evolution of Cooperation*, revised edition (Cambridge, MA: Perseus, 2006), 3, 126–134 [1984].
11 Alexis de Tocqueville, "The Americans Combat Individualism by the Principle of Interest Right Understood," *Democracy in America* (New York: Colonial Press, 1899), Vol. II, Book II, chapter VII, 129–132 [1840].
12 "Our Common Future," Report of the World Commission on Environment and Development (1987), I.2.27, at https://sustainabledevelopment.un.org/content/documents/5987our-common-future.pdf.
13 Goal 10, "Transforming Our World." (emphasis added)
14 Target 10.1, "Transforming Our World."
15 Target 10.2, "Transforming Our World."
16 Target 10.3, "Transforming Our World."
17 Target 10.4, "Transforming Our World."
18 United Nations, "The Sustainable Development Goals Report 2020," at 44.
19 Paragraph 2, "Transforming Our World."
20 United Nations, "The Sustainable Development Goals Report 2021," 47, at https://unstats.un.org/sdgs/report/2021/The-Sustainable-Development-Goals-Report-2021.pdf.

21 Zia Qureshi, "Tackling the inequality pandemic: is there a cure?" Brookings Institution (November 17, 2020), at www.brookings.edu/research/tackling-the-inequality-pandemic-is-there-a-cure.

22 United Nations, "The Sustainable Development Goals Report 2020," at 44.

23 David Ignatius, "After Covid-19, It Will Be a Different World," *Washington Post* (October 9, 2020).

24 Frank J. Garcia has made this same point in Frank J. Garcia, *Trade, Inequality, and Justice: Toward a Liberal Theory of Just Trade* (Ardsley, NY: Transnational Publishers, 2003), 1.

25 Branko Milanovic, *Global Inequality: A New Approach for the Age of Globalization* (Cambridge, MA: Harvard University Press, 2016), 161–176.

26 Michael Spence, *The Next Convergence: The Future of Economic Growth in a Multispeed World* (New York: Farrar, Straus and Giroux, 2011).

27 Christopher Ingraham, "World's Richest Men Add Billions to Their Fortunes as Others Struggle," *Washington Post* (January 2, 2012).

28 Ibid.

29 Matthew C. Klein and Michael Pettis, *Trade Wars Are Class Wars: How Rising Inequality Distorts the Global Economy and Threatens International Peace* (New Haven: Yale University Press, 2020).

30 Ibid. at 221.

31 Pettis is quoted in Adam Tooze, "Trade Wars Are Class Wars," *Phenomenal World* (June 13, 2020), at https://phenomenalworld.org/interviews/trade-wars-are-class-wars.

32 Oisin Suttle, *Distributive Justice and World Trade Law: A Political Theory of International Trade Regulation* (Cambridge: Cambridge University Press, 2018), 5–6.

33 David Hume, *A Treatise of Human Nature* (London: Penguin Books, 1985) [1748], book III, part II, section II; *see* Jonathan Harris, *Hume's Theory of Justice* (Oxford: Oxford University Press, 1980) and Simon Hope, "The Circumstances of Justice," *Hume Studies*, Vol. 36, No. 2 (2010), 125–148, at https://philpapers.org/rec/HO) PTCO-3.

34 David Hume, "Of Justice," section III in *An Enquiry Concerning the Principles of Morals* (1751).

35 Frank J. Garcia, *Trade, Inequality, and Justice*, at 104–107, quoting from 107.

36 Rafael Leal-Arcas, *Solutions for Sustainability*, at 47 note 2.

37 Paragraph 4, introduction, "Transforming Our World."

38 Goal 16, "Transforming Our World."

39 Goal 4, "Transforming Our World."

40 Goal 8, "Transforming Our World."

41 Goal 9, "Transforming Our World."

42 Target 10.2, "Transforming Our World."

43 United Nations, "The Sustainable Development Goals Report 2020," at 56.

44 United Nations, "The Sustainable Development Goals Report 2021," at 58.

45 Amartya Sen, *Development as Freedom* (New York: Anchor Books, 1999).

46 Ibid. at 12.

47 Ibid.

48 Ibid. at 3.

49 Ibid. at 18.

50 Martha C. Nussbaum, *Creating Capabilities: The Human Development Approach* (Cambridge, MA: Harvard University Press, 2011), 18. (emphasis in original)

51 Ibid. (emphasis in original)

52 Amartya Sen, "The Ends and Means of Sustainability," *Journal of Human Development and Capabilities*, Vol. 14, No. 1 (2013), 6–20, 13, at https://doi.org/10.1080/19452829.2012.747492.

53 Ibid.

54 William Easterly, *The Tyranny of Experts: Economists, Dictators, and the Forgotten Rights of the Poor* ((New York: Basic Books, 2013), 7.

55 Amartya Sen, *Development as Freedom*, at 87.

56 Ibid. at 112.

57 Ibid. at 269.

58 Amartya Sen, *The Idea of Justice* (Cambridge, MA: Harvard University Press, 2009), 249.

59 Ibid. at 251–252. (emphasis added)

60 *See* the annual United Nations Human Development Reports, at www.hdr.undp.org/en/global-reports.

61 Ibid.

62 UNDP, "Trade and Human Development: A Practical Guide to Mainstreaming Trade" (Vienna: United Nations Development Program, 2011), 9.

63 Ibid. at 10.

64 Ibid.

65 Ibid.

66 Ibid.

67 *See* James Bacchus, *Trade and Freedom*, at 262, and James Bacchus, *The Willing World*, at 81.

68 See Cathleen Cimino-Isaacs and Gary Clyde Hufbauer, "The Fate of Trade Adjustment Assistance: The Basics," Peterson Institute for International Economics (June 11, 2015), at www.piie.com/blogs/trade-investment-policy-watch/fate-trade-adjustment-assistance-basics?gclid=CjwKCAiAl4WABhAJEiwATUnEFyZhfPB45p2s1W385WjjEjtkR3KGk6ZfDH1AekFcFIx4BEZhs3f5yBoC9rUQAvD_BwE.

69 Gary Clyde Hufbauer and Zhiyao (Lucy) Lu, "The Payoff to America from Globalization: A Fresh Look with a Focus on Costs to Workers," Peterson Institute for International Economics, policy brief 17-16 (May 2017), 21, at www.piie.com/publications/policy-briefs/payoff-america-globalization-fresh-look-focus-costs-workers.

70 United States Network of the United Nations Sustainable Development Solutions Network, "America's Zero Carbon Action Plan," at www.unsdsn.org/Zero-Carbon-Action-Plan. Here it may be appropriate to note that I am a member of the advisory board and of the Leadership Council for the US Network of the SDSN.

71 Ibid. at 59.

72 Ibid. at 60.

73 Ibid. at 75–80.

74 Ibid. at 80.

75 Ibid. at 82.

76 White House, "FACT SHEET: The American Jobs Plan (March 31, 2021), at www.whitehouse.gov/briefing-room/statements-releases/2021/03/31/fact-sheet-the-american-jobs-plan.

77 Robert Z. Lawrence, "Adjustment Challenges for US Workers," at 100.

78 Goal 8, "Transforming Our World."

79 Target 8.7, "Transforming Our World."

80 Target 8.8, "Transforming Our World."

81 Gregory Shaffer, "Retooling Trade Agreements for Social Inclusion," Legal Studies Research Paper Series No. 2018-54, University of California, Irvine School of Law, 35.

82 ILO, "History of the ILO," at https://libguides.ilo.org/c.php?g=657806&p=4649148.

83 ILO, "About the Declaration," at www.ilo.org/declaration/thedeclaration/lang–en/index.htm.

84 Gregory Shaffer, "Retooling Trade Agreements for Social Inclusion," at 35.

85 Chapter 19 and Chapter 28.20, CPTPP.

86 Priya Satia, *Time's Monster: How History Makes History* (Cambridge, MA: Harvard University Press, 2020), 3.

87 John Stuart Mill, *Principles of Political Economy*, ed. J. M. Robson (Toronto: Toronto University Press, 1965), 3: 693 [1848].

88 Target 10.a, "Transforming Our World." (emphasis added)

89 For a more extensive analysis of the need for reform of "special and differential treatment," *see* James Bacchus and Inu Manak, *The Development Dimension: Special and Differential Treatment in Trade* (London: Routledge Press, 2021); *see also* James Bacchus and Inu Manak, "The Development Dimension: What to Do about Differential Treatment in Trade," Cato Institute, Policy Analysis No. 887 (April 13, 2020), at www.cato.org/publications/policy-analysis/development-dimension-what-do-about-differential-treatment-trade.

90 Pallavi Kishore, "Special and Differential Treatment in the Multilateral Trading System," *Chinese Journal of International Law*, 13 (2014): 363–394, 366.

91 Ibid.

92 Emanuel Ornelas, "Special and Differential Treatment for Developing Countries Reconsidered," Center for Economic Policy Research (May 14, 2016) https://voxeu.org/article/special-and-differential-treatment-developing-countries-reconsidered.

93 Ibid. (emphasis in the original)

94 Patrick Low, Hamid Mamdouh, and Evan Rogerson, "Balancing Rights and Obligations in the WTO – A Shared Responsibility," Government Offices of Sweden (2018), 27.

95 James Bacchus and Inu Manak, *The Development Dimension*, at 58–69.

96 Ibid. at 61.

97 "Presentation of the WTO MSME Group's Package of Recommendations and Discussion with the Private Sector," at www.wto.org/english/forums_e/business_e/msme_dec20_e.htm.

98 WTO, "World Trade Report 2016: Levelling the Trading Field for SMEs," 3, at www.wto.org/english/res_e/publications_e/wtr16_e.htm.

99 Target 8.3, "Transforming Our World."

100 WTO, "Draft Ministerial Decision on Establishing a Work Programme for Micro, Small, and Medium Enterprises (MSMEs) in the WTO," (WT/MIN(17)/24/Rev.1).

101 WTO, "World Trade Report 2016," at 3.

102 Ibid.

103 Soledad Leal Campos, Sofia Balino, and Constantine Bartel, "Joint Statement on Micro, Small, and Medium-Sized Enterprises: History and Latest Developments in the Informal Working Group," International Institute for Sustainable Development and CUTS Geneva (May 2020), 9–15, at www.iisd.org/publications/joint-state ment-micro-small-and-medium-sized-enterprises-history-and-latest.

104 International Finance Corporation, "Strengthening Access to Finance for Women-Owned SMEs in Developing Countries" (Washington, DC: International Finance Corporation, 2011), at www.ifc.org/wps/wcm/connect/topics_ext_content/ ifc_external_corporate_site/sustainability-at-ifc/publications/publications_report_ accesstofinanceforwomensmes.

105 Joel Richards, "She Trades Initiative Aims to Connect Women-Owned Companies Globally," *CTGN America* (December 26, 2017), at https://america.ctgn.com/2017/ 12/26/she-trades-initiative-aims-to-connect-women-owned-companies-globally.

106 Arancha Gonzalez, "When She Trades, We All Benefit," in "Reshaping Trade through Women's Economic Empowerment: Special Report," Center for International Governance Innovation (2018), 13, at www.cigionline.org/publica tions/reshaping-trade-through-womens-economic-empowerment.

107 Linda Scott, "It's Time to End the Male Monopoly in International Trade," *Financial Times* (September 20, 2020).

108 World Economic Forum, "Global Gender Gap Report 2020," at www3.weforum .org/docs/WEF_GGGR_2020.pdf.

109 Jonathan Woetzel et al., "The Power of Parity: How Advancing Women's Equality Can Add $12 Trillion," Mckinsey Global Institute (September 2015), at www .mckinsey.com/~/media/McKinsey/Featured%20Insights/Employment%20and%20 Growth/How%20advancing%20womens%20equality%20can%20add%2012% 20trillion%20to%20global%20growth/MGI%20Power%20of%20parity_Full% 20report_September%202015.ashx.

110 Amrita Bahri, "Women at the Frontline of COVID-19: Can Gender Mainstreaming in Free Trade Agreements Help?" *Journal of International Economic Law* (September 2020), at www.ncbi.nlm.nih.gov/pmc/articles/ PMC7499601/#FN73.

111 Kristalina Georgieva, Stefania Fabrizio, Cheng Hoon Lim, and Marina M. Tavares, "The COVID-19 Gender Gap," International Monetary Fund (July 21, 2020), at https://blogs.imf.org/2020/07/21/the-covid-19-gender-gap.

112 Ibid. *See also* UN Women and the Gender and COVID-19 Working Group, "Will the Pandemic Derail Hard-Won Progress on Gender Equality?" (2020), at www .unwomen.org/en/digital-library/publications/2020/07/spotlight-on-gender-covid- 19-and-the-sdgs.

113 Ibid.

114 Carbon Brief, "Mapping How Climate Change Disproportionately Affects Women's Health," at www.carbonbrief.org/mapping-how-climate-change-dispro portionately-affects-womens-health.

115 Goal 5, "Transforming Our World."

116 Target 5.1, "Transforming Our World."
117 WTO, "Joint Declaration on Trade and Women's Economic Empowerment on the Occasion of the WTO Ministerial Conference in Buenos Aires in December 2017," at www.wto.org/english/thewto_e/minist_e/mc11_e/genderdeclarationmc11_e.pdf.
118 Ibid. at paragraph 4.
119 Oonagh E. Fitzgerald, "Reuniting Trade and Human Rights," in "Reshaping Trade through Women's Economic Empowerment: Special Report," at 3.
120 WTO RTA Database (2019), at https://rtais.wto.org/UI/PublicMaintainRTAHome.aspx.
121 *Acuerdo de Libre Comercio entre la República de Chile y la República Oriental del Uruguay* (October 4, 2016), at http://investmentpolicyhub.unctad.org/Download/TreatyFile/5408.
122 Canada-Chile Free Trade Agreement (December 5, 1996), at http://international.gc.ca/trade-commerce/trade-agreements-accords-commerciaux/agr-acc/chile-chili/fta-ale/index.aspx?lang=eng.
123 Article 23.4, CPTPP.
124 Article 23.9, United States-Mexico-Canada Agreement (November 30, 2018), at https://ustr.gov/trade-agreements/free-trade-agreements/united-states-mexico-canada-agreement/agreement-between.
125 Arjan de Haan, "Toward a 'Win-Win' for Gender Equity and Trade," in "Reshaping Trade through Women's Economic Empowerment: Special Report," at 36.
126 Julia Seiermann, "Trade's Impact on Women Is Multi-Faceted; Trade Policy Should Be, Too," in "Reshaping Trade through Women's Economic Empowerment: Special Report," at 51.
127 Maria Panezi, "The Case for Developing a Model Chapter on Gender and Trade," in "Reshaping Trade through Women's Economic Empowerment: Special Report," at 30.
128 World Bank, "Indigenous Peoples," at www.worldbank.org/en/topic/indigenouspeoples.
129 John Borrows, "Indigenous Diversities in International Investment and Trade," in John Borrows and Risa Schwartz, eds., *Indigenous Peoples and International Trade: Building Equitable and Inclusive International Trade and Investment Agreements* (Cambridge: Cambridge University Press, 2020), 11–42, 15.
130 William David, "Rights of Indigenous Peoples in International Trade and Environment," in John Borrows and Risa Schwartz, eds., *Indigenous Peoples and International Trade*, 133–163, 162.
131 United Nations, "The Impact of COVID-19 on Indigenous Peoples," UN/DESA Policy Brief Number 70, 1, at www.un.org/development/desa/dpad/publication/un-desa-policy-brief-70-the-impact-of-covid-19-on-indigenous-peoples.
132 Ibid.
133 Ibid.
134 United Nations, "Indigenous Peoples and the 2030 Agenda," at www.un.org/development/desa/indigenouspeoples/focus-areas/post-2015-agenda/the-sustainable-development-goals-sdgs-and-indigenous.html.
135 United Nations Declaration on the Rights of Indigenous Peoples, G.A. Res. 217A (III), U.N. Doc. A/810 at 71 (1948).

136 John Borrows and Risa Schwartz, "Introduction," in John Barrows and Risa Schwartz, eds., *Indigenous Peoples in International Trade*, 1–7, 2.

137 Preamble, CPTPP.

138 *See* "International Trade Agreements and Indigenous Peoples: The Canadian Approach," at www.international.gc.ca/trade-commerce/indigenous_peoples-peu ples_autochtones/approach-approche.aspx?lang=eng.

139 Article 32.5, USMCA.

140 John Borrows, "Indigenous Diversities in International Investment and Trade," at 36.

141 Winthrop D. Jordan, *White Over Black: American Attitudes toward the Negro, 1550–1812* (Baltimore: Pelican Books, 1969), 216–228.

142 George M. Frederickson, *The Black Image in the White Mind: The Debate on Afro-American Character and Destiny, 1817–1914* (New York: Harper Torchbooks, 1971), 71–96.

143 David Hume, "Of National Characters," in David Hume, *Selected Essays* (Oxford: Oxford University Press, 1993), 113–125, fn. at 360.

144 Article 4, Universal Declaration of Human Rights, G.A. Res. 217A (III), U.N. Doc. A/810 at 71 (1948).

145 Articles XX(a) and XX(e), General Agreement on Tariffs and Trade.

146 Walk Free Foundation, "Global Slavery Index 2018," ii, at www.globalslaveryindex.org.

147 *See* Charles W. Mills, "Racial and Global Justice," in Duncan Bell, ed., *Empire, Race and Global Justice* (Cambridge: Cambridge University Press, 2019), 94–119.

148 Frantz Fanon, *The Wretched of the Earth*, translated by Constance Farrington (New York: Grove Press, 1968), 40 [1961].

149 Anne Case and Angus Deaton, *Deaths of Despair and the Future of Capitalism* (Princeton, NJ: Princeton University Press, 2020).

150 Ibid. at 4.

151 Debra P. Steger, "Lessons from History: Trade and Peace," in Padideh Ala'i, Tomer Broude, and Colin Picker, eds., *Trade as Guarantor of Peace, Liberty and Security? Critical, Empirical and Historical Perspectives* (Washington, DC: The American Society of International Law, 2006), 13–17, at https://ssrn.com/abstract=2467530.

152 Target 4.7, "Transforming Our World."

153 Martin Luther King, Jr., *Stride toward Freedom: The Montgomery Story* (Boston: Beacon Press, 1958), 27, 193.

CONCLUSION

1 Goal 17, "Transforming Our World."

2 *See* James Bacchus, *The Willing World*, 196–201.

3 Adam Smith, "Of the Influence and Authority of Conscience," part III, chapter III, *The Theory of Moral Sentiments* (New York: Prometheus Books, 2000), 191–220, 192–193 [1759, 1790].

4 Ibid. at 193.

5 Ibid.

6 Carlo Ginzburg, "Killing a Chinese Mandarin: The Moral Implications of Distance," *Critical Inquiry*, Vol. 21, No. 1 (Autumn 1994), 46–60, at www.jstor .org/stable/1343886; Matthew W. Wylie, "Moral Crime and Moral Punishment; The Philosophical Implications of Distance and Time in *The Brothers Karamazov*," *Toronto Slavic Quarterly*, No. 3 (Winter 2003), at http://sites.utoronto.ca/tsq/03/ index03.shtml.

7 Adam Smith, *The Theory of Moral Sentiments*, at 193.

8 David Hume, "Of Contiguity and Distance in Space and Time," book II, part III, section VII, *A Treatise of Human Nature* (New York: Penguin Books, 1985), 474–479 [1737–1740].

9 As discussed in Chapter 9, the best statement of this enlightened view of self-interest is the "principle of interest rightly understood" of Alexis de Tocqueville. *See* James Bacchus, *The Willing World*, 75–76, 211–212.

10 Francis Thompson, "The Mistress of Vision," in Francis Thompson, *The Mistress of Vision* (Aylesford: St. Albert's Press, 1966) [1896].

Index

Printed in the United States
by Baker & Taylor Publisher Services